Explorations in
LITERATURE

AMERICA READS　　　　　　　**CLASSIC EDITION**

AMERICA READSCLASSIC EDITION

BEGINNINGS IN LITERATURE
Alan L. Madsen
Sarah Durand Wood
Philip M. Connors

DISCOVERIES IN LITERATURE
L. Jane Christensen
Edmund J. Farrell

EXPLORATIONS IN LITERATURE
Nancy C. Millett
Raymond J. Rodrigues

PATTERNS IN LITERATURE
Edmund J. Farrell
Ouida H. Clapp
Karen J. Kuehner

TRADITIONS IN LITERATURE
Helen McDonnell
James E. Miller, Jr.
Russell J. Hogan

THE UNITED STATES IN LITERATURE
The Red Badge of Courage EDITION
Three Long Stories EDITION
James E. Miller, Jr.
Kerry M. Wood
Carlota Cárdenas de Dwyer

ENGLAND IN LITERATURE
Macbeth EDITION
Hamlet EDITION
John Pfordresher
Gladys V. Veidemanis
Helen McDonnell

CLASSICS IN WORLD LITERATURE
Kerry M. Wood
Helen McDonnell
John Pfordresher
Mary Alice Fite
Paul Lankford

The authors and editors wish to thank the following consultants for reading and teaching editorial material and proposed selections for America Reads:
■ Barbara E. Anderson, Junior Level Coordinator and Teacher, James B. Conant High School, Hoffman Estates, Illinois
■ Anita Arnold, Chairman, English Department, Thomas Jefferson High School, San Antonio, Texas
■ Pat Dudley, Principal, Long Elementary School, Abilene, Texas
■ Dr. V. Pauline Hodges-McLain, Coordinator, Language Arts, Jefferson County Public Schools, Golden, Colorado
■ Rance Howe, English/Language Arts Consultant K–12, Anoka-Hennepin ISD 11, Coon Rapids, Minnesota
■ Lisbeth Johnson, English Teacher, Capital High School, Olympia, Washington
■ Daniel Lane, Supervisor of Humanities, Holmdel Twp. Public Schools, Holmdel, New Jersey
■ May Lee, English Teacher, Baldwin Senior High School, Baldwin, New York
■ Richard T. Martin, English Department Chairman, Burrillville Junior-Senior High School, Harrisville, Rhode Island
■ Barbara McCormick, English Department Chairperson, Greenville High School, Greenville, Mississippi
■ James McCullough, English Teacher, Carmel High School for Boys, Mundelein, Illinois
■ Cathy Nufer, Teacher, Grade 6, Elm School, Hinsdale, Illinois
■ Marlyn Payne, Teacher, Grade 7, Nichols Middle School, Evanston, Illinois
■ Sally P. Pfeifer, English Department Chair, Lewis and Clark High School, Spokane, Washington
■ James B. Phillips, Instructor in English and Reading, Norwood Senior High School, Norwood, Massachusetts
■ John Pratt, Language Arts Chairperson, Edison High School, Stockton, California
■ Cora Wolfe, English Department Chairperson, Antelope Union High School, Wellton, Arizona

Explorations in LITERATURE

AMERICA READS   **CLASSIC EDITION**

Nancy C. Millett
Raymond J. Rodrigues

S C O T T,   F O R E S M A N

Scott, Foresman and Company   Editorial Offices: Glenview, Illinois
Regional Offices:
Sunnyvale, California Tucker, Georgia Glenview, Illinois Oakland, New Jersey Dallas, Texas

Nancy C. Millett Professor of Secondary Education, Wichita State University. Coauthor of *How to Read a Poem* and *How to Read a Short Story*. Coauthor of literature, grammar, and composition textbooks for secondary and elementary schools. Formerly teacher of English at the University of Rochester and Wichita High School East. Consultant on writing in grades K–12.

Raymond J. Rodrigues Associate Vice President for Academic Affairs at Colorado State University, Ft. Collins. Coauthor of *Teaching Writing with a Word Processor, Grades 7–13*. Formerly Director of Teacher Education at New Mexico State University and at the University of Colorado, Colorado Springs; high school teacher of English in Nevada and New Mexico. Past President of the Southern Nevada Teachers of English and the Utah Council of Teachers of English. Currently a member of the National Council of Teachers of English Editorial Board.

Cover: William Bradford, "Clark's Point Light, New Bedford" (detail), 1854. *Old Dartmouth Historical Society and Whaling Museum, New Bedford, Massachusetts*

Pronunciation key and dictionary entries are from *Scott, Foresman Advanced Dictionary* by E. L. Thorndike and Clarence L. Barnhart. Copyright © 1988 Scott, Foresman and Company.

ISBN: 0-673-29378-5

CONTENTS

UNIT 4   POETRY

UNIT 5   SHORT STORY 2

UNIT 8   NOVEL

THINKING CRITICALLY ABOUT LITERATURE

READING LITERATURE

COMMENT ARTICLES

THE WRITER'S CRAFT

HANDBOOK OF LITERARY TERMS

WRITER'S HANDBOOK

GLOSSARY OF LITERARY TERMS *720*

★ *Explorations in Literature* has six units containing short stories, poetry, plays, and nonfiction. A seventh unit is made up of Greek myths. The eighth unit consists of a novel, *The Call of the Wild*.

UNIT ORGANIZATION

Units begin with an illustration and a unit preview to help you see what each unit contains. Many selections are preceded by a wide yellow bar at the top of a page. This bar directs you to the Handbook of Literary Terms at the back of the text, where you will learn about an essential literary term before you read the selection.

Think and Discuss questions follow each selection or group of selections. You may want to read the questions before you read the selection as a way of guiding your reading.

Applying/Reviewing questions about the literary term you have studied also appear after literary works. These are to help you make certain you understand how an author has developed plot, used figurative language, or made use of other techniques.

Reading Literature Skillfully lessons appear from time to time. Here you will see short exercises on topics such as cause-and-effect relationships, predicting outcomes, and summarizing. You will be able to do most of these lessons rather quickly and without your teacher's help.

Vocabulary exercises throughout the book will help you understand words or meanings new to you. They will also show you how to determine the meanings of words from context or from the parts of a word. You may be tested on the words in these exercises.

Thinking Skills lessons will help you learn to think about literature in some new ways by practicing *classifying, generalizing, synthesizing* (putting together parts and elements to form new ideas) and *evaluating*.

Composition assignments and ideas follow most selections. You will find it useful to refer to the Writer's Handbook at the back of this text for more help with some of these assignments.

Enrichment selections are also included and provide ideas for class projects and speaking and listening activities.

OTHER FEATURES

Three types of articles can be found throughout this anthology. Comment articles provide interesting sidelights on a work, an author, or a related subject. (See, for example, Chinatown, page 56.)

Articles titled "The Writer's Craft" focus on how writers achieve their effects and help you to achieve similar effects in your writing. Finally, there are articles such as "Reading a Full-Length Play," page 450, that will give you some helpful hints on reading various types of literature.

UNIT REVIEWS

Each unit ends with a three-part review titled "Thinking Critically About Literature." Here you will be asked to read a new, short work and answer questions to help you apply what you have learned. You will also review the selection or selections in the unit and complete a writing assignment related to the unit material.

END-OF-BOOK MATERIAL

At the back of this text on page 657 is a Handbook of Literary Terms. There is also a Writer's Handbook. You will be referred to the Handbook of Literary Terms and the Writer's Handbook throughout earlier parts of the book. The Writer's Handbook is followed by a Glossary of Literary Terms and a Glossary that looks like a dictionary. The Glossary contains all words featured in Vocabulary exercises, plus other words you will encounter in your reading.

The stories, poems, and plays in this book were written by a wide variety of authors. Although some lived long ago, their work has survived because it is both meaningful and interesting. The work of those writers who are living today is included not only because it is well-written but because it provides insights into life today—and even into the future.

SHORT STORY 1

John F. Kensett, "Tree Reaching Out Over a Lake" (detail), *Private Collection*

UNIT 1

PREVIEW

UNIT 1 SHORT STORY 1

The Moustache / Robert Cormier
The Last Specimen / Joan Aiken
The Treasure of Lemon Brown / Walter Dean Myers
The Inspiration of Mr. Budd / Dorothy Sayers
Paw-Paw / Laurence Yep
A Christmas Memory / Truman Capote
To Build a Fire / Jack London
Top Man / James Ramsey Ullman
Rain, Rain, Go Away / Isaac Asimov
The Tell-Tale Heart / Edgar Allan Poe
Charles / Shirley Jackson
Mr. Mendelsohn / Nicholasa Mohr
The Drummer Boy of Shiloh / Ray Bradbury

Features
Reading a Short Story
Comment: Hair of Gold—and Other Colors
The Writer's Craft: Be Specific
Comment: Chinatown

Application of Literary Terms
plot
characterization
setting
point of view
inference

Reading Literature Skillfully
cause/effect

Vocabulary Skills
dictionary
affixes and roots
context

Thinking Skills
classifying   generalizing

Composition Assignments Include
Writing a Description
Writing a Narrative
Writing a Dialogue
Writing Advertisements
Reading/Writing Log
Writing a Story
Writing an Essay

Enrichment
Speaking and Listening
Role Playing

Thinking Critically About Literature
Concept Review
Content Review
Composition Review

The Moustache

Robert Cormier

My poor, poor grandmother. Old People aren't supposed to have those kinds of memories.

At the last minute Annie couldn't go. She was invaded by one of those twenty-four-hour flu bugs that sent her to bed with a fever, moaning about the fact that she'd also have to break her date with Handsome Harry Arnold that night. We call him Handsome Harry because he's actually handsome, but he's also a nice guy, cool, and he doesn't treat me like Annie's kid brother, which I am, but like a regular person. Anyway, I had to go to Lawnrest alone that afternoon. But first of all I had to stand inspection. My mother lined me up against the wall. She stood there like a one-man firing squad, which is kind of funny because she's not like a man at all, she's very feminine, and we have this great relationship—I mean, I feel as if she really likes me. I realize that sounds strange, but I know guys whose mothers love them and cook special stuff for them and worry about them and all but there's something missing in their relationship.

Anyway. She frowned and started the routine.

"That hair," she said. Then admitted: "Well, at least you combed it."

I sighed. I have discovered that it's better to sigh than argue.

"And that moustache." She shook her head. "I still say a seventeen-year-old has no business wearing a moustache."

"It's an experiment," I said. "I just wanted to see if I could grow one." To tell the truth, I had proved my point about being able to grow a decent moustache, but I also had learned to like it.

"It's costing you money, Mike," she said.

"I know, I know."

The money was a reference to the movies. The Downtown Cinema has a special Friday night offer—half-price admission for high school couples, seventeen or younger. But the woman in the box office took one look at my moustache and charged me full price. Even when I showed her my driver's license. She charged full admission for Cindy's ticket, too, which left me practically broke and unable to take Cindy out for a hamburger with the crowd afterward. That didn't help mat-

Cormier (côr mē ā′).

ters, because Cindy has been getting impatient recently about things like the fact that I don't own my own car and have to concentrate on my studies if I want to win that college scholarship, for instance. Cindy wasn't exactly crazy about the moustache, either.

Now it was my mother's turn to sigh.

"Look," I said, to cheer her up. "I'm thinking about shaving it off." Even though I wasn't. Another discovery: You can build a way of life on postponement.

"Your grandmother probably won't even recognize you," she said. And I saw the shadow fall across her face.

Let me tell you what the visit to Lawnrest was all about. My grandmother is seventy-three years old. She is a resident—which is supposed to be a better word than *patient*—at the Lawnrest Nursing Home. She used to make the greatest turkey dressing in the world and was a nut about baseball and could even quote batting averages, for crying out loud. She always rooted for the losers. She was in love with the Mets until they started to win. Now she has arteriosclerosis,[1] which the dictionary says is "a chronic disease characterized by abnormal thickening and hardening of the arterial walls." Which really means that she can't live at home anymore or even with us, and her memory has betrayed her as well as her body. She used to wander off and sometimes didn't recognize people. My mother visits her all the time, driving the thirty miles to Lawnrest almost every day. Because Annie was home for a semester break from college, we had decided to make a special Saturday visit. Now Annie was in bed, groaning theatrically—she's a drama major—but I told my mother I'd go, anyway.

I hadn't seen my grandmother since she'd been admitted to Lawnrest. Besides, the place is located on the Southwest Turnpike, which meant I could barrel along in my father's new Le Mans.[2] My ambition was to see the speedometer hit seventy-five. Ordinarily, I used the old station wagon, which can barely stagger up to fifty.

Frankly, I wasn't too crazy about visiting a nursing home. They reminded me of hospitals and hospitals turn me off. I mean, the smell of ether makes me nauseous, and I feel faint at the sight of blood. And as I approached Lawnrest—which is a terrible cemetery kind of name, to begin with—I was sorry I hadn't avoided the trip. Then I felt guilty about it. I'm loaded with guilt complexes. Like driving like a madman after promising my father to be careful. Like sitting in the parking lot, looking at the nursing home with dread and thinking how I'd rather be with Cindy. Then I thought of all the Christmas and birthday gifts my grandmother had given me and I got out of the car, guilty, as usual.

Inside, I was surprised by the lack of hospital smell, although there was another odor or maybe the absence of an odor. The air was antiseptic, sterile. As if there was no atmosphere at all or I'd caught a cold suddenly and couldn't taste or smell.

A nurse at the reception desk gave me directions—my grandmother was in East Three. I made my way down the tiled corridor and was glad to see that the walls were

---

1. **arteriosclerosis** (är tir′ē ō sklə rō′sis), a disease of the arteries, tubes which carry blood from the heart to all parts of the body. In this disease, the arterial walls harden, interfering with blood circulation.
2. **Le Mans** (lə mänz′).

painted with cheerful colors like yellow and pink. A wheelchair suddenly shot around a corner, self-propelled by an old man, white-haired and toothless, who cackled merrily as he barely missed me. I jumped aside—here I was, almost getting wiped out by a two-mile-an-hour wheelchair after doing seventy-five on the pike. As I walked through the corridor seeking East Three, I couldn't help glancing into the rooms, and it was like some kind of wax museum—all these figures in various stances and attitudes, sitting in beds or chairs, standing at windows, as if they were frozen forever in these postures. To tell the truth, I began to hurry because I was getting depressed. Finally, I saw a beautiful girl approaching, dressed in white, a nurse or an attendant, and I was so happy to see someone young, someone walking and acting normally, that I gave her a wide smile and a big hello and I must have looked like a kind of nut. Anyway, she looked right through me as if I were a window, which is about par for the course whenever I meet beautiful girls.

I finally found the room and saw my grandmother in bed. My grandmother looks like Ethel Barrymore. I never knew who Ethel Barrymore was until I saw a terrific movie, *None But the Lonely Heart,* on TV, starring Ethel Barrymore and Cary Grant. Both my grandmother and Ethel Barrymore have these great craggy faces like the side of a mountain and wonderful voices like syrup being poured. Slowly. She was propped up in bed, pillows puffed behind her. Her hair had been combed out and fell upon her shoulders. For some reason, this flowing hair gave her an almost girlish appearance, despite its whiteness.

She saw me and smiled. Her eyes lit up and her eyebrows arched and she reached out her hands to me in greeting. "Mike, Mike," she said. And I breathed a sigh of relief. This was one of her good days. My mother had warned me that she might not know who I was at first.

I took her hands in mine. They were fragile. I could actually feel her bones, and it seemed as if they would break if I pressed too hard. Her skin was smooth, almost slippery, as if the years had worn away all the roughness the way the wind wears away the surfaces of stones.

"Mike, Mike, I didn't think you'd come," she said, so happy, and she was still Ethel Barrymore, that voice like a caress. "I've been waiting all this time." Before I could reply, she looked away, out the window. "See the birds? I've been watching them at the feeder. I love to see them come. Even the blue jays. The blue jays are like hawks—they take the food that the small birds should have. But the small birds, the chickadees, watch the blue jays and at least learn where the feeder is."

She lapsed into silence, and I looked out the window. There was no feeder. No birds. There was only the parking lot and the sun glinting on car windshields.

She turned to me again, eyes bright. Radiant, really. Or was it a medicine brightness? "Ah, Mike. You look so grand, so grand. Is that a new coat?"

"Not really," I said. I'd been wearing my Uncle Jerry's old army-fatigue jacket[3] for

---

3. *army-fatigue jacket,* military work clothing worn in the field or whenever dress uniform is not required.

months, practically living in it, my mother said. But she insisted that I wear my raincoat for the visit. It was about a year old but looked new because I didn't wear it much. Nobody was wearing raincoats lately.

"You always loved clothes, didn't you, Mike?" she said.

I was beginning to feel uneasy because she regarded me with such intensity. Those bright eyes. I wondered—are old people in places like this so lonesome, so abandoned that they go wild when someone visits? Or was she so happy because she was suddenly lucid and everything was sharp and clear? My mother had described those moments when my grandmother suddenly emerged from the fog that so often obscured her mind. I didn't know the answers, but it felt kind of spooky, getting such an emotional welcome from her.

"I remember the time you bought the new coat—the Chesterfield," she said, looking away again, as if watching the birds that weren't there. "That lovely coat with the velvet collar. Black, it was. Stylish. Remember that, Mike? It was hard times, but you could never resist the glitter."

I was about to protest—I had never heard of a Chesterfield, for crying out loud. But I stopped. Be patient with her, my mother had said. Humor her. Be gentle.

We were interrupted by an attendant who pushed a wheeled cart into the room. "Time for juices, dear," the woman said. She was the standard forty- or fifty-year-old woman: glasses, nothing hair, plump cheeks. Her manner was cheerful but a businesslike kind of cheerfulness. I'd hate to be called "dear" by someone getting paid to do it. "Orange or grape or cranberry, dear? Cranberry is good for the bones, you know."

My grandmother ignored the interruption. She didn't even bother to answer, having turned away at the woman's arrival, as if angry about her appearance.

The woman looked at me and winked. A conspiratorial kind of wink. It was kind of horrible. I didn't think people winked like that anymore. In fact, I hadn't seen a wink in years.

"She doesn't care much for juices," the woman said, talking to me as if my grandmother weren't even there. "But she loves her coffee. With lots of cream and two lumps of sugar. But this is juice time, not coffee time." Addressing my grandmother again, she said, "Orange or grape or cranberry, dear?"

"Tell her I want no juices, Mike," my grandmother commanded regally, her eyes still watching invisible birds.

The woman smiled, patience like a label on her face. "That's all right, dear. I'll just leave some cranberry for you. Drink it at your leisure. It's good for the bones."

She wheeled herself out of the room. My grandmother was still absorbed in the view. Somewhere a toilet flushed. A wheelchair passed the doorway—probably that same old driver fleeing a hit-run accident. A television set exploded with sound somewhere, soap-opera voices filling the air. You can always tell soap-opera voices.

I turned back to find my grandmother staring at me. Her hands cupped her face, her index fingers curled around her cheeks like parenthesis marks.

Frederick Carl Frieseke, "Portrait of a Lady at Piano"
Campanile Galleries, Chicago

"But you know, Mike, looking back, I think you were right," she said, continuing our conversation as if there had been no interruption. "You always said, 'It's the things of the spirit that count, Meg.' The spirit! And so you bought the baby-grand piano—a baby grand in the middle of the Depression.[4] A knock came on the door and it was the deliveryman. It took five of them to get it into the house." She leaned back, closing her eyes. "How I loved that piano, Mike. I was never that fine a player, but you loved to sit there in the parlor, on Sunday evenings, Ellie on your lap, listening to me play and sing." She hummed a bit, a fragment of melody I didn't recognize. Then she drifted into silence. Maybe she'd fallen asleep. My mother's name is Ellen, but everyone always calls her Ellie. "Take my hand, Mike," my grandmother said suddenly. Then I remembered— my grandfather's name was Michael. I had been named for him.

"Ah, Mike," she said, pressing my hands with all her feeble strength. "I thought I'd lost you forever. And here you are, back with me again. . . ."

Her expression scared me. I don't mean scared as if I were in danger but scared because of what could happen to her when she realized the mistake she had made. My mother always said I favored her side of the family. Thinking back to the pictures in the old family albums, I recalled my grandfather as tall and thin. Like me. But the resemblance ended there. He was thirty-five when he died, almost forty years ago. And he wore a moustache. I brought my hand to my face. I also wore a moustache now, of course.

"I sit here these days, Mike," she said, her voice a lullaby, her hand still holding mine, "and I drift and dream. The days are fuzzy sometimes, merging together. Sometimes it's like I'm not here at all but somewhere else altogether. And I always think of you. Those years we had. Not enough years, Mike, not enough. . . ."

Her voice was so sad, so mournful that I made sounds of sympathy, not words exactly but the kind of soothings that mothers murmur to their children when they awaken from bad dreams.

"And I think of that terrible night, Mike, that terrible night. Have you ever really forgiven me for that night?"

"Listen . . ." I began. I wanted to say: "Nana, this is Mike your grandson, not Mike your husband."

"Sh . . . sh . . ." she whispered, placing a finger as long and cold as a candle against my lips. "Don't say anything. I've waited so long for this moment. To be here. With you. I wondered what I would say if suddenly you walked in that door like other people have done. I've thought and thought about it. And I finally made up my mind—I'd ask you to forgive me. I was too proud to ask before." Her fingers tried to mask her face. "But I'm not proud anymore, Mike." That great voice quivered and then grew strong again. "I hate you to see me this way—you always said I was beautiful. I didn't believe it. The Charity Ball when we led the grand march and you said I was the most beautiful girl there . . ."

"Nana," I said. I couldn't keep up the pretense any longer, adding one more burden to

---

4. *the Depression,* a period during the 1930s when the stock market crashed, banks failed, and many people lost their jobs.

my load of guilt, leading her on this way, playing a pathetic game of make-believe with an old woman clinging to memories. She didn't seem to hear me.

"But that other night, Mike. The terrible one. The terrible accusations I made. Even Ellie woke up and began to cry. I went to her and rocked her in my arms and you came into the room and said I was wrong. You were whispering, an awful whisper, not wanting to upset little Ellie but wanting to make me see the truth. And I didn't answer you, Mike. I was too proud. I've even forgotten the name of the girl. I sit here, wondering now—was it Laura or Evelyn? I can't remember. Later, I learned that you were telling the truth all the time, Mike. That I'd been wrong . . ." Her eyes were brighter than ever as she looked at me now, but tear-bright, the tears gathering. "It was never the same after that night, was it, Mike? The glitter was gone. From you. From us. And then the accident . . . and I never had the chance to ask you to forgive me . . ."

My grandmother. My poor, poor grandmother. Old people aren't supposed to have those kinds of memories. You see their pictures in the family albums and that's what they are: pictures. They're not supposed to come to life. You drive out in your father's Le Mans doing seventy-five on the pike and all you're doing is visiting an old lady in a nursing home. A duty call. And then you find out that she's a person. She's *somebody*. She's my grandmother, all right, but she's also herself. Like my own mother and father. They exist outside of their relationship to me. I was scared again. I wanted to get out of there.

"Mike, Mike," my grandmother said. "Say it, Mike."

I felt as if my cheeks would crack if I uttered a word.

"Say you forgive me, Mike. I've waited all these years . . ."

I was surprised at how strong her fingers were.

"Say, '*I forgive you, Meg.*'"

I said it. My voice sounded funny, as if I were talking in a huge tunnel. "I forgive you, Meg."

Her eyes studied me. Her hands pressed mine. For the first time in my life, I saw love at work. Not movie love. Not Cindy's sparkling eyes when I tell her that we're going to the beach on a Sunday afternoon. But love like something alive and tender, asking nothing in return. She raised her face, and I knew what she wanted me to do. I bent and brushed my lips against her cheek. Her flesh was like a leaf in autumn, crisp and dry.

She closed her eyes and I stood up. The sun wasn't glinting on the cars any longer. Somebody had turned on another television set, and the voices were the show-off voices of the panel shows. At the same time you could hear the soap-opera dialogue on the other television set.

I waited awhile. She seemed to be sleeping, her breathing serene and regular. I buttoned my raincoat. Suddenly she opened her eyes again and looked at me. Her eyes were still bright, but they merely stared at me. Without recognition or curiosity. Empty eyes. I smiled at her, but she didn't smile back. She made a kind of moaning sound and turned away on the bed, pulling the blankets around her.

I counted to twenty-five and then to fifty and did it all over again. I cleared my throat and coughed tentatively. She didn't move; she didn't respond. I wanted to say, "Nana, it's me." But I didn't. I thought of saying, "Meg, it's me." But I couldn't.

Finally I left. Just like that. I didn't say goodbye or anything. I stalked through the corridors, looking neither to the right nor the left, not caring whether that wild old man with the wheelchair ran me down or not.

On the Southwest Turnpike I did seventy-five—no, eighty—most of the way. I turned the radio up as loud as it could go. Rock music—anything to fill the air. When I got home, my mother was vacuuming the living-room rug. She shut off the cleaner, and the silence was deafening. "Well, how was your grandmother?" she asked.

I told her she was fine. I told her a lot of things. How great Nana looked and how she seemed happy and had called me Mike. I wanted to ask her—hey, Mom, you and Dad really love each other, don't you? I mean—there's nothing to forgive between you, is there? But I didn't.

Instead I went upstairs and took out the electric razor Annie had given me for Christmas and shaved off my moustache.

THINK AND DISCUSS
Understanding
1. Why does Mike go to Lawnrest Nursing Home?
2. How does he feel about the old people he sees in the corridors of the nursing home?
3. How does Mike describe his grandmother?
4. What does his grandmother say to indicate that she thinks she is living in another place and time?
5. Why does his grandmother ask Mike to say, "I forgive you, Meg"?

Analyzing
6. Why does he do as his grandmother asks?

7. What new understanding about his grandmother does Mike gain from this visit?
8. In what way is Cindy's love for Mike different from the way his grandmother feels about his grandfather?
9. What might be the reason Mike shaves his moustache?

Extending
10. When he arrives home, Mike does not tell his mother everything that happened at the nursing home. Discuss why Mike might have acted this way and whether you agree or disagree with his action.

BIOGRAPHY

Robert Cormier

1925–

Cormier wanted to become a fiction writer from the time he was in eighth grade, but he spent his early career working as a journalist. His reporting for New England newspapers won him numerous awards before he turned to writing fiction full-time.

Although his books are enjoyed by young adults, Cormier maintains that he writes books with young adults in them, not books for young adults. His stories do not have pat endings but portray life realistically— often harshly. *The Chocolate War* (1974), *I Am the Cheese* (1977), and *After the First Death* (1979) each won the *New York Times* Outstanding Book of the Year Award.

A short story must quickly introduce the elements important to its development. **Plot** is one of these elements. Plot refers to the series of related events selected by the author to present and bring about the resolution of some conflict. Conflict may be external, in which a character struggles against nature, an opponent, or some other outside force, or conflict may be internal, in which the struggle occurs within the character.

In a carefully constructed plot, details and incidents are selected and arranged in a cause-and-effect relationship so that each detail is a necessary link leading to the outcome of the story. The events in a plot usually follow this pattern: a situation is established; a conflict or problem arises; certain events bring about a climax, or a character takes some decisive action; the resolution occurs, followed by the conclusion. For example, in "The Moustache," the climax occurs when Mike kisses his grandmother and says, "I forgive you."

Characters are another important element. In fiction, people are characterized by what they say, what they do, and what others say about them. Review the first two pages of "The Moustache." In what ways do you learn about Mike? Later in the story, how do you learn about Mike's grandmother?

The **setting** is the time and place in which events in a story occur. In "The Moustache" what details tell you that the setting is modern times? Where does most of the story take place?

The contents of this unit are arranged so that you can talk about these and other elements important to understanding the stories you read. As you work on the first group of stories, which emphasizes plot, keep in mind that your ability to recognize **cause-and-effect relationships** can help you better understand what you are reading. An **effect** is what happens. A **cause** is what makes it happen. As a plot unfolds, look at each event. Ask yourself what has caused it and what it in turn might cause. In the story you just read, what causes Mike to go to the nursing home alone? What action does the visit cause Mike to take when he gets home?

From now on, when you read a story, ask yourself who is telling that story, or from whose **point of view** it is being told. Point of view in a story determines what you are told and the way in which you are told it.

All of the elements discussed in this article provide ways to help you read and understand what you have read. In addition, they offer you a vocabulary, a means of talking about your reading with your classmates and teacher. This special vocabulary allows you to say more than, "I liked the story" or "I didn't like it." You will still have a chance to voice your opinion, of course. But you will also be able to support that opinion.

See PLOT in the Handbook of Literary Terms, page 677.

The Last Specimen

Joan Aiken

Her hair had a greenish tint, and her horse had claws. Still, the minister felt there was no harm in her.

---

he Reverend Matthew Pentecost, aged seventy, had a regular monthly habit. On his way to conduct Evensong[1] in the tiny church of St.-Anthony-under-the-Downs, he invariably parked his aged Rover for ten minutes by the side of a small patch of woodland about ten minutes' drive from the church.

Services at St. Anthony's took place only once a month; for the rest of the time the isolated building with its Saxon stonework, Douai font,[2] willful hand organ, and two massive yew trees, drowsed undisturbed, save by casual tourists who occasionally wandered in, looked around, dropped a ten-pence piece[3] into the box that begged help for the fabric of the roof, and inspected the small overgrown churchyard with its nineteen graves.

At the monthly services the congregation seldom exceeded half a dozen, and in wet weather or snow Mr. Pentecost and Miss Sedom, who played the organ, had the place to themselves. St. Anthony's lay three quarters of a mile from any house; the mild slopes of the Berkshire downs enfolded it as sometimes after a falling tide a cup of sand will hold a single pebble.

One of the rector's favorite views was that of the church's swaybacked stone roof, bracketed between its two majestic dark yew trees, with the leisurely gray-green of the hillsides beyond. This was one reason for his

---

Aiken (ā′kən).
1. *Evensong,* vespers; an evening prayer, hymn, or service.
2. *Saxon stonework, Douai font,* the Saxons ruled England in A.D. 400s and 500s. Douai (dü′ā), a town in northern France, was a prosperous trading center in the Middle Ages. This description suggests the age and the history of the chapel.
3. *ten-pence piece,* a British coin.

pre-Evensong period of meditation beside the little wood. The second reason was the tactful desire to allow his parishioners time to assemble, sit down, and rest from their cross-country walk for a few minutes before he appeared among them. Except for the trees on his left, the countryside thereabouts lay bare as an open hand, so that the members of the congregation could be seen from a great distance, making their way along the footpath that led to the church from Compton Druce, the nearest hamlet.

On this evening in mid-April Mr. Pentecost sat in his rusty Rover with an especially happy and benign expression on his face. After a rainy afternoon the sky had cleared: thrushes, larks, and blackbirds were singing in fervent appreciation of the sun's last rays, which turned the greenish-white pearls of the budding hawthorn to a silvery dazzle. In this light the down grass and the young wheat shone with an almost luminous intensity of color.

"Interesting," mused Mr. Pentecost, "how these early greens of the year, dog's mercury and elder leaves, and the green of bluebells, contain such a strong mixture of blue in their color."

Mr. Pentecost's hobby was painting delicate watercolor landscapes, and he was minutely observant of such niceties.

"Then, later in the spring, in May and June, the brighter, more yellow greens appear: young beech and oak leaves with their buttery rich color; doubtless the extra degree of light from the sun has something to do with it."

Mr. Pentecost watched fondly as Ben Tracey, the farmer who owned the enormous pasture on his right, arrived in a Land-Rover with sacks of feed for the sheep. The spring had been an unusually cold one, and the grass remained unseasonably scanty. Sighting Ben, the sheep and lambs, well acquainted with the object of his daily visit, began purposefully making toward him from all corners of the vast field, lambs following their mothers like iron filings drawn to a magnet in regular converging lines, only broken at one point by the presence of a massive oak tree covered with reddish buds that grew toward the middle of the field. Mr. Pentecost eyed the tree thoughtfully. Was it not unusually advanced in its growth for such a cold season? And why had he not noticed it last month?

Farmer and rector waved to one another, then Mr. Pentecost, observing the last of his congregation pass through the churchyard and enter St. Anthony's porch, was about to start his motor again, when, in the rearview mirror, he noticed a girl, who had been slowly riding her pony along the road behind the car. At this moment she dismounted, tethered the pony to a tree, and vanished through a gate into the little wood.

Normally such a sight would have aroused no particular curiosity in Mr. Pentecost, but two unusual factors here caught his attention. First, neither girl nor mount were familiar to him; yet Mr. Pentecost was certain that he knew every girl and every pony within a ten-mile radius. So where had she come from? Second, the girl carried a trowel and a basket.

Without apparent haste, yet acting with remarkable calm and dispatch for a man of his age, Mr. Pentecost backed the Rover a hundred yards to the point where the pony stood tethered to a young ash tree. The rector got out of his car, studied the pony thoughtfully for a moment, then walked into the wood. The gate stood open: another factor worthy of note. Slightly compressing his lips, Mr. Pentecost closed it behind him and took the path that bisected the wood. The girl ahead of him was easily visible because of her bright-blue anorak; she was, in any case, walking slowly, glancing from side to side as if in search of something.

Mr. Pentecost could easily guess at the object of her quest. He caught up with her just as she had reached it: a patch of delicate spindly plants, each of them nine inches to a foot high, growing in a small sunny clearing. They had bell-shaped flowers the size of small, upside-down tulips—odd, elegant, mysterious flowers, white, with a pinkish-purple tracery over the fluted petals.

The girl knelt beside them and took her trowel from the basket.

"No, no. You mustn't," said Mr. Pentecost gently behind her. The girl gasped and spun around, gazing up at him with wide, frightened eyes.

"My dear child, believe me, you *mustn't*," repeated the rector, the seriousness of his tone mitigated to some degree by the mild expression in his blue eyes. The girl gazed at him, nonplussed, embarrassed, temporarily speechless, it seemed.

She was, he noticed, a very pretty girl, about seventeen, perhaps, in the accustomed uniform of jeans and T-shirt and riding boots. On her head, though, she sported a slightly absurd and certainly unusual article of headgear—not a crash helmet, but a strapped furry hat with a cylindrical top, like the shakoes[4] worn by cavalry in the Crimean War. Could she have inherited it from some great-great-grandfather? Or perhaps, thought the vicar indulgently, it was a prop borrowed from some local theatrical venture; the young loved to dress up in fancy dress. But, now that he saw her close to, he was certain that he did not know this girl; she was a total stranger. Her eyes were a clear beautiful greenish gold—like the color of the young oak leaves he had been thinking about a few minutes earlier. Her hair, what could be seen of it under the shako, was the same color, with a decided greenish tint; punk, no doubt, thought Mr. Pentecost knowledgeably. The children nowadays dyed their hair extraordinary colors; green was nothing out of the common. He had seen pink, orange, and lilac.

The girl continued to gaze at him in silence, abashed and nervous, grasping her trowel.

"Wild fritillaries are so rare, so very rare," Mr. Pentecost mildly explained to her, "that it is wrong, it is most dreadfully wrong to dig them up; besides, of course, being against the law. Did you not know that? And why, do you suppose, are they so rare?" he went on, considerately giving her time to recover her composure. "Why, because of people like yourself, my dear, finding out about where they grow and coming to dig up specimens. I know the temptation—believe me, I know it!—but you really must *not*, you know."

"Oh, dear," murmured the girl, finding her voice at last, it seemed. "I'm—I'm very sorry. I—I didn't know."

---

4. *shakoes,* high, stiff military hats with plumes or other ornament.

These are Imperial fritillaries, much brighter in color than those the Reverend Pentecost protects. Vincent Van Gogh, "Still Life, Fritillaires in Copper Vase," *Musee D'Orsay, Paris*

"No? You really didn't know? Where are you from?" he inquired, gently veiling his disbelief. "You are certainly not from anywhere around here, or I should have known you. And your steed," he added thoughtfully.

"No, I—I come from—from quite a long way away. I was sent"—she hesitated, looking sheepish and contrite—"sent to—to collect a specimen, as you say. It is the last, you see—we already have one of everything else."

Good gracious, thought Mr. Pentecost, in surprise and a certain amount of disapproval. *Everything* else? Aloud he said,

"It is for a school project, I conclude? Well, I am sorry to disappoint you, but you really must *not* remove the flowers from this precious patch. I will tell you what you can do, though—" as her face fell. "If you care to accompany me to Evensong in St. Anthony's—or, of course, wait outside the church if you prefer," he added kindly, "you may then come with me to my rectory in Chilton Parsley. I am fortunate enough to have quite a large number of fritillaries growing in my flower border, and I shall be happy to give you a specimen for your collection. How about that, my dear?"

"Why," said the girl slowly, "that—that is very kind of Your Reverence. I am indeed greatly obliged to you." She spoke with considerable formality; although English enough in appearance, she could, judging from her accent, have been a foreigner who had learned the language very correctly from some aristocratic old lady with nineteenth-century intonations. "I have instructions to be back though"—she glanced at the sky, then at the watch on her wrist—"by seven. Will that——?"

"Plenty of time," he assured her, smiling. "The evening service is never a long one. . . . Strict about that sort of thing, are they, at your school?"

She blushed.

Mr. Pentecost began walking back toward the gate, anxious, without making it too obvious that he was in a hurry, to join his patient parishioners, but also wishful to be certain that the girl accompanied him. She, however, showed no sign of intending to disobey his prohibition and came with him docilely enough. Once outside the copse gate—"You must *always* close gates, you know," Mr. Pentecost reminded her amiably but firmly— she remounted, and he got into his car. "Just follow behind," he told her, poking his white-haired head out of the window. She nodded, kicking the shaggy pony into a walk; perhaps it was the late light filtered through the young hawthorns, but the pony, too, Mr. Pentecost thought, showed a decided touch of green in its rough coat. "Only a very short way to the church," he called, swerving his car erratically across the road as he put his head out again to impart this information.

The girl nodded and kicked her pony again. For its diminutive size—a Shetland cross, perhaps?—the pony certainly showed a remarkable turn of speed.

Mr. Pentecost had not expected that the girl would be prepared to attend his service, but she quietly tied her pony to the lych-gate, murmured some exhortation into its ear, and followed him through the churchyard, glancing about her with interest. Then a doubt seemed to overtake her: "Am I dressed suitably to come inside?" she asked in a low, worried tone, pausing at the church door.

"Perfectly," he assured her, smiling at the glossy shako. "Our congregation at St. Anthony is quite informal."

So she slipped in after him and demurely took her place in a pew at the back.

After the service—which, as he had promised, lasted no longer than twenty-five minutes—the rector exchanged a few friendly words with the six members of his congregation, stood waving good-bye to them as they set off on their return walk across the fields, and then said to the girl, who had remounted and was waiting by the gate:

"Now, if you will follow me again, my dear, I will drive slowly and I do not think the journey should take more than about fifteen minutes for that excellent little animal of yours."

She nodded, and they proceeded as before, the vicar driving at twenty miles an hour, not much less than his normal speed, while horse and rider followed with apparent ease.

As he drove, Mr. Pentecost reflected. During Evensong his mind, as always, had been entirely given over to the service, but he had, with some part of it, heard the girl's voice now and then, particularly in the hymn, Miss Sedom's favorite, "Glory to Thee My God This Night." So the girl was, at least, familiar with Christian ritual. Or was a remarkably speedy learner. Or was it conceivable that she could be coached, as it were, continuously by—whatever agency had sent her? There were so many things wrong with her—and yet, mused the rector, he could swear that there was no harm about her, not an atom.

When they reached the damp and crumbling laurel-girt rectory, Mr. Pentecost drove around, as was his habit, to the mossy yard at the rear, and parked there.

"You can tie your pony to the mounting block—" He gestured to the old stable. "Now, I will just leave my cassock inside the back door—so—and fetch a trowel—ah, no, of course there is no need for that, you already have one." It was a bricklayer's trowel, but no matter. "Follow me, then."

The rectory garden, beyond the overgrown laurel hedge, was a wonderful wilderness of old-fashioned flowers and shrubs that had grown, proliferated, and battled for mastery during the last hundred years. Smaller and more delicate plants had, on the whole, fared badly; but Mr. Pentecost adored his fritillaries and had cherished them as carefully as he was able: frail and beautiful, both speckled and white, they drooped their magic bells among a drift of pale blue anemones and a fringe of darker blue grape hyacinths.

"Aren't they extraordinary?" he said, fondly looking down at them. "It is so easy to believe in a benevolent Creator when one considers these and the anemones—which, I believe, are the lilies of the field referred to in St. Matthew. Now, this little clump, still in bud, would, I think, transfer without too much harm, my dear—er—what did you say your name was?"

She hesitated. Then: "My name is Anjla," she answered, with a slight, uneasy tremor of her voice. And she knelt to dig up the clump of plants he had indicated. The rector fetched her a grimy plastic bag from the toolshed, but she shook her head.

"Thank you, but I can't take it. Only the flowers. This is—this is truly very kind of you."

A faint warning hum sounded in the air—like that of a clock before it strikes.

The vicar glanced across the wide meadow that lay alongside his garden. A large oak, leafless still, covered with reddish buds, grew in the middle of the grassy space. Mr. Pentecost eyed it thoughtfully. Beyond it, pale and clear, shone the evening star.

Mr. Pentecost said, "My dear—where do you really come from?"

The girl stood, tucking the plants into her basket. She followed the direction of his glance, but said defensively, "You would not know the name of the place."

It was, however, remarkably hard to evade Mr. Pentecost when he became as serious as he was now.

"Forgive my curiosity," he said, "but I do think it important that I should know—precisely why are you collecting specimens?"

She was silent for a moment; for too long. Mr. Pentecost went on, "You see—I am an absentminded, vague old man, but even *I* could not help noticing that your pony has claws on its hoofs. *Moropus!* A prehistoric horse not seen in these parts for thirty million years! And, well, there were various other things——"

She blushed furiously.

"That was the trouble!" she burst out. "For such a small errand—just one flower—they wouldn't allocate enough research staff. I *knew* there were details they had skimped on——"

"But why," he persisted mildly, "why are you collecting?"

Anjla looked at him sorrowfully. Then she said, "Well—as you seem to have spotted us, and it is so very late, in any case, I suppose it won't matter now if I tell you——"

"Yes, my dear?"

"This planet"—she glanced round at the stable yard—"is due to blow up—oh, very, very soon. Our scientists have calculated it to within the next three chronims——"

"Chronims?"

"Under one hundred of your hours, I think. Naturally, therefore, we were checking the contents of our own Terrestrial Museum——"

"Ah, I see." He stood thinking for a few minutes, then inquired with the liveliest interest, "And you really do have one of everything? Even—for instance—a rector of the Church of England?"

"I'm afraid so." Her tone was full of regret. "I *wish* I could take you with me. You have been so kind. But we have a vicar, a dean, a bishop, a canon—we have them all. Even an archbishop."

"My dear child! You mistook my meaning. I would not, not for one moment, consider leaving. My question was prompted by—by a simple wish to know."

The low hum was audible again. Anjla glanced at the sky.

"I'm afraid that now I really have to go."

"Of course you must, my dear. Of course."

They crossed the yard and found the shaggy Moropus demolishing, with apparent relish, the last of a bunch of carrots that had been laid on the mounting block for Mr. Pentecost's supper.

Anjla checked and stared, aghast. *"Sphim! What have you done?"*

She burst into a torrent of expostulation, couched in a language wholly unlike any earthly tongue; it appeared to have no consonants at all, to consist of pure sound, like the breathy note of an ocarina.

The Moropus guiltily hung its head and shuffled its long-clawed feet.

Mr. Pentecost stood looking at the pair in sympathy and perplexity.

The warning hum sounded in the air again.

"Do I understand that your—um—companion has invalidated his chance of departure by the consumption of those carrots?"

"I don't know what *can* have come over him—we were briefed so carefully—told to touch nothing, to take in nothing except—over and over again they told us——"

"Perhaps it was a touch of Method,"[5] suggested Mr. Pentecost. "He was really getting into the skin of his part." And he added something about Dis and Persephone[6] that the girl received with the blankness of noncomprehension. She had placed her hands on either side of the pony's hairy cheekbones; she bent forward until her forehead touched the other's. Thus she stood for a couple of moments in silence. Then she straightened and walked across the yard in the direction of the meadow. Her eyes swam with tears. Following her, interested and touched, Mr. Pentecost murmured,

"I will, of course, be glad to take care of your friend. During what little time remains."

"I am sure that you will. Thank you. I—I am glad to have met you."

"You could not—I suppose—show me what you both really look like?" he asked with a touch of wistfulness.

"I'm afraid that would be quite impossible. Your eyes simply aren't adapted, you see——"

He nodded, accepting this. Just the same, for a single instant he did receive an impression of hugeness, brightness, speed. Then the girl vaulted the fence and, carefully carrying her basket, crossed the meadow to the large oak tree in the center.

"Good-bye," called Mr. Pentecost. The Moropus lifted up its head and let out a soft groaning sound.

Beside the oak tree, Anjla turned and raised her hand with a grave, formal gesture. Then she stepped among the low-growing branches of the tree, which immediately folded like an umbrella, and with a swift flash of no-colored brilliance, shot upward, disintegrating into light.

Mr. Pentecost remained for a few moments, leaning with his forearms on the wooden fence, gazing pensively at the star Hesperus, which, now that the tree was gone, could be seen gleaming in radiance above the horizon.

The rector murmured:

---

5. **Method,** Method Acting, theory and technique of acting in which actors identify as closely as they can with the characters they are portraying in order to better create the illusion of reality.

6. **Dis and Persephone.** Dis (dis) is the Roman god of the lower world, or Hades. Persephone (pər sef'ə nē) in Greek mythology was made queen of Hades but was allowed to spend part of each year on the earth.

Earth's joys grow dim, its glories pass
  away
Change and decay in all around I see;
O Thou, Who changest not, abide with
  me.

Then, pulling a juicy tussock of grass from beside one of the fence posts, he carried it back to the disconsolate Moropus.

"Here, my poor friend; if we are to wait for Armageddon together, we may as well do so in comfort. Just excuse me for a moment while I fetch a deck chair and a steamer rug from the house. And do, pray, finish those carrots. I will be with you again directly."

He stepped inside the back door. The Moropus, with a carrot top and a hank of juicy grass dangling from its hairy lips, gazed after him sadly but trustfully.

THINK AND DISCUSS
Understanding
1. At the beginning of the story, why is Reverend Pentecost sitting in his Rover?
2. What does the girl carry in her basket?
3. Why does Reverend Pentecost approach her?
4. What things about the girl does the minister find odd?
5. Why does she go to Evensong and then to the rectory?
6. What does the girl say is about to happen?
7. Why can't the horse leave with the girl? What does it do instead?

Analyzing
8. The minister describes himself as "an absent-minded, vague old man." Do you agree or disagree with this description? Give reasons for your answer.
9. How does the girl feel about leaving the horse behind?

10. Reread the last sentence in the story. Explain why the horse might feel both sad and trustful.

Extending
11. Predict how the girl might behave when she reports home. How might she describe the minister? What might she say about the Moropus?

APPLYING: Plot HZ
See Handbook of Literary Terms, p. 677.

The **plot** of a story refers to the related events that present and eventually resolve some problem or conflict.
1. Which of the following states the problem, or conflict, in "The Last Specimen": (a) the minister's feelings about the girl; (b) the girl's loss of the Moropus; (c) the identity of the girl and the reason for her presence?
2. At what point does the climax of the story occur? *when reverend sees girl*
3. Is the conflict resolved in a way that you find satisfactory? Explain.
yes

The Last Specimen 21

COMPOSITION

Writing a Description

Describe a place you consider peaceful and lovely, one that you love as much as Reverend Pentecost does the English countryside. Make sure that your description tells how you feel about the place. See "Writing a Clear Description" in the Writer's Handbook before you begin to plan your composition.

Writing a Narrative

Pretend that one other person in the world shares the secret that Reverend Pentecost has learned from the girl. That person is you. How would you spend the last evening the world may ever see? Write a narrative in which you tell in detail how you spend the evening.

BIOGRAPHY

Joan Aiken

1924–

Joan Aiken had her first poem published when she was sixteen. She has written short stories and novels that contain horror, humor, and fantasy. She believes that writers should write as they wish, without worrying about what people will think of their writing. While Aiken's fiction often illustrates that life may contain some harsh or unpleasant moments, her work is also optimistic. Her books include *The Whispering Mountain* (1968), *Night Fall* (1969), *A Touch of the Chill; Tales for Sleepless Nights* (1979), and *The Trouble with Product X* (1985).

The Treasure of Lemon Brown

Walter Dean Myers

He was an eerie sight, a bundle of rags standing at the top of the stairs, his shadow on the wall looming over him.

he dark sky, filled with angry, swirling clouds, reflected Greg Ridley's mood as he sat on the stoop of his building. His father's voice came to him again, first reading the letter the principal had sent to the house, then lecturing endlessly about his poor efforts in math.

"I had to leave school when I was thirteen," his father had said, "that's a year younger than you are now. If I'd had half the chances that you have, I'd . . . ."

Greg had sat in the small, pale green kitchen listening, knowing the lecture would end with his father saying he couldn't play ball with the Scorpions. He had asked his father the week before, and his father had said it depended on his next report card. It wasn't often the Scorpions took on new players, especially fourteen-year-olds, and this was a chance of a lifetime for Greg. He hadn't been allowed to play high-school ball, which he had really wanted to do, but playing for the Community Center team was the next best thing. Report cards were due in a week, and Greg had been hoping for the best. But the principal had ended the suspense early when she sent that letter saying Greg would probably fail math if he didn't spend more time studying.

"And you want to play *basketball?*" His father's brows knitted over deep brown eyes. "That must be some kind of a joke. Now you just get into your room and hit those books."

That had been two nights before. His father's words, like the distant thunder that now echoed through the streets of Harlem, still rumbled softly in his ears.

It was beginning to cool. Gusts of wind made bits of paper dance between the parked cars. There was a flash of nearby lightning, and soon large drops of rain splashed onto his jeans. He stood to go upstairs, thought of the lecture that probably awaited him if he did anything except shut himself in his room with his math book, and started walking down the street instead. Down the block there was an old tenement that had been abandoned for some months. Some of the guys had held an impromptu checker tournament there the week before, and Greg had noticed that the door, once boarded over, had been slightly ajar.

Pulling his collar up as high as he could, he checked for traffic and made a dash across the street. He reached the house just as another flash of lightning changed the night to day for an instant, then returned the graffiti-scarred building to the grim shadows. He vaulted over the outer stairs and pushed tentatively on the door. It was open, and he let himself in.

The inside of the building was dark except for the dim light that filtered through the dirty windows from the streetlamps. There was a room a few feet from the door, and from where he stood at the entrance, Greg could see a squarish patch of light on the floor. He entered the room, frowning at the musty smell. It was a large room that might have been someone's parlor at one time. Squinting, Greg could see an old table on its side against one wall, what looked like a pile of rags or a torn mattress in the corner, and a couch, with one side broken, in front of the window.

He went to the couch. The side that wasn't broken was comfortable enough, though a little creaky. From this spot he could see the blinking neon sign over the bodega[1] on the corner. He sat a while, watching the sign blink first green then red, allowing his mind to drift to the Scorpions, then to his father. His father had been a postal worker for all Greg's life, and was proud of it, often telling Greg how hard he had worked to pass the test. Greg had heard the story too many times to be interested now.

For a moment Greg thought he heard something that sounded like a scraping against the wall. He listened carefully, but it was gone.

Outside the wind had picked up, sending the rain against the window with a force that shook the glass in its frame. A car passed, its tires hissing over the wet street and its red tail lights glowing in the darkness.

Greg thought he heard the noise again. His stomach tightened as he held himself still and listened intently. There weren't any more scraping noises, but he was sure he had heard something in the darkness—something breathing!

He tried to figure out just where the breathing was coming from; he knew it was in the room with him. Slowly he stood, tensing. As he turned, a flash of lightning lit up the room, frightening him with its sudden brilliance. He saw nothing, just the overturned table, the pile of rags and an old newspaper on the floor. Could he have been imagining the sounds? He continued listening, but heard nothing and thought that it might have just been rats. Still, he thought, as soon

---

1. *bodega* (bō dä′gə), a neighborhood grocery store. [Spanish]

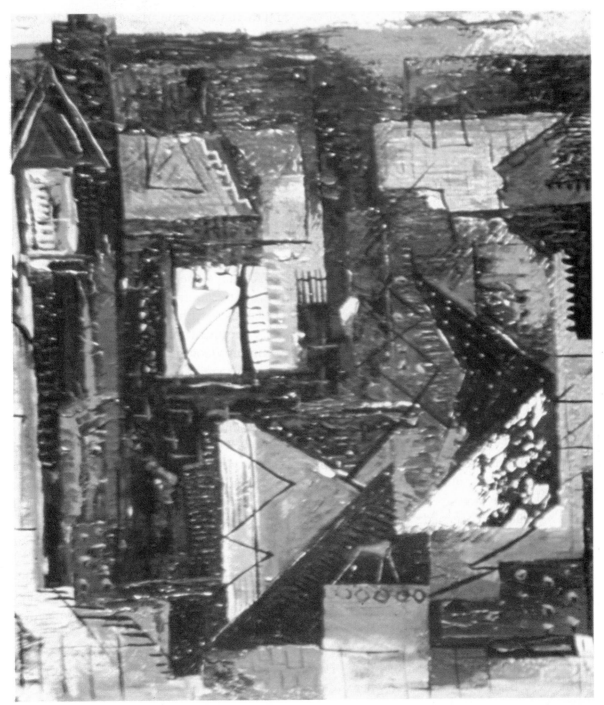

Richard Dempsey, "Cityscape," 1958
Private Collection

as the rain let up he would leave. He went to the window and was about to look out when he heard a voice behind him.

"Don't try nothin' 'cause I got a razor here sharp enough to cut a week into nine days!"

Greg, except for an involuntary tremor in his knees, stood stock still. The voice was high and brittle, like dry twigs being broken, surely not one he had ever heard before. There was a shuffling sound as the person who had been speaking moved a step closer. Greg turned, holding his breath, his eyes straining to see in the dark room.

The upper part of the figure before him was still in darkness. The lower half was in the dim rectangle of light that fell unevenly from the window. There were two feet, in cracked, dirty shoes from which rose legs that were wrapped in rags.

"Who are you?" Greg hardly recognized his own voice.

"I'm Lemon Brown," came the answer. "Who're you?"

"Greg Ridley."

"What you doing here?" The figure shuffled forward again, and Greg took a small step backward.

"It's raining," Greg said.

"I can see that," the figure said.

The person who called himself Lemon Brown peered forward, and Greg could see him clearly. He was an old man. His black, heavily wrinkled face was surrounded by a halo of crinkly white hair and whiskers that seemed to separate his head from the layers of dirty coats piled on his smallish frame. His pants were bagged to the knee, where they were met with rags that went down to the old shoes. The rags were held on with strings, and there was a rope around his middle. Greg relaxed. He had seen the man before, picking through the trash on the corner and pulling clothes out of a Salvation Army box. There was no sign of the razor that could "cut a week into nine days."

"What are you doing here?" Greg asked.

"This is where I'm staying." Lemon Brown said. "What you here for?"

"Told you it was raining out," Greg said, leaning against the back of the couch until he felt it give slightly.

"Ain't you got no home?"

"I got a home," Greg answered.

"You ain't one of them bad boys looking for my treasure, is you?" Lemon Brown cocked his head to one side and squinted one eye. "Because I told you I got me a razor."

"I'm not looking for your treasure," Greg answered, smiling. "*If* you have one."

"What you mean, *if* I have one," Lemon Brown said. "Every man got a treasure. You don't know that, you must be a fool!"

"Sure," Greg said as he sat on the sofa and put one leg over the back. "What do you have, gold coins?"

"Don't worry none about what I got," Lemon Brown said. "You know who I am?"

"You told me your name was orange or lemon or something like that."

"Lemon Brown," the old man said, pulling back his shoulders as he did so, "they used to call me Sweet Lemon Brown."

"Sweet Lemon?" Greg asked.

"Yessir. Sweet Lemon Brown. They used to say I sung the blues so sweet that if I sang at a funeral, the dead would commence to rocking with the beat. Used to travel all over Mississippi and as far as Monroe, Louisiana, and east on over to Macon, Georgia. You mean you ain't never heard of Sweet Lemon Brown?"

"Afraid not," Greg said. "What . . . what happened to you?"

"Hard times, boy. Hard times always after a poor man. One day I got tired, sat down to rest a spell and felt a tap on my shoulder. Hard times caught up with me."

"Sorry about that."

"What you doing here? How come you didn't go on home when the rain come. Rain don't bother you young folks none."

"Just didn't," Greg looked away.

"I used to have a knotty-headed boy just like you." Lemon Brown had half walked, half shuffled back to the corner and sat down against the wall. "Had them big eyes like you got. I used to call them moon eyes. Look into them moon eyes and see anything you want."

"How come you gave up singing the blues?" Greg asked.

"Didn't give it up," Lemon Brown said. "You don't give up the blues; they give you up. After a while you do good for yourself, and it ain't nothing but foolishness singing about how hard you got it. Ain't that right?"

"I guess so."

"What's that noise?" Lemon Brown asked, suddenly sitting upright.

Greg listened, and he heard a noise outside. He looked at Lemon Brown and saw the old man was pointing toward the window.

Greg went to the window and saw three men, neighborhood thugs, on the stoop. One was carrying a length of pipe. Greg looked back toward Lemon Brown, who moved quietly across the room to the window. The old

man looked out, then beckoned frantically for Greg to follow him. For a moment Greg couldn't move. Then he found himself following Lemon Brown into the hallway and up darkened stairs. Greg followed as closely as he could. They reached the top of the stairs, and Greg felt Lemon Brown's hand first lying on his shoulder, then probing down his arm until he finally took Greg's hand into his own as they crouched in the darkness.

"They's bad men," Lemon Brown whispered. His breath was warm against Greg's skin.

"Hey! Rag man!" A voice called. "We know you in here. What you got up under them rags? You got any money?"

Silence.

"We don't want to have to come in and hurt you, old man, but we don't mind if we have to."

Lemon Brown squeezed Greg's hand in his own hard, gnarled fist.

There was a banging downstairs and a light as the men entered. They banged around noisily, calling for the rag man.

"We heard you talking about your treasure," the voice was slurred. "We just want to see it, that's all."

"You sure he's here?" One voice seemed to come from the room with the sofa.

"Yeah, he stays here every night."

"There's another room over there; I'm going to take a look. You got that flashlight?"

"Yeah, here, take the pipe too."

Greg opened his mouth to quiet the sound of his breath as he sucked it in uneasily. A beam of light hit the wall a few feet opposite him, then went out.

"Ain't nobody in that room," a voice said. "You think he gone or something?"

"I don't know," came the answer. "All I know is that I heard him talking about some kind of treasure. You know they found that shopping bag lady with that money in her bags."

"Yeah. You think he's upstairs?"

"HEY, OLD MAN, ARE YOU UP THERE?"

Silence.

"Watch my back, I'm going up."

There was a footstep on the stairs, and the beam from the flashlight danced crazily along the peeling wallpaper. Greg held his breath. There was another step and a loud crashing noise as the man banged the pipe against the wooden banister. Greg could feel his temples throb as the man slowly neared them. Greg thought about the pipe, wondering what he would do when the man reached them—what he *could* do.

Then Lemon Brown released his hand and moved toward the top of the stairs. Greg looked around and saw stairs going up to the next floor. He tried waving to Lemon Brown, hoping the old man would see him in the dim light and follow him to the next floor. Maybe, Greg thought, the man wouldn't follow them up there. Suddenly, though, Lemon Brown stood at the top of the stairs, both arms raised high above his head.

"There he is!" A voice cried from below.

"Throw down your money, old man, so I won't have to bash your head in!"

Lemon Brown didn't move. Greg felt himself near panic. The steps came closer, and still Lemon Brown didn't move. He was an eerie sight, a bundle of rags standing at the top of the stairs, his shadow on the wall looming over him. Maybe, the thought came to Greg, the scene could be even eerier.

Greg wet his lips, put his hands to his mouth and tried to make a sound. Nothing came out. He swallowed hard, wet his lips once more and howled as evenly as he could.

"What's that?"

As Greg howled, the light moved away from Lemon Brown, but not before Greg saw him hurl his body down the stairs at the men who had come to take his treasure. There was a crashing noise, and then footsteps. A rush of warm air came in as the downstairs door opened, then there was only an ominous silence.

Greg stood on the landing. He listened, and after a while there was another sound on the staircase.

"Mr. Brown?" he called.

"Yeah, it's me," came the answer. "I got their flashlight."

Greg exhaled in relief as Lemon Brown made his way slowly back up the stairs.

"You O.K.?"

"Few bumps and bruises," Lemon Brown said.

"I think I'd better be going," Greg said, his breath returning to normal. "You'd better leave, too, before they come back."

"They may hang around outside for a while," Lemon Brown said, "but they ain't getting their nerve up to come in here again. Not with crazy old rag men and howling spooks. Best you stay awhile till the coast is clear. I'm heading out West tomorrow, out to East St. Louis."

"They were talking about treasures," Greg said. "You *really* have a treasure?"

"What I tell you? Didn't I tell you every man got a treasure?" Lemon Brown said. "You want to see mine?"

"If you want to show it to me," Greg shrugged.

"Let's look out the window first, see what them scoundrels be doing," Lemon Brown said.

They followed the oval beam of the flashlight into one of the rooms and looked out the window. They saw the men who had tried to take the treasure sitting on the curb near the corner. One of them had his pants leg up, looking at his knee.

"You sure you're not hurt?" Greg asked Lemon Brown.

"Nothing that ain't been hurt before," Lemon Brown said. "When you get as old as me all you say when something hurts is, 'Howdy, Mr. Pain, sees you back again.' Then when Mr. Pain see he can't worry you none, he go on mess with somebody else."

Greg smiled.

"Here, you hold this." Lemon Brown gave Greg the flashlight.

He sat on the floor near Greg and carefully untied the strings that held the rags on his right leg. When he took the rags away, Greg saw a piece of plastic. The old man carefully took off the plastic and unfolded it. He revealed some yellowed newspaper clippings and a battered harmonica.

"There it be," he said, nodding his head. "There it be."

Greg looked at the old man, saw the distant look in his eye, then turned to the clippings. They told of Sweet Lemon Brown, a blues singer and harmonica player who was appearing at different theaters in the South. One of the clippings said he had been the hit of the show, although not the headliner. All of the clippings were reviews of shows Lemon Brown had been in more than fifty years ago. Greg looked at the harmonica. It was dented badly on one side, with the reed holes on one end nearly closed.

"I used to travel around and make money for to feed my wife and Jesse—that's my boy's name. Used to feed them good, too. Then his mama died, and he stayed with his mama's sister. He growed up to be a man, and when the war come he saw fit to go off and fight in it. I didn't have nothing to give him except these things that told him who I was, and what he come from. If you know your pappy did something, you know you can do something too.

"Anyway, he went off to war, and I went off still playing and singing. 'Course by then I wasn't as much as I used to be, not without somebody to make it worth the while. You know what I mean?"

"Yeah," Greg nodded, not quite really knowing.

"I traveled around, and one time I come home, and there was this letter saying Jesse got killed in the war. Broke my heart, it truly did.

"They sent back what he had with him over there, and what it was is this old mouth fiddle and these clippings. Him carrying it around with him like that told me it meant something to him. That was my treasure, and when I give it to him he treated it just like that, a treasure. Ain't that something?"

"Yeah, I guess so," Greg said.

"You *guess* so?" Lemon Brown's voice rose an octave as he started to put his treasure back into the plastic. "Well, you got to guess 'cause you sure don't know nothing. Don't know enough to get home when it's raining."

"I guess . . . I mean, you're right."

"You O.K. for a youngster," the old man said as he tied the strings around his leg, "better than those scalawags what come here looking for my treasure. That's for sure."

"You really think that treasure of yours was worth fighting for?" Greg asked. "Against a pipe?"

"What else a man got 'cepting what he can pass on to his son, or his daughter, if she be his oldest?" Lemon Brown said. "For a big-headed boy you sure do ask the foolishest questions."

Lemon Brown got up after patting his rags in place and looked out the window again.

"Looks like they're gone. You get on out of here and get yourself home. I'll be watching from the window so you'll be all right."

Lemon Brown went down the stairs behind Greg. When they reached the front door the old man looked out first, saw the street was clear and told Greg to scoot on home.

"You sure you'll be O.K.?" Greg asked.

"Now didn't I tell you I was going to East St. Louis in the morning?" Lemon Brown asked. "Don't that sound O.K. to you?"

"Sure it does," Greg said. "Sure it does. And you take care of that treasure of yours."

"That I'll do," Lemon said, the wrinkles about his eyes suggesting a smile. "That I'll do."

The night had warmed and the rain had stopped, leaving puddles at the curbs. Greg didn't even want to think how late it was. He thought ahead of what his father would say and wondered if he should tell him about Lemon Brown. He thought about it until he reached his stoop, and decided against it. Lemon Brown would be O.K., Greg thought, with his memories and his treasure.

Greg pushed the button over the bell marked Ridley, thought of the lecture he knew his father would give him, and smiled.

THINK AND DISCUSS
Understanding
1. Why does Greg leave home?
2. Where does Greg go to get away from home?
3. Why do the three thugs come after Lemon Brown?
4. How do Greg and Lemon get rid of the thugs?
5. What is Lemon Brown's treasure?

Analyzing
6. When Greg asks about Lemon Brown's treasure, Lemon replies, "Every man got a treasure. You don't know that, you must be a fool!" What does he mean?
7. Why does Lemon consider his treasure a treasure?
8. At the beginning of the story, Greg is tired of his father's lectures. At the end, he smiles when he thinks of the lecture

he will receive when he gets home. What has caused this change?

Extending

9. Write a definition for the word *treasure* as it is used in this story.

READING LITERATURE SKILLFULLY
Cause-and-Effect Relationships

An **effect** is a result or an outcome. A **cause** is the event that produces a particular effect. Recognizing cause-and-effect relationships can help you follow the plot of a story. For each pair of items, tell which is a cause and which an effect.

1. (a) The bad men hear about Lemon's treasure.
   (b) The bad men come to rob Lemon.
2. (a) Greg's father will not allow him to play ball with the Scorpions.
   (b) Greg meets Lemon Brown.
3. (a) Greg howls from the upper floors of the house.
   (b) One of the thugs follows Lemon Brown and Greg up the stairs.

4. (a) Lemon's son goes to war.
   (b) Lemon gives his son the clippings and the harmonica.

COMPOSITION
Writing a Description

Do you have something that is important to you for personal or sentimental reasons, but that others might not consider important at all? Describe your treasure in such a way that your readers will wish they had one too.

Writing a Dialogue

Write a one- to two-page dialogue between Greg and his father after Greg gets home on the night of the story. Consider the emotions each character will show when they begin to talk. (Greg is glad to go home and get a lecture. What will his father be feeling?) Then consider how each character's emotions may change as the dialogue continues. Read "Writing Dialogue" in the Writer's Handbook before you begin your composition.

BIOGRAPHY

Walter Dean Myers
1937–

Claiming that life is "the best thing I've ever known," Walter Dean Myers has written of life in short stories collected in the anthologies *We Must See: Young Black Storytellers* and *We Be Word Sorcerers, 25 Stories by Black Americans.* He has also written numerous books for young people, including *Mojo and the Russians* and *fast sam, cool clyde, and stuff.* In 1968, his book *Where Does the Day Go?* won the Interracial Council Award for Children's Books.

Review PLOT in the Handbook of Literary Terms, page 677

The Inspiration of Mr. Budd

Dorothy Sayers

"Are you prepared to die?" The question threw Mr. Budd off balance, so alarmingly did it chime in with his thoughts about murder.

£500 REWARD

The *Evening Messenger*, ever anxious to further the ends of justice, has decided to offer the above reward to any person who shall give information leading to the arrest of the man, William Strickland, alias Bolton, who is wanted by the police in connection with the murder of the late Emma Strickland at 59 Acacia Crescent, Manchester.

DESCRIPTION OF THE WANTED MAN

The following is the official description of William Strickland: Age 43; height 6 ft. 1 or 2; complexion rather dark; hair silver-gray and abundant, may dye same; full gray mustache and beard, may now be clean-shaven; eyes light gray, rather close-set; hawk nose; teeth strong and white, displays them somewhat prominently when laughing, left upper eye-tooth stopped with gold; left thumbnail disfigured by a recent blow.

Speaks in rather loud voice; quick, decisive manner. Good address.

May be dressed in a gray or dark blue lounge suit, with stand-up collar (size 15) and soft felt hat.

Absconded 5th inst., and may have left, or will endeavor to leave, the country.

Mr. Budd read the description through carefully once again and sighed. It was in the highest degree unlikely that William Strickland should choose his small and unsuccessful saloon, out of all the barbers' shops in London, for a haircut or a shave, still less for "dyeing same"; even if he was in London, which Mr. Budd saw no reason to suppose.

Three weeks had gone by since the murder, and the odds were a hundred to one that William Strickland had already left a country too eager with its offer of free hospitality. Nevertheless, Mr. Budd committed the description, as well as he could, to memory. It was a chance—just as the Great Crossword Tournament had been a chance, just as the Ninth Rainbow Ballot had been a chance, and the Bunko Poster Ballot, and the Monster Treasure Hunt organized by the *Evening Clarion*. Any headline with money in it could attract Mr. Budd's fascinated eye in these lean days, whether it offered a choice between fifty thousand pounds down and ten pounds a week for life, or merely a modest hundred or so.

It may seem strange, in an age of shingling and bingling,[1] Mr. Budd should look enviously at Complete Lists of Prizewinners. Had not the hairdresser across the way, who only last year had eked out his mean ninepences with the yet meaner profits on cheap cigarettes and comic papers, lately bought out the greengrocer next door, and engaged a staff of exquisitely coiffed assistants to adorn his new "Ladies' Hairdressing Department" with its purple and orange curtains, its two rows of gleaming marble basins, and an apparatus like a Victorian chandelier for permanent waving?

Had he not installed a large electric sign surrounded by a scarlet border that ran round and round perpetually, like a kitten chasing its own tail? Was it not his sandwich-man[2] even now patrolling the pavement with a luminous announcement of Treatment and Prices? And was there not at this moment an endless stream of young ladies hastening into those heavily-perfumed parlors in the desperate hope of somehow getting a shampoo and a wave "squeezed in" before closing-time?

If the reception clerk shook a regretful head, they did not think of crossing the road to Mr. Budd's dimly lighted window. They made an appointment for days ahead and waited patiently, anxiously fingering the bristly growth at the back of the neck and the straggly bits behind the ears that so soon got out of hand.

Day after day Mr. Budd watched them flit in and out of the rival establishment, willing, praying even, in a vague, ill-directed manner, that some of them would come over to him; but they never did.

And yet Mr. Budd knew himself to be the finer artist. He had seen shingles turned out from over the way that he would never have countenanced, let alone charged three shillings and sixpence for. Shingles with an ugly hard line at the nape, shingles which were a slander on the shape of a good head or brutally emphasized the weak points of an ugly one; hurried, conscienceless shingles, botched work, handed over on a crowded afternoon to a girl who had only served a three years' apprenticeship and to whom the final mysteries of "tapering" were a sealed book.

And then there was the "tinting"—his own pet subject, which he had studied *con amore*[3]—if only those too-sprightly matrons would come to him! He would gently dissuade them from that dreadful mahogany dye that made them look like metallic robots—he

---

1. *shingling and bingling*, methods of cutting women's hair. A shingle is a tapered haircut; a bingle is a somewhat shorter cut.
2. *sandwich-man*, a man carrying two advertising boards hung from his shoulders, one in front and one behind.
3. *con amore* (kōn ä mōr′ä), an Italian expression meaning "with love, with tenderness."

Isabel Bishop, "On the Street," 1934
Whitney Museum of American Art

would warn them against that widely advertised preparation which was so incalculable in its effects; he would use the cunning skill which long experience had matured in him—tint them with the infinitely delicate art which conceals itself.

Yet nobody came to Mr. Budd but the navvies[4] and the young loungers and the men who plied their trade beneath the naphtha flares[5] in Wilton Street.

And why could not Mr. Budd also have burst out into marble and electricity and

swum to fortune on the rising tide?

The reason is very distressing, and, as it fortunately has no bearing on the story, shall be told with merciful brevity.

Mr. Budd had a younger brother, Richard, whom he had promised his mother to look after. In happier days Mr. Budd had owned a flourishing business in their native town of

---

4. *navvies* (nav′ēz), unskilled laborers, especially those who work on canals, railways, etc.
5. *naphtha-flares*, street lamps fueled by naphtha (naf′thə), a flammable liquid.

Northampton, and Richard had been a bank clerk. Richard had got into bad ways (poor Mr. Budd blamed himself dreadfully for this). There had been a sad affair with a girl, and a horrid series of affairs with bookmakers, and then Richard had tried to mend bad with worse by taking money from the bank. You need to be very much more skillful than Richard to juggle successfully with bank ledgers.

The bank manager was a hard man of the old school: he prosecuted. Mr. Budd paid the bank and the bookmakers, and saw the girl through her trouble while Richard was in prison, and paid for their fares to Australia when he came out, and gave them something to start life on.

But it took all the profits of the hairdressing business, and he couldn't face all the people in Northampton any more, who had known him all his life. So he had run to vast London, the refuge of all who shrink from the eyes of their neighbors, and bought this little shop in Pimlico, which had done fairly well, until the new fashion which did so much for other hairdressing businesses killed it for lack of capital.

That is why Mr. Budd's eye was so painfully fascinated by headlines with money in them.

He put the newspaper down, and as he did so, caught sight of his own reflection in the glass and smiled, for he was not without a sense of humor. He did not look quite the man to catch a brutal murderer single-handed. He was well on in the middle forties— a trifle paunchy, with fluffy pale hair, getting a trifle thin on top (partly hereditary, partly worry, that was), five feet six at most, and soft-handed, as a hairdresser must be.

Even razor in hand, he would hardly be a match for William Strickland, height six feet one or two, who had so ferociously battered his old aunt to death, so butcherly hacked her limb from limb, so horribly disposed of her remains in the copper.[6] Shaking his head dubiously, Mr. Budd advanced to the door, to cast a forlorn eye at the busy establishment over the way, and nearly ran into a bulky customer who dived in rather precipitately.

"I beg your pardon, sir," murmured Mr. Budd, fearful of alienating ninepence; "just stepping out for a breath of fresh air, sir. Shave, sir?"

The large man tore off his overcoat without waiting for Mr. Budd's obsequious hands.

"Are you prepared to die?" he demanded abruptly.

The question chimed in so alarmingly with Mr. Budd's thoughts about murder that for a moment it quite threw him off his professional balance.

"I beg your pardon, sir," he stammered, and in the same moment decided that the man must be a preacher of some kind. He looked rather like it, with his odd, light eyes, his bush of fiery hair and short, jutting chin-beard. Perhaps he even wanted a subscription. That would be hard, when Mr. Budd had already set him down as ninepence, or, with tip, possibly even a shilling.

"Do you do dyeing?" said the man impatiently.

"Oh!" said Mr. Budd, relieved, "yes, sir, certainly, sir."

---

6. *copper,* a large kettle used for cooking or for boiling laundry.

A stroke of luck, this. Dyeing meant quite a big sum—his mind soared to seven-and-sixpence.

"Good," said the man, sitting down and allowing Mr. Budd to put an apron about his neck. (He was safely gathered in now—he could hardly dart away down the street with a couple of yards of white cotton flapping from his shoulders.)

"Fact is," said the man, "my young lady doesn't like red hair. She says it's conspicuous. The other young ladies in her firm make jokes about it. So, as she's a good bit younger than I am, you see, I like to oblige her, and I was thinking perhaps it could be changed into something quieter, what? Dark brown, now—that's the color she has a fancy for. What do you say?"

It occurred to Mr. Budd that the young ladies might consider this abrupt change of coat even funnier than the original color, but in the interests of business he agreed that dark brown would be very becoming and a great deal less noticeable than red. Besides, very likely there was no young lady. A woman, he knew, will say frankly that she wants different colored hair for a change, or just to try, or because she fancies it would suit her, but if a man is going to do a silly thing he prefers, if possible, to shuffle the responsibility on to someone else.

"Very well, then," said the customer, "go ahead. And I'm afraid the beard will have to go. My young lady doesn't like beards."

"A great many young ladies don't, sir," said Mr. Budd. "They're not so fashionable nowadays as they used to be. It's very fortunate that you can stand a clean shave very well, sir. You have just the chin for it."

"Do you think so?" said the man, examining himself a little anxiously. "I'm glad to hear it."

"Will you have the mustache off as well, sir?"

"Well, no—no, I think I'll stick to that as long as I'm allowed to, what?" He laughed loudly, and Mr. Budd approvingly noted well-kept teeth and a gold stopping. The customer was obviously ready to spend money on his personal appearance.

In fancy, Mr. Budd saw this well-off and gentlemanly customer advising all his friends to visit "his man"—"wonderful fellow—wonderful—round at the back of Victoria Station—you'd never find it by yourself—only a little place, but he knows what he's about—I'll write it down for you." It was imperative that there should be no fiasco. Hair-dyes were awkward things—there had been a case in the paper lately.

"I see you have been using a tint before, sir," said Mr. Budd with respect. "Could you tell me——?"

"Eh?" said the man. "Oh, yes—well, fact is, as I said, my fiancée's a good bit younger than I am. As I expect you can see I began to go gray early—my father was just the same—all our family—so I had it touched up—streaky bits restored, you see. But she doesn't take to the color, so I thought, if I have to dye it at all, why not a color she does fancy while we're about it, what?"

It is a common jest among the unthinking that hairdressers are garrulous. This is their wisdom. The hairdresser hears many secrets and very many lies. In his discretion he occupies his unruly tongue with the weather and the political situation, lest, restless with inaction, it plunge unbridled into a mad career of inconvenient candor.

Lightly holding forth upon the caprices of the feminine mind, Mr. Budd subjected his customer's locks to the scrutiny of trained eye and fingers. Never—never in the process of Nature could hair of that texture and quality have been red. It was naturally black hair, prematurely turned, as some black hair will turn, to a silvery gray. However that was none of his business. He elicited the information he really needed—the name of the dye formerly used, and noted that he would have to be careful. Some dyes do not mix kindly with other dyes.

Chatting pleasantly, Mr. Budd lathered his customer, removed the offending beard, and executed a vigorous shampoo, preliminary to the dyeing process. As he wielded the roaring drier, he reviewed Wimbledon, the Silk-tax and the Summer Time Bill—at that moment threatened with sudden strangulation—and passed naturally on to the Manchester murder.

"The police seem to have given it up as a bad job," said the man.

"Perhaps the reward will liven things up a bit," said Mr. Budd, the thought being naturally uppermost in his mind.

"Oh, there's a reward, is there? I hadn't seen that."

"It's in tonight's paper, sir. Maybe you'd like to have a look at it."

"Thanks, I should."

Mr. Budd left the drier to blow the fiery bush of air at its own wild will for a moment, while he fetched the *Evening Messenger*. The stranger read the paragraph carefully and Mr. Budd, watching him in the glass, after the disquieting manner of his craft, saw him suddenly draw back his left hand, which was resting carelessly on the arm of the chair, and thrust it under the apron.

But not before Mr. Budd had seen it. Not before he had taken conscious note of the horny, misshapen thumbnail. Many people had such an ugly mark, Mr. Budd told himself hurriedly—there was his friend, Bert Webber, who had sliced the top of his thumb right off in a motorcycle chain—his nail looked very much like that. Mr. Budd thought and thought.

The man glanced up, and the eyes of his reflection became fixed on Mr. Budd's face with a penetrating scrutiny—a horrid warning that the real eyes were steadfastly interrogating the reflection of Mr. Budd.

"Not but what," said Mr. Budd, "the man is safe out of the country, I reckon. They've put it off too late."

The man laughed in a pleasant, conversational way.

"I reckon they have," he said. Mr. Budd wondered whether many men with smashed left thumbs showed a gold left upper eyetooth. Probably there were hundreds of people like that going about the country. Likewise with silver-gray hair ("may dye same") and aged about forty-three. Undoubtedly.

Mr. Budd folded up the drier and turned off the gas. Mechanically he took up a comb and drew it through the hair that never, never in the process of Nature had been that fiery red.

There came back to him, with an accuracy which quite unnerved him, the exact number and extent of the brutal wounds inflicted upon the Manchester victim—an elderly lady, rather stout, she had been. Glaring through the door, Mr. Budd noticed that his rival over the way had closed. The streets were full of people. How easy it would be—

"Be as quick as you can, won't you?" said the man, a little impatiently, but pleasantly enough. "It's getting late. I'm afraid it will keep you overtime."

"Not at all, sir," said Mr. Budd. "It's of no consequence—not the least."

No—if he tried to bolt out of the door, his terrible customer would leap upon him, drag him back, throttle his cries, and then with one frightful blow like the one he had smashed in his aunt's skull with—

Yet surely Mr. Budd was in a position of advantage. A decided man would do it. He would be out in the street before the customer could disentangle himself from the chair. Mr. Budd began to edge round towards the door.

"What's the matter?" said the customer.

"Just stepping out to look at the time, sir," said Mr. Budd, meekly pausing. (Yet he might have done it then, if he only had the courage to make the first swift step that would give the game away.)

"It's five-and-twenty past eight," said the man, "by tonight's broadcast. I'll pay extra for the overtime."

"Not on any account," said Mr. Budd. Too late now, he couldn't make another effort. He vividly saw himself tripping on the threshold—falling—the terrible fist lifted to smash him into a pulp. Or, perhaps, under the familiar white apron, the disfigured hand was actually clutching a pistol.

Mr. Budd retreated to the back of the shop, collecting his materials. If only he had been quicker—more like a detective in a book—he would have observed that thumbnail, that tooth, put two and two together, and run out to give the alarm while the man's beard was wet and soapy and his face buried in the towel. Or he could have dabbed lather in his eyes—nobody could possibly commit a murder or even run away down the street with his eyes full of soap.

Even now—Mr. Budd took down a bottle, shook his head and put it back on the shelf—even now, was it really too late? Why could he not take a bold course? He had only to open a razor, go quietly up behind the unsuspecting man and say in a firm, loud, convincing voice: "William Strickland, put up your hands. Your life is at my mercy. Stand up till I take your gun away. Now walk straight out to the nearest policeman." Surely, in his position, that was what Sherlock Holmes would do.

But as Mr. Budd returned with a little trayful of requirements, it was borne in upon him that he was not of the stuff of which great man-hunters are made. For he could not seriously see that attempt "coming off." Because if he held the razor to the man's throat and said: "Put up your hands," the man would probably merely catch him by the wrists and take the razor away. And greatly as Mr. Budd feared his customer unarmed, he felt it would be a perfect crescendo of madness to put a razor in his hands.

Or supposing he said, "Put up your hands," and the man just said, "I won't." What was he to do next? To cut his throat then and there would be murder, even if Mr. Budd could possibly have brought himself to do such a thing. They could not remain there, fixed in one position, till the boy came to do out the shop in the morning.

Perhaps the policeman would notice the light on and the door unfastened and come in? The he would say, "I congratulate you, Mr. Budd, on having captured a very dangerous criminal." But supposing the policeman didn't happen to notice—and Mr. Budd would have to stand all the time, and he would get exhausted and his attention would relax, and then—

After all, Mr. Budd wasn't called upon to arrest the man himself. "Information leading to arrest"—those were the words. He would be able to tell them the wanted man had been there, that he would now have dark-brown hair and mustache and no beard. He might even shadow him when he left—he might—

It was at this moment that the great Inspiration came to Mr. Budd.

As he fetched a bottle from the glass-fronted case he remembered with odd vividness, an old-fashioned wooden paper-knife that had belonged to his mother. Between sprigs of blue forget-me-not, hand-painted, it bore the inscription "Knowledge Is Power."

A strange freedom and confidence were vouchsafed to Mr. Budd; his mind was alert; he removed the razors with an easy, natural movement, and made nonchalant conversation as he skillfully applied the dark brown tint.

The streets were less crowded when Mr. Budd let his customer out. He watched the tall figure cross Grosvenor Place and climb on to a 24 bus.

"But that was only his artfulness," said Mr. Budd, as he put on his hat and coat and extinguished the lights carefully, "he'll take another at Victoria, like as not, and be making tracks from Charing Cross or Waterloo."[7]

He closed the shop door, shook it, as was his wont, to make sure that the lock had caught properly, and in his turn made his way, by means of a 24, to the top of Whitehall.

The policeman was a little condescending at first when Mr. Budd demanded to see "somebody very high up," but finding the little barber insist so earnestly that he had news of the Manchester murderer, and that there wasn't any time to lose, he consented to pass him through.

Mr. Budd was interviewed first by an important-looking inspector in uniform, who listened very politely to his story and made him repeat very carefully about the gold tooth and the thumbnail and the hair which had been black before it was gray or red and now dark brown.

The inspector then touched a bell, and said, "Perkins, I think Sir Andrew would like to see this gentleman at once," and he was taken to another room where sat a very shrewd, genial gentleman in mufti,[8] who heard him with even greater attention, and called in another inspector to listen too, and to take down a very exact description of— yes, surely the undoubted William Strickland as he now appeared.

"But there's one thing more," said Mr. Budd—"and I'm sure to goodness," he added, "I hope, sir, it is the right man, because if it isn't it'll be the ruin of me—"

---

7. **Charing Cross or Waterloo,** major railroad stations in London.
8. **mufti** (muf′tē), ordinary "civilian" clothes. Sir Andrew was not in uniform.

He crushed his soft hat into an agitated ball as he leaned across the table, breathlessly uttering the story of his great betrayal.

"Tzee—z-z-z—tzee—tzee—z-z—tzee—z-z——"

"Dzoo—dz-dz-dz—dzoo—dz—dzoo—dzoo—dz."

"Tzee—z—z."

The fingers of the wireless operator on the packet *Miranda* bound for Ostend[9] moved swiftly as they jotted down the messages of the buzzing wireless mosquito-swarms.

One of them made him laugh.

"The Old Man'd better have this, I suppose," he said.

The Old Man scratched his head when he read and rang a little bell for the steward. The steward ran down to the little round office where the purser was counting his money and checking it before he locked it away for the night. On receiving the Old Man's message, the purser put the money quickly into the safe, picked up the passenger list and departed aft. There was a short consultation, and the bell was rung again—this time to summon the head steward.

"Tzee—z-z—tzeez-z-z—tzee—tzee—z—tzee."

All down the Channel, all over the North Sea, up to the Mersey Docks, out into the Atlantic soared the busy mosquito-swarms. In ship after ship the wireless operator sent his message to the captain, the captain sent for the purser, the purser sent for the head steward and the head steward called his staff about him. Huge liners, little packets, destroyers, sumptuous private yachts—every floating thing that carried aerials—every port in England, France, Holland, Germany, Denmark, Norway, every police center that could interpret the mosquito message, heard, between laughter and excitement, the tale of Mr. Budd's betrayal. Two Boy Scouts at Croydon, practicing their Morse with a home-made valve set,[10] decoded it laboriously into an exercise book.

"Cripes," said Jim to George, "what a joke! D'you think they'll get the beggar?"

The *Miranda* docked at Ostend at 7 A.M. A man burst hurriedly into the cabin where the wireless operator was just taking off his headphones.

"Here!" he cried; "this is to go. There's something up and the Old Man's sent over for the police. The Consul's coming on board."

The wireless operator groaned, and switched on his valves.

"Tzee—z—tzee——" a message to the English police.

"Man on board answering to description. Ticket booked name of Watson. Has locked himself in cabin and refuses to come out. Insists on having hairdresser sent out to him. Have communicated Ostend police. Await instructions."

The Old Man with sharp words and authoritative gestures cleared a way through the excited little knot of people gathered about First Class Cabin No. 36. Several passengers had got wind of "something up." Magnificently he herded them away to the gangway

---

9. *wireless . . . Ostend,* the wireless telegraph operator on the *Miranda,* a boat carrying mail, passengers, goods, etc., to Ostend (os tend'), a seaport in northwest Belgium.

10. *Morse . . . valve set.* Morse code is a system in which letters, etc., are represented by dots and dashes or short and long sounds. A valve set is a wireless telegraph set that uses vacuum tubes.

with their bags and suitcases. Sternly he bade the stewards and the boy, who stood gaping with his hands full of breakfast dishes, to stand away from the door. Terribly he commanded them to hold their tongues. Four or five sailors stood watchfully at his side. In the restored silence, the passenger in No. 36 could be heard pacing up and down the narrow cabin, moving things, clattering, splashing water.

Presently came steps overhead. Somebody arrived, with a message. The Old Man nodded. Six pairs of Belgian police boots came tip-toeing down the companion. The Old Man glanced at the official paper held out to him and nodded again.

"Ready?"

"Yes."

The Old Man knocked at the door of No. 36.

"Who is it?" cried a harsh, sharp voice.

"The barber is here, sir, that you sent for."

"Ah!" There was relief in the tone. "Send him in alone if you please. I—I have had an accident."

"Yes, sir."

At the sound of the bolt being cautiously withdrawn, the Old Man stepped forward. The door opened a chink, and was slammed to again, but the Old Man's boot was firmly wedged against the jamb. The policemen surged forward. There was a yelp and a shot which smashed harmlessly through the window of the first-class saloon, and the passenger was brought out.

"Strike me pink!" shrieked the boy, "strike me pink if he ain't gone green in the night!"

Green!

Not for nothing had Mr. Budd studied the intricate mutual reactions of chemical dyes. In the pride of his knowledge he had set a mark on his man, to mark him out from the billions of this overpopulated world. Was there a port in all Christendom where a murderer might slip away, with every hair on him green as a parrot—green mustache, green eyebrows, and that thick, springing shock of hair, vivid, flaring midsummer green?

Mr. Budd got his five hundred pounds. The *Evening Messenger* published the full story of his great betrayal. He trembled, fearing this sinister fame. Surely no one would ever come to him again.

On the next morning an enormous blue limousine rolled up to his door, to the immense admiration of Wilton Street. A lady, magnificent in musquash[11] and diamonds, swept into the saloon.

"You are Mr. Budd, aren't you?" she cried. "The great Mr. Budd? Isn't it too wonderful? And now, dear Mr. Budd, you must do me a favor. You must dye my hair green, at once. Now. I want to be able to say I'm the very first to be done by you. I'm the Duchess of Winchester, and that awful Melcaster woman is chasing me down the street—the cat!"

If you want it done, I can give you the number of Mr. Budd's parlors in Bond Street.[12] But I understand it is a terribly expensive process.

---

11. *musquash* (mus'kwosh), a coat made of the fur of muskrats.

12. *Bond Street.* Mr. Budd's move from his Pimlico shop to the very fashionable Bond Street indicates the change in his fortunes and how much he has come up in the world.

THINK AND DISCUSS

Understanding

1. Describe Mr. Budd's circumstances at the beginning of the story and why he is so "painfully fascinated" by any offer of a reward.
2. What reason does the man give Mr. Budd for wanting his hair colored?
3. Why doesn't Mr. Budd try to catch the man before he leaves the shop?
4. Does Mr. Budd collect the reward?

Analyzing

5. Mr. Budd considers himself a "fine artist" in his profession. He decides, however, that he is not the sort to "catch a brutal murderer singlehanded." Do the events of the story bear out either of these opinions? Explain.
6. "The hairdresser hears many secrets and very many lies," states the narrator. Which of the customer's comments does Mr. Budd think may be lies? Which comment is Mr. Budd convinced is a lie?
7. At what point in the story did you realize the nature of Mr. Budd's "inspiration"? What details and hints throughout the story prepare readers for this outcome?
8. In what sense does Mr. Budd "betray" his profession?
9. What does he fear after he gets the reward?

10. What happens that is the opposite of what he expects?

Extending

11. Mr. Budd recalls the old inscription "Knowledge Is Power." Would it make a good title for this story?

REVIEWING: Plot HT

See Handbook of Literary Terms, p. 677.

Plot is a series of events selected by an author to present and bring about the resolution of an **internal** or **external conflict.**

1. What conflicts does Mr. Budd experience as he reads the newspaper?
2. What internal conflict does he undergo while working on the customer?
3. The point at which Mr. Budd starts to take a decisive action to end this conflict is one climax of the story. Locate the paragraphs in which he does so. What causes Mr. Budd finally to act?
4. Trace the events from the time Strickland leaves until he is arrested. What external conflict is there in the story?
5. What events come after the resolution of all conflicts and form the conclusion?

VOCABULARY

Dictionary

A dictionary contains many kinds of information besides definitions. Use your Glossary to answer these questions.

1. Which definition of *capital* best fits the context (page 35, column 1, paragraph 2) in which it appears?

2. The entry word *mean*[1] has a number, telling you to look also at *mean*[2] and *mean*[3]. In which entry do you find a definition that fits its context on page 33, column 1, paragraph 1?

3. Pronunciations are given in parentheses after an entry word. The pronunciation key at the top of the page tells how to pronounce the sound symbols. What three words from the key represent the vowel sounds in *fiasco?*

4. When more than one syllable in a word is accented, the primary accent mark (′) indicates the most stress or emphasis, while the secondary accent (′) indicates lesser stress. Which syllable of *authoritative* receives the primary stress? Which receives secondary stress?

5. What verb is *borne* a form of?

6. What part of a *shilling* is ninepence?

7. A word's origin is often explained in brackets at the end of an entry. From what language does *sinister* come? What is the original meaning in that language?

8. What definition of *saloon* best fits the context (page 32, column 2, paragraph 4)?

9. *Dubiously* does not have an entry of its own, but it is included as a run-on entry at the end of another entry. Under what entry word do you find *dubiously?*

10. Under what entry do you find *artfulness?* Copy the context sentence (page 39, column 1, paragraph 7), substituting the definition. Change words in the context sentence or in the definition in order to make it read smoothly.

THINKING SKILLS
Classifying

To classify things is to arrange them into categories according to some system. For example, all conflict can be classified as either internal or external.

All the important events in this story can be classified as either (a) events brought about by chance or (b) events caused by Mr. Budd. Classify all important events in the story.

COMPOSITION
Telling What Happened

Imagine that you are Mr. Budd. You want to tell your brother and his family in Australia about your adventure. Write a letter in which you tell about the event. Then tell what, if anything, you learned from it. Keep in mind that because you are writing a letter, your first and last paragraphs will not be the same as they would be if you were writing a report. See "Writing as a Story Character" in the Writer's Handbook before you begin your composition.

Writing Advertisements

Pretend Mr. Budd has hired you to write advertisements for his new beauty shop. Write four advertisements to be run in a London newspaper. Review the story to be sure you use the correct terms. You may illustrate your ads if you wish.

BIOGRAPHY

Dorothy Sayers
1893–1957

One of the first women ever to receive a degree from Oxford University in England, Dorothy Sayers is best known as a writer of mysteries. Her detective novels are noteworthy not only for their literary style but for their exacting use of background research and for their well-developed characters. In one book, *Murder Must Advertise,* Sayers used her own experiences as copywriter for an advertising agency to provide this background. In her later writings, she abandoned fiction in favor of religious and scholarly topics.

Comment

Hair of Gold—and Other Colors

Men and women have been tinting their hair from earliest times. Gold dust was used in many different countries. Powders such as starch, tinted white, yellow, and red were widely used. In ancient Greece, some women dyed their hair fashionably blue.

In ancient Rome, people used a lead comb dipped in vinegar to deposit lead salts on the hair that would gradually darken it. In 15th century Italy, both men and women tried to achieve blond hair by using either bleach or saffron (an orange-yellow color, also used in cooking, made from dried flowers), or dye made from onion skins. In Elizabethan England hair was dusted with powder or flour in colors like iris, violet, or white.

For centuries, only natural ingredients were used for coloring, such as powders made from ground minerals or vegetable dyes made from herbs, berries, and roots. One of the earliest dyes known, for example, is henna, a reddish-brown dye made from the leaves of a thorny shrub of Asia and Africa. Henna is still in wide use today.

Then in the late 1800s, it was discovered that hydrogen peroxide will take the color out of hair, turning it a strawlike yellow that can then be dyed any other color. This discovery was followed by a number of other, more sophisticated dyes created not in nature, but in chemical laboratories. It took researchers some time to learn about the ways different chemicals react in combination. The wrong combinations often produced severe effects—from allergic skin rashes to loss of hair to strange colors like the bright green with which Mr. Budd catches his murderer.

Writer's Craft

Be Specific

Good writers use specifics, individual details and particular pieces of information, to capture their readers' attention, to get them involved, and to hold their interest. They use specific words instead of generalities: "mahogany-brown penny loafers" instead of *shoes;* "a 1972 Volvo" instead of *an old foreign car;* "shouts and screams" instead of *a lot of noise;* "a two-foot Northern Pike" instead of *a big fish.*

In "The Inspiration of Mr. Budd," the ship's captain does not *ask* the onlookers to *move, tell* the stewards and the boy to *get away* from *in front of* the door or *tell* them to be *quiet.* Instead

> magnificently he herded them away to the gangway with their bags and suitcases. Sternly he bade the stewards and the boy, who stood gaping with his hands full of breakfast dishes, to stand away from the door. Terribly he commanded them to hold their tongues.

Nor are we simply told that Mr. Budd had *colored the man's hair bright green.* The man came out of the cabin with

> every hair on him green as a parrot—green mustache, green eyebrows, and that thick, springing shock of hair, vivid, flaring mid-summer green.

Good writers also use specifics to support generalities. Thus, in "The Moustache," after telling us that an old woman's hands are fragile—a word that labels but does not create a definite picture—Robert Cormier writes specifics that make us see and feel those frail hands.

> I took her hands in mine. They were fragile. I could actually feel her bones, and it seemed as if they would break if I pressed too hard. Her skin was smooth, almost slippery, as if the years had worn away all the roughness the way the wind wears away the surfaces of stones.

Similarly, after telling us that Lemon Brown is old, Walter Dean Myers gives specifics:

> His black, heavily wrinkled face was surrounded by a halo of crinkly white hair and whiskers that seemed to separate his head from the layers of dirty coats piled on his smallish frame.

An article on writer's craft appears in each unit of this book. Each article covers a different technique used by good writers.

As you study this book, you might keep a reading/writing log. In it, you record examples from your reading of the writing technique discussed in "The Writer's Craft." Reviewing your log before you write will help you use these techniques to improve your composition. Suggestions about what to record are found in some Composition assignments in each unit.

When you read, look for specifics.
When you write, use specifics.

See CHARACTERIZATION in the Handbook of Literary Terms, page 659

Paw-Paw

Laurence Yep

Casey Young is twelve years old. Her mother is dead; her father is in the hospital after an accident. She has spent an uncomfortable time with the family of her Uncle Phil and is now being taken to live with her grandmother in San Francisco's Chinatown.

t was like we'd gone through an invisible wall into another world. There was a different kind of air in Chinatown, lighter and brighter. I mean, on the north side there were the American bars and joints; on the west, the mansions and hotels of Nob Hill; and on the other two sides were the tall skyscrapers where insurance men or lawyers spent the day. And they were pushing all the sunshine and all the buildings of Chinatown together—like someone had taken several square miles of buildings and squeezed it until people and homes were compressed into a tiny little half of a square mile. I didn't know what to make of the buildings either. They were mostly three- or four-story stone buildings but some had fancy balconies, and others had decorations on them like curved tile roofs—one building had bright yellow balconies decorated with shiny, glazed purple dolphins—and there was a jumble of neon signs, dark now in the daytime, jammed all together. Most of the buildings, though, had some color to them—bright reds and rich golds with some green thrown in.

But it was the people there that got me. I don't think I'd ever seen so many Chinese in my life before this. Some were a rich, dark tan while others were as pale as Caucasians. Some were short with round faces and wide, full-lipped mouths and noses squashed flat, and others were tall with thin faces and high cheekbones that made their eyes look like the slits in a mask. Some were dressed in regular

American style while others wore padded silk jackets. All of them crowding into one tiny little patch of San Francisco.

Funny, but I felt embarrassed. Up until then I had never thought about skin colors because in the different places where we had lived, there were just poor people in all different colors. But now all of a sudden I saw all these funny brown people running around, a lot of them gabbling away at one another. I started to roll up the car window to try to shut out the sound and I noticed that my hand on the window handle was colored a honey kind of tan like some of the people outside. I took my hand off the handle and stared at it.

"What's the matter now?" Uncle Phil asked. We'd gotten caught in a momentary traffic snarl. I turned to see that Phil's face was brown as my hand. Phil adjusted his tie uneasily and growled, "What're you looking at?"

I looked ahead, keeping my eyes on the glove compartment. My father and I had never talked much about stuff like this. I knew more about race horses than I knew about myself—I mean myself as a Chinese. I looked at my hands again, thinking they couldn't be my hands, and then I closed my eyes and felt their outline, noticing the tiny fold of flesh at the corners. Maybe it was because I thought of myself as an American and all Americans were supposed to be white like on TV or in books or in movies, but now I felt like some mad scientist had switched bodies on me like in all those monster movies, so that I had woken up in the wrong one.

Suddenly I felt like I was lost. Like I was going on this trip to this place I had always heard about and I was on the only road to that place but the signs kept telling me I was going to some other place. When I looked in the glove compartment to check my maps, I found I'd brought the wrong set of maps. And the road was too narrow to turn around in and there was too much traffic anyway so I just had to keep on going . . . and getting more and more lost. It gave me the creeps so I kept real quiet.

Phil headed up Sacramento Street—a steep, slanting street that just zoomed on and on up to the top of Nob Hill, where the rich people lived and where they had the swanky hotels. Phil turned suddenly into a little dead-end alley wide enough for only one car. On one side was a one-story Chinese school of brick so old or so dirty that the bricks were practically a purple color. On the other side as we drove by was a small parking lot with only six spaces for cars. Phil stopped the car in the middle of the alley and I could see the rest of it was filled with apartment houses. Somewhere someone had a window open and the radio was blaring out. I couldn't find the place where it was coming from but I did see someone's diapers and shirts hung in the windows and on the fire escape of one apartment.

"Why do they hang their laundry in the windows?" I asked Phil.

"That's what people from Hong Kong use for curtains," Phil grumbled.

The sidewalk in front of the house was cracked like someone had taken a sledgehammer to it, and there were iron grates over the lower windows. The steps up to the doorway were old, worn concrete painted red. To the left were the mailboxes, which had Chinese words for the names or had no labels at all.

Chinatown,
San Francisco

To the right were the doorbells to all the nine apartments. Phil picked out the last and rang. He jabbed his thumb down rhythmically. Three short. Three long. Three short.

"Why are you doing that?" I asked.

"Signaling your grandmother," he grumbled. "She never answers just one buzz like any normal person, or even just three bursts. It's got to be nine buzzes in that way or she doesn't open the door. She says her friends know what she means."

So did I. It was Morse code for SOS.[1] The buzzer on the door sounded like an angry bee. Phil opened the door, putting his back against it and fighting against the heavy spring that tried to swing it shut. "Go on. Up three flights. Number nine. Remember now. You call her Paw-Paw."

"What's Paw-Paw?"

"Maternal grandmother. Chinese have a different word for every relation. Like I'm your *kauh-fu*—your maternal uncle. Actually your grandmother's name is *Ah Paw* but when you're close to someone, you repeat the word, so it's Paw-Paw."

"I don't know any Chinese," I said.

Phil grunted. "You don't have to worry about talking to her. She learned pretty good English when she was a maid to some rich Americans."

"When did she do that?"

"Just after your grandfather died. I was only a baby then. But she quit once Jeanie finished high school. She got tired of leaving Chinatown."

I walked into an old, dim hallway and climbed up the wooden steps. As I turned an angle on the stairs, I saw light burning fierce and bright from a window. When I came to

it, I looked out at the roof of the Chinese school next door. Someone had thrown some old 45s and a pair of sneakers down there. If I were some kind of kid that felt sorry for herself, I would almost have said that was the way I felt: like some piece of old ugly junk that was being kicked around on the discard pile.

I didn't stay by the window long, though, because Phil was coming up the stairs and I didn't want to act like his kids' stories about Paw-Paw had scared me. Anybody could be better than Uncle Phil and his family . . . I hoped. I stopped by the number-nine room, afraid to knock. It could not be the right place because I could hear rock music coming through the doorway. I scratched my head and checked the numbers on the other doors on the landing. Phil was still a flight down, huffing and puffing up the steps with my duffel bag—it wasn't that heavy; Phil was just that much out of shape. "Go on. Go on. Knock, you little idiot," he called up the stairwell.

I shrugged. It wasn't any of my business. I knocked at the door. I heard about six bolts and locks being turned. Finally the door swung open and I saw a tiny, pleasant, round-faced woman smiling at me. Her cheeks were a bright red. Her gray hair was all curly and frizzy around her head and a pair of rimless, thick eyeglasses perched on her nose. She was round and plump, wearing a sweater even on a hot day like this, a pair of cotton black slacks, and a pair of open heeled, flat slippers.

"Paw-Paw?" I asked.

---

1. **SOS.** These three letters, in telegraphic code, are the international signal for help.

"Hello. Hello." She opened up her arms and gave me a big hug, almost crushing me. It was funny, but I suddenly found myself holding on to her. Underneath all the soft layers of clothing I could feel how hard and tough she was. She patted me on the back three times and then left me for a moment to turn down her radio. It really was her old, white, beat-up radio playing rock music.

"Hey, how about a hand?" Phil puffed as he finally got to the landing.

Paw-Paw shuffled out to the landing in her slippered feet and made shooing motions. "You can go home now. We can do all right by ourselves."

Phil heaved his shoulders up and down in a great sigh and set the bag down. "Now, Momma——"

"Go on home," she said firmly. "We need time by ourselves."

I saw that Phil must have had some fine speech all prepared, probably warning Paw-Paw about me and warning me about ingratitude. He was not about to give up such an opportunity to make a speech.

"Now, Momma——"

"Go on. You're still not too old for a swat across the backside."

Phil ran his hand back and forth along the railing. "Really, Momma. You oughtn't——"

"Go on," Paw-Paw raised her hand.

Phil gulped. The thought of having a former district president of the lawyers spanked by his own mother must have been too much for him. He turned around and started down the steps. He still had to get in the last word though.

"You mind your Paw-Paw, young lady. You hear me?" he shouted over his shoulder.

I waited till I heard the door slam. "Do you know what those buzzes stand for?"

"Do you?" Her eyes crinkled up.

"It stands for SOS. But where did you learn it?"

"When I worked for the American lady, her boy had a toy . . . what do you call it?" She made a tapping motion with her finger.

"Telegraph?"

"Yes. It's a good joke on such a learned man, no?" Her round red face split into a wide grin and then she began to giggle and when she put her hand over her mouth, the giggle turned into a laugh.

I don't think that I had laughed in all that time since my father's accident a month ago. It was like all the laughter I hadn't been able to use came bubbling up out of some hidden well—burst out of the locks and just came up. Both of us found ourselves slumping on the landing, leaning our heads against the banister, and laughing.

Finally Paw-Paw tilted up her glasses and wiped her eyes. "Philip always did have too much dignity for one person. Ah." She leaned back against the railing on the landing before the stairwell, twisting her head to look at me. "You'll go far," she nodded. "Yes, you will. Your eyebrows are beautifully curved, like silkworms. That means you'll be clever. And your ears are small and close to your head and shaped a certain way. That means you're adventurous and win much honor."

"Really?"

She nodded solemnly. "Didn't you know? The face is the map of the soul." Then she leaned forward and raised her glasses and pointed to the corners of her eyes where there were two small hollows, just shadows, really. "You see those marks under my eyes?"

"Yes." I added after a moment, "Paw-Paw."

"Those marks, they mean I have a temper."

"Oh." I wondered what was to happen next.

She set her glasses back on her nose. "But I will make a deal with you. I can keep my temper under control if you can do the same with your love of adventure and intelligence. You see, people, including me, don't always understand a love of adventure and intelligence. Sometimes we mistake them for troublemaking."

"I'll try." I grinned.

I went and got my bag then and brought it inside Paw-Paw's place and looked around, trying to figure out where I'd put it. Her place wasn't more than ten by fifteen feet and it was crowded with her stuff. Her bed was pushed lengthwise against the wall next to the doorway leading out to the landing. To the right of the door was another doorway, leading to the small little cubicle of a kitchen, and next to that door was her bureau. The wall opposite the bed had her one window leading out to the fire escape and giving a view of the alley, which was so narrow that it looked like we could have shaken hands with the people in the apartment house across from us. Beneath the window was a stack of newspapers for wrapping up the garbage. Next to the window was a table with a bright red-and-orange-flower tablecloth. Paw-Paw pulled aside her chair and her three-legged stool and told me to put my bag under the table. A metal cabinet and stacks of boxes covered the rest of the wall and the next one had hooks from which coats and other stuff in plastic bags hung.

In the right corner of the old bureau were some statues and an old teacup with some dirt in it and a half-burnt incense stick stuck into it. The rest of the top, though, was covered with old photos in little cardboard covers. They filled the bureau top and the mirror too, being stuck into corners of the mirror or actually taped onto the surface.

Next to the photos were the statues. One was about eight inches high in white porcelain of a pretty lady holding a flower and with the most patient, peaceful expression on her face. To her left was a statue of a man with a giant-sized, bald head. And then there were eight little statues, each only about two inches high. "Who are they?" I asked.

"Statues of some holy people," Paw-Paw said reluctantly.

There was something familiar about the last statue on Paw-Paw's bureau. It was of a fat, balding god with large ears, who had little children crawling over his lap and climbing up his shoulders. "Hey," I said. "Is that the happy god?"

Paw-Paw looked puzzled. "He's not the god of happiness."

"But they call him the happy god. See?" I pulled my father's little plastic charm out of my pocket and pointed to the letters on the back. *Happy God—Souvenir of Chinatown.*

Paw-Paw didn't even try to read the lettering. Maybe my father had already shown it to her long ago. "He's not the god of happiness. He just looks happy. He's the Buddha—the Buddha who will come in the future. He's smiling because everyone will be saved by that time and he can take a vacation. The children are holy people who become like children again."

"What about the others, Paw-Paw?"

"I don't have the words to explain," Paw-Paw said curtly, like the whole thing was embarrassing her.

I sat down by the table on the stool, which was painted white with red flowers. "Sure you do. I think your English is better than mine."

"You don't want to know any of that stuff." With her index finger Paw-Paw rubbed hard against some spot on the table-cloth. "That stuff's only for old people. If I tell you any more, you'll laugh at it like all other young people do." There was bitter hurt and anger in her voice.

I should have left her alone, I guess; but we had been getting close to one another and suddenly I'd found this door between us—a door that wouldn't open. I wasn't so much curious now as I was desperate: I didn't want Paw-Paw shutting me out like that. "I won't laugh, Paw-Paw. Honest."

"That stuff's only for old people who are too stupid to learn American ways," she insisted stubbornly.

"Well, maybe I'm stupid too."

"No." Paw-Paw pressed her lips together tightly; and I saw that no matter how much I pestered her, I wasn't going to get her to tell me any more about the statues on her bureau. We'd been getting along so great before that I was sorry I'd ever started asking questions.

We both sat, each in our own thoughts, until almost apologetically Paw-Paw picked up a deck of cards from the table. "Do you play cards?"

"Some," I said. "Draw poker. Five-card stud. Things like that."

Paw-Paw shuffled the cards expertly. "Poker is for old men who like to sit and think too much. Now I know a game that's for the young and quick."

"What's that?"

"Slapjack." She explained that each of us took half of a deck and stacked it in front without looking at it. Then we would take turns taking the top card off and putting it down in the middle. Whenever a jack appeared, the first one to put her hand over the pile of cards got it. She then mixed the new cards with all the cards she still had in front of her. The first one to get all the cards won the game. It would sound like the advantage was with the person who was putting out the card at the time, but she was supposed to turn up the card away from her so she couldn't see it before the other player.

Paw-Paw had played a lot of card games, since she lived by herself, so she seemed to know when the jacks were going to come up. For a while all you could hear was the *slap-slap-slap*ping of cards and sometimes our hands smacking one another trying to get the pile. And sometimes I'd have more cards and sometimes Paw-Paw would. Eventually, though, she beat me. She shuffled the deck again. "You're a pretty good player," she grudged.

"Not as good as you, though."

Paw-Paw shuffled the cards, tapping them against the table so the cards in the pack were all even. "We used to play all the time. Your mother, Phil, everyone. We'd hold big contests and make plenty of noise. Only when Phil got older, he only wanted to play the games fancy Americans played like—what's that word for a road that goes over water?"

"A bridge? Phil wanted to play bridge."

"Yes." Paw-Paw put the deck on the table. I wandered over to the bed.

The radio was in a little cabinet built into the headboard of the bed. I lay down on the bed and looked at the radio dial. "Do you like rock music, Paw-Paw?"

"It's fun to listen to," Paw-Paw said, "and besides, *Chinese Hour* is on that station every night."

"Chinese Hour?"

"An hour of news and songs all in Chinese." Paw-Paw slipped the cards back carefully into their box. "They used to have some better shows on that station like mystery shows."

"I bet I could find some." I started to reach for the dial.

"Don't lose that station." Paw-Paw seemed afraid suddenly.

"Don't worry, Paw-Paw, I'll be able to get your station back for you." It was playing "Monster Mash" right then. I twisted the dial to the right and the voices and snatches of song slid past and then I turned the dial back to her station, where "Monster Mash" was still playing. "See?"

"As long as you could get it back," Paw-Paw said reluctantly.

I fiddled with the dial some more until I got hold of *Gunsmoke*. It'd gone off the air years ago but some station was playing reruns. Paw-Paw liked that, especially the deep voice of the marshal. It was good to sit there in the darkening little room, listening to Marshal Dillon inside your head and picturing him as big and tall and striding down the dusty streets of Dodge City. And I got us some other programs too, shows that Paw-Paw had never been able to listen to before.

Don't get the idea that Paw-Paw was stupid. She just didn't understand American machines that well. She lived with them in a kind of truce where she never asked much of them if they wouldn't ask much of her.

"It's getting near eight," Paw-Paw said anxiously. It was only when I got the station back for her that she began to relax. "I was always so worried that I would not be able to get back the station, I never tried to listen to others. Look what I missed."

"But you have me now, Paw-Paw," I said.

"Yes," Paw-Paw smiled briefly, straightening in her chair. "I guess I do."

THINK AND DISCUSS
Understanding
1. What has happened to Casey's father?
2. Who has she been staying with?
3. As Casey and Uncle Phil drive through Chinatown, what makes Casey conscious of her Chinese origins?
4. After he carries Casey's bag upstairs, what is Uncle Phil told to do? Does he do it?
5. How do Paw-Paw and Casey spend the rest of the day?

Analyzing
6. How does Casey feel as she becomes aware of the physical characteristics that identify her as Chinese?
7. Why is Casey going to live with Paw-Paw? Support your answer with evidence from the story.
8. How is Paw-Paw able to make Casey feel more comfortable and accepted?
9. What shows that Casey knows little about the customs, culture, or beliefs of Chinese people?

Extending
10. It is possible to interpret Paw-Paw's final remark in the story in several ways. What do you think she means? Explain your answer.

APPLYING: Characterization H𝕫
See Handbook of Literary Terms, p. 659.
   Characterization refers to the methods an author uses to acquaint the reader with characters. An author may describe a character's physical traits and personality, report the character's speech and actions, give opinions and reactions of other characters to this individual, or reveal the character's thoughts and feelings.

1. What do readers learn about Casey from Casey herself? from Paw-Paw? from Uncle Phil?
2. How does Paw-Paw characterize her son Phil?
3. Do you think Phil's speech and actions justify Paw-Paw's characterization?
4. How does Paw-Paw characterize herself?
5. Do you agree with this characterization? Explain your answer.

COMPOSITION ◀━●▬
Reading/Writing Log
   Laurence Yep is very specific in his descriptions of the world Casey discovers when she goes to Chinatown. One example of this is given below. Copy the heading and this example in your reading/writing log. Then find at least four other examples in the story and add them to your log.
Specific Descriptions of Chinatown
I didn't know what to make of the buildings either. They were mostly three- or four-story stone buildings but some had fancy balconies, and others had decorations on them like curved tile roofs—one building had bright yellow balconies decorated with shiny, glazed purple dolphins—and there was a jumble of neon signs, dark now in the daytime, jammed all together. Most of the buildings, though, had some color to them—bright reds and rich golds with some green thrown in.

Writing a Story

With the exception of Native Americans, everybody in the United States, or their ancestors, originally came from somewhere else. What is it like to be a newcomer? Write a story about an immigrant to this country. You may choose the time and place of your story as well as where your character has come from. If you or some living member of your family has not had this experience, recall what you have read or what you have learned in history class about immigrants. Make your story clear and interesting by using specific details in it. Review your reading/writing log before you begin. You may also find it helpful to read "Writing a Story" in the Writer's Handbook before you write this composition.

Writing a Description

Describe somebody who has made a strong impression on you. Tell what the person looks like and how he or she speaks and acts. Be sure to use specific details to help your readers understand why this person made such an impression. You may find the article, "Writing a Clear Description," in the Writer's Handbook to be helpful in writing this composition.

 BIOGRAPHY

Laurence Yep
1948–

Laurence Yep was born in San Francisco and attended grammar school in Chinatown. Having been influenced by a variety of cultures, Yep says, "I have no one culture to call my own. . . . However, in my writing, I can create my own." This variety of cultures shows in much of his writing, as it does in *Child of the Owl*, from which "Paw-Paw" is taken. Laurence Yep has written several novels for young people and a number of short stories.

Comment

Chinatown

There are Chinatowns in many cities, but San Francisco's Chinatown has the largest Chinese population of any city outside Asia. Today it is one of the major tourist attractions in the San Francisco area. Shops, restaurants, and even school buildings have been constructed especially to imitate a picturesque Oriental-style architecture—upward-curving tiled roofs which are supposed to throw back to the skies any bad luck or misfortune that may rain down from heaven. Oriental clothing, art, furniture, porcelain, and toys fill the shops, and food of all descriptions is available for tourists as well as residents.

Although there are historical records to show that people from China settled in the Americas more than 2500 years ago, the first large group of Chinese immigrants came to California as a result of the discovery of gold in the 1840s. These adventurous pioneers came to mine gold, along with the other "forty-niners" who flocked to the state from all over the world hoping to make their fortunes.

Later, when the first transcontinental railroad was being constructed, the railroad companies recruited and imported men from China as laborers. Soon the Chinese made up a large percentage of the work crews; they often did the most hazardous work and were an important reason why the railroad was completed in record time. But they were always isolated because of differences in language and culture, and there was no effective communication between the Chinese and other workers.

After the railroad was completed in 1869, thousands of Chinese men were left without a way to earn a living. Since there was a financial depression in California at the time, many unemployed Americans were quick to blame the Chinese workers for allegedly accepting a lower pay scale and for taking jobs away from them. Such anti-Chinese feeling produced many discriminatory state laws and local ordinances. These laws not only prevented other Chinese from entering the United States but also prevented the men who were here from bringing their families, from owning land, from attending public schools, and from applying for United States citizenship. Mob violence occasionally occurred during this time; some Chinese were abused physically and even killed, and others were ruined financially when crowds invaded Chinatowns and destroyed their shops and burned their homes. In 1943, 1952, and 1965 the discriminatory laws against the Chinese were repealed. Equality of rights and opportunities became law in the United States.

Review **CHARACTERIZATION** in the Handbook of Literary Terms, page 659

A Christmas Memory

Truman Capote

He was only seven; she was sixty-something. They were distant cousins who had only each other. Now grown, Buddy recalls Christmas and his unusual friend.

I magine a morning in late November. A coming of winter morning more than twenty years ago. Consider the kitchen of a spreading old house in a country town. A great black stove is its main feature; but there is also a big round table and a fireplace with two rocking chairs placed in front of it. Just today the fireplace commenced its seasonal roar.

A woman with shorn white hair is standing at the kitchen window. She is wearing tennis shoes and a shapeless gray sweater over a summery calico dress. She is small and sprightly, like a bantam hen; but, due to a long youthful illness, her shoulders are pitifully hunched. Her face is remarkable—not unlike Lincoln's, craggy like that, and tinted by sun and wind; but it is delicate too, finely boned, and her eyes are sherry-colored and timid. "Oh my," she exclaims, her breath smoking the windowpane, "it's fruitcake weather!"

The person to whom she is speaking is myself. I am seven; she is sixty-something. We are cousins, very distant ones, and we have lived together—well, as long as I can remember. Other people inhabit the house, relatives; and though they have power over us, and frequently make us cry, we are not, on the whole, too much aware of them. We are each other's best friend. She calls me Buddy, in memory of a boy who was formerly her best friend. The other Buddy died in the 1880s, when she was still a child. She is still a child.

"I knew it before I got out of bed," she says, turning away from the window with a

Capote (kə pō′tē).

A Christmas Memory **57**

purposeful excitement in her eyes. "The courthouse bell sounded so cold and clear. And there were no birds singing; they've gone to warmer country, yes indeed. Oh, Buddy, stop stuffing biscuit and fetch our buggy. Help me find my hat. We've thirty cakes to bake."

It's always the same: a morning arrives in November, and my friend, as though officially inaugurating the Christmas time of year that exhilarates her imagination and fuels the blaze of her heart, announces: "It's fruitcake weather! Fetch our buggy. Help me find my hat."

The hat is found, a straw cartwheel corsaged with velvet roses out-of-doors has faded: it once belonged to a more fashionable relative. Together, we guide our buggy, a dilapidated baby carriage, out to the garden and into a grove of pecan trees. The buggy is mine; that is, it was bought for me when I was born. It is made of wicker, rather unraveled, and the wheels wobble like a drunkard's legs. But it is a faithful object; springtimes, we take it to the woods and fill it with flowers, herbs, wild fern for our porch pots; in the summer, we pile it with picnic paraphernalia and sugar-cane fishing poles and roll it down to the edge of a creek; it has its winter uses, too: as a truck for hauling firewood from the yard to the kitchen, as a warm bed for Queenie, our tough little orange and white rat terrier who has survived distemper and two rattlesnake bites. Queenie is trotting beside it now.

Three hours later we are back in the kitchen hulling a heaping buggyload of windfall pecans. Our backs hurt from gathering them: how hard they were to find (the main crop having been shaken off the trees and sold by the orchard's owners, who are not us) among the concealing leaves, the frosted, deceiving grass. Caarackle! A cheery crunch, scraps of miniature thunder sound as the shells collapse and the golden mound of sweet oily ivory meat mounts in the milk-glass bowl. Queenie begs to taste, and now and again my friend sneaks her a mite, though insisting we deprive ourselves. "We mustn't, Buddy. If we start, we won't stop. And there's scarcely enough as there is. For thirty cakes." The kitchen is growing dark. Dusk turns the window into a mirror: our reflections mingle with the rising moon as we work by the fireside in the firelight. At last, when the moon is quite high, we toss the final hull into the fire and, with joined sighs, watch it catch flame. The buggy is empty, the bowl is brimful.

We eat our supper (cold biscuits, bacon, blackberry jam) and discuss tomorrow. Tomorrow the kind of work I like best begins: buying. Cherries and citron, ginger and vanilla and canned Hawaiian pineapple, rinds and raisins and walnuts and whiskey and oh, so much flour, butter, so many eggs, spices, flavorings: why, we'll need a pony to pull the buggy home.

But before these purchases can be made, there is the question of money. Neither of us has any. Except for skinflint sums persons in the house occasionally provide (a dime is considered very big money); or what we earn ourselves from various activities: holding rummage sales, selling buckets of hand-picked blackberries, jars of homemade jam and apple jelly and peach preserves, rounding up flowers for funerals and weddings.

Once we won seventy-ninth prize, five dollars, in a national football contest. Not that we know a fool thing about football. It's just that we enter any contest we hear about: at the moment our hopes are centered on the fifty-thousand-dollar Grand Prize being offered to name a new brand of coffee (we suggested "A.M."; and after some hesitation, for my friend thought it perhaps sacrilegious, the slogan "A.M.! Amen!"). To tell the truth, our only *really* profitable enterprise was the Fun and Freak Museum we conducted in a backyard woodshed two summers ago. The Fun was a stereopticon with slide views of Washington and New York lent us by a relative who had been to those places (she was furious when she discovered why we'd borrowed it); the Freak was a three-legged biddy chicken hatched by one of our own hens. Everybody hereabouts wanted to see that biddy: we charged grownups a nickel, kids two cents. And took in a good twenty dollars before the museum shut down due to the decease of the main attraction.

But one way and another we do each year accumulate Christmas savings, a Fruitcake Fund. These moneys we keep hidden in an ancient bead purse under a loose board under the floor under a chamber pot under my friend's bed. The purse is seldom removed from this safe location except to make a deposit, or, as happens every Saturday, a withdrawal; for on Saturdays I am allowed ten cents to go to the picture show. My friend has never been to a picture show, nor does she intend to: "I'd rather hear you tell the story, Buddy. That way I can imagine it more. Besides, a person my age shouldn't squander their eyes. When the Lord comes, let me see

him clear." In addition to never having seen movie, she has never: eaten in a restaurant, traveled more than five miles from home, received or sent a telegram, read anything except funny papers and the Bible, worn cosmetics, cursed, wished someone harm, told a lie on purpose, let a hungry dog go hungry. Here are a few things she has done, does do: killed with a hoe the biggest rattlesnake ever seen in this county (sixteen rattles), dip snuff (secretly), tame hummingbirds (just try it) till they balance on her finger, tell ghost stories (we both believe in ghosts) so tingling they chill you in July, talk to herself, take walks in the rain, grow the prettiest japonicas in town, know the recipe for every sort of old-time Indian cure, including a magical wart-remover.

Now, with supper finished, we retire to the room in a faraway part of the house where my friend sleeps in a scrap-quilt-covered iron bed painted rose pink, her favorite color. Silently, wallowing in the pleasures of conspiracy, we take the bead purse from its secret place and spill its contents on the scrap quilt. Dollar bills, tightly rolled and green as May buds. Somber fifty-cent pieces, heavy enough to weight a dead man's eyes. Lovely dimes, the liveliest coin, the one that really jingles. Nickels and quarters, worn smooth as creek pebbles. But mostly a hateful heap of bitter-odored pennies. Last summer others in the house contracted to pay us a penny for every twenty-five flies we killed. Oh, the carnage of August: the flies that flew to heaven! Yet it was not work in which we took pride. And, as we sit counting pennies, it is as though we were back tabulating dead flies. Neither of us has a head for figures; we count slowly, lose track, start again. According to her calculations, we have $12.73. According to mine, exactly $13. "I do hope you're wrong, Buddy. We can't mess around with thirteen. The cakes will fall. Or put somebody in the cemetery. Why, I wouldn't dream of getting out of bed on the thirteenth." This is true: she always spends thirteenths in bed. So, to be on the safe side, we subtract a penny and toss it out the window.

Of the ingredients that go into our fruitcakes, whiskey is the most expensive, as well as the hardest to obtain: state laws forbid its sale. But everybody knows you can buy a bottle from Mr. Haha Jones. And the next day, having completed our more prosaic shopping, we set out for Mr. Haha's business address, a "sinful" (to quote public opinion) fish-fry and dancing café down by the river. We've been there before, and on the same errand; but in previous years our dealings have been with Haha's wife, an iodine-dark Indian woman with brassy peroxided hair and a dead-tired disposition. Actually, we've never laid eyes on her husband, though we've heard that he's an Indian too. A giant with razor scars across his cheeks. They call him Haha because he's so gloomy, a man who never laughs. As we approach his café (a large log cabin festooned inside and out with chains of garish-gay naked lightbulbs and standing by the river's muddy edge under the shade of river trees where moss drifts through the branches like gray mist) our steps slow down. Even Queenie stops prancing and sticks close by. People have been murdered in Haha's café. Cut to pieces. Hit on the head. There's a case coming up in court next month. Naturally these goings-on happen at night when the colored lights cast crazy patterns and the Victrola wails. In the daytime Haha's is shabby and deserted. I knock at the door, Queenie barks, my friend calls: "Mrs. Haha, ma'am? Anyone to home?"

Footsteps. The door opens. Our hearts overturn. It's Mr. Haha Jones himself! And he *is* a giant; he *does* have scars; he *doesn't* smile. No, he glowers at us through Satan-tilted eyes and demands to know: "What you want with Haha?"

For a moment we are too paralyzed to tell. Presently my friend half-finds her voice, a whispery voice at best: "If you please, Mr. Haha, we'd like a quart of your finest whiskey."

His eyes tilt more. Would you believe it? Haha is smiling! Laughing, too. "Which one of you is a drinkin' man?"

"It's for making fruitcakes, Mr. Haha. Cooking."

This sobers him. He frowns. "That's no way to waste good whiskey." Nevertheless, he retreats into the shadowed café and seconds later appears carrying a bottle of daisy yellow unlabeled liquor. He demonstrates its sparkle in the sunlight and says: "Two dollars."

We pay him with nickels and dimes and pennies. Suddenly, jangling the coins in his hand like a fistful of dice, his face softens. "Tell you what," he proposes, pouring the money back into our bead purse, "just send me one of them fruitcakes instead."

"Well," my friend remarks on our way home, "there's a lovely man. We'll put an extra cup of raisins in *his* cake."

The black stove, stoked with coal and fire-

Buddy, his friend, and Queenie look for a Christmas tree.
Illustration by Franz Altschuler

wood, glows like a lighted pumpkin. Egg-beaters whirl, spoons spin round in bowls of butter and sugar, vanilla sweetens the air, ginger spices it; melting, nose-tingling odors saturate the kitchen, suffuse the house, drift out to the world on puffs of chimney smoke. In four days our work is done. Thirty-one cakes, dampened with whiskey, bask on window sills and shelves.

Who are they for?

Friends. Not necessarily neighbor friends: indeed, the larger share are intended for persons we've met maybe once, perhaps not at all. People who've struck our fancy. Like President Roosevelt. Like the Reverend and Mrs. J. C. Lucey, Baptist missionaries to Borneo who lectured here last winter. Or the little knife grinder who comes through town twice a year. Or Abner Packer, the driver of the six o'clock bus from Mobile, who exchanges waves with us every day as he passes in a dust-cloud whoosh. Or the young Wistons, a California couple whose car one afternoon broke down outside the house and who spent a pleasant hour chatting with us on the porch (young Mr. Wiston snapped our picture, the only one we've ever had taken). Is it because my friend is shy with everyone *except* strangers that these strangers, and merest acquaintances, seem to us our truest friends? I think yes. Also, the scrapbooks we keep of thank-you's on White House stationery, time-to-time communications from California and Borneo, the knife grinder's penny post cards, make us feel connected to eventful worlds beyond the kitchen with its view of a sky that stops.

Now a nude December fig branch grates against the window. The kitchen is empty, the cakes are gone; yesterday we carted the last of them to the post office, where the cost of stamps turned our purse inside out. We're broke. That rather depresses me, but my friend insists on celebrating—with two inches of whiskey left in Haha's bottle. Queenie has a spoonful in a bowl of coffee (she likes her coffee chicory-flavored and strong). The rest we divide between a pair of jelly glasses. We're both quite awed at the prospect of drinking straight whiskey; the taste of it brings screwed-up expressions and sour shudders. But by and by we begin to sing, the two of us singing different songs simultaneously. I don't know the words to mine, just: *Come on along, come on along, to the dark-town strutters' ball.* But I can dance: that's what I mean to be, a tap dancer in the movies. My dancing shadow rollicks on the walls; our voices rock the chinaware; we giggle: as if unseen hands were tickling us. Queenie rolls on her back, her paws plow the air, something like a grin stretches her black lips. Inside myself, I feel warm and sparky as those crumbling logs, carefree as the wind in the chimney. My friend waltzes round the stove, the hem of her poor calico skirt pinched between her fingers as though it were a party dress: *Show me the way to go home,* she sings, her tennis shoes squeaking on the floor. *Show me the way to go home.*

Enter: two relatives. Very angry. Potent with eyes that scold, tongues that scald. Listen to what they have to say, the words tumbling together into a wrathful tune: "A child of seven! whiskey on his breath! are you out of your mind? feeding a child of seven! must be loony! road to ruination! remember Cousin Kate? Uncle Charlie? Uncle Charlie's brother-in-law? shame! scandal! humiliation! kneel, pray, beg the Lord!"

Queenie sneaks under the stove. My friend gazes at her shoes, her chin quivers, she lifts her skirt and blows her nose and runs to her room. Long after the town has gone to sleep and the house is silent except for the chimings of clocks and the sputter of fading fires, she is weeping into a pillow already as wet as a widow's handkerchief.

"Don't cry," I say, sitting at the bottom of her bed and shivering despite my flannel nightgown that smells of last winter's cough syrup, "don't cry," I beg, teasing her toes, tickling her feet, "you're too old for that."

"It's because," she hiccups, "I *am* too old. Old and funny."

"Not funny. Fun. More fun than anybody. Listen. If you don't stop crying you'll be so tired tomorrow we can't go cut a tree."

She straightens up. Queenie jumps on the bed (where Queenie is not allowed) to lick her cheeks. "I know where we'll find pretty trees, Buddy. And holly, too. With berries big as your eyes. It's way off in the woods. Farther than we've ever been. Papa used to bring us Christmas trees from there: carry them on his shoulder. That's fifty years ago. Well, now: I can't wait for morning."

Morning. Frozen rime lusters the grass; the sun, round as an orange and orange as hot-weather moons, balances on the horizon, burnishes the silvered winter woods. A wild turkey calls. A renegade hog grunts in the undergrowth. Soon, by the edge of knee-deep, rapid-running water, we have to abandon the buggy. Queenie wades the stream first, paddles across barking complaints at the swiftness of the current, the pneumonia-making coldness of it. We follow, holding our shoes and equipment (a hatchet, a burlap sack) above our heads. A mile more: of chastising thorns, burs and briers that catch at our clothes; of rusty pine needles brilliant with gaudy fungus and molted feathers. Here, there, a flash, a flutter, an ecstasy of shrillings reminds us that not all the birds have flown south. Always, the path unwinds through lemony sun pools and pitch vine tunnels. Another creek to cross: a disturbed armada of speckled trout froths the water round us, and frogs the size of plates practice belly flops; beaver workmen are building a dam. On the farther shore, Queenie shakes herself and trembles. My friend shivers, too: not with cold but enthusiasm. One of her hat's ragged roses sheds a petal as she lifts her head and inhales the pine-heavy air. "We're almost there; can you smell it, Buddy?" she says, as though we were approaching an ocean.

And, indeed, it is a kind of ocean. Scented acres of holiday trees, prickly-leafed holly. Red berries shiny as Chinese bells: black crows swoop upon them screaming. Having stuffed our burlap sacks with enough greenery and crimson to garland a dozen windows, we set about choosing a tree. "It should be," muses my friend, "twice as tall as a boy. So a boy can't steal the star." The one we pick is twice as tall as me. A brave handsome brute that survives thirty hatchet strokes before it keels with a creaking, rending cry. Lugging it like a kill, we commence the long trek out. Every few yards we abandon the struggle, sit down and pant. But we have the strength of triumphant huntsmen; that and the tree's virile, icy perfume revive us, goad us on. Many compliments accompany our sunset return along the red clay road to town; but my friend is sly and noncommittal when passers-by praise the treasure perched on our buggy: what a fine tree and where did it come from? "Yonderways," she murmurs vaguely. Once a car stops and the rich mill owner's lazy wife leans out and whines: "Give ya two-bits cash for that ol' tree." Ordinarily my friend is afraid of saying no; but on this occasion she promptly shakes her head: "We wouldn't take a dollar." The mill owner's wife persists. "A dollar, my foot! Fifty cents. That's my last offer. Goodness, woman, you can get another one." In answer, my friend gently reflects: "I doubt it. There's never two of anything."

Home: Queenie slumps by the fire and sleeps till tomorrow, snoring loud as a human.

A trunk in the attic contains: a shoebox of ermine tails (off the opera cape of a curious lady who once rented a room in the house), coils of frazzled tinsel gone gold with age, one silver star, a brief rope of dilapidated, undoubtedly dangerous candylike light bulbs. Excellent decorations, as far as they go, which isn't far enough: my friend wants our tree to blaze "like a Baptist window," droop with weighty snows of ornament. But we can't afford the made-in-Japan splendors at the five-and-dime. So we do what we've always done: sit for days at the kitchen table with scissors and crayons and stacks of colored paper. I make sketches and my friend cuts them out: lots of cats, fish too (because they're easy to draw), some apples, some watermelons, a few winged angels devised from saved-up sheets of Hershey-bar tin foil. We use safety pins to attach these creations to the tree; as a final touch, we sprinkle the branches with shredded cotton (picked in August for this purpose). My friend, surveying the effect, clasps her hands together. "Now honest, Buddy. Doesn't it look good enough to eat?" Queenie tries to eat an angel.

After weaving and ribboning holly wreaths for all the front windows, our next project is the fashioning of family gifts. Tie-dye scarves for the ladies, for the men a home-brewed lemon and licorice and aspirin syrup to be taken "at the first Symptoms of a Cold and after Hunting." But when it comes time for making each other's gifts, my friend and I separate to work secretly. I would like to buy her a pearl-handled knife, a radio, a whole pound of chocolate-covered cherries (we tasted some once, and she always swears: "I could live on them, Buddy, Lord yes I could—

and that's not taking His name in vain"). Instead, I am building her a kite. She would like to give me a bicycle (she's said so on several million occasions: "If only I could, Buddy. It's bad enough in life to do without something *you* want: but confound it, what gets my goat is not being able to give somebody something you want *them* to have. Only one of these days I will, Buddy. Locate you a bike. Don't ask how. Steal it, maybe"). Instead, I'm fairly certain that she is building me a kite—the same as last year, and the year before: the year before that we exchanged slingshots. All of which is fine by me. For we are champion kite-fliers who study the wind like sailors; my friend, more accomplished than I, can get a kite aloft when there isn't enough breeze to carry clouds.

Christmas Eve afternoon we scrape together a nickel and go to the butcher's to buy Queenie's traditional gift, a good gnawable beef bone. The bone, wrapped in funny paper, is placed high in the tree near the silver star. Queenie knows it's there. She squats at the foot of the tree staring up in a trance of greed: when bedtime arrives she refuses to budge. Her excitement is equaled by my own. I kick the covers and turn my pillow as though it were a scorching summer's night. Somewhere a rooster crows: falsely, for the sun is still on the other side of the world.

"Buddy, are you awake?" It is my friend, calling from her room, which is next to mine; and an instant later she is sitting on my bed holding a candle. "Well, I can't sleep a hoot," she declares. "My mind's jumping like a jack rabbit. Buddy, do you think Mrs. Roosevelt will serve our cake at dinner?" We huddle in the bed, and she squeezes my hand

I-love-you. "Seems like your hand used to be so much smaller. I guess I hate to see you grow up. When you're grown up, will we still be friends?" I say always. "But I feel so bad, Buddy. I wanted so bad to give you a bike. I tried to sell my cameo Papa gave me. Buddy"—she hesitates, as though embarrassed—"I made you another kite." Then I confess that I made her one, too; and we laugh. The candle burns too short to hold. Out it goes, exposing the starlight, the stars spinning at the window like a visible caroling that slowly, slowly daybreak silences. Possibly we doze; but the beginnings of dawn splash us like cold water: we're up, wide-eyed and wandering while we wait for others to waken. Quite deliberately my friend drops a kettle on the kitchen floor. I tap-dance in front of closed doors. One by one the household emerges, looking as though they'd like to kill us both; but it's Christmas, so they can't. First, a gorgeous breakfast: just everything you can imagine—from flapjacks and fried squirrel to hominy grits and honey-in-the-comb. Which puts everyone in a good humor except my friend and I. Frankly, we're so impatient to get at the presents we can't eat a mouthful.

Well, I'm disappointed. Who wouldn't be? With socks, a Sunday school shirt, some handkerchiefs, a hand-me-down sweater and a year's subscription to a religious magazine for children. *The Little Shepherd*. It makes me boil. It really does.

My friend has a better haul. A sack of Satsumas,[1] that's her best present. She is proudest, however, of a white wool shawl knitted by her married sister. But she *says* her favorite gift is the kite I built her. And it *is* very beautiful; though not as beautiful as the one she made me, which is blue and scattered with gold and green Good Conduct stars; moreover, my name is painted on it, "Buddy."

"Buddy, the wind is blowing."

The wind is blowing, and nothing will do till we've run to a pasture below the house where Queenie has scooted to bury her bone (and where, a winter hence, Queenie will be buried, too). There, plunging through the healthy waist-high grass, we unreel our kites, feel them twitching at the string like sky fish as they swim into the wind. Satisfied, sun-warmed, we sprawl in the grass and peel Satsumas and watch our kites cavort. Soon I forget the socks and hand-me-down sweater. I'm as happy as if we'd already won the fifty-thousand-dollar Grand Prize in that coffee-naming contest.

"My, how foolish I am!" my friend cries, suddenly alert, like a woman remembering too late she has biscuits in the oven. "You know what I've always thought?" she asks in a tone of discovery, and not smiling at me but a point beyond. "I've always thought a body would have to be sick and dying before they saw the Lord. And I imagined that when He came it would be like looking at the Baptist window: pretty as colored glass with the sun pouring through, such a shine you don't know it's getting dark. And it's been a comfort: to think of that shine taking away all the spooky feeling. But I'll wager it never happens. I'll wager at the very end a body realizes the Lord has already shown Himself. That things as they are"—her hand circles in

_____

1. *Satsumas*, a type of oranges.

a gesture that gathers clouds and kites and grass and Queenie pawing earth over her bone—"just what they've always seen, was seeing Him. As for me, I could leave the world with today in my eyes."

This is our last Christmas together.

Life separates us. Those who Know Best decide that I belong in a military school. And so follows a miserable succession of bugle-blowing prisons, grim reveille-ridden summer camps. I have a new home too. But it doesn't count. Home is where my friend is, and there I never go.

And there she remains, puttering around the kitchen. Alone with Queenie. Then alone. ("Buddy dear," she writes in her wild hard-to-read script, "yesterday Jim Macy's horse kicked Queenie bad. Be thankful she didn't feel much. I wrapped her in a Fine Linen sheet and rode her in the buggy down to Simpson's pasture where she can be with all her Bones . . . .") For a few Novembers she continues to bake her fruitcakes single-handed; not as many, but some: and, of course, she always sends me "the best of the batch." Also, in every letter she encloses a dime wadded in toilet paper: "See a picture show and write me the story." But gradually in her letters she tends to confuse me with her other friend, the Buddy who died in the 1880s; more and more thirteenths are not the only days she stays in bed: a morning arrives in November, a leafless birdless coming of winter morning, when she cannot rouse herself to exclaim: "Oh my, it's fruitcake weather!"

And when that happens, I know it. A message saying so merely confirms a piece of news some secret vein had already received, severing from me an irreplaceable part of myself, letting it loose like a kite on a broken string. That is why, walking across a school campus on this particular December morning, I keep searching the sky. As if I expected to see, rather like hearts, a lost pair of kites hurrying toward heaven.

THINK AND DISCUSS
Understanding
1. Who tells this story?
2. At what time of year does the story take place?
3. Who receives the fruitcakes?
4. Why do the narrator and his friend get in trouble with the rest of the family?
5. What gifts does each receive?
6. At the end of the story, what happens to the narrator? his friend? Queenie?

Analyzing
7. How do Buddy and his friend feel about each other? Find passages to support your answer.
8. In what ways are they different from the rest of the household?

Extending
9. This story deals with a series of rather ordinary events. Why do you think they make such a lasting impression on the boy?

REVIEWING: Characterization

See Handbook of Literary Terms, p. 659.

Methods of **characterization** include describing a character's physical traits and personality, reporting speech and actions, giving opinions and reactions of other characters, and revealing a character's inner thoughts and feelings.

1. Characterize Buddy's friend. In doing this, consider the following: (**a**) her appearance; (**b**) her baking the fruitcakes and giving them only to certain people; (**c**) her teaching Buddy both how to make the cakes and—more important—how to earn money for ingredients; (**d**) what she has and has not done in her life; (**e**) her reaction to the scolding; (**f**) her ability to enjoy life. Find examples from the story to support your characterization.
2. Characterize Buddy. As you do, consider (**a**) his feelings about and treatment of his friend and (**b**) his ability to describe the people, places, and events in the story.

COMPOSITION

Writing a Personal Essay

In an essay of two paragraphs, give your feeling about a particular event. In the first paragraph, describe the event; in the second paragraph, describe your reaction to that event. Your essay need not be about a sad or upsetting event. You might choose a joyful happening such as the kite-flying on Christmas Day. Has anyone you've been afraid of turned out to be a kind person, as Haha Jones does in the story? Before you begin, review the Writer's Craft article and (if you are keeping one) your reading/ writing log. Doing this will help you use specific details in your essay.

Supporting an Opinion

When the woman in the car says Buddy's friend should sell the tree because it's always possible to "get another one," Buddy's friend replies, "I doubt it. There's never two of anything." Write an essay in which you either agree or disagree with the statement that there is "never two of anything." In this essay, first explain the meaning of the statement. Then state your opinion, providing reasons to support it. Your audience will be your teacher.

BIOGRAPHY

Truman Capote

1924–1984

Truman Capote began writing when he was still a child; in fact, while he was in school nothing *but* writing interested him. After publishing many stories in local newspapers, he wrote his first major prizewinning story at the age of nineteen. He later wrote numerous stories and novels ranging in scope from nightmarish tragedy to light comedy. Much of his writing reflects his Southern background.

See **SETTING** in the **Handbook of Literary Terms, page 686**

To Build a Fire

Jack London

He was alone, and it was seventy-five degrees below zero. Could he make it to camp before the cold conquered him?

---

 ay had broken cold and gray, exceedingly cold and gray, when the man turned aside from the main Yukon trail[1] and climbed the high earth bank, where a dim and little-traveled trail led eastward through the fat spruce timberland. It was a steep bank, and he paused for breath at the top, excusing the act to himself by looking at his watch. It was nine o'clock. There was no sun or hint of sun, though there was not a cloud in the sky. It was a clear day, and yet there seemed an intangible pall over the face of things, a subtle gloom that made the day dark and that was due to the absence of sun. This fact did not worry the man. He was used to the lack of sun. It had been days since he had seen the sun, and he knew that a few more days must pass before that cheerful orb, due south, would just peep above the skyline and dip immediately from view.

The man flung a look back along the way he had come. The Yukon lay a mile wide and hidden under three feet of ice. On top of this ice were as many feet of snow. It was all pure white, rolling in gentle undulations where the ice jams of the freeze-up had formed. North and south, as far as his eye could see, it was unbroken white, save for a dark hairline that curved and twisted from around the spruce-covered island to the south and that curved and twisted away into the north, where it disappeared behind another spruce-covered is-

---

1. **Yukon** (yü′kon) **trail,** a trail which runs through the Yukon, a territory in northwestern Canada.

Slightly abridged from *Lost Faces* by Jack London. Published by The Macmillan Company (1909).

land. This dark hairline was the trail—the main trail—that led south five hundred miles to the Chilcoot Pass, Dyea,[2] and salt water, and that led north seventy miles to Dawson, and still on to the north a thousand miles to Nulato, and finally to St. Michael on the Bering Sea,[3] a thousand miles and half a thousand more.

But all this—the mysterious, far-reaching hairline trail, the absence of sun from the sky, the tremendous cold, and the strangeness and weirdness of it all—made no impression on the man. It was not because he was long used to it. He was a newcomer in the land, a *chechaquo*,[4] and this was his first winter. The trouble with him was that he was without imagination. He was quick and alert in the things of life, but only in the things, not in the significances. Fifty degrees below zero meant eighty-odd degrees of frost. Such a fact impressed him as being cold and uncomfortable, and that was all. It did not lead him to meditate upon his frailty as a creature of temperature, and upon man's frailty in general, able only to live within certain narrow limits of heat and cold; and, from there on, it did not lead him to the conjectural field of immortality and man's place in the universe. Fifty degrees below zero stood for a bite of frost that hurt and that must be guarded against by the use of mittens, ear flaps, warm moccasins, and thick socks. Fifty degrees below zero was to him just precisely fifty degrees below zero. That there should be anything more to it than that was a thought that never entered his head.

As he turned to go on, he spat speculatively. There was a sharp, explosive crackle that startled him. He spat again. And again,

in the air, before it could fall to the snow, the spittle crackled. He knew that at fifty below spittle cracked on the snow, but this spittle had cracked in the air. Undoubtedly it was colder than fifty below—how much colder he did not know. But the temperature did not matter. He was bound for the old claim on the left fork of Henderson Creek where the boys were already. They had come over across the divide from the Indian Creek country, while he had come the roundabout way to take a look at the possibilities of getting out logs in the spring from the islands in the Yukon. He would be in to camp by six o'clock; a bit after dark, it was true, but the boys would be there, a fire would be going, and a hot supper would be ready. As for lunch, he pressed his hand against the protruding bundle under his jacket. It was also under his shirt, wrapped up in a handkerchief and lying against the naked skin. It was the only way to keep the biscuits from freezing. He smiled agreeably to himself as he thought of those biscuits, each cut open and sopped in bacon grease, and each enclosing a generous slice of fried bacon.

He plunged in among the big spruce trees. The trail was faint. A foot of snow had fallen since the last sled had passed over, and he was glad he was without a sled, traveling light. In fact, he carried nothing but the

---

2. **Chilcoot** (chil′küt) **Pass, Dyea** (dī′ā). Chilcoot Pass is a mountain pass in British Columbia, the territory just south of the Yukon. At the time of the story, Dyea was a town in western British Columbia, south of Chilcoot Pass.

3. **Dawson . . . Bering Sea.** Dawson is a city in the western part of the Yukon. Nulato (nü lä′tō) is a city in western Alaska. St. Michael is a port city on the western coast of Alaska.

4. **chechaquo** (chē chä′kō), a newcomer; greenhorn; tenderfoot. *[Spanish]*

lunch wrapped in the handkerchief. He was surprised, however, at the cold. It certainly was cold, he concluded, as he rubbed his numb nose and cheekbones with his mittened hand. He was a warm-whiskered man, but the hair on his face did not protect the high cheekbones and the eager nose that thrust itself aggressively into the frosty air.

At the man's heels trotted a dog, a big native husky, the proper wolf dog, gray-coated and without any visible or temperamental difference from its brother, the wild wolf. The animal was depressed by the tremendous cold. It knew that it was no time for traveling. Its instinct told it a truer tale than was told to the man by the man's judgment. In reality, it was not merely colder than fifty below zero; it was colder than sixty below, than seventy below. It was seventy-five below zero. Since the freezing point is thirty-two above zero, it meant that one hundred and seven degrees of frost obtained. The dog did not know anything about thermometers. Possibly in its brain there was no sharp consciousness of a condition of very cold such as was in the man's brain. But the brute had its instinct. It experienced a vague but menacing apprehension that subdued it and made it slink along at the man's heels, and that made it question eagerly every unwonted movement of the man as if expecting him to go into camp or to seek shelter somewhere and build a fire. The dog had learned fire, and it wanted fire, or else to burrow under the snow and cuddle its warmth away from the air.

The frozen moisture of its breathing had settled on its fur in a fine powder of frost, and especially were its jowls, muzzle, and eyelashes whitened by its crystalled breath. The man's red beard and mustache were likewise frosted, but more solidly, the deposit taking the form of ice and increasing with every warm, moist breath he exhaled. Also, the man was chewing tobacco, and the muzzle of ice held his lips so rigidly that he was unable to clear his chin when he expelled the juice. The result was that a crystal beard of the color and solidity of amber was increasing its length on his chin. If he fell down it would shatter itself, like glass, into brittle fragments. But he did not mind the appendage. It was the penalty all tobacco chewers paid in that country, and he had been out before in two cold snaps. They had not been so cold as this, he knew, but by the spirit thermometer at Sixty Mile[5] he knew they had been registered at fifty below and at fifty-five.

He held on through the level stretch of woods for several miles, crossed a wide flat, and dropped down a bank to the frozen bed of a small stream. This was Henderson Creek, and he knew he was ten miles from the forks. He looked at his watch. It was ten o'clock. He was making four miles an hour, and he calculated that he would arrive at the forks at half-past twelve. He decided to celebrate that event by eating his lunch there.

The dog dropped in again at his heels, with a tail drooping discouragement, as the man swung along the creek bed. The furrow of the old sled trail was plainly visible, but a dozen inches of snow covered the marks of the last runners. In a month no man had come up or down that silent creek. The man held steadily on. He was not much given to thinking, and

---

5. **Sixty Mile,** a village in the western part of the Yukon near the Alaskan border.

just then, particularly, he had nothing to think about save that he would eat lunch at the forks and that at six o'clock he would be in camp with the boys. There was nobody to talk to, and, had there been, speech would have been impossible because of the ice muzzle on his mouth. So he continued monotonously to chew tobacco and to increase the length of his amber beard.

Once in a while the thought reiterated itself that it was very cold and that he had never experienced such cold. As he walked along he rubbed his cheekbones and nose with the back of his mittened hand. He did this automatically, now and again changing hands. But, rub as he would, the instant he stopped his cheekbones went numb, and the following instant the end of his nose went numb. He was sure to frost his cheeks; he knew that, and experienced a pang of regret that he had not devised a nose strap of the sort Bud wore in cold snaps. Such a strap passed across the cheeks as well and saved them. But it didn't matter much, after all. What were frosted cheeks? A bit painful, that was all; they were never serious.

Empty as the man's mind was of thoughts, he was keenly observant, and he noticed the changes in the creek, the curves and bends and timber jams, and always he sharply noted where he placed his feet. Once, coming around a bend, he shied abruptly, like a startled horse, curved away from the place where he had been walking, and retreated several paces back along the trail. The creek he knew was frozen clear to the bottom—no creek could contain water in that arctic winter—but he knew also that there were springs that bubbled out from the hillsides and ran along under the snow and on top of the ice of the creek. He knew that the coldest snaps never froze these springs, and he knew likewise their danger. They were traps. They hid pools of water under the snow that might be three inches deep, or three feet. Sometimes a skin of ice half an inch thick covered them, and in turn was covered by the snow. Sometimes there were alternate layers of water and ice skin, so that when one broke through, he kept on breaking through for a while, sometimes wetting himself to the waist.

That was why he had shied in such panic. He had felt the give under his feet and heard the crackle of a snow-hidden ice skin. And to get his feet wet in such a temperature meant trouble and danger. At the very least it meant delay, for he would be forced to stop and build a fire, and, under its protection, to bare his feet while he dried his socks and moccasins. He stood and studied the creek bed and its banks and decided that the flow of water came from the right. He reflected awhile, rubbing his nose and cheeks, then skirted to the left, stepping gingerly and testing the footing for each step. Once clear of the danger, he took a fresh chew of tobacco and swung along at his four-mile gait.

In the course of the next two hours he came upon several similar traps. Usually the snow above the hidden pools had a sunken, candied appearance that advertised the danger. Once again, however, he had a close call, and once, suspecting danger, he compelled the dog to go on in front. The dog did not want to go. It hung back until the man shoved it forward, and then it went quickly across the white, unbroken surface. Suddenly it broke through, floundered to one side, and got away to firmer footing. It had wet its forefeet and legs, and almost immediately the water that clung to it turned to ice. It made quick efforts to lick the ice off its legs, then dropped down in the snow and began to bite out the ice that had formed between the toes. This was a matter of instinct. To permit the ice to remain would mean sore feet. It did not know this. It merely obeyed the mysterious prompting that arose from the deep crypts of its being. But the man knew, having achieved a judgment on the subject, and he removed the mitten from his right hand and helped tear out the ice particles. He did not expose his fingers more than a minute, and was astonished at the swift numbness that smote them. It certainly was cold. He pulled on the mitten hastily, and beat the hand savagely across his chest.

At twelve o'clock the day was at its brightest. Yet the sun was too far south on its winter journey to clear the horizon. The bulge of the earth intervened between it and Henderson Creek, where the man walked under a clear sky at noon and cast no shadow. At half-past twelve, to the minute, he arrived at the forks of the creek. He was pleased at the speed he had made. If he kept it up, he would certainly be with the boys by six. He unbuttoned his jacket and shirt and drew forth his lunch. The action consumed no more than a quarter of a minute, yet in that brief moment the numbness laid hold of the exposed fingers. He did not put the mitten on, but, instead, struck the fingers a dozen sharp smashes against his leg. Then he sat down on a snow-covered log to eat. The sting that followed upon the striking of his fingers against his leg ceased so quickly that he was startled.

He had no chance to take a bite of biscuit. He struck the fingers repeatedly and returned them to the mitten, baring the other hand for the purpose of eating. He tried to take a mouthful but the ice muzzle prevented. He had forgotten to build a fire and thaw out. He chuckled at his foolishness, and as he chuckled he noted the numbness creeping into the exposed fingers. Also, he noted that the stinging which had first come to his toes when he sat down was already passing away. He wondered whether the toes were warm or numb. He moved them inside the moccasins and decided that they were numb.

He pulled the mitten on hurriedly and stood up. He was a bit frightened. He stamped up and down until the stinging returned into the feet. It certainly was cold, was his thought. That man from Sulphur Creek had spoken the truth when telling how cold it sometimes got in the country. And he had laughed at him at the time! That showed one must not be too sure of things. There was no mistake about it, it *was* cold. He strode up and down, stamping his feet and threshing his arms, until reassured by the returning warmth. Then he got out matches and proceeded to make a fire. From the undergrowth, where high water of the previous spring had lodged a supply of seasoned twigs, he got his firewood. Working carefully from a small beginning, he soon had a roaring fire, over which he thawed the ice from his face and in the protection of which he ate his biscuits. For the moment the cold of space was outwitted. The dog took satisfaction in the fire, stretching out close enough for warmth and far enough away to escape being singed.

When the man had finished, he filled his

Sheila Gardner, "Emeralds," 1986
Tatistcheff Gallery, New York

pipe and took his comfortable time over a smoke. Then he pulled on his mittens, settled the ear flaps of his cap firmly about his ears, and took the creek trail up the left fork. The dog was disappointed and yearned back toward the fire. This man did not know cold. Possibly all the generations of his ancestry had been ignorant of cold, of real cold, of cold one hundred and seven degrees below freezing point. But the dog knew; all its ancestry knew, and it had inherited the knowledge. And it knew that it was not good to walk abroad in such fearful cold. It was the time to lie snug in a hole in the snow and wait for a curtain of cloud to be drawn across the face of outer space whence this cold came. On the other hand, there was no keen intimacy between the dog and the man. The one was the toil slave of the other, and the only caresses it had ever received were the caresses of the whip lash and of harsh and menacing throat sounds that threatened the whip lash. So the dog made no effort to communicate its apprehension to the man. It was not concerned in the welfare of the man; it was for its own sake that it yearned back toward the fire. But the man whistled and spoke to it with the sound of whip lashes, and the dog swung in at the man's heels and followed after.

The man took a chew of tobacco and proceeded to start a new amber beard. Also, his moist breath quickly powdered with white his mustache, eyebrows, and lashes. There did not seem to be so many springs on the left fork of the Henderson, and for half an hour the man saw no signs of any. And then it happened. At a place where there were no signs, where the soft, unbroken snow seemed to advertise solidity beneath, the man broke through. It was not deep. He wet himself halfway to the knees before he floundered out to the firm crust.

He was angry and cursed his luck aloud. He had hoped to get into camp with the boys at six o'clock, and this would delay him an hour, for he would have to build a fire and dry out his footgear. This was imperative at that low temperature—he knew that much; and he turned aside to the bank which he climbed. On top, tangled in the underbrush about the trunks of several small spruce trees, was a high-water deposit of dry firewood—sticks and twigs, principally, but also larger portions of seasoned branches and fine, dry, last year's grasses. He threw down several large pieces on top of the snow. This served for a foundation and prevented the young flame from drowning itself in the snow it otherwise would melt. The flame he got by touching a match to a small shred of birch bark that he took from his pocket. This burned even more readily than paper. Placing it on the foundation, he fed the young flame with wisps of dry grass and with the tiniest dry twigs.

He worked slowly and carefully, keenly aware of his danger. Gradually, as the flame grew stronger, he increased the size of the twigs with which he fed it. He squatted in the snow, pulling the twigs out from their entanglement in the brush and feeding directly to the flame. He knew there must be no failure. When it is seventy-five below zero, a man must not fail in his first attempt to build a fire—that is, if his feet are wet. If his feet are dry, and he fails, he can run along the trail for half a mile and restore his circulation. But the circulation of wet and freezing feet cannot be restored by running when it is seventy-five below. No matter how fast he runs, the wet feet will freeze the harder.

All this the man knew. The old-timer on Sulphur Creek had told him about it the previous fall, and now he was appreciating the advice. Already all sensation had gone out of his feet. To build a fire he had been forced to remove his mittens, and the fingers had quickly gone numb. His pace of four miles an hour had kept his heart pumping blood to the surface of his body and to all the extremities. But the instant he stopped, the action of the pump eased down. The cold of space smote the unprotected tip of the planet, and he, being of that unprotected tip, received the full force of the blow. The blood of his body recoiled before it. The blood was alive, like the dog, and like the dog it wanted to hide away and cover itself up from the fearful cold. So long as he walked four miles an hour, he pumped that blood, willy-nilly, to the surface, but now it ebbed away and sank down into the recesses of his body. The extremities were the first to feel its absence. His wet feet froze the faster, and his exposed fingers numbed the faster, though they had not yet begun to freeze. Nose and cheeks were already freezing, while the skin of all his body chilled as it lost its blood.

But he was safe. Toes and nose and cheeks would be only touched by the frost, for the fire was beginning to burn with strength. He was feeding it with twigs the size of his finger. In another minute he would be able to feed it with branches the size of his wrist, and then he could remove his wet footgear, and, while it dried, he could keep his naked feet warm by the fire, rubbing them at first, of course, with snow. The fire was a success. He was safe. He remembered the advice of the old-timer on Sulphur Creek and smiled. The old-timer had been very serious in laying down the law that no man must travel alone in the Klondike[6] after fifty below. Well, here he was; he had had the accident; he was alone; and he had saved himself. Those old-timers were rather womanish, some of them, he thought. All a man had to do was to keep his head, and he was all right. Any man who was a man could travel alone. But it was surprising, the rapidity with which his cheeks and nose were freezing. And he had not thought his fingers could go lifeless in so short a time. Lifeless they were, for he could scarcely make them move together to grip a twig, and they seemed remote from his body and from him. When he touched a twig, he had to look and see whether or not he had hold of it. The wires were pretty well down between him and his finger ends.

All of which counted for little. There was the fire, snapping and crackling and promising life with every dancing flame. He started to untie his moccasins. They were coated with ice; the thick German socks were like sheaths of iron halfway to the knees; and the moccasin strings were like rods of steel all twisted and knotted as by some conflagration. For a moment he tugged with his numb fingers; then, realizing the folly of it, he drew his sheath knife.

But before he could cut the strings, it happened. It was his own fault or, rather, his mistake. He should not have built the fire

6. **Klondike** (klon′dīk), a region in the western part of the Yukon territory.

under the spruce tree. He should have built it in the open. But it had been easier to pull the twigs from the brush and drop them directly on the fire. Now the tree under which he had done this carried a weight of snow on its boughs. No wind had blown for weeks, and each bough was fully freighted. Each time he had pulled a twig he had communicated a slight agitation to the tree—an imperceptible agitation, so far as he was concerned, but an agitation sufficient to bring about the disaster. High up in the tree one bough capsized its load of snow. This fell on the boughs beneath, capsizing them. This process continued, spreading out and involving the whole tree. It grew like an avalanche, and it descended without warning upon the man and the fire, and the fire was blotted out! Where it had burned was a mantle of fresh and disordered snow.

The man was shocked. It was as though he had just heard his own sentence of death. For a moment he sat and stared at the spot where the fire had been. Then he grew very calm. Perhaps the old-timer on Sulphur Creek was right. If he had only had a trail mate he would have been in no danger now. The trail mate could have built the fire. Well, it was up to him to build the fire over again, and this second time there must be no failure. Even if he succeeded, he would most likely lose some toes. His feet must be badly frozen by now, and there would be some time before the second fire was ready.

Such were his thoughts, but he did not sit and think them. He was busy all the time they were passing through his mind. He made a new foundation for a fire, this time in the open, where no treacherous tree could blot it out. Next he gathered dry grasses and tiny twigs from the high-water flotsam. He could not bring his fingers together to pull them out, but he was able to gather them by the handful. In this way he got many rotten twigs and bits of green moss that were undesirable, but it was the best he could do. He worked methodically, even collecting an armful of the larger branches to be used later when the fire gathered strength. And all the while the dog sat and watched him, a certain yearning wistfulness in its eyes, for it looked upon him as the fire provider, and the fire was slow in coming.

When all was ready, the man reached in his pocket for a second piece of birch bark. He knew the bark was there, and, though he could not feel it with his fingers, he could hear its crisp rustling as he fumbled for it. Try as he would, he could not clutch hold of it. And all the time, in his consciousness, was the knowledge that each instant his feet were freezing. This thought tended to put him in a panic, but he fought against it and kept calm. He pulled on his mittens with his teeth, and threshed his arms back and forth, beating his hands with all his might against his sides. He did this sitting down, and he stood up to do it; and all the while the dog sat in the snow, its wolf brush of a tail curled around warmly over its forefeet, its sharp wolf ears pricked forward intently as it watched the man. And the man, as he beat and threshed with his arms and hands, felt a great surge of envy as he regarded the creature that was warm and secure in its natural covering.

After a time he was aware of the first faraway signals of sensation in his beaten fingers. The faint tingling grew stronger till it evolved

Photograph by Lisa Ebright

into a stinging ache that was excruciating but which the man hailed with satisfaction. He stripped the mitten from his right hand and fetched forth the birch bark. The exposed fingers were quickly going numb again. Next he brought out his bunch of sulphur matches. But the tremendous cold had already driven the life out of his fingers. In his effort to separate one match from the others, the whole bunch fell in the snow. He tried to pick it out of the snow, but failed. The dead fingers could neither touch nor clutch. He was very careful. He drove the thought of his freezing feet, and nose, and cheeks, out of his mind, devoting his whole soul to the matches. He watched, using the sense of vision in place of that of touch, and when he saw his fingers on each side of the bunch, he closed them—that is, he willed to close them, for the wires were down, and the fingers did not obey. He pulled the mitten on the right hand, and beat it fiercely against his knee. Then, with both mittened hands, he scooped the bunch of matches, along with much snow, into his lap. Yet he was no better off.

After some manipulation he managed to get the bunch between the heels of his mittened hands. In this fashion he carried it to his mouth. The ice crackled and snapped when, by a violent effort, he opened his mouth. He drew the lower jaw in, curled the upper lip out of the way, and scraped the bunch with his upper teeth in order to separate a match. He succeeded in getting one, which he dropped on his lap. He was no better off. He could not pick it up. Then he devised a way. He picked it up in his teeth and scratched it on his leg. Twenty times he scratched before he succeeded in lighting it. As it flamed he held it with his teeth to the birch bark. But the burning brimstone went up his nostrils and into his lungs, causing him to cough spasmodically. The match fell into the snow and went out.

The old-timer on Sulphur Creek was right, he thought in the moment of controlled despair that ensued: after fifty below, a man should travel with a partner. He beat his hands but failed in exciting any sensation. Suddenly he bared both hands, removing the mittens with his teeth. He caught the whole bunch between the heels of his hands. His arm muscles not being frozen enabled him to press the hand heels tightly against the matches. Then he scratched the bunch along his leg. It flared into flame, seventy sulphur matches at once! There was no wind to blow them out. He kept his head to one side to escape the fumes, and held the blazing bunch to the birch bark. As he so held it, he became aware of sensation in his hand. His flesh was burning. He could smell it. Deep down below the surface he could feel it. The sensation developed into pain that grew acute. And still he endured it, holding the flame of the matches clumsily to the bark that would not light readily because his own burning hands were in the way, absorbing most of the flame.

At last, when he could endure no more, he jerked his hands apart. The blazing matches fell sizzling into the snow, but the birch bark was alight. He began laying dry grasses and the tiniest twigs on the flame. He could not pick and choose, for he had to lift the fuel between the heels of his hands. Small pieces of rotten wood and green moss clung to the twigs, and he bit them off as well as he could with his teeth. He cherished the flame carefully and awkwardly. It meant life, and it must not perish. The withdrawal of blood from the surface of his body now made him begin to shiver, and he grew more awkward. A large piece of green moss fell squarely on the little fire. He tried to poke it out with his fingers, but his shivering frame made him poke too far, and he disrupted the nucleus of the little fire, the burning grasses and tiny twigs separating and scattering. He tried to poke them together again, but in spite of the tenseness of the effort, his shivering got away with him, and the twigs were hopelessly scattered. Each twig gushed a puff of smoke and went out. The fire provider had failed. As he looked apathetically about him, his eyes chanced on the dog, sitting across the ruins of the fire from him, in the snow, making restless, hunching movements, slightly lifting one forefoot and then the other, shifting its weight back and forth on them with wistful eagerness.

The sight of the dog put a wild idea into his head. He remembered the tale of the man, caught in a blizzard, who killed a steer and crawled inside the carcass and so was saved. He would kill the dog and bury his hands in the warm body until the numbness went out of them. Then he could build another fire.

He spoke to the dog, calling it to him, but in his voice was a strange note of fear that frightened the animal, who had never known the man to speak in such a way before. Something was the matter, and its suspicious nature sensed danger—it knew not what danger, but somewhere, somehow, in its brain arose an apprehension of the man. It flattened its ears down at the sound of the man's voice, and its restless, hunching movements and the liftings and shiftings of its forefeet became more pronounced; but it would not come to the man. He got on his hands and knees and crawled toward the dog. This unusual posture again excited suspicion, and the animal sidled mincingly away.

The man sat up in the snow for a moment and struggled for calmness. Then he pulled on his mittens, by means of his teeth, and got up on his feet. He glanced down at first in order to assure himself that he was really standing up, for the absence of sensation in his feet left him unrelated to the earth. His erect position in itself started to drive the webs of suspicion from the dog's mind, and when he spoke peremptorily, with the sound of whip lashes in his voice, the dog rendered its customary allegiance and came to him. As it came within reaching distance, the man lost his control. His arms flashed out to the dog, and he experienced genuine surprise when he discovered that his hands could not clutch, that there was neither bend nor feeling in the fingers. He had forgotten for the moment that they were frozen and that they were freezing more and more. All this happened quickly, and before the animal could get away, he encircled its body with his arms. He sat down in the snow and in this fashion held the dog, while it snarled and whined and struggled.

But it was all he could do, hold its body encircled in his arms and sit there. He realized that he could not kill the dog. There was no way to do it. With his helpless hands he could neither draw nor hold his sheath knife nor throttle the animal. He released it, and it plunged wildly away, with tail between its legs and still snarling. It halted forty feet away and surveyed him curiously, with ears sharply pricked forward.

The man looked down at his hands in order to locate them, and found them hanging on the ends of his arms. It struck him as curious that one should have to use his eyes in order to find out where his hands were. He began threshing his arms back and forth, beating the mittened hands against his sides. He did this for five minutes, violently, and his heart pumped enough blood up to the surface to put a stop to his shivering. But no sensation was aroused in the hands. He had an impression that they hung like weights on the ends of his arms, but when he tried to run the impression down, he could not find it.

A certain fear of death, dull and oppressive, came to him. This fear quickly became poignant as he realized that it was no longer a mere matter of freezing his fingers and toes, or of losing his hands and feet, but that it was a matter of life and death with the chances against him. This threw him into a panic, and he turned and ran up the creek bed along the old, dim trail. The dog joined in behind and kept up with him. He ran blindly, without intention, in fear such as he had never known in his life. Slowly, as he plowed and floundered through the snow, he began to see things again—the banks of the creek, the old timber jams, the leafless aspens, and the sky. The running made him feel better. He did not shiver. Maybe, if he ran on, his feet would thaw out, and, anyway, if he ran far enough, he would reach camp and the boys. Without doubt he would lose some fingers and toes and some of his face, but the boys would take care of him, and save the rest of him when he got there. And at the same time there was another thought in his mind that said he would never get to the camp and the boys, that it was too many miles away, that the freezing had too great a start on him, and that he would soon be stiff and dead. This thought he kept in the background and refused to consider. Sometimes it pushed itself forward and demanded to be heard, but he thrust it back and strove to think of other things.

It struck him as curious that he could run at all on feet so frozen that he could not feel them when they struck the earth and took the weight of his body. He seemed to himself to skim along above the surface and to have no connection with the earth. Somewhere he had once seen a winged Mercury,[7] and he wondered if Mercury felt as he felt when skimming over the earth.

His theory of running until he reached camp and the boys had one flaw in it: he lacked the endurance. Several times he stumbled, and finally he tottered, crumpled up, and fell. When he tried to rise, he failed. He must sit and rest, he decided, and next time he would merely walk and keep on going. As he sat and regained his breath, he noted that he was feeling quite warm and comfortable. He was not shivering, and it even seemed

that a warm glow had come to his chest and trunk. And yet, when he touched his nose or cheeks, there was no sensation. Running would not thaw them out. Nor would it thaw out his hands and feet. Then the thought came to him that the frozen portions of his body must be extending. He tried to keep this thought down, to forget it, to think of something else; he was aware of the panicky feeling that it caused, and he was afraid of the panic. But the thought asserted itself and persisted, until it produced a vision of his body totally frozen. This was too much, and he made another wild run along the trail. Once he slowed down to a walk, but the thought of the freezing extending itself made him run again.

And all the time the dog ran with him, at his heels. When he fell down a second time, it curled its tail over its forefeet and sat in front of him, facing him, curiously eager and intent. The warmth and security of the animal angered him, and he cursed it till it flattened down its ears appeasingly. This time the shivering came more quickly upon the man. He was losing in his battle with the frost. It was creeping into his body from all sides. The thought of it drove him on, but he ran no more than a hundred feet when he staggered and pitched headlong. It was his last panic. When he had recovered his breath and control, he sat up and entertained in his mind the conception of meeting death with dignity. However, the conception did not come to him in such terms. His idea of it was that he

---

7. *Mercury,* in Roman mythology, the messenger of the gods. He is usually depicted as having wings on his sandals.

had been making a fool of himself, running around like a chicken with its head cut off—such was the simile that occurred to him. Well, he was bound to freeze anyway, and he might as well take it decently. With this new-found peace of mind came the first glimmerings of drowsiness. A good idea, he thought, to sleep off to death. It was like taking an anesthetic. Freezing was not so bad as people thought. There were lots worse ways to die.

He pictured the boys finding his body next day. Suddenly he found himself with them, coming along the trail and looking for himself. And, still with them, he came around a turn in the trail and found himself lying in the snow. He did not belong with himself any more, for even then he was out of himself, standing with the boys and looking at himself in the snow. It certainly was cold, was his thought. When he got back to the States he could tell the folks what real cold was. He drifted on from this to a vision of the old-timer on Sulphur Creek. He could see him quite clearly, warm and comfortable, and smoking a pipe.

"You were right, old hoss; you were right," the man mumbled to the old-timer of Sulphur Creek.

Then the man drowsed off into what seemed to him the most comfortable and satisfying sleep he had ever known. The dog sat facing him and waiting. The brief day drew to a close in a long, slow twilight. There were no signs of a fire to be made, and, besides, never in the dog's experience had it known a man to sit like that in the snow and make no fire. As the twilight drew on, its eager yearning for the fire mastered it, and with a great lifting and shifting of forefeet, it whined softly, then flattened its ears down in anticipation of being chidden by the man. But the man remained silent. Later the dog whined loudly. And still later it crept close to the man and caught the scent of death. This made the animal bristle and back away. A little longer it delayed, howling under the stars that leaped and danced and shone-brightly in the cold sky. Then it turned and trotted up the trail in the direction of the camp it knew, where were the other food providers and fire providers.

THINK AND DISCUSS
Understanding
1. Why is the man traveling with only the dog?
2. Where and when is he to join his companions?
3. What advice did the Old Timer give the man before the journey?
4. How did the man react to this advice?
5. Near the end of the story, what does the man think about this advice?
6. According to medical research,

prolonged exposure to cold can have a deadly effect on the mind, as well as on the body: one can lose awareness, memory, and the ability to think clearly. Does the man show any symptoms of exposure?

Analyzing

7. In what ways are the dog's reactions to the cold different from the man's?
8. What purpose does the description of the dog's reactions serve in the story?
9. The narrator says that the man's basic problem is his lack of imagination. What examples of the man's thoughts and behavior support this statement?

Extending

10. Do you think that the man's basic problem is lack of imagination? Explain.
11. Do you think the ending is appropriate? Why or why not?

APPLYING: Setting H𝓩
See Handbook of Literary Terms, p. 686.

Setting is the time and place in which the events of a narrative occur. The setting may be specific and detailed and introduced at the very beginning of the story, or it may be merely suggested through the use of details scattered throughout the story. In some stories the setting is vital to the narrative: it may have an effect on the events of the plot, reveal character, or create a certain atmosphere. In other stories, the setting is relatively unimportant: the story could happen almost anywhere or at any time.

1. In this story the author uses a variety of ways to establish the setting and describe it in detail. Find two or more passages in which the setting is described directly.
2. Find two or more passages in which the setting is suggested through details.
3. In "To Build a Fire," is setting vital to the narrative? Give reasons to support your answer.

COMPOSITION ✒
Reading/Writing Log

In this story Jack London gives many specific examples of the murderous cold. One of these is given below. Copy the heading and this example in your reading/writing log. Then find at least two additional examples in the story and add them to the log.

Specific Examples of Cold

Also, the man was chewing tobacco, and the muzzle of ice held his lips so rigidly that he was unable to clear his chin when he expelled the juice. The result was that a crystal beard of the color and solidity of amber was increasing its length on his chin.

Describing a Place

Jack London helps readers experience the setting by using specific details. Now you use specifics to describe to your classmates and teacher the most intense heat, wind, storm, dust, flood, or dryness that you have experienced. You might begin with a sentence describing your topic. ("It was the worst flood in seven years.") Write two paragraphs that support this idea with specific details. In one paragraph describe how the flood affected animals, plant life, and buildings. In the other paragraph, show how it affected you or someone else. Before you begin to write, list details for both paragraphs. If you are keeping a reading/writing log, note the specific details that you have recorded in it. Try to be just as specific as you write your own list. Keep your list with you as you write.

Telling an Event

Imagine that you are the Old Timer who gave the man advice. You have just learned how the man died, and you write a three-paragraph letter about the man to a friend.

First, briefly describe your advice and the man's reaction to it. Then tell what happened to the man. Conclude your letter by giving your own feelings. Use specific details to make your friend see and feel what you are describing. You may find the article "Writing as a Story Character" in the Writer's Handbook helpful as you write this letter.

BIOGRAPHY

Jack London

1876–1916

The financial problems of his family forced Jack London to leave school and go to work at the age of fourteen. For several years, he wandered around the country. Then he returned home to San Francisco, completed high school, and later enrolled at the University of California for a short time.

In 1896, after the gold rush to the Klondike had begun, he went to Alaska. He found no gold, but the experiences of the prospectors and trappers of the region gave him the materials for the stories he was to write. Back in San Francisco, he supported himself and his family by working at odd jobs, writing and studying in his spare time. By 1913 he was one of the best-known writers in the country.

Jack London's stories about Alaska during the gold rush are still widely read. His best-known novel is *The Call of the Wild*, which you will read in Unit 8.

Review SETTING in the Handbook of Literary Terms, page 686

Top Man

James Ramsey Ullman

The mountain, to all us us, was no longer a mere giant of ice: it had become a living thing, an enemy, watching us, waiting for us, hostile, relentless.

---

he gorge bent. The walls fell suddenly away and we came out on the edge of a bleak, boulder-strewn valley. And there it was.

Osborn saw it first. He had been leading the column, threading his way slowly among the huge rock masses of the gorge's mouth. Then he came to the first flat, bare place and stopped. He neither pointed nor cried out, but every man behind him knew instantly what it was. The long file sprang taut, like a jerked rope. As swiftly as we could, but in complete silence, we came out into the open ground where Osborn stood, and raised our eyes with his. In the records of the Indian Topographical Survey it says:

Kalpurtha: a mountain in the Himalayas, altitude 28,900 ft. The highest peak in British India and fourth highest in the world. Also known as K3. A Tertiary formation of sedimentary limestone——

There were men among us who had spent months of their lives—in some cases, years—reading, thinking, planning about what now lay before us, but at that moment statistics and geology, knowledge, thought and plans, were as remote and forgotten as the faraway western cities from which we had come. We were men bereft of everything but eyes, everything but the single, electric perception: There it was!

Before us the valley stretched away into miles of rocky desolation. To right and left it was bounded by low ridges which, as the eye

---

The Assault on K3

Camp VI
Camp V
Camp IV
Camp III
glaciers
Camp II
Camp I
Base Camp
valley

A diagram of the stages in the expedition's efforts to conquer K3

followed them, slowly mounted and drew closer together until the valley was no longer a valley at all, but a narrowing, rising corridor between the cliffs. What happened then I can describe only as a single, stupendous crash of music. At the end of the corridor and above it—so far above it that it shut out half the sky—hung the blinding white mass of K3.

It was like the many pictures I had seen, and at the same time utterly unlike them. The shape was there, and the familiar distinguishing features—the sweeping skirt of glaciers; the monstrous vertical precipices of the face and the jagged ice line of the east ridge; finally the symmetrical summit pyramid that transfixed the sky. But whereas in the pictures the mountain had always seemed unreal—a dream image of cloud, snow and crystal—it was now no longer an image at all. It was a mass, solid, imminent, appalling. We were still too far away to see the windy whipping of its snow plumes or to hear the cannonading of its avalanches, but in that sudden silent moment every man of us was for the first time aware of it, not as a picture in his mind but as a thing, an antagonist. For all its twenty-eight thousand feet of lofty grandeur, it seemed, somehow, less to tower than to crouch—a white-hooded giant, secret and remote, but living. Living and on guard.

I turned my eyes from the dazzling glare and looked at my companions. Osborn still stood a little in front of the others. He was absolutely motionless, his young face tense and shining, his eyes devouring the mountain as a lover's might devour the face of his beloved. One could feel in the very set of his body the overwhelming desire that swelled in him to act, to come to grips, to conquer. A little behind him were ranged the other men of the expedition: Randolph, our leader, Wittmer and Johns, Doctor Schlapp and Bixler. All were still, their eyes cast upward. Off to one side a little stood Nace, the Englishman, the only one among us who was not staring at K3 for the first time. He had been the last to come up out of the gorge and stood now with arms folded on his chest, squinting at the great peak he had known so long and fought so tirelessly and fiercely. His lean British face, under its mask of stubble and windburn, was expressionless. His lips were a colorless line, and his eyes seemed almost shut. Behind the sahibs ranged the porters, bent over their staffs, their brown, seamed faces straining upward from beneath their loads.

For a long while no one spoke or moved. The only sounds between earth and sky were the soft hiss of our breathing and the pounding of our hearts.

Through the long afternoon we wound slowly between the great boulders of the valley and at sundown pitched camp in the bed of a dried-up stream. The porters ate their rations in silence, wrapped themselves in their blankets and fell asleep under the stars. The rest of us, as was our custom, sat close about the fire that blazed in the circle of tents, discussing the events of the day and the plans for the next. It was a flawlessly clear Himalayan night and K3 tiered up into the blackness like a monstrous sentinel lighted from within. There was no wind, but a great tide of cold air crept down the valley from the ice fields above, penetrating our clothing, pressing gently against the canvas of the tents.

"Another night or two and we'll be needing the sleeping bags," commented Randolph.

Osborn nodded. "We could use them tonight, would be my guess."

Randolph turned to Nace. "What do you say, Martin?"

The Englishman puffed at his pipe a moment. "Rather think it might be better to wait," he said at last.

"Wait? Why?" Osborn jerked his head up.

"Well, it gets pretty nippy high up, you know. I've seen it thirty below at twenty-five thousand on the east ridge. Longer we wait for the bags, better acclimated we'll get."

Osborn snorted. "A lot of good being acclimated will do if we have frozen feet."

"Easy, Paul, easy," cautioned Randolph. "It seems to me Martin's right."

Osborn bit his lip, but said nothing. The other men entered the conversation, and soon it had veered to other matters: the weather, the porters and pack animals, routes, camps and strategy—the inevitable, inexhaustible topics of the climber's world.

There were all kinds of men among the eight of us, men with a great diversity of background and interest. Sayre Randolph, whom the Alpine Club had named leader of our expedition, had for years been a well-known explorer and lecturer. Now in his middle fifties, he was no longer equal to the grueling physical demands of high climbing, but served as planner and organizer of the enterprise. Wittmer was a Seattle lawyer, who had recently made a name for himself by a series of difficult ascents in the Coast Range of British Columbia. Johns was an Alaskan, a fantastically strong, able sourdough, who had been a ranger in the U.S. Forest Service and had accompanied many famous Alaskan expeditions. Schlapp was a practicing physician from Milwaukee, Bixler a government meteorologist with a talent for photography. I, at the time, was an assistant professor of geology at an eastern university.

Finally, and preeminently, there were Osborn and Nace. I say "preeminently," because even at this time, when we had been together as a party for little more than a month, I believe all of us realized that these were the two key men of our venture. None, to my knowledge, ever expressed it in words, but the conviction was there, nevertheless, that if any of us were eventually to stand on the hitherto unconquered summit of K3, it would be one of them, or both. They were utterly dissimilar men. Osborn was twenty-three and a year out of college, a compact, buoyant mass of energy and high spirits. He seemed to be wholly unaffected by either the physical or mental hazards of mountaineering and had already, by virtue of many spectacular ascents in the Alps and Rockies, won a reputation as the most skilled and audacious of younger American climbers. Nace was in

his forties—lean, taciturn, introspective. An official in the Indian Civil Service, he had explored and climbed in the Himalayas for twenty years. He had been a member of all five of the unsuccessful British expeditions to K3, and in his last attempt had attained to within five hundred feet of the summit, the highest point which any man had reached on the unconquered giant. This had been the famous tragic attempt in which his fellow climber and lifelong friend, Captain Furness, had slipped and fallen ten thousand feet to his death. Nace rarely mentioned his name, but on the steel head of his ice ax were engraved the words: To MARTIN FROM JOHN. If fate were to grant that the ax of any one of us should be planted upon the summit of K3, I hoped it would be his.

Such were the men who huddled about the fire in the deep, still cold of that Himalayan night. There were many differences among us, in temperament as well as in background. In one or two cases, notably that of Osborn and Nace, there had already been a certain amount of friction, and as the venture continued and the struggles and hardships of the actual ascent began, it would, I knew, increase. But differences were unimportant. What mattered—all that mattered—was that our purpose was one—to conquer the monster of rock and ice that now loomed above us in the night; to stand for a moment where no man, no living thing, had ever stood before. To that end we had come from half a world away, across oceans and continents to the fastnesses of inner Asia. To that end we were prepared to endure cold, exhaustion and danger, even to the very last extremity of human endurance. Why? There is no answer, and at the same time every man among us knew the answer; every man who has ever looked upon a great mountain and felt the fever in his blood to climb and conquer, knows the answer. George Leigh Mallory, greatest of mountaineers, expressed it once and for all when he was asked why he wanted to climb unconquered Everest. "I want to climb it," said Mallory, "because it's there."

Day after day we crept on and upward. The naked desolation of the valley was unrelieved by any motion, color, or sound, and, as we progressed, it was like being trapped at the bottom of a deep well or in a sealed court between great skyscrapers. Soon we were thinking of the ascent of the shining mountain not only as an end in itself but as an escape.

In our nightly discussions around the fire, our conversation narrowed more and more to the immediate problems confronting us, and during them I began to realize that the tension between Osborn and Nace went deeper than I had at first surmised. There was rarely any outright argument between them—they were both far too able mountain men to disagree on fundamentals—but I saw that at almost every turn they were rubbing each other the wrong way. It was a matter of personalities chiefly. Osborn was talkative, enthusiastic, optimistic, always chafing to be up and at it, always wanting to take the short, straight line to the given point. Nace, on the other hand, was matter-of-fact, cautious, slow. He was the apostle of trial-and-error and watchful waiting. Because of his far greater experience and intimate knowledge of K3, Randolph almost invariably followed his advice,

rather than Osborn's, when a difference of opinion arose. The younger man usually capitulated with good grace, but I could tell that he was irked.

During the days in the valley I had few occasions to talk privately with either of them, and only once did either mention the other in any but the most casual manner. Even then, the remarks they made seemed unimportant, and I remember them only in view of what happened later.

My conversation with Osborn occurred first. It was while we were on the march, and Osborn, who was directly behind me, came up suddenly to my side.

"You're a geologist, Frank," he began without preamble. "What do you think of Nace's theory about the ridge?"

"What theory?" I asked.

"He believes we should traverse under it from the glacier up. Says the ridge itself is too exposed."

"It looks pretty mean through the telescope."

"But it's been done before. He's done it himself. All right, it's tough—I'll admit that. But a decent climber could make it in half the time the traverse will take."

"Nace knows the traverse is longer," I said, "but he seems certain it will be much easier for us."

"Easier for him is what he means." Osborn paused, looking moodily at the ground. "He was a great climber in his day. It's a shame a man can't be honest enough with himself to know when he's through." He fell silent and a moment later dropped back into his place in line.

It was that same night, I think, that I

awoke to find Nace sitting up in his blanket and staring at the mountain.

"How clear it is," I whispered.

The Englishman pointed. "See the ridge?"

I nodded, my eyes fixed on the great, twisting spine of ice that climbed into the sky. I could see now, more clearly than in the blinding sunlight, its huge indentations and jagged, wind-swept pitches.

"It looks impossible," I said.

"No, it can be done. Trouble is, when you've made it, you're too done in for the summit."

"Osborn seems to think its shortness would make up for its difficulty."

Nace was silent a long moment before answering. Then for the first and only time I heard him speak the name of his dead companion. "That's what Furness thought," he said quietly. Then he lay down and wrapped himself in his blanket.

For the next two weeks the uppermost point of the valley was our home and workshop. We established our base camp as close to the mountain as we could, less than half a mile from the tongue of its lowest glacier, and plunged into the arduous tasks of preparation for the ascent. Our food and equipment were unpacked, inspected, and sorted, and finally repacked in lighter loads for transportation to more advanced camps. Hours on end were spent poring over maps and charts and studying the monstrous heights above us through telescope and binoculars. Under Nace's supervision, a thorough reconnaissance of the glacier was made and the route across it laid out; then began the backbreaking labor of moving up supplies and establishing the advance stations.

Camps I and II were set up on the glacier itself, in the most sheltered sites we could find. Camp III we built at its upper end, as near as possible to the point where the great rock spine of K3 thrust itself free of ice and began its precipitous ascent. According to our plans, this would be the advance base of operations during the climb; the camps to be established higher up, on the mountain proper, would be too small and too exposed to serve as anything more than one or two nights' shelter. The total distance between the base camp and Camp III was only fifteen miles, but the utmost daily progress of our porters was five miles, and it was essential that we should never be more than twelve hours' march from food and shelter. Hour after hour, day after day, the long file of men wound up and down among the hummocks and crevasses of the glacier, and finally the time arrived when we were ready to advance.

Leaving Doctor Schlapp in command of eight porters at the base camp, we proceeded easily and on schedule, reaching Camp I the first night, Camp II the second and the advance base the third. No men were left at Camps I and II, inasmuch as they were designed simply as caches for food and equipment; and, furthermore, we knew we would need all the man power available for the establishment of the higher camps on the mountain proper.

For more than three weeks now the weather had held perfectly, but on our first night at the advance base, as if by malignant prearrangement of Nature, we had our first taste of the supernatural fury of a high Himalayan storm. It began with great streamers of lightning that flashed about the mountain like a halo; then heavily through the weird glare snow began to fall. The wind howled about the tents with hurricane frenzy, and the wild flapping of the canvas dinned in our ears like machine-gun fire.

There was no sleep for us that night or the next. For thirty-six hours the storm raged without lull, while we huddled in the icy gloom of the tents. At last, on the third morning, it was over, and we came out into a world transformed by a twelve-foot cloak of snow. No single landmark remained as it had been before, and our supplies and equipment were in the wildest confusion. Fortunately, there had not been a single serious injury, but it was another three days before we had regained our strength and put the camp in order.

Then we waited. The storm did not return, and the sky beyond the ridges gleamed flawlessly clear, but night and day we could hear the roaring thunder of avalanches on the mountain above us. To have ventured so much as one step into that savage, vertical wilderness before the new-fallen snow froze tight would have been suicidal. We chafed or waited patiently, according to our individual temperaments, while the days dragged by.

It was late one afternoon that Osborn returned from a short reconnaissance up the ridge. His eyes were shining and his voice jubilant.

"It's tight!" he cried. "Tight as a drum! We can go!" All of us stopped whatever we were doing. His excitement leaped like an electric spark from one to another. "I went about a thousand feet, and it's sound all the way. What do you say, Sayre? Tomorrow?"

Randolph hesitated a moment, then looked at Nace.

"Better give it another day or two," said the Englishman.

Osborn glared at him. "Why?" he challenged.

"It's generally safer to wait until——"

"Wait! Wait!" Osborn exploded. "Don't you ever think of anything but waiting? The snow's firm, I tell you!"

"It's firm down here," Nace replied quietly, "because the sun hits it only two hours a day. Up above it gets the sun twelve hours. It may not have frozen yet."

"The avalanches have stopped."

"That doesn't necessarily mean it will hold a man's weight."

"It seems to me, Martin's point——" Randolph began.

Osborn wheeled on him. "Sure," he snapped. "I know. Martin's right. The cautious bloody English are always right. Let him have his way, and we'll be sitting here twiddling our thumbs until the mountain falls down on us." His eyes flashed to Nace. "Maybe with a little less of that bloody cautiousness, you English wouldn't have made such a mess of Everest. Maybe your pals Mallory and Furness wouldn't be dead."

"Osborn!" commanded Randolph sharply.

The youngster stared at Nace for another moment, breathing heavily. Then, abruptly, he turned away.

The next two days were clear and windless, but we still waited, following Nace's advice. There were no further brushes between him and Osborn, but an unpleasant air of restlessness and tension hung over the camp. I found myself chafing almost as impatiently as Osborn himself for the moment when we would break out of that maddening inactivity and begin the assault.

At last the day came. With the first paling of the sky, a roped file of men, bent almost double beneath heavy loads, began slowly to climb the ice slope just beneath the jagged line of the great east ridge. In accordance with prearranged plan, we proceeded in relays; this first group consisting of Nace, Johns, myself and eight porters. It was our job to ascend approximately two thousand feet in a day's climbing and establish Camp IV at the most level and sheltered site we could find. We would spend the night there and return to the advance base next day, while the second relay, consisting of Osborn, Wittmer and eight more porters, went up with their loads. This process was to continue until all necessary supplies were at Camp IV, and then the whole thing would be repeated between Camps IV and V, and V and VI. From VI, at an altitude of about 26,000 feet, the ablest and fittest men—presumably Nace and Osborn—would make the direct assault on the summit. Randolph and Bixler were to remain at the advance base throughout the operations, acting as directors and coordinators. We were under the strictest orders that any man, sahib or porter, who suffered illness or injury should be brought down immediately.

How shall I describe those next two weeks beneath the great ice ridge of K3? In a sense, there was no occurrence of importance, and at the same time everything happened that could possibly happen, short of actual disaster. We established Camp IV, came down again, went up again, came down again.

Then we crept laboriously higher. The wind increased, and the air grew steadily colder and more difficult to breathe. One morning two of the porters awoke with their feet frozen black; they had to be sent down. A short while later Johns developed an uncontrollable nosebleed and was forced to descend to a lower camp. Wittmer was suffering from splitting headaches and I from a continually dry throat. But providentially, the one enemy we feared the most in that icy, gale-lashed hell did not again attack us—no snow fell. And day by day, foot by foot, we ascended.

It is during ordeals like this that the surface trappings of a man are shed and his secret mettle laid bare. There were no shirkers or quitters among us—I had known that from the beginning—but now, with each passing day, it became more manifest which were the strongest and ablest among us. Beyond all argument, these were Osborn and Nace.

Osborn was magnificent. All the boyish impatience and moodiness which he had exhibited earlier were gone, and, now that he was at last at work in his natural element, he emerged as the peerless mountaineer he was. His energy was inexhaustible, and his speed, both on rock and ice, almost twice that of any other man in the party. He was always discovering new routes and short cuts; and there was such vigor, buoyancy and youth in everything he did that it gave heart to all the rest of us.

In contrast, Nace was slow, methodical, unspectacular. Since he and I worked in the same relay, I was with him almost constantly, and to this day I carry in my mind the clear image of the man—his tall body bent almost double against endless, shimmering slopes of ice; his lean brown face bent in utter concentration on the problem in hand, then raised searchingly to the next; the bright prong of his ax rising, falling, rising, falling with tireless rhythm, until the steps in the glassy incline were so wide and deep that the most clumsy of the porters could not have slipped from them had he tried. Osborn attacked the mountain, head on. Nace studied it, sparred with it, wore it down. His spirit did not flap from his sleeve like a pennon; it was deep inside him, patient, indomitable.

The day came soon when I learned from him what it is to be a great mountaineer. We were making the ascent from Camp IV to V, and an almost perpendicular ice wall had made it necessary for us to come out for a few yards on the exposed crest of the ridge. There were six of us in the party, roped together, with Nace leading, myself second, and four porters bringing up the rear. The ridge at this particular point was free of snow, but razor-thin, and the rocks were covered with a smooth glaze of ice. On either side the mountain dropped away in sheer precipices of five thousand feet.

Suddenly the last porter slipped. In what seemed to be the same instant I heard the ominous scraping of boot nails and, turning, saw a wildly gesticulating figure plunge sideways into the abyss. There was a scream as the next porter followed him. I remember trying frantically to dig into the ridge with my ax, realizing at the same time it would no more hold against the weight of the falling men than a pin stuck in a wall. Then I heard Nace shout, "Jump!" As he said it, the rope went tight about my waist, and I went hur-

tling after him into space on the opposite side of the ridge. After me came the nearest porter.

What happened then must have happened in five yards and a fifth of a second. I heard myself cry out, and the glacier, a mile below, rushed up at me, spinning. Then both were blotted out in a violent spasm, as the rope jerked taut. I hung for a moment, an inert mass, feeling that my body had been cut in two; then I swung in slowly to the side of the mountain. Above me the rope lay tight and motionless across the crest of the ridge, our weight exactly counterbalancing that of the men who had fallen on the far slope.

Nace's voice came up from below. "You chaps on the other side!" he shouted. "Start climbing slowly! We're climbing too!"

In five minutes we had all regained the ridge. The porters and I crouched panting on the jagged rocks, our eyes closed, the sweat beading our faces in frozen drops. Nace carefully examined the rope that again hung loosely between us.

"All right, men," he said presently. "Let's get on to camp for a cup of tea."

Above Camp V the whole aspect of the ascent changed. The angle of the ridge eased off, and the ice, which lower down had covered the mountain like a sheath, lay only in scattered patches between the rocks. Fresh enemies, however, instantly appeared to take the place of the old. We were now laboring at an altitude of more than 25,000 feet—well above the summits of the highest surrounding peaks—and day and night, without protection or respite, we were buffeted by the savage fury of the wind. Worse than this was that the atmosphere had become so rarefied it

Porters on the Way to K2
Galen Rowell/Mountain Light

could scarcely support life. Breathing itself was a major physical effort, and our progress upward consisted of two or three painful steps, followed by a long period of rest in which our hearts pounded wildly and our burning lungs gasped for air. Each of us carried a small cylinder of oxygen in our pack, but we used it only in emergencies, and found that, though its immediate effect was salutary, it left us later even worse off than before.

But the great struggle was now mental rather than physical. The lack of air induced a lethargy of mind and spirit; confidence and the powers of thought and decision waned. The mountain, to all of us, was no longer a mere giant of rock and ice; it had become a living thing, an enemy, watching us, waiting for us, hostile, relentless.

On the fifteenth day after we had first left the advance base, we pitched Camp VI at an altitude of 26,500 feet. It was located near the uppermost extremity of the great east ridge, directly beneath the so-called shoulder of the mountain. On the far side of the shoulder the stupendous north face of K3 fell sheer to the glaciers, two miles below. Above it and to the left rose the symmetrical bulk of the summit pyramid. The topmost rocks of its highest pinnacle were clearly visible from the shoulder, and the intervening fifteen hundred feet seemed to offer no insuperable obstacles.

Camp VI, which was in reality no camp at all but a single tent, was large enough to accommodate only three men. Osborn established it with the aid of Wittmer and one porter; then, the following morning, Wittmer and the porter descended to Camp V, and

Nace and I went up. It was our plan that Osborn and Nace should launch the final assault—the next day, if the weather held—with myself in support, following their progress through binoculars and going to their aid or summoning help from below if anything went wrong. As the three of us lay in the tent that night, the summit seemed already within arm's reach, victory securely in our grasp.

And then the blow fell. With fiendishly malignant timing, which no power on earth could have made us believe was a simple accident of nature, the mountain hurled at us its last line of defense. It snowed.

For a day and a night the great flakes drove down upon us, swirling and swooping in the wind, blotting out the summit, the shoulder, everything beyond the tiny white-walled radius of our tent. At last, during the morning of the following day, it cleared. The sun came out in a thin blue sky, and the summit pyramid again appeared above us, now whitely robed in fresh snow. But still we waited. Until the snow either froze or was blown away by the wind, it would have been the rashest courting of destruction for us to have ascended a foot beyond the camp. Another day passed. And another.

By the third nightfall our nerves were at the breaking point. For hours on end we had scarcely moved or spoken, and the only sounds in all the world were the endless moaning of the wind outside and the harsh, sucking noise of our breathing. I knew that, one way or another, the end had come. Our meager food supply was running out; even with careful rationing, there was enough left for only two more days.

Presently Nace stirred in his sleeping bag

and sat up. "We'll have to go down tomorrow," he said quietly.

For a moment there was silence in the tent. Then Osborn struggled to a sitting position and faced him.

"No," he said.

"There's still too much loose snow above. We can't make it."

"But it's clear. As long as we can see—"

Nace shook his head. "Too dangerous. We'll go down tomorrow and lay in a fresh supply. Then we'll try again."

"Once we go down we're licked. You know it."

Nace shrugged. "Better to be licked than——" The strain of speech was suddenly too much for him and he fell into a violent paroxysm of coughing. When it had passed, there was a long silence.

Then, suddenly, Osborn spoke again. "Look, Nace," he said, "I'm going up tomorrow."

The Englishman shook his head.

"I'm going—understand?"

For the first time since I had known him, I saw Nace's eyes flash in anger. "I'm the senior member of this group," he said. "I forbid you to go!"

With a tremendous effort, Osborn jerked himself to his feet. "You forbid me? This may be your sixth time on this mountain, and all that, but you don't own it! I know what you're up to. You haven't got it in you to make the top yourself, so you don't want anyone else to get the glory. That's it, isn't it? Isn't it?" He sat down again suddenly, gasping for breath.

Nace looked at him with level eyes. "This mountain has licked me five times," he said

softly. "It killed my best friend. It means more to me to lick it than anything else in the world. Maybe I'll make it and maybe I won't. But if I do, it will be as a rational, intelligent human being, not as a fool throwing my life away——"

He collapsed into another fit of coughing and fell back in his sleeping bag. Osborn, too, was still. They lay there inert, panting, too exhausted for speech.

It was hours later that I awoke from dull, uneasy sleep. In the faint light I saw Nace fumbling with the flap of the tent.

"What is it?" I asked.

"Osborn. He's gone."

The words cut like a blade through my lethargy. I struggled to my feet and followed Nace from the tent.

Outside, the dawn was seeping up the eastern sky. It was very cold, but the wind had fallen and the mountain seemed to hang suspended in a vast stillness. Above us the summit pyramid climbed bleakly into space, like the last outpost of a spent lifeless planet. Raising my binoculars, I swept them over the gray waste. At first I saw nothing but rock and ice; then, suddenly, something moved.

"I've got him," I whispered.

As I spoke, the figure of Osborn sprang into clear focus against a patch of ice. He took three or four slow upward steps, stopped, went on again. I handed the glasses to Nace.

The Englishman squinted through them a moment, returned them to me, and re-entered the tent. When I followed, he had already laced his boots and was pulling on his outer gloves.

"He's not far," he said. "Can't have been

gone more than half an hour." He seized his ice ax and started out again.

"Wait," I said. "I'm going with you."

Nace shook his head. "Better stay here."

"I'm going with you," I said.

He said nothing further, but waited while I made ready. In a few moments we left the tent, roped up, and started off.

Almost immediately we were on the shoulder and confronted with the paralyzing two-mile drop of the north face, but we negotiated the short exposed stretch without mishap and in ten minutes were working up the base of the summit pyramid. Our progress was creepingly slow. There seemed to be literally no air at all to breathe, and after almost every step we were forced to rest.

The minutes crawled into hours, and still we climbed. Presently the sun came up. Its level rays streamed across the clouds far below, and glinted from the summits of distant peaks. But, although the pinnacle of K3 soared a full five thousand feet above anything in the surrounding world, we had scarcely any sense of height. The stupendous wilderness of mountains and glaciers that spread beneath us to the horizon was flattened and remote, an unreal, insubstantial landscape seen in a dream. We had no connection with it, or it with us. All living, all awareness, purpose and will, was concentrated in the last step and the next—to put one foot before the other; to breathe; to ascend. We struggled on in silence.

I do not know how long it was since we had left the camp—it might have been two hours, it might have been six—when we suddenly sighted Osborn. We had not been able to find him again since our first glimpse through the binoculars, but now, unexpectedly and abruptly, as we came up over a jagged outcropping of rock, there he was. He was at a point, only a few yards above us, where the mountain steepened into an almost vertical wall. The smooth surface directly in front of him was obviously unclimbable, but two alternate routes were presented. To the left, a chimney cut obliquely across the wall, forbiddingly steep, but seeming to offer adequate holds. To the right was a gentle slope of snow that curved upward and out of sight behind the rocks. As we watched, Osborn ascended to the edge of the snow, stopped and tested it with his foot; then, apparently satisfied that it would bear his weight, he stepped out on the slope.

I felt Nace's body tense. "Paul!" he cried out.

His voice was too weak and hoarse to carry. Osborn continued his ascent.

Nace cupped his hands and called his name again, and this time Osborn turned. "Wait!" cried the Englishman.

Osborn stood still, watching us, as we struggled up the few yards to the edge of the snow slope. Nace's breath came in shuddering gasps, but he climbed faster than I had ever seen him climb before.

"Come back!" he called. "Come off the snow!"

"It's all right! The crust is firm!" Osborn called back.

"But it's melting! There's"—Nace paused, fighting for air—"there's nothing underneath!"

In a sudden, horrifying flash I saw what he meant. Looked at from directly below, at the point where Osborn had come to it, the slope on which he stood appeared as a harmless covering of snow over the rocks. From where we were now, however, a little to one side, it could be seen that it was in reality no covering at all, but merely a cornice or unsupported platform clinging to the side of the mountain. Below it was not rock, but ten thousand feet of blue air.

"Come back!" I cried. "Come back!"

Osborn hesitated, then took a downward step. But he never took the next. For in that same instant the snow directly in front of him disappeared. It did not seem to fall or to break away. It was just soundlessly and magically no longer there. In the spot where Osborn had been about to set his foot there was now revealed the abysmal drop of the north face of K3.

I shut my eyes, but only for a second, and when I reopened them Osborn was still, miraculously, there.

Nace was shouting, "Don't move! Don't move an inch!"

"The rope," I heard myself saying.

The Englishman shook his head. "We'd have to throw it, and the impact would be too much. Brace yourself and play it out." As we spoke, his eyes were traveling over the rocks that bordered the snow bridge. Then he moved forward.

I wedged myself into a cleft in the wall and let out the rope which extended between us. A few yards away, Osborn stood in the snow, transfixed, one foot a little in front of the other. But my eyes now were on Nace. Cautiously, but with astonishing rapidity, he edged along the rocks beside the cornice. There was a moment when his only support was an inch-wide ledge beneath his feet, an-

other where there was nothing under his feet at all and he supported himself wholly by his elbows and hands. But he advanced steadily, and at last reached a shelf wide enough for him to turn around on. At this point he was perhaps six feet away from Osborn.

"It's wide enough here to hold both of us," he said in a quiet voice. "I'm going to reach out my ax. Don't move until you're sure you have a grip on it. When I pull, jump."

He searched the wall behind him and found a hold for his left hand. Then he slowly extended his ice ax, head foremost, until it was within two feet of Osborn's shoulder.

"Grip it!" he cried suddenly. Osborn's hands shot out and seized the ax. "Jump!"

There was a flash of steel in the sunlight and a hunched figure hurtled inward from the snow to the ledge. Simultaneously another figure hurtled out. The haft of the ax jerked suddenly from Nace's hand, and he lurched forward and downward. A violent, sickening spasm convulsed my body as the rope went taut. Then it was gone. Nace did not seem to hit the snow; he simply disappeared through it, soundlessly. In the same instant the snow itself was gone. The frayed, yellow end of broken rope spun lazily in space.

Somehow my eyes went to Osborn. He was crouched on the ledge where Nace had been a moment before, staring dully at the ax he held in his hands. Beyond his head, not two hundred feet above, the white, untrodden pinnacle of K3 stabbed the sky.

Perhaps ten minutes passed, perhaps a half hour. I closed my eyes and leaned forward motionless against the rock, my face against my arm. I neither thought nor felt; my body and mind alike were enveloped in a suffocating numbness. Through it at last came the sound of Osborn moving. Looking up, I saw he was standing beside me.

"I'm going to try to make the top," he said tonelessly.

I merely stared at him.

"Will you come?"

I shook my head slowly. Osborn hesitated a moment, then turned and began slowly climbing the steep chimney above us. Halfway up he paused, struggling for breath. Then he resumed his laborious upward progress and presently disappeared beyond the crest.

I stayed where I was, and the hours passed. The sun reached its zenith above the peak and sloped away behind it. And at last I heard above me the sound of Osborn returning. As I looked up, his figure appeared at the top of the chimney and began the descent. His clothing was in tatters, and I could tell from his movements that only the thin flame of his will stood between him and collapse. In another few minutes he was standing beside me.

"Did you get there?" I asked.

He shook his head slowly. "I couldn't make it," he answered. "I didn't have what it takes."

We roped together silently and began the descent to the camp. There is nothing more to be told of the sixth assault on K3—at least not from the experiences of the men who made it. Osborn and I reached Camp V in safety, and three days later the entire expedition gathered at the advance base. It was decided, in view of the appalling tragedy that had occurred, to make no further attempt on the summit, and we began the evacuation of the mountain.

It remained for another year and other men to reveal the epilogue.

The summer following our attempt a combined English-Swiss expedition stormed the peak successfully. After weeks of hardship and struggle, they attained the topmost pinnacle of the giant, only to find that what should have been their great moment of triumph was, instead, a moment of the bitterest disappointment. For when they came out at last upon the summit, they saw that they were not the first. An ax stood there. Its haft was embedded in rock and ice, and on its steel head were the engraved words: To MARTIN FROM JOHN.

They were sporting men. On their return to civilization they told their story, and the name of the conqueror of K3 was made known to the world.

THINK AND DISCUSS

Understanding

1. Why are the men climbing the mountain?
2. Of the two men who are chosen to climb to the summit of K3, which is the younger? the more impatient?
3. Who is killed near the summit of K3? How is he killed?

Analyzing

4. What incident in Nace's past might explain his approach to mountaineering?
5. What **internal conflicts** are present in "Top Man"? What **external conflicts**?
6. Do the internal and external conflicts influence each other? Explain.
7. Find camps V and VI on the diagram on page 85. What important events take place in or near each camp?
8. Whose ax does the English-Swiss team find at the summit of K3? How did it get there?
9. When Osborn returns from the summit of K3, he tells the narrator, "I didn't have what it takes." What does he mean?

Extending

10. Who do you think is the "top man"? Explain.

REVIEWING: Setting H7

See **Handbook of Literary Terms, p. 686.**

Setting is the time and place in which events in a narrative occur. In some cases setting is specific and detailed; in others, it is merely suggested. Setting may be vital to plot, or it may be unimportant.

1. To what extent does the setting influence the characters' thoughts and actions?
2. To what extent does the setting influence the events of the plot?

VOCABULARY

Affixes and Roots

Many words in English are made up of smaller parts. Recognizing the arrangement and meaning of these parts—the structure of a word—may help you understand the whole word.

The *root* is the main part of a word and carries the word's basic meaning. To the root may be added one or more parts:

prefix	*root*	*suffix*
pre-	arrange	-ment

A *prefix* is a word part added to the beginning of a root to change the meaning in some way. The prefix *pre-*, for example, means "before."

A *suffix* is a word part added to the end of a root. Sometimes suffixes change the meaning, but more importantly they determine the function of the new word. In the example, the suffix *-ment* is added to the verb *arrange* to form the noun *arrangement*.

Now put together the meanings of all the parts to get the meaning of *prearrangement*: "the way or order in which persons or things are arranged beforehand."

The general name for both prefixes and suffixes is *affixes*. A word formed from a root plus one or more affixes is called a *derivative*.

Look closely at the structure of the

italicized derivatives in the following material. (If necessary, look up the meanings of prefixes, roots, or suffixes in the Glossary.) Then answer these questions on a sheet of paper.

1. The prefix *dis-* belongs to a group of prefixes (also including *de-*, *in-*, *non-*, and *un-*) called negative prefixes that mean "not" or have other negative meanings. If something is *dissimilar*, is it the same as or different from something else?

2. What is the root in *inactivity?* How does the negative prefix change the meaning of the root? What part of speech is *inactivity?*

3. If *peerless* means "without a peer, or equal," what does *flawless* mean?

4. When suffixes are added to certain roots, the spelling of the root changes. Common spelling changes include dropping a final *e*, changing a final *y* to *i*, and doubling a final consonant. What is the root in *supernatural?* What spelling change has taken place?

5. What is the root in *counterbalancing?* What does the prefix *counter-* mean? Use the word in a sentence.

COMPOSITION

Portraying a Setting as a Living Thing

Many characters in the story describe K3 as a killer, saying it takes conscious and "fiendish" delight in spoiling their plans. Write a paragraph in which you describe a setting as if it were a living thing. The setting you choose does not have to be one you consider an evil enemy.

Writing to Persuade

In a composition of one or two pages, tell whether (and why) you agree or disagree with this statement: *"Top Man" is ruined by its ending; nobody would ever actually behave as Nace and Osborn did.* Begin with a paragraph containing the statement and telling whether you agree with it. The paragraphs following should contain reasons for your opinion and examples from the story to support those reasons. Use the final paragraph to summarize.

BIOGRAPHY

James Ramsey Ullman
1907–1971

Born in New York in 1907, James Ramsey Ullman grew up to become a world traveler, more familiar with faraway places than with his native city. He climbed mountains on all continents, and in 1963 he was a member of the successful American Mount Everest Expedition. Among his best-known books are *The White Tower, Banner in the Sky, The Age of Mountaineering, Tiger of the Snows,* and *Americans on Everest.*

See POINT OF VIEW in the Handbook of Literary Terms, page 680

Rain, Rain, Go Away

Isaac Asimov

The new neighbors seemed to be sweet, but they were also a little strange.

---

here she is again," said Lillian Wright as she adjusted the venetian blinds carefully. "There she is, George."

"There who is?" asked her husband, trying to get satisfactory contrast on the TV so that he might settle down to the ball game.

"Mrs. Sakkaro," she said, and then, to forestall her husband's inevitable "Who's that?" added hastily, "The new neighbors, for goodness sake."

"Oh."

"Sunbathing. Always sunbathing. I wonder where her boy is. He's usually out on a nice day like this, standing in that tremendous yard of theirs and throwing the ball against the house. Did you ever see him, George?"

"I've heard him. It's a version of the Chinese water torture.[1] Bang on the wall, biff on the ground, smack in the hand. Bang, biff, smack, bang, biff——"

"He's a *nice* boy, quiet and well-behaved. I wish Tommie would make friends with him. He's the right age, too, just about ten, I should say."

"I didn't know Tommie was backward about making friends."

"Well, it's hard with the Sakkaros. They keep so to themselves. I don't even know what Mr. Sakkaro does."

"Why should you? It's not really anyone's business what he does."

"It's odd that I never see him go to work."

---

1. ***Chinese water torture***, a form of torture in which the victim is driven mad by the constant, measured drip of water on his or her head.

"No one ever sees me go to work."

"You stay home and write. What does *he* do?"

"I dare say Mrs. Sakkaro knows what Mr. Sakkaro does and is all upset because she doesn't know what *I* do."

"Oh, George." Lillian retreated from the window and glanced with distaste at the television. (Schoendienst was at bat.) "I think we should make an effort; the neighborhood should."

"What kind of an effort?" George was comfortable on the couch now, with a kingsize Coke in his hand, freshly opened and frosted with moisture.

"To get to know them."

"Well, didn't you, when she first moved in? You said you called."

"I said hello but, well, she'd just moved in and the house was still upset, so that's all it could be, just hello. It's been two months now and it's still nothing more than hello, sometimes. —She's so odd."

"Is she?"

"She's always looking at the sky; I've seen her do it a hundred times and she's never been out when it's the least bit cloudy. Once, when the boy was out playing, she called to him to come in, shouting that it was going to rain. I happened to hear her and I thought, wouldn't you know and me with a wash on the line, so I hurried out and, you know, it was broad sunlight. Oh, there were some clouds, but nothing, really."

"Did it rain, eventually?"

"Of course not. I just had to run out in the yard for nothing."

George was lost amid a couple of base hits and a most embarrassing bobble that meant a run. When the excitement was over and the pitcher was trying to regain his composure, George called out after Lillian, who was vanishing into the kitchen, "Well, since they're from Arizona, I dare say they don't know rainclouds from any other kind."

Lillian came back into the living room with a patter of high heels. "From where?"

"From Arizona, according to Tommie."

"How did Tommie know?"

"He talked to their boy, in between ball chucks, I guess, and he told Tommie they came from Arizona and then the boy was called in. At least, Tommie says it might have been Arizona, or maybe Alabama or some place like that. You know Tommie and his nontotal recall. But if they're that nervous about the weather, I guess it's Arizona and they don't know what to make of a good rainy climate like ours."

"But why didn't you ever tell me?"

"Because Tommie only told me this morning and because I thought he must have told you already and, to tell the absolute truth, because I thought you could just manage to drag out a normal existence even if you never found out. Wow——"

The ball went sailing into the right field stands and that was that for the pitcher.

Lillian went back to the venetian blinds and said, "I'll simply just have to make her acquaintance. She looks *very* nice. —Oh, look at that, George."

George was looking at nothing but the TV.

Lillian said, "I know she's staring at that cloud. And now she'll be going in. Honestly."

George was out two days later on a reference search in the library and came home with a load of books. Lillian greeted him jubilantly.

She said, "Now, you're not doing anything tomorrow."

"That sounds like a statement, not a question."

"It *is* a statement. We're going out with the Sakkaros to Murphy's Park."

"With——"

"With the next-door neighbors, George. *How* can you never remember the name?"

"I'm gifted. How did it happen?"

"I just went up to their house this morning and rang the bell."

"That easy?"

"It wasn't easy. It was hard. I stood there, jittering, with my finger on the doorbell, till I thought that ringing the bell would be easier than having the door open and being caught standing there like a fool."

"And she didn't kick you out?"

"No. She was sweet as she could be. Invited me in, knew who I was, said she was so glad I had come to visit. *You* know."

"And you suggested we go to Murphy's Park."

"Yes. I thought if I suggested something that would let the children have fun, it would be easier for her to go along with it. She wouldn't want to spoil a chance for her boy."

"A mother's psychology."

"But you should see her home."

"Ah. You had a reason for all this. It comes out. You wanted the Cook's tour.[2] But, please, spare me the color-scheme details. I'm not interested in the bedspreads, and the size of the closets is a topic with which I can dispense."

It was the secret of their happy marriage that Lillian paid no attention to George. She went into the color-scheme details, was most meticulous about the bedspreads, and gave him an inch-by-inch description of closet-size.

"And *clean?* I have never seen any place so spotless."

"If you get to know her, then, she'll be setting you impossible standards and you'll have to drop her in self-defense."

"Her kitchen," said Lillian, ignoring him, "was so spanking clean you just couldn't believe she ever used it. I asked for a drink of water and she held the glass underneath the tap and poured slowly so that not one drop fell in the sink itself. It wasn't affectation. She did it so casually that I just knew she always did it that way. And when she gave me the glass she held it with a clean napkin. Just hospital-sanitary."

"She must be a lot of trouble to herself. Did she agree to come with us right off?"

"Well—not right off. She called to her husband about what the weather forecast was, and he said that the newspapers all said it would be fair tomorrow but that he was waiting for the latest report on the radio."

"*All* the newspapers said so, eh?"

"Of course, they all just print the official weather forecast, so they would all agree. But I think they do subscribe to all the newspapers. At least I've watched the bundle the newsboy leaves——"

"There isn't much you miss, is there?"

"Anyway," said Lillian severely, "she called up the weather bureau and had them

---

2. **Cook's tour,** a quick, well-organized tour in which attractions are viewed only briefly, so-called after a British travel agent.

tell her the latest and she called it out to her husband and they said they'd go, except they said they'd phone us if there were any unexpected changes in the weather."

"All right. Then we'll go."

The Sakkaros were young and pleasant, dark and handsome. In fact, as they came down the long walk from their home to where the Wright automobile was parked, George leaned toward his wife and breathed into her ear. "So *he*'s the reason."

"I wish he were," said Lillian. "Is that a handbag he's carrying?"

"Pocket-radio. To listen to weather forecasts, I bet."

The Sakkaro boy came running after them, waving something which turned out to be an aneroid barometer,[3] and all three got into the back seat. Conversation was turned on and lasted, with neat give-and-take on impersonal subjects, to Murphy's Park.

The Sakkaro boy was so polite and reasonable that even Tommie Wright, wedged between his parents in the front seat, was subdued by example into a semblance of civilization. Lillian couldn't recall when she had spent so serenely pleasant a drive.

She was not the least disturbed by the fact that, barely to be heard under the flow of the conversation, Mr. Sakkaro's small radio was on, and she never actually saw him put it occasionally to his ear.

It was a beautiful day at Murphy's Park; hot and dry without being too hot; and with a cheerfully bright sun in a blue, blue sky. Even Mr. Sakkaro, though he inspected every quarter of the heavens with a careful eye and then stared piercingly at the barometer, seemed to have no fault to find.

Lillian ushered the two boys to the amusement section and bought enough tickets to allow one ride for each on every variety of centrifugal thrill that the park offered.

"Please," she had said to a protesting Mrs. Sakkaro, "let this be my treat. I'll let you have your turn next time."

When she returned, George was alone. "Where——" she began.

"Just down there at the refreshment stand. I told them I'd wait here for you and we would join them." He sounded gloomy.

"Anything wrong?"

"No, not really, except that I think he must be independently wealthy."

"What?"

"I don't know what he does for a living. I hinted——"

"Now who's curious?"

"I was doing it for you. He said he's just a student of human nature."

"How philosophical. That would explain all those newspapers."

"Yes, but with a handsome, wealthy man next door, it looks as though I'll have impossible standards set for me, too."

"Don't be silly."

"And he doesn't come from Arizona."

"He doesn't?"

"I said I heard he was from Arizona. He looked so surprised, it was obvious he didn't.

---

3. *aneroid* (an'ə roid') *barometer,* an instrument in which changes in air pressure are registered on a dial, used in predicting probable changes in the weather. The "falling" barometer, mentioned later, means that the air pressure is increasing and that rain is likely.

Alex Katz, "The Blue Umbrella #2," 1972
Private Collection

Then he laughed and asked if he had an Arizona accent."

Lillian said thoughtfully, "He has some kind of accent, you know. There are lots of Spanish-ancestry people in the Southwest, so he could still be from Arizona. Sakkaro could be a Spanish name."

"Sounds Japanese to me. —Come on, they're waving. Oh, look what they've bought."

The Sakkaros were each holding three sticks of cotton candy, huge swirls of pink foam consisting of threads of sugar dried out of frothy syrup that had been whipped about in a warm vessel. It melted ¯sweetly in the mouth and left one feeling sticky.

The Sakkaros held one out to each Wright, and out of politeness the Wrights accepted.

They went down the midway, tried their hand at darts, at the kind of poker game where balls were rolled into holes, at knocking wooden cylinders off pedestals. They took pictures of themselves and recorded their voices and tested the strength of their handgrips.

Eventually they collected the youngsters, who had been reduced to a satisfactorily breathless state of roiled-up insides, and the

Sakkaros ushered theirs off instantly to the refreshment stand. Tommie hinted the extent of his pleasure at the possible purchase of a hot-dog and George tossed him a quarter. He ran off, too.

"Frankly," said George. "I prefer to stay here. If I see them biting away at another cotton candy stick I'll turn green and sicken on the spot. If they haven't had a dozen apiece, I'll eat a dozen myself."

"I know, and they're buying a handful for the child now."

"I offered to stand Sakkaro a hamburger and he just looked grim and shook his head. Not that a hamburger's much, but after enough cotton candy, it ought to be a feast."

"I know. I offered her an orange drink and the way she jumped when she said no, you'd think I'd thrown it in her face. —Still, I suppose they've never been to a place like this before and they'll need time to adjust to the novelty. They'll fill up on cotton candy and then never eat it again for ten years."

"Well, maybe." They strolled toward the Sakkaros. "You know, Lil, it's clouding up."

Mr. Sakkaro had the radio to his ear and was looking anxiously toward the west.

"Uh-oh," said George, "he's seen it. One gets you fifty, he'll want to go home."

All three Sakkaros were upon him, polite but insistent. They were sorry, they had had a wonderful time, a marvelous time, the Wrights would have to be their guests as soon as it could be managed, but now, really, they had to go home. It looked stormy. Mrs. Sakkaro wailed that all the forecasts had been for fair weather.

George tried to console them. "It's hard to predict a local thunderstorm, but even if it

were to come, and it mightn't, it wouldn't last more than half an hour on the outside."

At which comment, the Sakkaro youngster seemed on the verge of tears, and Mrs. Sakkaro's hand, holding a handkerchief, trembled visibly.

"Let's go home," said George in resignation.

The drive back seemed to stretch interminably. There was no conversation to speak of. Mr. Sakkaro's radio was quite loud now as he switched from station to station, catching a weather report every time. They were mentioning "local thundershowers" now.

The Sakkaro youngster piped up that the barometer was falling, and Mrs. Sakkaro, chin in the palm of her hand, stared dolefully at the sky and asked if George could not drive faster, please.

"It does look rather threatening, doesn't it?" said Lillian in a polite attempt to share their guests' attitude. But then George heard her mutter, "Honestly!" under her breath.

A wind had sprung up, driving the dust of the weeks-dry road before it, when they entered the street on which they lived, and the leaves rustled ominously. Lightning flickered.

George said, "You'll be indoors in two minutes, friends. We'll make it."

He pulled up at the gate that opened onto the Sakkaros' spacious front yard and got out of the car to open the back door. He thought he felt a drop. They were *just* in time.

The Sakkaros tumbled out, faces drawn with tension, muttering thanks, and started off toward their long front walk at a dead run.

"Honestly," began Lillian, "you would think they were——"

The heavens opened and the rain came down in giant drops as though some celestial dam had suddenly burst. The top of their car was pounded with a hundred drum sticks, and halfway to their front door the Sakkaros stopped and looked despairingly upward.

Their faces blurred as the rain hit; blurred and shrank and ran together. All three shriveled, collapsing within their clothes, which sank down into three sticky-wet heaps.

And while the Wrights sat there, transfixed with horror, Lillian found herself unable to stop the completion of her remark: "—made of sugar and afraid they would melt."

THINK AND DISCUSS
Understanding
1. What things has Lillian Wright noticed about the new neighbors?
2. How does George view her curiosity?
3. What do the Sakkaros worry about?
4. Why do the Wrights and Sakkaros leave Murphy's Park?
5. What happens to the Sakkaros?

Analyzing
6. In what ways is the Sakkaros' behavior in keeping with their main concern?
7. Is Lillian's last observation about the Sakkaros accurate? Explain.
8. Where are the Sakkaros probably from?
9. Throughout the story, are readers given any hints about how it will end?

Extending
10. Do you think the story is tragic, comic, or something else? Explain.

APPLYING: Point of View HT
See Handbook of Literary Terms, p. 680.
Point of view refers to the relationship between the narrator and the story he or she tells. The author's choice of narrator for a story determines the amount of information a reader will be given.
1. From what point of view is this story told?
2. In what ways would the story have been different if it had been narrated by Lillian Wright? by Mrs. Sakkaro?

VOCABULARY
Context
Look up the following words in the Glossary to determine their meaning. Then decide which would best complete each of the sentences. Write that word on your paper.

affectation   resignation
attitude   semblance
composure

1. Daniel had spent only two weeks in London, so his friends in Florida knew his English accent was a temporary _____.

2. When the children begged her to ride

with them on the roller coaster, Janet sighed in _____ and went with them.

3. The diving champion was known for her ability to keep her _____ in tensely competitive situations.

4. By shoving clothes, books, and toys under the bed, Randy was able to create a _____ of order in his room.

5. Todd's casual _____ toward dress was shown especially when he arrived at the formal dinner in tennis shoes.

THINKING SKILLS
Generalizing

To generalize is to draw a general conclusion from particular information. For example, a scientist studies a planet through powerful telescopes, analyzes material brought back from the planet by unmanned space vehicles, and looks at satellite photos. Then he or she generalizes about whether the planet can sustain human life.

Make a generalization about the place the Sakkaros come from. Review the story to find the specific information you need in order to make this generalization.

COMPOSITION
Reporting the News

Write a newspaper account of events in this story. In the first paragraph, tell what happened. In the second paragraph, describe the reactions of the people who knew the Sakkaro family and saw what happened, quoting at least two members of the Wright family. In the third paragraph, report what the police are saying and doing. In the fourth, give the opinion of a scientist you interviewed.

Convincing Your Readers

Pretend that you are a member of the Wright family. Friends, neighbors, and even strangers think that you played some sinister part in what happened to the Sakkaros. Write a letter to the editor of your local newspaper. In your letter tell why you are writing, state that you did nothing wrong, and provide all the evidence you can to persuade your readers that you are telling the truth. Be sure to add a conclusion, one that you hope will impress readers. You may find "Writing as a Story Character" in the Writer's Handbook helpful as you write your letter.

BIOGRAPHY

Isaac Asimov
1920–

Born in Russia, Isaac Asimov came to New York City, where his family lived above his father's candy store. By the time he was five, he had taught himself to read; at nine he knew he was hooked on science fiction. For years he combined teaching at Boston University with a prolific writing career. His best-known science fiction includes the *Foundation* series and a collection of stories called *I, Robot*. Today he lives in New York City and devotes all his time to writing.

Review POINT OF VIEW in the Handbook of Literary Terms, page 680.

The Tell-Tale Heart

Edgar Allan Poe

What is it about the old man's eye that makes the narrator's blood run cold?

rue!—nervous—very dreadfully nervous I had been and am; but why *will* you say that I am mad? The disease had sharpened my senses—not destroyed—not dulled them. Above all was the sense of hearing acute. I heard all things in the heavens and in the earth. I heard many things in hell. How, then, am I mad? Hearken! and observe how healthily—how calmly I can tell you the whole story.

It is impossible to say how first the idea entered my brain; but once conceived, it haunted me day and night. Object there was none. Passion there was none. I loved the old man. He had never wronged me. He had never given me insult. For his gold I had no desire. I think it was his eye! Yes, it was this! One of his eyes resembled that of a vulture—a pale blue eye, with a film over it. Whenever it fell upon me, my blood ran cold; and so by degrees—very gradually—I made up my mind to take the life of the old man, and thus rid myself of the eye forever.

Now this is the point. You fancy me mad. Madmen know nothing. But you should have seen *me*. You should have seen how wisely I proceeded—with what caution—with what foresight—with what dissimulation I went to work! I was never kinder to the old man than during the whole week before I killed him. And every night, about midnight, I turned the latch of his door and opened it—oh, so gently! And then, when I had made an opening sufficient for my head, I put in a dark lantern,[1] all closed, closed, so that no light shone out, and then I thrust in my head. Oh,

---

1. *dark lantern*, a lantern whose light can be hidden by a cover over the opening.

From *The Complete Works of Edgar Allan Poe*, edited by James A. Harrison (17 vols.). New York: AMS Press, 1902.

you would have laughed to see how cunningly I thrust it in! I moved it slowly—very, very slowly, so that I might not disturb the old man's sleep. It took me an hour to place my whole head within the opening so far that I could see him as he lay upon his bed. Ha!—would a madman have been so wise as this? And then, when my head was well in the room, I undid the lantern cautiously—oh, so cautiously—cautiously (for the hinges creaked)—I undid it just so much that a single thin ray fell upon the vulture eye. And this I did for seven long nights—every night just at midnight—but I found the eye always closed; and so it was impossible to do the work; for it was not the old man who vexed me, but his Evil Eye. And every morning, when the day broke, I went boldly into the chamber, and spoke courageously to him, calling him by name in a hearty tone, and inquiring how he had passed the night. So you see he would have been a very profound old man, indeed, to suspect that every night, just at twelve, I looked in upon him while he slept.

Upon the eighth night I was more than usually cautious in opening the door. A watch's minute hand moves more quickly than did mine. Never before that night had I *felt* the extent of my own powers—of my sagacity. I could scarcely contain my feelings of triumph. To think that there I was, opening the door, little by little, and he not even to dream of my secret deeds or thoughts. I fairly chuckled at the idea; and perhaps he heard me; for he moved on the bed suddenly, as if startled. Now you may think that I drew back—but no. His room was as black as pitch with the thick darkness (for the shut-

ters were close fastened, through fear of robbers), and so I knew that he could not see the opening of the door, and I kept pushing it on steadily, steadily.

I had my head in, and was about to open the lantern, when my thumb slipped upon the tin fastening, and the old man sprang up in the bed, crying out—"Who's there?"

I kept quite still and said nothing. For a whole hour I did not move a muscle, and in the meantime I did not hear him lie down. He was still sitting up in the bed listening—just as I have done, night after night, hearkening to the death watches[2] in the wall.

Presently I heard a slight groan, and I knew it was the groan of mortal terror. It was not a groan of pain or of grief—oh, no!—it was the low stifled sound that arises from the bottom of the soul when overcharged with awe. I knew the sound well. Many a night, just at midnight, when all the world slept, it has welled up from my own bosom, deepening, with its dreadful echo, the terrors that distracted me. I say I knew it well. I knew what the old man felt, and pitied him, although I chuckled at heart. I knew that he had been lying awake ever since the first slight noise, when he had turned in the bed. His fears had been ever since growing upon him. He had been trying to fancy them causeless, but could not. He had been saying to himself: "It is nothing but the wind in the chimney—it is only a mouse crossing the floor," or "It is merely a cricket which has made a single chirp." Yes, he had been trying to comfort himself with these suppositions;

---

2. **death watches,** small beetles that live in wood and make a ticking sound.

Construction
by George Suyeoka

but he had found all in vain. *All in vain;* because Death, in approaching him, had stalked with his black shadow before him, and enveloped the victim. And it was the mournful influence of the unperceived shadow that caused him to feel—although he neither saw nor heard—to *feel* the presence of my head within the room.

When I had waited a long time, very patiently, without hearing him lie down, I resolved to open a little—a very, very little crevice in the lantern. So I opened it—you cannot imagine how stealthily, stealthily—until, at length, a single dim ray, like the thread of the spider, shot from out the crevice and full upon the vulture eye.

It was open—wide, wide open—and I grew furious as I gazed upon it. I saw it with perfect distinctness—all a dull blue, with a hideous veil over it that chilled the very marrow in my bones; but I could see nothing else of the old man's face or person, for I had directed the ray as if by instinct, precisely upon the spot.

And now have I not told you that what you mistake for madness is but overacuteness of the senses?—now, I say, there came to my ears a low, dull, quick sound, such as a watch makes when enveloped in cotton. I knew *that* sound well too. It was the beating of the old man's heart. It increased my fury, as the beating of a drum stimulates the soldier into courage.

But even yet I refrained and kept still. I scarcely breathed. I held the lantern motionless. I tried how steadily I could maintain the ray upon the eye. Meantime the hellish tattoo of the heart increased. It grew quicker and quicker, and louder and louder every instant.

The old man's terror *must* have been extreme! It grew louder, I say, louder every moment!—do you mark me well? I have told you that I am nervous: so I am. And now at the dead hour of the night, amid the dreadful silence of that old house, so strange a noise as this excited me to uncontrollable terror. Yet, for some minutes longer I refrained and stood still. But the beating grew louder, louder! I thought the heart must burst. And now a new anxiety seized me—the sound would be heard by a neighbor! The old man's hour had come! With a loud yell, I threw open the lantern and leaped into the room. He shrieked once—once only. In an instant I dragged him to the floor, and pulled the heavy bed over him. I then smiled gaily, to find the deed so far done. But, for many minutes, the heart beat on with a muffled sound. This, however, did not vex me; it would not be heard through the wall. At length it ceased. The old man was dead. I removed the bed and examined the corpse. Yes, he was stone, stone dead. I placed my hand upon the heart and held it there many minutes. There was no pulsation. He was stone dead. His eye would trouble me no more.

If still you think me mad, you will think so no longer when I describe the wise precautions I took for the concealment of the body. The night waned, and I worked hastily, but in silence. First of all I dismembered the corpse. I cut off the head and the arms and the legs.

I then took up three planks from the flooring of the chamber, and deposited all between the scantlings. I then replaced the boards so cleverly, so cunningly, that no human eye—not even *his*—could have detected anything wrong. There was nothing to wash out—no stain of any kind—no bloodspot whatever. I had been too wary for that. A tub had caught all—ha! ha!

When I had made an end of these labors, it was four o'clock—still dark as midnight. As the bell sounded the hour, there came a knocking at the street door. I went down to open it with a light heart—for what had I *now* to fear? There entered three men, who introduced themselves, with perfect suavity, as officers of the police. A shriek had been heard by a neighbor during the night; suspicion of foul play had been aroused; information had been lodged at the police office, and they (the officers) had been deputed to search the premises.

I smiled—for *what* had I to fear? I bade the gentlemen welcome. The shriek, I said, was my own in a dream. The old man, I mentioned, was absent in the country. I took my visitors all over the house. I bade them search—search *well*. I led them, at length, to *his* chamber. I showed them his treasures, secure, undisturbed. In the enthusiasm of my confidence, I brought chairs into the room, and desired them *here* to rest from their fatigues, while I myself, in the wild audacity of my perfect triumph, placed my own seat upon the very spot beneath which reposed the corpse of the victim.

The officers were satisfied. My *manner* had convinced them. I was singularly at ease. They sat, and while I answered cheerily, they chatted of familiar things. But, ere long, I felt myself getting pale and wished them gone. My head ached, and I fancied a ringing in my ears: but still they sat and still chatted. The ringing became more distinct; it continued and became more distinct; I talked more freely to get rid of the feeling; but it continued and gained definiteness—until, at length, I found that the noise was *not* within my ears.

No doubt I now grew *very* pale—but I talked more fluently, and with a heightened voice. Yet the sound increased—and what could I do? It was *a low, dull, quick sound—much such a sound as a watch makes when enveloped in cotton*. I gasped for breath—and yet the officers heard it not. I talked more quickly—more vehemently; but the noise steadily increased. I arose and argued about trifles, in a high key and with violent gesticulations, but the noise steadily increased. Why *would* they not be gone? I paced the floor to and fro with heavy strides, as if excited to fury by the observation of the men—but the noise steadily increased. Oh, what *could* I do? I foamed—I raved—I swore! I swung the chair upon which I had been sitting, and grated it upon the boards, but the noise arose over all and continually increased. It grew louder—louder—*louder!* And still the men chatted pleasantly, and smiled. Was it possible they heard not? No, no! They heard!—they suspected!—they *knew!*—they were making a mockery of my horror!—this I thought, and this I think. But anything was better than this agony! Anything was more tolerable than this derision! I could bear those hypocritical smiles no longer! I felt that I must scream or die!—and now—again!—hark! louder! louder! louder! *louder!*——

"Villains!" I shrieked, "dissemble no more! I admit the deed!—tear up the planks!—here, here!—it is the beating of his hideous heart!"

THINK AND DISCUSS
Understanding
1. Why does the narrator want to kill the old man?
2. How does he go about carrying out his plans?
3. Why do his plans go wrong?
4. What does the narrator do when the police come to question him?

Analyzing
5. Throughout the story, the narrator insists he is not mad. What proofs of his sanity does he offer?
6. Is the narrator characterized as sane or insane? Cite passages from the story to support your answer.

Extending
7. This story was written over one hundred years ago. Why do you think it is still widely read?
8. Edgar Allan Poe believed that a short story should create a "single emotional effect." What emotional effect do you think Poe created in this story? Pick out specific details that help create this effect.

REVIEWING: Point of View HT
See Handbook of Literary Terms, p. 680.

Point of view refers to the author's choice of narrator. The major points of view are (a) **first person,** in which a character from the story is the narrator; (b) **third-person objective,** in which the narrator is an outsider who can report only what he or she sees and hears; (c) **third-person limited,** in which the narrator is an outsider who can see into the mind of one character; (d) **third-person omniscient,** in which the narrator is an all-knowing outsider.

1. What is the point of view in "The Tell-Tale Heart"?
2. Who is the narrator?
3. What does Poe's use of this point of view and narrator cause the reader to experience?

COMPOSITION
Changing the Point of View
Imagine that you are one of the police officers who come to investigate the shriek heard in the night. When you return to the station, you write a report of a page or two on the incident. Use the pronoun *I*. Describe the appearance of the house during your search. Describe the man's appearance and behavior. Do you notice anything strange about him? What are your thoughts during the chat "about familiar things" that leads to the confession? What happens after that?

Describing an Emotion
Imagine that you are Edgar Allan Poe. "The Tell-Tale Heart" has just been published, and one reader has written you a letter. This reader has confused you, Edgar Allan Poe, with your creation, the narrator of the story. The letter says—in the cruelest words imaginable—that you are horribly and criminally mad, so insane that you don't even know that you are. It goes on to suggest various things that should be done to you, each of these more horrible than the last. Write a diary entry

for the day you receive the letter. In the entry, briefly describe what has happened; then tell how you feel about it.

ENRICHMENT
Speaking and Listening

Volunteer either to give an oral reading of "The Tell-Tale Heart," or to work with a classmate who has volunteered. Groups consisting of the student who will read and three or four helpers should meet several times to listen to the reading and make suggestions for improvement. Share the results of group work by presenting all readings to the entire class. Listeners should evaluate each reader according to the suggestions for improvement discussed in the small-group sessions.

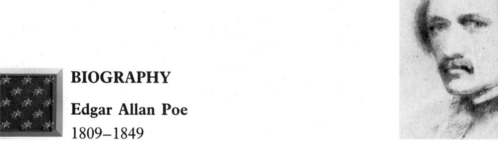

BIOGRAPHY

Edgar Allan Poe
1809–1849

The life of Edgar Allan Poe was, for the most part, a tragic one. Orphaned at an early age, Poe was taken in by the wealthy Allan family of Virginia. Following his attendance at English schools and instruction by private tutors, Poe attended the University of Virginia for a year. He also attended the military academy at West Point for a short time but was expelled. Increasing friction between Poe and his foster father led to a final break between the two when Poe was twenty-three.

Forced to make his own living, Poe turned to writing and editing. He achieved success as a poet, literary critic, and especially as a short-story writer. Poe believed that a short story should be written to produce a single emotional effect within the reader: all events, characters, ideas, and words should be chosen and manipulated solely for the purpose of achieving this effect. Few writers have used this formula more effectively than did Poe himself. Among his most famous short stories are "The Pit and the Pendulum," "The Cask of Amontillado," "The Fall of the House of Usher," and his detective stories "The Gold Bug" and "The Purloined Letter."

See INFERENCE in the Handbook of Literary Terms, page 671

Charles

Shirley Jackson

Charles was certainly a bad influence. But just who was he?

The day my son Laurie started kindergarten he renounced corduroy overalls with bibs and began wearing blue jeans with a belt. I watched him go off the first morning with the older girl next door, seeing clearly that an era of my life was ended, my sweet-voiced nursery-school tot replaced by a long-trousered, swaggering character who forgot to stop at the corner and wave goodbye to me.

He came home the same way, the front door slamming open, his hat on the floor, and the voice suddenly become raucous shouting, "Isn't anybody *here?*"

At lunch he spoke insolently to his father, spilled his baby sister's milk, and remarked that his teacher said we were not to take the name of the Lord in vain.

"How *was* school today?" I asked, elaborately casual.

"All right," he said.

"Did you learn anything?" his father asked.

Laurie regarded his father coldly. "I didn't learn nothing," he said.

"Anything," I said. "Didn't learn anything."

"The teacher spanked a boy, though," Laurie said, addressing his bread and butter. "For being fresh," he added, with his mouth full.

"What did he do?" I asked. "Who was it?"

Laurie thought. "It was Charles," he said. "He was fresh. The teacher spanked him and made him stand in a corner. He was awfully fresh."

"What did he do?" I asked again, but Laurie slid off his chair, took a cookie, and left, while his father was still saying, "See here, young man."

The next day Laurie remarked at lunch, as soon as he sat down, "Well, Charles was bad again today." He grinned enormously and

"Charles" from *The Lottery* by Shirley Jackson. Copyright 1948, 1949 by Shirley Jackson. Copyright renewed © 1976, 1977 by Lawrence Hyman, Barry Hyman, Mrs. Sara Webster, and Mrs. Joanne Schurer. *The Lottery* originally appeared in *The New Yorker*. Reprinted by permission of Farrar, Straus & Giroux, Inc. and Brandt & Brandt Literary Agents.

said, "Today Charles hit the teacher."

"Good heavens," I said, mindful of the Lord's name. "I suppose he got spanked again?"

"He sure did," Laurie said. "Look up," he said to his father.

"What?" his father said, looking up.

"Look down," Laurie said. "Look at my thumb. Gee, you're dumb." He began to laugh insanely.

"Why did Charles hit the teacher?" I asked quickly.

"Because she tried to make him color with red crayons," Laurie said. "Charles wanted to color with green crayons so he hit the teacher and she spanked him and said nobody play with Charles but everybody did."

The third day—it was Wednesday of the first week—Charles bounced a see-saw on the head of a little girl and made her bleed, and the teacher made him stay inside all during recess. Thursday Charles had to stand in a corner during story-time because he kept pounding his feet on the floor. Friday Charles was deprived of blackboard privileges because he threw chalk.

On Saturday I remarked to my husband, "Do you think kindergarten is too unsettling for Laurie? All this toughness and bad grammar, and this Charles boy sounds like such a bad influence."

"It'll be all right," my husband said reassuringly. "Bound to be people like Charles in the world. Might as well meet them now as later."

On Monday Laurie came home late, full of news. "Charles," he shouted as he came up the hill; I was waiting anxiously on the front steps. "Charles," Laurie yelled all the way up the hill. "Charles was bad again."

"Come right in," I said, as soon as he came close enough. "Lunch is waiting."

"You know what Charles did?" he demanded, following me through the door. "Charles yelled so in school they sent a boy in from first grade to tell the teacher she had to make Charles keep quiet, and so Charles had to stay after school. And so all the children stayed to watch him."

"What did he do?" I asked.

"He just sat there," Laurie said, climbing into his chair at the table. "Hi, Pop, y'old dust mop."

"Charles had to stay after school today," I told my husband. "Everyone stayed with him."

"What does this Charles look like?" my husband asked Laurie. "What's his other name?"

"He's bigger than me," Laurie said. "And he doesn't have any rubbers and he doesn't ever wear a jacket."

Monday night was the first Parent-Teachers meeting, and only the fact that the baby had a cold kept me from going; I wanted passionately to meet Charles's mother. On Tuesday Laurie remarked suddenly, "Our teacher had a friend come to see her in school today."

"Charles's mother?" my husband and I asked simultaneously.

"Naaah," Laurie said scornfully. "It was a man who came and made us do exercises, we had to touch our toes. Look." He climbed down from his chair and squatted down and touched his toes. "Like this," he said. He got solemnly back into his chair and said, picking up his fork, "Charles didn't even *do* exercises."

"That's fine," I said heartily. "Didn't Charles want to do the exercises?"

Paul Klee, "Senecio," 1922
Kunstmuseum, Basle

"Naaah," Laurie said. "Charles was so fresh to the teacher's friend he wasn't *let* do exercises."

"Fresh again," I said.

"He kicked the teacher's friend," Laurie said. "The teacher's friend told Charles to touch his toes like I just did and Charles kicked him."

"What are they going to do about Charles, do you suppose?" Laurie's father asked him.

Laurie shrugged elaborately. "Throw him out of school, I guess," he said.

Wednesday and Thursday were routine; Charles yelled during story hour and hit a boy in the stomach and made him cry. On Friday Charles stayed after school again and so did all the other children.

With the third week of kindergarten Charles was an institution in our family; the baby was being a Charles when she cried all afternoon; Laurie did a Charles when he filled his wagon full of mud and pulled it through the kitchen; even my husband, when he caught his elbow in the telephone cord and pulled telephone, ashtray, and a bowl of flowers off the table, said, after the first minute, "Looks like Charles."

During the third and fourth weeks it looked like a reformation in Charles; Laurie reported grimly at lunch on Thursday of the third week, "Charles was so good today the teacher gave him an apple."

"What?" I said, and my husband added warily, "You mean Charles?"

"Charles," Laurie said. "He gave the crayons around and he picked up the books afterward and the teacher said he was her helper."

"What happened?" I asked incredulously.

"He was her helper, that's all," Laurie said, and shrugged.

"Can this be true, about Charles?" I asked my husband that night. "Can something like this happen?"

"Wait and see," my husband said cynically. "When you've got a Charles to deal with, this may mean he's only plotting."

He seemed to be wrong. For over a week Charles was the teacher's helper; each day he handed things out and he picked things up; no one had to stay after school.

"The PTA meeting's next week again," I told my husband one evening. "I'm going to find Charles's mother there."

"Ask her what happened to Charles," my husband said. "I'd like to know."

"I'd like to know myself," I said.

On Friday of that week things were back to normal. "You know what Charles did today?" Laurie demanded at the lunch table, in a voice slightly awed. "He told a little girl to say a word and she said it and the teacher washed her mouth out with soap and Charles laughed."

"What word?" his father asked unwisely, and Laurie said, "I'll have to whisper it to you, it's so bad." He got down off his chair and went around to his father. His father bent his head down and Laurie whispered joyfully. His father's eyes widened.

"Did Charles tell the little girl to say *that?*" he asked respectfully.

"She said it *twice,*" Laurie said. "Charles told her to say it *twice.*"

"What happened to Charles?" my husband asked.

"Nothing," Laurie said. "He was passing out the crayons."

Monday morning Charles abandoned the little girl and said the evil word himself three or four times, getting his mouth washed out with soap each time. He also threw chalk.

My husband came to the door with me that evening as I set out for the PTA meeting. "Invite her over for a cup of tea after the meeting," he said. "I want to get a look at her."

"If only she's there," I said prayerfully.

"She'll be there," my husband said. "I don't see how they could hold a PTA meeting without Charles's mother."

At the meeting I sat restlessly, scanning each comfortable matronly face, trying to determine which one hid the secret of Charles. None of them looked to me haggard enough. No one stood up in the meeting and apologized for the way her son had been acting. No one mentioned Charles.

After the meeting I identified and sought out Laurie's kindergarten teacher. She had a plate with a cup of tea and a piece of chocolate cake; I had a plate with a cup of tea and a piece of marshmallow cake. We maneuvered up to one another cautiously, and smiled.

"I've been so anxious to meet you," I said. "I'm Laurie's mother."

"We're all so interested in Laurie," she said.

"Well, he certainly likes kindergarten," I said. "He talks about it all the time."

"We had a little trouble adjusting, the first week or so," she said primly, "but now he's a fine little helper. With occasional lapses, of course."

"Laurie usually adjusts very quickly," I said. "I suppose this time it's Charles's influence."

"Charles?"

"Yes," I said, laughing, "you must have your hands full in that kindergarten, with Charles."

"Charles?" she said. "We don't have any Charles in the kindergarten."

THINK AND DISCUSS
Understanding
1. Give some examples of how Laurie treats his parents.
2. Describe Charles's behavior in the kindergarten class.

Analyzing
3. In what ways are Laurie's actions similar to those of Charles?
4. Describe the ways Laurie's teacher tries to change Charles's behavior. Which of these methods seems to work best?
5. Who do you think the troublemaker in Laurie's class is?

Extending
6. What do you think Laurie's parents say to Laurie the day after the PTA meeting?

APPLYING: Inference H
See Handbook of Literary Terms, p. 671.
One way to make correct **inferences** about characters is to pay close attention to what those characters say and do.
1. Why are Laurie's parents so eager to meet Charles's mother?
2. Laurie describes Charles in these words: "He's bigger than me. And he doesn't

have any rubbers, and he doesn't even wear a jacket." Once you discover who Charles is, what inference about Laurie can you make from this description?

VOCABULARY
Context

Use context clues to figure out the meanings of the italicized words in these sentences.

1. He talks back to the teacher, ignores his father, and makes fun of his mother—he certainly is an *insolent* child. (a) clever; (b) loud; (c) friendly; (d) rude.
2. The crows' cawing sounded loud and *raucous;* especially in contrast to the doves' gentle cooing. (a) sweet; (b) harsh; (c) distant; (d) pleasant.
3. Even though he had loved and cared for the stray dog, Greg *renounced* his claim to the animal when its former owner appeared. (a) gave up; (b) announced; (c) demanded; (d) renewed.
4. Because she was unsure whether or not the thief had a gun, the policewoman approached him *warily*. (a) kindly; (b) cautiously; (c) angrily; (d) clumsily.

COMPOSITION
Writing a Narrative

Have you ever baby-sat for a child like Laurie? Write a composition of at least two paragraphs telling about your experience.

Writing a Story

Readers love surprise endings. Write a story that has one. Your classmates and teacher are your audience.

ENRICHMENT
Role Playing

By the second PTA meeting, the teacher is able to describe Laurie's behavior objectively and without emotion (page 120, column 2, paragraph 4), but she probably had had stronger feelings about Laurie earlier. How do you suppose she felt after the first day of school? the first week?

Working in small groups, take turns playing the part of the kindergarten teacher at the end of the first week of classes. Others in your group should act as the teacher's friends or family, offering sympathy and suggestions.

BIOGRAPHY

Shirley Jackson
1919–1965

Laurie, the child in "Charles," is modeled on a real person—Shirley Jackson's first child. The story appears, among other places, in Jackson's *Life Among the Savages*, which she called "a disrespectful memoir of my children." At the time of Jackson's death at the age of forty-six, she had published six novels, a collection of stories, two fictionalized accounts of her experiences with her husband and children, and three works for children, one of these a play.

Review INFERENCE in the Handbook of Literary Terms, page 671.

Mr. Mendelsohn

Nicholasa Mohr

"Man, I don't get you. You got a whole apartment next door all to yourself—six rooms! And you gotta come here to eat in this crowded kitchen. Why?"

---

sst . . . psst, Mr. Mendelsohn, wake up. Come on now!" Mrs. Suárez[1] said in a low quiet voice. Mr. Mendelsohn had fallen asleep again, on the large armchair in the living room. He grasped the brown shiny wooden cane and leaned forward, his chin on his chest. The small black skullcap that was usually placed neatly on the back of his head had tilted to one side, covering his right ear. "Come on now. It's late, and time to go home." She tapped him on the shoulder and waited for him to wake up. Slowly, he lifted his head, opened his eyes, and blinked.

"What time is it?" he asked.

"It's almost midnight. Caramba![2] I didn't even know you was still here. When I came to shut off the lights, I saw you was sleeping."

"Oh . . . I'm sorry. O.K., I'm leaving." With short, slow steps he followed Mrs. Suárez over to the front door.

"Go on now," she said, opening the door. "We'll see you tomorrow."

He walked out into the hallway, stepped about three feet to the left, and stood before the door of his apartment. Mrs. Suárez waited, holding her door ajar, while he carefully searched for the right key to each lock. He had to open seven locks in all.

A small fluffy dog standing next to Mrs. Suárez began to whine and bark.

"Shh—sh, Sporty! Stop it!" she said. "You had your walk. Shh."

"O.K.," said Mr. Mendelsohn, finally opening his door. "Good night." Mrs. Suárez smiled and nodded.

---

1. **Mrs. Suárez** (swä′res).
2. **caramba!** (kä räm′bä), goodness!
Nicholasa Mohr (nē kô lä′sä môr).

"Mr. Mendelsohn" from *El Bronx Remembered* by Nicholasa Mohr. Copyright © 1975 by Nicholasa Mohr. Reprinted by permission of Harper & Row, Publishers, Inc.

"Good night," she whispered, as they both shut their doors simultaneously.

Mr. Mendelsohn knocked on the door and waited; then tried the doorknob. Turning and pushing, he realized the door was locked, and knocked again, this time more forcefully. He heard Sporty barking and footsteps coming toward the door.

"Who's there?" a child's voice asked.

"It's me—Mr. Mendelsohn! Open up, Yvonne." The door opened, and a young girl, age nine, smiled at him.

"Mami! It's el Señor[3] Mr. Mendelsohn again."

"Tell him to come on in, muchacha!"[4] Mrs. Suárez answered.

"My mother says come on in."

He followed Yvonne and the dog, who leaped up, barking and wagging his tail. Mr. Mendelsohn stood at the kitchen entrance and greeted everyone.

"Good morning to you all!" He had just shaved and trimmed his large black mustache. As he smiled broadly, one could see that most of his teeth were missing. His large bald head was partially covered by his small black skullcap. Thick dark grey hair grew in abundance at the lower back of his head, coming around the front above his ears into short sideburns. He wore a clean white shirt, frayed at the cuffs. His worn-out pinstripe trousers were held up by a pair of dark suspenders. Mr. Mendelsohn leaned on his brown shiny cane and carried a small brown paper bag.

"Mr. Mendelsohn, come into the kitchen," said Mrs. Suárez, "and have some coffee with us." She stood by the stove. A boy of eleven, a young man of about seventeen, and a young pregnant woman were seated at the table.

"Sit here," said the boy, vacating a chair. "I'm finished eating." He stood by the entrance with his sister Yvonne, and they both looked at Mr. Mendelsohn and his paper bag with interest.

"Thank you, Georgie," Mr. Mendelsohn said. He sat down and placed the bag on his lap.

The smell of freshly perked coffee and boiled milk permeated the kitchen.

Winking at everyone, the young man asked, "Hey, what you got in that bag you holding onto, huh, Mr. Mendelsohn?" They all looked at each other and at the old man, amused. "Something special, I bet!"

"Well," the old man replied. "I thought your mama would be so kind as to permit me to make myself a little breakfast here today . . . so." He opened the bag, and began to take out its contents. "I got two slices of rye bread, two tea bags. I brought one extra, just in case anybody would care to join me for tea. And a jar of herring in sour cream."

"Sounds delicious!" said the young man, sticking out his tongue and making a face. Yvonne and Georgie burst out laughing.

"Shh . . . sh." Mrs. Suárez shook her head and looked at her children disapprovingly. "Never mind, Julio!" she said to the young man. Turning to Mr. Mendelsohn, she said, "You got the same like you brought last Saturday, eh? You can eat with us anytime. How about some fresh coffee? I just made it.

---

3. *Mami* (mä'mē) . . . *el Señor* (el sä nyôr').
4. *muchacha* (mü chä'chä), girl.

Yes?" Mr. Mendelsohn looked at her, shrugging his shoulders. "Come on, have some," she coaxed.

"O.K.," he replied. "If it's not too much bother."

"No bother," she said, setting out a place for the old man. "You gonna have some nice fresh bread with a little butter—it will go good with your herring." Mrs. Suárez cut a generous slice of freshly baked bread with a golden crust and buttered it. "Go on, eat. There's a plate and everything for your food. Go on, eat . . ."

"Would anyone care for some?" Mr. Mendelsohn asked. "Perhaps a tea bag for a cup of tea?"

"No . . . no thank you. Mr. Mendelsohn," Mrs. Suárez answered. "Everybody here already ate. You go ahead and eat. You look too skinny; you better eat. Go on, eat your bread."

The old man began to eat vigorously.

"Can I ask you a question?" Julio asked the old man. "Man, I don't get you. You got a whole apartment next door all to yourself—six rooms! And you gotta come here to eat in this crowded kitchen. Why?"

"First of all, today is Saturday, and I thought I could bring in my food and your mama could turn on the stove for me. You know, in my religion you can't light a fire on Saturday."[5]

"You come here anytime; I turn on the stove for you, don't worry," Mrs. Suárez said.

"Man, what about other days? We been living here for about six months, right?" Julio persisted. "And you do more cooking here than in your own place."

"It doesn't pay to turn on the gas for such a little bit of cooking. So I told the gas company to turn it off . . . for good! I got no more gas now, only an electric hot plate," the old man said.

Julio shook his head and sighed. "I don't know——"

"Julio, chico!" snapped Mrs. Suárez, interrupting him, "Basta[6]—it doesn't bother nobody." She looked severely at her son and shook her head. "You gotta go with your sister to the clinic today, so you better get ready now. You too, Marta."

"O.K., Mama," she answered, "but I wanted to see if I got mail from Ralphy today."

"You don't got time. I'll save you the mail; you read it when you get back. You and Julio better get ready; go on." Reluctantly, Marta stood up and yawned, stretching and arching her back.

"Marta," Mr. Mendelsohn said, "you taking care? . . . You know, this is a very delicate time for you."

"I am, Mr. Mendelsohn. Thank you."

"I raised six sisters," the old man said. "I ought to know. Six . . . and married them off to fine husbands. Believe me, I've done my share in life." Yvonne and Georgie giggled and poked each other.

"He's gonna make one of his speeches," they whispered.

". . . I never had children. No time to get

---

5. *in my religion . . . on Saturday.* Saturday is the Jewish Sabbath, a day of rest and worship. For many Jews, the restrictions against work on the Sabbath apply to such tasks as the lighting of stoves.

6. *chico* (chē'kô) . . . *basta* (bäs'tä), boy . . . stop; enough.

married. My father died when I was eleven. I went to work supporting my mother and six younger sisters. I took care of them, and today they are all married, with families. They always call and want me to visit them. I'm too busy and I have no time. . . ."

"Too busy eating in our kitchen," whispered Julio. Marta, Georgie, and Yvonne tried not to laugh out loud. Mrs. Suárez reached over and with a wooden ladle managed a light but firm blow on Julio's head.

". . . Only on the holidays, I make some time to see them. But otherwise, I cannot be bothered with all that visiting." Mr. Mendelsohn stopped speaking and began to eat again.

"Go on, Marta and Julio, you will be late for the clinic," Mrs. Suárez said. "And you two? What are you doing there smiling like two monkeys? Go find something to do!"

Quickly, Georgie and Yvonne ran down the hallway, and Julio and Marta left the kitchen.

Mrs. Suárez sat down beside the old man. "Another piece of bread?" she asked.

"No, thank you very much. . . . I'm full. But it was delicious."

"You too skinny—you don't eat right, I bet." Mrs. Suárez shook her head. "Come tomorrow and have Sunday supper with us."

"I really couldn't."

"Sure, you could. I always make a big supper and there is plenty. All right? Mr. Suárez and I will be happy to have you."

"Are you sure it will be no bother?"

"What are you talking for the bother all the time? One more person is no bother. You come tomorrow. Yes?"

The old man smiled broadly and nodded.

This was the first time he had been invited to Sunday supper with the family.

Mrs. Suárez stood and began clearing away the dishes. "O.K., you go inside; listen to the radio or talk to the kids or something. I got work to do."

Mr. Mendelsohn closed his jar of herring and put it back into the bag. "Can I leave this here till I go?"

"Leave it; I put it in the refrigerator for you."

Leaning on his cane, Mr. Mendelsohn stood up and walked out of the kitchen and down the long hallway into the living room. It was empty. He went over to a large armchair by the window. The sun shone through the window, covering the entire armchair and Mr. Mendelsohn. A canary cage was also by the window, and two tiny yellow birds chirped and hopped back and forth energetically. Mr. Mendelsohn felt drowsy; he shut his eyes. So many aches and pains, he thought. It was hard to sleep at night, but here, well . . . the birds began to chirp in unison and the old man opened one eye, glancing at them, and smiled. Then he shut his eyes once more and fell fast asleep.

When Mr. Mendelsohn opened his eyes, Georgie and Yvonne were in the living room. Yvonne held a deck of playing cards and Georgie read a comic book. She looked at the old man and, holding up the deck of cards, asked "Do you wanna play a game of War? Huh, Mr. Mendelsohn?"

"I don't know how to play that," he answered.

"It's real easy. I'll show you. Come on . . . please!"

"Well," he shrugged, "sure, why not? Maybe I'll learn something."

Yvonne took a small maple end table and a wooden chair, and set them next to Mr. Mendelsohn. "Now . . ." she began, "I'll shuffle the cards and you cut, and then I throw down a card and you throw down a card and the one with the highest card wins. O.K.? And then, the one with the most cards of all wins the game. O.K.?"

"That's all?" he asked.

"That's all. Ready?" she asked, and sat down. They began to play cards.

"You know, my sister Jennie used to be a great card player," said Mr. Mendelsohn.

"Does she still play?" asked Yvonne.

"Oh . . ." Mr. Mendelsohn laughed. "I don't know any more. She's already married and has kids. She was the youngest in my family—like you."

"Did she go to P.S. 39? On Longwood Avenue?"

"I'm sure she did. All my sisters went to school around here."

"Wow! You must be living here a long time, Mr. Mendelsohn."

"Forty-five years!" said the old man.

"Wowee!" Yvonne whistled. "Georgie, did you hear? Mr. Mendelsohn been living here for forty-five whole years!"

Georgie put down his comic book and looked up.

"Really?" he asked, impressed.

"Yes, forty-five years this summer we moved here. But in those days things were different, not like today. No sir! The Bronx has changed. Then, it was the country. That's right! Why, look out the window. You see the elevated trains on Westchester Ave-nue? Well, there were no trains then. That was once a dirt road. They used to bring cows through there."

"Oh, man!" Georgie and Yvonne both gasped.

"Sure. These buildings were among the first apartment houses to go up. Four stories high, and that used to be a big accomplishment in them days. All that was here was mostly little houses, like you still see here and there. Small farms, woodlands . . . like that."

"Did you see any Indians?" asked Georgie.

"What do you mean, Indians?" laughed the old man. "I'm not that old, and this here was not the Wild West." Mr. Mendelsohn saw that the children were disappointed. He added quickly, "But we did have carriages with horses. No cars and lots of horses."

"That's what Mami says they have in Puerto Rico—not like here in El Bronx," said Yvonne.

"Yeah," Georgie agreed. "Papi[7] says he rode a horse when he was a little kid in Puerto Rico. They had goats and pigs and all them things. Man, was he lucky."

"Lucky?" Mr. Mendelsohn shook his head. "You—you are the lucky one today! You got school and a good home and clothes. You don't have to go out to work and support a family like your papa and I had to do, and miss an education. You can learn and be somebody someday."

"Someday," said Yvonne, "we are gonna get a house with a yard and all. Mami says that when Ralphy gets discharged from the Army, he'll get a loan from the government

---

7. *Papi* (pä′pē).

Photo by Rodney Smith, from *In the Land of Light: Israel, a Portrait of Its People*

and we can pay to buy a house. You know, instead of rent."

Mrs. Suárez walked into the living room with her coat on, carrying a shopping bag.

"Yvonne, take the dog out for a walk, and Georgie come on! We have to go shopping. Get your jacket."

Mr. Mendelsohn started to rise. "No," she said, "stay . . . sit down. It's O.K. You can stay and rest if you want."

"All right, Mrs. Suárez," Mr. Mendelsohn said.

"Now don't forget tomorrow for Sunday supper, and take a nap if you like."

Mr. Mendelsohn heard the front door slam shut, and the apartment was silent. The warmth of the bright sun made him drowsy once more. It was so nice here, he thought, a house full of people and kids—like it used to be. He recalled his sisters and his parents . . . the holidays . . . the arguments . . . the laughing. It was so empty next door. He would have to look for a smaller apartment, near Jennie, someday. But not now. Now, it was just nice to sleep and rest right here. He heard the tiny birds chirping and quietly drifted into a deep sleep.

Mr. Mendelsohn rang the bell, then opened the door. He could smell the familiar cooking odors of Sunday supper. For two years he had spent every Sunday at his neighbors'. Sporty greeted him, jumping affectionately and barking.

"Shh—sh . . . down. Good boy," he said, and walked along the hallway toward the kitchen. The room was crowded with people and the stove was loaded with large pots of food, steaming and puffing. Mrs. Suárez was busy basting a large roast. Looking up, she saw Mr. Mendelsohn.

"Come in," she said, "and sit down." Motioning to Julio, who was seated, she continued, "Julio, you are finished, get up and give Mr. Mendelsohn a seat." Julio stood up.

"Here's the sponge cake," Mr. Mendelsohn said, and handed the cake box he carried to Julio, who put it in the refrigerator.

"That's nice. . . . Thank you," said Mrs. Suárez, and placed a cup of freshly made coffee before the old man.

"Would anyone like some coffee?" Mr. Mendelsohn asked. Yvonne and Georgie giggled, looked at one another, and shook their heads.

"You always say that!" said Yvonne.

"One of these days," said Ralphy, "I'm gonna say, 'Yes, give me your coffee,' and you won't have none to drink." The children laughed loudly.

"Don't tease him," Mrs. Suárez said, half smiling. "Let him have his coffee."

"He is just being polite, children," Mr. Suárez said, and shifting his chair closer to Mr. Mendelsohn, he asked, "So . . . Mr. Mendelsohn, how you been? What's new? You O.K.?"

"So-so, Mr. Suárez. You know, aches and pains when you get old. But there's nothing you can do, so you gotta make the best of it."

Mr. Suárez nodded sympathetically, and they continued to talk. Mr. Mendelsohn saw the family every day, except for Mr. Suárez and Ralphy, who both worked a night shift.

Marta appeared in the entrance, holding a small child by the hand.

"There he is, Tato,"[8] she said to the child, and pointed to Mr. Mendelsohn.

"Oh, my big boy! He knows, he knows he's my best friend," Mr. Mendelsohn said, and held the brown shiny cane out toward Tato. The small boy grabbed the cane and, shrieking with delight, walked toward Mr. Mendelsohn.

"Look at that, will you?" said Ralphy. "He knows Mr. Mendelsohn better than me, his own father."

"That's because they are always together," smiled Marta. "Tato is learning to walk with his cane!"

Everyone laughed as they watched Tato climbing the old man's knee. Bending over, Mr. Mendelsohn pulled Tato onto his lap.

"Oh . . . he's getting heavy," said Mrs. Suárez. "Be careful."

"Never mind," Mr. Mendelsohn responded, hugging Tato. "That's my best boy. And look how swell he walks, and he's not even nineteen months."

"What a team," Julio said. "Tato already walks like Mr. Mendelsohn and pretty soon he's gonna complain like him, too. . . ." Julio continued to tease the old man, who responded good-naturedly, as everyone laughed.

After coffee, Mr. Mendelsohn sat on the large armchair in the living room, waiting for supper to be ready. He watched with delight as Tato walked back and forth with the cane. Mr. Mendelsohn held Tato's blanket, stuffed bear, and picture book.

"Tato," he called out, "come here. Let me read you a book—come on. I'm going to read you a nice story."

Tato climbed onto the chair and into Mr. Mendelsohn's lap. He sucked his thumb and waited. Mr. Mendelsohn opened the picture book.

"O.K. Now. . . ." He pointed to the picture. "A is for Alligators. See that? Look at that big mouth and all them teeth. . . ." Tato yawned, nestled back, and closed his eyes. The old man read a few more pages and shut the book.

The soft breathing and sucking sound that Tato made assured Mr. Mendelsohn that the child was asleep. Such a smart kid. What a great boy, he said to himself. Mr. Mendelsohn was vaguely aware of a radio program, voices, and the small dog barking now and then, just before he too fell into a deep sleep.

This Sunday was very much like all the others; coffee first, then he and Tato would play a bit before napping in the large armchair. It had become a way of life for the old man. Only the High Holy Days and an occasional invitation to a family event, such as a marriage or funeral and so on, would prevent the old man from spending Sunday next door.

It had all been so effortless. No one ever asked him to leave, except late at night when he napped too long. On Saturdays, he tried to observe the Sabbath and brought in his meal. They lit the stove for him.

Mrs. Suárez was always feeding him, just like Mama. She also worried about me not eating, the old man had said to himself, pleased. At first, he had been cautious and had wondered about the food and the people that he was becoming so involved with. That

---

8. *Tato* (tä′tô).

first Sunday, the old man had looked suspiciously at the food they served him.

"What is it?" he had asked. Yvonne and Georgie had started giggling, and had looked at one another. Mrs. Suárez had responded quickly and with anger, cautioning her children; speaking to them in Spanish.

"Eat your food, Mr. Mendelsohn. You too skinny," she had told him.

"What kind of meat is it?" Mr. Mendelsohn insisted.

"It's good for you, that's what it is," Mrs. Suárez answered.

"But I——" Mr. Mendelsohn started.

"Never mind—it's good for you. I prepare everything fresh. Go ahead and eat it," Mrs. Suárez had interrupted. There was a silence as Mr. Mendelsohn sat still, not eating.

"You know, I'm not allowed to eat certain things. In my religion we have dietary laws. This is not—pork or something like it, is it?"

"It's just . . . chicken. Chicken! That's what it is. It's delicious . . . and good for you," she had said with conviction.

"It doesn't look like chicken to me."

"That's because you never ate no chicken like this before. This here is—is called Puerto Rican chicken. I prepare it special. So you gonna eat it. You too skinny."

Mr. Mendelsohn had tried to protest, but Mrs. Suárez insisted. "Never mind. Now I prepare everything clean and nice. You eat the chicken; you gonna like it. Go on!"

And that was all.

Mr. Mendelsohn ate his Sunday supper from then on without doubt or hesitation, accepting the affection and concern that Mrs. Suárez provided with each plateful.

That night in his own apartment, Mr. Mendelsohn felt uneasy. He remembered that during supper, Ralphy had mentioned that his G.I. loan had come through. They would be looking for a house soon, everyone agreed. Not in the Bronx; farther out, near Yonkers: It was more like the country there.

The old man tossed and turned in his bed. That's still a long way off. First, they have to find the house and everything. You don't move just like that! he said to himself. It's gonna take a while, he reasoned, putting such thoughts out of his mind.

Mr. Mendelsohn looked at his quarters.

"I told you, didn't I? See how nice this is?" his sister Jennie said. She put down the large sack of groceries on the small table.

It was a fair-sized room with a single bed, a bureau, a wooden wardrobe closet, a table, and two chairs. A hot plate was set on a small white refrigerator, and a white metal kitchen cabinet was placed alongside.

"We'll bring you whatever else you need, Louis," Jennie went on. "You'll love it here. I'm sure. There are people your own age, interested in the same things. Here—let's get started. We'll put your things away and you can get nicely settled."

Mr. Mendelsohn walked over to the window and looked out. He saw a wide avenue with cars, taxis, and buses speeding by. "It's gonna take me two buses, at least, to get back to the old neighborhood," he said.

"Why do you have to go back there?" Jennie asked quickly. "There is nobody there any more, Louis. Everybody moved!"

"There's shul. . . ."[9]

---

9. **shul** (shül), synagogue; a Jewish place of worship and religious study.

"There's shul right here. Next door you have a large temple. Twice you were robbed over there. It's a miracle you weren't hurt! Louis, there is no reason for you to go back. There is nothing over there, nothing," Jennie said.

"The trouble all started with that rooming house next door. Those people took in all kinds. . . ." He shook his head. "When the Suárez family lived there we had no problems. But nobody would talk to the landlord about those new people—only me. Nobody cared."

"That's all finished," Jennie said, looking at her watch. "Now look how nice it is here. Come on, let's get started." She began to put the groceries away in the refrigerator and cabinet.

"Leave it, Jennie," he interrupted. "Go on. . . . I'll take care of it. You go on home. You are in a hurry."

"I'm only trying to help," Jennie responded.

"I know, I know. But I lived in one place for almost fifty years. So don't hurry me." He looked around the room. "And I ain't going nowhere now. . . ."

Shaking her head, Jennie said, "Look— this weekend we have a wedding, but next weekend Sara and I will come to see you. I'll call the hotel on the phone first, and they'll let you know. All right?"

"Sure." He nodded.

"That'll be good, Louis. This way you will get a chance to get settled and get acquainted with some of the other residents." Jennie kissed Mr. Mendelsohn affectionately. The old man nodded and turned away. In a moment, he heard the door open and shut.

Slowly, he walked to the sack of groceries and finished putting them away. Then, with much effort, he lifted a large suitcase onto the bed. He took out several photographs. Then he set the photographs upright, arranging them carefully on the bureau. He had pictures of his parents' wedding and of his sisters and their families. There was a photograph of his mother taken just before she died, and another one of Tato.

That picture was taken when he was about two years old, the old man said to himself. Yes, that's right, on his birthday. . . . There was a party. And Tato was already talking. Such a smart kid, he thought, smiling. Last? Last when? he wondered. Time was going fast for him. He shrugged. He could hardly remember what year it was lately. Just before they moved! He remembered. That's right, they gave him the photograph of Tato. They had a nice house around Gunhill Road someplace, and they had taken him there once. He recalled how exhausted he had been after the long trip. No one had a car, and they had had to take a train and buses. Anyway, he was glad he remembered. Now he could let them know he had moved, and tell them all about what happened to the old neighborhood. That's right, they had a telephone now. Yes, he said to himself, let me finish here, then I'll go call them. He continued to put the rest of his belongings away.

Mr. Mendelsohn sat in the lobby holding onto his cane and a cake box. He had told the nurse at the desk that his friends were coming to pick him up this Sunday. He looked eagerly toward the revolving doors. After a short while, he saw Ralphy, Julio, and Georgie walk through into the lobby.

"Deliveries are made in the rear of the building," he heard the nurse at the desk say as they walked toward him.

"These are my friends, Mrs. Read," Mr. Mendelsohn said, standing. "They are here to take me out."

"Oh, well," said the nurse. "All right; I didn't realize. Here he is then. He's been talking about nothing else but this visit." Mrs. Read smiled.

Ralphy nodded, then spoke to Georgie. "Get Mr. Mendelsohn's overcoat."

Quickly, Mr. Mendelsohn put on his coat, and all four left the lobby.

"Take good care of him now . . ." they heard Mrs. Read calling. "You be a good boy now, Mr. Mendelsohn."

Outside, Mr. Mendelsohn looked at the young men and smiled.

"How's everyone?" he asked.

"Good," Julio said. "Look, that's my pickup truck from work. They let me use it sometimes when I'm off."

"That's a beautiful truck. How's everyone? Tato? How is my best friend? And Yvonne? Does she like school? And your Mama and Papa? . . . Marta? . . ."

"Fine, fine. Everybody is doing great. Wait till you see them. We'll be there in a little while," said Julio. "With this truck, we'll get there in no time."

Mr. Mendelsohn sat in the kitchen and watched as Mrs. Suárez packed food into a shopping bag. Today had been a good day for the old man; he had napped in the old armchair and spent time with the children.

Yvonne was so grown up, he almost had not recognized her. When Tato remembered him, Mr. Mendelsohn had been especially pleased. Shyly, he had shaken hands with the old man. Then he had taken him into his room to show Mr. Mendelsohn all his toys.

"Now I packed a whole lotta stuff in this shopping bag for you. You gotta eat it. Eat some of my Puerto Rican chicken—it's good for you. You too skinny. You got enough for tomorrow and for another day. You put it in the refrigerator. Also I put some rice and other things."

He smiled as she spoke, enjoying the attention he received.

"Julio is gonna drive you back before it gets too late," she said. "And we gonna pick you up again and bring you back to eat with us. I bet you don't eat right." She shook her head. "O.K.?"

"You shouldn't go through so much bother," he protested mildly.

"Again with the bother? You stop that! We gonna see you soon. You take care of yourself and eat. Eat! You must nourish yourself, especially in such cold weather."

Mr. Mendelsohn and Mrs. Suárez walked out into the living room. The family exchanged good-byes with the old man. Tato, feeling less shy, kissed Mr. Mendelsohn on the cheek.

Just before leaving, Mr. Mendelsohn embraced Mrs. Suárez for a long time, as everybody watched silently.

"Thank you," he whispered.

"Thank you? For what?" Mrs. Suárez said. "You come back soon and have Sunday supper with us. Yes?" Mr. Mendelsohn nodded and smiled.

It was dark and cold out. He walked with effort. Julio carried the shopping bag. Slowly, he got into the pickup truck. The ride back was bumpy and uncomfortable for Mr. Mendelsohn. The cold wind cut right through into the truck, and the old man was aware of the long winter ahead.

His eyelids were so heavy he could hardly open them. Nurses scurried about busily. Mr. Mendelsohn heard voices.

"Let's give him another injection. It will help his breathing. Nurse! Nurse! The patient needs. . . ."

The voices faded. He remembered he had gone to sleep after supper last—last when? How many days have I been here . . . here in the hospital? Yes, he thought, now I know where I am. A heart attack, the doctor had said, and then he had felt even worse. Didn't matter; I'm too tired. He heard voices once more, and again he barely opened his eyes. A tall thin man dressed in white spoke to him.

"Mr. Mendelsohn, can you hear me? How do you feel now? More comfortable? We called your family. I spoke to your sister, Mrs. Wiletsky. They should be here very soon. You feeling sleepy? Good. . . . Take a little nap—go on. We'll wake you when they get here, don't worry. Go on now. . . ."

He closed his eyes, thinking of Jennie. She'll be here soon with Esther and Rosalie and Sara. All of them. He smiled. He was so tired. His bed was by the window and a bright warm sash of sunshine covered him almost completely. Nice and warm, he thought, and felt comfortable. The pain had lessened, practically disappeared. Mr. Mendelsohn heard the birds chirping and Sporty

barking. That's all right, Mrs. Suárez would let him sleep. She wouldn't wake him up, he knew that. It looked like a good warm day; he planned to take Tato for a walk later. That's some smart kid, he thought. Right now he was going to rest.

"This will be the last of it, Sara."

"Just a few more things, Jennie, and we'll be out of here."

The two women spoke as they packed away all the items in the room. They opened drawers and cabinets, putting things away in boxes and suitcases.

"What about these pictures on the bureau?" asked Sara.

Jennie walked over and they both looked at the photographs.

"There's Mama and Papa's wedding picture. Look, there's you, Sara, when Jonathan was born. And Esther and . . . look, he's got all the pictures of the entire family." Jennie burst into tears.

"Come on, Jennie; it's all over, honey. He was sick and very old." The older woman comforted the younger one.

Wiping her eyes, Jennie said, "Well, we did the best we could for him, anyway."

"Who is this?" asked Sara, holding up Tato's photo.

"Let me see," said Jennie. "Hummm . . . that must be one of the people in that family that lived next door in the old apartment on Prospect Avenue. You know—remember that Spanish family? He used to visit with them. Their name was . . . Díaz or something like that, I think. I can't remember."

"Oh, yes," said Sara. "Louis mentioned them once in a while, yes. They were nice to him. What shall we do with it? Return it?"

"Oh," said Jennie, "that might be rude. What do you think?"

"Well, I don't want it, do you?"

"No," Jennie hesitated. ". . . But let's just put it away. Maybe we ought to tell them what happened. About Louis." Sara shrugged her shoulders. "Maybe I'll write to them," Jennie went on, "if I can find out where they live. They moved. What do you say?"

"I don't care, really," Sara sighed. "I have a lot to do yet. I have to meet Esther at the lawyer's to settle things. And I still have to make supper. So let's get going."

Both women continued to pack, working efficiently and with swiftness. After a while, everything was cleared and put away in boxes and suitcases.

"All done!" said Sara.

"What about this?" asked Jennie, holding up Tato's photograph.

"Do what you want," said Sara. "I'm tired. Let's go."

Looking at the photograph, Jennie slipped it into one of the boxes. "I might just write and let them know."

The two women left the room, closing the door behind them.

THINK AND DISCUSS
Understanding

1. According to Mr. Mendelsohn, why does he spend so much time with the Suárez family?
2. Why did Mr. Mendelsohn never marry?
3. Why does the Suárez family leave the Bronx?
4. Describe Mr. Mendelsohn's new room.
5. How do you learn that he has died?
6. What does Jennie do with the picture of Tato?

Analyzing

7. How do Mrs. Suárez and her husband treat Mr. Mendelsohn?
8. Trace the development of these relationships: Mr. Mendelsohn and the older Suárez children; Mr. Mendelsohn and Tato.
9. When Mr. Mendelsohn is leaving the new house, he hugs Mrs. Suárez for a long time, and then thanks her. In what ways is this scene different from all the other times he has thanked her for her hospitality?
10. Do Jennie and Sara have any idea how important their brother's friends were to him? Give reasons for your answer.

Extending

11. After their brother is dead, Jennie tells Sara, "We did the best we could for him." In your opinion, is her statement accurate?
12. Do you think Jennie will ever even try to locate the Suárez family to tell them of her brother's death? Explain.

REVIEWING: Inference

See Handbook of Literary Terms, p. 671.

An **inference** is a reasonable and intelligent conclusion drawn from hints or other information provided by an author.

1. Why does Mr. Mendelsohn spend so much time with the Suárez family?
2. Mr. Mendelsohn says there's no point in having gas in his apartment because he usually eats with his neighbors. What other reasons might there be for his having no gas?
3. Mr. Mendelsohn always offers to share food with the Suárez family. Given the way he is characterized, what can you infer about why he does this?
4. What can you infer about the relationship between Mr. Mendelsohn and his sisters?

COMPOSITION

Supporting Your Opinion

In the course of his adult life, Mr. Mendelsohn had two "families" that he felt close to—his sisters and their families and Mr. and Mrs. Suárez and their family.

Complete this statement: "At the time of the story, Mr. Mendelsohn probably considers his family to be _____." (Fill in the name of one family or the other.) Then write a paragraph explaining your choice.

Expressing Your Feelings

Pretend you are Mrs. Suárez and have just learned that Mr. Mendelsohn is dead. Write a letter to his sister Jennie. First explain how you regarded Mr. Mendelsohn and how you felt when he died. Then describe your fondest memory of him. Conclude your letter with a paragraph offering your condolences to Jennie and the rest of the family. As you plan your letter, ask yourself what Mrs. Suárez might feel about Jennie's treatment of Mr. Mendelsohn, whether she would state these feelings in the letter, and—if she were to state them—whether she would do so calmly, furiously, or in some other way. Before you begin to write, see "Writing as a Story Character" in the Writer's Handbook.

BIOGRAPHY

Nicholasa Mohr

1935–

Nicholasa Mohr turned to writing only after she had earned a reputation as a painter and printmaker. Her first book, *Nilda,* which she illustrated herself, received many awards. *El Bronx Remembered, In Nueva York,* and *Felita,* also award-winning books, established Mohr's reputation as an accomplished writer and as a spokeswoman for the Puerto Rican people.

THINKING CRITICALLY
ABOUT LITERATURE

UNIT 1   SHORT STORY 1

■ CONCEPT REVIEW

The story that ends this unit contains many of the important ideas and literary terms found in the stories you have just studied. It also contains notes and questions designed to help you think critically about your reading. Page numbers in these notes refer to an Application. For a more extensive discussion of literary terms, see the Handbook of Literary Terms.

The Drummer Boy of Shiloh

Ray Bradbury

In the April night, more than once, blossoms fell from the orchard trees and lighted with rustling taps on the drumhead. At midnight a peach stone left miraculously on a branch through winter, flicked by a bird, fell swift and unseen; it struck once, like panic, and jerked the boy upright. In silence he listened to his own heart ruffle away, away— at last gone from his ears and back in his chest again.

After that he turned the drum on its side, where its great lunar face peered at him whenever he opened his eyes.

His face, alert or at rest, was solemn. It was a solemn time and a solemn night for a boy just turned fourteen in the peach orchard near Owl Creek not far from the church at Shiloh.

■ *Shiloh* (shī′lō). Now a national park in S.W. Tennessee, Shiloh was the site in 1862 of a major battle of the Civil War.

■ setting (page 82): The place is peaceful until the reader learns the boy's reaction to it.

■ If the drum makes no sound, he might forget about it and go to sleep.
■ characterization (page 54): Note additional details of setting and characterization.

Slightly abridged from "The Drummer Boy of Shiloh" by Ray Bradbury. Copyright © 1960 by Ray Bradbury. Reprinted by permission of Don Congdon Associates, Inc.

". . . thirty-one . . . thirty-two . . . thirty-three." Unable to see, he stopped counting.

Beyond the thirty-three familiar shadows forty thousand men, exhausted by nervous expectation and unable to sleep for romantic dreams of battles yet unfought, lay crazily askew in their uniforms. A mile farther on, another army was strewn helterskelter, turning slowly, basting themselves with the thought of what they would do when the time came—a leap, a yell, a blind plunge their strategy, raw youth their protection and benediction.

Now and again the boy heard a vast wind come up that gently stirred the air. But he knew what it was—the army here, the army there, whispering to itself in the dark. Some men talking to others, others murmuring to themselves, and all so quiet it was like a natural element arisen from South or North with the motion of the earth toward dawn.

What the men whispered the boy could only guess and he guessed that it was "Me, I'm the one, I'm the one of all the rest who won't die. I'll live through it. I'll go home. The band will play. And I'll be there to hear it."

Yes, thought the boy, *that's all very well for them, they can give as good as they get!*

For with the careless bones of the young men, harvested by night and bindled around campfires, were the similarly strewn steel bones of their rifles with bayonets fixed like eternal lightning lost in the orchard grass.

Me, thought the boy, *I got only a drum, two sticks to beat it, and no shield.*

There wasn't a man-boy on this ground tonight who did not have a shield he cast, riveted, or carved himself on his way to his first attack, compounded of remote but nonetheless firm and fiery family devotion, flag-blown patriotism, and cocksure immortality strengthened by the touchstone of very real gunpowder, ramrod, Minié ball, and flint. But without these last, the boy felt his family move yet farther off in the dark, as if one of those great prairie-burning trains had chanted them away, never to return—leaving him with this drum which was worse than a toy in the game to be played tomorrow or someday much too soon.

The boy turned on his side. A moth brushed his face, but it was peach blossom. A peach blossom flicked him, but it was a moth.

■ **classifying:** The thoughts and feelings of all the soldiers are similar, yet each has been put into one of two opposing categories depending on which army he belongs to.

■ **point of view** (page 107): Readers are told the boy's thoughts and feelings.

■ The other soldiers have weapons. The boy has only his drum.

■ *Minié* (min′ē) *ball*, a cone-shaped bullet that expands when fired.

Nothing stayed put. Nothing had a name. Nothing was as it once was.

If he stayed very still, when the dawn came up and the soldiers put on their bravery with their caps, perhaps they might go away, the war with them, and not notice him living small here, no more than a toy himself.

"Well, by thunder now," said a voice. The boy shut his eyes to hide inside himself, but it was too late. Someone, walking by in the night, stood over him. "Well," said the voice quietly, "here's a soldier crying *before* the fight. Good. Get it over. Won't be time once it all starts."

And the voice was about to move on when the boy, startled, touched the drum at his elbow. The man above, hearing this, stopped. The boy could feel his eyes, sense him slowly bending near. A hand must have come down out of the night, for there was a little *rat-tat* as the fingernails brushed and the man's breath fanned the boy's face.

"Why, it's the drummer boy, isn't it?"

The boy nodded, not knowing if his nod was seen. "Sir, is that you?" he said.

"I assume it is." The man's knees cracked as he bent still closer. He smelled as all fathers should smell, of salt-sweat, tobacco, horse and boot leather, and the earth he walked upon. He had many eyes. No, not eyes, brass buttons that watched the boy.

He could only be, and was, the general. "What's your name, boy?" he asked.

"Joby, sir," whispered the boy, starting to sit up.

"All right, Joby, don't stir." A hand pressed his chest gently, and the boy relaxed. "How long you been with us, Joby?"

"Three weeks, sir."

"Run off from home or join legitimate, boy?"

Silence.

"Fool question," said the general. "Do you shave yet, boy? Even more of a fool. There's your cheek, fell right off the tree overhead. And the others here, not much older. Raw, raw, the lot of you. You ready for tomorrow or the next day, Joby?"

"I think so, sir."

"You want to cry some more, go on ahead. I did the same last night."

"You, sir?"

"It's the truth. Thinking of everything ahead. Both sides figuring

■ inference (page 120): From his silence, you can infer that the boy ran off to war.

the other side will just give up, and soon, and the war done in weeks and us all home. Well, that's not how it's going to be. And maybe that's why I cried."

"Yes, sir," said Joby.

The general must have taken out a cigar now, for the dark was suddenly filled with the Indian smell of tobacco unlighted yet, but chewed as the man thought what next to say.

"It's going to be a crazy time," said the general. "Counting both sides, there's a hundred thousand men—give or take a few thousand—out there tonight, not one as can spit a sparrow off a tree, or knows a horse clod from a Minié ball. Stand up, bare the breast, ask to be a target, thank them and sit down, that's us, that's them. We should turn tail and train four months, they should do the same. But here we are, taken with spring fever and thinking it blood lust, taking our sulphur with cannons instead of with molasses, as it should be—going to be a hero, going to live forever. And I can see all them over there nodding agreement, save the other way around. It's wrong, boy, it's wrong as a head put on hindside front and a man marching backward through life. Sometime this week more innocents will get shot out of pure Cherokee enthusiasm than ever got shot before. Owl Creek was full of boys splashing around in the noonday sun just a few hours ago. I fear it will be full of boys again, just floating, at sundown tomorrow, not caring where the current takes them."

The general stopped and made a little pile of winter leaves and twigs in the dark as if he might at any moment strike fire to them to see his way through the coming days when the sun might not show its face because of what was happening here and just beyond.

The boy watched the hand stirring the leaves and opened his lips to say something, but did not say it. The general heard the boy's breath and spoke himself.

"Why am I telling you this? That's what you wanted to ask, eh? Well, when you got a bunch of wild horses on a loose rein somewhere, somehow you got to bring order, rein them in. These lads, fresh out of the milkshed, don't know what I know; and I can't tell them—men actually die in war. So each is his own army. I got to make one army of them. And for that, boy, I need you."

"Me!" The boy's lips barely twitched.

"You, boy," said the general quietly. "You are the heart of the

■ As it is used here, *save* means "except."

■ You can infer that the boys in the creek will be dead tomorrow.

This boy is identified as John F. P. Robie; he is thought to be the drummer boy of Shiloh. *Courtesy Chicago Historical Society*

army. Think about that. You are the heart of the army. Listen to me, now."

And lying there, Joby listened. And the general spoke. If he, Joby, beat slow tomorrow, the heart would beat slow in the men. They would lag by the wayside. They would drowse in the fields on their muskets. They would sleep forever after that—in those same fields, their hearts slowed by a drummer boy and stopped by enemy lead.

But if he beat a sure, steady, ever faster rhythm, then, then, their knees would come up in a long line down over that hill, one knee after the other, like a wave on the ocean shore. Had he seen the ocean ever? Seen the waves rolling in like a well-ordered cavalry charge to the sand? Well, that was it, that's what he wanted, that's what was needed. Joby was his right hand and his left. He gave the orders, but Joby set the pace.

So bring the right knee up and the right foot out and the left knee

■ The boy is the heart of the army. His drum is the heartbeat.

up and the left foot out, one following the other in good time, in brisk time. Move the blood up the body and make the head proud and the spine stiff and the jaw resolute. Focus the eye and set the teeth, flare the nostril and tighten the hands, put steel armor all over the men, for blood moving fast in them does indeed make men feel as if they'd put on steel. He must keep at it, at it! Long and steady, steady and long! Then, even though shot or torn, those wounds got in hot blood—in blood he'd helped stir—would feel less pain. If their blood was cold, it would be more than slaughter, it would be murderous nightmare and pain best not told and no one to guess.

The general spoke and stopped, letting his breath slack off. Then, after a moment, he said, "So there you are, that's it. Will you do that, boy? Do you know now you're general of the army when the general's left behind?"

The boy nodded mutely.

"You'll run them through for me then, boy?"

"Yes, sir."

"Good. And, maybe, many nights from tonight, many years from now, when you're as old or far much older than me, when they ask you what you did in this awful time, you will tell them—one part humble and one part proud—I was the drummer boy at the battle of Owl Creek or the Tennessee River, or maybe they'll just name it after the church there. I was the drummer boy at Shiloh. Good grief, that has a beat and sound to it fitting for Mr. Longfellow. 'I was the drummer boy at Shiloh.' Who will ever hear those words and not know you, boy, or what you thought this night, or what you'll think tomorrow or the next day when we must get up on our legs and move."

The general stood up. "Well, then. God bless you, boy. Good night."

"Good night, sir." And tobacco, brass, boot polish, salt-sweat, and leather, the man moved away through the grass.

Joby lay for a moment staring, but unable to see where the man had gone. He swallowed. He wiped his eyes. He cleared his throat. He settled himself. Then, at last, very slowly and firmly he turned the drum so it faced up toward the sky.

He lay next to it, his arm around it, feeling the tremor, the touch, the muted thunder as all the rest of the April night in the year 1862, near the Tennessee River, not far from the Owl Creek, very close to the church named Shiloh, the peach blossoms fell on the drum.

■ **plot** (page 21): Turning the drum so it faces the sky is the **climax** of the story.

■ Note that readers are never told which side the General's troops are fighting.

THINK AND DISCUSS
Understanding
1. What is the setting of this story?
2. What will Joby carry into battle?
3. Give reasons why the General is worried about the upcoming battle.
4. What does he ask Joby to do?

Analyzing
5. Why has Joby been crying?
6. Do Joby's feelings change after his talk with the General? Explain.

Extending
7. Both characters cry on the night before the battle. Who do you think has reason to cry—Joby? the General? both? neither? Explain.

REVIEWING LITERARY TERMS
Plot
1. What are the internal conflicts in the story?
2. What is the external conflict?

Characterization
3. Tell what you learn about Joby from how he looks, what he says and thinks, what he does, and what the General says about him.

Setting
4. Is the setting of this story essential to the development of the plot, or could the story take place almost anywhere? Explain.

Point of View
5. From what point of view is "The Drummer Boy of Shiloh" told? Give reasons for your answer.

Inference
6. Why does the General speak to Joby as he does? Is it only because his troops need a drumbeat to march to? Explain.

■ CONTENT REVIEW
THINKING SKILLS
Classifying
1. Classify the stories you have read in this unit according to their points of view.
2. Put stories from the unit into these categories: Has Clever or Surprise Ending; Features an Old Person; Contains Elements of Fantasy. You will not use all of the stories.

Generalizing
3. In both "To Build a Fire" and "Top Man," setting influences the actions of the characters and contributes to the development of the plot. Consider the importance of setting in the stories that follow. Could each story have taken place anywhere else? Does the setting—either the time or the place—contribute to the development of the plot? Explain your choices. (a) "The Inspiration of Mr. Budd"; (b) "Paw-Paw"; (c) "The Tell-Tale Heart."
4. Imagine that the following pairs of characters have gotten together to write books on the topics given. For one of the pairs, explain why the characters are qualified to write on that topic. What might they say about it? (a) Paw-Paw and Buddy's friend in "A Christmas Memory": *Joy is where you find it.* (b) Buddy and Mr. Mendelsohn: *Your family is made up of the people who love*

you. (**c**) Lemon Brown and Reverend Pentecost in "The Last Specimen": *What's really important.* (**d**) the man in "To Build a Fire" and Mrs. Sakkaro in "Rain, Rain, Go Away": *Survival.*

■ COMPOSITION REVIEW

Supporting Your Opinion

Which story in this unit would make the best movie? Which well-known actors and actresses should play the leading roles? Write a composition in which you do the following: State your choice of story and give reasons for that choice. State your choice of actor or actress to play two of the main characters. Support these choices by briefly describing each character and then telling why the actor or actress is suitable for the role.

Writing a Story

Decide what kind of story you want to write. Possibilities include a story that is funny, sad, exciting, fantastic, or frightening. Or you might choose to write a story that is fantastic and frightening, sad and exciting, or some other combination. Write your story, keeping in mind what you have learned about plot, character, setting, point of view, and inference. Evaluate your first draft by asking yourself how well you handled these. Then revise your draft and write your final copy.

Analyzing Likenesses and Differences

Both Mike's grandmother ("The Moustache") and Mr. Mendelsohn live in places that are exclusively for the elderly. In a composition of three paragraphs, analyze likenesses and differences in their situation and give your opinion of it. In your first paragraph, describe each place and tell why the character is there. In the second paragraph, describe the attitude of some staff members toward the elderly as indicated by the behavior of the woman who brings the juice and the woman at the desk the day Mr. Mendelsohn visits the Suárez family. In the third paragraph, give your opinion of this treatment.

Reviewing Writer's Craft: Specific Details

In this unit you have seen how writers use specific details. You may have read examples, copied some, and found examples on your own. Now try your hand at creating your own specific details. Imagine that you are writing a story about someone your own age. In two paragraphs that could be used in your story, describe this character. In the first paragraph, describe the character's appearance. In the second paragraph, describe what he or she says and does. Before you begin, review how writers in this unit use specific details to describe characters. Consult your reading/writing log if you have been keeping one. Then make a list of details about your character to use as you write your composition.

DRAMA 1

Edward Hopper, "New York Movie," 1939, *The Museum of Modern Art, New York*

Page 145, Edward Hopper, drawing for painting "New York Movie," *Whitney Museum of American Art, New York*

PREVIEW

UNIT 2   DRAMA 1

Plays
The Legend of Sleepy Hollow / Margaret Blackburn
  From a story by Washington Irving
Back There / Rod Serling
The Three Garridebs / Michael and Mollie Hardwick
  From a story by Sir Arthur Conan Doyle
from **The Ugly Duckling** / A. A. Milne

Features
Reading Radio, Television, and
  Stage Plays
Comment: Traveling in Time
The Writer's Craft: Use Precise,
  Active Verbs
Comment: Writer and Character—
  Who Becomes Famous?

Application of Literary Terms
irony
stereotype

Reading Literature Skillfully
comparison and contrast

Vocabulary Skills
idioms

Thinking Skills
synthesizing

Composition
Writing a Narrative
Writing as a Story Character
Writing a Dialogue

Enrichment
Creative Project
Readers Theater

Thinking Critically About Literature
Concept Review
Content Review
Composition Review

The Legend of Sleepy Hollow

Margaret Blackburn

From a story by Washington Irving

What did happen to Ichabod Crane? Did the headless horseman get him?

CHARACTERS

ANNOUNCER

ICHABOD CRANE, village schoolteacher

MASTER YOST VAN HUTEN, pupil

KATRINA VAN TASSEL, daughter of a wealthy Dutch farmer

FROW VAN TASSEL, Katrina's mother

MYNHEER VAN TASSEL, Katrina's father

BROM VAN BRUNT, Ichabod's rival

HANS VAN RIPPER, farmer

FROW VAN RIPPER, his wife

FARMER VAN TIL, a neighbor

TWO MEN, a WOMAN, several CHILDREN, a MINISTER

Music: "Memories." Fade in, establish, and out slowly under.

ANNOUNCER. Washington Irving's famous "Legend of Sleepy Hollow" was first read by a delighted public over one hundred and twenty-five years ago, but the church still stands today as Irving described it, and automobiles rattle over the Headless Horseman's Bridge near Tarrytown, New York.

(Music: Time bridge. Weird and uncanny.)

ANNOUNCER *(lowering voice)*. Long ago the valley called *Sleepy Hollow* was a place bewitched.

(Sound: Indian war whoops. Fade into background and hold.)

ANNOUNCER. Some say that an old Indian Chief held his pow-wows there before Master Henry Hudson discovered the spot.

(Sound: War whoops up briefly and fade out.)

ANNOUNCER. Some say it was a meeting place of witches. . . .

(Sound: Eerie shrieks and laughter. Fade into background and hold.)

ANNOUNCER. . . . after they were driven out of New England . . . and you can still hear

---

from *Doorways to Discovery* of *The Ginn Basic Readers* by David H. Russell and others. Copyright 1952 by Silver Burdett & Ginn, Inc. Used with permission.

their voices in the air . . . high above the treetops.

(*Sound: Shrieks and laughter up briefly. Include voices in next cue. Then fade out.*)

VOICES. Greymalkin! Brimstone! Meet me in the forest.

ANNOUNCER. But everyone in Sleepy Hollow agreed on one thing. . . . and that was the headless ghost of a Hessian trooper[1] on horseback.

(*Sound: Wind. Horse's hoofs on turf. Fade out into background and hold.*)

ANNOUNCER. His head had been shot off by a cannon ball, and he roamed the valley on windy nights.

(*Sound: Wind and hoofs up briefly. Fade slowly under. Out.*)

ANNOUNCER. Many worthy citizens had heard the Headless Horseman, and not a few had actually seen him with their own eyes. Of all the legends that hung about—this was the favorite legend of Sleepy Hollow.

(*Music: Quaint pastoral. Up and under. Out.*)

ANNOUNCER. The schoolhouse in Sleepy Hollow was presided over by Ichabod Crane. He was tall and lank, with hands that dangled a mile out of his sleeves, and feet that might have served for shovels. He had huge ears, large glassy-green eyes, and a long snipe nose like a weathercock. When he strode along the profile of a hill on a windy day, one might have taken him for a scarecrow eloped from the cornfield. But in his small empire of the schoolroom (*Fading*) bounded with log walls, he ruled supreme. . . .

(*Sound: Gabble of children, up and under. Up briefly between next three cues.*)

VOICE. Sixty seconds make a minute, sixty minutes make an hour, twenty-four hours make a day. . . .

VOICE. The state of Connecticut is bounded on the north by Massachusetts, on the east by Rhode Island. . . .

VOICE. The fat cat ate the rat. Run, cat, run.

(*Sound: Rapping of ruler on desk. Children's gabble fades out quickly.*)

ICHABOD (*comedy voice, very nasal and shrill*). Silence, children. I observe that Master Yost Van Huten is more than usually industrious with his slate. Come forward, Master Yost, and let us all admire your handiwork.

YOST (*sulkily*). Please, teacher, I don't wanna.

ICHABOD. You will bring me your slate at once, Master Yost. Thank you . . . Hmmm . . . What have we here?

(*Sound: Children laughing and snickering.*)

ICHABOD (*rapping*). You would draw a caricature of your teacher, would you, Master Yost? Read aloud what you have written.

YOST (*sulkily*). Teacher's mad and I'm glad,
    And I know what'll please him. . . .

ICHABOD. Go on.

YOST. A bottle of wine to make him shine,
    And Katrina Van Tassel to tease him.

(*Sound: Laughter and snickers.*)

ICHABOD. I have ever borne in mind the golden maxim: "Spare the rod and spoil the child." I would not on any account have Master Yost Van Huten spoiled. You will hold out your hand, Master Yost.

YOST. Aw, I don't wanna!

---

1. **Hessian trooper.** Hessians (hesh'ɔns) were German soldiers hired by England to fight on the English side in the Revolutionary War.

Ichabod Crane and the Headless Horseman is thought to have been painted by William John Wilgus around 1835. *National Gallery of Art, Washington, D.C.*

(*Sound: Ruler on child's hand and child yelps intermittently. Out. Then child crying softly to end of scene.*)

ICHABOD. I am only doing my bounden duty by your good parents, Master Yost! There! It may smart now, my poetic young friend, but you will remember it and thank me for it the longest day you have to live.

(*Music: Bridge to close scene, then under. Out.*)

ANNOUNCER. Despite his stern discipline and his peculiar appearance, this schoolteacher was regarded as a man of great learning. He would quote long passages from Cotton Mather's history of New England witch-craft. He was the singing master of Sleepy Hollow and led the choir earnestly on Sundays. These accomplishments gave him an advantage over the country bumpkins in wooing the blooming Katrina Van Tassel, daughter of the wealthiest Dutch farmer in the neighborhood. On afternoons, when his scholarly duties were over, Ichabod would repair to the Van Tassel farmhouse situated (*Fading*) on the banks of the Hudson in a green and fertile nook. . . .

ICHABOD. And how are you, Miss Katrina? Hmmmm! Always busy spinning, weaving, or baking some of your delicious little cakes, ahem—such delicious little cakes!

KATRINA. It's nice of you to praise 'em, Master Crane. Won't you try some of today's baking? This honey loaf and these doughnuts. And a bit of the new cheese and a glass of father's cider.

ICHABOD (*with mouth too full, smacking lips*). Mmm! Just a morsel! Just a trifle! Just a drop! I'm a light eater, Miss Katrina. I take only enough to keep soul and body together!

KATRINA. But you must taste my apple cake, Master Crane. And a bit of this coffee-kuchen. Here, let me fill up your glass, too!

ICHABOD (*speaking with difficulty through a full mouth*). Miss Katrina, your charms have made a deep impression on my heart!

KATRINA (*giggling*). Oh, Master Crane, how you do talk!

ICHABOD (*mouth full*). Katrina, there is something I must tell you. . . . I'll thank you to pass the peach preserves. . . . Something I have been long hoping . . . Well, if you insist, just a drop more cider. . . . Katrina, I love you!

KATRINA. Hist! Here comes Mother! I'll be singing.

ICHABOD. Here's my tuning fork![2]
(*Sound: Tuning fork sounds "A."*)

KATRINA. Do-re-mi. . . . (*Sings scale. Breaks off.*)

MOTHER (*fade on*). Good day to you, Master Crane! I see you're giving my girl a singing lesson.

ICHABOD. Yes, indeed, Frow Van Tassel. Now give me "A," Miss Katrina.
(*Sound: Tuning fork sounds "A."*)

KATRINA. Ahhhh!

ICHABOD (*bleating*). Ahhh!

KATRINA (*up one tone*). Oh-h-h.

ICHABOD (*nasally*). Ohhh! And now for the psalm for next Sabbath.

BOTH. By Babel's streams we sat and wept,
    While memory still to Zion clung.

ICHABOD (*through nose*). The winds alone our harpstrings swept,

BOTH. Which on the weeping willows hung-g-g . . .

MOTHER. Very nice, I'm sure. . . . Well, I must run along to my poultry. Geese and ducks are foolish things, but girls can look after themselves. . . . (*Fading*) Do a good lesson, Katrina.

ICHABOD. Miss Katrina, as I was saying . . . (*Singing scale*) do-re-mi-fa-so-la-I love you-u-u.

KATRINA (*singing scale*). Do-re-mi-fa-so-la. This is so sudden, Master Crane!

ICHABOD. Your virtues exceed my fondest hopes. . . . Just how large is this farm, Miss Katrina?

KATRINA. Three hundred acres. Ahhh!

ICHABOD (*gloatingly*). Three hundred acres! Miss Katrina, I adore you! Tell me you'll be Missus Ichabod Crane!

KATRINA (*demurely*). You must give me time to think it over. I'll give you your answer——

ICHABOD. When?

KATRINA. Come next Friday week—at our quilting frolic! Do-re-mi-fa-so-la-a-a.
(*Music: Up fast then fade slowly under. Out.*)

ANNOUNCER (*musing*). Next Friday week.

---

2. **tuning fork**, a small, two-pronged instrument used to find pitch.

. . . The days passed slowly for our impatient lover. Already in anticipation, Ichabod saw himself master of the rich fields, the vast barn, sleek porkers, snowy geese, regiments of turkeys! He knew he had a rival in Brom Van Brunt, a burly young farmer, who won all the neighborhood races and cockfights, and was leader of a gang of mischief-makers. Brom had boasted that he would "double the schoolmaster up, and lay him on a shelf of his own schoolhouse," but Ichabod did not take his threats very seriously. To pass the time until the quilting bee, he reread Cotton Mather's book on witchcraft from cover to cover. He remained at his desk in the log schoolhouse one evening so late that it was pitch dark when at last he started homeward. As he walked along through the Hollow, his teeth began to chatter and the ordinary sounds of the night took on ghostly terrors.
(Music: Atmospheric bridge.)

(Sound: Footsteps on gravel. Crickets in broadcast. Hold under.)
ICHABOD *(to self)*. Ooo . . . what a spooky night. . . . J-j-just the night for the h-h-headless horseman to ride. Wh-w-what if I should m-m-meet him?
(Sound: Hoot of owl.)
ICHABOD. It sounds like an owl . . . but it might be a witch. There was old Nance Dinwiddie of Salem and Bess o'Bedlam . . . she that curdled the cow's milk and put burrs in the baby's hair. O-oo-h.
(Sound: Hoot of owl.)
ICHABOD. Mercy on us! What a dreadful sound! Some poor homeless ghost, I make

no doubt. *(Pleading)* Get back to your grave, do, that's a good ghost!
(Sound: Hoot of owl at distance.)
ICHABOD. What a black night! Not a single star. Ooooooooooo-ooooooh! there goes one now . . . shooting across the sky. A falling star means death. Then there was that black cat I met yesterday, that's a sure sign of trouble.
(Sound: Bullfrogs croaking.)
ICHABOD. Ahhh! Is that a bullfrog or a hant?
(Sound: Fade footsteps and crickets to distant background.)
(Music: Transition bridge. Fade out under.)
ANNOUNCER. Finally came the evening of the quilting frolic at Mynheer Van Tassel's. Ichabod wanted to arrive in style at the home of his lady love; so he borrowed an old plow horse called Gunpowder from Hans Van Ripper, the farmer in whose home he was boarding. On this steed he presented a curious figure indeed. He rode with short stirrups which brought his bony knees up to the pommel of the saddle, and the motion of his arms was like the flapping of great black wings. Such was the romantic figure that arrived presently at Mynheer Van Tassel's farmhouse *(Fading)* to find the merrymaking in full swing!
(Music: Fade in dance tune of the period.)
(Sound: Fade in sounds of country dance and small crowd noise. Sounds and music to background and hold.)
ICHABOD. Ah, Mynheer Van Tassel *(Nasally)*, this is indeed a salubrious occasion!
VAN TASSEL. Evenin,' Ichabod, evenin'! Fall to and help yourself to the vittles!
ICHABOD *(smacking lips)*. What a bounteous repast! Apple and pumpkin pies . . .

broiled shad . . . roasted chickens . . . preserved plums and peaches from my own trees . . . ah, I should say your own trees, Mynheer Van Tassel!

(*Music: Dance tune ending.*)

VOICES (*calling*). Ichabod. Ichabod Crane! Show us how you dance the shake-down!

ICHABOD (*gallantly*). If Miss Katrina will be my partner!

KATRINA. Yes, here I am.

(*Music: Jig music into background and hold.*)
(*Sound: Clapping hands and stamping feet to time of music.*)

VOICES OF CROWD (*ad lib*). Go to it, Ichabod! Hooray! See the schoolmaster!

(*Sound: All sound and music fade to distant broadcast.*)

ANNOUNCER. But Brom Van Brunt, Ichabod's rival for the hand of Katrina, did not feel so gay as the rest of the party.

(*Sound: All sound and music up to immediate broadcast and hold.*)

VAN BRUNT (*over voices, viciously*). You'd think it was St. Vitus himself clattering around the floor. He's put together so loose he'll fall apart if he don't watch out!

MAN'S VOICE (*laughing*). Aha, Brom Van Brunt, you've got a pretty rival for Katrina's hand, eh!

WOMAN'S VOICE (*laughing*). The schoolmaster is counting his chickens afore they're hatched.

ANOTHER MAN'S VOICE. Look at him ogle her!

VAN BRUNT (*between teeth*). You wait and see. I'll fix him! I'll fix him!

(*Music: Jig ending.*)
(*Sound: Clapping and stamping out with music. Hold crowd to broadcast.*)

CHORUS OF VOICES (*ad lib*). Bravo, Ichabod Crane! Bravo!

VAN TASSEL (*shouting*). Bring the mulled cider. Fall to, neighbors. You've got a cold ride home!

(*Sound: Glasses and dishes rattle into broadcast.*)

MAN (*smacking lips*). Ahhhh! This is the stuff to put heart into a man! Eh, Van Til?

VAN TIL. Give me a few bumpers of friend Van Tassel's cider, and I'll laugh at the Headless Horseman himself!

ICHABOD (*nasally quavering*). The Headless Horseman! (*Lowering voice*) Has he been seen of late?

MAN. Yes, just t'other night old Brower met the horseman. "I hear you don't believe in me?" says the ghost. "That I don't," said old Brower. "I think you're a humbug." With that the phantom caught him for such a ride as never was. Then with a clap of thunder he turned into a skeleton and flung Brower into the brook. "That'll teach you not to believe in honest ghosts," says he as he disappeared.

CHORUS (*ad lib*). Do tell! I hadn't heard that! Do you mean? . . . (*Etc.*)

ICHABOD (*chattering of teeth and stammering*). W-w-what a thing to happen to a body!

VAN BRUNT. Ah, that's nothing! I met the Headless Horseman myself t'other night coming from Tarrytown. . . .

MAN (*laughing*) (*ad lib*). Coming back from the Flowing Bowl Tavern you'd see anything!

VAN BRUNT. No, I was sober enough. I offered to race the ghost to the inn for a bowl of punch, and I'd have won the race too, but just as we got to the bridge by the churchyard (*Pause*) he vanished in a ball of fire!

ICHABOD (*low*). A ball of fire! The Sleepy Hollow Bridge, you say! And tonight I have to cross it!

VAN BRUNT (*taunting*). If you get by Major Andre's hanging tree alive, you mean, schoolmaster. They do say the goings-on around that tree, the wailings and the groanings, are terrible these nights.

VAN TIL. Well, ghosts or no ghosts, I've got to be getting home! I've got a barn full of cows to milk at cockcrow!

ALL (*ad lib*). That's right. Me, too. Good-by neighbor Van Tassel! (*Fade*) Thank you. A fine party, neighbor.

VAN TASSEL. Good-by, friends!

FROW VAN TASSEL. Thanks for your help with the quilting!

(*Sound: Crowd noises fade out under.*)

ICHABOD. I want to speak a word to your lovely daughter before I depart, Van Tassel. You—ah—give in pretty much to her wishes, I take it?

VAN TASSEL (*laughing*). I love that lass even better than my pipe, schoolmaster, and I've had just one rule bringing her up. Let her have her own way!

ICHABOD. Good! Ah! (*Calling*) Miss Katrina! Miss Katrina! May I speak with you apart?

KATRINA (*fade on*). Have you brought your tuning fork, Master Crane? I don't know as we know how to talk without that! (*Giggles . . . fade out*)

(*Music: Bridge. Up, then under. Out.*)

ANNOUNCER. What passed at this interview, I wouldn't pretend to say. But something must have gone very wrong, for Ichabod stole forth after awhile with a crestfallen air. Ah, these women! Ichabod went to the barn without any of his former airs, kicked poor Gunpowder awake, and set off through the hills. . . . The hour was as dismal as himself. Driving clouds hid the stars and the moon.

(*Music: Weird, atmospheric.*)

(*Sound: Crickets. One horse at walk. Crack of whip. Fade crickets and horse to background and hold.*)

ICHABOD. Get up, you crow's bait. Heaven have mercy on us! What's the matter with the critter?

(*Sound: Horse at walk. Horse stops. Crack of whip.*)

ICHABOD. Giddap! Consarn you, you one-eyed, knock-kneed, sway-backed son of Bala-am!

(*Sound: Horse whinnies. Hoofbeats at walk again, hold briefly and stop.*)

ICHABOD (*in whisper*). It's the hanging tree! He sees the tree where they hanged Andre. Come, come, Gunpowder. If we're to get home afore cockcrow, we must get by this tree somehow. I'll whistle to keep our courage up.

(*Sound: Whistling of "Yankee Doodle." Horse at walk again. Add whistling of "Yankee Doodle" in higher key and out of time with first. Then whistling stops. Horse held to background.*)

ICHABOD. Ooooo . . . even the echo mocks me tonight!

(*Sound: Groans.*)

ICHABOD. Ohhhh! What was that?

VOICE (*ghostly*). Ichabod! Ichabod Crane!

ICHABOD (*in whisper*). W-w-who wants Ichabod Crane?

(*Sound: Weird laughter.*)

ICHABOD (*in whisper*). I see it now, waiting beside the road—a man on horseback. Perhaps it's just one of the revelers going home from Van Tassel's. I'll speak to him. (*In loud, cheerful tone*) Good evening, friend!

(*Sound: Add hoofbeats of second horse at walk in distance.*)

ICHABOD (*fearfully*). W-w-who are you? Whoa, Gunpowder!

(*Sound: First horse stops. Second horse approaches.*)

ICHABOD. If he's more than mortal, a psalm tune ought to drive him away. (*Singing nasally and quaveringly*) Praise God from whom all blessings flow. . . .

VOICE (*distant*). H-hark from the tombs a mournful sound. . . .

ICHABOD. There goes that echo again, mocking me! Oh, mercy! Mercy! He's riding alongside.

(*Sound: As second horse comes into immediate broadcast, first horse begins walking again. Hold both in broadcast.*)

ICHABOD (*in loud tone*). Friend, since you don't seem disposed to be civil, I'll just take my leave of you. Giddap, Gunpowder!

(*Sound: Horse one, then horse two, breaks into trot.*)

ICHABOD (*dismally*). He's close on my heels! (*Calling*) Very well, friend, I have no mind to be sociable myself, so I'll just drop behind, if you don't mind.

(*Sound: Horse one, then horse two, slows pace to walk.*)

ICHABOD. He won't let me lag behind. Well, here comes the moon out from under the cloud. Now I'll get a glimpse of his face! Bless me, he hasn't any head! He's the headless horseman himself! And he's carrying his head afore him on the saddle! Giddap, Gunpowder!

(*Sound: Horses break into gallop. Fade into distance.*)

ANNOUNCER. Away then they dashed, stones flying at every bound. Ichabod's flimsy garments fluttered in the wind as he stretched his long lank body over the horse's head in the eagerness of his flight.

(*Sound: Two horses at gallop fade into broadcast and hold.*)

ICHABOD (*gasping . . . over*). There's the church bridge ahead, Gunpowder! . . . Ghosts can't abide . . . churches! Reach the bridge, we're safe!

(*Sound: Two horses galloping on dirt road, then on bridge, then on road again. Distant cockcrow. Hold horses in broadcast.*)

ICHABOD. Cockcrow! Ghosts always vanish at cockcrow. Let's see . . . if he's gone.

ICHABOD (*gasp*). He hasn't vanished! He's right behind! (*Shout*) He's going to throw his head at me. (*Scream*) Ahhhh!

(*Sound: Horses fade quickly with scream to silence. Dead air: five seconds.*)

ANNOUNCER. The next morning the old horse was found without his saddle, and with the bridle under his feet, soberly cropping the grass at his master's gate. And where was Ichabod Crane? That worried Frow Van Ripper, too (*Fade*) as she said. . . .

FROW VAN RIPPER (*fade in*). Hans Van Ripper, please to call Master Crane to breakfast. He's late for school now. And breakfast is spoiling. Hurry now!

HANS. Ja, ja.

(*Sound: Chair scraped on wood floor.*)

HANS (*surprised*). Why, Frow, look out the

window, yet. That's Gunpowder. But where's my saddle? And look at the bridle. (*Sound: Footsteps on wood. Door opens.*)

HANS (*calling*). Ichabod Crane, why didn't you put Gunpowder in the barn last night? (*Short pause*) Ichabod, Ichabod, why don't you answer?

FROW VAN RIPPER. But Hans, has something happened to the schoolmaster? Where is he? (*Music: Bridge. Fade out under.*)

ANNOUNCER. Over at the schoolhouse the boys and girls gathered at the usual hour. As time went by, and Master Crane did not appear, groups formed on the steps and in the yard. Several of the older boys strolled about the banks of the brook while the younger ones played in the schoolyard. But still no schoolmaster! Later in the day small groups of neighbors gathered (*Fading*) to discuss the strange disappearance.

MAN 1. Ach, the poor schoolmaster. He's a strange one!

MAN 2. Wasn't Ichabod over at Van Tassel's for the quilting last night?

MAN 1. Wasn't he, now? You should'a seen him doing the shakedown with Miss Katrina. And eat—where does he put it?

VAN TIL. Well, then, he would have had to come home by the bridge and the church road. He was on Gunpowder, wasn't he, Hans?

HANS. Ja, neighbor. I lent him my horse and my best saddle to help him woo Miss Katrina. (*Laughter from the group*) And it looks as if we both lost! (*Laughter up and under*)

MAN 2. Let's walk down to see the bridge how. Maybe we can see the nag's footprints.

(*Music: Bridge. Fade out under.*)

ANNOUNCER. And so the neighbors followed slowly after Ichabod's landlord, Hans Van Ripper, as he walked with bent head and searching eyes toward the Sleepy Hollow bridge. Hans noticed that the horses' hoofs were deeply dented in the road, evidently because of furious speed. When he found his best saddle trampled in the mud, he was speechless with anger. (*Fading*) But as the men reached the bridge. . . .

MAN 1 (*excited*). Hans! There! On the bank near the water. It's Ichabod's hat!

VAN TIL. And that smashed pumpkin. Where did it come from?

HANS (*shocked*). Ichabod's hat! And so close to the water, too. We must look for his body. . . . (*Voice fading*) He must have a decent burial. . . .

ANNOUNCER. And so the good neighbors searched the brook, but the body of the schoolmaster was not to be found. When Hans Van Ripper got home, he went to Ichabod's room. His pitch pipe, his books, clothes—all were there. As he was a bachelor and in nobody's debt, no one troubled his head any more about him. But as winter approached and the time came for stories by the fireside, the story of Ichabod's disappearance was told again and again. (*Fading*) And the legend grew until one day. . . .

(*Music: Wedding march up and under.*)

MINISTER. Brom Van Brunt, wilt thou have this woman to be thy wedded wife . . . (*Fading to murmur, then up*) so long as ye both shall live?

VAN BRUNT. I will.

MINISTER. Katrina Van Tassel, wilt thou have

this man to be . . . (*Fading, then up*) I now pronounce that they are man and wife.

(*Music: Wedding march up, fade slowly and out under.*)

ANNOUNCER. At the wedding breakfast at the Van Tassel home, the conversation naturally turned to Ichabod (*Fading*) as the guests reminisced.

(*Sound: Small crowd at breakfast. Fade into background and hold.*)

WOMAN. Have another piece of cake, Hans.

HANS. That I will. Say, wasn't this Ichabod's favorite cake? Wonder what's become of him?

VAN TIL. Why, I saw Ichabod Crane in New York when I was in the city last week.

HANS (*unbelievingly*). No. . . . Van Til. You mean our Ichabod? Yi, yi, yi.

VAN TIL. You know, Hans, I've been thinking about that ride of Ichabod's. Seems to me that pumpkin we found beside his hat was more important than we thought. Whenever we tell that story and Brom Van Brunt is within earshot, he always laughs fit to kill. I'm not so sure about this headless horseman. (*Fade*)

(*Sound: Fade crowd noise to silence. Five seconds.*)

ANNOUNCER. Although Hans Van Ripper and Farmer Van Til questioned the method of Ichabod's disappearance, the old country wives maintained for years that the schoolmaster was spirited away by supernatural means. The bridge became more than ever an object of superstitious awe. The schoolhouse, deserted and fallen to decay, was reported as haunted by Ichabod's ghost. And the plowboy would swear·that of a still summer evening he could hear Ichabod Crane's voice chanting melancholy psalm tunes among the tranquil solitude of Sleepy Hollow.

(*Music: Up.*)

(*Curtain.*)

THINK AND DISCUSS
Understanding
1. What is the **setting** of this play?
2. We learn about **characters** from what they say, what they do, and what others say about them. At the beginning of the play (page 148, column a, paragraph eight), what do we learn from the Announcer about Ichabod Crane?
3. How do the townspeople of Sleepy Hollow regard the schoolmaster?

4. What happens to Katrina Van Tassel and Brom Van Brunt?

Analyzing
5. What **inference** can you make about Ichabod's character from the way he behaves? Back up your answer with specific examples from the play.
6. What do you think happens when Ichabod and Katrina meet after the quilting party? Give reasons for your answer.

7. Which of the following is not important in the development of the **plot** of this play? (**a**) Ichabod tries to outrun the Headless Horseman; (**b**) a quilting party is held at the Van Tassel farm; (**c**) Ichabod punishes Yost Van Huten; (**d**) Ichabod proposes to Katrina.
8. What is suggested by the presence of a broken pumpkin at the spot where Ichabod disappeared?

Extending

9. What do you think has happened to Ichabod Crane? Why do you think as you do?

BIOGRAPHY

Washington Irving

1783–1859

Ichabod Crane was not the only character to be ridiculed by the pen of writer Washington Irving. The title of Irving's first book, published in 1809 under the name Diedrich Knickerbocker, was a mouthful: *A History of New York from the Beginning of the World to the End of the Dutch Dynasty*. In it Irving satirized the history of New York state, both during its colonial days and during his lifetime. The book enraged, amused, and offended New Yorkers; it is considered a comic masterpiece.

Washington Irving was born in New York City. At various times during his life, he practiced law, ran a family business, and served as United States ambassador to England and Spain. But he was always happiest writing. His famous *Sketch Book* contains his best known tales— "Rip Van Winkle" and "The Legend of Sleepy Hollow."

Plays are written to be performed. A playwright creates a story and tells it through dialogue, the words spoken by the actors. Playwrights also give stage directions to provide additional information about the setting, characters, and actions in the play. Reading a play requires imagination on the part of the reader. As you read, you must visualize what you would be seeing or hearing if the play were being performed.

Some plays are written to be played on stage by actors before a live audience. Others are written to be filmed for movies or television. Still others are written to be performed for an audience listening to the radio. *The Legend of Sleepy Hollow* is an example of the last kind of play.

In reading any play, you call on the same kinds of skills you use in reading other types of literature. You look for details indicating setting and character, you examine the structure of the plot, you make inferences about characters and situations, and so forth. In addition, looking for points of **comparison and contrast** will help you as you read. When you compare and contrast, you tell how things are alike and how they are different. For example, the next play you will read, *Back There*, was written for television. You might compare it with *The Legend of Sleepy Hollow*, noting that while both plays contain stage directions and dialogue, the stage directions in each are very different.

Because *The Legend of Sleepy Hollow* is a radio play, all stage directions in it refer to sound. Changes in scene are all suggested by changes in sound, and the particular mood, or overall feeling, of a scene must be created with sound effects. For example, Ichabod makes his way to the quilting party, and the stage directions help us know when he arrives.

(Music: Fade in dance tune of the period.)
(Sound: Fade in sounds of country dance music to background and hold.)

Review the stage directions in *The Legend of Sleepy Hollow* and contrast them with those you will read in *Back There*. Note that, in the television play, the camera can be used to carry the audience from scene to scene or to direct attention to a particular place in a scene.

Then, when you read the third play in the unit, note how the stage directions are used to help create a set for a play written to be performed for a live audience. Ask yourself how the directions in *The Three Garridebs* are like those in the other two plays and how they are different.

As you read the plays, remember that the most important ingredient that you, the reader, can bring to them is your imagination. The more you use your imagination to see and hear the characters, settings, and actions, the more you will enjoy your reading.

See IRONY in the Handbook of Literary Terms, page 672

Back There

Rod Serling

If you could return to the past, what would you change?
What *could* you change?

CHARACTERS

PETER CORRIGAN, a young man
JACKSON, member of the Washington Club
MILLARD, member of the Washington Club
WHITAKER, member of the Washington Club
WILLIAM, attendant at the Washington Club
ATTENDANT ONE, at the Washington Club
ATTENDANT TWO, at the Washington Club
MRS. LANDERS, landlady of a rooming house
LIEUTENANT
LIEUTENANT'S WIFE
POLICE CAPTAIN
POLICEMAN
TURNKEY
POLICE OFFICER
JONATHAN WELLINGTON
LANDLADY
NARRATOR

ACT ONE

SCENE ONE

Exterior of club at night. Near a large front entrance of double doors is a name plaque in brass which reads "The Washington Club, Founded 1858." In the main hall of the building is a large paneled foyer with rooms leading off on either side. An attendant, WILLIAM, *carrying a tray of drinks, crosses the hall and enters one of the rooms. There are four men sitting around in the aftermath of a card game.* PETER CORRIGAN *is the youngest, then two middle-aged men named* WHITAKER *and* MILLARD, *and* JACKSON, *the oldest, a white-haired man in his sixties, who motions the tray from the attendant over to the table.*

JACKSON. Just put it over here, William, would you?

WILLIAM. Yes, sir. *(He lays the tray down and walks away from the table.)*

CORRIGAN. Now what's your point? That if it were possible for a person to go back in time there'd be nothing in the world to prevent him from altering the course of history—is that it?

MILLARD. Let's say, Corrigan, that you go back in time. It's October, 1929. The day before the stock market crashed.[1] You know on the following morning that the securities are going to tumble into an abyss. Now using that prior knowledge, there's a hundred things you can do to protect yourself.

CORRIGAN. But I'm an anachronism back there. I don't really belong back there.

MILLARD. You could sell out the day before the crash.

CORRIGAN. But what if I did and that started the crash earlier? Now history tells us that on October 24th, 1929, the bottom dropped out of the stock market. That's a fixed date. October 24th, 1929. It exists as an event in the history of our times. It *can't* be altered.

MILLARD. And I say it can. What's to prevent it? What's to prevent me, say, from going to a broker[2] on the morning of October 23rd?

CORRIGAN. Gentlemen, I'm afraid I'll have to leave this time travel to H. G. Wells.[3] I'm much too tired to get into any more metaphysics[4] this evening. And since nobody has ever gone back in time, the whole blamed thing is much too theoretical. I'll probably see you over the weekend.

WHITAKER. Don't get lost back in time now, Corrigan.

CORRIGAN. I certainly shall not. Good night, everybody.

VOICES. Good night, Pete. Good night, Corrigan. See you tomorrow.

(CORRIGAN walks out into the hall and heads toward the front door.)

WILLIAM *(going by)*. Good night, Mr. Corrigan.

---

1. *stock market crashed.* In October, 1929, stocks suddenly became greatly devalued, leading to a nationwide financial disaster and the ruin of many people.
2. *broker,* a person who buys and sells stocks and bonds for a client.
3. *H. G. Wells,* 1866–1946, an English writer known particularly for his prophetic science fiction. One of his best-known novels is *The Time Machine,* about traveling in time.
4. *metaphysics* (met′ə fiz′iks), the philosophical study of such concepts as time, space, and reality.

CORRIGAN. Good night, William. (*Then he looks at the elderly man a little more closely.*) Everything all right with you, William? Looks like you've lost some weight.

WILLIAM (*with a deference built of a forty-year habit pattern*). Just the usual worries, sir. The stars and my salary are fixed. It's the cost of living that goes up. (CORRIGAN *smiles, reaches in his pocket, starts to hand him a bill.*)

WILLIAM. Oh no, sir, I couldn't.

CORRIGAN (*forcing it into his hand*). Yes, you can, William. Bless you and say hello to your wife to me.

WILLIAM. Thank you so much, sir. (*A pause*) Did you have a coat with you?

CORRIGAN. No. I'm rushing the season a little tonight, William. I felt spring in the air. Came out like this.

WILLIAM (*opening the door*). Well, April *is* spring, sir.

CORRIGAN. It's getting there. What is the date, William?

WILLIAM. April 14th, sir.

CORRIGAN. April 14th. (*Then he turns and grins at the attendant.*) 1965—right?

WILLIAM. I beg your pardon, sir? Oh, yes, sir. 1965.

CORRIGAN (*going out*). Good night, William. Take care of yourself. (*He goes out into the night.*)

SCENE TWO

Exterior of the club. The door closes behind CORRIGAN. *He stands there near the front entrance. The light from the street light illuminates the steps. There's the sound of chimes from the distant steeple clock.* CORRIGAN *looks at his wristwatch, holding it out toward the light so it can be seen more clearly. Suddenly his face takes on a strange look. He shuts his eyes and rubs his temple. Then he looks down at his wrist again. This time the light has changed. It's a wavery, moving light, different from what it had been.* CORRIGAN *looks across toward the light again. It's a gaslight*[5] *now. He reacts in amazement. The chimes begin to chime again, this time eight times. He once again looks at the watch, but instead of a wristwatch there is just a fringe of lace protruding from a coat. There is no wristwatch at all. He grabs his wrist, pulling at the lace and coat. He's dressed now in a nineteenth-century costume. He looks down at himself, looks again toward the gaslight that flickers, and then slowly backs down from the steps staring at the building from which he's just come. The plaque reads "Washington Club." He jumps the steps two at a time, slams against the front door, pounding on it. After a long moment the door opens. An* ATTENDANT, *half undressed, stands there peering out into the darkness.*

ATTENDANT ONE. Who is it? What do you want?

CORRIGAN. I left something in there.

(*He starts to push his way in and the* ATTENDANT *partially closes the door on him.*)

ATTENDANT ONE. Now here you! The Club is closed this evening.

CORRIGAN. The devil it is. I just left here a minute ago.

ATTENDANT ONE (*peers at him*). You did what?

---

5. *gaslight.* Gas was used for lighting on streets and in buildings, chiefly during the nineteenth century.

You drunk, young man? That it? You're drunk, huh?

CORRIGAN. I am not drunk. I want to see Mr. Jackson or Mr. Whitaker, or William. Let me talk to William. Where is he now?

ATTENDANT ONE. Who?

CORRIGAN. William. What's the matter with you? Where did *you* come from? (*Then he looks down at his clothes.*) What's the idea of this? (*He looks up. The door has been shut. He pounds on it again, shouting.*) Hey! Open up!

VOICE (*from inside*). You best get away from here or I'll call the police. Go on. Get out of here.

(CORRIGAN *backs away from the door, goes down to the sidewalk, stands there, looks up at the gaslight, then up and down the street, starts at the sound of noises. It's the clip-clop of horses' hooves and the rolling, squeaky sound of carriage wheels. He takes a few halting, running steps out into the street. He bites his lip, looks around.*)

CORRIGAN (*under his breath*). I'll go home. That's it. Go home. I'll go home. (*He turns and starts to walk and then run down the street, disappearing into the night.*)

SCENE THREE

Hallway of rooming house. There is the sound of a doorbell ringing. MRS. LANDERS, *the landlady, comes out from the dining room and goes toward the door.*

MRS. LANDERS. All right. All right. Have a bit of patience. I'm coming. (*Opening door*) Yes?

CORRIGAN. Is this 19 West 12th Street?

MRS. LANDERS. That's right. Whom did you wish to see?

CORRIGAN. I'm just wondering if . . .

(*He stands there trying to look over her shoulder.* MRS. LANDERS *turns to look behind her and then suspiciously back toward* CORRIGAN.)

MRS. LANDERS. Whom did you wish to see, young man?

CORRIGAN. I . . . I used to live here. It's the oldest building in this section of town.

MRS. LANDERS (*stares at him*). How's that?

CORRIGAN (*wets his lips*). What I mean is . . . as I remember it . . . it was the oldest——

MRS. LANDERS. Well now really, young man. I can't spend the whole evening standing here talking about silly things like which is the oldest building in the section. Now if there's nothing else——

CORRIGAN (*blurting it out*). Do you have a room?

MRS. LANDERS (*opens the door just a little bit wider so that she can get a better look at him; looks him up and down and appears satisfied*). I have a room for acceptable boarders. Do you come from around here?

CORRIGAN. Yes. Yes, I do.

MRS. LANDERS. Army veteran?

CORRIGAN. Yes. Yes, as a matter of fact I am.

MRS. LANDERS (*looks at him again up and down*). Well, come in. I'll show you what I have.

(*She opens the door wider and* CORRIGAN *enters. She closes it behind him. She looks expectantly up toward his hat and* CORRIGAN *rather hurriedly and abruptly removes it. He grins, embarrassed.*)

CORRIGAN. I'm not used to it.

MRS. LANDERS. Used to what?

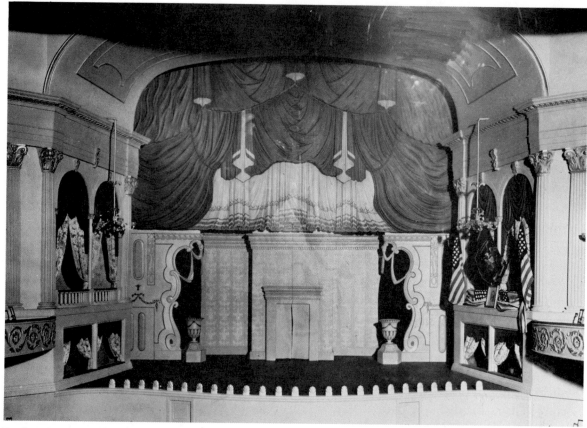

Replica of stage of Ford's Theater. Presidential box is at right.
Photo from Frederick Lewis/Thornton Collection

CORRIGAN (*points to the hat in his hand*). The hat. I don't wear a hat very often.

MRS. LANDERS (*again gives him her inventory look, very unsure of him now*). May I inquire as to what your business is?

CORRIGAN. I'm an engineer.

MRS. LANDERS. Really. A professional man. Hmmm. Well, come upstairs and I'll show you.

(*She points to the stairs that lead off the hall and* CORRIGAN *starts up as an army officer and his wife come down them.*)

MRS. LANDERS (*smiling*). Off to the play?

LIEUTENANT. That's right, Mrs. Landers.

Dinner at The Willard and then off to the play.

MRS. LANDERS. Well, enjoy yourself. And applaud the President for me!

LIEUTENANT. We'll certainly do that.

LIEUTENANT'S WIFE. Good night, Mrs. Landers.

MRS. LANDERS. Good night, my dear. Have a good time. This way, Mr. Corrigan.

(*The* LIEUTENANT *and* CORRIGAN *exchange a nod as they pass on the stairs. As they go up the steps,* CORRIGAN *suddenly stops and* MRS. LANDERS *almost bangs into him.*)

MRS. LANDERS. Now what's the trouble?

CORRIGAN (*whirling around*). What did you say?

MRS. LANDERS. What did I say to whom? When?

CORRIGAN. To the lieutenant. To the officer. What did you just say to him?
(*The* LIEUTENANT *has turned. His wife tries to lead him out, but he holds out his hand to stop her so that he can listen to the conversation from the steps.*)

CORRIGAN. You just said something to him about the President.

LIEUTENANT (*walking toward the foot of the steps*). She told me to applaud him. Where might your sympathies lie?

MRS. LANDERS (*suspiciously*). Yes, young man. Which army *were* you in?

CORRIGAN (*wets his lips nervously*). The Army of the Republic,[6] of course.

LIEUTENANT (*nods, satisfied*). Then why make such a thing of applauding President Lincoln? That's his due, we figure.

MRS. LANDERS. That and everything else, may the good Lord bless him.

CORRIGAN (*takes a step down the stairs, staring at the* LIEUTENANT). You're going to a play tonight?
(*The* LIEUTENANT *nods.*)

LIEUTENANT'S WIFE (*at the door*). We may or we may not, depending on when my husband makes up his mind to get a carriage in time to have dinner and get to the theater.

CORRIGAN. What theater? *What* play?

LIEUTENANT. Ford's Theater, of course.

CORRIGAN (*looking off, his voice intense*). Ford's Theater. Ford's Theater.

LIEUTENANT. Are you all right? I mean do you feel all right?

CORRIGAN (*whirls around to stare at him*). What's the name of the play?

LIEUTENANT (*exchanges a look with his wife*). I beg your pardon?

CORRIGAN. The play. The one you're going to tonight at Ford's Theater. What's the name of it?

LIEUTENANT'S WIFE. It's called "Our American Cousin."

CORRIGAN (*again looks off thoughtfully*). "Our American Cousin" and Lincoln's going to be there. (*He looks from one to the other, first toward the landlady on the steps, then down toward the soldier and his wife.*) And it's April 14th, 1865, isn't it? Isn't it April 14th, 1865? (*He starts down the steps without waiting for an answer. The* LIEUTENANT *stands in front of him.*)

LIEUTENANT. Really, sir, I'd call your actions most strange.
(CORRIGAN *stares at him briefly as he goes by, then goes out the door, looking purposeful and intent.*)

SCENE FOUR

Alley at night. On one side is the stage door with a sign over it reading "Ford's Theater." CORRIGAN *turns the corridor into the alley at a dead run. He stops directly under the light, looks left and right, then vaults over the railing and pounds on the stage door.*

CORRIGAN (*shouting*). Hey! Hey, let me in! President Lincoln is going to be shot tonight!
(*He continues to pound on the door and shout.*)

---

6. *Army of the Republic*, the northern army, or Federal Army, in the United States Civil War.

ACT TWO

SCENE ONE

Police station at night. It's a bare receiving room with a POLICE CAPTAIN at a desk. A long bench on one side of the room is occupied by sad miscreants awaiting disposition. There is a line of three or four men standing in front of the desk with several policemen in evidence. One holds onto CORRIGAN who has a bruise over his eye and his coat is quite disheveled. The POLICE CAPTAIN looks up to him from a list.

CAPTAIN. Now what's this one done? (*He peers up over his glasses and eyes CORRIGAN up and down.*) Fancy Dan with too much money in his pockets, huh?

CORRIGAN. While you idiots are sitting here, you're going to lose a President!

(*The CAPTAIN looks inquiringly toward the POLICEMAN.*)

POLICEMAN. That's what he's been yellin' all the way over to the station. And that's what the doorman at Ford's Theater popped him on the head for. (*He nods toward CORRIGAN.*) Tried to pound his way right through the stage door. Yellin' some kind of crazy things about President Lincoln goin' to get shot.

CORRIGAN. President Lincoln *will* be shot! Tonight. In the theater. A man named Booth.

CAPTAIN. And how would you be knowin' this? I suppose you're clairvoyant or something. Some kind of seer or wizard or something.

CORRIGAN. I only know what I know. If I told you *how* I knew, you wouldn't believe me.

Look, keep me here if you like. Lock me up.

CAPTAIN (*motions toward a TURNKEY,[7] points to cell block door*). Let him sleep it off.

(*The TURNKEY grabs CORRIGAN'S arm and starts to lead him out of the room.*)

CORRIGAN (*shouting as he's led away*). Well, you better hear me out. Somebody better get to the President's box at Ford's Theater. Either keep him out of there or put a cordon of men around him. A man named John Wilkes Booth is going to assassinate him tonight!

(*He's pushed through the door leading to the cell block. A tall man in cape and black moustache stands near the open door at the other side. He closes it behind him, takes a step into the room, then with a kind of very precise authority, he walks directly over to the CAPTAIN'S table, shoving a couple of people aside as he does so with a firm gentleness. When he reaches the CAPTAIN'S table he removes a card from his inside pocket, puts it on the table in front of the CAPTAIN.*)

WELLINGTON. Wellington, Captain. Jonathan Wellington.

(*The CAPTAIN looks at the card, peers at it over his glasses, then looks up toward the tall man in front of him. Obviously the man's manner and dress impresses him. His tone is respectful and quiet.*)

CAPTAIN. What can I do for you, Mr. Wellington?

WELLINGTON. That man you just had incarcerated. Mr. Corrigan I believe he said his name was.

---

7. *turnkey*, jailer.

CAPTAIN. Drunk, sir. That's probably what he is.

WELLINGTON. Drunk or . . . (*He taps his head meaningfully.*) Or perhaps, ill. I wonder if he could be remanded in my custody. He might well be a war veteran and I'd hate to see him placed in jail.

CAPTAIN. Well, that's real decent of you, Mr. Wellington. You say you want him remanded in *your* custody?

WELLINGTON. Precisely. I'll be fully responsible for him. I think perhaps I might be able to help him.

CAPTAIN. All right, sir. If that's what you'd like. But I'd be careful of this one if I was you! There's a mighty bunch of crackpots running the streets these days and many of them his like, and many of them dangerous too, sir. (*He turns toward* TURNKEY.) Have Corrigan brought back out here. This gentleman's going to look after him. (*Then he turns to* WELLINGTON.) It's real decent of you, sir. Real decent indeed.

WELLINGTON. I'll be outside. Have him brought out to me if you would.

CAPTAIN. I will indeed, sir.

(WELLINGTON *turns. He passes the various people who look at him and make room for him. His walk, his manner, his positiveness suggest a commanding figure and everyone reacts accordingly. The* CAPTAIN *once again busies himself with his list and is about to check in the next prisoner, when a young* POLICE OFFICER *alongside says:*)

POLICE OFFICER. Begging your pardon, Captain.

CAPTAIN. What is it?

POLICE OFFICER. About that Corrigan, sir.

CAPTAIN. What about him?

POLICE OFFICER. Wouldn't it be wise, sir, if——

CAPTAIN (*impatiently*). If what?

POLICE OFFICER. He seemed so positive, sir. So sure. About the President, I mean.

CAPTAIN (*slams on the desk with vast impatience*). What would you have us do? Send all available police to Ford's Theater? And on what authority? On the word of some demented fool who probably left his mind someplace in Gettysburg.[8] If I was you, mister, I'd be considerably more thoughtful at sizing up situations or you'll not advance one-half grade the next twenty years. Now be good enough to stand aside and let me get on with my work.

POLICE OFFICER (*very much deterred by all this, but pushed on by a gnawing sense of disquiet*). Captain, it wouldn't hurt.

CAPTAIN (*interrupting with a roar*). It wouldn't hurt if what?

POLICE OFFICER. I was going to suggest, sir, that if perhaps we place extra guards in the box with the President——

CAPTAIN. The President has all the guards he needs. He's got the whole Federal Army at his disposal and if they're satisfied with his security arrangements, then I am too and so should you. Next case!

(*The young* POLICE OFFICER *bites his lip and looks away, then stares across the room thoughtfully. The door opens and the* TURNKEY *leads* CORRIGAN *across the room and over to the door. He opens it and points out:* CORRIGAN *nods and walks outside. The*

---

8. **Gettysburg** (get′iz bèrg′), a town in Pennsylvania, the site of one of the major battles of the Civil War in July, 1863.

door closes behind him. The young POLICE OFFICER *looks briefly at the* CAPTAIN, *then puts his cap on and starts out toward the door.*)

SCENE TWO

Lodging-house, WELLINGTON'S *room.* WELLINGTON *is pouring wine into two glasses.* CORRIGAN *sits in a chair, his face in his hands. He looks up at the proffered drink and takes it.*

WELLINGTON. Take this. It'll make you feel better. (CORRIGAN *nods his thanks, takes a healthy swig of the wine, puts it down, then looks up at the other man.*) Better?

CORRIGAN (*studying the man*). Who are you, anyway?

WELLINGTON (*with a thin smile*). At the moment I'm your benefactor and apparently your only friend. I'm in the Government service, but as a young man in college I dabbled in medicine of a sort.

CORRIGAN. Medicine?

WELLINGTON. Medicine of the mind.

CORRIGAN (*smiles grimly*). Psychiatrist.

WELLINGTON (*turning to him*). I don't know the term.

CORRIGAN. What about the symptoms?

WELLINGTON. They *do* interest me. This story you were telling about the President being assassinated.

CORRIGAN (*quickly*). What time *is* it?

WELLINGTON. There's time. (*Checks a pocket watch*) A quarter to eight. The play won't start for another half hour. What gave you the idea that the President would be assassinated?

CORRIGAN. I happen to know, that's all.

WELLINGTON (*again the thin smile*). You have a premonition?

CORRIGAN. I've got a devil of a lot more than a premonition. Lincoln *will* be assassinated. (*Then quickly*) Unless somebody tries to prevent it.

WELLINGTON. *I* shall try to prevent it. If you can convince me that you're neither drunk nor insane.

CORRIGAN (*on his feet*). If I told you what I was, you'd be convinced I *was* insane. So all I'm *going* to tell you is that I happen to know for a fact that a man named John Wilkes Booth will assassinate President Lincoln in his box at Ford's Theater. I don't know what time it's going to happen . . . that's something I forgot—but——

WELLINGTON (*softly*). Something you forgot?

CORRIGAN (*takes a step toward him*). Listen, please—— *He stops suddenly, and begins to waver. He reaches up to touch the bruise on his head.*)

WELLINGTON (*takes out a handkerchief and hands it to* CORRIGAN). Here. That hasn't been treated properly. You'd best cover it.

CORRIGAN (*very, very shaky, almost faint, takes the handkerchief, puts it to his head and sits back down weakly*). That's . . . that's odd. (*He looks up, still holding the handkerchief.*)

WELLINGTON. What is?

CORRIGAN. I'm so . . . I'm so faint all of a sudden. So weak. It's almost as if I were——

WELLINGTON. As if you were what?

CORRIGAN (*with a weak smile*). As if I'd suddenly gotten drunk or some—(*He looks up, desperately trying to focus now as his vision starts to become clouded.*) I've never . . . I've never felt like this before. I've never—

(His eyes turn to the wine glass on the table. As his eyes open wide, he struggles to his feet.) You . . . you devil! You drugged me, didn't you! *(He reaches out to grab* WELLINGTON, *half struggling in the process.)* You drugged me, didn't you!

WELLINGTON. I was forced to, my young friend. You're a very sick man and a sick man doesn't belong in jail. He belongs in a comfortable accommodation where he can sleep and rest and regain his . . . *(He smiles a little apologetically.)* his composure, his rationale. Rest, Mr. Corrigan. I'll be back soon.

(He turns and starts toward the door. CORRIGAN *starts to follow him, stumbles to his knees, supports himself on one hand, looks up as* WELLINGTON *opens the door.)*

CORRIGAN. Please . . . please, you've got to believe me. Lincoln's going to be shot tonight.

WELLINGTON *(smiling again)*. And *that's* odd! Because . . . perhaps I'm *beginning* to believe you! Good night, Mr. Corrigan. Rest well. *(He turns and goes out of the room, closing the door behind him. We hear the sound of the key being inserted, the door locked.)*

*(*CORRIGAN *tries desperately to rise and then weakly falls over on his side. He crawls toward the door. He scrabbles at it with a weak hand.)*

CORRIGAN *(almost in a whisper)*. Please . . . please . . . somebody . . . let me out. I wasn't kidding . . . I know . . . *the President's going to be assassinated!* (*His arm, supporting him, gives out and he falls to his face, then in a last effort, he turns himself over so that he's lying on his back.)*

(There is a sound of a heavy knocking on the door. Then a LANDLADY'S *voice from outside.)*

LANDLADY. There's no need to break it open, Officer. I've got an extra key. Now if you don't mind, stand aside.

(There's the sound of the key inserted in the lock and the door opens. The young POLICE OFFICER *from earlier is standing there with an angry-faced* LANDLADY *behind him. The* POLICE OFFICER *gets down on his knees, props up* CORRIGAN'S *head.)*

POLICE OFFICER. Are you all right? What happened?

CORRIGAN. What time is it? *(He grabs the* OFFICER, *almost pulling him over.)* You've got to tell me what time it is.

POLICE OFFICER. It's ten-thirty-five. Come on, Corrigan. You've got to tell me what you know about this. You may be a madman or a drunk or I don't know what—but you've got me convinced and I've been everywhere from the Mayor's office to the Police Commissioner's home trying to get a special guard for the President.

CORRIGAN. Then go yourself. Find out where he's sitting and get right up alongside of him. He'll be shot from behind. That's the way it happened. Shot from behind. And then the assassin jumps from the box to the stage and he runs out of the wings.

POLICE OFFICER *(incredulous)*. You're telling me this as if, as if it has already happened.

CORRIGAN. It *has* happened. It happened a hundred years ago and I've come back to see that it *doesn't* happen. *(Looking beyond the* POLICE OFFICER) Where's the man who brought me in here? Where's Wellington?

LANDLADY *(peering into the room)*. Wellington? There's no one here by that name.

CORRIGAN (*waves a clenched fist at her, still holding the handkerchief*). Don't tell me there's no one here by that name. He brought me in here. He lives in this room.

LANDLADY. There's no one here by that name.

CORRIGAN (*holds the handkerchief close to his face, again waving his fist*). I tell you the man who brought me here was named—— (*He stops abruptly, suddenly caught by something he sees on the handkerchief. His eyes slowly turn to stare at it in his hand. On the border are the initials J.W.B.*)

CORRIGAN. J.W.B.?

LANDLADY. Of course! Mr. John Wilkes Booth who lives in this room and that's who brought you here.

CORRIGAN. He said his name was Wellington! And *that's* why he drugged me. (*He grabs the* POLICE OFFICER *again.*) He gave me wine and he drugged me. He didn't want me to stop him. He's the one who's going to do it. Listen, you've got to get to that theater. You've got to stop him. John Wilkes Booth! He's going to kill Lincoln. Look, get out of here now! Will you stop him? Will you——

(*He stops abruptly, his eyes look up. All three people turn to look toward the window. There's the sound of crowd noises building, suggestive of excitement, and then almost a collective wail, a mournful, universal chant that comes from the streets, and as the sound builds we suddenly hear intelligible words that are part of the mob noise.*)

VOICES. The President's been shot. President Lincoln's been assassinated. Lincoln is dying.

(*The* LANDLADY *suddenly bursts into tears. The* POLICE OFFICER *rises to his feet, his face white.*)

POLICE OFFICER. Oh my dear God! You were right. You *did* know. Oh . . . my . . . dear . . . God!

(*He turns almost trance-like and walks out of the room. The* LANDLADY *follows him.* CORRIGAN *rises weakly and goes to the window, staring out at the night and listening to the sounds of a nation beginning its mourning. He closes his eyes and puts his head against the window pane and with fruitless, weakened smashes, hits the side of the window frame as he talks.*)

CORRIGAN. I tried to tell you. I tried to warn you. Why didn't anybody listen? Why? Why didn't anyone listen to me?

(*His fist beats a steady staccato on the window frame.*)

SCENE THREE

The Washington Club at night. CORRIGAN *is pounding on the front door of the Washington Club.* CORRIGAN *is standing there in modern dress once again. The door opens. An* ATTENDANT *we've not seen before appears.*

ATTENDANT TWO. Good evening. Mr. Corrigan. Did you forget something, sir?

(CORRIGAN *walks past the* ATTENDANT, *through the big double doors that lead to the card room as in Act One. His three friends are in the middle of a discussion. The fourth man at the table, sitting in his seat, has his back to the camera.*)

MILLARD (*looking up*). Hello, Pete. Come on over and join tonight's bull session. It has to do with the best ways of amassing a fortune. What are your tried-and-true methods?

CORRIGAN (*his voice intense and shaky*). We were talking about time travel, about going back in time.

JACKSON (*dismissing it*). Oh that's old stuff. We're on a new tack now. Money and the best ways to acquire it.

CORRIGAN. Listen . . . listen, I want to tell you something. This is true. If you go back into the past you can't change anything. (*He takes another step toward the table.*) Understand? You can't change anything. (*The men look at one another, disarmed by the intensity of* CORRIGAN'S *tone.*)

JACKSON (*rises, softly*). All right, old man, if you say so. (*Studying him intensely*) Are you all right?

CORRIGAN (*closing his eyes for a moment*). Yes . . . yes, I'm all right.

JACKSON. Then come on over and listen to a lot of palaver from self-made swindlers. William here has the best method.

CORRIGAN. William?

(*He sees the attendant from Act One but now meticulously dressed, a middle-aged millionaire obviously, with a totally different manner, who puts a cigarette in a holder with manicured hands in the manner of a man totally accustomed to wealth.* WILLIAM *looks up and smiles.*)

WILLIAM. Oh yes. My method for achieving security is by far the best. You simply inherit it. It comes to you in a beribboned box. I was telling the boys here, Corrigan. My great-grandfather was on the police force here in Washington on the night of Lincoln's assassination. He went all over

town trying to warn people that something might happen. (*He holds up his hands in a gesture.*) How he figured it out, nobody seems to know. It's certainly not recorded any place. But because there was so much publicity, people never forgot him. He became a police chief, then a councilman, did some wheeling and dealing in land and became a millionaire. What do you say we get back to our bridge, gentlemen?

(JACKSON *takes the cards and starts to shuffle.* WILLIAM *turns in his seat once again.*)

WILLIAM. How about it, Corrigan? Take a hand?

CORRIGAN. Thank you, William, no. I think I'll . . . I think I'll just go home.

(*He turns very slowly and starts toward the exit. Over his walk we hear the whispered, hushed murmurings of the men at the table.*)

VOICES. Looks peaked, doesn't he? Acting so strangely. I wonder what's the matter with him.

(CORRIGAN *walks into the hall and toward the front door.*)

NARRATOR'S VOICE. Mr. Peter Corrigan, lately returned from a place "Back There"; a journey into time with highly questionable results. Proving, on one hand, that the threads of history are woven tightly and the skein of events cannot be undone; but, on the other hand, there are small fragments of tapestry that *can* be altered. Tonight's thesis, to be taken as you will, in *The Twilight Zone!*[9]

---

9. *The Twilight Zone*, the name of the television program on which "Back There" was originally produced.

THINK AND DISCUSS
Understanding
1. What is the geographic setting of the play?
2. In what way does the **setting** change in the course of the play?
3. Early in the play, does Corrigan believe that history can be altered?
4. When Corrigan warns of the danger to the President, most people think he is insane. Who are the only people who believe him? What does each person do?
5. When Corrigan returns to 1965, what one change does he discover?

Analyzing
6. Why does Corrigan give William money?
7. Why is Wellington so interested in Corrigan?
8. What does Corrigan try to tell his friends when he returns to the present?

Extending
9. If *Back There* had been written for radio rather than for television, how might each of the changes in setting have been indicated using only sound?

APPLYING: Irony H⫶
See Handbook of Literary Terms, p. 672.
Irony is the contrast between what is expected, or what appears to be, and what actually is. **Verbal irony** is the contrast between what is said and what is actually meant. **Irony of situation** refers to a happening that is the opposite of what is expected or intended. **Dramatic irony** occurs when the audience or reader knows more than the characters do. Now answer these questions about the use of irony in *Back There*.

1. At the beginning of the play, Corrigan insists that history "*can't* be altered." In light of his opinion, what is ironic about Corrigan's situation throughout most of the play?
2. Why is it ironic that Jonathan Wellington helps release Corrigan from prison and calls himself Corrigan's benefactor and friend?
3. Throughout the play, Corrigan tries to convince people that Lincoln is about to be assassinated. How are these encounters examples of dramatic irony?
4. When Corrigan tells the police captain that a man named Booth will shoot Lincoln, the captain replies, "I suppose you're clairvoyant or something. Some kind of seer or wizard or something." What kind of irony is this? Explain.

READING LITERATURE SKILLFULLY
Comparison and Contrast
In this unit you have learned to use points of **comparison and contrast** as you read and discuss short plays. As you read, you note ways in which the plays are alike and ways in which they are different. You can also make use of comparison and contrast to help your understanding of a single work. For example, in *Back There*, you might compare and contrast two characters, telling how those characters are alike and how they are different.

Use comparison and contrast to answer these questions about *Back There*.

1. Compare and contrast the Washington of Act One, Scene One, with the same city in Act One, Scene Two. In what ways are the two settings alike? How are they different?

2. Compare and contrast the group at the Washington Club at the beginning of the play with the group gathered there at the end. In comparing and contrasting, consider both the characters present and how they speak and act.

COMPOSITION ◆━━
Writing a Narrative

Imagine that you could improve the course of history by changing the fate of one person. Who would that person be? Would you prevent an assassination? Would you keep a Hitler or a Napoleon from coming to power? Might you have Eleanor Roosevelt run for and win the office of President of the United States? What effects would your change in history have on the world? Write a composition to explain how you would change history and what the results would be. Support your choice by explaining the positive effects the change would have.

Writing as a Story Character

Imagine that you are the police officer who believes Corrigan's story. Pretend that ten years have passed since that night when Corrigan tried to stop the assassination of President Lincoln. Write an autobiographical account starting with that night. Describe Corrigan—how he looked and what he said; then tell why you believed him and what you did about it.

Write about the reactions people had to you as you tried to warn of the assassination. Tell about how you became a police chief, a dealer in real estate, and a millionaire. You might even wonder whatever became of Corrigan. You may find it useful to review the article "Writing as a Story Character" in the Writer's Handbook before beginning your composition.

ENRICHMENT
Creative Project

Divide into small groups. Each group then pretends to be the camera crew for filming *Back There*. The director has left the shots up to you. First, pick one of the scenes from the play. Then decide how you would film the scene. Start by finding the definitions of some basic motion picture vocabulary, such as *zooming, panning, long shot, medium shot, overhead shot,* and *close-up*. You can do research in the library to find this and other information about camera work.

When you have completed your research, sit down as a group and write a set of camera directions for your scene. Be sure each camera shot contributes in some way to the meaning of what is going on in the scene. Will you want to have a close-up of a character's face, or perhaps pull in for a medium shot over his shoulder as he is talking, to show the reactions of the characters he is talking to? Might you call for a long shot in a certain scene to show a large group of characters at once? Maybe you'll wish to follow one character with the camera (*pan*) throughout an exchange to show that he is the most important person in the scene. Be very specific about what kinds of directions you write.

BIOGRAPHY

Rod Serling
1924–1975

"There is a fifth dimension beyond that which is known to man. . . . It is the dimension of imagination. It is an area which we call the Twilight Zone." These words served to introduce and conclude the weekly television series, *The Twilight Zone*, which ran from 1959 to 1964.

The narrator was Rod Serling, an American playwright who wrote almost exclusively for television. Born in Syracuse, New York, Serling edited his high school paper and then joined the Army, where he became a prizefighter and eventually served for three years in the Philippines. His first forty scripts were rejected, but he eventually became the most prolific scriptwriter in television.

Serling won six Emmy Awards for excellence in original dramatic writing for television between 1955 and 1964. Two of these were for "The Twilight Zone."

Comment

Traveling in Time

"Where does time go?" This question, so commonly asked by small children, is something most of us have wondered about. It seems that people have always been interested in the passage of time and the possibility of traveling through time. Many writers have used this theme. Washington Irving's story "Rip Van Winkle," published in 1819, is about a man who falls asleep in New York's Catskill Mountains and awakens twenty years later. Not only has his beard grown a foot, but the Revolutionary War has been fought and won by the Americans. The reactions of the townspeople to Rip's return and Rip's own reactions to the changes he sees provide many amusing scenes.

In *A Connecticut Yankee in King Arthur's Court*, a novel by Mark Twain published in 1889, a nineteenth-century American mechanic is knocked unconscious. He awakens under a tree near legendary Camelot in the England of a much earlier

Newell Convers Wyeth, *Rip Van Winkle*, 1921. Private Collection. *Courtesy Brandywine River Museum*

century and proceeds to outdo Merlin the magician and King Arthur's best knights.

In 1895 H. G. Wells's celebrated *The Time Machine* appeared. The novel concerns a man who travels by time machine into the distant future. The novel was among the first to link events of fantasy or fiction with believable—if not actual—scientific background. It remains enormously popular, and was made into a film in 1960.

Time travel is a favorite theme of science fiction writer Ray Bradbury, author of the *Martian Chronicles*. In a short story entitled "A Sound of Thunder," hunters travel back into prehistoric times to "bag" dinosaurs who are scheduled to die in their own niche of history. The travelers are absolutely forbidden to do anything to change the setting or sequence of events—they may not even touch a blade of grass—so that they do not inadvertently change the future. One character disobeys the rules, with horrifying results that become apparent when the travelers return to the present. This story and Rod Serling's *Back There* are similar in that the reader is left not only with the question "Can we change the past, and therefore the future?" but also "Should we?"

The possibilities of time travel continue to fascinate scientists as well as writers and film makers. Whether time travel is scientifically possible or not, the topic holds a seemingly unlimited number of plots and possibilities.

Writer's Craft

Use Precise, Active Verbs

Writers choose words to make their writing lively and to affect the emotions of their readers. Good writers use precise, active verbs to help the reader see the actions taking place as well as to keep the story moving. Look at these sentences.

Alex *went* down the hill.
Alex *tore* down the hill.
Alex *drove* down the hill.
Alex *tumbled* down the hill.

Notice how dull the verb *went* is in the first sentence. It tells you little about how Alex moved or what he might have been feeling. The verbs *tore*, *drove*, and *tumbled* are much more precise and active, and they tell you, even in such short sentences, what might be going on in Alex's life or thoughts. For example, in which sentence is Alex probably in a hurry? In which sentence might he be in pain?

In *The Legend of Sleepy Hollow,* automobiles don't merely *cross* the Headless Horseman's Bridge, they *rattle* across it, allowing readers a clear picture of both bridge and automobile. When Ichabod Crane meets the "headless horseman," the announcer describes the scene.

Away then they dashed, stones flying at every bound. Ichabod's flimsy garments fluttered in the wind as he stretched his long lank body over the horse's head in the eagerness of his flight.

To appreciate the importance of precise and active verbs, try replacing *dashed, fluttered,* and *stretched* in the preceding paragraph with *went, moved,* and *put.*

Note the verbs in these sentences.

POLICEMAN: That's what he's been yellin' all the way over to the station. And that's what the doorman at the Ford Theater popped him on the head for. (*He nods toward* CORRIGAN.) Tried to pound his way right through the stage door . . .

The verbs show how frantic Corrigan has become; they suggest the noise and violence of the scene; they show Corrigan's despair as he tries to get through the door, to *pound through it* so that he can get into the theater to save Lincoln. The writer chose these precise verbs to draw concrete pictures of the actions. He also chose them to create a scene of tension and conflict.

In the play that follows, look for examples of precise, active verbs that tell you exactly what kind of action is taking place.

When you read, look for precise, active verbs.
When you write, use precise, active verbs.

See STEREOTYPE in the Handbook of Literary Terms, page 688

The Three Garridebs

Michael *and* **Mollie Hardwick**
From a story by **Sir Arthur Conan Doyle**

CHARACTERS

DR. WATSON

SHERLOCK HOLMES

MRS. HUDSON, Their housekeeper. Middle-aged and perhaps Scottish. She dotes on them, but despairs of Holmes's habits.

JOHN GARRIDEB, "A short, powerful man with the round, fresh, clean-shaven face characteristic of so many American men of affairs. The general effect was chubby and rather childlike, so that one received the impression of quite a young man with a broad set smile upon his face . . . His accent was American, but was not accompanied by any eccentricity of speech."

MRS. SAUNDERS, Nathan Garrideb's housekeeper. Perhaps young and rather blowsy, to contrast her with Mrs. Hudson.

NATHAN GARRIDEB, "A very tall, loose-jointed, round-backed person, gaunt and bald, some sixty-odd years of age. . . . Large round spectacles and a small projecting goat's beard combined with his stooping attitude to give him an expression of peering curiosity. The general effect, however, was amiable, though eccentric."

MR. HOLLOWAY'S CLERK, A very deferential young man.

MR. HOLLOWAY, Rather oily.

A UNIFORMED CONSTABLE, Portly and majestic.

INSPECTOR LESTRADE, "A quick and energetic worker, despite his adherence to conventional methods to the exclusion of inspiration." Sallow, rat-faced, dark-eyed. . . . In his forties. An unrefined accent.

SCENE ONE

The parlor of 221B Baker Street. The lamp is lit on the table, on which is a tray bearing glasses and a decanter. WATSON *is seated, contentedly puffing his pipe and reading a newspaper, occasionally refreshing himself from a glass. A telephone directory lies to hand. The picture-hook is occupied by a portrait of Queen Victoria.* HOLMES, *wearing his old dressing-gown over his clothes, enters, pipe in mouth and reading a letter which he has just taken from its envelope.*

WATSON. Ah, Holmes!

HOLMES. My dear Watson, here's a chance for you to make some money.

WATSON. Eh? Well, don't keep me waiting. What is it?

(HOLMES sits opposite WATSON, who fills a glass and passes it over.)

HOLMES. Have you ever heard the name Garrideb?

WATSON. Garrideb?

HOLMES. G-A-R-R-I-D-E-B.

WATSON. There is no such name.

HOLMES *(waving the letter at WATSON).* Let's hope there is, for your sake. If you can lay hands on a Garrideb, there is money in it. *(WATSON quickly picks up the telephone directory and turns pages.)*

WATSON. Soon see what the telephone directory has to offer. What's it all about, Holmes?

HOLMES. It's a long story—rather a whimsical one, too. I don't think that in all our adventures together we have ever come across anything more singular.

WATSON. Here you are! *(Reads)* "Garrideb, N. 136 Little Ryder Street."

HOLMES. Is he the only one?

WATSON. Er, yes.

HOLMES. Then I'm sorry to disappoint you. That is the man who has written me this letter. We want another to match him. *(Knock on door.)*

WATSON. Confound it, Holmes, I wish . . . Come in!

(MRS. HUDSON enters, carrying a card tray.) Yes, Mrs. Hudson?

MRS. HUDSON. A visitor, Mr. Holmes.

HOLMES *(taking the card and glancing at it).* Mr. John Garrideb.

WATSON. *John* Garrideb!

HOLMES. Ask him to step up, Mrs. Hudson.

MRS. HUDSON *(going).* Yes, sir.

(HOLMES passes WATSON the card.)

WATSON *(reads).* "John Garrideb, Counsellor at Law, Moorville, Kansas, United States of America!"

HOLMES *(chuckling).* A second Garrideb, Watson. But this gentleman is in the plot already, I'm afraid.

WATSON. Plot?

HOLMES. I certainly didn't expect to see him this evening, but he'll be able to tell us a good deal that I need to know.

MRS. HUDSON *(returning).* Mr. Garrideb, sir.

HOLMES. Come in, sir. Come in!

(MRS. HUDSON exits as JOHN GARRIDEB enters.)

JOHN GARRIDEB. Mr. Sherlock Holmes? Ah, yes! Your pictures aren't unlike you, if you don't mind my saying so.

(They shake hands.)

HOLMES. Not at all. This is my friend and colleague, Dr. Watson.

WATSON. How d'ye do?

(They shake hands, WATSON *gestures to the vacant chair.* GARRIDEB *sits.)*

The Three Garridebs 177

Holmes in Holmes's famous study. From a 1987 Broadway production starring
Frank Langella as Holmes and Donel Donnelly as Watson. *Photo by Paul B. Goode.*

JOHN GARRIDEB. Pleased to know you, gentlemen. Now, Mr. Holmes, I believe you've had a letter from my namesake, Mr. Nathan Garrideb?

HOLMES. I have had such a letter. *(Holding it up)* I take it you are the Mr. John Garrideb referred to in it?

JOHN GARRIDEB. Sure I am.

HOLMES. I see you have been in England for some time.

JOHN GARRIDEB *(suspiciously)*. What makes you say that?

HOLMES. Your clothes. Your whole outfit is English.

JOHN GARRIDEB *(laughs)*. Well, I've read of your tricks, Mr. Holmes, but I never guessed I'd be the subject of them. Now, how do you figure that out?

HOLMES. Quite simply. The shoulder cut of your coat, the toes of your boots—could anyone doubt it?

JOHN GARRIDEB. Well, well, well! Yes, business brought me over here some little time ago. But say, I guess we didn't meet to talk about the cut of my socks. *(Hardening)* What about getting down to that paper there in your hand?

HOLMES. Patience! Patience, Mr. Garrideb! Dr. Watson would tell you that these little digressions of mine sometimes have some bearing on the matter.

WATSON. Quite true.

HOLMES. Tell me, why did the other Mr. Garrideb—Mr. Nathan Garrideb—not come with you?

JOHN GARRIDEB *(flaring)*. That guy! Why did he ever drag you into it at all? Here was a bit of professional business between two gentlemen, and one of them goes and writes to a detective! I saw him this morning. He told me this fool-trick he'd played, and that's why I'm here now.

HOLMES. I fancy it was simply zeal on his part to help you both achieve your object. And I understand that's equally vital for you both.

JOHN GARRIDEB. Huh!

HOLMES. He knew I had means of getting information. So it was very natural that he should apply to me.

JOHN GARRIDEB *(mollified)*. Well, if you're content just to help us find the man we're seeking, then there's no harm.

HOLMES. That is just how it does stand. Now perhaps we may have a clear account from your own lips. My friend here knows none of the details yet.

WATSON. Quite so!

JOHN GARRIDEB. Does he need to?

HOLMES. We usually work together.

JOHN GARRIDEB. Well—O.K. Dr. Watson, if you came from Kansas you wouldn't need me to tell you who Alexander Hamilton Garrideb was.

WATSON. Oh, really?

JOHN GARRIDEB. No sir! He made his pile in real estate in Chicago. But he spent it buying up land along the Arkansas River, west of Fort Dodge. It's grazing land and lumber land and arable land and mineralized land, and just every sort of land that brings dollars to the guy that owns it.

WATSON. I see.

JOHN GARRIDEB. Alexander Hamilton Garrideb had no kith or kin. But he took a kind of pride in the unusual name he had. I was in the law at Topeka, and he was tickled to death to meet another guy with that same name. "Find me another, anywhere in the world," said he, "and you won't regret it." I told him I was a busy man. I couldn't spend my life hiking round the world in search of Garridebs. "Nonetheless," he said, "that's just what you will do, if things pan out as I've planned them."

HOLMES. What happened, Mr. Garrideb?

JOHN GARRIDEB. Alexander Hamilton Garrideb died—that's what happened, Mr. Holmes. He left a will behind him that was the queerest ever filed in the State of Kansas. His property was divided into three parts. I was to have one of them—on condition that I found two more Garridebs to share the remainder. We can't lay a finger on a cent of it until we all three stand in a row. But when we do it's five million dollars for each!

WATSON (whistles). Remarkable!

JOHN GARRIDEB. Well, it was a chance in a lifetime. I let my legal practice slide and set forth looking for Garridebs.

WATSON. Can't say I blame you.

JOHN GARRIDEB. You can take my word for it, there isn't another one in the whole United States. I went through it with a fine-tooth comb. So I thought I'd try the old country. Sure enough, there was the name in the London telephone directory. I went after this Nathan Garrideb and explained the whole matter to him. But he's a lone man, like me.

HOLMES. With no relatives?

JOHN GARRIDEB. Some women, but no men. The will says three adult men. So there you are, Mr. Holmes. We still have a vacancy, and if you can help fill it we'll be very ready to pay your charges.

HOLMES. Well, Watson, I said it was a whimsical business, didn't I?

WATSON. That's the word for it. I should have thought your obvious course was to advertise in the agony columns[1] of the newspapers, Mr. Garrideb.

JOHN GARRIDEB. Oh, I've done that. No replies.

HOLMES. Dear me! Well, it is certainly a most curious little problem. Yes, I may take a glance at it at my leisure.

JOHN GARRIDEB (rising). I'd be mighty grateful, Mr. Holmes.

HOLMES. You'll let me know how you are progressing, Mr. Garrideb?

(HOLMES and WATSON rise.)

JOHN GARRIDEB. Oh, sure, sure.

HOLMES. By the way, you come from Topeka, you say. I used to correspond with a gentleman there. He's dead now—old Dr. Lysander Starr. He was Mayor in 1890 or thereabouts.

JOHN GARRIDEB. Old Dr. Starr! His name is still honored in Topeka, Mr. Holmes. Well, good day, gentlemen. I reckon you'll hear from me in a day or two.

HOLMES. ⎫
⎬ Good day, Mr. Garrideb.
WATSON. ⎭

(He exits. HOLMES returns to his chair, lapsing into deep thought. WATSON remains standing.)

WATSON (chuckling). Well, Holmes—what a business! So you think that if I can lay hands on a Garrideb, these other two will pay a reward. It'd certainly help my wound

---

1. *agony columns*, newspaper columns of personal advertisements for lost objects, missing friends and relatives, and marriage separations.

pension! (*He rubs his leg.*) Eh, Holmes? Holmes?

HOLMES (*back from thought*). I beg your pardon, Watson?

WATSON. Oh, never mind. What do you think?

HOLMES. I'm wondering, Watson—just wondering what on earth could the man's object be in telling us such a rigmarole of lies.

WATSON. Lies!

HOLMES. I nearly asked him outright. There are times when a brutal frontal attack is the best policy. But I thought it better to let him believe he had fooled us.

WATSON. How on earth do you mean?

HOLMES. Here is a man with an English coat frayed at the elbow and trousers bagged at the knee with a year's wear—and yet by this document and his own account he's a provincial American not long in London. There have been no such advertisements in the agony columns. You know I never miss anything there.

WATSON. But he is from Topeka, evidently. He knew of your old friend, Dr. . . . whatsisname?

HOLMES. Lysander Starr? Well, *I* never knew such a gentleman.

WATSON. You didn't!

HOLMES. I invented him on the spur of the moment. So you see, Watson—touch this fellow where you would, he was false.

WATSON. You think he isn't even an American then?

HOLMES. No, I wouldn't go so far as that. But he's worn his accent smooth with years of London.

WATSON. Then what's his game? What's the meaning of this search for Garridebs?

HOLMES. Whatever it is, it's worth our attention. Granting that the man's a rascal, he's certainly a complex and ingenious one. We must now find out if our other correspondent is a fraud also.

WATSON. Nathan Garrideb?

HOLMES. Exactly. (*Jumping up*) Come, Watson. I fancy we may well find him at home at this time of the evening.

(*They exit.* MRS. HUDSON *enters. She replaces* WATSON'S *glass on the tray, together with the letter and envelope, turns the lamp lower and exits, carrying the tray. The stage remains empty for a few moments.*)

SCENE TWO

(*The stage as before.* MRS. SAUNDERS *enters from the side opposite to that used by* MRS. HUDSON. *She carries two or three learned-looking books. She places the books on the table, turns up the lamp, shifts the chairs a little more, then goes to the portrait of Queen Victoria, turning it back to front to reveal a picture of the Sphinx. We are now in* NATHAN GARRIDEB'S *study. As* MRS. SAUNDERS *completes these tasks,* NATHAN GARRIDEB *enters slowly, shuffling rather than walking, peering short-sightedly through his spectacles at an ancient vase he is holding.*)

MRS. SAUNDERS. Ow, there you are, Mr. Garrideb!

NATHAN GARRIDEB (*peering at her*). Eh? What? Oh, Mrs. Saunders!

MRS. SAUNDERS. Been looking for you all over the 'ouse, I 'ave. There's two gents to see you.

NATHAN GARRIDEB. Gents . . . Er, gentlemen? See me? Goodness gracious!

(*He resumes his scrutiny of the vase.*)

MRS. SAUNDERS. Well, will I show 'em in, then?

NATHAN GARRIDEB. Eh? Show . . . ? Ah, yes, yes. To be sure.

(MRS. SAUNDERS *exits, rolling her eyes despairingly at the audience as she goes.* GARRIDEB *is lost again in the study of his vase.* MRS. SAUNDERS *ushers in* HOLMES *and* WATSON *in street clothes.*)

MRS. SAUNDERS. Mr. Sherlock 'olmes, Dr. Wilson.

WATSON. Watson.

(MRS. SAUNDERS *gives him a malevolent look and exits.* GARRIDEB *takes no notice of them. They exchange a glance.* WATSON *clears his throat noisily.* GARRIDEB *looks up, surprised.*)

NATHAN GARRIDEB. Ah! Gentlemen! Mr. Holmes, wasn't it? And Dr. . . . ?

WATSON (*with a sigh*). Watson.

NATHAN GARRIDEB. To be sure! I wrote to you earlier today. (HOLMES *and* WATSON *exchange an amused glance*) Do sit down, gentlemen.

(HOLMES *takes one chair.* WATSON *is about to take the other when* GARRIDEB *alarms him by springing forward with a cry and picking something off the seat, to hold it aloft. It is a coin.* WATSON, *relieved, sits down.*)

NATHAN GARRIDEB. There! I've been searching for that coin all day. Syracusan of the best period. They degenerated greatly towards the end, and some prefer the Alexandrian school. But I hold these supreme. (*He puts the vase and the coin on the table and stands back to admire the former.*) You see my little interests in life, gentle-

men. My doctor lectures me about never going out, never taking exercise. But why should I go anywhere, when I have so much to keep me here? I can assure you, the adequate cataloguing of my cabinets of fossils alone would take me a good three months.

HOLMES. But do you *never* go out, sir?

NATHAN GARRIDEB. Mm? Oh, now and again I drive down to the auction rooms. Otherwise, no. I very seldom leave these rooms. My researches are too absorbing. But you can imagine, Mr. Holmes, what a terrific shock—pleasant, mind you, but terrific— it was for me when I heard of this unparalleled good fortune. It only needs one more Garrideb to complete the matter! And surely we can find one?

HOLMES. It is possible.

NATHAN GARRIDEB. I had heard that you handled strange cases, Mr. Holmes, and that was why I sent to you. Of course, this American gentleman is quite right. I should have taken his advice before doing so. But I acted for the best.

HOLMES. Mr. Garrideb, are you really anxious to acquire an estate in America?

NATHAN GARRIDEB. Certainly not, sir! But this gentleman has assured me that he will buy me out as soon as we have established our claim. Five million dollars was the sum named. There are a dozen specimens in the market at the present moment which would fill gaps in my collection, and which I am unable to purchase for want of a few hundred pounds. Just think what I could do with five million dollars!

WATSON. Quite understandable.

NATHAN GARRIDEB. But, forgive me, may I ask the purpose of your visit this evening, gentlemen?

HOLMES. Purely in order to make your acquaintance, Mr. Garrideb. There are a few questions I need to ask.

NATHAN GARRIDEB. I shall be happy to answer any there are.

(*He sits.*)

HOLMES. This American gentleman—Mr. John Garrideb. I understand from your letter that up to this week you were unaware of his existence.

NATHAN GARRIDEB. That is so. He called last Tuesday.

HOLMES. Has he told you of our interview with him today?

NATHAN GARRIDEB. Yes, he came straight back to me. He had been very angry before. He seemed to think my writing to you was some reflection on his honor. But he was quite cheerful when he returned.

HOLMES. Did he suggest any course of action?

NATHAN GARRIDEB. He did not.

HOLMES. Has he had, or asked for, any money from you?

NATHAN GARRIDEB. Never.

HOLMES. You see no possible object he has in view?

NATHAN GARRIDEB. None, except what he states.

HOLMES (*thoughtfully*). I see. Mr. Garrideb, have you any articles of great value in your collection?

NATHAN GARRIDEB. No, sir. I am not a rich man. It is a good collection, but not a very valuable one.

HOLMES. You have no fear of burglars?

NATHAN GARRIDEB. Not the least.

HOLMES. How long have you been in these rooms?

NATHAN GARRIDEB. Nearly five years.

(JOHN GARRIDEB *enters hastily.*)

Oh! Mr. Garrideb! Do step in, sir.

JOHN GARRIDEB. Thank *you*, Mr. Garrideb. (*He quickly approaches* NATHAN GARRIDEB, *waving a scrap of newspaper at him.*) Here we are! Here we are! Mr. Garrideb, my congratulations, sir!

NATHAN GARRIDEB. Congrat . . . ? Mr. Garrideb! You don't . . . you don't say . . . !

JOHN GARRIDEB. You're a rich man, Mr. Garrideb. We're both rich men!

NATHAN GARRIDEB. Oh!

JOHN GARRIDEB. Mr. Holmes, Dr. Watson—we can only say we're sorry we've troubled you unnecessarily.

WATSON. Really?

JOHN GARRIDEB. Here, Doctor. Read this. It's an advertisement from a newspaper in Birmingham. My agent there sent me it.

HOLMES. Birmingham Warwickshire, or Birmingham Alabama?

JOHN GARRIDEB. Warwickshire, of course! Right here in your own Midlands. Go on, Doctor—read it!

(WATSON *takes the paper.*)

WATSON (*reads*). Howard Garrideb . . . Good heavens! Howard Garrideb, Constructor of Agricultural Machinery. Binders, reapers, steam and hand plows . . . Hah! Spelt P-L-O-W-S! These provincial newspapers! Nathan

NATHAN GARRIDEB. Oh, do go on, sir!

WATSON. Sorry! (*Reads*) . . . plows, drills, harrows, farmers' carts, buckboards . . .

Buckboards?[2] . . . and all other appliances. Estimates for Artesian Wells. Apply Grosvenor Buildings, Aston.

NATHAN GARRIDEB. Glorious! Wonderful! The third Garrideb!

JOHN GARRIDEB. You said it! And now we must hustle. I've written to this guy and told him you'll be at his office tomorrow afternoon at four.

NATHAN GARRIDEB. You—you want *me* to see him?

JOHN GARRIDEB. That's the idea. Don't you agree, Mr. Holmes? Here am I, a wandering Yank with a wonderful tale. Why should he believe me? But a Britisher with solid references . . . He's bound to take notice of you, Mr. Garrideb. Mind, I wish I could go along with you, but I have a pretty busy day ahead tomorrow.

NATHAN GARRIDEB. But . . . but I haven't made such a journey for years!

JOHN GARRIDEB. Aw, it's nothing, Mr. Garrideb. I've figured out your connections for you. You leave at twelve and you can be back here the same night.

NATHAN GARRIDEB. But . . .

JOHN GARRIDEB. All you have to do is see this guy, explain the matter, and get an affidavit of his existence. Gee whiz! Here I've come, all the way from the States! You surely don't figure a hundred miles or so too much trouble for your share?

HOLMES. I quite agree, Mr. Garrideb. I think that what Mr. John Garrideb says is quite true.

JOHN GARRIDEB. You see!

NATHAN GARRIDEB (*disconsolately*). Well . . . If you insist, I shall go. It is certainly hard for me to refuse you any request, sir, considering the hope you have brought into my life.

HOLMES. Then that is agreed. No doubt you will let me have a report as soon as you can? I must complete my records of the case, you understand?

JOHN GARRIDEB. Sure, sure. I'll see to that. And now, I'll have to get on. I'll call tomorrow and see you off to Birmingham, Mr. Garrideb. (*Going*) Good night, gentlemen. Good night, Mr. Garrideb. (*He exits.*)

NATHAN GARRIDEB. Good night, Mr. Garrideb. (*Sighs*) Ah, dear me! Dear me!

HOLMES. Mr. Garrideb, I should very much appreciate a glance over your collection. In my profession all sorts of odd knowledge come in useful.

NATHAN GARRIDEB (*brightening*). Ah! I'd always heard you were a very intelligent man, Mr. Holmes. I could show you it now, if you have the time?

HOLMES. Unfortunately, no. But supposing I should be able to look in tomorrow while you are away, I presume there would be no objection to my looking round?

NATHAN GARRIDEB. None at all, my dear sir. Most welcome! Mrs. Saunders is in the basement up to four o'clock. I will say a word to her, and she will be ready to let you in.

HOLMES. Capital! (*He moves as if to go, but pauses*) Oh, by the way—who is your house agent?[3]

NATHAN GARRIDEB. My . . . ? Oh, I rent

---

2. *plows . . . buckboards.* The British spell "plow" *plough.* A buckboard is a type of wagon.
3. *house agent,* a real estate agent or broker.

these rooms from, let me see, Holloway and Steele, in the Edgware Road. But if I may ask . . . ?

HOLMES. No matter, my dear Mr. Garrideb. No matter at all. Come along, Watson.

WATSON. Good evening, Mr. Garrideb.

NATHAN GARRIDEB (*puzzled*). Good . . . good evening, gentlemen.

(HOLMES *and* WATSON *exit.* GARRIDEB *stares after them for a moment, then shrugs, picks up the vase and wanders off examining it in the direction from which he first entered.* MRS. SAUNDERS *enters from the opposite side, flicking at things with a feather mop. She takes down the hanging picture, picks up the books from the table, and exits opposite. The stage remains empty for a few moments.*)

SCENE THREE

The stage as before. MR. HOLLOWAY'S CLERK *enters, carrying a ledger and a poster about a property for sale and bearing the name of* HOLLOWAY AND STEELE. *He places the ledger and poster on the table, then moves the chairs so that the table is set like a desk, with one chair at one side of it and two at the other. Then he hangs the poster from the picture hook and has just completed doing so when* HOLMES *and* WATSON *enter from the opposite side. They still wear street clothes, and* WATSON *carries a walking-cane. The* CLERK *sketches a bow.*

CLERK. Good morning, gentlemen. Mr. Holmes? Dr. Watson?

WATSON. The same.

CLERK. Mr. Holloway received your message for an appointment and will be most pleased to see you. If you'll just take a seat . . . ?

(*He gestures towards the two chairs.* HOLMES *and* WATSON *sit.*)

I'll tell him you're here and he'll be out directly, I'm sure.

WATSON. Thank you.

(*The* CLERK *exits with another little bow.* WATSON *waits until he has gone.*)

Holmes, will you kindly stop being so secretive and tell me why it's necessary to come to these estate agents?

HOLMES. For a little information, that is all. Now that our little problem is drawing to a close . . .

WATSON. Drawing to a close!

HOLMES. Surely you've outlined the solution in your own mind?

WATSON. I can't make head nor tail of it!

HOLMES. Oh, the head is clear enough. We should see the tail before today is out.

WATSON. Holmes, what *are* you talking about?

HOLMES (*sighing*). What struck you as curious about that advertisement our American friend produced?

WATSON. The advertisement? Why, only that spelling mistake. (*Chuckles*) P-L-O-W for plough!

HOLMES. Nothing else?

WATSON. No. Well . . .

HOLMES. Ah!

WATSON. There was a word new to me. *Buckboard.*

HOLMES. Watson, you improve all the time. A buckboard is a wagon seat—in America. P-L-O-W is bad English—but good American.

WATSON. I see!

HOLMES. And Artesian wells, which were also mentioned, are commoner in America than with us. In other words it was a typical American advertisement, but purporting to be from an English firm.

WATSON. Then—you mean to suggest this American lawyer had it printed himself?

HOLMES. What else do you make of it?

WATSON. But why?

HOLMES. There are other possibilities, of course. But he wanted to get that good old fossil up to Birmingham at all costs—that is clear.

WATSON. But you urged him to go!

HOLMES. I might have told him he was on a wild-goose chase; but on second thoughts it seemed better to clear the stage by letting him go. You see, Watson . . .
(*He breaks off suddenly and nudges* WATSON *as* HOLLOWAY *enters briskly, to take his seat at the other side of the desk.*)

HOLLOWAY. Mr. Holmes, Dr. Watson? *Too* pleased to be of service, gentlemen. Some enquiry about a house in Little Ryder Street, I understand?

HOLMES. Number one hundred and thirty-six.

HOLLOWAY. Ah, I know it well. Very well. It has been on our books for many years.
(*He taps the ledger.*)

HOLMES. A friend of mine, Mr. Garrideb, is your tenant.

HOLLOWAY. Quite so, quite so.

HOLMES (*with a glance at* WATSON). He, er, suggested we call on you in our efforts to find out whether an acquaintance of mine—whose name I have unfortunately forgotten—lived there before Mr. Garrideb himself. If you could possibly be so kind . . . ?

HOLLOWAY. Think nothing of it, sir.
(*He opens the ledger and begins riffling through the pages.*)
Let me see, Mr. Garrideb has been there five years. Now . . .
(*He pauses at a page.*)
Ah, but of course! The house was empty before that.

HOLMES. Empty!

HOLLOWAY. For about a year, that is—while we were trying to trace the previous tenant. Did a flit,[4] as we say. (*Suspiciously*) Not *your* friend, I trust, Mr. Holmes?

HOLMES (*with mock indignation*). Really, sir!

HOLLOWAY. Dear me, sir, no offense intended, I'm sure!
(*He begins to turn more pages.*)

HOLMES (*casually*). I suppose you suffer a good many cases of that sort of thing in your business, Mr. Holloway? People leaving owing you money?

HOLLOWAY. All too many, sir, all too many. There one day, gone the next, and never seen again. Mind you, this particular person was paid up six months in advance, so we'd no cause to complain at first. But then the arrears began mounting and, well, we just had to re-let.

WATSON. Disgraceful! Sheer lack of consideration!

HOLMES. Do you know, Mr. Holloway, although I'm almost ashamed to admit it, what you are saying does remind me somehow of this acquaintance of mine—oh, a very slight acquaintance, I assure you. Irresponsible, inclined to be haphazard . . .

---

4. *did a flit*, left in secret while owing money.

Holmes and Watson portrayed by actors Frank Langella and Donel Donnelly. *Photo by Paul B. Goode.*

HOLLOWAY. Well, Mr. Holmes, if you run across him again, you might do *us* the favor of letting us know.

HOLMES. With pleasure. Now, let me try to remember . . . about medium height with light-colored hair?

HOLLOWAY. Oh, no. Tall. Very dark features. And a beard. I remember him well.

HOLMES. Ah! And I think I begin to do so too, from your description. Now, if I could just catch his name . . .

(*He bangs his forehead with his fist.*)

HOLLOWAY. Waldron. Mr. Joseph Waldron.

HOLMES. Of course!

(*He leaps to his feet.* WATSON *and* HOLLOWAY *rise more slowly.*)

Mr. Holloway, I really am obliged to you. Clearly I cannot trace this person, and my reason for wishing to do so was, in any case, only slight. But you have shown me every courtesy, and if I hear further of him you may count upon me to let you know. My dear Watson . . .

WATSON (*bewildered*). Yes, Holmes?

HOLMES. We are taking up this gentleman's valuable time. (*To* HOLLOWAY) Good-day, sir, and thank you.

(*He marches off.* WATSON *hesitates, then nods to* HOLLOWAY *and follows.* HOLLOWAY *bows deeply, closes the ledger and turns to go. He catches sight of the poster.*)

HOLLOWAY (*calling*). Mr. Jenkins!

HOLLOWAY'S CLERK (*off-stage*). Sir?

(*He appears.*)

HOLLOWAY (*pointing to the poster*). It's sold.

(*He marches off with the ledger. The* CLERK *takes down the poster and walks off after him. The stage remains empty for a few moments.*)

SCENE FOUR

The stage as before. A POLICE CONSTABLE *enters, carrying a rolled poster, which he proceeds to hang from the picture-hook. It comprises many head-and-shoulders portraits of men. He stands, hands behind his back, beside the poster.* HOLMES, WATSON *and* INSPECTOR LESTRADE *enter.*

LESTRADE. There's just a few more, Mr. Holmes, and then I'm afraid the searching gets harder. Ah, Constable, you've found 'em, then.

CONSTABLE (*nodding towards the poster*). Yes-sir.

HOLMES. Inspector Lestrade, I'm deeply indebted. It isn't the first time this Rogues' Gallery of yours has helped me.

(*He goes and examines the portraits on the poster.*)

LESTRADE. You're welcome any time.

(HOLMES *stabs his finger suddenly at one of the portraits.*)

HOLMES. Ah!

LESTRADE. Got him, have you?

HOLMES. See, Watson.

WATSON. Great heavens! John Garrideb!

LESTRADE. Garrideb? That's "Killer" Evans! Alias Morecroft. Real name, James Winter.

HOLMES. Excellent! Any more details?

LESTRADE. Suppose you tell me first what you want with him? And what's all this talk about a Garrideb, or something?

HOLMES. Oh, nothing. Nothing at all. Just a course of enquiry I've chosen to pursue.

LESTRADE. You wouldn't hold anything back?

HOLMES. My dear Lestrade!

LESTRADE (*chuckling*). Oh, well, I should know better than to ask. Now, let's see— "Killer" Evans. Yes. (*Enumerating on his fingers*) Native of Chicago. Known to have shot three men in the States, but got out of prison through political influence. Came to London—let's see, 1893. Shot a man over cards in a nightclub in the Waterloo Road in January '95. Got manslaughter. Came out last year and hasn't been in trouble since.

WATSON. A dangerous customer, Inspector.

LESTRADE. Very. Carries arms and ready to use 'em.

HOLMES. Hm! This man he shot in London— who was he?

LESTRADE. Prescott. Roger Prescott. Came from Chicago, too. Quite a name there as a forger and counterfeiter.

HOLMES. Have you his picture?

LESTRADE. Once they're dead we file 'em away. Take weeks to find.

HOLMES. Can you remember what he looked like?

LESTRADE. Tall chap. Very dark features— and a beard.

HOLMES. Ah!

LESTRADE. Here! You *do* know something, Mr. Holmes!

HOLMES. No, no. Lestrade, you've been as helpful as ever. I will say this for Scotland Yard—there may be an occasional want of imagination, but for thoroughness and method you lead the world.

(*The* CONSTABLE *is trying not to laugh.*)

LESTRADE. Now, then, Mr. Holmes!

(*He sees the* CONSTABLE *grinning and glares*

at him. LESTRADE *turns to exit, jerking his thumb at the* CONSTABLE *who takes down the poster.)*

You can find your own way out, gentlemen?

HOLMES. Thank you, Lestrade.

WATSON. Good-day, Inspector.

(LESTRADE *exits, followed by the* CONSTABLE.*)*

WATSON. So, Holmes, our American lawyer is none other than "Killer" Evans!

HOLMES. With another alias to add to his list— John Garrideb. Well, the picture begins to define itself now. Our client, as he told us, has lived in that house for five years. It was empty for a year before that, because the previous tenant, a man named Waldron, had unaccountably disappeared. Waldron was a tall, bearded man with very dark features. So was Prescott, the man "Killer" Evans shot in 1895, which would be about the time Waldron disappeared.

WATSON. Then—you think that Prescott and Waldron were the same man?

HOLMES. As a working hypothesis, I think we may take it that Prescott, the American forger and counterfeiter, used to live in the very rooms which our innocent friend Nathan Garrideb now devotes to his museum. And "Killer" Evans, alias John Garrideb, is clearly interested in those rooms.

WATSON. And our next move?

HOLMES. We must go there this afternoon, while our friend is absent in Birmingham. In the meantime, I should devote an hour to cleaning your service revolver. (*They move towards the exit.*) If our Wild West friend tries to live up to his nickname, we must be ready for him.

(*They exit. The stage remains empty for a few moments.*)

SCENE FIVE

The stage as before. MRS. SAUNDERS *enters, carrying the picture of the Sphinx and polishing its glass with a duster. She hangs it from the hook and straightens it. Then she rearranges the furniture, flicking at it with her duster. There is a knock at the door at the opposite side to that from which she entered. She goes to answer it, disappears from sight for a moment, then re-enters with* HOLMES *and* WATSON.

MRS. SAUNDERS. Mr. Garrideb left word you would be calling, sir. Said you was to look at anything you wanted.

HOLMES. Thank you, Mrs. Saunders.

(*He produces a coin.*)

I am sure you have more than enough work calling you.

MRS. SAUNDERS (*with a little bob*). Thank *you,* sir. You've only to ring if you want anything. I'll be in the basement.

WATSON. Thank you.

(*She bobs again and exits, with a last flick of her duster at a chair as she goes.* WATSON *runs his finger along a chair back, looks distastefully at the dust on it and holds it up to* HOLMES.*)*

HOLMES. Never mind, my dear fellow. A more conscientious servant would not have left us alone—and I fancy our American friend will be coming visiting shortly. We do not want other company.

WATSON. What shall we do when he comes? (HOLMES *glances round, looking for a place of concealment, then points to one of the exits.*)

HOLMES. That alcove will do. There's room in it for us both.

WATSON. What makes you think he'll come?

HOLMES. He wanted to get Nathan Garrideb out of these rooms—that is very clear. As the old fellow never goes out of his own accord, it took some planning to arrange it.

WATSON. Then the whole of this Garrideb invention was apparently for no other end?

HOLMES. I must say there is a certain devilish ingenuity about it.

WATSON. Lucky for him the rooms are tenanted by someone with such an outlandish name.

HOLMES. That undoubtedly gave him his opening. But he wove his plot with remarkable cunning.

WATSON. What's he after, then?

HOLMES. That is what we are here to find out. As far as I can see, it has nothing at all to do with Nathan Garrideb. It is something connected with the man who was shot—Prescott. There's some guilty secret in this room, or so I read it.

WATSON. Maybe there's something valuable in the collection. Something the old man doesn't realize he owns.

HOLMES. No. The fact that Roger Prescott, of evil memory, once lived in these rooms points to some deeper reason than that. (*Lower*) Listen!

(*They listen.*)

He's at the door! Quickly!

(*They hasten into the alcove.* WATSON *remains peeping out and draws his revolver.* JOHN GARRIDEB *enters cautiously from the opposite side. After a glance round he goes straight to the piece of matting and throws it aside. He takes out a knife and works for some moments, as though prizing up the small trapdoor. It gives, and he lays the knife aside. He lifts the trapdoor and kneels, staring down.* WATSON *comes stealthily forward, brandishing the revolver, followed by* HOLMES.)

HOLMES. You have found what you are seeking, I trust, Mr. Garrideb?

JOHN GARRIDEB. Holmes!

(*He rises slowly, his hand going cautiously to his pocket.*)

Well, well! I guess you've been one too many for me. Saw through my game, eh, and played me for a sucker from the first. Well, sir, I sure hand it to you, but . . .

(*He whips out a revolver.* HOLMES *leaps forward and brings* JOHN GARRIDEB *to the floor, but the gun fires as he falls and* WATSON *drops his own revolver as he crumples to the ground.* HOLMES *strikes* GARRIDEB, *who goes still.*)

HOLMES. Watson!

(WATSON *groans.*)

HOLMES. Watson! Tell me you're not hurt, my dear old friend.

WATSON. I . . . I don't think it's much, Holmes. My calf . . .

(HOLMES *pounces on* WATSON's *trouser leg, pulling it up to examine the wound. He pulls out a vast handkerchief and quickly dresses it.*)

HOLMES. You'll live, Watson. A mere scratch.

WATSON (*sitting up rather quickly*). Oh!

HOLMES (*hard*). By the Lord Harry, it's as well for that devil there. If he'd killed you he would never have left this room alive.

(WATSON *struggles to rise.* HOLMES *tries to restrain him, but* WATSON *insists. He tests his leg and finds he can stand perfectly well.*)

WATSON. Quite all right, Holmes. Just went down with the shock.

HOLMES. Then come along, my dear fellow, and let us see what it is beneath the floorboards that so interested this scoundrel. (*They lift the trap.* WATSON *peers down.*)

WATSON. A cellar. Machinery . . . bottles . . . paper . . .

HOLMES. The late Prescott's outfit.

(JOHN GARRIDEB *groans and raises himself on to an elbow.*)

JOHN GARRIDEB. The greatest forger and counterfeiter England ever saw. No man could tell a Prescott from a Bank of England.

WATSON. You killed him.

JOHN GARRIDEB. Yes, and got five years for it. Five years, when I should by rights have had a medal the size of a soup plate. If I hadn't fixed him he'd have flooded London with his fake notes. But I got five years—the only man who knew where he made them.

HOLMES. You served your sentence and waited to get back here.

JOHN GARRIDEB. And then what? I find this crazy old boob of a collector squatting right on top of a fortune, and never going out. I had to shift him somehow. You may think my scheme was far-fetched, but how *do* you shift a guy out of his own home?

WATSON. With your record, Evans, I am surprised you didn't use a more direct method.

(JOHN GARRIDEB *gets up and spreads his open hands.*)

JOHN GARRIDEB. No, sir. I'm a soft-hearted sucker that can't start shooting unless the other guy has a gun. If you hadn't waved yours at me just now I'd have given up like a lamb. I . . . I'm sorry, Doctor.

WATSON. Well . . . it was only a scratch.

JOHN GARRIDEB. Swell. But say, Mr. Holmes, what have I done wrong, anyways? I've not used this plant. I never hurt the old geezer. What do you get me on?

HOLMES (*grimly*). Attempted murder of my greatest friend will do for the moment.
(*He gives* JOHN GARRIDEB *a long, severe stare; then, suddenly, he smiles.*)
But who knows—when Scotland Yard hear that you have led them to a fortune in counterfeit money, they may even give you that medal you seek.
(*Curtain begins to fall.*)
You can wear it on your prison uniform.

THINK AND DISCUSS
Understanding
1. Why does John Garrideb say he is looking for others with the same last name?
2. In Scene One, what reasons does Holmes give for his belief that John Garrideb is lying?
3. How does Holmes know that the ad listing the name of the third Garrideb is a fake?
4. What does Holmes learn from the estate agent?
5. Who is John Garrideb?

Analyzing
6. Why does Holmes ask Nathan about the value of his collection?
7. How many Garridebs are there?

Extending
8. Review the stage directions for the play. How many different settings are there? How is each change of scene indicated?
9. What are the advantages to a stage set such as this one?

APPLYING: Stereotype HT
See Handbook of Literary Terms, p. 688.

A **stereotype** is a fixed, generalized idea about a character or a situation. An example of a stereotypical character is the wicked stepmother in a fairy tale or the absent-minded professor in a story about a school. A stereotypical situation is a plot about a small boy and his brave dog or the prairie widow who fights to save her farm. The character of Watson in *The Three Garridebs* is a good example of a

stereotype. He is the typical foil—that is, a character who sets up or plays off another character to allow the latter to show knowledge, wit, or other special talent. Notice that many of Watson's speeches are merely short statements such as "I see," "But why?" and "Oh, really?" which allow Holmes to perform and explain something that only he is capable of figuring out.

Answer the following questions about use of stereotype in the play.

1. A common stereotype is the isolated scholar, someone who studies the world by reading books or collecting things such as coins or pottery rather than going out *into* the world. Which character in the play fits this stereotype? What details does the playwright use to characterize him?
2. Is John Garrideb a stereotype? Back up your answer with examples from the play. Be sure to look at both dialogue and stage directions.

VOCABULARY
Idioms
An idiom is a phrase whose meaning is different from the meanings of the individual words in the phrase. When John Garrideb says of another character, "He *made his pile* in real estate," he means the character became very rich. Idioms add color and character to writing. You can often figure out the meaning of an idiom through context, just as you would figure out the meaning of an unfamiliar word. Read the sentences below and notice the

italicized idioms. Each is from *The Three Garridebs*. Use context to decide what each idiom means and write the letter of the correct answer on your paper.

1. If things don't *pan out* with this job, I'll have to hunt for another one.
   (**a**) fit in the pan; (**b**) turn out well; (**c**) last a short time; (**d**) become amusing.
2. "The suspect has an ironclad alibi," muttered the captain. "We can't *lay a finger on him.*"
   (**a**) take his fingerprints; (**b**) hit him; (**c**) accuse him; (**d**) give him a manicure.
3. Sarah went over the flower bed *with a fine-tooth comb*, but she could find no clues to the robbery.
   (**a**) very closely; (**b**) by raking with a comb; (**c**) while combing her hair; (**d**) on her hands and knees.
4. After I *let my history homework slide*, I started getting low grades.
   (**a**) threw away my history homework; (**b**) failed; (**c**) neglected my history homework; (**d**) slipped on the ice.
5. I tried to tell Luis he was on a *wild goose chase* when he waded in to search the pond for his keys.
   (**a**) was wasting his time; (**b**) was not listening; (**c**) would not see any geese; (**d**) would catch cold.
6. Rosa had to *hand it* to her little sister Maria; the kid had won the race without any head start.
   (**a**) give credit; (**b**) hit with her hand; (**c**) hand over all her own trophies; (**d**) shake hands.

THINKING SKILLS
Synthesizing

To synthesize is to put together parts and elements to form a new pattern or structure, one that was not there before. For example, if an actress is to play the part of a wealthy teenage girl in the South at the time of the Civil War, costumes and makeup will help her become that character. But to play the part, she will also use her own knowledge of that period in history. For example, she must discover how a teenage girl would have moved or stood or behaved.

In *The Three Garridebs*, John Garrideb gives himself away because he is not careful about details—he says he has come from America but the cut of his clothing is British. He presents Holmes with an ad that he has supposedly cut from a British newspaper, but the ad is full of American spellings and words common to American— but not British—English.

Suppose you were to be transported into the past to the time of the American Revolution. You want to "pass" as a citizen of the time and not be recognized as a visitor from the future. What things about yourself would you have to change? Work with a small group of classmates to list all the changes in dress, speech, and behavior that would be necessary. Then share your lists with the rest of the class.

COMPOSITION
Reading/Writing Log

Review this play for examples of precise, active verbs. Record your findings in your reading/writing log. Write the sentence in which a precise, active verb appears, and then underline the verb. Finally, choose five of these verbs and use them in sentences of your own.

Explaining a Process

Notice that in investigating the affair of the Garridebs, Sherlock Holmes relies on his own thinking, information given by people involved in the case, and information obtained from other sources. In a five-paragraph essay, describe Holmes's way of working on a case. In the first paragraph, introduce the detective and the method. In each of the next three paragraphs, describe one of the three areas above and give examples from the play to make your description more clear. In the final paragraph, summarize the results obtained by this method.

ENRICHMENT
Readers Theater

Plan to participate as either a speaker or listener in a Readers Theater presentation of *The Three Garridebs*. Those assigned parts should practice reading their lines as actors might speak them. After individual practice, work together in small groups. Listen to others read their lines and make suggestions for improvement. On the day of the reading, listeners should decide whether each reader is reading loudly enough to be heard and clearly enough to be understood. In addition, listeners should decide whether the tone of voice of the reader is in keeping with that of the character whose part is being read.

BIOGRAPHY

Sir Arthur Conan Doyle
1859–1930

Sherlock Holmes is considered by many to be the most famous character in fiction. Ironically, although his creator enjoyed writing the Holmes stories and became world famous because of them, he would have probably preferred to be remembered for his historical novels or for his medical writing and research.

Conan Doyle was born in Edinburgh, Scotland, where he studied medicine. He served as a doctor with the British forces in the Boer War in South Africa. Unlike the bachelor Holmes, Conan Doyle enjoyed two happy marriages. He died on July 7, 1930, while holding the hand of his second wife.

Comment

Writer and Character—Who Becomes Famous?

Fictional characters often become more well-known then their human creators. Sometimes readers actually confuse the character with the author who created that character. Although most readers feel familiar with Robinson Crusoe, Huckleberry Finn, and the March girls in *Little Women*, many cannot name the writers who created them. And many readers think those who created the characters were just like the characters themselves.

Sherlock Holmes and Sir Arthur Conan Doyle were no exception to this phenomenon. Lovers of the Holmes stories flocked to Baker Street seeking the famous address, 221B, which did not exist at the time the stories were written. Readers wrote letters to Holmes that were delivered automatically to Conan Doyle and that, it is said, he answered personally.

Readers and publishers refused to allow the death of Holmes, which occurred in a story Conan Doyle published in 1893. Readers pleaded with him, threatened him, and even offered him bribes to resurrect Holmes. Finally, he brought the detective back to life. His hero again appeared in a series of stories that began in 1903.

Perhaps nothing is as indicative of the link between character and creator than the fact that Conan Doyle was often asked to assist in real criminal cases, usually to remedy an unjust conviction. In 1903 in London, an Indian man named George Edalji was accused of a particularly gruesome series of crimes. Tried and convicted, he was sentenced to seven years in prison. Even though the crimes continued while he was in prison, the authorities showed no interest in releasing him or finding the real culprit. Suddenly in 1906, with no explanation, Edalji was released. However, no restitution was offered, he could not continue his law practice, and he was expected to report regularly to the police. In despair Edalji wrote to Conan Doyle and asked his help.

Doyle read the trial transcripts and other documents. When he met Edalji he saw immediately that the man was half blind in the daylight and almost totally so at night. He could never have traveled to the scenes of the crimes, which were far from lights and civilization. Conan Doyle found many other examples of faulty evidence or no evidence at all. Doyle, using many of Sherlock Holmes's methods, cut the case against Edalji to shreds. At the same time, he proved beyond doubt, though not in court, who the real criminal was. The man was never brought to trial, but Edalji's name was finally cleared.

Who was acting in this case, Conan Doyle or his creation, Sherlock Holmes? Does it matter? Do you think it mattered to Edalji who had his life and respectability restored to him? Not every writer can walk out into the real world as a character. But perhaps all beloved fictional characters are composed of some element—either large or small—of their creators.

THINKING CRITICALLY ABOUT LITERATURE

UNIT 2   DRAMA 1

■ CONCEPT REVIEW

At the end of each unit in this textbook is a selection that contains many of the important ideas and literary terms found in the literature you have just studied. This final selection also contains notes designed to help you think critically about your reading. Page numbers in the notes refer to an Application. A more extensive discussion of these terms is in the Handbook of Literary Terms.

The King and Queen of this tale fear they will never find a suitable husband for their daughter, the Princess Camilla. In their eyes, Camilla is not beautiful. Unfortunately, all fairy-tale princesses are supposed to be beautiful. So, the King and Queen have concocted a plan in which Simon, a visiting prince, will be introduced to Dulcibella, a beautiful woman who is one of Camilla's ladies-in-waiting. Camilla's parents plan to tell Simon that Dulcibella is the Princess Camilla. After he is sufficiently in love with Dulcibella to marry her, Camilla, hidden under a wedding veil, will take her rightful place at the marriage ceremony.

Prince Simon has arrived at the castle.

from The Ugly Duckling

A. A. Milne

PRINCE SIMON *wanders in from the back unannounced. He is a very ordinary-looking young man in rather dusty clothes. He gives a deep sigh of relief as he sinks into the King's Throne.* CAMILLA, *a new and strangely beautiful* CAMILLA, *comes in.*

PRINCESS (*surprised*). Well!

PRINCE. Oh, hello!

PRINCESS. Ought you?

PRINCE (*getting up*). Do sit down, won't you?

PRINCESS. Who are you, and how did you get here?

PRINCE. Well, that's rather a long story. Couldn't we sit down? You could sit here if you liked, but it isn't very comfortable.

PRINCESS. That is the King's Throne.

PRINCE. Oh, is that what it is?

PRINCESS. Thrones are not meant to be comfortable.

PRINCE. Well, I don't know if they're meant to be, but they certainly aren't.

PRINCESS. Why were you sitting on the King's Throne, and who are you?

PRINCE. My name is Carlo.

PRINCESS. Mine is Dulcibella.

PRINCE. Good. And now couldn't we sit down?

PRINCESS (*sitting down on the long seat to the left of the throne, and, as it were, wafting him to a place next to her*). You may sit here, if you like. Why are you so tired? (*He sits down.*)

PRINCE. I've been taking very strenuous exercise.

PRINCESS. Is that part of the long story?

PRINCE. It is.

PRINCESS (*settling herself*). I love stories.

PRINCE. This isn't a story, really. You see, I'm attendant on Prince Simon, who is visiting here.

PRINCESS. Oh? I'm attendant on Her Royal Highness.

PRINCE. Then you know what he's here for.

PRINCESS. Yes.

PRINCE. She's very beautiful, I hear.

PRINCESS. Did you hear that? Where have you been lately?

PRINCE. Traveling in distant lands—with Prince Simon.

PRINCESS. Ah! All the same, I don't understand. Is Prince Simon in the Palace now? The drawbridge *can't* be down yet!

PRINCE. I don't suppose it is. *And* what noise it makes coming down!

PRINCESS. Isn't it terrible?

PRINCE. I couldn't stand it any more. I just had to get away. That's why I'm here.

PRINCESS. But how?

■ Camilla is very direct—almost rude—here, unlike the typical polite and prim princess.

■ Camilla has no illusions about the perfect world of a fairy tale.

■ Both characters are pretending to be someone else.

■ irony (page 171): Simon is planning a deception the same as the King and Queen's.

■ Have you ever replied, "Where have *you* been?" when someone says something naïve or questionable? Camilla is more tactful, but this is what she means.

PRINCE. Well, there's only one way, isn't there? That beech tree, and then a swing and a grab for the battlements, and don't ask me to remember it all— *(He shudders.)*

PRINCESS. You mean you came across the moat by that beech tree?

PRINCE. Yes. I got so tired of hanging about.

PRINCESS. But it's terribly dangerous!

PRINCE. That's why I'm so exhausted. Nervous shock. *(He lies back.)*

PRINCESS. Of course, it's different for *me*.

PRINCE *(sitting up)*. Say that again. I must have got it wrong.

PRINCESS. It's different for me, because I'm used to it. Besides, I'm so much lighter.

PRINCE. You don't mean that *you*—

PRINCESS. Oh yes, often.

PRINCE. And I thought I was a brave man! At least, I didn't until five minutes ago, and now I don't again.

PRINCESS. Oh, but you are! And I think it's wonderful to do it straight off the first time.

PRINCE. Well, *you* did.

PRINCESS. Oh no, not the first time. When I was a child.

PRINCE. You mean that you crashed?

PRINCESS. Well, you only fall into the moat.

PRINCE. Only! Can you *swim?*

PRINCESS. Of course.

PRINCE. So you swam to the castle walls, and yelled for help, and they fished you out and walloped you. And next day you tried again. Well, if *that* isn't pluck—

PRINCESS. Of course I didn't. I swam back, and did it at once; I mean I tried again at once. It wasn't until the third time that I actually did it. You see, I was afraid I might lose my nerve.

PRINCE. Afraid she might lose her nerve!

PRINCESS. There's a way of getting over from this side, too; a tree grows out from the wall and you jump into another tree—I don't think it's quite so easy.

PRINCE. Not quite so easy. Good. You must show me.

PRINCESS. Oh, I will.

PRINCE. Perhaps it might be as well if you taught me how to swim first. I've often heard about swimming, but never—

PRINCESS. You can't swim?

PRINCE. No. Don't look so surprised. There are a lot of other things

■ *battlements,* the defensive walls at the top of a castle.

■ **stereotype** (page 192): The humor here is based on the fact that fairy-tale princesses are not supposed to go about swinging across moats.

■ *pluck,* nerve or courage.

■ The tables are turned here. Camilla, a princess, has been swinging across the moat since childhood; the prince is grown up and he still can't do it without great fear.

■ **verbal irony** (page 171): Simon obviously does not really mean this; he would prefer not to ever *think* about crossing the moat again.

which I can't do. I'll tell you about them as soon as you have a couple of years to spare.

PRINCESS. You can't swim and yet you crossed by the beech tree! And you're *ever* so much heavier than I am! Now who's brave?

PRINCE (*getting up*). You keep talking about how light you are. I must see if there's anything in it. Stand up! (*She stands obediently and he picks her up.*) You're right, Dulcibella. I could hold you here forever. (*Looking at her*) You're very lovely. Do you know how lovely you are?

PRINCESS. Yes. (*She laughs suddenly and happily.*)

PRINCE. Why do you laugh?

PRINCESS. Aren't you tired of holding me?

PRINCE. Frankly, yes. I exaggerated when I said I could hold you forever. When you've been hanging by the arms for ten minutes over a very deep moat, wondering if it's too late to learn how to swim—(*He puts her down.*)—What I meant was that I should *like* to hold you forever. Why did you laugh?

PRINCESS. Oh, well, it was a little private joke of mine.

PRINCE. If it comes to that, I've got a private joke too. Let's exchange them.

PRINCESS. Mine's very private. One other woman in the whole world knows, and that's all.

PRINCE. Mine's just as private. One other man knows, and that's all.

PRINCESS. What fun. I love secrets. . . . Well, here's mine. When I was born, one of my godmothers promised that I should be very beautiful.

PRINCE. How right she was.

PRINCESS. But the other one said this:

> *I give you with this kiss*
> *A wedding day surprise.*
> *Where ignorance is bliss*
> *'Tis folly to be wise.*

And nobody knew what it meant. And I grew up very plain. And then, when I was about ten, I met my godmother in the forest one day. It was my tenth birthday. Nobody knows this—except you.

PRINCE. Except us.

PRINCESS. Except us. And she told me what her gift meant. It meant

■ Simon is the first to see something in Camilla that others have not seen.

■ By now, you can probably infer the nature of each character's private joke.

■ Notice how the playwright gives you a very clear picture of a character whom you will never meet in the play.

that I *was* beautiful—but everybody else was to go on being ignorant, and thinking me plain, until my wedding day. Because, she said, she didn't want me to grow up spoilt and wilful and vain, as I should have done if everybody had always been saying how beautiful I was; and the best thing in the world, she said, was to be quite sure of yourself, but not to expect admiration from other people. So ever since then my mirror has told me I'm beautiful, and everybody else thinks me ugly, and I get a lot of fun out of it.

PRINCE. Well, seeing that Dulcibella is the result, I can only say that your godmother was very, very wise.

PRINCESS. And now tell me *your* secret.

PRINCE. It isn't such a pretty one. You see, Prince Simon was going to woo Princess Camilla, and he'd heard that she was beautiful and haughty and imperious—all *you* would have been if your godmother hadn't been so wise. And being a very ordinary-looking fellow himself, he was afraid she wouldn't think much of him, so he suggested to one of his attendants, a man called Carlo, of extremely attractive appearance, that *he* should pretend to be the Prince, and win the Princess's hand; and then at the last moment they would change places—

PRINCESS. How would they do that?

PRINCE. The Prince was going to have been married in full armor—with his visor down.

PRINCESS (*laughing happily*). Oh, what fun!

PRINCE. Neat, isn't it?

PRINCESS (*laughing*). Oh, very . . . very . . . very.

PRINCE. Neat, but not so terribly *funny*. Why do you keep laughing?

PRINCESS. Well, that's another secret.

PRINCE. If it comes to that, *I've* got another one up my sleeve. Shall we exchange again?

PRINCESS. All right. You go first this time.

PRINCE. Very well. I am not Carlo. (*Standing up and speaking dramatically.*) I am Simon!—ow! (*He sits down and rubs his leg violently.*)

PRINCESS (*alarmed*). What is it?

PRINCE. Cramp. (*In a mild voice, still rubbing*) I was saying that I was Prince Simon.

PRINCESS. Shall I rub it for you? (*She rubs.*)

PRINCE (*still hopefully*). I am Simon.

PRINCESS. Is that better?

■ *imperious*, overbearing.

■ Compare Simon's feelings about himself with the King and Queen's feelings about Camilla.

■ A *visor* is a face plate on a suit of armor. It can be raised to reveal the face or clamped down to conceal it.

■ Camilla and the audience know that the wedding veil was to serve the same purpose for Camilla as the visor was to serve for Simon.

■ Notice here and elsewhere that Simon is an inept prince; he cannot swing across moats, and he gets leg cramps.

PRINCE (*despairingly*). I am Simon.

PRINCESS. I know.

PRINCE. How did you know?

PRINCESS. Well, you told me.

PRINCE. But oughtn't you to swoon or something?

PRINCESS. Why? History records many similar ruses.

PRINCE (*amazed*). Is that so? I've never read history. I thought I was being profoundly original.

PRINCESS. Oh, no! Now I'll tell you *my* secret. For reasons very much like your own the Princess Camilla, who is held to be extremely plain, feared to meet Prince Simon. Is the draw-bridge down yet?

PRINCE. Do your people give a faint, surprised cheer every time it gets down?

PRINCESS. Naturally.

PRINCE. Then it came down about three minutes ago.

PRINCESS. Ah! Then at this very moment your man Carlo is declaring his passionate love for my maid, Dulcibella. That, I think, is funny. (*So does the* PRINCE. *He laughs heartily.*) Dulcibella, by the way, is in love with a man she calls Eg, so I hope Carlo isn't getting carried away.

PRINCE. Carlo is married to a girl he calls "the little woman," so Eg has nothing to fear.

PRINCESS. By the way, I don't know if you heard, but I said, or as good as said, that I am the Princess Camilla.

PRINCE. I wasn't surprised. History, of which I read a great deal, records many similar ruses.

PRINCESS (*laughing*). Simon!

PRINCE (*laughing*). Camilla! (*He stands up.*) May I try holding you again? (*She nods. He takes her in his arms and kisses her.*) Sweetheart!

PRINCESS. You see, when you lifted me up before, you said, "You're very lovely," and my godmother said that the first person to whom I would seem lovely was the man I should marry; so I knew then that you were Simon and I should marry you.

PRINCE. I knew directly when I saw you that I should marry you, even if you were Dulcibella. By the way, which of you *am* I marrying?

PRINCESS. When she lifts her veil, it will be Camilla. (*Voices are heard outside.*) Until then it will be Dulcibella.

PRINCE (*in a whisper*). Then goodbye, Camilla, until you lift your veil.

PRINCESS. Goodbye, Simon, until you raise your visor.

■ To *swoon* is to "faint," something princesses and other traditional fictional females do regularly.

■ Notice how much humor the playwright derives from a broken drawbridge.

THINK AND DISCUSS
Understanding
1. When they first meet, who do Simon and Camilla say they are?
2. How has Simon entered the castle?
3. How does Camilla know that Simon is the one she will marry?

Analyzing
4. What do their reactions to swinging across the moat tell you about the characters of Simon and Camilla?
5. Will the godmother who gave Camilla the rhyme be happy with Camilla's choice of husband? Explain.

Extending
6. In the original tale, "The Ugly Duckling," a baby swan is raised in a family of ducks. Because the baby swan doesn't look like the ducklings, it is considered ugly. It spends a miserable childhood, teased about its "ugliness." Then one day it sees itself in the water and realizes that it is beautiful; it looks just like the swans swimming nearby. Compare and contrast the tale with the events of the play you just read.

REVIEWING LITERARY TERMS
Irony
1. What is ironic about Simon's saying to Camilla, "You're very lovely. Do you know how lovely you are?"
2. What is ironic about Simon's saying that he'd planned to wear his visor down at the wedding?

Stereotype
3. What are some qualities of Simon and Camilla that demonstrate that they are not stereotypes?
4. Simon tells Camilla, "Simon was going to woo Princess Camilla, and he'd heard that she was beautiful, haughty, and imperious . . ." In what ways does this statement illustrate both irony and stereotype?

■ CONTENT REVIEW
THINKING SKILLS
Classifying
1. Review the casts of characters for the three plays in this unit. Then classify each character as either stereotypical or fully drawn. Be prepared to explain your reasons for each classification.

Generalizing
2. The character of the country schoolteacher in the one-room schoolhouse is a familiar one in American history and literature. Based on the way the villagers treat Ichabod Crane throughout the play, how do you think these teachers were regarded by those whose children they taught? Were teachers respected? Were they considered important members of the community? Were they given special treatment? Did they have much power?
3. Over the years, both Ichabod Crane and Sherlock Holmes have won a fame that seems almost independent of the literature they appear in. Their names are often used when the topic of conversation is not literature. For example, it is not uncommon to hear

someone described as having a mind like Sherlock Holmes's and another person as looking like Ichabod Crane. What qualities of each character might account for this popularity?

Synthesizing

4. Both *The Legend of Sleepy Hollow* and *Back There* contain elements of fantasy or the supernatural. Consider the following statement: "Good literature deals with real people and events. Literature that contains fantasy or science fiction is just not worth reading." Do you agree? Why or why not? Which of the two plays proves your point better? Explain.

Evaluating

5. Of the three plays you have just read, which one would you most like to produce, direct, or act in? Why?

■ COMPOSITION REVIEW

Writing a Dialogue

Write a scene to follow the play that explains what you think happened to Ichabod Crane. Choose any two characters from the play—two of the farmers, Katrina and Van Brunt, or two schoolchildren. Have the characters discuss the disappearance and come to a conclusion about what really happened. Perhaps one or more of the characters was directly involved; perhaps not. You decide. Write your scene in play form, using *The Legend of Sleepy Hollow* as a model.

Writing a Narrative

Imagine that the "headless horseman" *is* a real ghost. Write a short composition from his point of view describing how he became a ghost and why he stays in Sleepy Hollow. Perhaps he does not mean to frighten anyone, but is only looking for company. Or perhaps he is searching for the person who killed him.

Reviewing Writer's Craft: Precise, Active Verbs

Write a composition about something that has happened to you or someone you know that was frightening, puzzling, or mysterious. As you describe the situation and reaction to it, be sure to use precise, active verbs that help your readers to visualize what you are describing. If you are keeping a reading/writing log, review it as you plan your composition.

ONFICTION

Quiltmaker Celestine Bacheller (1850–1900), "Crazy Quilt" (detail), *The Museum of Fine Arts, Boston*

PREVIEW

UNIT 3   NONFICTION

Features
Reading Nonfiction
Comment: Books Become Movies
Writer's Craft: Write Good
   Beginnings

Application of Literary Terms
hyperbole
connotation/denotation

Review of Literary Terms
stereotype
irony

Reading Literature Skillfully
graphic aids
fact/opinion

Vocabulary Skills
dictionary
compound words

Thinking Skills
evaluating

Composition
Describing a Mood
Responding to a Quotation
Writing a Diary Entry
Defining an Abstract Word
Writing a Letter
Writing About Nonfiction
Explaining a Choice
Writing to Compare and Contrast
Using Hyperbole in Description
Writing a Poem
Reading/Writing Log

Enrichment
Oral Research Report
Oral Interpretation

Thinking Critically About Literature
Concept Review
Content Review
Composition Review

Kin

James S. Kunen *and* **Jane Sims Podesta**

As long as one of us lives, everyone who lived before us lives.

---

hen it was over, those who had been there called it one of the most extraordinary reunions in American history. Actually it wasn't a reunion at all, since most of those present were strangers to one another. Call it a reconnecting, then—a reconciliation. "When I drove past these cypress tress planted two hundred years ago and looked across the land, I knew I was home," said Dorothy Spruill Redford [in the summer of 1986]. "I felt it deep inside."

Two hundred summers after their ancestors had been dragged there in chains—eighty of them shipped from Africa aboard the brig *Camden*—Redford and perhaps two thousand other people had come home to Somerset Place, once one of the largest slave-holding plantations in North Carolina. They were descendants of the black men and women who had carved the magnificent estate from the Great Alligator Swamp in the eastern part of the state, who had dug by hand a canal six miles long and twenty feet wide to drain the malarial swamp, who had built a fourteen-room mansion, sawmills, a gristmill. They had cleared and farmed the plantation's 5,870 acres, and many of them had died in the process. Their descendants had come to pay them homage from as far away as California and West Germany. They were doctors, lawyers, teachers, farmers, politicians and musicians, carrying the variously spelled surnames of their ancestors' original slave masters: Lee and Leigh, Horniblue and Honeyblue, Blunt and Blount. Among them was one Clarence W. Blount, 65, Democratic majority leader of the Maryland state senate, who sat in the elegant study of Josiah Collins III searching for his family name in a slave record book. "I feel somber," he said quietly. "Slavery—it's the worst punishment man can inflict on man." Another descendant, retired farmer Ludie Bennett, 83, of Creswell, North Carolina, knew it intimately: His father, Darious, had been born into bondage on the Somerset estate in 1854.

The reunion was the culmination of nine years' meticulous research by Redford, 43, a social services supervisor in Portsmouth, Va. After watching the TV miniseries version of Alex Haley's *Roots* in 1977 with her only child, Deborah, now 23, Redford embarked on the search for her own family origins. "I felt this overwhelming need to know about my past," she says. "I used to think of slavery as ancient history, but I'm only the third generation that wasn't born slave. That's amazing to me."

Written by James S. Kunen, reported by Jane Sims Podesta, *People Weekly*, September 15, 1986. Copyright © 1986 Time Inc. Reprinted by permission.

Working nights, weekends and vacations, Redford pored through faded local court records for three years before she discovered her link to Somerset Place. In the Chowan County Courthouse, she found a bill of sale showing that her great-great-great-grandmother, Elsy Littlejohn, and Littlejohn's six children had been sold in 1826 by the Littlejohn plantation to the owner of Somerset, Josiah Collins Jr., who already owned Elsy's husband, Peter.

Four years later Redford unearthed a 5,000-page collection of Collins family records in the state archives, which provided the names of 21 slave families that had worked the rice-and-corn plantation from its founding in 1785 to the end of the Civil War. In 1865, 328 men, women and children labored in bondage at Somerset. The indefatigable Redford was able to trace several thousand of their living descendants. Through hundreds of phone calls and letters, she invited them all to this remarkable gathering.

For the most part, the day was festive. By remembering their ancestors' slavery the descendants were celebrating their own freedom. They picnicked on the lawns, listened to speeches and spirituals and watched a reenactment of a slave wedding. They heard North Carolina Governor James G. Martin proclaim August 30 Somerset Homecoming Day, and enjoyed a surprise visit by author Alex Haley, who had heard that *Roots* had inspired Redford. Two others who returned were silver-haired, blue eyed Josiah Collins VI, 78, a retired real estate appraiser from Seattle, and Frances Inglis, 57, a potter from Edenton, North Carolina, both descendants of the plantation owners. "I deplore the institution of slavery," said Inglis. "It brought the downfall of our family."

Others remarked that the achievement and endurance of their shackled forebears had outlived the pain and degradation of slavery. "Think about the strength it took to build this place," said State Senator Blount. "Talk about true grit. Talk about the right stuff. They had it, and so do we."

Their graves are unmarked. Their one-room, eighteen-foot-square wooden cabins, in each of which as many as fifteen slaves lived, have long since been torn down. All that remains of the slaves are some broken bricks from the slave hospital. But that seemed not to matter. On August 30 the whole plantation had been transformed into their monument. "As long as one of us lives, everyone who lived before us lives," Redford told the crowd. "Until the day Somerset plantation crumbles, the slaves will be remembered." The slaves' descendants stood and applauded, and a few whispered, "Amen."

THINK AND DISCUSS
Understanding
1. What first inspired Dorothy Redford to learn about her heritage?

2. What event had occurred two hundred years before the reunion?

3. About how many people attended the reunion?

Reading NONFICTION

In this unit you will find excerpts from autobiographies; you will read articles, essays, and a famous speech. All these selections are nonfiction; that is, they are based on true happenings—not made-up ones—but since the forms and purposes of the selections are different, they are called by different names.

An **autobiography** is the story of a person's life told by the person who lived it. (A **biography** is the story of a person's life written by someone else.) Both are usually book-length.

Articles are found in newspapers and magazines. Their main purpose is to give information about a particular person, place, topic, or event. **Essays** are also found in magazines and newspapers. However, the main purpose of an essay is not only to give information but also to convince readers to accept the author's opinion.

Speeches are written for a particular occasion—graduation, a memorial service, a group that has gathered to hear the views of someone running for office.

All of these various types of nonfiction are blends of **fact and opinion.** Which is which? Facts can be proved true or not true. If someone says that the temperature is 85 degrees, we can check this statement by looking at a thermometer. Opinions, on the other hand, cannot be proved. If someone remarks, "It's hot today," the statement cannot be proved because what is hot to one person may not seem hot to another.

When reading any nonfiction, it is wise to be aware not only of fact and opinion but of opinion disguised as fact. The statement "Women are not as interested in sports as men are" may be opinion stated as if it were fact. If the writer or speaker can quote numerous surveys showing this to be true, fine. If not, view the statement with suspicion.

It would be wrong, however, to think that all opinions are bad. Suppose an expert in agriculture and population growth expresses the opinion that hunger will continue to be a major problem in developing nations in the next century. He cannot prove this because the next century isn't here yet. But his opinion should carry some weight because he is experienced in dealing with the problems of world hunger today.

As you read, use any visual aids provided for you. Some types of nonfiction —particularly factual articles or books containing much factual material—are accompanied by photos, charts, maps, diagrams, or graphs. Studying these **graphic aids** will often make an idea clear, a sequence of events plain, or complex directions simple. Study any accompanying illustrations to help you better understand what you read.

It is estimated that most people read more nonfiction than fiction during their lives. Learning to read as an expert does will increase your knowledge and the enjoyment you get from reading nonfiction.

Music Inside My Head

Gordon Parks

**In this autobiographical selection Parks, a renowned photographer
and film maker, tells how he became interested in music and
how he tried to get the world of music interested in him.**

---

t was natural that we hoped for
an early spring. But winter was
deep in the earth and unwilling
to be hurried. So spring would
sneak in a bit at a time, breathe upon the
cold, and then retreat. It gnawed at the snow,
dwindling it with rain and sun, but the cold
wind never slept. It roamed the nights, re-
pairing the damage that had been done during the day. It was good when finally the icicles fell and melted into the earth and the
smoke left our breath and the frozen Mississippi moved again.

By now the land was stricken with poverty.[1] Every newspaper and magazine I read
showed photographs of men queued up at
breadlines[2] and employment halls seeking
food and work. And this poverty attacked my
family wherever it caught us. Yet hunger, I
learned, was less frightening in the summer.
I could walk slower and give more freely of

what energy I had. And it was easier when
the moon shone and the stars twinkled over
the warm evenings, and love was close at
hand.

July brought such evenings and also my
first quarrel with Sally.[3] It happened over
some minor thing, but it kept us apart for
months. And during those hours I worried
and worked at a composition that spoke my
feelings. The song was called "No Love,"
and I wrote it at an upright piano my sister
inherited with the house. And now that I had
started writing songs again, I worked at it late
into the nights and on weekends; music was

---

1. *By now . . . poverty.* The author is referring to the
great depression of the 1930s.
2. *breadlines,* lines of people waiting to receive food given
as charity or relief.
3. *Sally,* the girl who later became Parks's wife.

the one thing that kept me hopeful. A peculiar experience had kindled my love for it long before Casamala[4] decided that I should become a composer.

I was seven at the time. The Kansas day was hot and I was hunting June bugs in our cornfield when I heard a murmuring in the cornstalks. The murmuring grew into music, and I stood there, my mouth full of mulberries, puzzled, looking up at the slow-drifting clouds to see if they were the music's source. The violins, horns, and drums were as true to me as the sunlight, and I had a feeling that the music was trapped inside my head, that it would be there even if I had no ears. I covered them with my hands, and the sounds were still there and they continued until all the clouds moved away and there was nothing but pale sky. Then it was gone as mysteriously as it had come, and I ran toward the house a little frightened, a little joyful, eager to tell my experience. But no one was around and I scooted up on the piano stool and started banging our old Kimball upright—trying to reproduce the sounds I had heard. The noise reached my father in another part of the field and he dropped his hoe and rushed to the house. He opened the door and watched me with astonishment; I was screaming as loud as I could.

"Have you gone batty, boy?"

I jumped down and started telling my story, but he only looked at me, at the mulberry stains around my mouth, and shook his head. "I declare, if you don't quit fondin' yourself on those mulberries, you're goin' to be swearin' you saw the devil. Now stop that bangin' and git to your chores."

Perhaps I never forgave my father's reactions to those delirious moments, for never again did we talk about things bordering on fantasy—not even a bedtime story. On that day, however (and to the woe of my good father), I began to play the piano. Several years later, Earl McCray, a music professor at the white school, offered me free music lessons. I was assigned a trombone and placed in our junior-high-school orchestra. But by now I was accustomed to playing by ear, and the slow process of learning to read music seemed unnecessary. I indulged in trickery. Each Saturday morning, before my appointment with Mr. McCray, my sister fingered my lesson on the piano and I memorized it; then I went off to astonish the professor with my "sight reading." He recommended me as soloist at the graduation concert. And everyone said I played "The Rosary" with great feeling that night. Only my sister knew I couldn't read a note.

This was long past. But now at nineteen, five years later, I regretted the tricks I had played upon the professor. I had never learned to read or write music, though I was determined to compose; it seemed the one way to avoid a less-than-ordinary existence. I worked out a notation system of my own by referring to the piano keys as numbers instead of notes—a process that proved more complicated then the conventional way.

The next consideration was a publisher; it was disheartening to discover that all the important ones were in Chicago or farther east. And there were warnings against dishonest publishers who stole songs; but this

---

4. *Casamala,* a girl of Parks's acquaintance, who encouraged him in his musical studies.

didn't bother me. It would have been flattering, I thought, to have composed something worthy of a professional's theft. The difficulty would be to get someone to transpose my numbers to notes and then have the final work accepted. But I knew I couldn't depend on music alone. That first winter[5] had taught me that I would have to fight with everything that came to hand. Learning, I knew, would be the most effective weapon against the coming years. So once again I seized upon books. After school I searched the local library shelves for authors who might help me in different ways. I pushed my mind into the foreign worlds of Thomas Mann, Dostoevski, James Joyce[6] and others whom I had never read before. I tried stone sculpture, short-story writing, poetry and, when I could hustle the material, painting. I did everything I could to protect myself against another such winter. Somewhere in between I played basketball for the Diplomats[7] and my high school as well.

A collapse was inevitable, and it came during a basketball game in October, 1931. I had dribbled past two guards and arched the ball perfectly, knowing it would swish through the hoop. But a blackness suddenly covered the court and the ball disappeared into it like a balloon into a cloud, and I felt myself falling. The coach had my teammates carry me to the locker room, where I was examined by the school nurse. Her only comment was that I looked awful hungry and thin to be playing such a strenuous game. But at home later that evening a doctor whom my sister called said I was on the verge of a physical breakdown. I had wasted from 165 pounds to 124 in less than three months. If I was to regain my

health, he said, I would have to leave school for the remainder of the year and rest.

So at twenty I found myself an invalid. There was no chance of graduating with my class. I was already too far behind. In fact, I knew that I would never go back to school. For the next five months I sat in the dark of my room rejecting time, light, and reason. I never heard from Sally during that time, but my sister helped me through the long convalescence and tried to get me to read, to write, to do anything that would divert my eyes from the blank wall opposite my bed. I finally opened a book one rainy afternoon. And gradually I began to read, think, and hope again. One thing was clear. I couldn't escape my fate by trying to outrun it. I would have to take my time from now on, and grow in the light of my own particular experience— and accept the slowness of things that were meant to be slow. Spring was back again, but I was afraid to look upon its coming with any pleasure. It had deceived me once too often.

By April I had regained my weight and strength. And before long I was hanging out at Jim's pool hall again, for it was a good place to get back into the stream of things. Arguments were always going; they flared, blossomed, and faded by the dozens. Some of them were senseless, some were heated, some were comical.

During one argument, one man claimed that Glen Gray, the band leader, had a mustache. The other denied it. My interest was

5. *That first winter,* 1928–1929. When his mother died the previous year, Parks had come to live with his sister and her family in St. Paul, Minnesota.
6. *Thomas Mann, Dostoevski* (dos′tə yef′skē), *James Joyce,* important novelists of the 19th and 20th centuries.
7. *the Diplomats,* a boys' club.

casual until one of the men, a waiter at the Hotel St. Paul, boasted that he should know since he "rubbed shoulders with Gray every night." He was lying of course about the shoulder rubbing, but he did see the orchestra leader regularly; anyone working there had the same opportunity. I wondered why I hadn't thought of this before. Many of the best orchestras played at the large Twin City hotels;[8] if only I could get one of them to broadcast my songs. The thought grew and I hurried home, sorted out several of my compositions, and set my alarm clock for six o'clock. And by seven-thirty the next morning I was at the Hotel St. Paul servants' entrance, the songs tucked in my pocket, applying for a waiter's job.

The timekeeper, an old gray-haired man, looked me over and asked me to wait around until he saw the day's work schedule. And for the next four hours I paced the corridor, looking expectantly at him now and then. At eleven-thirty, he motioned for me.

"Are you an experienced waiter?"

"Yessir. Yessir." (I had never waited on table in my life.)

"You ever work here before?"

"Not yet, no, sir."

"Where have you worked?"

"The Minnesota Club, the Lowry, the ——"

"Okay, okay. There's a Rotary[9] luncheon today, nothing steady. You want to work it?"

"Is that where the orchestra plays?"

"Orchestra? What's the orchestra got to do with it?" he asked.

"Oh nothing, nothing. Just thought I'd ask." My heart thumped like a drum.

"Well, do you want it or not?" he snapped.

"Yessir, I'll take it." I stepped up to his table and signed in.

The banquet captain changed my status from waiter to bus boy the instant he saw me pick up a tray. And as I trudged back and forth between the kitchen and the banquet hall, under the weight of the trays of drinks, I could hear the music coming from the main dining room. It was frustrating to have Glen Gray so close and not to be able to talk with him. But the driving captain kept his eye on me, pointing to tray after tray. And only once, when the dining-room door swung open, did I glimpse the tall, debonair orchestra leader directing his orchestra. And I noticed then that he did have a mustache.

Much later, the Rotarians were enjoying coffee, puffing cigars and asking silly questions of a mind reader they had hired for entertainment. I hung around, clearing dirty dishes from the tables—and listening to the questions and answers.

"Who's going to be most famous in this room?" someone asked.

"Good question," the mind reader said. He then covered his eyes and turned his back to the audience. There was snickering as he supposedly searched the future. Whomever he chose was in for a good razzing. The laughter was already building.

"Gentlemen." There was a momentary quiet. "There is a boy in the back of this room in a white uniform" (every eye in the room turned on me). "He will be more widely acclaimed than any——"

---

8. *Twin City hotels*. Minneapolis and St. Paul, Minnesota, are known as the Twin Cities.
9. *Rotary*. The Rotary Club is a men's service organization.

That was enough. Bedlam broke loose. "Boy! Boy! Come up here!" It was the mind reader's voice screaming over the others. "Bring him up, somebody!"

Two men started toward me, but I grabbed a tray of dishes, and, fleeing the banquet hall, I tripped and threw the dishes in all directions. But I got to my feet and kept going until I reached the dressing room.

In spite of that fiasco, I was hired three days later as a regular bus boy, and assigned to the main dining room.

Glen Gray left soon after, without my having had a chance to speak to him. But Kay Kyser, Bert Lown, Jack Teagarden and others, who came later, didn't get off so easy. Each of them suffered through my inexhaustible efforts—and they encouraged me. But none of them acted as though Tin Pan Alley[10] was overlooking a great talent.

Late that summer, I was offered the head bus boy job at the Hotel Lowry, by the *maître d'hôtel*,[11] a former wrestler whose name was Gleason. I took it. And for nearly three hours each day, after the luncheon crowd left, I had the main dining room and the huge grand piano all to myself. Once the tables were set for the evening, I played away before an imagined audience—using the light-control switches for color combinations that added to the mood. On one such afternoon I was playing and singing "No Love" when I felt someone was behind me. Embarrassed, I stopped, turned and looked into the shadows. It was Larry Duncan, the orchestra leader who was currently engaged by the hotel.

"Is that your music?" he asked.

"Yes."

"Go ahead. Play it again."

I played it again and he listened attentively. When I finished he asked me if I would like to have it orchestrated.

"I sure would," I said, and it was probably the understatement of my lifetime. The orchestra's arranger spent the rest of that afternoon with me, taking the piece down as I played it. And, as I watched him work, I hoped that my afternoons of fantasy were coming to an end.

This happened on a Wednesday.

During dinner on the following Friday night, Larry motioned me toward the bandstand. "We're broadcasting 'No Love' on the network show tomorrow night—with your permission, of course," he said.

I got Sally on the telephone and, without knowing whether she cared or not, I excitedly spilled out the good news. "I composed it for you—don't forget to listen." Her voice didn't reveal the slightest interest. She said, very casually, that she would listen—but, I found out later, she spent the next two hours telephoning all her friends. And I spent the rest of that evening and the next day drifting about in a trance.

On the night of the broadcast, Abby, the drummer, congratulated me and showed a group of waiters and myself the program. Fate had arranged things. There was my name among those of Irving Berlin, Duke Ellington, Cole Porter and Jerome Kern.[12] Now, in spite of my imagining the worst—a broken microphone, a broken promise, a

---

10. *Tin Pan Alley*, the body of composers and publishers of popular music.
11. *maître d'hôtel* (me'trə dō tel'), headwaiter. *[French]*
12. *Irving Berlin . . . Jerome Kern*, well-known songwriters.

canceled broadcast—it was going to happen. I knew that Gleason kept a death watch on unfilled water glasses, so I went about filling them to the brim. I wanted to hear every word, every note, without being disturbed.

When at last the moment came, people continued to eat, drink, and talk, as if they were unaware of the miracle taking place. I wanted to shout, to command everyone to listen, to ascend with me—far above ordinary things. But they kept on eating, drinking, laughing, and talking. And, just before the vocalist approached the microphone, I took refuge near the bandstand where I could hear him sing my lyrics. But now, at such a moment, a drunk started rapping his glass with a spoon. He wanted more water. I ignored him. He rapped louder and I hated him for it.

"What is it, sir?" A shiver went up my back. It was Gleason's voice.

"Water! Water! Tell that boy our party wants water!"

Such was my lot, I thought, and I turned toward the table only to have Gleason wave me away. He was filling the glasses and proudly explaining that the music the orchestra was playing was mine. The drunk whispered the news to his party, and his party whispered the news to the next table, and soon everyone in the entire dining room was looking toward me. When the orchestra finished, a burst of applause filled the air. I smiled nervously, picked up a tray of dirty dishes and left the room amidst the ovation. Then, slipping into an empty room, I telephoned Sally. "Yes I listened," she said, "and it was beautiful. Would you like to come over sometime, maybe tonight?"

"As soon as I can get out of here," I answered. The sky was overcast and it was chilly when I boarded the street car; but I couldn't accept such a night. There were stars and a moon instead, and a ridiculous hint of spring in the fall air. My heart, in its joy, would have it no other way.

THINK AND DISCUSS
Understanding
1. What is Parks's financial condition at the time he writes "No Love"?
2. Why does he write "No Love"?
3. What causes his physical breakdown?
4. Why does Parks apply for work at the Hotel St. Paul?
5. Describe how he meets Larry Duncan, the bandleader.

Analyzing
6. Describe the personal qualities of Gordon Parks that you discover in this selection.
7. What do you think Parks means by his statement " . . . learning, I knew, would be the most effective weapon against the coming years."
8. Reread the first and last paragraphs of this selection. What different feeling is created by each? Explain.

Extending

9. Which do you think plays the strongest role in Parks's success: talent, hard work, or good luck? Explain.
10. This selection is from an **autobiography,** told in Parks's own words. How do you think the passage would be different if the events had been told biographically, that is, by another person?

COMPOSITION

Describing a Mood

Parks described the way he felt in the first and last paragraphs of his autobiography by referring to the weather. In the first paragraph, his mood is cold and dreary. In the last, it is joyful. Write two paragraphs in which you describe your mood before or after an event by comparing it to the season, time of day, and weather. Try to make your two paragraphs as different in mood as possible. See "Writing a Clear Description" in the Writer's Handbook.

Responding to a Quotation

Parks calls learning a "weapon against the coming years." Do you agree? Others have called learning a lamp, a tool, a key. In a two-paragraph essay, respond to this quotation. In the first paragraph explain why you agree or disagree that learning is a weapon. In the second paragraph, develop your own comparison for learning.

BIOGRAPHY

Gordon Parks
1912–

The talents of Gordon Parks seem unlimited: he is a composer, an award-winning photographer, a film director, a novelist, and a poet.

He was born in Fort Scott, Kansas, in 1912, and moved to St. Paul, Minnesota, where he attended high school. After trying a number of jobs, he became a photographer. His work led to various government assignments during World War II, a career with *Life* magazine, and many international awards. Along with a reputation in photography, Parks gained recognition for his musical compositions and his writing. The range of his abilities is most evident in *The Learning Tree,* an autobiographical novel published in 1963. He then wrote the screenplay for the movie of the same title, directed it, and composed the musical score.

Review STEREOTYPE in the Handbook of Literary Terms, page 688

Hyacinth Drift

from **Cross Creek**

Marjorie Kinnan Rawlings

Marjorie Rawlings has left New York City and a successful career as a journalist to live on a farm near Cross Creek in northern Florida. There she grows oranges and devotes the rest of her energy to her writing. She loves her new life, but a time comes when she just has to get away. . . .

nce I lost touch with the Creek. I had had hardships that seemed to me more than one could bear alone. I loved the Creek, I loved the grove, I loved the shabby farmhouse. Suddenly they were nothing. The difficulties were greater than the compensations. I talked morosely with my friend Dessie. I do not think she understood my torment, for she is simple and direct and completely adjusted to all living. She knew only that a friend was in trouble.

She said, "We'll take one of those river trips we've talked about. We'll take that eighteen-foot boat of yours with a couple of outboard motors and put in at the head of the St. John's River. We'll go down the river for several hundred miles."

I agreed, for the Creek was torture.

Men protested.

"Two women alone? The river runs through some of the wildest country in Florida. You'll be lost in the false channels. No one ever goes as far as the head of the river." Then, passionately, betraying themselves, "It will be splendid. What if you do get lost? Don't let any one talk you out of it."

The river was a blue smear through the marsh. The marsh was tawny. It sprawled to the four points of the compass; flat; interminable; meaningless.

I thought, "This is fantastic. I am about to deliver myself over to a nightmare."

But life was a nightmare. The river was at least of my own choosing.

The St. John's River flows from south to north and empties into the Atlantic near the Florida-Georgia line. Its great mouth is salt and tidal, and ocean-going vessels steam into it as far as Jacksonville. It rises in a chain of small lakes near the Florida east coast, south of Melbourne. The lakes are linked together by stretches of marsh through which, in times of high water, the indecisive course of the young river is discernible. Two years of drought had shrunken the stream and dried the marshes. The southernmost sources were overgrown with marsh grass. Water hyacinths had filled the channels. The navigable head of the St. John's proved to be near Fort Christmas, where the highway crosses miles of wet prairie and cypress swamp between Orlando and Indian River City.

There is a long high fill across the marsh, with a bridge over the slight blue twisting that is the river. We drove car and trailer down an embankment and unloaded the small boat in the backwaters. The bank was of black muck, smelling of decay. It sucked at our feet as we loaded our supplies. We took our places in the boat and drifted slowly into mid-channel.

Water hyacinths began to pass us, moving with a faint anxiety in their lifted leaves. The river was no more than a path through high grass. We swung under the bridge and the boy at the wheel of our car lifted his hand in parting and shot away. Something alive and potent gripped the flat bottom of the boat. The hyacinths moved more rapidly. The river widened to a few yards and rounded a bend, suddenly decisive. Dess started the outboard motor. I hunched myself together amidships and spread the U. S. Coast and Geodetic Survey river chart on my knees and clicked open my compass. I noticed disconsolately, "Lights, Beacons, Buoys and Dangers Corrected for Information Received to Date of Issue." There would be neither lights, beacons nor buoys for at least a hundred miles. Bridge and highway disappeared, and there was no longer any world but this incredible marsh, this unbelievable amount of sky.

Half a mile beyond the bridge a fisherman's shack leaned over the river. For sociability, we turned in by the low dock. The fisherman and his wife squatted on their haunches and gave us vague directions. We pointed to Bear Island on our chart.

He said, "You won't never see Bear Island. Where they got a channel marked on your map it's plumb full o' hyacinths. Down the river a ways you'll see a big ol' sugar-berry tree stickin' up in the marsh. That's your mark. You keep to the left. The next mark you'll get is a good ways down the river. You go left by a pertickler tall piece o' grass."

The woman said, "You just got to keep tryin' for the main channel. You'll get so you can tell."

The man said, "I ain't never been as far as you-all aim to go. From what I hear, if you oncet get through Puzzle Lake, you got right clare river."

The woman said, "You'll some kind of enjoy yourselves. The river life's the finest kind of life. You couldn't get you no better life than the river."

We pushed away from the dock.

Winslow Homer, "Homosassa River,"
The Brooklyn Museum

The man said, "I'd be mighty well obliged if you'd send me a postcard when you get where you're goin'. That-a-way I won't have to keep on worryin' about you."

Dess cranked the motor and they waved after us. Dess began to whistle, shrilly and tunelessly. She is an astonishing young woman. She was born and raised in rural Florida and guns and campfires and fishing-rods and creeks are corpuscular in her blood. She lives a sophisticate's life among worldly people. At the slightest excuse she steps out of civilization, naked and relieved, as I should step out of a soiled chemise. She is ten years my junior, but she calls me, with much tenderness, pitying my incapabilities, "Young un."

"Young un," she called, "it's mighty fine to be traveling."

I was prepared for marsh. It was startling to discover that there was in sight literally nothing else. Far to the west, almost out of sight to the east, in a dark line like cloud banks was the distant swamp that edged this fluid prairie. We may have taken the wrong channel for a mile or so, for we never saw the sugar-berry tree; nothing but river grass, brittle and gold, interspersed, where the ground was highest, with butter-yellow flowers like tansy. By standing up in the boat I could see the rest of the universe. And the universe was yellow marsh, with a pitiless blue infinity over it, and we were lost at the bottom.

At five o'clock in the afternoon the river dissolved without warning into a two-mile spread of flat confusion. A mile of open water lay ahead of us, neither lake nor river nor slough. We advanced into the center. When we looked over our shoulders, the marsh had closed in over the channel by which we had come. We were in a labyrinth. The stretch of open water was merely the fluid heart of a maze. Channels extended out of it in a hundred directions—some shallow, obviously no outlets; others as broad as the stream we had left behind us, and tempting. We tried four. Each widened in a deceptive sweep. A circling of the shore line showed there was no channel. Each time we returned to the one spot we could again identify—a point of marsh thrust into the water like a swimming moccasin.

Dess said, "That map and compass don't amount to much."

That was my fault. I was totally unable to follow the chart. I found later, too late for comfort, that my stupidity was not entirely to blame, for, after the long drought, half the channels charted no longer existed. The sun had become a prodigious red disc dropping into a distant slough. Blue herons flew over us to their night's quarters. Somewhere the river must continue neatly out of this desolation. We came back once more to the point of land. It was a foot or two out of water and a few square yards of the black muck were comparatively dry. We beached the rowboat and made camp.

There was no dry wood. We carried a bag of fat pine splinters but it occurred to me desperately that I would save them. I laid out a cold supper while Dess set up our two camp cots side by side on the open ground. As the sun slid under the marsh to the west, the full moon surged out of it to the east. The marsh was silver and the water was steel, with ridges of rippled ebony where ducks swam in the twilight. Mosquitoes sifted against us like a drift of needles. We were exhausted. We propped our mosquito bar over the cots on crossed oars, for there was no bush, no tree, from which to hang it.

We did not undress, but climbed under the blankets. Three people had had a hand in loading our cots and the wooden endpieces were missing. The canvas lay limp instead of taut, and our feet hung over one end and our heads over the other, so that we were disposed like corpses on inadequate stretchers. The crossed oars slid slowly to the muck, the mosquito bar fluttered down and mosquitoes were about us in a swarm. Dess reached under her cot for her light rifle, propped it between us, and balanced the mosquito bar accurately on the end of its barrel.

"You can get more good out of a .22 rifle than any other kind of gun," she informed me earnestly.

I lay on my back in a torment of weariness, but there was no rest. I had never lain in so naked a place, bared so flatly to the sky. The moon swung high over us and there was no sleeping for the brightness. Toward morning dewdrops collected over the netting as though the moonlight had crystallized. I fell asleep under a diamond curtain and wakened with warm full sunlight on my face. Cranes and herons were wading the shore near me and Dess was in the rowboat a few hundred yards away, casting for bass.

Marsh and water glittered iridescent in the sun. The tropical March air was fresh and wind-washed. I was suddenly excited. I made campfire with fatwood splinters and cooked bacon and toast and coffee. Their fragrance eddied across the water and I saw Dess lift her nose and put down her rod and reel. She too was excited.

"Young un," she called, "where's the channel?"

I pointed to the northeast and she nodded vehemently. It had come to both of us like a revelation that the water hyacinths were drifting faintly faster in that direction. From that instant we were never very long lost. Forever after, where the river sprawled in confusion, we might shut off the motor and study the floating hyacinths until we caught, in one direction, a swifter pulsing, as though we put our hands closer and closer to the river's heart. It was very simple. Like all simple facts, it was necessary to discover it for oneself.

We had, in a moment, the feel of the river; a wisdom for its vagaries. When the current took us away that morning, we gave ourselves over to it. There was a tremendous exhilaration, an abandoning of fear. The new channel was the correct one, as we knew it should be. The river integrated itself again. The flat golden banks closed in on both sides of us, securing a snug safety. The strangeness of flowing water was gone, for it was all there was of living.

In midmorning, solid land made its way here and there toward us, and then in time withdrew. For a mile we had a low rolling hill for company, with traces of ancient habitation at its peak: a few yards of rotting fence, a crepe myrtle, an orange tree.

We passed a lone fisherman hauling his seine. His legs were planted cranelike in the water. His long arms looped up folds of the gray net with the rhythm of a man swinging a sickle. We told him our origin and our destination. Because we were now a part of the river he offered us a fish. His catch was meager and we refused it. We passed cattle, wild on the marsh. They loomed startlingly above us, their splotched black and brown and red and white luminous against the blue sky, like cattle in Bonheur pictures hung high above the eye-level.

The river dissolved into shallow pools and was interspersed with small islands, palm-crowded and lonely. It was good to see trees, lifting the eyes from so many miles of flatness. The pools gathered themselves together and there was under us again a river, confined between obvious banks. Sometimes the low-lying land was dry for a great distance, specked with soapberry bushes, and the wild cattle cropped a short grass that grew there.

We had Puzzle Lake and then Lake Harney, we knew, somewhere ahead of us. We came out from a canal-like stretch of river into a body of open water. Dess and I stiffened. She shut off the motor.

Far away across the marsh there was a long white rolling as though all the sheep in the world were being driven through prehistoric dust clouds. The mad thought came to me that we had embarked on the wrong river and had suddenly reached the ocean, that the vast billowing in the distance was surf. But something about the thing was familiar. That distant line was a fill, a forty-foot sand embankment across the marsh between the St. John's River and the east coast town of Mimms, and I had driven its one-rut grade two weeks before. The marsh had been even more desolate from the height of that untraveled, unfinished roadway. The fill ended, I remembered, in a forty-foot drop to a decrepit ferry

that crossed the river. The billowing we now saw was loose white sand moving along the embankment ahead of a high wind. I ran my finger along the chart. There was no ferry mapped for the far side of Puzzle Lake. A ferry was indicated, however, on the far side of Lake Harney.

I said, "Dess, we've come through Puzzle Lake and didn't know it. We've reached Lake Harney."

She did not question my surety. She spun the motor.

"All right, young un. Which way across?"

I compared chart and compass. I pointed. She headed the boat as I directed. I split nautical points to keep our position exactly. I took her across water so shoal we had to pole through it; under overhanging banks and through dense stiff sedge, when often a plainly better channel swung a few feet away in another direction. The extreme low water, I called, had evidently dried Lake Harney to this confused alternating of open lake and maze. Dess whistled dubiously but asked no questions. We struck deep water at last and were at the ferry I had indeed remembered. The old ferryman peered from his hut and came down to meet us, shading his eyes. He seemed to find us very strange indeed. Where had we come from?

"We put in yesterday at Fort Christmas," I answered him, "and I'm glad to say we've just finished navigating Lake Harney."

He stared in earnest.

"Lady," he said, "you haven't even reached Lake Harney. You've just come through Puzzle Lake."

The ferry here simply was not charted, and the episode proves anything one may wish it to prove. I felt contentedly that it proved a harmony with the river so complete that not even the mistaking of whole lakes could lose us. Others of more childish faith were sure it proved the goodness of God in looking after imbeciles. I know only that we were congratulated by fishermen the entire length of the river on navigating Puzzle Lake successfully.

"I brought our boat through Puzzle Lake," I told them with simple dignity, "by the sternest use of chart and compass."

And it was only in Dess's more evil moments that she added, "—in the firm belief that she was crossing Lake Harney."

Lake Harney itself was four miles long, unmistakably broad and open. We crossed it in late afternoon with the westerly sun on our left cheeks and a pleasant March wind ruffling the blue water. Passing out of the lake we bought roe shad, fresh and glistening from the seine. The current quickened. The hyacinths plunged forward. The character of the river changed the instant the lake was left behind. It was deep and swift, the color of fine clear coffee that is poured with the sun against it. It was mature. All its young torture was forgotten, and its wanderings in the tawny marsh. The banks had changed. They were high. Tall palms crowded great live oaks and small trees grew humbly in their shadows. Toward sunset we swung under the western bank at one of those spots a traveler recognizes instinctively as, for the moment, home.

If I could have, to hold forever, one brief place and time of beauty, I think I might choose the night on that high lonely bank above the St. John's River. We found there a deserted cabin, gray and smooth as only cypress weathers. There was no door for its doorway, no panes or shutters for its windows, but the roof was whole, with lichens thick across the shingles. Dess built me a fire of red cedar. She sat on the sagging steps and whittled endpieces for our cots, and I broiled shad and shad roe over fragrant coals, and French-fried potatoes, and found I had the ingredients for Tartar sauce.

Dess nailed a board between low rafters in the cabin from which to hang the mosquito bar over our cots, and said, "Young un, Christopher Columbus had nothing on us. He had a whole ocean to fool around in, and a what-do-you-call-it:—a continent, to come out on. Turn that boy loose in the St. John's marsh, and he'd have been lost as a hound puppy."

We had hot baths out of a bucket that night, and sat on the cabin steps in pajamas while the fire died down. Suddenly the soft night turned silver. The moon was rising. We lay on our cots a long time wakeful because of beauty. The moon shone through the doorway and windows and the light was patterned with the shadows of Spanish moss waving from the live oaks. There was a deserted grove somewhere behind the cabin, and the incredible sweetness of orange bloom drifted across us.

A mockingbird sang from a palm tree at sunrise. We found by daylight that the cabin sat among guava trees higher than the roof. The yard was pink and white with periwinkles. Dess shot a wild duck on the wing with the .22 and I roasted it in the Dutch oven for breakfast. We lay all morning on the bank in the strong sunlight, watching the mullet jumping in the river. At noon we went reluctantly to the water's edge to load the boat and move on. The boat was half filled with water and was resting with an air of permanence on the river bottom.

My first thought was of pure delight that it was no longer necessary to leave this place. But Dess was already stepping out of her sailor trousers. I too removed superfluous clothing. We bailed the boat and found two streams of water gushing in steadily under bow and stern seats. We managed to drag the boat on shore and turn it upside down. We found that the caulking had worked loose out of two seams. Dess donated a shirt, and for two hours with pocket knives we stuffed strips of cloth into treacherous cracks. When we put the boat in the river again, the caulking held.

I begged to stay another night, but Dess was restless. We pushed on for the few hours left of daylight. The shore line narrowed to thin strips of sand with tall twisted palms along them. The clear brown river was glassy in the windless evening. The palms were mirrored along both banks, so that when white ibises flew over in a rosy sunset, the river might have been the Nile.

We camped that night in comparative comfort under an upturned tree root. The spot was not tempting from the water, but once we were snugged down, it proved cavelike and cozy. A moccasin slithered from under my feet at the edge of camp and went harmlessly about his business. Dess cut down a young palmetto and we had swamp cabbage for dinner. I cooked it with a piece of white bacon and baked corn sticks in the Dutch oven to go with it.

In the morning we watched the hyacinth drift closely to be sure of taking the cut to Prairie Landing instead of wandering into Lake Jessup. A highway crossed the river here and folk waved down to us. In the cut a woman was running a catfish line. She was gaunt and suntanned, ragged and dirty. She pulled in the line, hand over hand, with a quick, desperate accuracy. She lifted a shaggy head when we called "Howdy" and said "Hey," and bent again to her line with a terrifying absorption. Something about her shamed all soft, clean women.

We cut across the south end of Lake Monroe and found that it was Sunday in the city of Sanford. We had reached the outpost of large-vessel traffic on the St. John's, and we put-putted under the bow of an incoming freight steamer. We had meant to bathe and put on clean shirts and slacks that morning, but there had been no landing place among the marshes. Dess strapped around her waist the leather belt that held her bowie knife at one hip and her revolver at the other, and felt better prepared for Sanford than if we had been clean. She landed us neatly at the city dock, in the lee of an immaculate pleasure yacht from Long Island Sound. The owner, trim in double-breasted blue, came to the rail and looked down at us. We had also intended to do a better job of stowing. The bow end of our boat was piled untidily with our supplies, our folded cots, our extra outboard motor and our gasoline tins. Dess stood up in the stern and stretched and shifted her armored belt.

She called up to the yacht owner, "Safe to come into this town?"

"That depends on what you are coming

for," he said, and smiled.

"Not a thing but gasoline. Where's the nearest place a fellow can fuel up?"

"All the filling stations near the docks are closed this morning. But I'm having my yacht refuelled, and a station is opening for me. How much do you need?"

Dess checked our tins with her eye.

"Five gallons is about right."

He smiled again.

"I'm sending my car to the station. If you will bring your tins up, I'll be very happy to have my man take you along and bring you back."

"Thanks, fellow," Dess said. . . .

There was a sound inside the yacht. There simmered up the companionway a woman, magnificent in pink spectator sports costume. The crew jumped almost to attention and escorted her down the yacht's gangplank.

The woman snapped over her shoulders, "I must have the car at once. I cannot be late to church for this nonsense."

Our . . . man turned rosy and made a comradely gesture to us.

He leaned over and whispered, "The car will be back in just a moment. If you don't mind waiting—. Please wait."

"O.K., fellow," Dess said.

The pink spectator sports swept into a limousine. In a few minutes the car had returned. We were driven in style to a filling station and our tins filled with gasoline. We bought the New York Sunday papers. The yacht crew brought the tins down to us and helped us re-stow our duffle. Dess outlined our trip briefly to the owner. She cranked up and we were off again.

"Good luck!" called the yacht owner. "The very best of good luck!"

He waved after us as far as we could see him, as though reluctant to break a mystic thread. His face was wistful.

. . . . Dess said pityingly and indignantly, "I'll bet he'd give his silk shirt to go down the river with us instead of with Pink Petticoats."

We used the gasoline and forgot to read the papers.

Out of Lake Monroe we began to see fishermen pulling seines every few miles along the river. Here and there was a camp. Once a palmetto thatching made a tip-tilted shelter and a startlingly pretty girl in overalls looked out with a placid face. We passed an old fisherman and a little girl in a boat. The child was rowing. We encountered a tall lumber steamer in mid-stream. The book of Pilot Rules on my lap provided that the boat in our position should swing to starboard, passing to port, and should give two short distinct blasts on the boat's whistle to signify its intention. Two lusty blasts on my dog whistle brought no answering blow from the steamer, but the cook, paring potatoes in the open stern, waved to us as we angled to cross their wake.

We had "right clare river" now, the river life was indeed the finest of lives, and there was no hurry left in the world. We put up a golden-brown deep creek and fished all afternoon. A white egret fished companionably with us a few yards away, and water turkeys flapped their wings lazily from high cypresses. A water moccasin arched his six feet of magnificent mottled hide between a spider lily and a swamp laurel. The laurel was in full bloom and the sunny creek was a wedge of fragrance. We found a white sand bar and had a swim in water clear as amber.

Camp that night was on a pine bluff, very high and dry and decent after the tree root and the moccasin. Storm threatened for the first time and we stretched a tarpaulin between slash pines to make a shelter. We were on the east bank. The moon and sun rose behind us. In the morning we found that small animals had dug holes all about us while we slept.

We pushed the motor that day. The river was deep and narrow. The banks were dense swamp, black with undergrowth. A landing would have been, for the most, impossible. We ate a cold lunch as we traveled. Beyond Deland Landing we called at a houseboat tethered to the bank. Its owner had been captain of the old Clyde River Line, and he received our request for advice on crossing Lake George with the old-school graciousness of large craft meeting small. He took my compass well forward of the houseboat, away from its metal stanchions, to chart our course across the fourteen-mile lake the more precisely. I made the mental note that perhaps I had better move the cast iron Dutch oven from under my seat. He gave us a set of distance cards and a choice of courses. The more sporting course was the main channel used by large steamers. In a boat as small as ours we should be out of sight of land for nearly an hour. The west channel never entirely lost the land, but if it came on to blow, we would do best by taking neither, and hugging the west shore. He bowed us courteously on our way.

We planned to camp as close as possible that night to the Volusia bar. We wanted to cross Lake George in the early morning before the wind rose. Beyond the village of Astor the scrub reared high against the west. Cypress swamp bordered the river. There was scarcely a patch of ground large enough to step out on. We pushed on to a cluster of fishing huts at the junction of lake and river. Hyacinths moved here in vast green flexible sheets. The huts were on stakes over the river and were not inviting.

Only one stood on enough ground to offer camping facilities. We poled through the hyacinths and called from the rickety small dock. A sullen-faced woman spoke curtly from the doorway. We could see the interior of the shack. There were pallets on the floor; a table; a chair or two. A dirty child peered from her skirts. We were not wanted here, it was plain, but she was a squatter, with no right to refuse us. Dess and I debated the matter in low voices. The woman, the place, seemed to me preferable to the dark swamp to which we must return. But the wind was freshening from the west. Even now, hyacinths were piling in behind us.

Dess said, "I'd rather sleep with a moccasin over each shoulder than get caught in a hyacinth block."

We swung about to turn back up the river. As we pushed away, the child dropped to the doorsill and began to pat his hands together. He chanted with shrill delight, "They're going away! They're going away!" I wondered what life had done to this woman and this child, that, among a friendly fisher-folk, they should know such fear and hate of strangers.

When the sun dropped behind the scrub,

swamp and river were in darkness. At twilight we had retraced several miles. When we landed at the only promising opening, we found a comfortable square of high ground. As we were making camp three fishermen hailed us excitedly. Were we the women who had put in at Fort Christmas nearly a week before? If so, they must know. Word had been sent down the river from other fishermen to watch for us and to report our safety. The three were camped across the river from us. They had a trail cut into the swamp to a spot of sound dry earth. Their campfire flickered sociably all night.

The course for the main channel was, simply, north by east. But there was fog at daylight, and when the fog lifted a little the wind came freshly from its week-long westerly quarter. Boats twice our size had been in trouble on Lake George. Its squalls were notably dangerous. It seemed needlessly heroic to deny ourselves the comfort of the sight of land. We had no intention of hugging the safe shore, so we compromised on the west channel. We left the great channel markers behind and a gust of wind twisted our stern. There was a half hour when the haze threatened to obscure all visible shore lines. Then Drayton's Island lifted ahead.

Midway, the wind was blowing the whitecaps off the waves, but it was helpfully behind us. With both arms braced against the steering handle of the motor, Dess kept the boat headed when water that rolled like surf lifted our stern. The propeller churned high out of the water. When it dropped again the boat lunged and turned.

I called, "She's sluing badly!"

Dess shouted, "Young un, if you had this wind under your stern, you'd slue, too!"

The distant shore seemed stationary. We passed the north point of Drayton's Island, where the main channel joined the west, with the lake boiling after us. At the first sheltered dock we stopped to rest and an old Negro gave us fresh drinking water. We had been some two and a half hours in crossing the lake.

The river resumed its broad quiet way as though it had left no tumult behind it. It had the dignity of age, was not now in that dark hurry to reach the sea. At Welaka one afternoon we left the hyacinths swirling leisurely and turned up our home river, the Ocklawaha. I thought in a panic, I shall never be happy on land again. I was afraid once more of all the painful circumstances of living.

But when the dry ground was under us, the world no longer fluid, I found a forgotten loveliness in all the things that have nothing to do with men. Beauty is pervasive, and fills, like perfume, more than the object that contains it. Because I had known intimately a river, the earth pulsed under me. The Creek was home. Oleanders were sweet past bearing, and my own shabby fields, weed-tangled, were newly dear. I knew, for a moment, that the only nightmare is the masochistic human mind.

THINK AND DISCUSS

Understanding

1. Why does Dess suggest the river trip?
2. Who was in charge of the maps and compass? Why were these of little use?

Analyzing

3. Which of the two women seems more at home on the river? Explain.
4. At what point does the trip change from an ordeal to a pleasant adventure? What key discovery causes the change?
5. How does the river journey affect Rawlings's state of mind?

Extending

6. In your opinion, is this selection mainly about escaping from problems, the value of friendship, or the beauty of nature?

REVIEWING: Stereotype H✗

See Handbook of Literary Terms, p. 688.

Stereotypes are fixed, generalized ideas about characters or situations.

1. At first, men protest when they learn that Dess and Rawlings plan the river trip. What stereotype is implied by their question, "Two women alone?"
2. How do the actions of the women on the trip disprove this stereotype?

COMPOSITION

Writing a Diary Entry

Imagine that you are Dess. Write a diary entry describing one day's events that Rawlings wrote about. Try to capture Dess's speaking style as you write.

Describing a Place

Where do you go (or where do you wish you could go) when you need to "get away from it all"? In a short composition, describe a real or imaginary place that would relax you and improve your mood.

BIOGRAPHY

Marjorie Kinnan Rawlings
1896–1953

At the age of thirty-two, Marjorie Kinnan Rawlings bought an orange grove sight unseen in central Florida and left city lights and a life as a journalist behind. She planned to produce oranges and short stories. Her project almost failed. The grove was run-down; the buildings in shambles. Rawlings could hire only a few workers and did much of the backbreaking labor herself. Her writing efforts were slow to bear fruit as well. It was years before her stories, based on the people and the land she had come to love, began to be published.

Rawlings did well with her oranges, too. The grove didn't make her rich, but it produced enough to keep her on the land she loved.

Comment

Books Become Movies

Marjorie Kinnan Rawlings's best known book, *The Yearling,* won a Pulitzer Prize for Literature in 1938. The book tells the story of the Baxter family and their struggle to survive in the Florida scrub country. Young Jody Baxter's efforts to keep a tame fawn have tragic consequences. The book, which quickly became a modern classic, was made into a movie in 1946 by Metro-Goldwyn-Mayer. Gregory Peck played Jody's father; Jane Wyman, his mother; and Claude Jarman, Jr., played Jody.

Another of Rawlings's books was made a film in 1983. *Cross Creek,* published in 1942, is a collection of essays, character sketches, and stories. The book was filmed as a continuous story about Marjorie Rawlings's departure from New York, arrival in Cross Creek, Florida, and achievement as a farmer and writer there. Mary Steenbergen played Rawlings; Rip Torn, her neighbor; and Peter Coyote, Norman—the man who was to become her second husband. The film was nominated for an Oscar for Best Picture of the Year.

Jody and the fawn. *The Museum of Modern Art Film Stills Archives*

Review IRONY in the Handbook of Literary Terms, page 672

Not Poor, Just Broke

Dick Gregory

The teacher thought he was a troublemaker, but he just wanted someone to know he was there.

never learned hate at home, or shame. I had to go to school for that. I was about seven years old when I got my first big lesson. I was in love with a little girl named Helene Tucker, a light-complected little girl with pigtails and nice manners. She was always clean and she was smart in school. I think I went to school then mostly to look at her. I brushed my hair and even got me a little old handkerchief. It was a lady's handkerchief, but I didn't want Helene to see me wipe my nose on my hand. The pipes were frozen again, there was no water in the house, but I washed my socks and shirt every night. I'd get a pot, and go over to Mister Ben's grocery store, and stick my pot down into his soda machine. Scoop out some chopped ice. By evening the ice melted to water for washing. I got sick a lot that winter because the fire would go out at night before the clothes were dry. In the morning I'd put them on, wet or dry, because they were the only clothes I had.

Everybody's got a Helene Tucker, a symbol of everything you want. I loved her for her goodness, her cleanness, her popularity. She'd walk down my street and my brothers and sisters would yell, "Here comes Helene," and I'd rub my tennis sneakers on the back of my pants and wish my hair wasn't so nappy and the white folks' shirt fit me better. I'd run out on the street. If I knew my place and didn't come too close, she'd wink at me and say hello. That was a good feeling. Sometimes I'd follow her all the way home, and shovel the snow off her walk and try to make friends with her Momma and her aunts. I'd drop money on her stoop late at night on my

From *Nigger: An Autobiography* by Dick Gregory with Robert Lipsyte. Copyright © 1984 by Dick Gregory Enterprises, Inc. Reprinted by permission of the publisher, E. P. Dutton, a division of NAL Penguin Inc., and Dick Gregory.

way back from shining shoes in the taverns. And she had a Daddy, and he had a good job. He was a paper hanger.

I guess I would have gotten over Helene by summertime, but something happened in that classroom that made her face hang in front of me for the next twenty-two years. When I played the drums in high school it was for Helene and when I broke track records in college it was for Helene and when I started standing behind microphones and heard applause I wished Helene could hear it, too. It wasn't until I was twenty-nine years old and married and making money that I finally got her out of my system. Helene was sitting in that classroom when I learned to be ashamed of myself.

It was on a Thursday. I was sitting in the back of the room, in a seat with a chalk circle drawn around it. The idiot's seat, the troublemaker's seat.

The teacher thought I was stupid. Couldn't spell, couldn't read, couldn't do arithmetic. Just stupid. Teachers were never interested in finding out that you couldn't concentrate because you were so hungry, because you hadn't had any breakfast. All you could think about was noontime, would it ever come? Maybe you could sneak into the cloakroom and steal a bite of some kid's lunch out of a coat pocket. A bite of something. Paste. You can't really make a meal of paste, or put it on bread for a sandwich, but sometimes I'd scoop a few spoonfuls out of the paste jar in the back of the room. Pregnant people get strange tastes. I was pregnant with poverty. Pregnant with dirt and pregnant with smells that made people turn away, pregnant with cold and pregnant with shoes that were never bought for me, pregnant with five other people in my bed and no Daddy in the next room, and pregnant with hunger. Paste doesn't taste too bad when you're hungry.

The teacher thought I was a troublemaker. All she saw from the front of the room was a little black boy who squirmed in his idiot's seat and made noises and poked the kids around him. I guess she couldn't see a kid who made noises because he wanted someone to know he was there.

It was on a Thursday, the day before the Negro payday. The eagle always flew on Friday. The teacher was asking each student how much his father would give to the Community Chest.[1] On Friday night, each kid would get the money from his father, and on Monday he would bring it to the school. I decided I was going to buy me a Daddy right then. I had money in my pocket from shining shoes and selling papers, and whatever Helene Tucker pledged for her Daddy I was going to top it. And I'd hand the money right in. I wasn't going to wait until Monday to buy me a Daddy.

I was shaking, scared to death. The teacher opened her book and started calling out names alphabetically.

"Helene Tucker?"

"My Daddy said he'd give two dollars and fifty cents."

"That's very nice, Helene. Very, very nice indeed."

That made me feel pretty good. It

---

1. **Community Chest,** fund of money contributed voluntarily by people to support charity and welfare in their community.

wouldn't take too much to top that. I had almost three dollars in dimes and quarters in my pocket. I stuck my hand in my pocket and held onto the money, waiting for her to call my name. But the teacher closed her book after she called everybody else in the class.

I stood up and raised my hand.

"What is it now?"

"You forgot me."

She turned toward the blackboard. "I don't have time to be playing with you, Richard."

"My Daddy said he'd . . . "

"Sit down, Richard, you're disturbing the class."

"My Daddy said he'd give . . . fifteen dollars."

She turned around and looked mad. "We are collecting this money for you and your kind, Richard Gregory. If your Daddy can give fifteen dollars you have no business being on relief."

"I got it right now, I got it right now, my Daddy gave it to me to turn in today, my Daddy said . . . "

"And furthermore," she said, looking right at me, her nostrils getting big and her lips getting thin and her eyes opening wide, "we know you don't have a Daddy."

Helene Tucker turned around, her eyes full of tears. She felt sorry for me. Then I couldn't see her too well because I was crying, too.

"Sit down, Richard."

And I always thought the teacher kind of liked me. She always picked me to wash the blackboard on Friday, after school. That was a big thrill, it made me feel important. If I didn't wash it, come Monday the school might not function right.

"Where are you going, Richard?"

I walked out of school that day, and for a long time I didn't go back very often. There was shame there.

Now there was shame everywhere. It seemed like the whole world had been inside that classroom, everyone had heard what the teacher had said, everyone had turned around and felt sorry for me. There was shame in going to the Worthy Boys' Annual Christmas Dinner for you and your kind, because everybody knew what a worthy boy was. Why couldn't they just call it the Boys' Annual Dinner, why'd they have to give it a name? There was shame in wearing the brown and orange and white plaid mackinaw the welfare gave to three thousand boys. Why'd it have to be the same for everybody so when you walked down the street the people could see you were on relief? It was a nice warm mackinaw and it had a hood, and my Momma beat me and called me a little rat when she found out I stuffed it in the bottom of a pail full of garbage way over on Cottage Street. There was shame in running over to Mister Ben's at the end of the day and asking for his rotten peaches, there was shame in asking Mrs. Simmons for a spoonful of sugar, there was shame in running out to meet the relief truck. I hated that truck, full of food for you and your kind. I ran into the house and hid when it came. And then I started to sneak through alleys, to take the long way home so the people going into White's Eat Shop wouldn't see me. Yeah, the whole world heard the teacher that day, we all know you don't have a Daddy.

THINK AND DISCUSS
Understanding
1. What reasons does Richard give for loving Helene?
2. Why is the class collecting money?
3. Describe Richard's plan for "buying a Daddy."

Analyzing
4. What do you think causes Richard to pledge far more money than he has?
5. Richard says that after this incident at school, "there was shame everywhere." Of all the shames that he mentions, which seems to have affected him the most? Explain.

Extending
6. If you had been the teacher, how would you have reacted when Richard pledged the fifteen dollars?

REVIEWING: Irony HT
See Handbook of Literary Terms, p. 672.

The word *ironic* is often used to describe a situation or happening that is the opposite of what is expected.
1. What did Richard intend to accomplish by pledging fifteen dollars?
2. What was the actual result of his pledge? Why is this situation ironic?

COMPOSITION
Defining an Abstract Word
Shame is an abstract word—you can't see, touch, hear, or smell something called *shame*. But in the last paragraph of this selection, Dick Gregory is able to make *shame* vividly real to readers by providing clear, specific, personal examples. Write a one-paragraph definition of an abstract word (such as *love, justice, disgust, beauty, fear,* and so on).

Writing a Letter
Imagine that you are Dick Gregory's teacher and that you have just read his autobiographical account. Write a letter to Gregory in which you explain why you talked to him the way you did, explain that you understand how he felt, and tell him whether you would react differently now that you understand his feelings.

BIOGRAPHY

Dick Gregory
1932–

Though first known as a comedian, Dick Gregory has since won national attention as a writer, civil rights leader, and political activist. He frequently publicizes his concerns not only through his writing (he is author of more than a half-dozen books), but also by demonstrations and long-distance running. In his books and in performances, Gregory combines an urgent sense of social justice with a sharp sense of humor.

Write Good Beginnings

What, then, is the American, this new man?

Hector St. John de Crèvecoeur

These are the times that try men's souls . . .

Thomas Paine

There are two names you would not have me mention, for you are sick of the sound of them.

Edna St. Vincent Millay

These three quotations have two things in common—each begins a work of nonfiction; each catches readers' attention and makes them want to read on.

Reread the beginning of "Not Poor, Just Broke."

I never learned hate at home, or shame. I had to go to school for that.

This beginning not only makes readers curious, but it also hints at what the mood, or overall feeling, of the selection will be.

Here is Marjorie Rawlings, introducing her narrative and conveying a different feeling.

Once I lost touch with the Creek. I had had hardships that seemed to me more than one could bear alone. I loved the Creek, I loved the grove, I loved the shabby farmhouse. Suddenly they were nothing.

We do not know what will follow, but we do know the writer is prepared to be brutally honest about her own feelings, and this makes us curious about and perhaps sympathetic to both her and the situation she describes.

Good beginnings are equally important in other types of writing. Read the beginning of the short story "In Another Country" by Ernest Hemingway. Does it arouse your curiosity? About what?

In the fall the war was always there, but we did not go to it any more.

At a time when most poets were singing the praises of their country, a landscape, or a flower, the poet Walt Whitman shocked readers by beginning a poem with this line:

I celebrate myself, and sing myself.

Good beginnings can arouse curiosity, hint at what is to come, jolt us into paying attention. As you read, watch for the various ways that writers begin. Then try beginning your own compositions in equally interesting ways.

When you read, look for good beginnings.

When you write, use good beginnings.

ARTICLE

Treasure Hunt

D'Arcy O'Connor

Will the mysterious treasure ever be found?　

AK ISLAND, Nova Scotia—
Daniel Blankenship, wiping
mud from his face, emerges
from the bowels of the earth. It
is 2:30 in the afternoon, and for the past six
hours he has been working 150 feet down in
an eight-foot-diameter shaft known as
Borehole 10-X.

He is tired, wet, and hungry. Still, he
smiles cheerfully. "We're almost there," he
shouts to a reporter over the din of an air
compressor, pump, and power generator.

The "there" he is speaking of is a subterranean chamber, possibly one of many dug several hundred years ago, perhaps to hide a
treasure of immense value on this uninhabited 140–acre island in Mahone Bay, about
forty miles southwest of Halifax. And the
rugged sixty-four-year-old Mr. Blankenship
has been doggedly pursuing that treasure for
the past twenty-two years.

"There" is also where, eleven years ago, he
came within about five seconds of being en-
tombed when the steel casing around the hole
started to buckle fifty feet above his head.
(With debris raining down on him, he was
winched out of the collapsing shaft moments

before it closed beneath his feet.)

That was but one of several brushes with
death the former Miami contractor has had
while serving his "obsession to be part of the
team that brings this crazy search to its conclusion."

The team is Triton Alliance Ltd., a Mon-
treal-based consortium of forty-eight partners, most of them wealthy Canadian and
U.S. businessmen, formed in 1969 to participate in the world's longest-running and most
expensive treasure hunt. Mr. Blankenship,
whose personal quest began in 1965, joined
the Triton group as a director and field manager after he had poured $97,000 (U.S.) of
his own money into the project.

Neither he nor Triton, which has invested
about $3 million in the search, has yet to
come up with a dime's worth of treasure.
Nevertheless, both are far from calling it
quits.

Triton is now prepared to spend up to
$10 million to sink an enormous steel and
concrete-encased shaft 180 feet southwest of

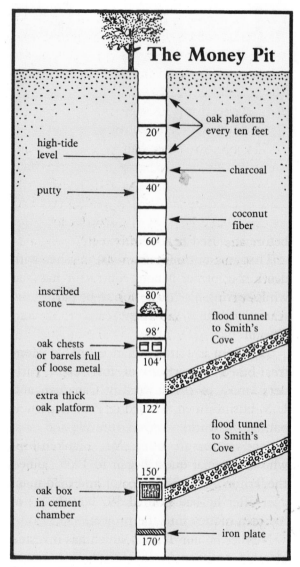

The Money Pit

oak platform every ten feet

20′

high-tide level

charcoal

putty

40′

coconut fiber

60′

inscribed stone

80′

flood tunnel to Smith's Cove

98′

oak chests or barrels full of loose metal

104′

extra thick oak platform

122′

flood tunnel to Smith's Cove

150′

oak box in cement chamber

iron plate

170′

Courtesy of *The Wall Street Journal*

Borehole 10-X. The hole, sixty to seventy feet in diameter and two hundred feet deep, will, according to Triton's president, David Tobias, "in all probability" be the "deepest and most expensive archaeological dig ever made in North America." And if that project, scheduled to begin next March, doesn't solve Oak Island's 197-year-old mystery, says Mr. Tobias, "then nothing will."

William Sobey, a Triton director and honorary chairman of Sobeys Stores Ltd., one of Canada's largest supermarket chains, has been waiting half a century for the solution. "I remember as a bug-eyed kid fifty years ago hearing stories about Oak Island," he says. "Finally, it looks like we might soon find the answer."

Another Triton director and major investor is Charles Brown III, a wealthy Boston real-estate investor who first learned of Oak Island in a front-page article in this newspaper [*The Wall Street Journal*] in July 1970. "I packed my wife and kids in the car and headed up soon after," he recalls. "I sat up past midnight talking to Dan [Blankenship] on the island, and I was hooked." He adds: "There's no doubt in my mind that the [original] workings exist. Whether there's a treasure there, we'll see."

The center of Triton's shaft will be in the so-called Money Pit, where the mystery was born on a summer day in 1795, when three farmboys rowed out from the mainland to explore the wooded island. Near the island's eastern end, they stumbled across an ancient clearing of rotted moss-covered stumps, at the center of which stood a single large oak tree with a sawed-off limb. Directly below the limb, the earth had sunk into a shallow saucerlike depression.

The boys spent the summer excavating beneath the limb, finding themselves in a filled-in shaft, thirteen feet in diameter, with tightly fitted log platforms placed across it at ten-foot intervals. With the assistance of others, they eventually dug the hole to 90 feet, where, atop yet another log platform, the workers found a large slab of rock bearing a hieroglyphic[1] inscription no one could decipher. Then, after the ninety-foot platform was removed, something very strange happened. Sea water began to percolate slowly through the bottom of the pit. It soon rose to within thirty feet of the surface, and attempts to bail it were unavailing.

Later search groups, convinced that a treasure vault lay just below the ninety-foot level, tried to circumvent the water problem by sinking shafts one hundred feet and deeper adjacent to the Money Pit, and then tunneling toward their goal. But in every case, water began seeping into their tunnels once they were within a few feet of the Money Pit. Those shafts also filled to thirty feet from the surface, which is sea level.

In 1850, it was discovered that the flooding was no mere geological event. Beneath the beach at Smith's Cove, five hundred feet east of the Money Pit, workers uncovered rock-walled tunnels leading from beyond the low-tide mark to the island's interior. The cove's drainage system had been carefully covered with layers of rock, eelgrass, and a bed of some mysterious brown fiber, all of which prevented the drains from clogging up with silt. The fiber was eventually analyzed by the Smithsonian Institution and found to be coir, or coconut fiber—this on an island fifteen hundred miles north of the nearest coconut tree. (Coir is still being found under various parts of the island by the Triton group.)

Still More Flood Traps?

The flooding system was apparently designed by the creators of the Money Pit as a booby trap to prevent anyone from digging more than ninety feet. When the tight log platforms, which acted as a hydraulic seal, were removed, the trap was sprung. A second similar system was later discovered leading out to sea on the island's south side. And Mr. Blankenship is convinced that other flood traps are yet to be found.

Through the latter half of the 1800s and well into this century, more than a dozen successive treasure syndicates tried to stem the flow of sea water and dig deeper into the area of the Money Pit. But group after group left the island frustrated, broke, and beaten by the ingenious designer of the underground workings.

Those failed treasure hunters left the eastern end of the island a rabbit warren of abandoned tunnels, drill holes, and shafts. The island has also claimed the lives of six searchers and has lured millions of dollars in fruitless investment. But their drill probes show evidence of metal, wood, and cement deep in the Money Pit.

It wasn't until 1967 that anyone realized just how deep and extensive the original workings are. That was when Triton's Mr. Tobias, then operating on his own, hired professional drillers. That effort and more recent ones have located a labyrinth of flooded tunnels and chambers, some with wood-cribbed roofs, below the 160-foot bedrock level. Some of the cavities are more than 200 feet deep.

Dating Artifacts

Core samples from those depths have

---

1. *hieroglyphic* (hī′ər əglif′ik), picture or symbol which stands for a word, sound, or idea.

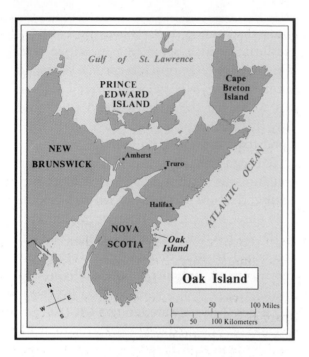

Gulf of St. Lawrence

PRINCE EDWARD ISLAND

Cape Breton Island

NEW BRUNSWICK

Amherst

Truro

ATLANTIC OCEAN

Halifax

NOVA SCOTIA

Oak Island

Oak Island

0   50   100 Miles
0   50   100 Kilometers

was never really interested in anything found above the 160-foot level." he says, "since that could be stuff from previous searchers' work." But Triton's drilling, he adds, has proved "beyond a doubt that there's an intricate maze of original manmade underground workings."

Borehole 10-X began as one of those experimental drill probes. In 1971, the water-filled hole was enlarged to twenty-seven inches in diameter, with the drill churning out bits of metal chain and wood from different levels. Several large cavities were encountered, including one 230 feet down. An underwater television camera was lowered into the chamber, and the observers above saw what appeared to be wooden beams, a pickax, and a severed human hand.

Narrow Escape

Wearing diving gear, Mr. Blankenship had himself lowered into the chamber. But because of the murky, fast-flowing sea water and the instability of the anhydrite rock walls, he was hauled out before he could retrieve any artifacts. (It was in that narrow shaft in 1976 that Mr. Blankenship barely escaped with his life when the entire hole collapsed.)

Today, Borehole 10-X is slowly being reopened with an eight-foot diameter steel and reinforced concrete casing. It is being kept reasonably dry with 24-hour-a-day pumping that spews out 650 gallons of water per minute. Mr. Blankenship says, "10-X could be a shortcut to solving the mystery. We may find

yielded pieces of wood, charcoal, cement, iron, brass, china, and hand-worked clay. Triton has had these findings examined by independent laboratories in Canada and the U.S. Carbon-14 analysis[2] of the wood dated it to the year 1575, plus or minus eighty-five years. The cement was found to be a primitive type common to the sixteenth and seventeenth centuries, and the metal was reported to have been smelted before 1800. Other Triton discoveries include an ancient set square and a pair of wrought-iron scissors. The Smithsonian Institution declared the scissors to be Spanish-American in origin and perhaps three hundred years old.

It is because of these clues that Mr. Tobias, a sixty-two-year-old self-made Montreal millionaire, has invested more than $500,000 in Oak Island during the past two decades. "I

---

2. **Carbon-14 analysis,** a method of dating geological formations or archaeological finds by measuring the amount of decayed carbon in them.

something when we get down to those voids, maybe even a tunnel" leading back to the Money Pit.

But Mr. Blankenship's determination to reach the original workings via Borehole 10-X is tempered by Mr. Tobias' conviction that a major excavation of the Money Pit itself is "the only sure way to find out what's down there, where it is, and what it is." He adds that the project, which will include the construction of large cofferdams[3] on the east and south sides of the island to control the water flow, will enable Triton to explore virtually all the areas where previous drilling and excavation indicated evidence of the original works. The flooding problem, he says, will be handled with large-capacity pumps and cement grouting, and, "We'll shore up and follow every single tunnel we encounter on the way down." The project is currently being designed and engineered by Cox Underground Research of Ottawa.

Figuring the Odds

Mr. Tobias predicts that Triton's chances "are nine out of ten of finding something of significant archaeological and historical value" during the four to six months that completing the shaft is expected to take. And, he adds, "I think we've got a fifty percent chance of finding a treasure," the value of which "may be hundreds of millions, maybe billions of dollars."

Almost all Oak Island investigators, past and present, agree that the underground complex (which modern engineers say involved at least 100,000 man-hours of work, given sixteenth- or seventeenth-century tools and technology) was designed to hide some-

thing of great value. "No other explanation makes sense," says Mr. Blankenship.

But the question remains: Did whoever buried something beneath Oak Island come back and retrieve it before the Money Pit was discovered in 1795? To this, Triton and others reply: If that were the case, surely the early discoverers would have found gaping holes rather than the carefully sealed-up workings.

As for the nature of the treasure-trove, theories range from the booty of individual pirates ("impossible, given the depth and complexity," says Mr. Blankenship) to the Crown Jewels of France, long-lost Inca gold, Spanish wealth plundered from the New World, and even the original manuscripts of William Shakespeare as written by Francis Bacon.

Circumstantial Evidence

Mr. Tobias, who for many years believed Oak Island was the site of a pirate communal bank, now has "a strong hunch" that the workings were designed and used by the British admiral and buccaneer Francis Drake as a temporary repository for the loot his ships seized in their frequent attacks on treasure-laden Spanish galleons during the 1570s and '80s. He notes that although no one has found documents to support any of the hypotheses, his own theory does comport well with Triton's carbon-dating results and other findings, as well as with the fact that the Spanish fleets routinely passed 300 to

---

3. *cofferdam*, a temporary dam made of wooden piles and steel which exposes an underwater area in order to build the foundation of a bridge or pier.

400 miles south of Mahone Bay on their homeward voyage via the Gulf Stream.

Mr. Blankenship, on the other hand, thinks the Spanish themselves might have engineered the project. "Why they did it, I don't know. But it fits the time frame, and the Spanish certainly had the wealth, manpower, and technology to do it."

To finance the shaft it intends to sink (and related on-site costs), Triton hopes to raise as much as $10 million in the next few months through a public share offering or some sort of limited partnership. "We're still not sure which route we'll take," Mr. Tobias says.

The current work in Borehole 10-X and the planned excavation of the Money Pit mark the end of a ten-year hiatus, during which very little has been accomplished on the island. Part of the delay, Mr. Tobias says, had to do with his own preoccupation with personal business affairs. But two years ago, he sold his packaging and label-manufacturing business, and he is now "prepared to devote all my time and energy to Oak Island." (Mr. Tobias and his family are currently the largest Triton shareholder, with 31%; Mr. Blankenship with 18.7%, has the second-largest stake.)

The Nolan Claim

The delay also resulted from protracted and messy litigation over ownership of the island. In 1977, Mr. Tobias purchased the island from its previous owner, M. R. Chappell of Sydney, Nova Scotia, for $125,000. However, a competing treasure hunter, Frederick Nolan of Bedford, Nova Scotia, has for many years laid claim to seven of the island's thirty-two lots; Mr. Tobias contested the claim. The case has dragged through the Nova Scotia courts for the past five years, costing the litigants almost $100,000. Last April, in appeals court, the contest was finally resolved in Mr. Nolan's favor.

Mr. Nolan, a fifty-nine-year-old land surveyor, has been looking for treasure on his property in a small-scale operation for the past twenty-eight years. He is convinced that the cache lies under his lots, most of which are in the swampy center of the island. "I'm close, really close, to finding it. Maybe this summer," he predicts.

Mr. Blankenship broodingly suggests that "Nolan has already found some treasure" on his lots. "I'm sure of it," he says. Mr. Nolan denies that.

There is a good chance the two sides may soon be back in court. They are currently arguing over access rights to the 600-foot causeway that now joins the island to the mainland, as well as over the location of the boundary line on Mr. Nolan's lot closest to the Money Pit. Indeed, that line, less than 600 feet west of the Money Pit, may someday prove crucial if Triton finds itself following a treasure tunnel in that direction.

Another Opinion

Meanwhile, in her home on the mainland overlooking Mahone Bay, Mildred Restall says the feuding treasure hunters will never "find any treasure on that damn island."

The seventy-two-year-old Mrs. Restall has good reason to feel bitter about Oak Island. She endured five hard years living there with her husband and two sons in a small construction shack without electricity or indoor plumbing while they desperately tried to find treasure. In August 1965, her husband and twenty-four-year-old son, as well as two other workers, drowned at the bottom of a twenty-seven-foot shaft. "And do you know what?" Mrs. Restall says with a sigh today, "I knew from the first day I stepped on that miserable island that there was no treasure there."

Mr. Tobias offers a different appraisal. "We'll probably at the very least uncover one of the most fascinating archaeological and historical sites in North America." And, he adds, "How many people in their lifetime get the opportunity to be associated with a project that may turn out to be as exciting as the discovery of King Tut's tomb or the City of Troy?"

It is that possibility, Mr. Tobias says, "that keeps me going." As for the chance that he will become extremely wealthy should Triton hit pay dirt, Mr. Tobias says, "I wouldn't start living like Adnan Khashoggi."[4]

But then he pauses, smiles and confesses, "Well, maybe just a little bit."

---

4. *Adnan Khashoggi* (adʹnon kä shōʹgī), wealthy Saudi businessman known for his extravagant lifestyle.

THINK AND DISCUSS
Understanding
1. Who are Blankenship and Tobias?
2. When was the money pit first discovered? Who discovered it?
3. What is *coir?* Why was it unusual to find *coir* in the tunnels?

Analyzing
4. What facts support the theory that there is something valuable in the pit?
5. Are there any facts to support Tobias's "strong hunch" that Francis Drake may have buried his loot there?
6. Why is Mrs. Restall bitter?

READING LITERATURE SKILLFULLY
Graphic Aids

The article states that rock-walled tunnels lead from Smith's Cove to the money pit. When the tight log platforms were removed, water flowed into the pit from the cove. Find the tunnels in the diagram of the money pit. At about what depth do they flow into the shaft? At what depth is the inscribed stone? What has probably kept the oak box from rotting?

Now look at the map, observe the directional key and the distance scale, and locate Oak Island. About how far is it from Amherst? In what direction does it lie from Halifax? Find Nova Scotia on a larger map.

VOCABULARY
Dictionary

This article contains words that have come into English from several other languages. Using your Glossary, tell what language each word is from.

debris hiatus hypothesis
buccaneer labyrinth galleon
cache

COMPOSITION
Writing a Letter

Suppose that a local organization is sponsoring a contest, the winner of which will get a free trip to Oak Island. In a two-paragraph letter to the President of the Oak Island Contest, tell why you are qualified and why you would like to go.

Writing about Nonfiction

In a two- or three-paragraph composition, tell whether you think this article is well-written. You will find the article "Writing About Nonfiction" in the Writer's Handbook helpful as you plan and write this composition.

BIOGRAPHY

D'Arcy O'Connor
1941–

D'Arcy O'Connor has been covering the story of Oak Island's subterranean vault for several years. He has written other articles about the subject for the *Wall Street Journal* and a book about the hidden treasure called *The Money Pit* (1978). He is presently working on a new book that will update the material he published in 1978.

O'Connor was born in Canada, but moved to South America with his family when he was a child. After attending high school in Buenos Aires, Argentina, he returned to Canada, where he completed his education. He now lives in Quebec, where he teaches journalism, writes screenplays as well as articles for magazines and newspapers, and sails.

The Voyage of the Phu Khanh[1]

Kathleen Kilgore

A boy shows the meaning of courage—and of loyalty.

n the first warm day in May my son Hong and I were cutting the pokeweed around the edges of my mother-in-law's backyard, while my daughter picked up the trash that had blown into the lilac bushes that winter. When I looked up, Hong was standing unusually still. At his feet, half buried in burdock and dandelion greens was a fiberglass boat about the size of a clawfoot bathtub. It was full of scummy water.

"It doesn't leak," he said hopefully.

"I think the owner would give it to you if you asked," I replied. "But what are you going to do with it?"

"I will get food for the family."

"Hong, it isn't big enough to go out in Boston Harbor. And there's no motor."

"My basket boat in Vietnam smaller than that! And I go out two, three miles at night, alone."

"It seems dangerous."

"I ran away when I thirteen and a half. They try to push me off the refugee boat, but I hang on. They try to kill me, but I get a gun. Then I live in the camp alone. If I worry about dangerous," he concluded, "then you have no son."

On the stern, Hong carefully painted in Chinese red the name of his home port, Nha Trang, and the province name, Phu Khanh ("rich enterprise"), just as it had been on the boat on which he had escaped.

Late spring evenings, he would sit in the boat in the backyard, assembling a mysterious collection of tin cans wound with fishing line, hooks, and weights. Occasionally he would yell at his sister, warning her that a virgin stepping over fishing gear was unlucky.

1. *Phu Khanh* (fü kän′ə).

Early one summer morning, when he judged the moon and tides to be right, a friend with a driver's license took him and the boat to Carson Beach. All day I worried about undertows and cold water. But in the afternoon, as I came back from the store, I found Hong setting up a table on two sawhorses for fish cleaning. In the plastic buckets were ninety-seven flounder.

When he turned sixteen and got a summer job, I thought the tiny boat would be replaced by something with an engine or at least a sail. But the money went into the bank for college. Every spring the cans, the tackle box, and the anchor come up from the basement to be carefully cleaned.

There are changes. His legs are so muscled from weight training he can't squat for long, but sits like a Westerner. He whistles a Lionel Richie tune instead of "Dark is the jungle path that leads to my lover's village" as he unwinds the tin cans, and no longer cares if little girls step over them. The moon is no longer a goddess who rules the sea, but a gray rock whose orbit he calculated in physics class. Soon the little boat will be too small for a grown American man.

The phrase "boat person" embarrasses him, and yet to me, that's what he'll always be. The skinny kid in the dinghy, setting out from home and family, from the safety of a predestined life, into the ocean, paddling madly toward an unknown shore. And I can only stand on the beach and wave good-bye.

THINK AND DISCUSS
Understanding
1. Where is Hong from? How old was he when he left his native country?
2. What is the Phu Khanh?
3. How does Hong earn money for college?

Analyzing
4. Why is Hong so confident about his ability to handle the dangers of his small boat?
5. Describe how Hong changes as he grows older.
6. Kilgore refers to Hong as "my son," yet she does not seem to know much about his early life. Explain why that might be so.

Extending
7. Do you think Kilgore used good judgment in allowing Hong to go out in the small boat? Explain.
8. Kilgore values the phrase "boat person" as a description of Hong. Explain why you agree or disagree that the term is appropriate to Hong.

VOCABULARY
Compound Words
A compound is a word formed by joining two or more words. *Bathtub* is a compound; so is *boat person* (though it is

spelled as two words). Sometimes the meaning of a compound is obvious in the combined meaning of the joined words. This is true of *bathtub*, but it is not the case with *boat person*.

Each of the words below is a compound found in "The Voyage of the Phu Khanh." Which of them have meanings that are easily understood by recognizing the joined words? For which words would you need dictionary help?

basket boat   undertow
backyard   sawhorse
clawfoot   boat person

COMPOSITION
Writing a Prediction
Imagine that twenty years have passed. What is Hong doing now? Where does he live? What is his work? What does he enjoy? Write a one-paragraph description of Hong's life in twenty years. Obviously you will be inventing all the details, but your prediction should be based on what you know about his character and abilities now.

Before beginning to write, make a list of Hong's character traits and abilities.

Explaining a Choice
Hong names his boat, *Rich Enterprise*, for the province he comes from. If you had a chance to name a boat, what would you call it and why? In a brief composition, describe a boat and what you would name it; then explain why you chose that particular name.

ENRICHMENT
Oral Research Report
Hong is only one of thousands of people who left Southeast Asia as "boat people." Why did these people leave their countries? What dangers did they face? To what countries did they travel? How were they received? How are they doing now? Prepare an oral report for your class, answering as many of the questions as you can. You will find news magazines in your local library a good source of information.

BIOGRAPHY

Kathleen Kilgore
1946–

Born in Washington, D.C., Kathleen Kilgore lived abroad with her parents, at one time acting as a translator for her father in Switzerland. After graduating from college, Kilgore planned a career in the U.S. Foreign Service, but instead she and her husband became involved in community political activities in Boston. They now live in Dorchester, Massachusetts, where Kilgore balances community work with her writing career. Among her novels for young adults are *The Wolfman of Beacon Hill* (1982) and *The Ghost Maker* (1984). In 1981 she and her husband became the parents of a fifteen-year-old Vietnamese refugee.

See HYPERBOLE in the Handbook of Literary Terms, page 669

My Boss the Cat

Paul Gallico

I once had a cat I suspected of being able to read.

---

f you are thinking of acquiring a cat at your house and would care for a quick sketch of what your life will be like under *Felis domesticus*,[1] you have come to the right party. I have figured out that, to date, I have worked for—and I mean *worked for*—thirty-nine of these four-legged characters, including one memorable period when I was doing the bidding of some twenty-three assorted resident felines all at the same time.

Cats are, of course, no good. They're chiselers and panhandlers, sharpers and shameless flatterers. They're as full of schemes and plans, plots and counterplots, wiles and guiles as any confidence man. They can read your character better than a $50-an-hour psychiatrist. They know to a milligram how much of the old oil to pour on to break you down. They are definitely smarter than I am, which is one reason why I love 'em.

Cat-haters will try to floor you with the old argument, "If cats are so smart, why can't they do tricks, the way dogs do?" It isn't that cats can't do tricks; it's that they *won't*. They're far too hep to stand up and beg for food when they know in advance you'll give it to them anyway. And as for rolling over, or playing dead, or "speaking," what's in it for pussy that isn't already hers?

Cats, incidentally, are a great warm-up for a successful marriage—they teach you your place in the household. The first thing Kitty does is to organize your home on a comfortable basis—*her* basis. She'll eat when she wants to; she'll go out at her pleasure. She'll come in when she gets good and ready, if at all.

She wants attention when she wants it and

---

1. *Felis domesticus* (fē'lis də mes'tə cus), the scientific classification for the domestic cat.

David Hockney, "Mr. and Mrs. Clark and Percy,"
The Tate Gallery

darned well means to be let alone when she has other things on her mind. She is jealous; she won't have you showering attentions or caresses on any other minxes, whether two- or four-footed.

She gets upset when you come home late and when you go away on a business trip. But when *she* decides to stay out a couple of nights, it is none of your darned business where she's been or what she's been up to. Either you trust her or you don't.

She hates dirt, bad smells, poor food, loud noises, and people you bring home unexpectedly to dinner.

Kitty also has her share of small-child obstinacy. She enjoys seeing you flustered, bussed, red in the face and losing your temper. Sometimes, as she hangs about watching, you get the feeling that it is all she can do to keep from busting out laughing. And she's got the darndest knack for putting the entire responsibility for everything on *you*.

For instance, Kitty pretends that she can neither talk nor understand you, and that she is therefore nothing but a poor helpless dumb animal. What a laugh! Any self-respecting racket-working cat can make you understand at all times exactly what she wants. She has one voice for "Let's eat," another for wanting out, still a third for "You don't happen to have seen my toy mouse around here, the one with the tail chewed off?" and a host of other easily identifiable speeches. She can also understand you perfectly, if she thinks there's profit in it.

I once had a cat I suspected of being able to read. This was a gent named Morris, a big tabby[2] with topaz eyes who lived with me when I was batching it in a New York apartment. One day I had just finished writing to a lady who at that time was the object of my devotion. Naturally I brought considerable of the writer's art into telling her this. I was called to the telephone for a few minutes. When I returned, Morris was sitting on my desk reading the letter. At least, he was staring down at it, looking a little ill. He gave me that long, baffled look of which cats are capable, and immediately meowed to be let out. He didn't come back for three days. Thereafter I kept my private correspondence locked up.

The incident reminds me of another highly discriminating cat I had down on the farm by the name of Tante[3] Hedwig. One Sunday a guest asked me whether I could make a cocktail called a Mexican.

I said I thought I could, and proceeded to to blend a horror of gin, pineapple juice, vermouth, bitters, and other ill-assorted ingredients. Pouring out a trial glass, I spilled it on the grass. Tante Hedwig came over, sniffed, and, with a look of shameful embarrassment, solicitously covered it over. Everybody agreed later that she had something there.

Let me warn you not to put too much stock in the theory that animals do not think and that they act only by instinct. Did you ever try to keep a cat out that wanted to come in, or vice versa? I once locked a cat in the cellar. *He* climbed a straight, smooth cement wall, hung on with his paws (I saw the claw marks to prove it); unfastened the window hook with his nose; and climbed out.

Cats have fabulous memories, I maintain, and also the ability to measure and evaluate what they remember. Take, for instance, our two Ukrainian grays, Chin and Chilla. My wife brought them up on a medicine dropper. We gave them love and care and a good home on a farm in New Jersey.

Eventually we had to travel abroad, so Chin and Chilla went to live with friends in Glenview, Illinois, a pretty, snazzy place. Back in the United States, we went out to spend Thanksgiving in Glenview. We looked forward, among other things, to seeing our two cats. When we arrived at the house, Chin and Chilla were squatting at the top of a broad flight of stairs. As we called up a tender greeting to them, we saw an expression of horror come over both their faces. "Great heavens! It's those *paupers!* Run!" With that, they vanished and could not be found for five hours. They were frightened to death we had come to take them back to the squalor of a country estate in New Jersey, and deprive them of a room of their own in Illinois, with glassed-in sun porch, screens for their toilets and similar superluxuries.

After a time they made a grudging appearance and consented to play the old games and talk over old times, guardedly. But when the

---

2. *tabby*, a grey or fawn-colored cat with dark stripes.
3. *Tante* (tän'tə), German for "aunt."

hour arrived for our departure, they vanished once more. Our hostess wrote us that apparently they got hold of a timetable somewhere and waited until our train was past Elkhart before coming out.

It was this same Chilla who, one day on the farm, after our big ginger cat, Wuzzy, had been missing for forty-eight hours led us to where he was, a half mile away, out of sight and out of hearing, caught in a trap. Every so often Chilla would look back to see if we were coming. Old Wuz was half dead when we got there, but when he saw Chilla he started to purr.

Two-Timing, or Leading the Double Life, is something you may be called upon to face with your cat. It means simply that Kitty manages to divide her time between two homes sufficiently far apart that each home-owner thinks she is his.

I discovered this when trying to check up on the unaccountable absences of Lulu II, a seal-point Siamese.[4] I finally located her at the other end of the bay, mooching on an amiable spinster. When I said, "Oh, I hope that my Lulu hasn't been imposing on you," she replied indignantly, "*Your* Lulu! You mean *our* dear little Pitipoo! We've been wondering where she went when she disappeared occasionally. We do hope she hasn't been annoying *you*."

The shocking part of this story, of course, is that, for the sake of a handout, Lulu, with a pedigree as long as your arm, was willing to submit to being called Pitipoo.

Of all things a smart cat does to whip you into line, the gift of the captured mouse is the cleverest and most touching. There was Limpy, the wild barn cat down on the farm who lived off what she caught in the fields. We were already supporting four cats, but in the winter, when we went to town, we brought her along.

We had not been inside the apartment ten minutes before Limpy caught a mouse, or probably *the* mouse, and at once brought it over and laid it at our feet. Now, as indicated before, Limpy had hunted to survive. To Limpy, a dead mouse was Big and Little Casino, touchdown, home run, and Grand Slam. Yet this one she gave to us.

How can you mark it up except as rent, or thanks, or "Here, looka; this is the most important thing I do. You take it because I like you"? You can teach a dog to retrieve and bring you game, but only a cat will voluntarily hand over its kill to you as an unsolicited gift.

How come Kitty acts not like the beast of prey she is but like a better-class human being? I don't know the answer. The point is, she does it—and makes you her slave ever after. Once you have been presented with a mouse by your cat, you will never be the same again. She can use you for a door mat. And she will, too.

---

4. *seal-point Siamese,* a Siamese cat with fawn-colored body and dark-brown extremities.

THINK AND DISCUSS
Understanding
1. Gallico's essay is based on his experiences with how many cats?
2. According to Gallico, why don't cats do tricks?
3. How does the cat named Limpy win the affection of the Gallicos?

Analyzing
4. Does Gallico like cats or not? Explain.
5. What seems to be Gallico's purpose in telling these cat stories?

Extending
6. Which cat mentioned in this essay would you choose as a pet? Why?

APPLYING: Hyperbole
See Handbook of Literary Terms, p. 669.
In speaking or writing, exaggerated statements can attract attention and add emphasis. **Hyperbole** can also be amusing.
1. Explain why the title of Gallico's essay is an example of hyperbole.
2. List three other examples of hyperbole in the essay.

THINKING SKILLS
Evaluating
When you evaluate, you make a judgment based on some sort of standard. Evaluate this essay by deciding whether it would encourage someone to get a cat.

COMPOSITION ◄━
Writing to Compare and Contrast
At one point Gallico briefly compares dogs and cats. Choose two other animals and compare them as household pets. Imagine that you are giving advice to a friend who is looking for a pet. Describe one animal in your first paragraph, the other in the second paragraph. In your final paragraph, present your conclusion about which animal would make the better pet. See "Writing to Compare and Contrast" in the Writer's Handbook for help in preparing and revising your paper.

Using Hyperbole in Description
Using Gallico's essay as a model, write an exaggerated description of your pet, or the pet of someone you know.

 ## BIOGRAPHY

Paul W. Gallico

1897–1976

Paul Gallico worked as a movie critic, sports writer, and war correspondent before turning full time to writing fiction. Among his works are *The Snow Goose* (1941), *Lou Gehrig: Pride of the Yankees* (1942), *Thomasina* (1957), and *The Poseidon Adventure* (1972).

Review HYPERBOLE in the Handbook of Literary Terms, page 669

A Celebration of Grandfathers

Rudolfo A. Anaya

I am glad I knew my grandfather.

uenos días le de Dios, abuelo."[1] God give you a good day, grandfather. This is how I was taught as a child to greet my grandfather, or any grown person. It was a greeting of respect, a cultural value to be passed on from generation to generation, this respect for the old ones.

The old people I remember from my childhood were strong in their beliefs, and as we lived daily with them we learned a wise path of life to follow. They had something important to share with the young, and when they spoke the young listened. These old *abuelos* and *abuelitas*[2] had worked the earth all their lives, and so they knew the value of nurturing, they knew the sensitivity of the earth. They knew the rhythms and cycles of time, from the preparation of the earth in the spring to the digging of the *acequias*[3] that brought the water to the dance of harvest in the fall. They shared good times and hard times. They helped each other through the epidemics and the personal tragedies, and they shared what little they had when the hot winds burned the land and no rain came. They learned that to survive one had to share in the process of life.

My grandfather was a plain man, a farmer from the valley called Puerto de Luna on the Pecos River.[4] He was probably a descendant of those people who spilled over the mountain from Taos, following the Pecos River in search of farmland. There in that river valley he settled and raised a large family.

Rudolfo A. Anaya (ä nä′yä).

1. *Buenos días le de Dios, abuelo* (bwe′nôs dē′äs le de dē′ôs ä bwe′lô). *[Spanish]*
2. *abuelos* (ä bwe′lôs) *and abuelitas* (ä bwe lē′täs), grandfathers and grandmothers.
3. *acequias* (ä se kwē′äs), irrigation ditches.
4. *Puerto de Luna* (pwer′tô de lü′nä) . . . *Pecos* (pe′kôs) *River.*

Bearded and walrus-mustached, he stood five feet tall, but to me as a child he was a giant. I remember him most for his silence. In the summers my parents sent me to live with him on his farm, for I was to learn the ways of a farmer. My uncles also lived in that valley, there where only the flow of the river and the whispering of the wind marked time. For me it was a magical place.

I remember once, while out hoeing the fields, I came upon an anthill, and before I knew it I was badly bitten. After he had covered my welts with the cool mud from the irrigation ditch, my grandfather calmly said: "Know where you stand." That is the way he spoke, in short phrases, to the point.

One very dry summer, the river dried to a trickle, there was no water for the fields. The young plants withered and died. In my sadness and with the impulse of youth I said, "I wish it would rain!" My grandfather touched me, looked up into the sky and whispered, "Pray for rain." In his language there was a difference. He felt connected to the cycles that brought the rain or kept it from us. His prayer was a meaningful action, because he was a participant with the forces that filled our world, he was not a bystander.

A young man died at the village one summer. A very tragic death. He was dragged by his horse. When he was found I cried, for the boy was my friend. I did not understand why death had come to one so young. My grandfather took me aside and said: "Think of the death of the trees and the fields in the fall. The leaves fall, and everything rests, as if dead. But they bloom again in the spring. Death is only this small transformation in life."

These are the things I remember, these fleeting images, few words.

I remember him driving his horse-drawn wagon into Santa Rosa in the fall when he brought his harvest produce to sell in the town. What a tower of strength seemed to come in that small man huddled on the seat of the giant wagon. One click of his tongue and the horses obeyed, stopped or turned as he wished. He never raised his whip. How unlike today when so much teaching is done with loud words and threatening hands.

I would run to greet the wagon, and the wagon would stop. *"Buenos días le de Dios, abuelo,"* I would say. *"Buenos días te de Dios, mi hijo,"*[5] he would answer and smile, and then I could jump up on the wagon and sit at his side. Then I, too, became a king as I rode next to the old man who smelled of earth and sweat and the other deep aromas from the orchards and fields of Puerto de Luna.

We were all sons and daughters to him. But today the sons and daughters are breaking with the past, putting aside *los abuelitos.*[6] The old values are threatened, and threatened most where it comes to these relationships with the old people. If we don't take the time to watch and feel the years of their final transformation, a part of our humanity will be lessened.

I grew up speaking Spanish, and oh! how difficult it was to learn English. Sometimes I would give up and cry out that I couldn't learn. Then he would say, *"Ten paciencia."*[7] Have patience. *Paciencia,* a word with the

---

5. *mi hijo* (mē ē′hô), my son.
6. *los abuelitos* (lôs ä bwe lē′tôs), grandparents.
7. *Ten paciencia* (ten pä sē en′sē ä).

strength of centuries, a word that said that someday we would overcome. "You have to learn the language of the Americanos," he said. "Me, I will live my last days in my valley. You will live in a new time."

A new time did come, a new time is here. How will we form it so it is fruitful? We need to know where we stand. We need to speak softly and respect others, and to share what we have. We need to pray not for material gain, but for rain for the fields, for the sun to nurture growth, for nights in which we can sleep in peace, and for a harvest in which everyone can share. Simple lessons from a simple man. These lessons he learned from his past which was as deep and strong as the currents of the river of life.

He was a man; he died. Not in his valley, but nevertheless cared for by his sons and daughters and flocks of grandchildren. At the end, I would enter his room which carried the smell of medications and Vicks. Gone were the aroma of the fields, the strength of his young manhood. Gone also was his patience in the face of crippling old age. Small things bothered him; he shouted or turned sour when his expectations were not met. It was because he could not care for himself, because he was returning to that state of childhood, and all those wishes and desires were now wrapped in a crumbling old body.

"*Ten paciencia,*" I once said to him, and he smiled. "I didn't know I would grow this old," he said.

I would sit and look at him and remember what was said of him when he was a young man. He could mount a wild horse and break it, and he could ride as far as any man. He could dance all night at a dance, then work

the *acequia* the following day. He helped the neighbors, they helped him. He married, raised children. Small legends, the kind that make up everyman's life.

He was ninety-four when he died. Family, neighbors, and friends gathered; they all agreed he had led a rich life. I remembered the last years, the years he spent in bed. And as I remember now, I am reminded that it is too easy to romanticize old age. Sometimes we forget the pain of the transformation into old age, we forget the natural breaking down of the body. My grandfather pointed to the leaves falling from the tree. So time brings with its transformation the often painful, wearing-down process. Vision blurs, health wanes; even the act of walking carries with it the painful reminder of the autumn of life. But this process is something to be faced, not something to be hidden away by false images. Yes, the old can be young at heart, but in their own way, with their own dignity. They do not have to copy the always-young image of the Hollywood star.

I returned to Puerto de Luna last summer, to join the community in a celebration of the founding of the church. I drove by my grandfather's home, my uncles' ranches, the neglected adobe washing down into the earth from whence it came. And I wondered, how might the values of my grandfather's generation live in our own? What can we retain to see us through these hard times? I was to become a farmer, and I became a writer. As I plow and plant my words, do I nurture as my grandfather did in his fields and orchards? The answers are not simple.

"They don't make men like that anymore," is a phrase we hear when one does honor to a man. I am glad I knew my grandfather. I am glad there are still times when I can see him in my dreams, hear him in my reverie. Sometimes I think I catch a whiff of that earthy aroma that was his smell. Then I smile. How strong these people were to leave such a lasting impression.

So, as I would greet my *abuelo* long ago, it would help us all to greet the old ones we know with this kind and respectful greeting: *"Buenos días le de Dios."*

THINK AND DISCUSS
Understanding
1. Describe the grandfather's appearance and manner of speaking.
2. When does the grandfather tell the narrator to have patience? When does the narrator return this advice?

Analyzing
3. Why do you think the narrator remembers Grandfather's lessons so well?
4. Does the narrator believe that his grandfather's lessons apply in our "new time"? Explain.
5. The narrator says, "The old values are threatened." What part of this threat seems to concern him most?

Extending
6. Do you agree that grandparents—and people their age—have valuable knowledge to share with the present time? Explain.

7. In your opinion, what is the best way values can be passed from one generation to the next?

REVIEWING: Hyperbole H⚡
See Handbook of Literary Terms, p. 669.
A writer may use **hyperbole** to emphasize a personal reaction. For example, Anaya says of his five-foot-tall grandfather, "to me as a child he was a giant." What does this hyperbole tell you about Anaya's attitude toward his grandfather?

READING LITERATURE SKILLFULLY
Fact and Opinion
As you learned in "Reading Nonfiction" (page 209), it is wise to keep track of the difference between facts and opinions when reading and to value those opinions that are supported by facts.

1. Is the following a statement of fact or a statement of opinion about the *abuelos* and *abuelitas* the narrator knew when he was a child?

   They helped each other through the epidemics and the personal tragedies, and they shared what little they had when the hot winds burned the land and no rains came.

2. Which of the following are statements of fact and which are statements of opinion?

   He was ninety-four when he died. Family, neighbors, and friends gathered; they all agreed he had led a rich life.

   But this process [aging] is something to be faced, not something to be hidden away by false images.

   I am glad I knew my grandfather.

   In the summer my parents sent me to live with him on his farm, for I was to learn the ways of a farmer.

3. Find at least two facts in the essay to support the narrator's opinion that "a part of our humanity will be lessened" if we do not take time to know the old people among us.

COMPOSITION
Expressing Your Opinion

Have you had a positive experience with an old person similar to the one described in this essay? If so, write a letter to the narrator in which you tell him that you agree with the opinion stated in the essay and telling why. Be sure you back up your opinion with facts.

Writing a Poem

Write a poem in praise of an old person. Choose someone you know or have read about. Before you begin to plan your poem, see "Writing a Poem" in the Writer's Handbook.

BIOGRAPHY

Rudolfo A. Anaya
1937–

Rudolfo Anaya was born into a Spanish-speaking family in Pastura, New Mexico, where, he says, "everyone tells stories. . . . I learned from the old storytellers how to recreate the narrative and pass it on."

Anaya currently teaches English and American literature at the University of New Mexico. In addition to teaching and writing, he has participated in workshops dealing with topics such as cultural awareness, Mexican culture, and Chicano culture.

HL**T** See **CONNOTATION/DENOTATION** in the Handbook of Literary Terms, page 661

One Land, Two Worlds

Jamake Highwater

Are all people the same? Should they be treated as if they were?

When I was five years old, I discovered a wonderful creature. It looked like a bird, but it was able to do things that many other birds cannot do. For instance, in addition to flying in the enormous sky that shelters the land where I grew up, it swam and dove in the lakes and, sometimes, it just floated majestically on the water's silver surface. It could also waddle, rather gracelessly, in the tall grass that grew along the edges of the water. The bird was called *méksikatsi*,[1] which, in the Blackfeet language, means "pink-colored feet." Méksikatsi seemed an ideal name for the versatile fly-swim bird, since it really did have bright pink feet.

When I was ten years old I was told by a teacher of the English language that *méksikatsi* was not really *méksikatsi*. It didn't matter that the word described the bird exactly or that the Blackfeet people had called it Méksikatsi for thousands of years. The bird, I was told, was called duck.

"DUCK?" I was extremely disappointed. The word "duck" didn't make any sense, for indeed Méksikatsi doesn't look like the word "duck." It doesn't even *sound* like the word "duck." So why do people call it duck?

This lesson was the first of many from which I slowly learned, to my amazement, that the people of white America don't *see* the same things that Indians see. America is one land, but it is two worlds.

As my education in the ways of white people progressed, I finally came to understand what duck means to them—but I could never forget that *méksikatsi* also has meaning, even though it means something *fundamentally* different from what duck means.

This lesson in words and the ideas they

Jamake (juh mah′kuh).

1. *méksikatsi* (mēk′sē kät′sē).

Preface from *Many Smokes, Many Moons* by Jamake Highwater (J.B. Lippincott). Copyright © 1978 by Jamake Highwater. Reprinted by permission of Harper & Row, Publishers, Inc. and the Fox Chase Agency for the author.

convey is very difficult to understand. In fact, it has been the most complicated lesson of my life. As I have gained more education in both the culture of the white man and that of the Indian, I have found it progressively more difficult to pass from one world to the other. It is not simply a matter of language, for, as everyone knows, it is possible to translate with accuracy from one language to another without losing too much of the original meaning. But there is no method for translating "alien ideas."

I am sometimes alienated by the way ideas find their way into English words. For instance, when an English word is descriptive—like the word "wilderness"—I am often appalled by what is implied by the description. After all, the forest is not "wild" in the sense that it is something that needs to be tamed. For Blackfeet Indians, the forest is the natural state of the world. It is the cities that are wild and need "taming." In a word like "universe" I find even more complicated problems, for Indians do not believe in a "*uni*-verse," but in a "*multi*-verse." Indians don't believe that there is only *one* truth, but think there are many truths.

I talked to my Indian friends at college about this situation, and we all agreed that it ought to be studied and understood by all people, because it surely contained a lesson that could benefit everybody.

If we can accept the paradox that the real humanity of people is understood through cultural *differences* rather than cultural similarities, then we can make profound sense of our differences. It is possible that there is not one truth, but many; not one *real* experience, but many realities; not one history,

but many different ways of looking at events.

At the core of each person's life is a package of beliefs that he or she learns and that has been culturally determined long in advance of the person's birth. That is equally true for Indians and for white people. The world is made coherent by our description of it. Language permits us to express ourselves, but it also places limits on what we are able to say. What we call things largely determines how we evaluate them. What we see when we speak of "reality" is simply that preconception—that cultural package we inherited at birth. For me it was *méksikatsi;* for an English-speaking child it was duck. Indian children are urged to see things and to name them in terms of the cultural package of the white man, but the children of white America are rarely given the opportunity to know the world as others know it.

I have become determined to clarify that Indians have a different way of looking at the world than white people do, and that that difference is *not* necessarily a matter of "error" or simply a variation in the words used to name things.

I discovered a sixteenth-century anonymous engraving that represented Columbus being greeted "by natives of the dominion of the Great Khan." I asked Choctaw Indian artist Asa Battles to make a drawing of the same event from the Indian perspective.

The old engraving depicts three sailing vessels anchored offshore and a landing party of elegantly dressed gentlemen erecting a cross on the new-found land while their leader, Columbus, flanked by two officers, is given a rich tribute by natives who do not

"Landing at Hispaniola,"
courtesy New York Public
Library, from Theodore
deBry, *Collectiones
Peregrinationum in Indiam
Orientalem et Indiam
Occidentalem*

look in the least like Indians. It is a familiar depiction of a famous scene from the white man's idealized history.

The other picture depicts an unfamiliar scene: an Indian gasping in amazement as a floating island carrying odd creatures with hairy faces and defoliated trees approaches.

When I showed the two pictures to white people they said, "Well, of course you realize that what those Indians thought they saw—if you *really* investigate the facts—was not really there at all." In other words, there were no island and no defoliated trees, but a ship with a party of Spaniards.

Indians, looking at the same pictures, pause with perplexity and then say, "Well, after all, a ship is a floating island, and what are the masts of a ship but the trunks of tall trees?" In other words, what the Indians saw

was real in terms of their own experience.

The artists of all races have known for years that "reality" depends on how you look at things. An Indian teacher has said it in another way: "The apple is very complicated, but for the apple tree it is easy."

The Indians saw a floating island while white men saw a ship. Isn't it also possible— if we use our imaginations—that another, more alien people with an utterly different way of seeing and thinking might see neither an island nor a ship? They might see the complex network of molecules that science tells us produce the outward shapes and colors that we *see* as objects. In that case, who *really* sees "reality"?

We see the world in terms of our cultural heritage. Among politically concerned people with a liberal dogma, there is a good-natured

Asa Battles

and pompous insistence that all people are fundamentally the same. What is *fundamental*, however, to people concerned with political idealism is sometimes rather superficial. Some libertarians seem to believe that even biology is democratic, but what they see when they refer to the homogeneous attributes of all human physiology is not blood or nerves, but things that are much more cultural. They do not like to notice that races and national groups tend to evolve distinctive stereotypes both emotionally and physically. They believe that *all* men are fundamentally the same because all men—they insist—need and want the same things. They do not take into consideration the reason a Navajo family may rip the toilet out of its newly built government house. Navajos believe it is disgusting to put a toilet under the same roof with

people rather than at a distance from the house. Many liberals also fail to take into account the great variety of ways in which people of a single culture respond to the same things, let alone the vaster differences that exist between cultures. There is no question that all people feel sorrow and happiness, but the things that evoke these responses and the manner in which such feelings may be expressed socially can be highly dissimilar from culture to culture.

Political idealists have overemphasized the uniformity of people. It is exceedingly dangerous to take democratic idealism out of politics and attempt to apply it to science and art. The *uniformity* that the biologist and physicist discover at the core of the material world is easily distorted into *conformity* when applied to less fundamental issues, and gradually we find that the very democratic process that is supposed to set us free has deprived cultures and individuals of the right to be dissimilar.

It is very unfashionable at the moment to suggest that all people are *not* the same. It is equally unpopular to insist that we can learn more about a culture from its differences than from its similarities to other cultures, and that the basis of human nature is probably more visible in human diversity than in the relatively few ways in which we are fundamentally the same. Political people usually strive for admirable but naïve political goals; one nation, one world. In the process of trying to unify the world we must be exceedingly careful not to destroy the diversity of the many cultures of man that give human life meaning, focus, and vitality.

I grew up in two Americas—the ancient one that existed for my ancestors for tens of thousands of years, and the new one that is written about in history books. Like the pictures of the Spanish landing, the tales of these two Americas are rarely compatible. It is for this reason that the arts of American Indians are precious—they provide a glimpse into their own history, into the world of the *other* America.

For a long time the viewpoint of primal peoples, such as Indians, was considered naïve and primitive, especially if the peoples kept their history alive through oral and pictorial traditions rather than by writing history books. Today we are learning that people are not the same, and that we cannot evaluate all experience the same way. We are also learning that everybody doesn't have to be the same in order to be equal. It is no longer realistic for dominant cultures to send out missionaries to convert everyone to their ideas of the "truth." Today we are beginning to look into the ideas of groups outside the dominant culture, and we are finding different kinds of "truth" that make the world we live in far bigger than we ever dreamed it could be—for the greatest distance between people is not geographical space, but culture.

THINK AND DISCUSS
Understanding
1. Why didn't Highwater like the word *duck?*
2. What are the "two Americas" that Highwater grew up in?

Analyzing
3. What does Highwater mean when he says Indians believe in a "*multi*-verse"?
4. Why does Highwater object to the emphasis on the sameness of all people?

Extending
5. Highwater writes, "America is one land, but it is two worlds." Explain why you agree or disagree with him.

APPLYING: H𝕏
Connotation/Denotation
See Handbook of Literary Terms, p. 661.
   Connotations of certain words play an important part in Highwater's essay.

1. What connotations does the word *wilderness* have for Highwater?
2. The literal meaning of *universe* is "everything there is; the whole of existing things." What additional meaning does Highwater find in the word? Why does he disagree with that connotation?

READING LITERATURE SKILLFULLY
Graphic Aids
To help make his point, Highwater uses graphic aids—the two pictures.

1. What is shown in each picture?
2. What important differences do you see in comparing the two pictures?
3. Would the essay be better if the pictures were omitted? Explain.

COMPOSITION
Reading/Writing Log
Copy the first paragraph of this essay in your reading/writing log. Is there a creature that appeals to your imagination? Jot down some of the characteristics that make it special to you. Write a description of it. Before you write, try describing the creature to some of your classmates, without telling the creature's name.

Renaming an Animal
Do you know of a creature that deserves a better name? Write a three-paragraph essay renaming it. In your first paragraph, describe the special qualities that make you interested in the creature, but do not name it. In the second, give the name and explain why you feel it's not suitable. In the third, choose a new name and give reasons for your choice.

Describing Two Points of View
Try describing a situation or event from two different points of view. (What would happen, for example, if a grandfather attended a rock concert with his grandchild?) Describe each person's experience in a paragraph.

BIOGRAPHY

Jamake Highwater
1942–

Jamake Highwater is the author of over twenty books, among these *Anpao: An American Indian Odyssey*, which was a Newbery Honor Book in 1978. Writing is not the only area in which he excels. He has been a professor of architecture, co-moderator and organizer of the Aspen Institutes' arts festivals, and contributor to publications on American music. In 1978 he was honored by the Blood Band of the Blackfeet Nation of Alberta, Canada, for his many achievements on behalf of Indian culture.

The Gettysburg Address

Abraham Lincoln

The Battle of Gettysburg, fought in Pennsylvania during the first three days of July, 1863, was one of the bloodiest of the Civil War. Thousands of soldiers were buried on the battlefield. On November 19, part of the field was made a national memorial. Lincoln gave this speech at the dedication of the memorial.

Four score and seven years ago our fathers brought forth on this continent a new nation, conceived in Liberty, and dedicated to the proposition that all men are created equal.

Now we are engaged in a great civil war, testing whether that nation, or any nation so conceived and so dedicated, can long endure. We are met on a great battle-field of that war. We have come to dedicate a portion of that field as a final resting place for those who here gave their lives that that nation might live. It is altogether fitting and proper that we should do this.

But, in a larger sense, we cannot dedicate— we cannot consecrate—we cannot hallow— this ground. The brave men, living and dead, who struggled here, have consecrated it, far above our poor power to add or detract. The world will little note, nor long remember what we say here, but it can never forget what they did here. It is for us the living, rather, to be dedicated here to the unfinished work which they who fought here have thus far so nobly advanced. It is rather for us to be here dedicated to the great task remaining before us—that from these honored dead we take increased devotion to that cause for which they gave the last full measure of devotion—that we here highly resolve that these dead shall not have died in vain—that this nation, under God, shall have a new birth of freedom—and that government of the people, by the people, for the people, shall not perish from the earth.

THINK AND DISCUSS

Understanding

1. What three important facts are given in the second paragraph of the address?
2. Who has "consecrated" the ground?
3. What is left for the living to do?

Analyzing

4. What will insure "that these dead shall not have died in vain"?

Extending

5. Which is better known today—the Battle of Gettysburg or the Gettysburg Address? Would Lincoln be pleased?

COMPOSITION

Writing a Summary

Imagine that you have been asked to explain the Address to a group of ten-year-olds. Write a summary of the speech for them, using no more than four sentences.

Writing a Letter

Imagine that you were in the audience when Lincoln gave his speech. Did you have a good view? Could you hear him clearly? Were you surprised when he sat down so quickly? How did the people around you react? Write a letter to a friend, describing your experience. In your last paragraph, make a prediction about how the newspapers will react.

ENRICHMENT

Oral Interpretation

Memorize Lincoln's speech and deliver it to your class. You might select some music that you feel would be appropriate to your oral presentation.

BIOGRAPHY

Abraham Lincoln
1809–1865

Sixteenth President of the United States, Abraham Lincoln attracted both fierce loyalties and bitter hatred during the four years of his presidency (1861–1865). In addition to steering the country through the Civil War, the Lincoln administration brought about significant and far-reaching legislation such as the abolition of slavery, the establishment of an income tax, and the beginning of compulsory military service. Few public figures have so frequently been celebrated in songs, poems, plays, and stories. The multi-volume biography of Lincoln by the twentieth-century poet Carl Sandburg has become a modern classic. Lincoln saw the end of the Civil War on April 9, 1865, but he was not able to put into effect his plans for reuniting the country. He was assassinated on April 14 of that year.

UNIT 3   NONFICTION

■ CONCEPT REVIEW

This unit ends with a selection from the autobiography of Margaret Mead, who is well known for her work in anthropology— the study of the origin and development of the human race. The selection contains many of the important ideas and literary terms found in the nonfiction you have just studied. It also contains notes and questions designed to help you think critically about your reading. Page numbers in the notes refer to an Application. For a more extensive discussion of literary terms, see the Handbook of Literary Terms.

On Being a Granddaughter

Margaret Mead

My paternal grandmother, who lived with us from the time my parents married until she died in 1927, while I was studying anthropological collections in German museums, was the most decisive influence in my life. She sat at the center of our household. Her room— and my mother always saw to it that she had the best room, spacious and sunny, with a fireplace if possible—was the place to which we immediately went when we came in from playing or home from school. There my father went when he arrived in the house. There we did our lessons on the cherrywood table with which she had begun housekeeping and which, later, was my dining room table for twenty-

Margaret Mead's paternal grandmother at the time of her wedding. *Institute for Intercultural Studies*

five years. There, sitting by the fire, erect and intense, she listened to us and to all of Mother's friends and to our friends. In my early childhood she was also very active—cooking, preserving, growing flowers in the garden, and attentive to all the activities of the country and the farm. . . .

My mother was trustworthy in all matters that concerned our care. Grandma was trustworthy in a quite different way. She meant exactly what she said, always. If you borrowed her scissors, you returned them. In like case, Mother would wail ineffectually, "Why does everyone borrow my scissors and never return them?" and Father would often utter idle threats. But Grandma never threatened. She never raised her voice. She simply commanded respect and obedience by her complete expectation that she would be obeyed. And she never gave silly orders . . . Grandma never said, "Do this because Grandma says so," or "because Grandma wants you to do it." She simply said, "Do it," and I knew from her tone of voice that it was necessary.

■ **hyperbole** (page 250): Mother uses exaggeration to make her point.

My grandmother grew up in the little town of Winchester, in Adams County, Ohio, which two of my great-great-grandfathers had founded. She was one of nine children who reached adulthood. . . .

My grandmother began school teaching quite young, at a time when it was still somewhat unusual for a girl to teach school. When my grandfather, who was also a teacher, came home from the Civil War, he married my grandmother and they went to college together. They also graduated together. She gave a graduation address in the morning and my grandfather, who gave one in the afternoon, was introduced as the husband of Mrs. Mead who spoke this morning.

■ **synthesizing:** Note the various ways in which Grandma's life has not been typical of the lives led by most women in the last half of the nineteenth century.

My grandfather was a school superintendent. . . . He died when my father was six. Two days later the principal took his place and my grandmother took the principal's place. From then on she taught, sometimes in high school, sometimes small children, until she came to live with us when my parents married. It was the small children in whom she was most interested, and I have the notes she took on the schools she observed during a visit to Philadelphia before my parents' marriage.

She understood many things that are barely recognized in the wider educational world even today. . . . She thought that memorizing mere facts was not very important and that drill was stultifying. The result was that I was not well drilled in geography or spelling. But I learned to observe the world around me and to note what I saw—to observe flowers and children and baby chicks. She taught me to read for the sense of what I read and to enjoy learning.

With the exception of the two years I went to kindergarten . . . and the year I was eight . . . she taught me until I went to high school and even then helped me with my lessons when my teachers were woefully inadequate, as they often were. I never expected any teacher to know as much as my parents or my grandmother did. . . .

Grandma was a wonderful storyteller, and she had a set of priceless, individually tailored anecdotes with which American grandparents of her day brought up children. There was the story of the little boys who had been taught absolute, quick obedience. One day when they were out on the prairie, their father shouted, "Fall down on your faces!" They did, and the terrible prairie fire swept over them *and they weren't hurt*. There was also the story of three boys at school, each of whom received a cake sent from home. One hoarded his, and the mice ate it; one ate all of his, and he got sick; and who do you think had the best time?—why, of course, the one who shared his cake with his friends. Then there was the little boy who ran away from home and stayed away all day. When he came home after supper, he found the family sitting around the fire and nobody said a word. Not a word. Finally, he couldn't stand it anymore and said, "Well, I see you have the same old cat!" And there was one about a man who was so lazy he would rather starve than work. Finally, his neighbors decided to bury him alive. On the way to the cemetery they met a man with a wagon-load of unshelled corn. He asked where they were going. When they told him that they were going to bury that no-good man alive, the owner of the corn took pity on him and said, "I tell you what. I will give you this load of corn. All you will have to do is shell it." But the lazy man said, "Drive on, boys!"

Because Grandma did so many things with her hands, a little girl could always tag after her, talking and asking questions and listening. Side by side with Grandma, I learned to peel apples, to take the skin off tomatoes by plunging them into scalding water, to do simple embroidery stitches, and to knit. Later, during World War I, when I had to cook for the whole household, she taught me a lot about cooking, for example, just when to add a lump of butter, something that always had to be concealed from Mother, who thought that cooking with butter was extravagant.

While I followed her about as she carried out the endless little

Margaret Mead's paternal grandmother in 1907. *Institute for Intercultural Studies*

■ Note the use of hyperbole in this anecdote.

household tasks that she took on, supplementing the work of the maids or doing more in between maids—and we were often in between—she told me endless tales about Winchester. She told me about her school days and about the poor children who used to beg the cores of apples from the rich children who had whole apples for lunch. She told me about Em Eiler, who pushed Aunt Lou off a rail fence into a flooded pasture lot; about Great-aunt Louisian, who could read people's minds and tell them everything they had said about her and who had been a triplet and was so small when she was born that she would fit into a quart cup; about Grace, who died from riding a trotting horse too hard, which wasn't good for girls; and about the time Lida cut off Anna Louise's curls and said, "Now they won't say 'pretty little girl' anymore." My great-grandfather used to say such a long grace, she told me, that one of her most vivid memories was of standing, holding a log she had started to put on the fire, for what seemed to be hours for fear of interrupting him. All this was as real to me as if I had lived it myself. . . .

■ Is Grace's fate an example of a fact or an opinion?

Mother never ceased to resent the fact that Grandma lived with us, but she gave her her due. Grandma never "interfered"—never tried to teach the children anything religious that had not previously been introduced by my mother, and in disagreements between my mother and father she always took my mother's side. When my father threatened to leave my mother, Grandma told him firmly that she would stay with her and the children.

When Grandma was angry, she sat and held her tongue. I used to believe that this involved some very mysterious . . . trick. She was so still, so angry, and so determined not to speak, not to lose her temper. And she never did. But not losing her temper came out of her eyes like fire. Years later, when I was given a picture of her as a young woman, I felt that I had looked very like her at the same age. But when I actually compared pictures of me with the one of her, I looked milky mild. Not until the birth of her great-great-granddaughter, my daughter's daughter Sevanne Margaret, did that flashing glance reappear in the family. . . .

I think it was my grandmother who gave me my ease in being a woman. She was unquestionably feminine—small and dainty and pretty. . . . She had gone to college when this was a very unusual thing for a girl to do, she had a firm grasp of anything she paid attention to, she had married and had a child, and she had a career of her

■ connotation/denotation (page 260): Mead here gives the connotation—not the denotation—of *feminine*.

own. All this was true of my mother, as well. But my mother was filled with passionate resentment about the condition of women, as perhaps my grandmother might have been had my grandfather lived and had she borne five children and had little opportunity to use her special gifts and training. As it was, the two women I knew best were mothers and had professional training. So I had no reason to doubt that brains were suitable for a woman. And as I had my father's kind of mind—which was also his mother's—I learned that the mind is not sex-typed.

The content of my conscience came from my mother's concern for other people and the state of the world, and from my father's insistence that the only thing worth doing is to add to the store of exactly known facts. But the strength of my conscience came from Grandma, who meant what she said. . . .

■ Note that Mead characterizes her mother and her grandmother by telling ways in which they were alike and ways in which they were different.

THINK AND DISCUSS
Understanding
1. What are some of the things Grandma does in the Mead household?
2. What job was Grandma trained for?
3. Why did the young Margaret Mead think her grandmother was trustworthy?
4. What does Grandma consider to be the best way to teach children?
5. What part of Grandma's face always gives away the fact that she is angry?

Analyzing
6. What is the purpose of the anecdotes about the boy who shared his cake and the two boys in the prairie fire?
7. Describe the Mead family, basing your description on information from the selection.

Extending
8. Do you think the kind of anecdote favored by Grandma is a useful tool to use in raising children? Explain.

REVIEWING LITERARY TERMS
Hyperbole
1. Cite examples of hyperbole in the tale of the lazy man and the wagon full of corn.

Connotation/Denotation
2. What connotation does the word *mother-in-law* have?
3. Of the people in this selection, who is most likely to agree with this connotation—Margaret Mead? her father? her mother? Give evidence to support your answer.

■ CONTENT REVIEW
THINKING SKILLS
Classifying
1. Of the three people you read about in the Autobiography section of this unit,

which one seems most real and alive to you? List the three main characters in order from most to least real. Be prepared to give reasons for your classification.

Generalizing

2. Which selection is humorous? Compare and contrast that selection with "A Celebration of Grandfathers."

3. Many of the people you have read about in Unit 3 have looked for and accepted challenges. Describe the challenges faced by the following people. What do all these situations have in common? Marjorie Rawlings; Gordon Parks; Daniel Blankenship and David Tobias ("Treasure Hunt"); and Kathleen Kilgore's son Hong ("Voyage of the Phu Khanh").

Synthesizing

4. The modern novelist and short story writer J. D. Salinger has one of his characters suggest that what Lincoln should have done at Gettysburg was stand up, shake his fist at the crowd, and sit back down. Based on what you learned about the Civil War in general and the Battle of Gettysburg in particular, explain what you think the character meant by the statement.

Evaluating

5. Imagine that you have a chance to interview one of the following people. Which one would you choose? Why? What questions would you ask? What comments would you make? Rudolfo Anaya; Abraham Lincoln; Jamake Highwater; Dorothy Redford (the organizer of the reunion in "Kin").

6. Why do you think most people read so much more nonfiction than fiction?

■ COMPOSITION REVIEW

Writing a Character Sketch

Who is the most admirable character you have encountered in this unit? In your judgment, what makes that character admirable? Write a character sketch in which you describe your choice in paragraph one, tell why you think the person is admirable in paragraph two, and conclude in paragraph three by telling whether you want to be like the person.

Writing About Yourself

Write an autobiographical narrative about something that taught you a lesson and might teach someone else something about life. Jot down your ideas first. Next, list what happened. Check to see that events are in the correct sequence, or order. Begin your composition by telling what happened; then, tell what you learned from this. Check your first draft for places you might substitute specific words for more general ones.

Reviewing Writer's Craft
Write Good Beginnings

Choose a topic that you find interesting and write a one- or two-paragraph beginning for an essay on the topic. Before you begin, review the Writer's Craft article in this unit. If you are keeping a reading/writing log, consult it before you begin your composition.

POETRY

Walter Ufer, "Where the Desert Meets the Mountains" (detail), *Anschulz Collection*

PREVIEW

UNIT 4   POETRY

Poets in this unit include
Stephen Vincent Benét
Robert Frost
Ralph Waldo Emerson
Henry Wadsworth Longfellow
Alfred Noyes
Alice Walker
Margaret Danner
Margaret Tsuda
Edna St. Vincent Millay
May Swenson
Langston Hughes

Features
Reading a Poem
Comment: Ballads
Comment: Highwaymen, Footpads,
    and Rufflers
The Writer's Craft: Appeal to the Senses

Application of Literary Terms
rhyme   symbol
rhythm   personification
simile   alliteration
metaphor   onomatopoeia
imagery   figurative language

Reading Literature Skillfully
judgments
author's purpose

Vocabulary Skills
context
affixes

Thinking Skills
classifying
generalizing

Composition Assignments Include
Writing a Rhyme
Writing About an Event
Writing to Compare and Contrast
Creating Metaphors
Writing an Explanation
Reading/Writing Log
Creating a Symbol
Writing About a Poem

Enrichment
Art Project
Oral Reading

Thinking Critically About Literature
Concept Review
Content Review
Composition Review

The Ballad of William Sycamore (1790–1871)

Stephen Vincent Benét

My father, he was a mountaineer,
His fist was a knotty hammer;
He was quick on his feet as a running
    deer,
And he spoke with a Yankee stammer.

5 My mother, she was merry and brave,
And so she came to her labor,
With a tall green fir for her doctor grave[1]
And a stream for her comforting neighbor.

And some are wrapped in the linen fine,
10 And some like a godling's scion;[2]
But I was cradled on twigs of pine
In the skin of a mountain lion.

And some remember a white, starched lap
And a ewer with silver handles;
15 But I remember a coonskin cap
And the smell of bayberry candles.

The cabin logs, with the bark still rough,
And my mother who laughed at trifles,
And the tall, lank visitors, brown as snuff,
20 With their long, straight squirrel-rifles.

I can hear them dance, like a foggy song,
Through the deepest one of my slumbers,
The fiddle squeaking the boots along
And my father calling the numbers.[3]

25 The quick feet shaking the puncheon-floor,
And the fiddle squealing and squealing,
Till the dried herbs rattled above the door
And the dust went up to the ceiling.

There are children lucky from dawn
    till dusk,
30 But never a child so lucky!
For I cut my teeth on "Money Musk"[4]
In the Bloody Ground of Kentucky![5]

When I grew tall as the Indian corn,
My father had little to lend me,
35 But he gave me his great, old powder-horn
And his woodsman's skill to befriend me.

With a leather shirt to cover my back,
And a redskin nose to unravel
Each forest sign, I carried my pack
40 As far as a scout could travel.

(Continued)

Benét, (bə nā′).

1. *for her doctor grave,* her grave (serious) doctor.
2. *like a godling's scion* (sī′ən), descendant of a god.
3. *calling out the numbers,* the steps for the dance.
4. *"Money Musk,"* a popular square-dance tune.
5. *Bloody Ground of Kentucky.* Kentucky was often referred to as "Dark and Bloody Ground" because of early Indian wars.

Till I lost my boyhood and found my wife,
A girl like a Salem clipper!
A woman straight as a hunting-knife
With eyes as bright as the Dipper!

45 We cleared our camp where the
     buffalo feed,
Unheard-of streams were our flagons;
And I sowed my sons like the apple-seed
On the trail of the Western wagons.

They were right, tight boys,
     never sulky or slow,
50 A fruitful, a goodly muster.
The eldest died at the Alamo.
The youngest fell with Custer.

The letter that told it burned my hand.
Yet we smiled and said, "So be it!"
55 But I could not live when they fenced
     the land,
For it broke my heart to see it.

I saddled a red, unbroken colt
And rode him into the day there;
And he threw me down like a thunderbolt
60 And rolled on me as I lay there.

The hunter's whistle hummed in my ear
As the city-men tried to move me,
And I died in my boots like a pioneer
With the whole wide sky above me.

65 Now I lie in the heart of the fat,
     black soil,
Like the seed of a prairie-thistle;
It has washed my bones with honey
     and oil
And picked them clean as a whistle.

And my youth returns, like the rains
     of Spring,
70 And my sons, like the wild-geese flying;
And I lie and hear the meadow-lark sing
And have much content in my dying.

Go play with the towns you have built
     of blocks,
The towns where you would have
     bound me!
75 I sleep in my earth like a tired fox,
And my buffalo have found me.

Frederic Remington, "The Bronco Buster,"
(large version) 1909 *The Art Institute of Chicago*

THINK AND DISCUSS

Understanding

1. What kind of boyhood did the speaker have?
2. What happened to his eldest and youngest sons?
3. How does the speaker die?

Analyzing

4. What is the **setting** for this ballad?

5. What is the **point of view** of the poem?
6. How does the speaker characterize his parents, himself, and his wife?
7. What was the one experience in his life that he could not endure?
8. How is this ballad like a short story?
9. Read the Comment article on this page. How many of the ballad characteristics does this poem have?

BIOGRAPHY

Stephen Vincent Benét

1898–1943

Stephen Vincent Benét's first volume of poems was published when he was seventeen, and in 1929 *John Brown's Body*, a long narrative poem on the Civil War, won a Pulitzer Prize for poetry. Many of his works display an intense feeling of patriotism.

Comment

Ballads

Poems that tell a story are called **narrative poems.** The earliest form of narrative poem, still popular today, is the folk **ballad.** The word *ballad* means "a simple song," "a story in verse." No one knows where or when folk ballads originated, but they have been sung for many hundreds of years. The authors of the old folk ballads are unknown, for ballads were sung long before printing was known. They were passed along from person to person and generation to generation and country to country.

The ballad has a quickly unfolding plot and a lively, lilting rhythm with a definite pattern. The old folk ballads usually treated a simple theme such as love, hate, and death.

Many modern authors have written ballads, styling them after the old folk ballad. When the author of a ballad is known, we call the work a **literary ballad.** You have already read one ballad. There are several more in this unit.

Nothing Gold Can Stay

Robert Frost

Nature's first green is gold,
Her hardest hue to hold.
Her early leaf's a flower;
But only so an hour.
5 Then leaf subsides to leaf.
So Eden sank to grief,
So dawn goes down to day.
Nothing gold can stay.

THINK AND DISCUSS

Understanding

1. The first line seems to be a contradiction. Think of the first new shoots of spring. What color are they?
2. What color is the dawn? What happens to dawn? (line 7)
3. Reread the title. What word could you substitute for *stay*?

Analyzing

4. In the biblical story in Genesis, Adam and Eve were driven from the Garden of Eden. How does this help explain line 6?

Extending

5. Think of something else that is gold-colored or gold. Does what you thought of "stay," or does it change?

BIOGRAPHY

Robert Frost
1874–1963

Long considered one of America's most important poets, Robert Frost was born in California but moved with his family to Massachusetts at the age of ten. Thus New England became the emotional background of Frost's poetic life. As a young man he attended Dartmouth College and Harvard but never graduated. He worked in a textile mill and at a number of odd jobs before settling down on a New Hampshire farm. Eleven years of farming and writing poetry brought little success, but then his first collection of poems was published in England, and he began to achieve recognition. During his life he received four Pulitzer Prizes, more than twenty honorary degrees, and numerous other awards.

Catalogue

Rosalie Moore

Cats sleep fat and walk thin.
Cats, when they sleep, slump;
When they wake, stretch and begin
Over, pulling their ribs in.
5 Cats walk thin.

Cats wait in a lump,
Jump in a streak.
Cats, when they jump, are sleek
As a grape slipping its skin—
10 They have technique.
Oh, cats don't creak.
They sneak.

Cats sleep fat.
They spread out comfort underneath them
15 Like a good mat,
As if they picked the place
And then sat;
You walk around one
As if he were the City Hall
20 After that.

If male,
A cat is apt to sing on a major scale;
This concert is for everybody, this
Is wholesale.
25 For a baton, he wields a tail.

(He is also found,
When happy, to resound
With an enclosed and private sound.)

A cat condenses.
30 He pulls in his tail to go under bridges,
And himself to go under fences.
Cats fit
In any size box or kit,
And if a large pumpkin grew under one,
35 He could arch over it.

When everyone else is just ready to go out,
The cat is just ready to come in.
He's not where he's been.
Cats sleep fat and walk thin.

Robert Amft, "Cat Tale"
Private Collection

THINK AND DISCUSS
Understanding
1. The speaker lists many habits of cats. Find lines in the poem that describe a cat's movements.
2. Find lines that describe a cat's personality.

Analyzing
3. What is the speaker describing in lines 26–28?
4. How does the speaker seem to feel about cats? What lines especially suggest these feelings?

 BIOGRAPHY

Rosalie Moore

1910–

Rosalie Moore and her husband, William Louis Brown, wrote several juvenile books under the names Bill and Rosalie Brown. When Moore wrote "Catalogue," her most reprinted poem, she had been trying to write about something else. But her cat, Jay Bird, sat either on her paper or on her typewriter. Every time she put him down, he simply climbed up again and sat there looking at her. Finally she decided to write about him.

Fifteen

William Stafford

South of the Bridge on Seventeenth
I found back of the willows one summer
day a motorcycle with engine running
as it lay on its side, ticking over
5 slowly in the high grass. I was fifteen.

I admired all that pulsing gleam, the
shiny flanks, the demure headlights
fringed where it lay; I led it gently
to the road and stood with that
10 companion, ready and friendly. I was fifteen.

We could find the end of a road, meet
the sky on out Seventeenth. I thought about
hills, and patting the handle got back a
confident opinion. On the bridge we indulged
15 a forward feeling, a tremble. I was fifteen.

Thinking, back farther in the grass I found
the owner, just coming to, where he had flipped
over the rail. He had blood on his hand, was pale—
I helped him walk to his machine. He ran his hand
20 over it, called me good man, roared away.

I stood there, fifteen.

Understanding

1. What is the **setting** in this poem?
2. From what point of view is the poem written?
3. What does the speaker find?

Analyzing

4. Summarize what the speaker does in each stanza of the poem.
5. Why do you think the line "I was fifteen" is repeated so many times in the poem?

Extending

6. If you had been the one to find the motorcycle, would you have been tempted to take it for a ride? Why or why not?
7. Can you think of a time when you, like the speaker in the poem, were inclined to follow a dream but did not? Explain.

BIOGRAPHY

William Stafford
1914–

Much of William Stafford's poetry is set in the Midwest and Northwest and conveys a distinct feeling of place; he describes his poetry as informal, almost narrative in style, "much like talk."

Born in Kansas in 1914, Stafford earned his B.A. and M.A. from the University of Kansas and his Ph.D. from the University of Iowa. He has received many awards for both poetry and prose, including the National Book Award for Poetry for *Traveling Through the Dark*.

Reading A POEM

Poetry is made from the things that concern all of us. Poems are written about universal experiences—love, hate, jealousy, fear, the drudgery of day-to-day existence, joy, delight. The four poems you have just read give you some idea of how varied poetry can be. In "The Ballad of William Sycamore," you heard the story of a man who might serve to represent an entire group of Americans—those who followed the frontier as it moved farther and farther west. Is William Sycamore a sympathetic character, one you can like and wish well? Is he an ancestor to be proud of? In "Nothing Gold Can Stay," Robert Frost creates a picture and through that picture makes a comment on the human condition. In "Catalogue" a creature common to everyday life is viewed in a way that makes readers take another look. In "Fifteen" a boy of that age finds a motorcycle—its motor running, ready to go—and you share that experience with him.

A poem's meaning is found not only in what a poet says but in how the poet says it. And no two voice their views in exactly the same way.

It is not easy to tell why a poet writes a particular poem. For a poet, it is natural to write, just as it is for a painter to paint and a composer to write music. Perhaps he or she felt compelled to write by an impression or a deeply felt experience. Or poets may want to share what they have seen and learned and thought about life. They have a longing, as we all do, to communicate with somebody who will understand.

In this unit, you will explore some of the ways poets achieve their purposes. They may use rhyme, rhythm, figurative language, imagery, and various sound devices. They may use symbols; that is, they will use one thing to stand for something else.

When you read a poem, begin by paying attention to the title, always a good clue to the meaning. Read the poem once, just to get the overall feel of it. Then reread it, noting any footnotes, and asking yourself as you read what the person who wrote the poem is telling you. Is the **author's purpose** to inspire you? to make you smile? to comfort you? to arouse a patriotic feeling? to share a view of nature? All these things are possible. Give a careful reading; don't decide too quickly.

Once you have determined author's purpose, you can make a judgment about whether the poem successfully carries out that purpose. In making a **judgment,** you look at all the information available and form an opinion based on that information. Again, a careful reading is a must—the poem itself contains the evidence you need.

Finally, you might be inspired to write your own poetry. Poems in this unit will help you see the many and varied forms poetry can take. And the article "How to Write a Poem" in the Writer's Handbook will give you a few pointers.

See RHYME in the Handbook of Literary Terms, page 682.

Concord Hymn

Ralph Waldo Emerson

On April 19, 1775, at Concord's North Bridge, farmers fired on
English troops for the second time that day; the first battle of the
Revolution had been in Lexington, only a few hours earlier and a few
miles away.

Sung at the Completion of the Battle Monument, July 4, 1837

By the rude bridge that arched the flood,
   Their flag to April's breeze unfurled,
Here once the embattled farmers stood
   And fired the shot heard round the world.

5 The foe long since in silence slept;
   Alike the conqueror silent sleeps;
And Time the ruined bridge has swept
   Down the dark stream which seaward creeps.

On this green bank, by this soft stream,
10   We set today a votive stone;
That memory may their deed redeem,
   When, like our sires, our sons are gone.

Spirit, that made those heroes dare
   To die, and leave their children free,
15 Bid Time and Nature gently spare
   The shaft we raise to them and thee.

"The Concord Hymn" by Ralph Waldo Emerson (1837).

Ralph Earle, "The Battle of Lexington, April 19, 1775" (copper engraving by Amos Doolittle)
Chicago Historical Society

THINK AND DISCUSS
Understanding
1. The purpose of each stanza in this poem is somewhat different. What is the purpose of stanza one?
2. In stanza two, what does the speaker say has happened?
3. What does the speaker wish for in stanza four?

Analyzing
4. *Votive* means "done or given because of a vow or solemn promise." To whom does "their" in line 11 refer? Why would they need a votive stone?
5. Line 4 has become a famous line. In what way is the meaning of this statement possible?

Extending
6. Why would this hymn have been sung on July 4?
7. There are many monuments in the United States to honor those who died in war. In what other ways do we honor war dead?

APPLYING: Rhyme   H2
See Handbook of Literary Terms, p. 682.
   End **rhymes** set up in a definite pattern of sounds are called **rhyme schemes**. What is the rhyme scheme of "Concord Hymn"?

Review RHYME in the Handbook of Literary Terms, page 682

The Wreck of the Hesperus

Henry Wadsworth Longfellow

This literary ballad may have been a favorite of your parents, your grandparents, and your great-grandparents! See if you can tell why. It was inspired by a newspaper account of an actual wreck.

It was the schooner Hesperus,[1]
    That sailed the wintry sea;
And the skipper had taken his
    little daughter,
    To bear him company.

5 Blue were her eyes as the fairy-flax,[2]
    Her cheeks like the dawn of day,
And her bosom white as the
    hawthorn buds,
    That ope in the month of May.

The skipper he stood beside the helm,
10   His pipe was in his mouth,
And he watched how the veering flaw
    did blow
    The smoke now West, now South.

Then up and spake an old Sailòr,
    Had sailed to the Spanish Main,
15 "I pray thee, put into yonder port,
    For I fear a hurricane.

"Last night, the moon had a golden ring,
    And tonight no moon we see!"
The skipper, he blew a whiff from his pipe,
20   And a scornful laugh laughed he.

Colder and louder blew the wind,
    A gale from the Northeast,
The snow fell hissing in the brine,
    And the billows frothed like yeast.

25 Down came the storm, and smote amain
    The vessel in its strength;
She shuddered and paused,
    like a frighted steed,
    Then leaped her cable's length.

"Come hither! come hither! my little
    daughter,
30   And do not tremble so;
For I can weather the roughest gale
    That ever wind did blow."

1. *Hesperus* (hes'pər əs).
2. *fairy-flax*, a flowering herb.

He wrapped her warm in his seaman's coat
    Against the stinging blast;
35 He cut a rope from a broken spar,
    And bound her to the mast.

"O father! I hear the church-bells ring,
    Oh say, what may it be?"
"'T is a fog bell on a rock-bound coast!"—
40   And he steered for the open sea.

"O father! I hear the sound of guns,
    Oh say, what may it be?"
"Some ship in distress, that cannot live
    In such an angry sea!"

45 "O father! I see a gleaming light,
    Oh say, what may it be?"
But the father answered never a word,
    A frozen corpse was he.

Lashed to the helm, all stiff and stark,
50   With his face turned to the skies,
The lantern gleamed through the
        gleaming snow
    On his fixed and glassy eyes.

Then the maiden clasped her hands
        and prayed
    That saved she might be;
55 And she thought of Christ, who stilled the
        wave
    On the Lake of Galilee.

And fast through the midnight
        dark and drear,
    Through the whistling sleet and snow,
Like a sheeted ghost, the vessel swept
60   Tow'rds the reef of Norman's Woe.

And ever the fitful gusts between
    A sound came from the land;
It was the sound of the trampling surf
    On the rocks and the hard sea-sand.

65 The breakers were right beneath her bows,
    She drifted a dreary wreck,
And a whooping billow swept the crew
    Like icicles from her deck.

She struck where the white and
        fleecy waves
70   Looked soft as carded wool,
But the cruel rocks, they gored her side
    Like the horns of an angry bull.

Her rattling shrouds, all sheathed in ice,
    With the masts went by the board;
75 Like a vessel of glass, she stove[3] and sank,
    Ho! ho! the breakers roared!

At daybreak, on the bleak sea-beach,
    A fisherman stood aghast,
To see the form of a maiden fair,
80   Lashed close to a drifting mast.

The salt sea was frozen on her breast,
    The salt tears in her eyes;
And he saw her hair, like the brown
        sea-weed,
    On the billows fall and rise.

85 Such was the wreck of the Hesperus,
    In the midnight and the snow!
Christ save us all from a death like this,
    On the reef of Norman's Woe!

---

3. *stove*, broke a hole in.

THINK AND DISCUSS
Understanding
1. Briefly, retell the **plot** of this ballad.

Analyzing
2. When does the climax occur?
3. Why do you think the skipper doesn't pay attention to the old Sailor's warnings?
4. What do you think was the author's purpose in writing this ballad?

Extending
5. Can you account for the popularity of this poem? If so, how?

REVIEWING: Rhyme HT
See Handbook of Literary Terms, p. 682.

This **rhyme scheme,** or pattern of sounds, is somewhat different from those of the other poems you have read so far. What is the rhyme scheme?

VOCABULARY
Context
Many of the words in "The Concord Hymn" have more than one meaning. In order to understand the words as used in the poem, you must pay attention to context. On your paper, write the letter of the correct meaning of each word, as it is used in the poem.

1. *rude:* (**a**) impolite; (**b**) roughly made or done
2. *flood:* (**a**) great flow of water over what is usually dry land; (**b**) large amount of water; ocean, sea, lake, or river
3. *flag:* (**a**) get tired; grow weak; (**b**) flagstone; (**c**) piece of cloth attached by one end to a staff
4. *bank:* (**a**) small container with a slot through which coins can be dropped; (**b**) a long pile or heap; (**c**) rising ground bordering a lake or river
5. *spare:* (**a**) refrain from harming or destroying; (**b**) thin; lean; (**c**) in reserve; extra

THINKING SKILLS
Generalizing
Longfellow and Emerson lived during the same period in American history, and both were extremely popular in their lifetime. Based on the two poems you have just read, can you make any generalizations about the kinds of poetry that people in nineteenth-century America liked to read?

COMPOSITION
Writing a Rhyme
The first stanza of "Concord Hymn" is engraved on the base of the monument. Assume that you have been asked to write four lines in honor of a person, place, or event. These lines will appear on a monument. Your rhyme scheme, or pattern, should be *abab*.

Writing About an Event
Read current newspapers to find an article you consider especially interesting. Use the events from the article as the subject for a story or poem.

BIOGRAPHIES

Ralph Waldo Emerson 1803–1882

Born in Boston, Ralph Waldo Emerson grew up in a poverty-stricken family. His father, a minister, died when Emerson was young. He was able to attend Harvard, however, and in 1829 he became associate pastor at the Unitarian Second Church in Boston and married Ellen Tucker. In 1832 his wife and two of his brothers died. Deeply grieved by these events, he traveled abroad for a while.

In 1835 he remarried and moved to Concord, where he read, wrote, prepared lectures, and influenced others in Transcendentalism, a philosophy popular in New England during the 1830s.

In the 1840s and 1850s, Emerson was in great demand as a lecturer. In a journal entry dated Kalamazoo, Michigan, February 1860, he wrote "My chief adventure was the necessity of riding in a buggy forty-eight miles to Grand Rapids; then, after the lecture, twenty more on the return; and the next morning getting back to Kalamazoo in time for the train at twelve. So I saw Michigan and its forests and wolverines pretty thoroughly."

One of his most famous essays is "Self-Reliance," which contains the famous line: "Trust thyself: every heart vibrates to that iron string."

Henry Wadsworth Longfellow 1807–1882

Emerson and Longfellow both lived at about the same time. During his lifetime, Longfellow was probably the best-loved of all American poets. He wrote chiefly about nature, family, and patriotism.

Longfellow was born in Portland, Maine, was educated at Bowdoin College and abroad, and taught both at Bowdoin and at Harvard. His poems about Paul Revere, Miles Standish, John and Priscilla Alden, and Hiawatha were once known to every schoolchild.

See RHYTHM in the Handbook of Literary Terms, page 683

The Highwayman

Alfred Noyes

Part One:

The wind was a torrent of darkness among the gusty trees;
The moon was a ghostly galleon tossed upon cloudy seas;
The road was a ribbon of moonlight over the purple moor;
And the highwayman came riding—
5   Riding—riding—
The highwayman came riding, up to the old inn door.

He'd a French cocked hat on his forehead, a bunch of lace at his chin,
A coat of the claret velvet, and breeches of brown doeskin;
They fitted with never a wrinkle; his boots were up to the thigh!
10 And he rode with a jeweled twinkle,
    His pistol butts a-twinkle,
His rapier hilt a-twinkle, under the jeweled sky.

Over the cobbles he clattered and clashed in the dark inn yard;
And he tapped with his whip on the shutters, but all was locked and barred;
15 He whistled a tune to the window, and who should be waiting there
But the landlord's black-eyed daughter,
    Bess, the landlord's daughter,
Plaiting a dark red love knot into her long black hair.

And dark in the dark old inn yard a stable-wicket creaked
20 Where Tim the ostler listened; his face was white and peaked;
His eyes were hollows of madness, his hair like moldy hay,
But he loved the landlord's daughter,
    The landlord's red-lipped daughter;
Dumb as a dog he listened, and he heard the robber say—

25 "One kiss, my bonny sweetheart; I'm after a prize tonight;
But I shall be back with the yellow gold before the morning light;
Yet, if they press me sharply, and harry me through the day,
Then look for me by moonlight,
    Watch for me by moonlight,
30 I'll come to thee by moonlight, though hell should bar the way."

He rose upright in the stirrups; he scarce could reach her hand,
But she loosened her hair i' the casement! His face burned like a brand
As the black cascade of perfume came tumbling over his breast;
And he kissed its waves in the moonlight
35   (Oh, sweet black waves in the moonlight!);
Then he tugged at his rein in the moonlight, and galloped away to the West.

Part Two:
He did not come in the dawning; he did not come at noon;
And out o' the tawny sunset, before the rise o' the moon,
When the road was a gypsy's ribbon, looping the purple moor,
40 A redcoat troop came marching—
    Marching—marching—
King George's men came marching, up to the old inn door.

They said no word to the landlord; they drank his ale instead;
But they gagged his daughter and bound her to the foot of her narrow bed;
45 Two of them knelt at her casement, with muskets at their side!
There was death at every window,
    And hell at one dark window,
For Bess could see, through her casement, the road that *he* would ride.

                                                              (Continued)

Alfred Noyes 289

Photograph by Dan Morrill

They had tied her up to attention, with many a sniggering jest;
50 They had bound a musket beside her, with the barrel beneath her breast!
"Now keep good watch!" and they kissed her.
She heard the dead man say:
Look for me by moonlight,
   Watch for me by moonlight,
55 *I'll come to thee by moonlight, though hell should bar the way!*

She twisted her hands behind her, but all the knots held good!
She writhed her hands till her fingers were wet with sweat or blood!
They stretched and strained in the darkness, and the hours crawled by like years,
Till, now, on the stroke of midnight,
60   Cold on the stroke of midnight,
The tip of one finger touched it! The trigger at least was hers!

The tip of one finger touched it; she strove no more for the rest!
Up she stood, to attention, with the barrel beneath her breast.
She would not risk their hearing; she would not strive again;
65 For the road lay bare in the moonlight,
   Blank and bare in the moonlight,
And the blood of her veins in the moonlight throbbed to her love's refrain.

Tlot-tlot; tlot-tlot! Had they heard it? The horse-hoofs ringing clear;
Tlot-tlot, tlot-tlot, in the distance! Were they deaf that they did not hear?
70 Down the ribbon of moonlight, over the brow of the hill,
The highwayman came riding—
   Riding—riding—
The redcoats looked to their priming! She stood up, straight and still!

Tlot-tlot, in the frosty silence! *Tlot-tlot,* in the echoing night!
75 Nearer he came and nearer! Her face was like a light!
Her eyes grew wide for a moment; she drew one last deep breath;
Then her finger moved in the moonlight,
   Her musket shattered the moonlight,
Shattered her breast in the moonlight and warned him—with her death.

(Continued)

80 He turned; he spurred to the westward; he did not know who stood
Bowed, with her head o'er the musket, drenched with her own red blood!
Not till the dawn he heard it; and slowly blanched to hear
How Bess, the landlord's daughter,
   The landlord's black-eyed daughter,
85 Had watched for her love in the moonlight, and died in the darkness there.

Back he spurred like a madman, shrieking a curse to the sky,
With the white road smoking behind him, and his rapier brandished high!
Blood-red were his spurs i' the golden noon; wine-red was his velvet coat,
When they shot him down on the highway,
90   Down like a dog on the highway,
And he lay in his blood on the highway, with the bunch of lace at his throat.

And still of a winter's night, they say, when the wind is in the trees,
When the moon is a ghostly galleon tossed upon cloudy seas,
When the road is a ribbon of moonlight over the purple moor,
95 *A highwayman comes riding—*
   Riding—riding—
A highwayman comes riding, up to the old inn door.

Over the cobbles he clatters and clangs in the dark inn yard;
And he taps with his whip on the shutters, but all is locked and barred;
100 *He whistles a tune to the window, and who should be waiting there*
But the landlord's black-eyed daughter,
   Bess, the landlord's daughter,
Plaiting a dark red love knot into her long black hair.

THINK AND DISCUSS

Understanding

1. What is the **setting** of the poem?
2. What are the major incidents in the plot?

Analyzing

3. What methods does the author use to characterize Bess, Tim, and the highwayman?
4. How do you infer the king's soldiers have learned where to set their trap to capture the highwayman?

Extending

5. Why do you think the last two stanzas are printed in italic type?

APPLYING: Rhythm HT
See Handbook of Literary Terms, p. 683.

Rhythm is a series of stressed and unstressed sounds in a group of words. Rhythm may be regular or it may be varied.

1. Read aloud the first stanza to get a sense of the rhythm of the whole poem. What sounds are suggested by the rhythm of lines 4–6?
2. Is the rhythm regular or irregular?
3. Does the rhythm seem appropriate to the meaning of the poem? Explain.

Comment

Highwaymen, Footpads, and Rufflers

If you were a wealthy person in eighteenth-century England, a journey of any kind could be an extremely dangerous venture. The streets and roads about London were infested with highwaymen, footpads (highwaymen without horses), and rufflers (today we would call them "muggers"). Highway robbery was an almost daily occurrence. The outlaws grew so bold, according to one source, that they once posted notices on the doors of the rich, warning everyone who ventured out of town to carry at least ten gold coins and a watch—or risk a penalty of death.

During this "golden age of crime" a Prime Minister, the Prince of Wales, and the Lord Mayor of London all had expensive encounters with robbers. Queen Anne once narrowly missed an ambush when her coach was delayed: a waiting band of highwaymen attacked another coach by mistake. A later monarch, George II, was not so fortunate. While walking in Kensington Gardens, he was confronted by a lone highwayman and was forced to give up his money, his watch, and the buckles of his shoes.

In a time when organized police forces were unheard of, the principal means of fighting crime was to offer large rewards for the capture of criminals. An unfortunate side effect of this system was that it made possible the extraordinary double career of Jonathan Wild. On one hand, Wild was a master criminal, plotting thefts, receiving stolen goods. On the other hand, Wild was the most successful "thief-taker" of all, and made an additional profit by returning stolen goods to their owners— for a fee. If a thief objected to Wild's leadership, he was quickly betrayed to the authorities, and Wild pocketed another reward. Like many of the highwaymen he dealt with, Wild eventually finished his career at the end of a rope, betrayed in his own turn.

There are many obvious parallels between the highwaymen of eighteenth-century England and the outlaws of the American West. A further parallel exists in the mysterious process by which brutal and greedy men of both eras have become figures of folklore and legend.

Women

Alice Walker

They were women then
My mama's generation
Husky of voice—Stout of
Step
5 With fists as well as
Hands
How they battered down
Doors
And ironed
10 Starched white
Shirts
How they led
Armies
Headragged Generals
15 Across mined
Fields
Booby-trapped
Ditches
To discover books
20 Desks
A place for us
How they knew what we
Must know
Without knowing a page
25 Of it
Themselves.

I shall write of the old men I knew
And the young men
I loved
30 And of the gold toothed women
Mighty of arm
Who dragged us all
To church.

Charles White, "Oh, Mary, Don't You Weep," 1956
Collection of Harry Belafonte

THINK AND DISCUSS
Understanding
1. What physical characteristics do the women have?

Analyzing
2. What does the speaker mean by saying the women had "fists as well as/ Hands"?
3. Who are the "Headragged Generals"?
4. For what reason have the women "battered down/Doors" and "led/Armies . . . Across mined/Fields"?
5. What is meant by lines 22–26?
6. Is the speaker's attitude toward these women admiring or critical, grateful or resentful? Explain.

Extending
7. Do you think the women of the speaker's generation will need to be as strong as their mothers were, or have their mothers already fought and won most of the battles for them?

REVIEWING: Rhythm HT
See Handbook of Literary Terms, p. 683.
Rhythm is a series of stressed and unstressed sounds. Reread "Women" aloud. Is the rhythm regular or varied?

The Texas Rangers

Traditional

Come all ye Texas Rangers wherever you may be,
I'll tell you of some troubles that happened unto me.
My name is nothin' extry and that I will not tell,
So here's to all you rangers, I'm sure I wish you well.

5 Was at the age of seventeen I joined the jolly band.
We marched from San Antonio down to the Rio Grande.
The captain he informed us, I guess he thought it right,
Before we reach the station we'll surely have to fight.

And when the bugles sounded, our captain gave command.
10 "To arms, to arms," he shouted, "and by your horses stand."
I saw the smoke ascending, it seemed to reach the sky,
And then the thought it struck me, my time had come to die.

I saw the Indians coming, I heard them give a yell.
My feelings at that moment no tongue can ever tell.
15 I saw their glittering lances, the arrows round me flew,
And all my strength it left me, and all my courage, too.

We fought for nine hours fully before the strife was o'er.
The like of dead and wounded I never saw before.
And when the smoke had risen and the Indians they had fled
20 We loaded up our rifles and counted up our dead.

And all of us were wounded, the noble captain slain.
The sun was shining sadly across the bloody plain.
Sixteen as brave a rangers as ever roamed the West
Were buried by their comrades with arrows in their breast.

25 And now my song is ended, I guess I sung enough.
The life of any ranger, you see, is very tough.
And if you have a mother who don't want you to roam,
I'll advise you by experience, you'd better stay at home.

THINK AND DISCUSS
Understanding
1. From whose point of view is the story told?
2. Briefly describe the events in the story.

Analyzing
3. What is the **rhyme scheme?**
4. Does the poem have a regular or varied **rhythm?** How do rhyme and rhythm contribute to the poem?

Extending
5. Reread lines 11–16. Does this seem to you an accurate description? Explain.

READING LITERATURE SKILLFULLY
Judgments
The purpose of a ballad is to tell a story, and most ballads deal with basic issues such as death, love, or hate. Make a **judgment** about "The Texas Rangers" by answering these questions.
1. The speaker tells us he isn't famous (line 3). Why then does he tell his story?

2. Find at least three examples in the poem of specific words and phrases that help you to visualize the action.
3. How does the speaker feel about his fellow rangers?
4. Is the poem successful in telling its story? Explain.

COMPOSITION ✒
Writing a Monologue
Imagine that you are Tim the ostler. It is after the events of "The Highwayman," and you are sitting alone in the stable yard. Write a one-page monologue, or speech to be spoken aloud to yourself, in which you review the events of the poem, tell what part in them you played, and describe your feelings now.

Writing to Compare and Contrast
Both "The Highwayman" and "Texas Rangers" tell a story. In what other ways are these poems alike? How are they different? Write a two-paragraph composition in which you compare and contrast the poems.

BIOGRAPHIES

Alfred Noyes 1880–1958

Alfred Noyes was born in Staffordshire, England. While still in his twenties, he became a successful poet, and he continued writing both poetry and prose throughout his life. Before his death in 1958, he wrote about "The Highwayman." "'The Highwayman' was written on the actual scene where the Golden Farmer, Jerry Abershaw, and other highwaymen used to lie in wait for the stagecoaches, about thirty miles from London. I was only just down from Oxford at the time and had taken rooms in a little cottage on the edge of the heath, which was still as unspoiled a bit of wild country as it was in the eighteenth century. I had gone there to finish my longer poem on Sir Francis Drake, who is himself sometimes described as a great buccaneer. But one night the wind blowing through the pines and the clatter of a horse's hoofs on the roads gave me the first line of 'The Highwayman'—'The wind was a torrent of darkness among the gusty trees.'

"The poem was written in a few hours, and shortly afterwards appeared in *Blackwood's Magazine*.

"The point of the poem is not that the highwayman was a highwayman, but that the heroine was a heroine."

Alice Walker 1944–

Alice Walker is known for her powerful portrayal of the experience of black people, especially families, in America. Her writing has been called "candid," "truthful," and "convincing." She is the author of a number of poetry and short story collections and novels. In 1983 her novel *The Color Purple* received an American Book Award and a Pulitzer Prize. Later, it was made into a film, starring Whoopie Goldberg.

Alice Walker grew up in Georgia, one of eight children of hardworking farmers. Since graduating from Sarah Lawrence College in 1965, she has done social work and has taught writing and black literature at several colleges and universities.

Writer's Craft

Appeal to the Senses

All writers want readers to experience their writing as fully as possible. And good writers help us do this by using words that appeal to one of the five senses.

The lines that follow are from the poems you just read. To what senses do they appeal?

But I remember a coonskin cap
And the smell of bayberry candles

Cats wait in a lump

By the rude bridge that arched the flood,
Their flag to April's breeze unfurled

The snow fell hissing on the brine,
And the billows frothed like yeast.

When you read "The Wreck of the Hesperus," you learned that Longfellow got the idea for the poem from a newspaper article about an actual occurrence. The poet imagined the horror of that night, and he wrote a poem that allows readers to feel it still. One reason for his success is that he used words and images that appeal to the senses.

The newspaper account probably told who, what, where, when, and how. What would such an account be like compared to the poem? Longfellow, by appealing to the senses, allows readers to see, hear, feel, taste, and smell—to be there for the event that he found so moving. We see the skipper's daughter, with "cheeks like the dawn of day." We taste and feel the salty, "stinging blast" of the storm's winds. We hear and see the snow fall "hissing on the brine." Later we see the lantern shining "through the gleaming snow on the fixed and glassy eyes" of the dead skipper. A "whooping billow" sweeps the frozen crew "like icicles from the deck" into the sea.

Note how Alfred Noyes appeals to readers' senses in "The Highwayman." We see Tim the stable lad, with his "white peaked face," his eyes that are "hollows of madness," and his hair "like moldy hay." We, like the landlord's daughter, hear "the horse-hoofs ringing clear." And we see the highwayman, dead on the road: "He lay in his blood on the highway, with the bunch of lace at his throat."

Although modern poetry may contain less description, it too makes use of words that appeal to the senses. Reread Alice Walker's "Women," noting how sensory words such as *husky, stout, battered, fists, mighty of arm,* help us to see and know the people to whom she pays tribute.

Because poems are, as a rule, shorter than other types of writing, poets put words that appeal to the senses to especially good use. Such words allow them to create pictures and impressions in very little space. However, these words can be found in good writing of all types.

When you read, look for words that
appeal to the senses.
When you write, use words that
appeal to the senses.

See SIMILE in the Handbook of Literary Terms, page 688

How Tuesday Began

Kathleen Fraser

Don't let me lose you,
lady. We're jogging up
First Avenue in the sun,
nursing morning with
5 our habits.
I must have boarded before
you, where the bus stops
and the dusty nightgowns
beckon from Orchard St.
10 I must have pulled out
my book, peeled off my gloves,
and settled among the fumes
for a poem or two,
my habit.
15 I didn't see you,
black, filling the aisle
with your green housedress,
lowering each part of you
gently, in front of me,
20 maybe heaving a sigh, your
sorrow and habit.
Still, my eyes pulled
sideways. Someone old
moved without moving,
25 veins, vague eyes resisting
the aisle in front
of her, a journey
to be mastered upright,
seat by seat.

30 We rolled with the bus,
easy as rubber lifeboats
on troubled water.
But she hung to the same
space, sensing the movement
35 around her, sinking
in her own flesh.
Then you reached out, lady,
and pulled her in
beside you.
40 You were fading
and full of troubles, lady,
and you saw her drowning
and you reached out
and said, "I don't see
45 so good myself."

Richard Estes, "Bus Reflections," 1972
Private Collection

THINK AND DISCUSS
Understanding
1. What is the **setting**—both time and place—of this poem?
2. What is the speaker's "habit" (line 14)?
3. How is the black woman described (lines 15–21)?
4. Describe the progress of the old woman (lines 23–36). What does the black woman do?

Analyzing
5. Has the action of the black woman affected the speaker in any particular way? How can you tell?

Extending
6. Do you think the title of this poem is appropriate? Why or why not?

APPLYING: Simile H⊅
See Handbook of Literary Terms, p. 688.
A **simile** is a figure of speech that involves a direct comparison between two unlike things, usually with the words *like* or *as*.
1. Note the simile in lines 30–32. Who are the "We" in line 30?
2. What two things are being compared? Is this an effective comparison? Explain.

Kathleen Fraser 301

Review SIMILE in the Handbook of Literary Terms, page 688

The Base Stealer

Robert Francis

Poised between going on and back, pulled
Both ways taut like a tightrope-walker,
Fingertips pointing the opposites,
Now bouncing tiptoe like a dropped ball
5 Or a kid skipping rope, come on, come on,
Running a scattering of steps sidewise,
How he teeters, skitters, tingles, teases,
Taunts them, hovers like an ecstatic bird,
He's only flirting, crowd him, crowd him,
10 Delicate, delicate, delicate, delicate—now!

THINK AND DISCUSS

Understanding

1. How does the title help explain what is happening in the poem?

Analyzing

2. Does the speaker in the poem seem to be expressing anger, indifference, admiration, or amusement toward the base stealer? How can you tell?

3. The phrases "come on" and "crowd him" are each repeated twice, and the word *delicate* is repeated four times. What effect do these repetitions have on the sense of the poem? At the final word *now!* what is happening?

Extending

4. If you had never seen a person trying to steal a base during a baseball game, could you understand the process after reading this poem? Explain.

REVIEWING: Simile

See Handbook of Literary Terms, p. 688.

A **simile** is a direct comparison using *like* or *as*, between two basically unlike things.

Think of a tightrope walker with arms outstretched for balance, delicately "poised between going on and back" and "pulled both ways taut" by being ready to move in any direction at an instant. Now mentally compare the tightrope walker with a baseball player trying to steal a base, "poised" and "pulled" in a similar way. Like most other figurative language, a simile can provide fresh insight into an idea or subject by giving the reader a new way of looking at something—in this case, the base stealer's acrobatic artistry.

1. What two similes in the poem describe the base stealer's bouncing on tip-toe?
2. What kind of movement is suggested by "hovers like an ecstatic bird"?

COMPOSITION
Describing an Event

The speaker in "How Tuesday Began" describes an event that lasted only a few seconds, yet made a lasting impression.

Think of an event in your experience that did the same thing. Then write either a poem or a short composition describing this event. Use two similes in your description.

Writing an Explanation

Choose a sport with which you are very familiar. Assume you must explain that sport to someone who now knows nothing about it. Your purpose is to give that person enough information to allow him or her to watch the sport with understanding and enjoyment. Narrow your topic by choosing something about the sport that you can explain in one or two paragraphs— how a player steals a base, for example. Then write your explanation.

BIOGRAPHIES

Kathleen Fraser 1937–

Author of several books of poetry for both children and adults, Kathleen Fraser has also taught poetry and creative writing in New York, at the University of Iowa, and in San Francisco.

Robert Francis 1901–1987

For over forty years Robert Francis lived in a two-room home in Amherst, Massachusetts, where he produced essays, poetry, fiction, and an autobiography, *The Trouble with Francis*. "My speciality has been not to earn much but to spend little," he once told an interviewer. After graduating from Harvard, he taught high school for one year and then devoted his life to writing poetry. In his honor, the University of Massachusetts Press established the Juniper Prize for poetry. In 1984 he was awarded the ten-thousand-dollar Fellowship of the Academy of American Poets.

See METAPHOR in the Handbook of Literary Terms, page 674

The clouds pass

Richard Garcia

The clouds pass in a blue sky
Too white to be true
Before winter sets in
The trees are spending all their money

5 I lie in gold
Above a green valley
Gold falls on my chest
I am a rich man.

Thomas Hart Benton, "Autumn" (detail)
Whitney Museum of American Art

THINK AND DISCUSS
Understanding
1. At what time of year is the poem set? How can you tell?

Analyzing
2. Why might the speaker say that he is rich?
3. What emotions does he seem to be feeling?

APPLYING: Metaphor
See Handbook of Literary Terms, p. 674.
   A **metaphor** is a figure of speech that involves an implied comparison between two relatively unlike things. What two activities are being compared in the metaphor in line 4?

METAPHOR

 Review METAPHOR in the Handbook of Literary Terms, page 674

I'll Walk the Tightrope

Margaret Danner

I'll walk the tightrope that's been stretched for me,
and though a wrinkled forehead, perplexed why,
will accompany me, I'll delicately
step along. For if I stop to sigh
5 at the earth-propped stride
of others, I will fall. I must balance high
without a parasol to tide
a faltering step, without a net below,
without a balance stick to guide.

"I'll Walk the Tightrope" by Margaret Danner. Reprinted by permission of Naomi Washington, for the Estate of Margaret Danner.

THINK AND DISCUSS
Understanding
1. What is a tightrope? Where does one usually see a tightrope walker?
2. The speaker mentions three things that tightrope walkers usually have. What are they?

Analyzing
3. Does the speaker have these three things? Does this make the situation less or more dangerous?
4. Is the speaker literally on a tightrope? Explain.

Extending
5. Have you ever been in a situation where you felt you were on a tightrope? What caused this situation?

REVIEWING: Metaphor

See Handbook of Literary Terms, p. 674.

A **metaphor** is a figure of speech that involves an implied comparison between two relatively unlike things.

1. This poem is really one long metaphor. Do you think the speaker means walking on a tightrope to be a metaphor for a particular situation in life or for all of life?
2. What does line 1 indicate about the speaker's feelings? What does line 2 indicate about the speaker's feelings?
3. Does the speaker feel that everyone is a tightrope walker? Explain.

COMPOSITION

Creating Metaphors

Imagine that you are in one of your favorite places. Write at least two metaphors that describe it. You might begin by thinking of what you hear, see, touch, taste, or smell in that place.

Writing About Poetry

Look at the poems you have already read in this unit for one containing metaphors. In a short composition, discuss the use of metaphor in this poem and whether each metaphor is effective. Before you begin, review "Writing About Poetry" in the Writer's Handbook.

BIOGRAPHY

Margaret Danner

1915–1984

Poet and teacher, Margaret Danner grew up in Chicago and for a time worked as an editor on the magazine, *Poetry*. In 1960 she became the first poet-in-residence at Wayne State University in Michigan. She also founded Boone House, a poetry and art center for black artists, at Wayne State.

See IMAGERY in the Handbook of Literary Terms, page 670

Snow Sculpture

Margaret Tsuda

There is nothing about
a snowplow
to suggest a
sculptor's mallet and chisel.
5 Nor does the
driver appear
unusually gifted.

Yet,
tutored by
10 rhythms of
sun-melt and
night-freeze,
blocks and mounds
heaped up by the
15 plow's dogged efforts
assume
shapes and forms
fantastic and beautiful,
abstract or figure-evoking,
20 turning both sides
of each street into
sculpture gardens.

Margaret Tsuda (tsü′dä).

"Snow Sculpture" from *Cry Love Aloud* by Margaret Tsuda.
Copyright © 1972 by Margaret Tsuda. Reprinted by permission.

THINK AND DISCUSS
Understanding
1. What materials and tools does a sculptor use? (line 4)

Analyzing
2. How is the snowplow like a sculptor's tool?
3. What do "sunmelt" and "night-freeze," accomplish?

Extending
4. What other large, powerful machines have you seen that do beautiful work? Suggest **similes** to describe their appearance or the work they do.

APPLYING: Imagery
See Handbook of Literary Terms, p. 670.
Imagery refers to concrete details that appeal to the senses. By using specific images, authors establish mood (the overall feeling in a literary work) and arouse emotion in their readers. To what sense does the imagery in this poem appeal?

Review IMAGERY in the Handbook of Literary Terms, page 670

Jukebox Showdown

Victor Hernández Cruz

Two men got into a fight with a jukebox
The air was night and warm
Splattered all over the avenue
Was screws and bolts
5 Broken 45's all over the place
The police came and arrested all three
The police asked the jukebox questions
Then dropped quarters in

Victor Hernández (er nän′des) *Cruz* (krüs).

Originally entitled "Side 15" by Victor Hernández Cruz. Copyright © 1976 by Victor Hernández Cruz. Reprinted by permission.

THINK AND DISCUSS
Understanding
1. What is the setting of this poem?

Analyzing
2. Why might the men have gotten into a fight with the jukebox?
3. Why do the police drop quarters in the jukebox?

Extending
4. Have you ever felt like "fighting" with a machine? Explain.

REVIEWING: Imagery HT
See Handbook of Literary Terms, p. 670.
   Imagery refers to concrete details that appeal to the senses of sight, sound, taste, touch, smell, and to internal feelings.
1. In descriptions of fights, what is usually "splattered all over"? To what would "45's" refer?
2. Contrast the images in this poem with those you created as you answered question 1.
3. What emotions does this poem arouse?

California Hills in August

Dana Gioia

I can imagine someone who found
these fields unbearable, who climbed
the hillside in the heat, cursing the dust,
cracking the brittle weeds underfoot,
5 wishing a few more trees for shade.

An Easterner especially, who would scorn
the meagreness of summer, the dry
twisted shapes of black elm,
scrub oak, and chaparral—a landscape
10 August has already drained of green.

One who would hurry over the clinging
thistle, foxtail, golden poppy,
knowing everything was just a weed,
unable to conceive that these trees
15 and sparse brown bushes were alive.

And hate the bright stillness of the noon,
without wind, without motion,
the only other living thing
a hawk, hungry for prey, suspended
20 in the blinding, sunlit blue.

And yet how gentle it seems to someone
raised in a landscape short of rain—
the skyline of a hill broken by no more
trees than one can count, the grass,
25 the empty sky, the wish for water.

Zoltan Szabo, "Thistle"
Private Collection

Gioia (joy′ə).

Reprinted by permission; © 1982 Dana Gioia. Originally in *The New Yorker*.

THINK AND DISCUSS
Understanding
1. What kinds of things does the speaker mention in describing the hills?
2. In what kind of landscape was the speaker raised?

Analyzing
3. How does the speaker seem to feel about the landscape described?
4. To what sense or senses do the images in this poem appeal?

READING LITERATURE SKILLFULLY
Author's Purpose
An author may write to amuse, to inspire, to praise, or for countless other reasons. Answer these questions about **author's purpose** in the poem you just read.
1. What is your overall impression of the landscape described?
2. Why do you think you have reacted this way?

COMPOSITION ◆━▶
Reading/Writing Log
Skim several of the poems you have read so far in this unit, and then list in your reading/writing log all the words or phrases in them that appeal to the senses. After each word or phrase, tell the sense or senses appealed to. One poem has been done for you.

Words That Appeal to the Senses
"Snow Sculpture"
sun-melt (touch, sight)
night-freeze (touch, sight)
blocks and mounds heaped up (sight)
shapes and forms fantastic and beautiful (sight)
abstract or figure-evoking (sight)
sculpture gardens (sight, touch)

Writing a Description
In a two- or three-paragraph composition, describe a scene you know well and enjoy but which might not appeal to everyone. Use images to help your audience (your classmates) appreciate what you see. Review your reading/writing log before you begin this composition.

Writing a Dialogue
Write an imaginary dialogue between a police officer and the jukebox after the fight in "Jukebox Showdown." The questions of the officer should be serious and straightforward; the answers from the jukebox should consist of appropriate titles or lyrics from current popular songs. (This assignment might be written as a group project, with each member contributing one or more questions and answers, which are then combined to form the dialogue.)

BIOGRAPHIES

Margaret Tsuda

Margaret Tsuda was born and raised in New York City, studied fine arts at Hunter College, and later made a career in textile design. She began publishing poetry in 1969. In much of her work, Tsuda forms thoughtful impressions of city life, looking beyond the dull, impersonal atmosphere to find scenes of simple beauty. Her poems, which have been translated into many languages, are collected in *Cry Love Aloud* and *Urban River*. The ink drawings with which she illustrates her own books reflect her heritage as a Nisei (one of the first generation of Japanese-Americans to be born in this country).

Victor Hernández Cruz 1949–

Born in Puerto Rico, Victor Hernández Cruz came to New York City at an early age. He lived in New York until he joined the English Department of the University of California at Berkeley. His poems have appeared in many publications, and he has published several collections of his work.

Dana Gioia 1950–

Dana Gioia successfully combines careers in business and writing. He is an executive at General Foods and his poetry has been published in *The New Yorker*, *The Paris Review*, *Poetry*, and *The Hudson Review*.

Gioia was raised in southern California; he now lives outside New York City. Gioia explains that "California Hills in August" was written when he went back to California after having lived in the Northeast for a number of years. On his last day in California, he took a walk in the hills. It was then that he realized "how foreign the sparse August hills of California seemed to most Americans who come from areas which are lushly green and overgrown during the summer." Of the last stanza, "where the speaker upsets everything said up to this point," Gioia asks, "Isn't one of the purposes of poetry to make us see the unexpected beauty of some person, place, or thing we previously took for granted or dismissed?"

See SYMBOL in the Handbook of Literary Terms, page 689

Caged Bird

Maya Angelou

A free bird leaps
on the back of the wind
and floats downstream
till the current ends
5 and dips his wing
in the orange sun rays
and dares to claim the sky.

But a bird that stalks
down his narrow cage
10 can seldom see through
his bars of rage
his wings are clipped and
his feet are tied
so he opens his throat to sing.

15 The caged bird sings
with a fearful trill
of things unknown
but longed for still
and his tune is heard
20 on the distant hill
for the caged bird
sings of freedom.

The free bird thinks of another breeze
and the trade winds[1] soft through the sighing trees
25 and the fat worms waiting on a dawn-bright lawn
and he names the sky his own.

But a caged bird stands on the grave of dreams
his shadow shouts on a nightmare scream
his wings are clipped and his feet are tied
30 so he opens his throat to sing.

The caged bird sings
with a fearful trill
of things unknown
but longed for still
35 and his tune is heard
on the distant hill
for the caged bird
sings of freedom.

---

1. *trade winds,* winds that blow almost continually on a course toward the equator.

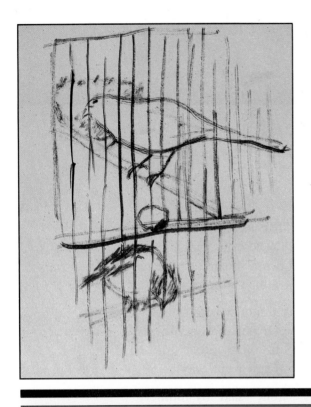

Pierre Bonnard "Canaries," *Phillips Memorial Gallery*

THINK AND DISCUSS
Understanding
1. Describe the free bird's surroundings (stanzas one and four). What is this bird doing? What is it thinking about?
2. Describe the caged bird's appearance (stanzas two and five). What is this bird doing?
3. According to the speaker, why does the caged bird sing?

Analyzing
4. In stanza one, the free bird "leaps" and "dares." What other words suggesting human actions and emotions does the speaker use to describe both birds?
5. Which two stanzas are the same? What purpose is served by this repetition?

APPLYING: Symbol H𝕏
See Handbook of Literary Terms, p. 689.

A **symbol** is a person, place, event, or object that has meaning in itself but suggests other meanings as well. The birds in the poem behave as normal birds might. There are suggestions, however, that the birds are also symbolic of something.
1. What kind of person might be symbolized by a bird with clipped wings?
2. What kinds of human actions might be symbolized by a free bird daring "to claim the sky"?
3. What circumstances could cause a person to feel "caged"?

Review SYMBOL in the Handbook of Literary Terms, page 689

The Ballad of the Harp-Weaver

Edna St. Vincent Millay

"Son," said my mother,
  When I was knee-high,
"You've need of clothes to cover you,
  And not a rag have I.

5 "There's nothing in the house
  To make a boy breeches,
Nor shears to cut a cloth with,
  Nor thread to take stitches.

"There's nothing in the house
10 But a loaf-end of rye,
And a harp with a woman's head
  Nobody will buy,"
  And she began to cry.

That was in the early fall.
15 When came the late fall,
"Son," she said, "the sight of you
  Makes your mother's blood crawl,—

"Little skinny shoulder-blades
  Sticking through your clothes!
20 And where you'll get a jacket from
  God above knows.

"It's lucky for me, lad,
  Your daddy's in the ground,
And can't see the way I let
25 His son go around!"
  And she made a queer sound.

That was in the late fall.
  When the winter came,
I'd not a pair of breeches
30 Nor a shirt to my name.

I couldn't go to school,
  Or out of doors to play.
And all the other little boys
  Passed our way.

35 "Son," said my mother,
  "Come, climb into my lap,
And I'll chafe your little bones
  While you take a nap."

And, oh, but we were silly
40 For half an hour or more,
Me with my long legs
  Dragging on the floor,

A-rock-rock-rocking
  To a mother-goose rhyme!
45 Oh, but we were happy
  For half an hour's time!

But there was I, a great boy,
  And what would folks say
To hear my mother singing me

50 To sleep all day,
In such a daft way?

Men say the winter
Was bad that year;
Fuel was scarce,
55 And food was dear.

A wind with a wolf's head
Howled about our door,
And we burned up the chairs
And sat upon the floor.

60 All that was left us
Was a chair we couldn't break,
And the harp with a woman's head
Nobody would take,
For song or pity's sake.

65 The night before Christmas
I cried with the cold,
I cried myself to sleep
Like a two-year-old.

And in the deep night
70 I felt my mother rise,
And stare down upon me
With love in her eyes.

I saw my mother sitting
On the one good chair,
75 A light falling on her
From I couldn't tell where,

Looking nineteen,
And not a day older,
And the harp with a woman's head
80 Leaned against her shoulder.

Her thin fingers, moving
In the thin, tall strings,
Were weav-weav-weaving
Wonderful things.

85 Many bright threads,
From where I couldn't see,
Were running through the harp-strings
Rapidly,

And gold threads whistling
90 Through my mother's hand.
I saw the web grow,
And the pattern expand.

She wove a child's jacket,
And when it was done
95 She laid it on the floor
And wove another one.

She wove a red cloak
So regal to see,
"She's made it for a king's son,"
100 I said, "and not for me."
But I knew it was for me.

She wove a pair of breeches
Quicker than that!
She wove a pair of boots
105 And a little cocked hat.

She wove a pair of mittens,
She wove a little blouse,
She wove all night
In the still, cold house.

110 She sang as she worked,
And the harp-strings spoke;
Her voice never faltered,
And the thread never broke.
And when I awoke,—

115 There sat my mother
With the harp against her shoulder,
Looking nineteen,
And not a day older,

(Continued)

Edna St. Vincent Millay 315

A smile about her lips,
120 And a light about her head,
And her hands in the harp-strings
    Frozen dead.

And piled up beside her
    And toppling to the skies,
125 Were the clothes of a king's son,
    Just my size.

THINK AND DISCUSS
Understanding
1. Describe the setting of this poem.
2. From what **point of view** is it told?
3. As the winter progresses, why do the mother and son keep the harp?

Analyzing
4. The ballad contains a fantastic element. Describe this.

REVIEWING: Symbol HT
See Handbook of Literary Terms, p. 689.

A **symbol** is a person, place, event, or object that has meaning in itself but suggests other meanings as well. What might the harp symbolize?

COMPOSITION
Creating a Symbol
Choose a symbol for something that your classmates are familiar with. Then write a paragraph describing your symbol and explaining why you chose it.

Writing a Description
In a composition of one or two paragraphs, describe a gift that you consider to be one of the most special that you have ever received.

 BIOGRAPHIES

Maya Angelou 1928–
After studying music, dance, and drama, Maya Angelou became an actress and singer. She is best known, however, for her short stories, novels, plays, poetry, songs, and screenplays, including a ten-part series for television on African traditions in American life.

Edna St. Vincent Millay 1892–1950
Edna St. Vincent Millay was born in Rockland, Maine. Her first poem, "Renascence," was published when she was only nineteen. Her collection of poems, *The Harp-Weaver*, won a Pulitzer Prize in 1923.

See **PERSONIFICATION** in the Handbook of Literary Terms, page 676

Check

James Stephens

The Night was creeping on the ground!
She crept, and did not make a sound

Until she reached the tree: and then
She covered it, and stole again

5 Along the grass behind the wall!
—I heard the rustling of her shawl

As she threw blackness everywhere
Along the sky, the ground, the air,

And in the room where I was hid!
10 But, no matter what she did

To everything that was without,
She could not put my candle out!

So I stared at the Night! and she
Stared back solemnly at me!

Reprinted with permission of Macmillan Publishing Company and
The Society of Authors on behalf of the copyright owner, Mrs. Iris
Wise, from *Collected Poems* by James Stephens. Copyright 1915 by
Macmillan Publishing Company, renewed 1943 by James Stephen.

THINK AND DISCUSS
Understanding
1. Describe the setting of the poem.
2. Where is the speaker?

Analyzing
3. What emotion is the speaker feeling in line 9?
4. Look up the word *check* in your Glossary. Which meaning best applies to the title of this poem?

APPLYING: Personification H𝓛
See Handbook of Literary Terms, p. 676.
  Personification is the giving of human characteristics to nonhuman things and events.
1. What is personified in this poem?
2. Is the thing personified made to seem friendly or frightening? Explain.
3. The situation described in the last two lines could be called a standoff. Explain how this has come about.

Review PERSONIFICATION in the Handbook of Literary Terms, page 676

The Walrus and the Carpenter

Lewis Carroll

The sun was shining on the sea,
    Shining with all his might:
He did his very best to make
    The billows smooth and bright—
5 And this was odd, because it was
    The middle of the night.

The moon was shining sulkily,
    Because she thought the sun
Had got no business to be there
10   After the day was done—
"It's very rude of him," she said,
    "To come and spoil the fun!"

The sea was wet as wet could be,
    The sands were dry as dry.
15 You could not see a cloud, because
    No cloud was in the sky:
No birds were flying overhead—
    There were no birds to fly.

The Walrus and the Carpenter
20   Were walking close at hand;
They wept like anything to see
    Such quantities of sand:
"If this were only cleared away,"
    They said, "it would be grand!"

25 "If seven maids with seven mops
    Swept it for half a year,
Do you suppose," the Walrus said,
    "That they could get it clear?"
"I doubt it," said the Carpenter,
30   And shed a bitter tear.

"Oysters, come and walk with us!"
    The Walrus did beseech.
"A pleasant walk, a pleasant talk,
    Along the briny beach;
35 We cannot do with more than four,
    To give a hand to each."

The eldest Oyster looked at him,
    But never a word he said:
The eldest Oyster winked his eye,
40   And shook his heavy head—
Meaning to say he did not choose
    To leave the oyster-bed.[1]

But four young Oysters hurried up,
    All eager for the treat:

---

1. oyster-bed, place such as a rock where many oysters attach themselves to live.

"The Walrus and the Carpenter" by Lewis Carroll from *Through the Looking-Glass* (Altemus, 1871).

⁴⁵ Their coats were brushed, their faces washed,
    Their shoes were clean and neat—
And this was odd, because, you know,
    They hadn't any feet.

Four other Oysters followed them,
⁵⁰   And yet another four;
And thick and fast they came at last,
    And more, and more, and more—
All hopping through the frothy waves,
    And scrambling to the shore.

⁵⁵ The Walrus and the Carpenter
    Walked on a mile or so,
And then they rested on a rock
    Conveniently low:
And all the little Oysters stood
⁶⁰   And waited in a row.

"The time has come," the Walrus said,
    "To talk of many things;
Of shoes—and ships—and sealing-wax[2]—
    Of cabbages—and kings—
⁶⁵ And why the sea is boiling hot—
    And whether pigs have wings."

"But wait a bit," the Oysters cried,
    "Before we have our chat;
For some of us are out of breath,
⁷⁰   And all of us are fat!"
"No hurry!" said the Carpenter.
    They thanked him much for that.

"A loaf of bread," the Walrus said,
    "Is what we chiefly need:
⁷⁵ Pepper and vinegar besides
    Are very good indeed—
Now if you're ready, Oysters dear,
    We can begin to feed."

"But not on us!" the Oysters cried,
⁸⁰   Turning a little blue.[3]
"After such kindness, that would be
    A dismal thing to do!"
"The night is fine," the Walrus said,
    "Do you admire the view?

⁸⁵ "It was so kind of you to come!
    And you are very nice!"
The Carpenter said nothing but
    "Cut us another slice:
I wish you were not quite so deaf—
⁹⁰   I've had to ask you twice!"

"It seems a shame," the Walrus said,
    "To play them such a trick,
After we've brought them out so far,
    And made them trot so quick!"
⁹⁵ The Carpenter said nothing but
    "The butter's spread too thick!"

"I weep for you," the Walrus said:
    "I deeply sympathize."
With sobs and tears he sorted out
¹⁰⁰   Those of the largest size,
Holding his pocket-handkerchief
    Before his streaming eyes.

"O Oysters," said the Carpenter,
    "You've had a pleasant run!
¹⁰⁵ Shall we be trotting home again?"
    But answer came there none—
And this was scarcely odd, because
    They'd eaten every one.

---

2. *sealing-wax,* a wax which is melted for use as a seal on letters, packages, etc. Often a design is made in the still-soft wax with a special stamp called a seal.
3. *blue,* a pun on *blue* meaning "sad" or—when referring to seafood—"spoiled."

THINK AND DISCUSS

THINK AND DISCUSS
Understanding
1. How do the Walrus and Carpenter persuade the young oysters to go with them?
2. What happens to the oysters who go?

Analyzing
3. What hints are there in stanzas one and two that the poem is not to be taken seriously?
4. What situations in lines 1–6 and lines 46–48 are called "odd"?
5. What occurs in lines 106–108 that is *not* ("scarcely") odd?

REVIEWING: Personification HL
See Handbook of Literary Terms, p. 676.
   Personification is the attributing of human characteristics to nonhuman things.

1. Find examples of personification in the first two stanzas of this poem.
2. Is the effect of this personification humorous, sad, horrifying, or something else?

COMPOSITION
Writing to Compare and Contrast
   Write a composition in which you describe a scene you know well at two different times. You might, for example, describe the view from your kitchen window at noon and in darkness. Try to use personification in your description.

Writing a Dialogue
   Choose a favorite food, and then personify it by giving it human characteristics as Lewis Carroll does with the oysters. Then write a dialogue between you and this food.

BIOGRAPHIES

James Stephens 1882–1950
   James Stephens was born in Ireland, where many of his tales and stories are set. He was also active in the Irish nationalist movement.

Lewis Carroll 1832–1898
   Charles Lutwidge Dodgson, who used the pen name *Lewis Carroll*, created *Alice in Wonderland* and then *Through the Looking Glass*, the book in which "The Walrus and the Carpenter" appears.

See ALLITERATION in the Handbook of Literary Terms, page 658

Still Life: Lady with Birds

Quandra Prettyman

She, in dowdy dress and dumpy,
clutching her black purse and brown paper bag,
comes bounty bearing and love bestows.

She, with birds for epaulets,[1]
5 thrusts such crusts as she has, such crumbs.
They cluster and grab and grabbing, sometimes, claw.

She, alone in this agony,
feeds them swiftly, firmly brushes them away,
speaking wild rantings to no one I see.

10 Sometimes one comes late,
finds no where to rest at her shoulders,
finds no crust to eat at her feet.

To that one, she
holds out her arm.
15 Him, she brings in.

---

1. *epaulets* (ep′ə lets), ornaments worn on the shoulders, usually of a uniform.

THINK AND DISCUSS

Understanding
1. What is the lady doing?
2. How do most of the birds behave?
3. How does the woman treat the bird that comes late?

Analyzing
4. Describe the woman's appearance. How do her actions contrast with her appearance?
5. To what might "this agony" (line 7) refer?
6. Several sentences in this poem are **inverted,** the words in them are not in the usual order. A sentence containing **inversion** shouldn't be hard to read if you concentrate on the meaning instead of the form. Who comes "bounty bearing and love bestows"? Put this and other sentences in the poem in normal order.

Extending
7. Can you see any similarities between the way the birds act and human behavior? Explain.

APPLYING: Alliteration HT
See Handbook of Literary Terms, p. 658.
   The use of repeated consonant sounds, especially at the beginnings of words, is called **alliteration.** The use of alliteration can link words that are similar in image, thought, and feeling. What examples of this kind of alliteration do you find in "Still Life: Lady with Birds"?

Zoltan Szabo, "The Flirt" (detail)
Private Collection

Review ALLITERATION in the Handbook of Literary Terms, page 658

Quilt

John Updike

The quilt that covers all of us, to date,
Has patches numbered 1 to 48,*
Five northern rents,[1] a crooked central seam,
    A ragged eastern edge, a way
5   Of bunching uglily, and a
Perhaps too energetic color scheme.

Though shaken every twenty years, this fine
Old quilt was never beaten on the line.
It took long making. Generations passed
10   While thread was sought, and calico
    And silk were coaxed from Mexico
And France. The biggest squares were added last.

Don't kick your covers, son. The bed is built
So you can never shake the clinging quilt
15 That blanketed your birth and tries to keep
    Your waking warm, impalpable
    As atmosphere. As earth it shall
Be tucked about you through your longest sleep.

*Since I composed this rather nifty
20   Couplet, the number rose to 50.

---

1. *rents,* holes or gaps.

Quiltmaker Judy Dales,
"America the Beautiful,"
Private Collection

THINK AND DISCUSS
Understanding
1. According to the speaker, when will we be able to "shake," or get rid of, the quilt?

Analyzing
2. What is the quilt? When did you realize this?
3. Explain the "five northern rents," the "crooked central seam," and the "ragged Eastern edge."

4. "Bunching uglily" is something cloth might do. What additional meaning does it take on in the context of this poem? When did we last "bunch uglily"?

Extending
5. Do you agree with the speaker that the quilt can't be kicked off? Explain.

REVIEWING: ALLITERATION H*

See Handbook of Literary Terms, p. 658.

Alliteration is the repetition of consonant sounds at the beginnings of words. It can create melody in a poem, call attention to certain words, and point out similarities and contrasts. Find examples of alliteration in "Quilt."

COMPOSITION

Writing About a Poem

Choose another poem for this unit and, in a short composition, discuss use of alliteration in it. Before you begin to plan your paper, see "Writing About Poetry" in the Writer's Handbook.

Writing About a Character

In a composition of one paragraph, write a description of the lady who feeds the birds as she performs some other activity such as preparing supper or watching television. Base your description on what you have learned about her from the poem.

ENRICHMENT

Art Project

Working in groups of three or four students, plan and execute a "patch" to represent your state on the quilt. After you have decided what symbols you'll use to represent your state, decide on a medium—cloth, paper, and paint, and any other ideas or combinations that will make your patch stand out. Finished patches might be displayed in the classroom.

BIOGRAPHIES

Quandra Prettyman 1933–

Born in Baltimore, Quandra Prettyman graduated from Antioch College and did graduate work at the University of Michigan. Now living in New York City, she has taught at the New School for Social Research, the New York College of Insurance, and Connecticut College.

John Updike 1932–

John Updike is an accomplished novelist and writer of short stories, poetry, and criticism. He has been awarded both the Pulitzer Prize and the National Book Award for fiction.

Born in a small town in Pennsylvania, he attended Harvard University. After graduation he worked on the staff of *The New Yorker*, to which he still contributes.

See ONOMATOPOEIA in the Handbook of Literary Terms, page 676

Dog at Night

Louis Untermeyer

At first he stirs uneasily in sleep
And, since the moon does not run off, unfolds
Protesting paws. Grumbling that he must keep
Both eyes awake, he whimpers; then he scolds
5 And, rising to his feet, demands to know
The stranger's business. You who break the dark
With insolent light, who are you? Where do you go?
But nothing answers his indignant bark.
The moon ignores him, walking on as though
10 Dogs never were. Stiffened to fury now,
His small hairs stand upright, his howls come fast,
And terrible to hear is the bow-wow
That tears the night. Stirred by this bugle-blast,
The farmer's hound grows active; without pause
15 Summons her mastiff and the cur that lies
Three fields away to rally to the cause.
And the next county wakes. And miles beyond
Throats ring themselves and brassy lungs respond
With threats, entreaties, bellowings and cries,
20 Chasing the white intruder down the skies.

THINK AND DISCUSS

Understanding

1. What disturbs the dog?
2. Why does he bark?
3. Why do the other dogs bark?

Analyzing

4. Find examples of **personification** in the poem.
5. Who is the "white intruder" of the last line?

APPLYING: Onomatopoeia HZ
See Handbook of Literary Terms, p. 676.

Onomatopoeia is the use of words whose sounds suggest their sense. Find words in the poem that suggest the different noises made by the dogs. How do these noises change from the beginning to the end of the poem?

VOCABULARY

Affixes

One way to find a root word is to remove what you think are prefixes or suffixes and see what is left. This doesn't always work, however. For example, *in-* can sometimes be a prefix, as it is in *insane*. But if you remove *in-* from *insolent*, you do not get an English root. For words like these, you may need to use the dictionary.

Some of the following words are made up of an English root plus affixes. For these words, separate the parts with plus signs; then write a definition, like this: *in + sane*, "not sane; crazy." For any word that does not have an English root, copy it whole; then look it up in the Glossary and write the definition after it, like this: *insolent*, "boldly rude; insulting."

1. uneasily   4. entreaty
2. indignant   5. intruder
3. active

BIOGRAPHY

Louis Untermeyer 1885–1977

Louis Untermeyer's first ambition was to become a composer, but at seventeen he gave up his dream and entered his father's jewelry-manufacturing business. Twenty years later, after having written eleven books, he left the family firm to give more time to his writing. Untermeyer was active in almost every field of literature; among his outstanding contributions are *Modern American Poetry* and *Modern British Poetry*, both highly respected anthologies.

Review **ONOMATOPOEIA** in the Handbook of Literary Terms, page 676

Dandelions

Deborah Austin

under cover of night and rain
the troops took over.
waking to total war in beleaguered houses
over breakfast we faced the batteries
5 marshalled by wall and stone, deployed
with a master strategy no one had suspected
and now all
firing

pow

10 all day, all yesterday
and all today
the barrage continued
deafening sight.
reeling now, eyes ringing from noise, from walking
15 gingerly over the mined lawns
exploded at every second
rocked back by the starshellfire
concussion of gold on green
bringing battle-fatigue
20 pow by lionface firefur pow by
goldburst shellshock pow by
whoosh   splat   splinteryellow   pow   by
pow   by   pow

---

tomorrow smoke drifts up
25 from the wrecked battalions,
all the ammunition, firegold fury, gone.
smoke
drifts
thistle-blown
30 over the war-zone, only
here and there, in the shade by the peartree
pow   in the crack by the
curbstone   pow   and back of the
35 ashcan, lonely
guerrilla snipers, hoarding
their fire shrewdly
never

pow

40 surrender

Charles Burchfield, "Dandelion
Seeds and the Moon"
Private Collection

THINK AND DISCUSS
Understanding
1. At the end of the poem, what is left of the invaders?

Analyzing
2. Why does the speaker think that dandelions in the lawn are exploding ammunition in a war zone?
3. Why do the people feel "beleaguered" (line 3) and have "battle-fatigue" (line 19)?
4. In line 13, the figurative expression "deafening sight" suggests an effect on the eyes similar to the effect of an explosion on the ears. Find other similar figurative expressions.

Extending
5. Who will win this war? Explain.

REVIEWING: Onomatopoeia H⟋
See Handbook of Literary Terms, p. 676.
   Onomatopoeia is the use of words with sounds that suggest meaning. Find onomatopoetic words in "Dandelions" and discuss whether they are effective.

COMPOSITION ◄▬▬
Creating Compound Words
   Make up five compound words (such as *firefur*) to describe a plant or animal. Then use each word in a sentence. If you are keeping a reading/writing log, review it before you begin.

Writing an Amusing Anecdote
   Have you ever felt "beseiged" by something—ants, autumn leaves, snow, junk mail? Write a brief composition telling about this experience.

BIOGRAPHY

Langston Hughes

1902–1967

Langston Hughes was born in Joplin, Missouri, and began writing poetry when he was a student at Central High School in Cleveland, Ohio. He worked as a farmer, cook, waiter, sailor, and doorman before his first book was published. He also studied at Columbia and Lincoln universities.

Hughes wrote novels, short stories, plays, song lyrics, and radio scripts. He is best known for his poetry. A leading figure in the Harlem Renaissance, a movement among young black writers to celebrate their race and its African heritage, he also wrote to "explain and illuminate" the condition of black people in America.

Dreams

Hold fast to dreams
For if dreams die
Life is a broken-winged bird
That cannot fly.

5 Hold fast to dreams
For when dreams go
Life is a barren field
Frozen with snow.

THINK AND DISCUSS
Analyzing
1. What kind of dreams do you think the speaker is talking about?
2. What two **metaphors** are used to describe a life without dreams? In what ways are the metaphors appropriate?

Extending
3. How important do you think dreams are? Suggest some metaphors of your own that could be applied to a life without dreams.

See **FIGURATIVE LANGUAGE** in the Handbook of Literary Terms, page 663

Dream Variations

To fling my arms wide
In some place of the sun,
To whirl and to dance
Till the white day is done.
5 Then rest at cool evening
Beneath a tall tree
While night comes on gently,
    Dark like me—
That is my dream!

10 To fling my arms wide
In the face of the sun,
Dance! Whirl! Whirl!
Till the quick day is done.
Rest at pale evening . . .
15 A tall, slim tree . . .
Night coming tenderly
    Black like me.

THINK AND DISCUSS
Understanding
1. Summarize what the speaker dreams of
   doing.

Analyzing
2. What does *variation* mean? How does it
   apply to this poem?

APPLYING: Figurative Language HandbookLT
See Handbook of Literary Terms, p. 663.
   Figurative language is any language that
goes beyond the literal meaning of words
to furnish new effects or fresh insights into
an idea or a subject.
1. Compare and contrast the figurative
   language in the two parts of the poem.
2. To what does the speaker compare
   himself?

Mother to Son

Well, son, I'll tell you:
Life for me ain't been no crystal stair.
It's had tacks in it,
And splinters,
5 And boards torn up,
And places with no carpet on the floor—
Bare.
But all the time
I'se been a-climbin' on,
10 And reachin' landin's,
And turnin' corners,
And sometimes goin' in the dark
Where there ain't been no light.
So boy, don't you turn back.
15 Don't you set down on the steps
'Cause you finds it's kinder hard.
Don't you fall now—
For I'se still goin', honey,
I'se still climbin',
20 And life for me ain't been no crystal stair.

THINK AND DISCUSS
Understanding
1. Who is the speaker?
2. According to the speaker, why can't the son "give up"?

Analyzing
3. What would a "crystal stair" be like?

4. What is the speaker's life like?
5. What is suggested by the pattern of **rhythm** in this poem?

Extending
6. Do you agree with the sentiment expressed in lines 14–20? Explain.

Review **FIGURATIVE LANGUAGE** in the Handbook of Literary Terms, page 663

The Negro Speaks of Rivers

I've known rivers:
I've known rivers ancient as the world and older than the
    flow of human blood in human veins.

My soul has grown deep like the rivers.

5 I bathed in the Euphrates[1] when dawns were young.
I built my hut near the Congo and it lulled me to sleep.
I looked upon the Nile and raised the pyramids above it.
I heard the singing of the Mississippi when Abe Lincoln
    went down to New Orleans, and I've seen its muddy
10   bosom turn all golden in the sunset.

I've known rivers:
Ancient, dusky rivers.

My soul has grown deep like the rivers.

John Wilson, "My Brother" 1942
Smith College Museum of Art

---

1. *Euphrates* (yü frā′tēz), a river in southwest Asia.

THINK AND DISCUSS
Understanding
1. What specific historical events are referred to in this poem?

Analyzing
2. Notice that the title uses the article *the*. What does this tell you about the speaker? Does it refer to just one person?
3. What was the condition of black people at the time "Abe Lincoln went down to New Orleans"? In what ways might this influence what the speaker sees?

REVIEWING: Figurative Language
See Handbook of Literary Terms, p. 663.

Any language that goes beyond the literal meanings of words to furnish new effects or fresh insights is **figurative language.** According to the speaker, what is the result of the experiences traced in the poem? What figurative expression is used to describe this result?

THINKING SKILLS
Classifying
Classify these poems by Langston Hughes according to whether the primary purpose of each is to "explain and illuminate the condition of black people in America."

COMPOSITION
Creating Figures of Speech
Think of some things your ancestors experienced that contribute to who and what you are today. Jot down five or six of these. Then, for each item you noted, write one sentence describing that experience. Each sentence should contain figurative language to help your reader visualize what you describe.

Writing a Letter
Imagine that you are the son (or daughter) being addressed in "Mother to Son." Write a letter to your mother giving your reaction to her statements. If you wish, you might write a poem rather than a letter. Before beginning to plan your composition, see "Writing as a Story Character," in the Writer's Handbook.

BIOGRAPHY

May Swenson
1919–1989

May Swenson was one of America's most famous modern poets. Born and raised in Logan, Utah, she lived for many years on Long Island. She received many grants, including Rockefeller, Guggenheim, and Ford Foundation grants. In 1987, she received a 130,000 dollar Fellowship from the MacArthur Foundation.

In much of her poetry, Swenson played with language—putting words together in unusual combinations and creating puns. Among her most popular books are *Poems to Solve* (1966), *More Poems to Solve* (1971), and *New and Selected Things Taking Place* (1979).

For Swenson, the enjoyment of poetry was "based in a craving to get through the curtains of things as they *appear*, to things as they *are*, and then into the larger, wilder space of things as they are *becoming*."

Cat and the Weather

Cat takes a look at the weather.
Snow.
Puts a paw on the sill.
His perch is piled, is a pillow.

5 Shape of his pad appears.
Will it dig? No.
Not like sand.
Like his fur almost.

But licked, not liked.
10 Too cold.
Insects are flying, fainting down.
He'll try

(Continued)

Nathaniel Currier, "The Favorite Cat," drawn about 1840
The Metropolitan Museum of Art

"Cat and the Weather" from *To Mix With Time* by May Swenson. Copyright © 1963 by May Swenson. Reprinted by permission of the author.

to bat one against the pane.
They have no body and no buzz.
15 And now his feet are wet;
it's a puzzle.

Shakes each leg,
then shakes his skin
to get the white flies off.
20 Looks for his tail,

tells it to come on in
by the radiator.
World's turned queer
somehow. All white,

25 no smell. Well, here
inside it's still familiar.
He'll go to sleep until
it puts itself right.

THINK AND DISCUSS
Understanding
1. Describe how the cat goes about exploring the snow.
2. What decision does the cat finally make (lines 27–28)?

Analyzing
3. To the cat, what are the snowflakes? Why does the cat find them unnerving?

4. Find examples of **alliteration** in "Cat and the Weather." Discuss ways in which they contribute to the overall feeling of the poem.
5. Poetry often lets us see everyday objects and happenings in a completely new way. Reread lines 20–23. What is literally happening? Compare your literal answer with the figurative language of the poem.

Over the Field

They have a certain beauty, those wheeled
        fish when, steel
        fins stiff out
        from their sides
5   they grope

over the field, then through cloud, slice
        silver snouts,
        and climb,

trailing glamorous veils like slime.
10 Their long abdomens cannot curve, but
        arrogantly cut
        blue,
        power enflaming
        their gills.

15   They claim
that sea where no fish swam, until they flew
        to minnow it
        with their metal.

Inflexible bellies carry, like roe,
20   Jonahs sitting row
        on row.
        I sit by the fin
        in

one of those whale-big fish, while
25 several silver minnows, lined up, wheel
        the runway
        way
        below.

THINK AND DISCUSS
Understanding
1. Where is the speaker?
2. What is she looking at?

Analyzing
3. To what are the planes compared? Is this a **simile** or a **metaphor**? Explain.
4. What is the "power" that enflames their gills?
5. What are *roe*? Who was *Jonah*?
6. The Jonahs sit "row on row." Why are they also like *roe*?
7. This is a concrete poem: its shape suggests its subject. What picture is created by the placement of words in this poem?

Waking from a Nap on the Beach

Sounds like big
rashers of bacon frying.
I look up from where I'm lying
expecting to see stripes

5 red and white. My eyes drop shut,
stunned by the sun.
Now the foam is flame, the long
troughs charcoal, but

still it chuckles and sizzles, it
10 burns and burns, it never gets done.
The sea is that
fat.

James Abbott McNeill Whistler, "Coast of Brittany (Alone
with the Tide)," 1861
Wadsworth Atheneum, Hartford

"Waking From a Nap on the Beach" by May Swenson.
Copyright © 1966 by May Swenson. Reprinted by
permission of the author. First appeared in *The Saturday
Review*.

THINK AND DISCUSS

Understanding

1. What has the speaker been doing?
2. What happens when she opens her eyes?

Analyzing

3. What is being compared in the **simile** in lines 1–2?
4. What are the red and white stripes the speaker expects to see? What has led her to expect this?
5. Foam appears on the highest part of a wave. Why is this foam "flame"? To what is the trough between each breaking wave compared?
6. Define the word *fat* as it is used in this poem.
7. Find examples of **onomatopoeia** in this poem. What sounds are suggested?

Extending

8. One reader of this poem argues that it gives those who have been in the described setting a wonderful new way of viewing it, but that if a reader has never actually been to the seashore it has no meaning. Do you agree or disagree with this opinion? Explain.

Fable for When There's No Way Out

Grown too big for his skin,
and it grown hard,

without a sea and atmosphere—
he's drunk it all up—

5 his strength's inside him now,
but there's no room to stretch.

He pecks at the top
but his beak's too soft;

though instinct or ambition shoves,
10 he can't get through.

Barely old enough to bleed
and already bruised!

In a case this tough
what's the use

15 if you break your head
instead of the lid?

Despair tempts him
to just go limp:

Maybe the cell's
20 already a tomb,

and beginning end
in this round room.

Still, stupidly he pecks
and pecks, as if from under

25 his own skull—
yet makes no crack . . .

No crack until
he finally cracks,

and kicks and stomps.
30 What a thrill

and shock to feel
his little gaff[1] poke

through the floor!
A way he hadn't known or meant.

35 Rage works if reason won't.
When locked up, bear down.

---

1. *gaff* (gaf), here the bony, sharp spine on the back of a bird's leg.

May Swenson

THINK AND DISCUSS
Understanding
1. What is the bird trying to do? What lines tell you so?
2. What lines suggest the bird is tempted to give up? What reason for giving up is suggested?
3. How does the bird finally succeed?

Analyzing
4. At what point did you realize who "he" is in the poem?
5. Most fables end with *morals*, statements that express a teaching or lesson. What lines in this poem serve as the moral?
6. In line 20 the shell is described figuratively as a "tomb." To what other things is the shell compared? What phrase in the last stanza reinforces the comparison between the shell and a cell?

Extending
7. How might this poem influence someone who is facing a situation in which there appears to be no way out?

COMPOSITION
Writing from Personal Experience
Write two paragraphs in which you tell about an unusual or surprising solution you found to some problem or predicament. Or, make up such a solution to some predicament. In one paragraph, describe the problem and the solutions that didn't work. In the second paragraph, describe the solution that finally worked and the way you arrived at it. Did you think for a long time, or did the solution come "out of the blue"?

Writing a Concrete Poem
First decide on a topic for a concrete poem. Then determine a shape for your poem that will suggest its topic. As you work to create that shape, keep in mind that you might write upside down, in circles, or any other way that will help you form a picture with words on a page. Completed poems might be displayed in the classroom.

ENRICHMENT
Oral Reading
Working in groups of four or five students, choose a "program" of poems to present to your classmates and teacher. You might use poems you've studied in this unit, giving—for example—a reading of the poetry of Langston Hughes or a reading of patriotic poems. Or you might ask your teacher or librarian for help in locating other poems to present—poems about animals, for example. Depending on your choice of poems, readings may be done individually or in groups. Practice reading aloud to your group before the day of your presentation.

THINKING CRITICALLY
ABOUT LITERATURE

UNIT 4   POETRY

■ CONCEPT REVIEW

This poem will help you review some of the important ideas and literary elements found in the unit. The sidenotes with the poem will help you think critically about your reading. A page number in the sidenotes refers to an Application. For a more thorough discussion, see the Handbook of Literary Terms.

Sea Lullaby

Elinor Wylie

The old moon is tarnished
With smoke of the flood,
The dead leaves are varnished
With color like blood,

5 A treacherous smiler
With teeth white as milk,
A savage beguiler
In sheathings of silk,

The sea creeps to pillage,
10 She leaps on her prey;
A child of the village
Was murdered today.

(*Continued*)

■ Note the irony of the title in light of events in the poem.

■ **imagery** (p. 308): The imagery in the first stanza sets the tone.

■ **personification** (p. 317): Note how the sea is personified.

■ Note the inversion in stanza two, all of which refers to *sea* in line 9.

■ Note the effect of *murdered* on the tone.

She came up to meet him
In a smooth golden cloak,
15 She choked him and beat him
To death, for a joke.

Her bright locks were tangled,
She shouted for joy,
With one hand she strangled
20 A strong little boy.

Now in silence she lingers
Beside him all night
To wash her long fingers
In silvery light.

■ **rhythm** (p. 293) and **rhyme scheme** (p. 283): Both rhyme and rhythm are in sharp contrast with subject and tone.

■ **figurative language** (p. 331): Note that the figurative language in this stanza is in sharp contrast to the way the sea is described earlier.

THINK AND DISCUSS
Understanding
1. Describe the setting of the poem.
2. How has the boy died?
3. Why did the sea treat the boy as she did?
4. Have people found his body yet? How do you know?

Analyzing
5. Characterize the sea. Support your answer with lines from the poem.

Extending
6. Do you think this poem gives an accurate picture of its subject? Explain.

REVIEWING LITERARY TERMS
Rhyme
1. What is the rhyme scheme of the poem?

Rhythm
2. Does "Sea Lullaby" have a regular pattern of rhythm, or is the pattern varied? Explain.
3. Are rhyme and rhythm in keeping with the tone of the poem? Explain.

Imagery
4. To what senses does the imagery in stanzas two and three appeal?

Personification
5. Contrast the behavior of the sea in stanza five with the way she acts in stanza six. What does the personification say about the sea's predictability? her trustworthiness?

Figurative Language
6. Choose one figurative expression from the poem, explain its literal meaning, and then tell whether you think it is appropriate and why.

■ CONTENT REVIEW
THINKING SKILLS
Classifying

1. Place poems in this unit into one of these classifications: those with fairly regular patterns of rhyme and rhythm; those with no end rhyme scheme and varied rhythm.

Generalizing

2. Look at your list for question 1. Is it possible to make any generalizations based on the classifying you did? Is there any similarity of theme among poems in the same group? Do modern poems tend to fall into one classification?

3. Animals appear in "Catalogue," "Still Life: Lady with Birds," "Dog at Night," and "Cat and the Weather." Compare the different attitudes about animals expressed in these poems.

4. Both "Quilt" and "The Negro Speaks of Rivers" deal with ties to the past and the influence of the past on the present. Compare and contrast the ways this subject is treated in each poem.

Synthesizing

5. Assume that "The Highwayman" is fairly typical of traditional poetry, and that "California Hills in August" is fairly typical of modern poetry. Compare and contrast these poems to come up with four or five statements about how traditional and modern poetry differ. As you compare and contrast, consider elements such as plot, character, point of view, rhyme, rhythm, and use of imagery and figures of speech.

Evaluating

6. If you could choose two poems from the unit to place in a time capsule that will be opened in one hundred years, which would you choose? Why?

■ COMPOSITION REVIEW
Writing a Fable

Decide on a lesson you'd like to express in the form of a fable. You might choose a familiar saying such as "Look before you leap" or else write a lesson of your own. Write a fable that is no more than one page in length. (If you wish, you may write this assignment as a poem.)

Writing About Literature

Choose either Langston Hughes or May Swenson as a topic for a paper in which you discuss that poet's use of rhyme, imagery, and any of the other tools available to poets as they write. Support your statements with lines from the poems.

Reviewing Writer's Craft: Appeal to the Senses

Many of the poems in this unit are about a person, place, or event that is not in itself very important—or at least not earthshaking (a dog howls at the moon, a cat encounters its first snowfall, a lady feeds pigeons). When seen through the poet's eyes, however, these events become something special—we see them as if we were seeing for the first time. Choose a commonplace event, place, or person, and write either a paragraph or a poem about it. Before you begin to write, review your reading/writing log. Be sure to use words that appeal to the senses in order to help readers experience your subject.

SHORT STORY 2

Will Barnet, "The Stairway" (detail), *Private Collection*

UNIT 5

PREVIEW

UNIT 5 SHORT STORY 2

Features
Reading Modern and Traditional Stories
The Writer's Craft: Use Comparisons

Application of Literary Terms
theme   satire
tone   foreshadowing
mood   flashback

Reading Literature Skillfully
predicting outcomes

Vocabulary Skills
dictionary
antonyms
combining forms

Thinking Skills
classifying
generalizing

Composition Assignments Include
Writing a Diary Entry
Supporting a Statement
Writing a Character Sketch
Writing a Letter
Writing an Interview
Writing a Personal Essay
Writing a News Story
Explaining a Choice
Changing Point of View
Writing as a Story Character

Enrichment
Creative Project
Speaking and Listening

Thinking Critically About Literature
Concept Review
Content Review
Composition Review

Southpaw

Judith Viorst

They used to be best friends, but now she hopes he gets cavities. What has he done?

Dear Richard,

Don't invite me to your birthday party because I'm not coming. And give back the Disneyland sweat shirt I said you could wear. If I'm not good enough to play on your team, I'm not good enough to be friends with.

Your former friend,
Janet

P.S. I hope when you go to the dentist he finds twenty cavities.

Dear Janet,

Here is your stupid Disneyland sweat shirt, if that's how you're going to be. I want my comic books now—finished or not. No girl has ever played on the Mapes Street baseball team, and as long as I'm captain, no girl ever will.

Your former friend,
Richard

P.S. I hope when you go for your checkup you need a tetanus shot.

Dear Richard,

I'm changing my goldfish's name from Richard to Stanley. Don't count on my vote for class president next year. Just because I'm a member of the ballet club doesn't mean I'm not a terrific ballplayer.

Your former friend,
Janet

P.S. I see you lost your first game, 28–0.

Dear Janet,

I'm not saving any more seats for you on the bus. For all I care you can stand the whole way to school. Why don't you forget about baseball and learn something nice like knitting?

Your former friend,
Richard

P.S. Wait until Wednesday.

Dear Richard,

My father said I could call someone to go with us for a ride and hot-fudge sundaes. In case you didn't notice, I didn't call you.

Your former friend,
Janet

P.S. I see you lost your second game, 34–0.

Dear Janet,

Remember when I took the laces out of my blue-and-white sneakers and gave them to you? I want them back.

Your former friend,
Richard

P.S. Wait until Friday.

George Wesley Bellows, "On the Porch" (detail), 1919
Columbus Museum of Art, Ohio

Dear Richard,

Congratulations on your unbroken record. Eight straight losses, wow! I understand you're the laughingstock of New Jersey.

Your former friend,
Janet

P.S. Why don't you and your team forget about baseball and learn something nice like knitting, maybe?

Dear Janet,

Here's the silver horseback-riding trophy that you gave me. I don't think I want to keep it anymore.

Your former friend,
Richard

P.S. I didn't think you'd be the kind who'd kick a man when he's down.

Dear Richard,

I wasn't kicking exactly. I was kicking *back.*

Your former friend,
Janet

P.S. In case you were wondering my batting average is .345.

Dear Janet,

Alfie is having his tonsils out tomorrow. We might be able to let you catch next week.

Richard

Dear Richard,

I pitch.

Janet

Dear Janet,

Joel is moving to Kansas and Danny sprained his wrist. How about a permanent place in the outfield?

Richard

Dear Richard,

I pitch.

Janet

Dear Janet,

Ronnie caught the chicken pox and Leo broke his toe and Elwood has these stupid violin lessons. I'll give you first base. That's my final offer.

Richard

Dear Richard,

Susan Reilly plays first base, Marilyn Jackson catches, Ethel Kahn plays center field, I pitch. It's a package deal.

Janet

P.S. Sorry about your 12-game losing streak.

Dear Janet,

Please! Not Marilyn Jackson.

Richard

Dear Richard,

Nobody ever said that I was unreasonable. How about Lizzie Martindale instead?

Janet

Dear Janet,

At least could you call your goldfish Richard again?

Your friend,
Richard

THINK AND DISCUSS

Understanding

1. How does Janet respond to Richard's refusal to let her play?
2. What does Richard say is his reason for not wanting Janet on the team?
3. What is Janet's attitude about girls and baseball?
4. Why does Richard agree to let Janet play?

Analyzing

5. What was the relationship of Richard and Janet before this conflict? How do you know?
6. Janet uses **hyberbole** in her letters. What examples can you find? What is the effect of the hyperbole?

Extending

7. What **connotations** do the words *baseball, ballet,* and *knitting* have? Do you think these connotations depend on whether you are a boy or girl?
8. If you were Janet, would you have wanted to play on Richard's team? Explain.

 BIOGRAPHY

Judith Viorst
1931–

Judith Viorst is a poet and journalist as well as a successful short-story writer. Her books for children deal with everyday events in a sensitive and humorous way. She often challenges traditional roles for boys and girls. Her male characters demonstrate affection, and her female characters are often athletic.

Viorst was born and educated in New Jersey. Her publications for young children include *Sunday Morning* (1968); *Alexander and the Terrible, Horrible, No Good, Very Bad Day* (1972); and *The Tenth Good Thing About Barney* (1971).

The main difference between traditional and modern stories is one of emphasis. All short stories contain the elements plot, character, and setting, and all are told from a particular point of view. But in a traditional story, stronger emphasis is placed on plot, while in a modern story emphasis is on character.

For example, in this unit you will read "The Ransom of Red Chief" by O. Henry and "The Lady, or the Tiger?" by Frank W. Stockton. These stories were written in the early twentieth and late nineteenth centuries. In both stories plot is far more important than character development. You continue to read these stories to see what events will follow. On the other hand, in "A Lesson in Discipline" by Teresa Foley and in "Thank You, Ma'am" by Langston Hughes, emphasis is on character. You read on to see ways in which the characters will change, how they will behave, and why. For example, in "A Lesson in Discipline," readers are told about a class that grows "stupider and lazier and fresher and more obnoxious" each school year and about the teacher who challenges this behavior. But more important than this pattern of events are the ways in which the students change because of this teacher and what later happens to her. In "Thank You, Ma'am," there is very little action. After the early attempt at a mugging, Roger's intended victim takes him to her house and gives him supper. Hughes's concern is not with creating an exciting, action-packed plot but rather with character motivation—why Roger behaves as he does at various points in the story—and psychology—how Roger's thinking changes as a result of his experiences.

As you read each story in this unit, ask yourself how it might turn out. **Predicting outcomes** means questioning yourself as you read as to what might happen next based on what has already occurred. For example, in your reading of "Southpaw," you might first have asked yourself how the team will perform, how Janet's attitude will change as the season progresses, and how Richard's behavior might also change. Partway through the story, you might predict that the losing streak will continue, and you read on to see both whether you are right and what may happen next.

Later in this unit, you will find yourself predicting outcomes in stories about a boy who experiences mixed emotions about his elderly grandfather, a girl who loves to tell her friends scary stories, a man whose intelligence is increased through surgery, and another man who is standing on the gallows. Predicting outcomes as you read will add to your enjoyment and understanding of both modern and traditional short stories.

See THEME in the Handbook of Literary Terms, page 690

A Lesson in Discipline

Teresa Foley

Every year for six years we grew stupider and lazier and fresher and more obnoxious.

We were a terrible class. Every class likes to remember that it was pure hellion,[1] but the thirty of us who started under Miss Gallagher at the Down School near the Buick garage really were terrible.

Child-centered psychology burgeoned[2] in our town at this time. We were allowed to do some ridiculous things in school because we wanted to. When our parents heard about them, they were furious at first. Then they decided that the school must know what it was doing, and they let us do the same things and worse at home.

Every year for six years we grew stupider and lazier and fresher and more obnoxious. No one ever separated any of us, or kept any of us back. We were a terrible package, referred to by certain members of the PTA as "*Les Misérables*."[3]

Then came the seventh year and Miss Barracombie.

She was new to the school that year, so we did not have the usual case studies on her from previous classes. Her looks might have given us a clue, but we had always known amateur, experimental teachers so we did not recognize the career teacher when we saw her. She was perhaps fifty, tall, square-shouldered, and erect; neither feminine nor mannish, merely healthy and strong. Her face was handsome but not pretty. She had no subtle expressions: she smiled outright, she frowned outright, or she concentrated. Her voice was not harsh but had a peculiar carrying quality, vibrating longer than most. Eugene Kent took off his hearing aid after the first day.

---

1. *hellion* (hel'yən), a mischievous, troublesome person.
2. *burgeoned* (bėr'jənd), grew quickly; flowered.
3. *Les Misérables* (lā mē'zä rà bl'), a novel by the French author Victor Hugo; the title means "the miserable ones."

"A Lesson in Discipline" by Teresa Foley, *Harper's*, December, 1956. Reprinted by permission of the author.

She greeted us that day as no teacher ever had. No talk of adjustment here, no plea for growth, no challenge to find ourselves. She said:

"My name is Virginia Barracombie and it will be Miss Barracombie to you indefinitely. One of these days you will meet someone from the last school in which I taught. The worst that he tells you about me will be true. It's a far cry from child to man, and it's not through games that we get there. You and I are bound together in a contract for one year. I teach; you learn. Behave yourselves and pay attention and this will be one of the good years of your lives. You have a minute to prepare yourself with ruler, compass, pencil, and paper for a review of the meaning and use of decimals."

It was the shock treatment all right—but with economy, with the clarity of piano keys struck singly, above all with authority. We had neither the opportunity nor the mind to look across the aisles at each other until recess. We were at work in the first five minutes—we, who always had a period in which to get ready to get ready. It was a blow to our unit pride, but we were less of a group after the long summer and temporarily distracted from getting together on what to do about it.

We thought at first that we were just going along with her in a momentary tolerance. She was novelty, and among teachers that was hard to find. Then we found ourselves bound in a work routine. At that point some of us tried to bolt.

In its reactions to Miss Barracombie the class divided into four groups. Several of the nicer girls and a couple of the boys who had strict scholastic accountability to professional parents went into her camp almost immediately when they saw that she was systematic, skillful, and just. Another group, whose names and faces are always hard to remember, went along with her because they sensed that she was a stronger personality; that balking would be tiring, involve exposure of weakness, and end in failure. These two groups accounted for perhaps two-thirds of the class. In the remaining third were the Idiot rebels and the Hard-nut rebels.

The Idiots moved in first, without seeing where they were going. For example:

Idiot: "Do we *have* to put our names on our compositions?" (looking around at the other Idiots for appreciative laughter)

Miss B.: "You don't *have* to."

Idiot: (next day after papers had been passed back) "I didn't get my paper back. I haven't no grade."

Miss B.: "Did you expect one?"

Idiot: "You said we didn't *have* to put our names on them."

Miss B.: "That's right. You don't *have* to walk around with your eyes open, either."

The Idiot sat down, uneasily. That afternoon his name was up with the absentees who had to make up the composition.

The Idiots were beaten from the start. She was indifferent to petty annoyances, and they did not dare try big ones.

The Hard-nuts, the long-time class heroes, waited more patiently, seeking their own ground. Their particular dragon in the case of Miss Barracombie was her good sense, which forced an antagonist to assume a role so foolish as to threaten his status among his classmates. This forced the Hard-nuts to try to operate outside the teaching periods, in the rather limited areas of truancy, ground rules, and personal relationships.

It was difficult to challenge her with truancy because there our parents were solidly on her side, and besides, the occasional absence or trumped-up tardiness of an individual did little to alter the steady civilizing routine. As for opportunities on the school grounds, Miss Barracombie supervised only in her turn, and was by some unexpected quirk more lenient than any of the other teachers, letting us proceed at games considerably rougher than we wished to be playing.

The worst of the Hard-nuts was Lennie Sopel. He was big and tough and bearded already, very much in the know about engines, baseball statistics, and older women. He had a way of muttering wisecracks half under his breath when girls recited. At first they reached only to people in the surrounding seats. Then one day as Lila Crocker went down the aisle, Lennie, in a loud whisper, made a smart remark that shook the room like an east wind.

Miss Barracombie stopped listening to a girl at the study table. The girl stopped talking. Lila fled to the waste basket and back to her seat, her face scarlet.

The room became as silent as a tomb in a pyramid.

Miss Barracombie looked at Lennie for a long time, and he locked eyes with her, ready for a showdown.

"What are you thinking about, Lennie?" she asked at last, rather softly for her.

"Nothin'." He could say that one word as though it were the nastiest in the language. "Absolutely nothin'."

"Well, I'm thinking about something," she said, still calm and relaxed. "You come in at three and I'll tell you about it. In the meantime, stand up."

"What for? What'd I do?"

"Stand up, please."

Lennie hesitated. Again it was one of her simple inescapable requests. He slid out into the aisle and stood up.

Miss Barracombie went back to her work with the girl at the table. Lennie started to sit down once, but she gave him a steady eye and he straightened up again. He had to stand by his seat throughout the rest of the afternoon. We kept looking at him, waiting for him to say something; Lennie couldn't seem to think of anything to say.

She kept him after school forty-five minutes every day for six months. He never spoke out of turn again in class and he never missed a session with her. It seemed a heavy punishment for one remark, and we couldn't get over either her giving it or his taking it. When we asked him what he had to do, all he would say was, "Nothin'. She just gives me the dickens."

"For forty hours, Lennie?"

"Who's countin'? And whose business?"

Then one day Alice Rowe gave us the lowdown. She had been helping in the inner office when the intercom was open to Miss Barracombie's room.

"She's teaching him to read."

Nobody would believe her. Lennie's in seventh grade, everybody said. He knows how to read.

"No, he doesn't," Alice said. "I heard him stumbling over the littlest words up there. Who's ever heard him read in class?"

We tried to remember when we had heard Lennie read. He was a transfer to us in the fourth grade, and there hadn't been much oral reading since then.

"How does he do his other work?" we asked.

"Who says he does?"

No wonder Lennie couldn't fight her. She taught him in secret the one thing he needed to have to give up cheating and pretending.

The truth was, no rebellion had a chance with her. She wasn't mean and she never struck anybody (although our parents queried us over and over again on this point, wanting, we thought, to be able to say, "Of course, she has order! She whips them."). No situation could come up that she would not know how to handle and without damage to her single drive: she would teach: we would learn.

Whatever we studied, we mastered. Of course, she knew the ones of us who could not connect with the main lines she was trolling,[4] but she put out other lines for them and they mastered them, too. Nobody was free not to learn. We were free to fail, but somehow a failure was not a separate thing, only a step in learning. She never assumed that we had achieved. She probed and exposed until she read it in the blood. A week later when we were not expecting it, she would check again. She was the only teacher whose grades on our report cards we never questioned. Nor would we let our indignant parents go to her. She knew.

This was no love affair between the class and Miss Barracombie, however. She was businesslike and not tender with us. She encouraged no intimacies, and the thought of confiding in her as we had in Miss Tondreau who used to love us in the third grade was wholly ridiculous. We were just different with her. When our special teachers came and Miss Barracombie left the room, Eugene Kent would replace his hearing aid, and we would be at once stalking a world of enemies. By the end of the period our specials would be limp and distraught.

We did no better left on our own. If Miss Barracombie stepped out of the room— something she wisely did rarely—we would have hit the ceiling. After all, we had been indulged for years. Thirty near-simians[5] don't forget that in a few stretching months. We had never been convinced that discipline comes from within, and when the restraining presence was removed we reverted to the barbarians that we were.

Miss Barracombie never mentioned our behavior with other teachers or when she was out of the room, although the specials must have complained bitterly. It seemed to be part of her code that she was responsible when she was with us and others were responsible when they took us. We liked that. Miss Barracombie did not lecture or make us feel guilty. There was nothing to lecture or feel guilty about. We behaved. We learned. We had to: it was the contract.

---

4. *trolling* (trōl′ing), fishing by drawing a baited hook through water.

5. *near-simians* (sim′ē ən), apelike creatures.

But the final lesson we learned from Miss Barracombie was one she did not try to teach us. It was during the last period. We were in the midst of a discussion on the use of quotation marks. The intercom box pinged on the wall and the principal said:

"A telegram has just arrived for you, Miss Barracombie. Will you send a boy down for it?"

She sent Herbert Harvey Bell. He was in the corner seat by the door. He went out running because she knew exactly how long it took to get to the office and back and he did not want to answer for loitering.

He returned with the telegram, gave it to her, and took his seat.

She opened the envelope calmly and neatly so as not to tear the inside sheet. Still reading it, she turned about slowly so that her back was toward the class. Her hands lowered. We could see that she was no longer looking at the telegram but at the bulletin board. She did not turn back to us. She kept looking at something on the board.

Then before the alerted, somehow apprehensive eyes of the class, Miss Barracombie began to grow smaller. It was in her shoulders first. They began to narrow, to go forward. Her back curved. Her head dropped. We waited, not knowing what to do. Herbert Harvey Bell seemed to feel the most responsible. He looked around at all of us with a question in his wide, stunned eyes. We had nothing for him. Herbert Harvey pulled himself up from his seat and ran across the hall to the teacher there.

Lennie Sopel had started down from his seat, but when he saw the other teacher, Mrs. Hamilton, coming, he turned and went back up the aisle.

Mrs. Hamilton went up to Miss Barracombie and peered into her face. Then she bent to the telegram still in her hands.

"Oh, my dear," she said and put her arm around Miss Barracombie. Miss Barracombie did not move. Her shoulders were gone, melted into her narrow back.

Mrs. Hamilton turned her in the direction of the door. Our teacher put both hands across her face and, huddled and small, walked out like a child under Mrs. Hamilton's arm.

No one breathed or moved. A few minutes later Mrs. Hamilton looked into our room.

"Miss Barracombie has lost someone dear to her, boys and girls. Try to finish the period quietly."

No one came near us for the rest of the afternoon, not even to dismiss us. But we did not behave as we usually did when left alone. Most of us took out our composition notebooks and pens. Some just sat there.

We were frightened—a little sad for Miss Barracombie, of course—but mainly frightened, and frightened for ourselves. If she could be struck down, who was so tall, so erect, with all things under control, what could not happen to the rest of us who never had any control on the inside, who had to be made by others to hold our shoulders back?

We were the best we had ever been until the bell rang that day. For a moment we could see our connection with adults. Through a maze of equivalent fractions and common denominators we could see other people, huddled and shrinking, being led out of strange rooms. And their faces were ours.

THINK AND DISCUSS

Understanding

1. Why was the class "terrible"?
2. What is the contract Miss Barracombie announces to the class?
3. What causes her to lose control?

Analyzing

4. From what **point of view** is the story told?
5. What is the "last thing" she teaches the class?

Extending

6. How would you have reacted if Miss Barracombie had been your teacher?

APPLYING: Theme HZ

See Handbook of Literary Terms, p. 690.

The main idea or underlying meaning of a literary work is its **theme.** A theme may be stated or implied.

1. What is the subject of this story?
2. In your own words, tell the theme of this story. Is the theme directly stated or is it implied?

COMPOSITION ◆

Writing a Diary Entry

Assume you are Miss Barracombie and you have been teaching this class for a few weeks. Write a diary entry in which you record some of your thoughts about the class.

Supporting a Statement

Reread the description of Miss Barracombie from the time she reads the telegram until she leaves the classroom. Then write a composition of three to five paragraphs on the use of figurative language in this description.

ENRICHMENT

Creative Project

One of the subjects of "A Lesson in Discipline" is the view children have of the adult world and what happens when they learn that their vision is not necessarily accurate. As a class, make two collages: one of the adult world as it appears to you now, and the other of the adult world as it appeared to you when you were younger.

 BIOGRAPHY

Teresa Foley

Teresa Foley is a former classroom teacher and director of curriculum for the public schools of Dover, New Hampshire. She has published many short stories in national magazines.

Thank You, Ma'am

Langston Hughes

He did not trust the woman *not* to trust him. And he did not want to be mistrusted now.

She was a large woman with a large purse that had everything in it but a hammer and nails. It had a long strap, and she carried it slung across her shoulder. It was about eleven o'clock at night, and she was walking alone, when a boy ran up behind her and tried to snatch her purse. The strap broke with the tug the boy gave it from behind. But the boy's weight and the weight of the purse caused him to lose his balance. Instead of taking off full blast, the boy fell on his back on the sidewalk, and his legs flew up. The large woman simply turned around and kicked him right square in his blue-jeaned sitter. She shook him until his teeth rattled. Then she reached down and picked the boy up by his shirt.

After that the woman said, "Pick up my pocketbook, boy, and give it here."

She still held him tightly. But she bent down enough to let him pick up her purse.

Then she said, "Now ain't you ashamed of yourself?"

Firmly gripped by his shirt front, the boy said, "Yes'm."

The woman said, "What did you want to do it for?"

The boy said, "I didn't aim to."

She said, "You lie!"

By that time two or three people passed, turned to look, and some stood watching.

"If I turn you loose, will you run?" asked the woman.

"Yes'm," said the boy.

"Then I won't turn you loose," said the woman. She did not release him.

"Lady, I'm sorry," whispered the boy.

"Um-hum! Your face is dirty. I got a great mind to wash your face for you. Ain't you got

"Thank You, Ma'am" from *The Langston Hughes Reader* by Langston Hughes. Published by George Braziller, Inc. Copyright © 1958 by Langston Hughes. Copyright renewed 1986 by George Houston Bass. Reprinted by permission of Harold Ober Associates Incorporated.

nobody home to tell you to wash your face?"

"No'm," said the boy.

"Then it will get washed this evening," said the large woman, starting up the street, dragging the frightened boy behind her.

He looked as if he were fourteen or fifteen, thin and wild, in tennis shoes and blue jeans.

The woman said, "You ought to be my son. I would teach you right from wrong. Least I can do right now is to wash your face. Are you hungry?"

"No'm," said the boy. "I just want you to turn me loose."

"Was I bothering you when I turned that corner?" asked the woman.

"No'm."

"But you put yourself in contact with *me*," said the woman. "If you think that contact is not going to last a while, you got another thought coming. When I get through with you, sir, you are going to remember Mrs. Luella Bates Washington Jones."

Sweat popped out on the boy's face, and he began to struggle. Mrs. Jones stopped, jerked him around in front of her, put a half nelson about his neck, and continued to drag him up the street. When she got to her door, she dragged the boy inside, down a hall, and into a large room at the rear of the house. She switched on the light and left the door open. The boy could hear other roomers laughing and talking. Some of their doors were open, too; so he knew he and the woman were not alone. The woman still had him by the neck in the middle of her room.

She said, "What is your name?"

"Roger," answered the boy.

"Then, Roger, you go to that sink and wash your face," said the woman. She turned him loose—at last. Roger looked at the door—and went to the sink.

"Let the water run until it gets warm," she said. "Here's a clean towel."

"You gonna take me to jail?" asked the boy, bending over the sink.

"Not with that face. I would not take you nowhere," said the woman. "Here I am trying to get home to cook me a bite to eat, and you snatch my pocketbook! Maybe you ain't been to your supper, either, late as it be. Have you?"

"There's nobody home at my house," said the boy.

"Then we'll eat," said the woman. "I believe you're hungry—or been hungry—to try to snatch my pocketbook!"

"I want a pair of suede shoes," said the boy.

"Well, you didn't have to snatch *my* pocketbook to get some suede shoes," said Mrs. Luella Bates Washington Jones. "You could of asked me."

"Ma'am?"

The water dripping from his face, the boy looked at her. There was a long pause. A very long pause. After drying his face and not knowing what else to do, the boy dried it again. Then he turned around. The door was open. He would make a dash for it down the hall. He would run, run, run, *run!*

The woman was sitting on the day bed. After a while she said, "I were young once and I wanted things I could not get."

There was another long pause. The boy's mouth opened. Then he frowned, not knowing he frowned.

The woman said, "Um-hum! You thought I was going to say, *but I didn't snatch people's*

pocketbooks. Well, I wasn't going to say that." Pause. Silence. "I have done things, too, which I would not tell you, son—neither tell God, if He didn't already know. Everybody's got something in common. Sit you down while I fix us something to eat. You might run that comb through your hair so you will look presentable."

In another corner of the room behind a screen was a gas plate and an icebox. Mrs. Jones got up and went behind the screen. The woman did not watch the boy to see if he was going to run now. She didn't watch her purse, which she left behind her on the day bed. But the boy took care to sit on the far side of the room, away from the purse. He thought she could easily see him out of the corner of her eye if she wanted to. He did not trust the woman *not* to trust him. And he did not want to be mistrusted now.

"Do you need somebody to go to the store," asked the boy, "to get some milk or something?"

"Don't believe I do," said the woman, "unless you want sweet milk yourself. I was going to make cocoa out of this canned milk I got here."

"That will be fine," said the boy.

She heated some lima beans and ham, made the cocoa, and set the table. The woman did not ask the boy anything about where he lived, or his folks, or anything else that would embarrass him. Instead, as they ate, she told him about her job in a hotel beauty shop, what the work was like, and how all kinds of women came in and out. Then she cut him half of her ten-cent cake.

"Eat some more, son," she said.

When they finished eating, she got up and said, "Now here, take this ten dollars and buy yourself some suede shoes. And, next time, do not make the mistake of latching onto my pocketbook nor nobody *else's*—because shoes got by devilish ways will burn your feet. I got to get my rest now. But from here on in, son, I hope you will behave yourself."

She led him down the hall to the front door and opened it. "Good night! Behave yourself, boy!" she said as he went down the steps.

The boy wanted to say something more than "Thank you, ma'am," to Mrs. Luella Bates Washington Jones. Although his lips moved, he couldn't even say that as he turned at the foot of the stairs and looked up at the large woman in the door. Then she shut the door.

THINK AND DISCUSS
Understanding
1. What happens to Roger as he grabs Mrs. Jones's purse?
2. How does Mrs. Jones react to the attempted purse snatching?
3. What reason does Roger give for trying to steal the purse?
4. How does Mrs. Jones treat Roger once they get to her home?

Analyzing
5. Why do you think Mrs. Jones tells Roger, "I have done some things, too, which I would not tell you, son. . . . Everybody's got something in common"?
6. What effect does her comment seem to have on Roger?
7. Why do you think Roger can't say, "Thank you, Ma'am" to Mrs. Jones?

Extending
8. Mrs. Jones "wins" with understanding, not revenge. How would you state the **theme** of the story?

READING LITERATURE SKILLFULLY
Predicting Outcomes

In "Thank You, Ma'am," the reader suspects from the start that Mrs. Jones is in control. It seems obvious that she will be teaching the boy a lesson, although it is unclear exactly what that lesson will be. How can you, the reader, predict the outcome of a story ahead of time? A good reader pays attention to clues in a story. These clues can help you predict outcomes, and so prepare you for events to come.

Answer these questions about "Thank You, Ma'am."

1. How does Mrs. Jones treat Roger after he attempts to snatch her purse?
2. Is Roger willing to listen to Mrs. Jones's criticism? How do you know?
3. At what point do you know that Mrs. Jones will not call the police but will leave Roger with an important lesson?

COMPOSITION
Writing a Character Sketch

Write a one- or two-paragraph composition about the two characters in this story. As you plan your composition, consider the following: At the conclusion of "Thank You, Ma'am," Roger wants to thank Mrs. Jones. Is he sincere in wanting to do this? What can you infer about both characters' past actions from clues given in the story? What can you infer about their future behavior? On what do you base your inferences?

Writing a Letter

Assume that you are Roger in "Thank You, Ma'am." Several months have passed since the episode with Mrs. Jones. Write her a letter expressing your gratitude. Begin by explaining specifically how your feelings changed from the moment you tried to rob her until she finally let you go. For additional help, see "Writing as a Story Character" in the Writer's Handbook.

For a biography of Langston Hughes, see page 330.

Use Comparisons

In "A Lesson in Discipline," Miss Barracombie, the new teacher, introduces herself to the class that has never been required to behave or to learn:

My name is Virginia Barracombie and it will be Miss Barracombie to you indefinitely. One of these days you will meet someone from the last school in which I taught. The worst that he tells you about me will be true. It's a far cry from child to man, and it's not through games that we get there. You and I are bound together in a contract for one year. I teach; you learn. Behave yourselves and pay attention and this will be one of the good years of your lives. You have a minute to prepare yourself with ruler, compass, pencil, and paper for a review of the meaning and use of decimals.

In this passage Miss Barracombie is completely straightforward. Then, however, the narrator tells readers the effect of the introduction on the class:

It was the shock treatment all right—but with economy, with the clarity of piano keys struck singly . . .

This description contains two comparisons—the teacher's introduction is a "shock treatment" that jolts the class to attention; then, each point is made "with the clarity of piano keys struck singly." Miss Barracombie has gotten the students' attention and allowed for no confusion about what she expects.

Good writers use comparisons to convey ideas and add interest to their writing. Now read these passages. In each, what two things are being compared?

The Hard-Nuts' . . . particular dragon in the case of Miss Barracombie was her good sense.

Of course, she knew the ones of us who could not connect with the main lines she was trolling, but she put out other lines for them . . .

She never assumed that we had achieved. She probed and exposed until she read it in the blood.

When our special teachers came and Miss Barracombie left the room, Eugene Kent would replace his hearing aid, and we would be at once stalking a world of enemies.

Our teacher put both hands across her face and, huddled and small, walked out like a child under Mrs. Hamilton's arm.

Note that each of these comparisons not only gives information but does so in a way that makes the writing lively, clear, and interesting.

When you read, look for comparisons.
When you write, use comparisons.

See TONE in the Handbook of Literary Terms, page 691

The Ransom of Red Chief

O. Henry

Bill was to be scalped at daybreak and Sam was to be broiled at the stake. At first neither took the idea seriously.

It looked like a good thing: but wait till I tell you. We were down South, in Alabama—Bill Driscoll and myself—when this kidnaping idea struck us. It was, as Bill afterward expressed it, "during a moment of temporary mental apparition";[1] but we didn't find that out till later.

There was a town down there, as flat as a flannel-cake, and called Summit, of course. It contained inhabitants of as undeleterious[2] and self-satisfied a class of peasantry as ever clustered around a Maypole.

Bill and me had a joint capital of about six hundred dollars, and we needed just two thousand dollars more to pull off a fraudulent town-lot scheme in western Illinois with. We talked it over on the front steps of the Hotel. Philoprogenitiveness,[3] says we, is strong in semi-rural communities; therefore, and for other reasons, a kidnaping project ought to do better there than in the radius of newspapers that send reporters out in plain clothes to stir up talk about such things. We knew that Summit couldn't get after us with anything stronger than constables and, maybe, some lackadaisical bloodhounds and a diatribe or two in the *Weekly Farmers' Budget*. So, it looked good.

We selected for our victim the only child of a prominent citizen named Ebenezer Dorset. The father was respectable and tight, a mortgage fancier and a stern, upright collection-plate passer and forecloser. The kid was a boy of ten, with bas-relief freckles, and hair the color of the cover of the magazine you buy at the newsstand when you want to catch a train. Bill and me figured that Ebenezer

---

1. *apparition,* Bill means *aberration,* a temporary disorder of the mind.
2. *undeleterious,* harmless.
3. *philoprogenitiveness,* love of offspring.

would melt down for a ransom of two thousand dollars to a cent. But wait till I tell you.

About two miles from Summit was a little mountain, covered with a dense cedar brake. On the rear elevation of this mountain was a cave. There we stored provisions.

One evening after sundown, we drove in a buggy past old Dorset's house. The kid was in the street, throwing rocks at a kitten on the opposite fence.

"Hey, little boy!" says Bill, "would you like to have a bag of candy and a nice ride?"

The boy catches Bill neatly in the eye with a piece of brick.

"That will cost the old man an extra five hundred dollars," says Bill, climbing over the wheel.

That boy put up a fight like a welterweight cinnamon bear; but, at last, we got him down in the bottom of the buggy and drove away. We took him up to the cave, and I hitched the horse in the cedar brake. After dark I drove the buggy to the little village, three miles away, where we had hired it, and walked back to the mountain.

Bill was pasting court-plaster over the scratches and bruises on his features. There was a fire burning behind the big rock at the entrance of the cave, and the boy was watching a pot of boiling coffee, with two buzzard tail-feathers stuck in his red hair. He points a stick at me when I come up, and says:

"Ha! cursed paleface, do you dare to enter the camp of Red Chief, the terror of the plains?"

"He's all right now," says Bill, rolling up his trousers and examining some bruises on his shins. "We're playing Indian. We're making Buffalo Bill's show look like magic-lantern views of Palestine in the town hall. I'm Old Hank, the Trapper, Red Chief's captive, and I'm to be scalped at daybreak. By Geronimo! that kid can kick hard."

Yes, sir, that boy seemed to be having the time of his life. The fun of camping out in a cave had made him forget that he was a captive himself. He immediately christened me Snake-eye, the Spy, and announced that, when his braves returned from the warpath, I was to be broiled at the stake at the rising of the sun.

Then we had supper; and he filled his mouth full of bacon and bread and gravy, and began to talk. He made a during-dinner speech something like this:

"I like this fine. I never camped out before; but I had a pet 'possum once, and I was nine last birthday. I hate to go to school. Rats ate up sixteen of Jimmy Talbot's aunt's speckled hen's eggs. Are there any real Indians in these woods? I want some more gravy. Does the trees moving make the wind blow? We had five puppies. What makes your nose so red, Hank? My father has lots of money. Are the stars hot? I whipped Ed Walker twice, Saturday. I don't like girls. You dassent catch toads unless with a string. Do oxen make any noise? Why are oranges round? Have you got beds to sleep on in this cave? Amos Murray has got six toes. A parrot can talk, but a monkey or a fish can't. How many does it take to make twelve?"

Every few minutes he would remember that he was a pesky redskin, and pick up his stick rifle and tiptoe to the mouth of the cave to rubber for the scouts of the hated paleface. Now and then he would let out a war-whoop that made Old Hank the Trapper shiver.

That boy had Bill terrorized from the start.

"Red Chief," says I to the kid, "would you like to go home?"

"Aw, what for?" says he. "I don't have any fun at home. I hate to go to school. I like to camp out. You won't take me back home again, Snake-eye, will you?"

"Not right away," says I. "We'll stay here in the cave awhile."

"All right!" says he. "That'll be fine. I never had such fun in all my life."

We went to bed about eleven o'clock. We spread down some wide blankets and quilts and put Red Chief between us. We weren't afraid he'd run away. He kept us awake for three hours, jumping up and reaching for his rifle and screeching: "Hist! pard," in mine and Bill's ears, as the fancied crackle of a twig or the rustle of a leaf revealed to his young imagination the stealthy approach of the outlaw band. At last, I fell into a troubled sleep, and dreamed that I had been kidnaped and chained to a tree by a ferocious pirate with red hair.

Just at daybreak, I was awakened by a series of awful screams from Bill. They weren't yells, or howls, or shouts, or whoops, or yawps, such as you'd expect from a manly set of vocal organs—they were simply indecent, terrifying, humiliating screams, such as women emit when they see ghosts or caterpillars. It's an awful thing to hear a strong, desperate, fat man scream incontinently in a cave at daybreak.

I jumped up to see what the matter was. Red Chief was sitting on Bill's chest, with one hand twined in Bill's hair. In the other he had the sharp case-knife we used for slicing bacon; and he was industriously and realistic-ally trying to take Bill's scalp, according to the sentence that had been pronounced upon him the evening before.

I got the knife away from the kid and made him lie down again. But, from that moment, Bill's spirit was broken. He laid down on his side of the bed, but he never closed an eye again in sleep as long as that boy was with us. I dozed off for a while, but along toward sun-up I remembered that Red Chief had said I was to be burned at the stake at the rising of the sun. I wasn't nervous or afraid; but I sat up and lit my pipe and leaned against a rock.

"What you getting up so soon for, Sam?" asked Bill.

"Me?" says I. "Oh, I got a kind of pain in my shoulder. I thought sitting up would rest it."

"You're a liar!" says Bill. "You're afraid. You was to be burned at sunrise, and you was afraid he'd do it. And he would, too, if he could find a match. Ain't it awful, Sam? Do you think anybody will pay out money to get a little imp like that back home?"

"Sure," said I. "A rowdy kid like that is just the kind that parents dote on. Now, you and the Chief get up and cook breakfast, while I go up on the top of this mountain and reconnoiter."

I went up on the peak of the little mountain and ran my eye over the contiguous vicinity. Over towards Summit I expected to see the sturdy yeomanry of the village armed with scythes and pitchforks beating the countryside for the dastardly kidnapers. But what I saw was a peaceful landscape dotted with one man ploughing with a dun mule. Nobody was dragging the creek; no couriers dashed hither and yon, bringing tidings of no news

Robert Henri, "Tom Cafferty," 1924, *Memorial Art Gallery of the University of Rochester*

to the distracted parents. There was a sylvan attitude of somnolent sleepiness pervading that section of the external outward surface of Alabama that lay exposed to my view. "Perhaps," says I to myself, "it has not yet been discovered that the wolves have borne away the tender lambkin from the fold. Heaven help the wolves!" says I, and I went down the mountain to breakfast.

When I got to the cave I found Bill backed up against the side of it, breathing hard, and the boy threatening to smash him with a rock half as big as a cocoanut.

"He put a red-hot boiled potato down my back," explained Bill, "and then mashed it with his foot; and I boxed his ears. Have you got a gun about you, Sam?"

I took the rock away from the boy and kind of patched up the argument. "I'll fix you," says the kid to Bill. "No man ever yet struck the Red Chief but he got paid for it. You better beware!"

After breakfast the kid takes a piece of leather with strings wrapped around it out of his pocket and goes outside the cave unwinding it.

"What's he up to now?" says Bill, anxiously. "You don't think he'll run away, do you, Sam?"

"No fear of it," says I. "He don't seem to be much of a home body. But we've got to fix up some plan about the ransom. There don't seem to be much excitement around Summit on account of his disappearance; but maybe they haven't realized yet that he's gone. His folks may think he's spending the night with Aunt Jane or one of the neighbors. Anyhow, he'll be missed today. Tonight we must get a message to his father demanding the two thousand dollars for his return."

Just then we heard a kind of war whoop, such as David might have emitted when he knocked out the champion Goliath.[4] It was a sling that Red Chief had pulled out of his pocket, and he was whirling it around his head.

I dodged, and heard a heavy thud and a kind of a sigh from Bill, like a horse gives out when you take his saddle off. A rock the size of an egg had caught Bill just behind his left ear. He loosened himself all over and fell in the fire across the frying pan of hot water for washing the dishes. I dragged him out and poured cold water on his head for half an hour.

By and by, Bill sits up and feels behind his ear and says: "Sam, do you know who my favorite biblical character is?"

"Take it easy," says I. "You'll come to your senses presently."

"King Herod,"[5] says he. "You won't go away and leave me here alone, will you, Sam?"

I went out and caught that boy and shook him until his freckles rattled.

"If you don't behave," says I, "I'll take you straight home. Now, are you going to be good, or not?"

"I was only funning," says he, sullenly. "I didn't mean to hurt Old Hank. But what did he hit me for? I'll behave, Snake-eye, if you won't send me home, and if you'll let me play the Black Scout today."

"I don't know the game," says I. "That's for you and Mr. Bill to decide. He's your playmate for the day. I'm going away for a while, on business. Now, you come in and make friends with him and say you are sorry for hurting him, or home you go, at once."

I made him and Bill shake hands, and then I took Bill aside and told him I was going to Poplar Grove, a little village three miles from the cave, and find out what I could about how the kidnaping had been regarded in Summit. Also, I thought it best to send a peremptory letter to old man Dorset that day, demanding the ransom and dictating how it should be paid.

"You know, Sam," says Bill, "I've stood by you without batting an eye in earthquakes, fire and flood—in poker games, dynamite outrages, police raids, train robberies, and cyclones. I never lost my nerve yet till we kidnaped that two-legged skyrocket of a kid. He's got me going. You won't leave me long with him, will you, Sam?"

---

4. Goliath, in the Bible, a Philistine giant whom David killed with a stone from a sling.

5. King Herod, King of Judea, a tyrant who at the time of Jesus Christ's birth ordered all the male infants of Bethlehem killed.

"I'll be back some time this afternoon," says I. "You must keep the boy amused and quiet till I return. And now we'll write the letter to old Dorset."

Bill and I got paper and pencil and worked on the letter while Red Chief, with a blanket wrapped around him, strutted up and down, guarding the mouth of the cave. Bill begged me tearfully to make the ransom fifteen hundred dollars instead of two thousand. "I ain't attempting," says he, "to decry the celebrated moral aspect of parental affection, but we're dealing with humans, and it ain't human for anybody to give up two thousand dollars for that forty-pound chunk of freckled wildcat. I'm willing to take a chance at fifteen hundred dollars. You can charge the difference up to me."

So, to relieve Bill, I acceded, and we collaborated a letter that ran this way:

EBENEZER DORSET, ESQ.:

We have your boy concealed in a place far from Summit. It is useless for you or the most skillful detectives to attempt to find him. Absolutely, the only terms on which you can have him restored to you are these: We demand fifteen hundred dollars in large bills for his return; the money to be left at midnight tonight at the same spot and in the same box as your reply—as hereinafter described. If you agree to these terms, send your answer in writing by a solitary messenger tonight at half-past eight o'clock. After crossing Owl Creek on the road to Poplar Grove, there are three large trees about a hundred yards apart, close to the fence of the wheat field on the right-hand side. At the bottom of the fence post, opposite the third tree, will be found a small pasteboard box.

The messenger will place the answer in this box and return immediately to Summit.

If you attempt any treachery or fail to comply with our demand as stated, you will never see your boy again.

If you pay the money as demanded, he will be returned to you safe and well within three hours. These terms are final, and if you do not accede to them no further communication will be attempted.

TWO DESPERATE MEN

I addressed this letter to Dorset, and put it in my pocket. As I was about to start, the kid comes up to me and says:

"Aw, Snake-eye, you said I could play the Black Scout while you was gone."

"Play it, of course," says I. "Mr. Bill will play with you. What kind of a game is it?"

"I'm the Black Scout," says Red Chief, "and I have to ride to the stockade to warn the settlers that the Indians are coming. I'm tired of playing Indian myself. I want to be the Black Scout."

"All right," says I. "It sounds harmless to me. I guess Mr. Bill will help you foil the pesky savages."

"What am I to do?" asks Bill, looking at the kid suspiciously.

"You are the hoss," says Black Scout. "Get down on your hands and knees. How can I ride to the stockade without a hoss?"

"You'd better keep him interested," said I, "till we get the scheme going. Loosen up."

Bill gets down on his all fours, and a look comes in his eye like a rabbit's when you catch it in a trap.

"How far is it to the stockade, kid?" he asks, in a husky manner of voice.

"Ninety miles," says the Black Scout. "And you have to hump yourself to get there on time. Whoa, now!"

The Black Scout jumps on Bill's back and digs his heels in his side.

"For Heaven's sake," says Bill, "hurry back, Sam, as soon as you can. I wish we hadn't made the ransom more than a thousand. Say, you quit kicking me or I'll get up and warm you good."

I walked over to Poplar Grove and sat around the post office and store, talking with the chaw-bacons that came in to trade. One whiskerando says that he hears Summit is all upset on account of Elder Ebenezer Dorset's boy having been lost or stolen. That was all I wanted to know. I bought some smoking tobacco, referred casually to the price of black-eyed peas, posted my letter surreptitiously, and came away. The postmaster said the mail-carrier would come by in an hour to take the mail to Summit.

When I got back to the cave Bill and the boy were not to be found. I explored the vicinity of the cave, and risked a yodel or two, but there was no response.

So I lighted my pipe and sat down on a mossy bank to await developments.

In about half an hour I heard the bushes rustle, and Bill wabbled out into the little glade in front of the cave. Behind him was the kid, stepping softly like a scout, with a broad grin on his face. Bill stopped, took off his hat, and wiped his face with a red handkerchief. The kid stopped about eight feet behind him.

"Sam," says Bill, "I suppose you'll think I'm a renegade, but I couldn't help it. I'm a grown person with masculine proclivities and habits of self-defense, but there is a time when all systems of egotism and predominance fail. The boy is gone. I sent him home. All is off. There was martyrs in old times," goes on Bill, "that suffered death rather than give up the particular graft they enjoyed. None of 'em ever was subjugated to such supernatural tortures as I have been. I tried to be faithful to our articles of depredation;[6] but there came a limit."

"What's the trouble, Bill?" I asks him.

"I was rode," says Bill, "the ninety miles to the stockade, not barring an inch. Then, when the settlers was rescued, I was given oats. Sand ain't a palatable substitute. And then, for an hour I had to try to explain to him why there was nothin' in holes, how a road can run both ways, and what makes the grass green. I tell you, Sam, a human can only stand so much. I takes him by the neck of his clothes and drags him down the mountain. On the way he kicks my legs black and blue from the knees down; and I've got to have two or three bites on my thumb and hand cauterized.

"But he's gone"—continues Bill—"gone home. I showed him the road to Summit and kicked him about eight feet nearer there at one kick. I'm sorry we lose the ransom; but it was either that or Bill Driscoll to the madhouse."

Bill is puffing and blowing, but there is a look of ineffable peace and growing content on his rose-pink features.

---

6. *articles of depredation.* Bill means *articles of confederation,* a contract or agreement. The constitution adopted by the thirteen original states was called the Articles of Confederation.

"Bill," says I, "there isn't any heart disease in your family, is there?"

"No," says Bill, "nothing chronic except malaria and accidents. Why?"

"Then you might turn around," says I, "and have a look behind you."

Bill turns and sees the boy, and loses his complexion and sits down plump on the ground and begins to pluck aimlessly at grass and little sticks. For an hour I was afraid of his mind. And then I told him that my scheme was to put the whole job through immediately and that we would get the ransom and be off with it by midnight if old Dorset fell in with our proposition. So Bill braced up enough to give the kid a weak sort of a smile and a promise to play the Russian in a Japanese war with him as soon as he felt a little better.

I had a scheme for collecting that ransom without danger of being caught by counterplots that ought to commend itself to professional kidnapers. The tree under which the answer was to be left—and the money later on—was close to the road fence with big, bare fields on all sides. If a gang of constables should be watching for anyone to come for the note, they could see him a long way off crossing the fields or in the road. But no, sirree! At half-past eight I was up in that tree as well hidden as a tree toad, waiting for the messenger to arrive.

Exactly on time, a half-grown boy rides up the road on a bicycle, locates the pasteboard box at the foot of the fencepost, slips a folded piece of paper into it, and pedals away again back toward Summit.

I waited an hour and then concluded the thing was square. I slid down the tree, got the note, slipped along the fence till I struck the woods, and was back at the cave in another half an hour. I opened the note, got near the lantern, and read it to Bill. It was written with a pen in a crabbed hand, and the sum and substance of it was this:

TWO DESPERATE MEN.

Gentlemen: I received your letter today by post, in regard to the ransom you ask for the return of my son. I think you are a little high in your demands, and I hereby make you a counter-proposition, which I am inclined to believe you will accept. You bring Johnny home and pay me two hundred and fifty dollars in cash, and I agree to take him off your hands. You had better come at night, for the neighbors believe he is lost, and I couldn't be responsible for what they would do to anybody they saw bringing him back. Very respectfully,

EBENEZER DORSET.

"Great Pirates of Penzance," says I; "of all the impudent——"

But I glanced at Bill, and hesitated. He had the most appealing look in his eyes I ever saw on the face of a dumb or a talking brute.

"Sam," says he, "what's two hundred and fifty dollars, after all? We've got the money. One more night of this kid will send me to a bed in Bedlam.[7] Besides being a thorough gentleman, I think Mr. Dorset is a spendthrift for making us such a liberal offer. You ain't going to let the chance go, are you?"

"Tell you the truth, Bill," says I, "this lit-

---

7. **Bedlam,** popular name for the hospital of St. Mary of Bethlehem, an insane asylum in London, England.

tle he ewe lamb has somewhat got on my nerves too. We'll take him home, pay the ransom, and make our getaway."

We took him home that night. We got him to go by telling him that his father had bought a silver-mounted rifle and a pair of moccasins for him, and we were to hunt bears the next day.

It was just twelve o'clock when we knocked at Ebenezer's front door. Just at the moment when I should have been abstracting the fifteen hundred dollars from the box under the tree, according to the original proposition, Bill was counting out two hundred and fifty dollars into Dorset's hand.

When the kid found out we were going to leave him at home he started up a howl like a calliope and fastened himself as tight as a leech to Bill's leg. His father peeled him away gradually, like a porous plaster.

"How long can you hold him?" asks Bill.

"I'm not as strong as I used to be," says old Dorset, "but I think I can promise you ten minutes."

"Enough," says Bill. "In ten minutes I shall cross the Central, Southern, and Middle Western States, and be legging it trippingly for the Canadian border."

And, as dark as it was, and as fat as Bill was, and as good a runner as I am, he was a good mile and a half out of Summit before I could catch up with him.

THINK AND DISCUSS
Understanding
1. Who is Red Chief?
2. Why do Bill and Sam decide to kidnap Ebenezer Dorset's son?
3. During their first night in the cave, what does Johnny almost do to Bill?
4. What do the kidnappers finally do with Red Chief?

Analyzing
5. Is there any indication in the first few pages of the story that the kidnapping may not succeed? If so, where?
6. How would you characterize Bill and Sam?
7. Near the middle of the story, who is in control? Why is this unusual?
8. What is unusual about Ebenezer Dorset's letter to the kidnappers?

9. What is unexpected about the outcome of the story?

Extending
10. Do you think this experience will cause Sam and Bill to change their ways?

APPLYING: Tone H⊼
See Handbook of Literary Terms, p. 691.

Practically any subject can be made to seem serious or silly, depending on how it is handled. An author's choice of words and details reveals his or her attitude toward that subject and establishes the **tone** of the work. Abduction is usually a serious topic. Think about how this topic is handled in "The Ransom of Red Chief." Then answer the questions that follow.

1. Do Bill and Sam take their kidnapping plot seriously?
2. Does the author seem to take Bill and Sam's plot seriously? How does the author's attitude influence the way you regard the two men and their activities?
3. Describe the tone of this story.

VOCABULARY
Dictionary
Use your Glossary to answer the following questions. Write the answers on your paper. Be sure you know the meaning of each vocabulary word.
1. Does the accent in *fraudulent* fall on the first, second, or third syllable?
2. Does the first syllable of *bas-relief* rhyme with *ha*, *lace*, or *glass?*
3. Does the first syllable of *stealthy* rhyme with *reel*, *tell*, or *mail?*
4. Does the syllable in *reconnoiter* that has a primary accent rhyme with *deck*, *boy*, or *her?*

5. Does the accented syllable in *contiguous* rhyme with *don*, *dig*, or *flu?*

COMPOSITION
Comparing and Contrasting
The humor of "The Ransom of Red Chief" lies in the contrast between what kidnappers are usually like and what Sam and Bill are like. Write a paragraph in which you compare and contrast most kidnappers with Sam and Bill.

Writing an Interview
Assume you are a journalist on the *Western Star.* You decide to interview Johnny, Sam, Bill, and Johnny's father. Write at least three questions to ask each of these people. Then write answers for these questions. Try to use the same tone in your questions that O. Henry uses in the story. Be sure that answers sound as if they were given by the characters interviewed.

BIOGRAPHY

O. Henry
1862–1910

O. Henry's real name was William Sydney Porter. He was born in Greensboro, North Carolina, but after a brief schooling there he drifted off to Texas, where he became a bank teller, began writing pieces for newspapers, and founded his own humor magazine called *The Rolling Stone* (1894–1895). He later settled in New York.

O. Henry's humorous stories with ingenious plots and surprise endings gained him enormous popularity. He wrote so many short stories that nine collections were published during his life and eight more after his death. In 1918 the O. Henry Memorial Awards were established. These are awarded each year to the authors of the best short stories.

Review TONE in the Handbook of Literary Terms, page 691

The Medicine Bag

Virginia Driving Hawk Sneve

We were afraid our friends would laugh because Grandpa wasn't tall and stately like TV Indians.

---

y kid sister Cheryl and I always bragged about our Sioux grandpa, Joe Iron Shell. Our friends, who had always lived in the city and only knew about Indians from movies and TV, were impressed by our stories. Maybe we exaggerated and made Grandpa and the reservation sound glamorous, but when we'd return home to Iowa after our yearly summer visit to Grandpa, we always had some exciting tale to tell.

We always had some authentic Sioux article to show our listeners. One year Cheryl had new moccasins that Grandpa had made. On another visit he gave me a small, round, flat, rawhide drum which was decorated with a painting of a warrior riding a horse. He taught me a real Sioux chant to sing while I beat the drum with a leather-covered stick that had a feather on the end. Man, that really made an impression.

We never showed our friends Grandpa's picture. Not that we were ashamed of him, but because we knew that the glamorous tales we told didn't go with the real thing. Our friends would have laughed at the picture because Grandpa wasn't tall and stately like TV Indians. His hair wasn't in braids but hung in stringy, gray strands on his neck, and he was old. He was our great-grandfather, and he didn't live in a teepee, but all by himself in a part log, part tar-paper shack on the Rosebud Reservation in South Dakota. So when Grandpa came to visit us, I was so ashamed and embarrassed I could've died.

There are a lot of yippy poodles and other fancy little dogs in our neighborhood, but they usually barked singly at the mailman from the safety of their own yards. Now it sounded as if a whole pack of mutts were barking together in one place.

I got up and walked to the curb to see what the commotion was. About a block away I saw a crowd of little kids yelling, with the dogs yipping and growling around someone who was walking down the middle of the street.

I watched the group as it slowly came closer and saw that in the center of the strange procession was a man wearing a tall black hat. He'd pause now and then to peer at something in his hand and then at the houses on either side of the street. I felt cold and hot at the same time as I recognized the man. "Oh, no!" I whispered. "It's Grandpa!"

I stood on the curb, unable to move even though I wanted to run and hide. Then I got mad when I saw how the yippy dogs were growling and nipping at the old man's baggy pant legs and how wearily he poked them away with his cane. "Stupid mutts," I said as I ran to rescue Grandpa.

When I kicked and hollered at the dogs to get away, they put their tails between their legs and scattered. The kids ran to the curb where they watched me and the old man.

"Grandpa," I said and felt pretty dumb when my voice cracked. I reached for his beat-up old tin suitcase, which was tied shut with a rope. But he set it down right in the street and shook my hand.

"*Hau, Takoza,* Grandchild," he greeted me formally in Sioux.

All I could do was stand there with the whole neighborhood watching and shake the hand of the leather-brown old man. I saw how his gray hair straggled from under his big black hat, which had a drooping feather in its crown. His rumpled black suit hung like a sack over his stooped frame. As he shook my hand, his coat fell open to expose a bright-red satin shirt with a beaded bolo tie under the collar. His get-up wasn't out of place on the reservation, but it sure was here, and I wanted to sink right through the pavement.

"Hi," I muttered with my head down. I tried to pull my hand away when I felt his bony hand trembling, and looked up to see fatigue in his face. I felt like crying. I couldn't think of anything to say so I picked up Grandpa's suitcase, took his arm, and guided him up the driveway to our house.

Mom was standing on the steps. I don't know how long she'd been watching, but her hand was over her mouth and she looked as if she couldn't believe what she saw. Then she ran to us.

"Grandpa," she gasped. "How in the world did you get here?"

She checked her move to embrace Grandpa and I remembered that such a display of affection is unseemly to the Sioux and would embarrass him.

"*Hau,* Marie," he said as he shook Mom's hand. She smiled and took his other arm.

As we supported him up the steps, the door banged open and Cheryl came bursting out of the house. She was all smiles and was so obviously glad to see Grandpa that I was ashamed of how I felt.

"Grandpa!" she yelled happily. "You came to see us!"

Grandpa smiled and Mom and I let go of him as he stretched out his arms to my ten-year-old sister, who was still young enough to be hugged.

"*Wicincala*, little girl," he greeted her and then collapsed.

He had fainted. Mom and I carried him into her sewing room, where we had a spare bed.

After we had Grandpa on the bed Mom stood there helplessly patting his shoulder.

"Shouldn't we call the doctor, Mom?" I suggested, since she didn't seem to know what to do.

"Yes, she agreed with a sigh. "You make Grandpa comfortable, Martin."

I reluctantly moved to the bed. I knew Grandpa wouldn't want to have Mom undress him, but I didn't want to, either. He was so skinny and frail that his coat slipped off easily. When I loosened his tie and opened his shirt collar, I felt a small leather pouch that hung from a thong around his neck. I left it alone and moved to remove his boots. The scuffed old cowboy boots were tight and he moaned as I put pressure on his legs to jerk them off.

I put the boots on the floor and saw why they fit so tight. Each one was stuffed with money. I looked at the bills that lined the boots and started to ask about them, but Grandpa's eyes were closed again.

Mom came back with a basin of water. "The doctor thinks Grandpa is suffering from heat exhaustion," she explained as she bathed Grandpa's face. Mom gave a big sigh, "*Oh, hinh*, Martin. How do you suppose he got here?"

We found out after the doctor's visit. Grandpa was angrily sitting up in bed while Mom tried to feed him some soup.

"Tonight you let Marie feed you, Grandpa," spoke my dad, who had gotten home from work just as the doctor was leaving. "You're not really sick," he said as he gently pushed Grandpa back against the pillows. "The doctor said you just got too tired and hot after your long trip."

Grandpa relaxed, and, between sips of soup, he told us of his journey. Soon after our visit to him Grandpa decided that he would like to see where his only living descendants lived and what our home was like. Besides, he admitted sheepishly, he was lonesome after we left.

I knew everybody felt as guilty as I did— especially Mom. Mom was all Grandpa had left. So even after she married my dad, who's a white man and teaches in the college in our city, and after Cheryl and I were born, Mom made sure that every summer we spent a week with Grandpa.

I never thought that Grandpa would be lonely after our visits, and none of us noticed how old and weak he had become. But Grandpa knew, and so he came to us. He had ridden on buses for two and a half days. When he arrived in the city, tired and stiff from sitting for so long, he set out, walking, to find us.

He had stopped to rest on the steps of some building downtown and a policeman found him. The cop, according to Grandpa, was a good man who took him to the bus stop and waited until the bus came and told the driver to let Grandpa out at Bell View Drive. After Grandpa got off the bus, he started walking again. But he couldn't see the house numbers on the other side when he walked on the sidewalk so he walked in the middle of the street.

Quill decorated bag from the Dakota Indians, a tribe of the Sioux nation. *Heye Foundation*

That's when all the little kids and dogs followed him.

I knew everybody felt as bad as I did. Yet I was so proud of this eighty-six-year-old man, who had never been away from the reservation, having the courage to travel so far alone.

"You found the money in my boots?" he asked Mom.

"Martin did," she answered, and roused herself to scold. "Grandpa, you shouldn't have carried so much money. What if someone had stolen it from you?"

Grandpa laughed. "I would've known if anyone tried to take the boots off my feet. The money is what I've saved for a long time—a hundred dollars—for my funeral. But you take it now to buy groceries so that I won't be a burden to you while I am here."

"That won't be necessary, Grandpa," Dad said. "We are honored to have you with us and you will never be a burden. I am only sorry that we never thought to bring you home with us this summer and spare you the discomfort of a long trip."

Grandpa was pleased. "Thank you," he answered. "But do not feel bad that you didn't bring me with you for I would not have come then. It was not time." He said this in such a way that no one could argue with him. To Grandpa and the Sioux, he once told me, a thing would be done when it was the right time to do it, and that's the way it was.

"Also," Grandpa went on, looking at me, "I have come because it is soon time for Martin to have the medicine bag."

We all knew what that meant. Grandpa thought he was going to die, and he had to follow the tradition of his family to pass the medicine bag, along with its history, to the oldest male child.

"Even though the boy," he said still looking at me, "bears a white man's name, the medicine bag will be his."

I didn't know what to say. I had the same hot and cold feeling that I had when I first saw Grandpa in the street. The medicine bag was the dirty leather pouch I had found around his neck. "I could never wear such a thing," I almost said aloud. I thought of having my friends see it in gym class or at the swimming pool and could imagine the smart things they would say. But I just swallowed hard and took a step toward the bed. I knew I would have to take it.

But Grandpa was tired. "Not now, Martin," he said, waving his hand in dismissal, "it is not time. Now I will sleep."

So that's how Grandpa came to be with us for two months. My friends kept asking to come see the old man, but I put them off. I told myself that I didn't want them laughing at Grandpa. But even as I made excuses I knew it wasn't Grandpa that I was afraid they'd laugh at.

Nothing bothered Cheryl about bringing her friends to see Grandpa. Every day after school started, there'd be a crew of giggling little girls or round-eyed little boys crowded around the old man on the patio, where he'd gotten in the habit of sitting every afternoon.

Grandpa would smile in his gentle way and patiently answer their questions, or he'd tell them stories of brave warriors, ghosts, animals, and the kids listened in awed silence. Those little guys thought Grandpa was great.

Finally, one day after school, my friends came home with me because nothing I said stopped them. "We're going to see the great Indian of Bell View Drive," said Hank, who was supposed to be my best friend. "My brother has seen him three times so he oughta be well enough to see us."

When we got to my house, Grandpa was sitting on the patio. He had on his red shirt, but today he also wore a fringed leather vest that was decorated with beads. Instead of his usual cowboy boots, he had solidly beaded moccasins on his feet that stuck out of his black trousers. Of course, he had his old black hat on—he was seldom without it. But it had been brushed, and the feather in the beaded headband was proudly erect, its tip a brighter white. His hair lay in silver strands over the red shirt collar.

I stared just as my friends did, and I heard one of them murmur, "Wow!"

Grandpa looked up, and, when his eyes met mine, they twinkled as if he were laughing inside. He nodded to me, and my face got all hot. I could tell that he had known all along I was afraid he'd embarrass me in front of my friends.

"*Hau, hoksilas*, boys," he greeted and held out his hand.

My buddies passed in a single file and shook his hand as I introduced them. They were so polite I almost laughed. "How, there, Grandpa," and even a "How-do-you-do, sir."

"You look fine, Grandpa," I said as the guys sat on the lawn chairs or on the patio floor.

"*Hanh*, yes," he agreed. "When I woke up this morning, it seemed the right time to dress in the good clothes. I knew that my grandson would be bringing his friends."

"You guys want some lemonade or something?" I offered. No one answered. They were listening to Grandpa as he started telling how he'd killed the deer from which his vest was made.

Grandpa did most of the talking while my friends were there. I was so proud of him and amazed at how respectfully quiet my buddies were. Mom had to chase them home at supper time. As they left, they shook Grandpa's hand again and said to me:

"Martin, he's really great!"

"Yeah, man! Don't blame you for keeping him to yourself."

"Can we come back?"

But after they left, Mom said, "No more visitors for a while, Martin. Grandpa won't admit it, but his strength hasn't returned. He likes having company, but it tires him."

That evening Grandpa called me to his room before he went to sleep. "Tomorrow," he said, "when you come home, it will be time to give you the medicine bag."

I felt a hard squeeze from where my heart is supposed to be and was scared, but I answered, "OK, Grandpa."

All night I had weird dreams about thunder and lightning on a high hill. From a distance I heard the slow beat of a drum. When I woke up in the morning, I felt as if I hadn't slept at all. At school it seemed as if the day would never end and, when it finally did, I ran home.

Grandpa was in his room, sitting on the bed. The shades were down, and the place was dim and cool. I sat on the floor in front of Grandpa, but he didn't even look at me. After what seemed a long time he spoke.

"I sent your mother and sister away. What you will hear today is only for a man's ears. What you will receive is only for a man's hands." He fell silent, and I felt shivers down my back.

"My father in his early manhood," Grandpa began, "made a vision quest to find a spirit guide for his life. You cannot understand how it was in that time, when the great Teton Sioux were first made to stay on the reservation. There was a strong need for guidance from *Wakantanka*, the Great Spirit. But too many of the young men were filled with despair and hatred. They thought it was hopeless to search for a vision when the glorious life was gone and only the hated confines of a reservation lay ahead. But my father held to the old ways.

"He carefully prepared for his quest with a purifying sweat bath, and then he went alone to a high butte top to fast and pray. After three days he received his sacred dream—in which he found, after long searching, the white man's iron. He did not understand his vision of finding something belonging to the white people, for in that time they were the enemy. When he came down from the butte to cleanse himself at the stream below, he found the remains of a campfire and the broken shell of an iron kettle. This was a sign which reinforced his dream. He took a piece of the iron for his medicine bag, which he had made of elk skin years before, to prepare for his quest.

"He returned to his village, where he told his dream to the wise old men of the tribe. They gave him the name *Iron Shell*, but neither did they understand the meaning of the dream. This first Iron Shell kept the piece of iron with him at all times and believed it gave him protection from the evils of those unhappy days.

"Then a terrible thing happened to Iron Shell. He and several other young men were taken from their homes by the soldiers and sent far away to a white man's boarding school. He was angry and lonesome for his parents and the young girl he had wed before he was taken away. At first Iron Shell resisted the teacher's attempts to change him, and he did not try to learn. One day it was his turn to work in the school's blacksmith shop. As he walked into the place he knew that his medicine had brought him there to learn and work with the white man's iron.

"Iron Shell became a blacksmith and worked at the trade when he returned to the reservation. All of his life he treasured the medicine bag. When he was old, and I was a man, he gave it to me, for no one made the vision quest any more."

Grandpa quit talking, and I stared in disbelief as he covered his face with his hands. His shoulders were shaking with quiet sobs, and I looked away until he began to speak again.

"I kept the bag until my son, your mother's father, was a man and had to leave us to fight in the war across the ocean. I gave him the bag, for I believed it would protect him in battle, but he did not take it with him. He was afraid that he would lose it. He died in a faraway place."

Again Grandpa was still, and I felt his grief around me.

"My son," he went on after clearing his throat, "had only a daughter and it is not proper for her to know of these things."

He unbuttoned his shirt, pulled out the leather pouch, and lifted it over his head. He held it in his hand, turning it over and over as if memorizing how it looked.

"In the bag," he said as he opened it and removed two objects, "is the broken shell of the iron kettle, a pebble from the butte, and a piece of the sacred sage." He held the pouch upside down and dust drifted down.

"After the bag is yours you must put a piece of prairie sage within and never open it again until you pass it on to your son." He replaced the pebble and the piece of iron, and tied the bag.

I stood up, somehow knowing I should. Grandpa slowly rose from the bed and stood upright in front of me holding the bag before my face. I closed my eyes and waited for him to slip it over my head. But he spoke.

"No, you need not wear it." He placed the soft leather bag in my right hand and closed my other hand over it. "It would not be right to wear it in this time and place where no one will understand. Put it safely away until you are again on the reservation. Wear it then, when you replace the sacred sage."

Grandpa turned and sat again on the bed. Wearily he leaned his head against the pillow. "Go," he said, "I will sleep now."

"Thank you, Grandpa," I said softly and left with the bag in my hands.

That night Mom and Dad took Grandpa to the hospital. Two weeks later I stood alone on the lonely prairie of the reservation and put the sacred sage in my medicine bag.

THINK AND DISCUSS
Understanding
1. Why does Grandpa come to Iowa? How does he get there?
2. Why doesn't Martin invite his friends to the house to visit Grandpa?
3. What is in the medicine bag?

Analyzing
4. When his friends visit Grandpa, Martin is proud instead of embarrassed. Why?
5. Summarize the family history that Grandpa tells Martin. In what ways does this change Martin's thinking about wearing the medicine bag?
6. In the last sentence, we see Martin placing the sacred sage in the bag. What can we **infer** has happened to Grandpa?

Extending
7. What kinds of things might young people learn from parents, grandparents, or older relatives? Of what value is this knowledge?

REVIEWING: Tone HʒT
See Handbook of Literary Terms, p. 691.
  Tone is the attitude of the writer toward the subject. Think about the way Grandpa and his medicine bag are presented; then answer the questions that follow.
1. How does Grandpa regard the medicine bag? How do you know?
2. Trace the change in Martin's feelings about the medicine bag.
3. Describe the subject of this story and the author's attitude toward that subject.

THINKING SKILLS
Generalizing
  When you generalize, you draw a general conclusion from particular information. In giving his grandson the medicine bag, Grandpa tells a family history that goes back several generations. From Grandpa's story, you might make some generalizations

about the history of the Sioux. Refer to Grandpa's story as you discuss the questions that follow.

1. What effect did being placed on reservations have on the Sioux?
2. How did the government regard the Sioux way of life? Explain.

COMPOSITION
Writing a Description

Throughout the story, we see Grandpa from Martin's point of view. Now write a comparison in which Grandpa describes Martin. Before you begin writing, list details that Grandpa would be likely to notice (Martin's modern dress, his various reactions to his grandfather). For additional help in writing this composition, see "Writing as a Story Character" in the Writer's Handbook.

Writing a Personal Essay

The vision quest undertaken by the young men of the Sioux nation both prepared them for the responsibilities of adulthood and helped them find a place in adult society. Does coming of age in modern society contain any ceremonies or events similar to the vision quest? Write a three- to five-paragraph essay in which you describe the vision quest and then tell ways in which it is similar to a ceremony or event in modern society.

ENRICHMENT
Speaking and Listening

Most families can identify their ethnic backgrounds, the heritages and cultures from which they originate. Many families are products of several different cultures. Ask family members to identify at least one of the cultures from which you are descended. Or choose a culture in which you are interested. Then either by talking to members of that culture or by looking up information in the library, choose an object or a custom that is important to that culture. Prepare a brief (three- to five-minute) speech that describes the object or custom and explains its significance. If you can, use an audio-visual aid in your speech. Then present your speech to your classmates.

BIOGRAPHY

Virginia Driving Hawk Sneve
1933–

Virginia Driving Hawk Sneve grew up on the Rosebud Sioux reservation in South Dakota. She was educated at South Dakota State University. While working as a teacher and counselor, she began to write history books and historical fiction. Sneve depicts American Indian life today and interprets history from the viewpoint of the American Indian. Her books include *Jimmy Yellow Hawk* (1972), *They Led a Nation* (1975), and *High Elk's Treasure* (1972).

See MOOD in the Handbook of Literary Terms, page 675

Old Man at the Bridge

Ernest Hemingway

The enemy was rapidly approaching the bridge, and the old man could go no further.

An old man with steel-rimmed spectacles and very dusty clothes sat by the side of the road. There was a pontoon bridge across the river and carts, trucks, and men, women, and children were crossing it. The mule-drawn carts staggered up the steep bank from the bridge with soldiers helping push against the spokes of the wheels. The trucks ground up and away heading out of it all and the peasants plodded along in the ankle deep dust. But the old man sat there without moving. He was too tired to go any farther.

It was my business to cross the bridge, explore the bridgehead beyond, and find out to what point the enemy had advanced. I did this and returned over the bridge. There were not so many carts now and very few people on foot, but the old man was still there.

"Where do you come from?" I asked him.

"From San Carlos," he said, and smiled.

That was his native town and so it gave him pleasure to mention it and he smiled.

"I was taking care of animals," he explained.

"Oh," I said, not quite understanding.

"Yes," he said, "I stayed, you see, taking care of animals. I was the last one to leave the town of San Carlos."

He did not look like a shepherd nor a herdsman and I looked at his black dusty clothes and his gray dusty face and his steel-rimmed spectacles and said, "What animals were they?"

"Various animals," he said, and shook his head. "I had to leave them."

Refugees along the route between Barcelona and the French border during the Spanish Civil War, January 1939. Photo by Robert Capa.

I was watching the bridge and the African-looking country of the Ebro Delta and wondering how long now it would be before we would see the enemy, and listening all the while for the first noises that would signal that ever-mysterious event called contact, and the old man still sat there.

"What animals were they?" I asked.

"There were three animals altogether," he explained. "There were two goats and a cat and then there were four pairs of pigeons."

"And you had to leave them?" I asked.

"Yes. Because of the artillery. The captain told me to go because of the artillery."

"And you have no family?" I asked, watching the far end of the bridge where a few last carts were hurrying down the slope of the bank.

"No," he said, "only the animals I stated. The cat, of course, will be all right. A cat can look out for itself, but I cannot think what will become of the others."

"What politics have you?" I asked.

"I am without politics," he said. "I am

seventy-six years old. I have come twelve kilometers now and I think now I can go no further."

"This is not a good place to stop," I said. "If you can make it, there are trucks up the road where it forks for Tortosa."

"I will wait a while," he said, "and then I will go. Where do the trucks go?"

"Towards Barcelona," I told him.

"I know no one in that direction," he said, "but thank you very much. Thank you again very much."

He looked at me very blankly and tiredly, then said, having to share his worry with someone, "The cat will be all right, I am sure. There is no need to be unquiet about the cat. But the others. Now what do you think about the others?"

"Why, they'll probably come through it all right."

"You think so?"

"Why not?" I said, watching the far bank where now there were no carts.

"But what will they do under the artillery when I was told to leave because of the artillery?"

"Did you leave the dove cage unlocked?" I asked.

"Yes."

"Then they'll fly."

"Yes, certainly they'll fly. But the others. It's better not to think about the others," he said.

"If you are rested I would go," I urged. "Get up and try to walk now."

"Thank you," he said and got to his feet, swayed from side to side and then sat down backwards in the dust.

"I was taking care of animals," he said dully, but no longer to me. "I was only taking care of animals."

There was nothing to do about him. It was Easter Sunday and the Fascists were advancing toward the Ebro. It was a gray overcast day with a low ceiling so their planes were not up. That and the fact that cats know how to look after themselves was all the good luck that old man would ever have.

THINK AND DISCUSS
Understanding
1. What are the weather conditions at the time of the story?
2. Why must the narrator go back across the bridge?
3. Why did the old man stay at home until the last minute?
4. Where is the old man at the end of the story?

Analyzing
5. Why are the peasants crossing the bridge?
6. Why doesn't the old man cross the bridge?

Extending
7. In what ways is the old man a **symbol** of civilians in wartime?

APPLYING: Mood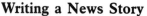
See Handbook of Literary Terms, p. 675.

The atmosphere and feeling that a writer creates in a work is its **mood.** A writer creates mood through setting, imagery, descriptions, and other evocative words. Think about how "Old Man at the Bridge" makes you feel.

1. What is the overall feeling of the first paragraph of "Old Man at the Bridge"? What words and images contribute to this feeling?

2. The old man was "taking care of animals." He is "without politics." Contrast these details with what is going on around him. In what ways does this contrast contribute to the mood of the story?

COMPOSITION
Writing a News Story

Write a news story of three to five paragraphs that describes the events that occur immediately after the events of "Old Man at the Bridge." Include the fate of the old man. Try not to alter the mood of Hemingway's story. Begin with a "lead," or quick opening sentence that presents the "who," "what," "where," "when," and "why" of the story.

Creating a Mood

Choose the kind of mood you want to create, and then write a paragraph that creates it. Before you begin, list details of setting, objects, and images to use in your paragraph.

BIOGRAPHY

Ernest Hemingway
1899–1961

Ernest Hemingway was one of the most influential American writers of this century. His deceptively simple literary style has influenced countless writers around the world. Hemingway grew up in Oak Park, Illinois. Before the United States entered World War I, he served in a French ambulance unit. He later fought in the Italian infantry. After the war, he went to Paris, where he worked as a correspondent for American newspapers.

His war experiences gave him material for many of his books and short stories. *For Whom the Bell Tolls*, considered by some to be his finest novel, grew out of his experiences in the Spanish Civil War. He won the Pulitzer Prize in 1953 for *The Old Man and the Sea*. In 1954, he was awarded the Nobel Prize for Literature.

Review MOOD in the Handbook of Literary Terms, page 675

Upon the Waters

Joanne Greenberg

It was a special day, one for which he had waited for over ten years.

It was a bright green day. The big trees on the side streets were raining seeds and the wind stirred in its second sleep. A long flatbed truck came rattling down Grant Street and stopped by the new steel, chrome, and glass building. The building's lines were so austere it made Cephas[1] wonder if anyone really worked in it. Then he saw some women going in. Good. He checked his appearance by hitching up to the rearview mirror. He was wearing a clean white shirt and a bow tie, and his thin grey hair had been slicked down with water. When he was sure he was presentable, he got down out of the cab of the truck, dusted himself off and began to walk slowly toward the building. It had been many years—perhaps they had moved. No, there was the sign: BOONE COUNTY DEPARTMENT OF WELFARE. The last time he had been here the building was a temporary shed and the people were lined up outside waiting for the relief trucks to come. That was in 1934, in the winter. His father had been proud of holding out till '34. He stopped and looked at the building again. Some secretaries came out, laughing and talking. They didn't look at him, being used to seeing people who came hesitantly to their offices to acknowledge failure in life. Cephas checked himself again in the big glass door and then went in. There was a large booth with a woman behind it and eight or nine rows of benches facing it. People were sitting quietly, staring at nothing, waiting. To the right there were a series of chutes with numbers over them. Cephas went up to the booth.

"Take a number," the woman said, without looking at him.

"Ma'am?"

---

1. *Cephas* (sē'fəs).

"You take a number and wait your turn. We'll call you."

He took one of the plastic number cards. It said 15. He went back, sat down and waited. "Five," the woman called. A heavy woman got up slowly and went to the booth and then to one of the chutes. Cephas waited. Minutes were born, ripened, aged, and died without issue. "Number six." Around him the springtime asthmatics whistled and gasped. He looked at the cracks in his fingers. "Number seven." An hour went by, another. A number, another. He was afraid to go out and check his truck lest the line speed up and he lose his place. "Number thirteen," the woman called.

So they came to his number at last and he went up to the desk, gave back the plastic card and was directed to his chute. Another woman was there at another desk. She took his name, Cephas Ribble, and his age, sixty-eight. Had he been given aid before? Yes. Had he been on General Assistance, Aid to the Needy Disabled? Tuberculosis?

"It was what they called Relief."

"Yes, but under what category was it?"

"It was for the people that was off their farms or else didn't have nothin' to eat. They called it Goin' On The County. It was back in 19 and 34. We held out till '34."

"I see. Now you are applying for the old age pension?" He said he wasn't.

"Are you married, Mr. Ribble?" She sighed. "Never had the pleasure," he said.

"Are you in emergency status?" He said he wasn't.

"All right, then, take this card and go to room 11, on your left." She pressed a little light or something and he felt the people shifting their weight on the benches behind him. Number sixteen, he expected. He made his way to room 11.

The lady there was nice; he could see it right off. She told him about the different kinds of what they called Aid, and then she had him sign some forms: permission to inquire into his bank account, acceptance of surplus or donated food, release of medical information, and several others. Then she said sympathetically, "In what way are you disabled?"

He thought about all the ways a man might be disabled and checked each one off. It was a proud moment, a man sixty-eight without one thing in the world to complain of in his health.

"I ain't disabled no way, but I'm pleased you asked me, though. A man don't take time to be grateful for things like his health. If the shoe don't pinch, you don't take notice, do you." He sat back, contented. Then he realized that the sun was getting hotter and what with everything in the truck, he'd better get on. The woman had put down her ball point pen. "Mr. Ribble, if you aren't disabled or without funds, what kind of aid do you want?" A shadow of irritation crossed her face.

"No aid at all," he said. "This is about somethin' different." He tried to hold down his excitement. It was his special day, a day for which he had waited for over a decade, but it was no use bragging and playing the boy, so he said no more. The woman was very annoyed. "Then why didn't you tell the worker at the desk?"

Tom Heflin, "The Sun Feels Good" *Private Collection*

"She didn't give me no chance, ma'am, an' neither did that other lady. I bet you don't have many repair men comin' in here to fix things—not above once, anyway."

"Well, Mr. Ribble, what is it you want?" She heard the noise of co-workers leaving and returning from their coffee breaks. She sighed and began to drum her fingers, but he wasn't aware of her impatience. He was be-

ginning back in 1934. She would have to listen to all of it!

"Thirty-four cleaned us out—cleaned us to bone. You wonder how *farmers* could go hungry. I don't know, but we did. After the drought hit there was nothin' to do but come in town an' sign up on the County. Twice a month my pa would come in an' bring back food. Sometimes I came with him. I seen them lines of hungry men just standin' out there like they was poleaxed an' hadn't fallen yet. I tell you, them days was pitiful, *pitiful*." He glanced up at her and then smiled. "I'm glad to see *you* done good since—got a new buildin' an' all. Yes, you come right up." He looked around with approval at the progress they had made.

"Mr. Ribble . . . ?" He returned. "See, we taken the Relief, but we never got to tell nobody the good it done for us. After that year, things got a little better, and soon we was on toward bein' a payin' farm again. In '46 we built us a new house—every convenience, an' in '56 we got some of them automated units for cattle care. Two years ago we was doin' good, an' last year, I knew it was time to think about My Plan for real. It was time to Thank The Welfare."

"Mr. Ribble, thanks are not necessary. . . ."

"Don't you mind, ma'am, you just get your men an' come with me."

"I beg your pardon. . . ."

"I do more than talk, ma'am. You come on out an' bring your men."

Mr. Morrissey had come back from his coffee break and was standing in the hall. She signaled him with her eyes as she followed Cephas Ribble, now walking proud and sure out to his truck. He sighed and followed, wondering why he was always around when somebody needed to make a madness plain. Why did it never happen to McFarland?

Cephas was reaching into his pocket and they thought: *gun*. He took out a piece of paper and turned to them as they stood transfixed and pale and thinking of violence. "I got it all here, all of what's in the truck. Get your men, ma'am; no use wastin' time. It's all in the truck and if it don't get unloaded soon, it's gonna spoil."

"What is this about, Mr. Ribble?"

"My donation, ma'am, I told you. I'm givin' the Relief six hundred chickens, thirty bushels of tomatoes, thirty bushels of apricots—I figured for variety, an' don't you think the apricots was a good idea, though?—ten bushels of beans, six firkins of butter—ma'am, you better get them chickens out, it don't do to keep 'em in this sun. I thought about milk, so I give two cans—that's one hundred gallons of milk, you know, for the babies."

They were dumbfounded. Cephas could see that. He wanted to tell them that he wasn't trying to be big. Everybody gives what he can. He's even signed a form right there in the office about promising to accept donated food and clothing. Their amazement at his gift embarrassed him. Then he realized that it was probably the only way they could thank him—by making a fuss. People on the state payroll must have to walk a pretty narrow line. They'd have to be on the lookout for people taking advantage. That was it. It was deep work, that welfare, mighty deep work.

"What are we supposed to do with all that food?" Mr. Morrissey said. Cephas saw that the man was making sure it wasn't a bribe. "Why, give it to the poor. Call 'em in an' let 'em get it. You can have your men unload it right now, an' I'd do it quick if I was you—like I said, it won't be long till it starts to turn in all this heat."

Mr. Morrissey tried to explain that modern welfare methods were different from those of

1934. Even then, the food had been U.S. surplus and not privately donated. It had come from government warehouses. Cephas spoke of the stupidity and waste of Government and rained invective on the Soil Bank and the Department of Agriculture. Mr. Morrissey tried again. "We don't give out any *food*. There hasn't been any *donated* since 1916!"

No doubt of it, these welfare people had to be awful careful. Cephas nodded. "The others do what they can—don't blame 'em if it don't seem like much," he said sympathetically. "I signed that slip in there about the donated food, so there must *be* some donated."

"It's done because of an obsolete law," Mrs. Traphagen argued, "one of the old Poor Laws that never got taken off the books."

"—an' here you folks are followin' it, right today," Cephas mused, "it must make you mighty proud."

"Mr. Ribble, *we have no place to store all this!*"

Cephas found his throat tightening with happiness. He had come in humility, waited all the morning just so he could show his small gratitude and be gone, and here were these people thunderstruck at the plenty. "Mister," he said, "I pay my taxes without complainin', but I never knowed how hard you people was workin' for your money. You got to guard against every kind of bribes and invitations to break the law; you got to find ways to get this food to the poor people so fast, you can't even store it! Mister, you make me proud to be an American!"

A policeman had stopped by the truck and was tranquilly writing a ticket. Cephas excused himself modestly and strode off to defend his situation. The two workers stood staring after him as he engaged the officer. It was, after all, state law that food could be donated. Had the department no parking place for donors? The policeman looked over at the stunned bearers of the state's trust. He had stopped writing.

"Could that truck fit in the workers' parking lot?" Morrissey murmured.

"What are we going to *do* with it all?" whimpered Mrs. Traphagen.

"All those chickens—six hundred chickens!"

"The poor will never stand for it," Mrs. Traphagen sighed.

"First things first," Mr. Morrissey decided, and went to confront the policeman.

Cephas's truck in the workers' parking lot blocked all their cars. As a consequence, the aid applications of eight families were held pending investigation. Six discharged inmates of the state hospital remained incarcerated for a week longer pending home checkups. Thirty-seven women washed floors and children's faces in the expectation of home visits which were not made. A meeting on disease at the Midtown Hotel was one speaker short, and high school students scheduled to hear Social Work, Career of Tomorrow, remained unedified. Applicants who came to apply for aid that afternoon were turned away. There was no trade in little plastic cards and the hive of offices was empty. But the people of the Boone County Department of Public Welfare were not idle. It was only that the action had moved from the desks and files and chutes to the workers' parking lot and into the hands of its glad tyrant, Cephas Ribble.

All afternoon Cephas lifted huge baskets of apricots and tomatoes into the arms of the welfare workers. All afternoon they went from his truck to their cars carrying the baskets, chickens festooned limply over their arms. When they complained to Mr. Morrissey, he waved them off. Were they to go to every home and deliver the food, they asked? Were big families to get the same amount as small families?

Cephas was a titan. He lifted smiling, and loaded with a strong arm. He never stopped for rest or to take a drink. The truck steamed in the hot spring light, but he was living at height, unbothered by the heat or the closeness or the increasing rankness of his chickens. Of course he saw that the welfare people weren't dressed for unloading food. They were dressed for church, looked like. It was deep work, very deep, working for the state. You had to set a good example. You had to dress up and talk very educated so as to give the poor a moral uplift.

You had to be honest. A poor man could lie—he'd been poor himself so he knew, but it must be a torment to deal with people free to lie and not be able to do it yourself.

By 3:30 the truck had been unloaded into the cars and Cephas was free to go home and take up his daily life again. He shook hands with the director and the casework supervisor, the head bookkeeper and the statistician. To them he presented his itemized list, carefully weighed and given the market value as of yesterday, in case they needed it for their records. Then he carefully turned the truck out of the parking lot, waved goodbye to the sweating group, nosed into the sluggish mass of afternoon traffic and began to head home.

The lot burst into a cacophony of high-pitched voices:

"I've got three mothers of dropouts to visit!"

"What am I going to *do* with all this stuff?"

"Who do we give this to? My people won't take the Lady Bountiful bit!"

"Does it count on their food allowance? Do we go down Vandalia and hand out apricots to every kid we see?"

"I don't have the time!"

"Which families get it?"

"Do we take the value off next month's check?"

"It's hopeless to try to distribute this fairly," the supervisor said.

"It will cost us close to a thousand dollars to distribute it at all," the statistician said.

"It would cost us close to two thousand to alter next month's checks," the bookkeeper said, "and the law specifies that we have to take extra income-in-kind off the monthly allowance."

"If I were you," Morrissey said, "I would take all this home and eat it and not let anyone know about it."

"Mr. Morrissey!" Mrs. Traphagen's face paled away the red of her exertion. "That is fraud! You know as well as I do what would happen if it got out that we had diverted welfare commodities to our own use! Can you imagine what the mayor would say, what the governor would say, the state legislature, the Department of Health, Education, and Welfare, the National Association of Social Workers!" She had begun to tremble and the two chickens that were hanging over her arm nodded to one another, with a kind of slow decorum, their eyes closed righteously against the thought. Motors started, horns sounded and cars began to clot the exit of the parking lot. The air was redolent.

As the afternoon wore on, apricots began to appear in the hands of children from Sixteenth and Vandalia Street all the way to the Boulevard. Tomatoes flamed briefly on the windowsills of the ghetto between Fourteenth and Kirk, and on one block, there was a chicken in every pot.

The complaints began early the next day. Sixteen people called the Mayor's Committee on Discrimination claiming that chickens, fruit, and vegetables had been given to others while they had received tomatoes, half of them rotten. A rumor began that the food had been impregnated with medicine to test on the poor and that three people had died from it. The Health Department finally issued a denial, which brought a score of reporters to its door. During the questioning by reporters, a chemist at the department called the whole affair "the blatherings of a bunch of pinheads on the lunatic fringe." On the following day, the department received complaints from the ACLU, the Black Muslims, and the Diocesan Council, all of whom demanded apologies. There were eighteen calls at the Department of Welfare protesting a tomato "bombing" which had taken place on Fourteenth and Vandalia, in which passersby had been hit with tomatoes dropped from the roofs of slum houses. The callers demanded that the families of those involved be stricken from the welfare rolls as relief cheaters, encouraging waste and damaging the moral fiber of the young. Twenty-two mothers on the Aid to Dependent Children program picketed the governor's mansion carrying placards saying *Hope, Not Handouts* and *Jobs, Not Charity*. Sixty-eight welfare clients called to say that they had received no food at all and demanded equal service. When they heard that the Vandalia Street mothers were picketing, a group of them went down to protest. Words were exchanged between the two groups and a riot ensued in which sixteen people were hospitalized for injuries, including six members of the city's riot squad. Seven of the leaders and four who were bystanders were jailed pending investigation. The FBI was called into the case in the evening to ascertain if the riot was Communist-inspired. At ten o'clock, the mayor went on TV with a plea for reason and patience. He stated that the riot was a reflection of the general decline in American morals and a lack of respect for the law. He ordered a six-man commission to be set up to hear testimony and make recommendations. A political opponent demanded a thorough investigation of the county welfare system and the local university's hippies. On the following day, Mrs. Traphagen was unable to go to work at the welfare office, having been badly scalded on the hand while canning a bushel of apricots.

Cephas Ribble remembered everyone at the Welfare Office in his prayers. After work he would think about the day he had spent in the city and of his various triumphs. The surprise and wonder on the faces of the workers, and the modest awe of the woman who had said, "Mr. Ribble, you don't need to thank us," humbled and moved him. It had been a wonderful day. He had given his plenty unto the poor, plenty that was the doing of his own hands. He rose refreshed into his work, marveling at the meaning and grandeur in which his simplest chores were suddenly invested. He said, as he checked his chickens, "A man has his good to do. I'm gonna do it every year. I'm gonna have a day for the poor. Yessir, every year!" And he smiled genially on the chickens, the outbuildings, and the ripening fields of a generous land.

THINK AND DISCUSS
Understanding
1. What do the workers at the Welfare Department assume that Cephas wants?
2. What does Cephas want to do? Why?
3. How do the welfare workers react to his presentation?

Analyzing
4. Why do the workers not want to accept Cephas's donation? Is their reaction reasonable or unreasonable? Why?
5. What happens when the workers distribute the food?

Extending
6. How do you think the welfare workers will react next year, when they see Cephas again?
7. The title of this story comes from the biblical quotation: "Cast your bread upon the waters and it will return a hundredfold." How does this quotation relate to the story?

REVIEWING: Mood HƵ
See Handbook of Literary Terms, p. 675.
   The atmosphere and feeling that a writer creates in a work through imagery and details is called **mood**.

1. Examine the first sentence. Is it serious, good-natured, or bitter?
2. What kind of a character is Cephas? Is he dangerous, likable, or pathetic?
3. Describe the mood of this story.

THINKING SKILLS
Classifying
   To classify things is to arrange them into categories or groups according to some system. The characters in this story might be divided into two groups, according to how they view the welfare system. First decide on a name for each group. For each, choose a word or phrase that sums up that group's attitude toward the system. Then put the characters in the story into one group or the other.

COMPOSITION ◄━●
Reading/Writing Log
   Throughout "Upon the Waters," Joanne Greenberg uses comparisons to make the writing clear, vivid, and interesting. These descriptions often contribute to the mood of the story as well. For example, when Cephas tells of the hungry men standing in line for welfare in 1934, he says they stood "like they was poleaxed and hadn't fallen yet." Your Glossary tells you the meaning

of *poleax,* and you see the hungry, dejected men through Cephas's eyes—they appear as men who have already been killed but who have not yet fallen. Not only does this comparison allow you to see what Cephas saw, it also tells you something about him. The comparison suggests Cephas's unique way of viewing the world.

Copy these examples of comparisons from the story in your reading/writing log. Then find at least two other examples and record them as well. After each example, note the things being compared.

Comparisons

Minutes were born, ripened, aged, and died without issue. (Time is compared to a person.)

There was no trading in little plastic cards, and the hive of offices was empty. (Offices compared to beehive.)

Describing a Person

Choose a person—real or imaginary—and write a paragraph describing that person to your classmates and teacher. Use at least two comparisons in your description. See "Writing a Clear Description" in the Writer's Handbook before you begin your paragraph.

Defending a Choice

To understand the title of this story, you have to first understand the biblical allusion on which it is based (see question 7). Think of another title for this story, one that makes use of a comparison. You might use personification (such as "The Generous Land"), a metaphor, or a simile. Then write a paragraph in which you explain why the title you have chosen is appropriate.

BIOGRAPHY

Joanne Greenberg

1932–

Joanne Greenberg has written novels, articles, reviews, and short stories. Much of her writing deals with social and psychological problems. Her most popular novel, *I Never Promised You a Rose Garden* (1964), is about a girl's battle against mental illness. This novel, which she published under the pseudonym Hannah Green, was made into a movie. Greenberg is also a professor of anthropology. She lives in Colorado with her family.

See SATIRE in the Handbook of Literary Terms, page 684

The Lady, or the Tiger?

Frank R. Stockton

**She loved the young man, but she could not have him. The choice
she had to make cost her days and nights of anguish.**

---

n the very olden time, there lived a semibarbaric king, whose ideas, though somewhat polished and sharpened by the progressiveness of distant Latin neighbors,[1] were still large, florid, and untrammeled, as became the half of him which was barbaric. He was a man of exuberant fancy, and, withal, of an authority so irresistible that, at his will, he turned his varied fancies into facts. He was greatly given to self-communing; and, when he and himself agreed upon anything, the thing was done. When every member of his domestic and political systems moved smoothly in its appointed course, his nature was bland and genial; but whenever there was a little hitch, and some of his orbs got out of their orbits, he was blander and more genial still, for nothing pleased him so much as to make the crooked straight, and crush down uneven places.

Among the borrowed notions by which his barbarism had become semifixed was that of the public arena, in which, by exhibitions of manly and beastly valor, the minds of his subjects were refined and cultured.

But even here the exuberant and barbaric fancy asserted itself. The arena of the king was built, not to give the people an opportunity of hearing the rhapsodies of dying gladiators, nor to enable them to view the inevitable conclusion of a conflict between religious opinions and hungry jaws, but for purposes far better adapted to widen and develop the mental energies of the people. This vast amphitheater, with its encircling galleries, its mysterious vaults, and its unseen passages, was an agent of poetic justice, in which crime was punished, or virtue rewarded, by the decrees of an impartial and incorruptible chance.

---

1. *Latin neighbors*, peoples of the ancient Roman empire.

From *The Lady, or the Tiger and Other Stories* by Frank R. Stockton (Charles Scribner's Sons, 1884).

When a subject was accused of a crime of sufficient importance to interest the king, public notice was given that on an appointed day the fate of the accused person would be decided in the king's arena, a structure which well deserved its name; for, although its form and plan were borrowed from afar, its purpose emanated solely from the brain of this man, who, every barleycorn a king,[2] knew no tradition to which he owed more allegiance than pleased his fancy, and who ingrafted on every adopted form of human thought and action the rich growth of his barbaric idealism.

When all the people had assembled in the galleries, and the king, surrounded by his court, sat high up on his throne of royal state on one side of the arena, he gave a signal, a door beneath him opened, and the accused subject stepped out into the amphitheater. Directly opposite him, on the other side of the enclosed space, were two doors, exactly alike and side by side. It was the duty and the privilege of the person on trial to walk directly to these doors and open one of them. He could open either door he pleased; he was subject to no guidance or influence but that of the aforementioned impartial and incorruptible chance. If he opened the one, there came out of it a hungry tiger, the fiercest and most cruel that could be procured, which immediately sprang upon him and tore him to pieces, as a punishment for his guilt. The moment that the case of the criminal was thus decided, doleful iron bells were clanged, great wails went up from the hired mourners posted on the outer rim of the arena, and the vast audience, with bowed heads and downcast hearts, wended slowly their homeward way, mourning greatly that one so young and fair, or so old and respected, should have merited so dire a fate.

But if the accused person opened the other door, there came forth from it a lady, the most suitable to his years and station that his majesty could select among his fair subjects; and to this lady he was immediately married, as a reward for his innocence. It mattered not that he might already possess a wife and family or that his affections might be engaged upon an object of his own selection; the king allowed no such subordinate arrangements to interfere with his great scheme of retribution and reward. The exercises, as in the other instance, took place immediately, and in the arena. Another door opened beneath the king, and a priest, followed by a band of choristers and dancing maidens blowing joyous airs on golden horns and treading an epithalamic measure, advanced to where the pair stood, side by side, and the wedding was promptly and cheerily solemnized. Then the gay brass bells rang forth their merry peals, the people shouted glad hurrahs, and the innocent man, preceded by children strewing flowers on his path, led his bride to his home.

This was the king's semibarbaric method of administering justice. Its perfect fairness is obvious. The criminal could not know out of which door would come the lady; he opened either he pleased, without having the slightest idea whether, in the next instant, he was to be devoured or married. On some occasions the tiger came out of one door, and on

---

2. *every barleycorn a king.* A barleycorn is a measurement used in former times equal to one-third of an inch. *Barleycorn* is here substituted in the usual phrase "every inch a king" to create a humorous effect of antiquity.

some out of the other. The decisions of this tribunal were not only fair, they were positively determinate; the accused person was instantly punished if he found himself guilty, and, if innocent, he was rewarded on the spot, whether he liked it or not. There was no escape from the judgments of the king's arena.

The institution was a very popular one. When the people gathered together on one of the great trial days, they never knew whether they were to witness a bloody slaughter or a hilarious wedding. This element of uncertainty lent an interest to the occasion which it could not otherwise have attained. Thus, the masses were entertained and pleased, and the thinking part of the community could bring no charge of unfairness against this plan; for did not the accused person have the whole matter in his own hands?

This semibarbaric king had a daughter as blooming as his most florid fancies and with a soul as fervent and imperious as his own. As is usual in such cases, she was the apple of his eye and was loved by him above all humanity. Among his courtiers was a young man of that fineness of blood and lowness of station common to the conventional heroes of romance who love royal maidens. This royal maiden was well satisfied with her lover, for he was handsome and brave to a degree unsurpassed in all this kingdom, and she loved him with an ardor that had enough of barbarism in it to make it exceedingly warm and strong. This love affair moved on happily for many months, until one day the king happened to discover its existence. He did not hesitate nor waver in regard to his duty in the premises. The youth was immediately cast into prison, and a day was appointed for his trial in the king's arena. This, of course, was an especially important occasion, and his majesty, as well as all the people, was greatly interested in the workings and development of this trial. Never before had such a case occurred; never before had a subject dared to love the daughter of the king. In afteryears such things became commonplace enough, but then they were, in no slight degree, novel and startling.

The tiger cages of the kingdom were searched for the most savage and relentless beasts, from which the fiercest monster might be selected for the arena, and the ranks of maiden youth and beauty throughout the land were carefully surveyed by competent judges, in order that the young man might have a fitting bride in case fate did not determine for him a different destiny. Of course, everybody knew that the deed with which the accused was charged had been done. He had loved the princess, and neither he, she, nor anyone else thought of denying the fact, but the king would not think of allowing any fact of this kind to interfere with the workings of the tribunal, in which he took such great delight and satisfaction. No matter how the affair turned out, the youth would be disposed of, and the king would take an aesthetic pleasure in watching the course of events, which would determine whether or not the young man had done wrong in allowing himself to love the princess.

The appointed day arrived. From far and near the people gathered and thronged the great galleries of the arena, and crowds, unable to gain admittance, massed themselves against its outside walls. The king and his

Mark Sabin, "Lady on a Tiger," 1978
Private Collection

court were in their places opposite the twin doors—those fateful portals so terrible in their similarity.

All was ready. The signal was given. A door beneath the royal party opened, and the lover of the princess walked into the arena. Tall, beautiful, fair, his appearance was greeted with a low hum of admiration and anxiety. Half the audience had not known so grand a youth had lived among them. No wonder the princess loved him! What a terrible thing for him to be there!

As the youth advanced into the arena, he turned, as the custom was, to bow to the king, but he did not think at all of that royal personage; his eyes were fixed upon the prin-

cess who sat to the right of her father. Had it not been for the moiety of barbarism in her nature, it is probable that lady would not have been there, but her intense and fervid soul would not allow her to be absent on an occasion in which she was so terribly interested.

From the moment that the decree had gone forth, that her lover should decide his fate in the king's arena, she had thought of nothing, night or day, but this great event and the various subjects connected with it. Possessed of more power, influence, and force of character than anyone who had ever before been interested in such a case, she had done what no other person had done—she had possessed

The Lady, or the Tiger? **399**

herself of the secret of the doors. She knew in which of the two rooms that lay behind those doors stood the cage of the tiger, with its open front, and in which waited the lady. Through these thick doors, heavily curtained with skins on the inside, it was impossible that any noise or suggestion should come from within to the person who should approach to raise the latch of one of them, but gold and the power of a woman's will had brought the secret to the princess.

And not only did she know in which room stood the lady ready to emerge, all blushing and radiant, should her door be opened, but she knew who the lady was. It was one of the fairest and loveliest of the damsels of the court who had been selected as the reward of the accused youth should he be proved innocent of the crime of aspiring to one so far above him, and the princess hated her. Often had she seen, or imagined that she had seen, this fair creature throwing glances of admiration upon the person of her lover, and sometimes she thought these glances were perceived and even returned. Now and then she had seen them talking together; it was but for a moment or two, but much can be said in a brief space; it may have been on most unimportant topics, but how could she know that? The girl was lovely, but she had dared to raise her eyes to the loved one of the princess, and, with all the intensity of the savage blood transmitted to her through long lines of wholly barbaric ancestors, she hated the woman who blushed and trembled behind that silent door.

When her lover turned and looked at her, and his eye met hers as she sat there paler and whiter than anyone in the vast ocean of anxious faces about her, he saw, by that power of quick perception which is given to those whose souls are one, that she knew behind which door crouched the tiger and behind which stood the lady. He had expected her to know it. He understood her nature, and his soul was assured that she would never rest until she had made plain to herself this thing, hidden to all other lookers-on, even to the king. The only hope for the youth in which there was any element of certainty was based upon the success of the princess in discovering this mystery, and the moment he looked upon her, he saw she had succeeded, as in his soul he knew she would succeed.

Then it was that his quick and anxious glance asked the question: "Which?" It was as plain to her as if he shouted it from where he stood. There was not an instant to be lost. The question was asked in a flash; it must be answered in another.

Her right arm lay on the cushioned parapet before her. She raised her hand, and made a slight, quick movement toward the right. No one but her lover saw her. Every eye but his was fixed on the man in the arena.

He turned, and with a firm and rapid step he walked across the empty space. Every heart stopped beating, every breath was held, every eye was fixed immovably upon that man. Without the slightest hesitation, he went to the door on the right and opened it.

Now, the point of the story is this: Did the tiger come out of that door, or did the lady?

The more we reflect upon this question, the harder it is to answer. It involves a study of the human heart which leads us through devious mazes of passion, out of which it is difficult to find our way. Think of it, fair reader, not as if the decision of the question depended upon yourself, but upon that hot-blooded, semibarbaric princess, her soul at a white heat beneath the combined fires of despair and jealousy. She had lost him, but who should have him?

How often, in her waking hours and in her dreams, had she started in wild horror and covered her face with her hands as she thought of her lover opening the door on the other side of which waited the cruel fangs of the tiger!

But how much oftener had she seen him at the other door! How in her grievous reveries had she gnashed her teeth and torn her hair, when she saw his start of rapturous delight as he opened the door of the lady! How her soul had burned in agony when she had seen him rush to meet that woman, with her flushing cheek and sparkling eye of triumph; when she had seen him lead her forth, his whole frame kindled with the joy of recovered life; when she had heard the glad shouts from the multitude, and the wild ringing of the happy bells; when she had seen the priest, with his joyous followers, advance to the couple and make them man and wife before her very eyes; and when she had seen them walk away together upon their path of flowers, followed by the tremendous shouts of the hilarious multitude, in which her one despairing shriek was lost and drowned!

Would it not be better for him to die at once, and go to wait for her in the blessed regions of semibarbaric futurity?

And yet, that awful tiger, those shrieks, that blood!

Her decision had been indicated in an instant, but it had been made after days and nights of anguished deliberation. She had known she would be asked, she had decided what she would answer, and without the slightest hesitation, she had moved her hand to the right.

The question of her decision is one not to be lightly considered, and it is not for me to presume to set myself up as the one person able to answer it. And so I leave it with all of you: Which came out of the opened door—the lady, or the tiger?

THINK AND DISCUSS
Understanding
1. When does this story take place?
2. How does the king determine the guilt or innocence of an accused person?
3. Why is the hero thrown in jail?

Analyzing
4. Describe the character of the princess.
5. What conflict does the princess face?
6. What is the climax of the story?
7. How does the author increase suspense at this point?

Extending
8. Some readers of this story have felt cheated because the author does not say what is behind the door that the princess chooses for the young man. Why do you suppose the author might have chosen to end the story in this way?
9. What choice do you think the princess makes? Give reasons for your view.

APPLYING: Satire H7
See Handbook of Literary Terms, p. 684.

In a **satire,** the author ridicules the vices or follies of people and society, usually for the purpose of producing some change in attitude or action. One common target of satire is a system of justice; another is literary form itself.

1. What are the chances of the person on trial choosing the tiger? the lady? What does this say about the king's system of justice?
2. In what ways is this story like a standard fairy tale? How is it different?

VOCABULARY
Antonyms

Look up each of the following words in the Glossary. Then match each word in Column A with its *antonym* (the word most opposite it in meaning) in Column B. Write the pairs of antonyms on your paper. Be sure you spell all the words correctly.

Column A	Column B
novel	fervid
subordinate	doleful
rapturous	commonplace
bland	genial
savage	imperious

COMPOSITION
Explaining a Choice

The expression "on the horns of a dilemma" is often used to refer to a situation in which one has to choose between two equally unpleasant alternatives. Have you ever found yourself in such a situation? In a two-paragraph composition, describe the choices and explain why your decision was a difficult one. Then explain which one you finally chose, and why.

Writing for Advice

Assume you are the princess, and you have decided to write to Adora, the advice columnist in your local newspaper, to get help in dealing with your dilemma. Write your letter, and then write Adora's response.

BIOGRAPHY

Frank Stockton
1834–1902

Frank Stockton was born, raised, and educated in Philadelphia. He was apprenticed as a wood-engraver and worked as an engraver until 1870. He then became a magazine editor and contributor. He wrote many short fantasies and tales for children. His collections include *Ting-a-Ling, The Floating Prince and Other Fairy Tales,* and *The Bee-Man of Orne and Other Fanciful Tales.* After his stories for adults won acclaim, he devoted his time exclusively to writing for them.

Review SATIRE in the Handbook of Literary Terms, page 684

My Delicate Heart Condition

Toni Cade Bambara

No wonder Aunt Hazel screamed so about my scary stories and Mary was always shushing me. We all had bad hearts.

---

y cousin Joanne has not been allowed to hang out with me for some time because she went and told Aunt Hazel that I scare her to death whenever she sleeps over at our house or I spend the weekend at hers. The truth is I sometimes like to tell stories about blood-thirsty vampires or ugly monsters that lurk in clothes closets or giant beetles that eat their way through the shower curtain, like I used to do at camp to entertain the kids in my bunk. But Joanne always cries and that makes the stories even weirder, like background music her crying. And too—I'm not going to lie about it—I get spookier on purpose until all the little crybabies are stuffing themselves under their pillows and throwing their sneakers at me and making such a racket that Mary the counselor has to come in and shine her flashlight around the bunkhouse. I play like I'm asleep. The rest of them are too busy blubbering and finding their way out from under the blankets to tell Mary that it's me. Besides, once they get a load of her standing against the moonlight in that long white robe of hers looking like a ghost, they just start up again and pretty soon the whole camp is awake. Anyway, that's what I do for fun. So Joanne hasn't been around. And this year I'll have to go to the circus by myself and to camp without her. My mother said on the phone to Aunt Hazel—"Good, keep Jo over there and maybe Harriet'll behave herself if she's got no one to show off to." For all the years my mother's known me, she still doesn't understand that my behaving has got nothing to do with who I hang out with. A private thing between me and me or maybe between me and the Fly family since they were the ones that first got

---

me to sit through monster movies and withstand all the terror I could take.

For four summers now, me and the Fly family have had this thing going. A battle of nerves, you might say. Each year they raise the rope closer and closer to the very top of the tent—I hear they're going to perform outdoors this year and be even higher—and they stretch the rope further across the rings where the clowns and the pony riders perform. Each year they get bolder and more daring with their rope dancing and the swinging by the legs and flinging themselves into empty space making everyone throw up their hands and gasp for air until Mr. Fly at the very last possible second swings out on his bar to catch them up by the tips of their heels. Everyone just dies and clutches at their hearts. Everybody but me. I sit there calmly. I've trained myself. Joanne used to die and duck her head under the benches and stay there till it was all over.

Last summer they really got bold. On the final performance just before the fair closed, and some revival type tent show[1] comes in and all the kids go off to camp, the Fly family performed without a net. I figured they'd be up to something so I made sure my stomach was like steel. I did ten push-ups before breakfast, twenty sit-ups before lunch, skipped dinner altogether. My brother Teddy kidded me all day—"Harriet's trying out for the Olympics." I passed up the icie man on the corner and the pizza and sausage stand by the schoolyard and the cotton candy and jelly apple lady and the pickle and penny candy boy, in fact I passed up all the stands that lead from the street down the little roadway to the fair grounds that used to be a swamp when we first moved from Baltimore to Jamaica, Long Island. It wasn't easy, I'm not going to lie, but I was taking no chances. Between the balloon man and the wheel of fortune was the usual clump of ladies from church who came night after night to try to win the giant punch bowl set on the top shelf above the wheel, but had to settle night after night for a jar of gumdrops or salt and pepper shakers or some other little thing from the bottom shelf. And from the wheel of fortune to the tent was at least a million stands selling B.B. bats and jawbreakers and gingerbread and sweet potato pie and frozen custard and—like I said it wasn't easy. A million ways to tempt you, to unsettle your stomach, and make you lose the battle to the Fly family.

I sat there almost enjoying the silly clowns who came tumbling out of a steamer trunk no bigger than the one we have in the basement where my mother keeps my old report cards and photographs and letters and things. And I almost enjoyed the fire eater and the knife thrower, but I was so close up I could see how there wasn't any real thrill. I almost enjoyed the fat-leg girls who rode the ponies two at a time and standing up, but their costumes weren't very pretty—just an ordinary polo shirt like you get if you run in the PAL[2] meets and short skirts you can wear on either side like the big girls wear at the roller rink. And I almost enjoyed the jugglers except that my Uncle Bubba can juggle the dinner plates better any day of the week so long as Aunt Hazel isn't there to stop him. I was impatient and started yawning. Finally all the clowns

---

1. *revival type tent show*, religious services peformed by a traveling minister.
2. *PAL*, Police Athletic League (New York).

hitched up their baggy pants and tumbled over each other out of the ring and into the dark, the jugglers caught all the things that were up in the air and yawning just like me went off to the side. The pony girls brought their horses to a sudden stop that raised a lot of dust, then jumped down into the dirt and bowed. Then the ringmaster stepped into the circle of light and tipped his hat which was a little raggedy from where I was sitting and said—"And now, Ladieeez and Gentlemen, what you've alll been waiting forrr, the Main aTTRACtion, the FLY FAMILEEE." And everyone jumped up to shout like crazy as they came running out on their toes to stand in the light and then climb the ropes. I took a deep breath and folded my arms over my chest and a kid next to me went into hiding, acting like she was going to tie her shoelaces.

There used to be four of them—the father, a big guy with a bald head and a bushy mustache and shoulders and arms like King Kong; a tall lanky mother whom you'd never guess could even climb into a high chair or catch anything heavier than a Ping-Pong ball to look at her; the oldest son who looked like his father except he had hair on his head but none on his face and a big face it was, so that no matter how high up he got you could always tell whether he was smiling or frowning or counting; the younger boy about thirteen, maybe, had a vacant stare like he was a million miles away feeding his turtles or something, anything but walking along a tightrope or flying through the air with his family. I had always liked to watch him because he was as cool as I was. But last summer the little girl got into the act. My grandmother says she's probably a midget 'cause no self-respecting mother would allow her child to be up there acting like a bird. "Just a baby," she'd say. "Can't be more than six years old. Should be home in bed. Must be a midget." My grandfather would give me a look when she started in and we'd smile at her together.

They almost got to me that last performance, dodging around with new routines and two at a time so that you didn't know which one Mr. Fly was going to save at the last minute. But he'd fly out and catch the little boy and swing over to the opposite stand where the big boy was flying out to catch them both by the wrists and the poor woman would be left kind of dangling there, suspended, then she'd do this double flip which would kill off everyone in the tent except me, of course, and swing out on the very bar she was on in the first place. And then they'd mess around two or three flying at once just to confuse you until the big drum roll started and out steps the little girl in a party dress and a huge blindfold wrapped around her little head and a pink umbrella like they sell down in Chinatown. And I almost—I won't lie about it—I almost let my heart thump me off the bench. I almost thought I too had to tie my shoelaces. But I sat there. Stubborn. And the kid starts bouncing up and down on the rope like she was about to take off and tear through the canvas roof. Then out swings her little brother and before you know it, Fly Jr. like a great eagle with his arms flapping grabs up the kid, her eyeband in his teeth and swoops her off to the bar that's already got Mrs. Mr. and Big Bro on it and surely there's no room for him. And everyone's standing on their feet clutching at their faces. Everyone but me. Cause I know from the getgo[3] that Mr. and Mrs. are going to leave the bar to give Jr. room and fly over to the other side. Which is exactly what they do. The lady in front of me, Mrs. Perez, who does all the sewing in our neighborhood, gets up and starts shaking

her hands like ladies do to get the fingernail polish dry and she says to me with her eyes jammed shut "I must go finish the wedding gowns. Tell me later who died." And she scoots through the aisle, falling all over everybody with her eyes still shut and never looks up. And Mrs. Caine taps me on the back and leans over and says, "Some people just can't take it." And I smile at her and at her twins who're sitting there with their mouths open. I fold my arms over my chest and just dare the Fly family to do their very worst.

The minute I got to camp, I ran up to the main house where all the counselors gather to say hello to the parents and talk with the directors. I had to tell Mary the latest doings with the Fly family. But she put a finger to her mouth like she sometimes does to shush me. "Let's not have any scary stuff this summer, Harriet," she said, looking over my shoulder at a new kid. This new kid, Willie, was from my old neighborhood in Baltimore so we got friendly right off. Then he told me that he had a romantic heart so I quite naturally took him under my wing and decided not to give him a heart attack with any ghost tales. Mary said he meant "rheumatic" heart, but I don't see any difference. So I told Mary to move him out of George's tent and give him a nicer counselor who'd respect his romantic heart. George used to be my play boyfriend when I first came to camp as a little kid and didn't know any better. But he's not a nice person. He makes up funny nicknames for people which aren't funny at all. Like

---

3. *getgo*, slang term meaning "beginning."

calling Eddie Michaels the Watermelon Kid or David Farmer Charcoal Plenty which I really do not appreciate and especially from a counselor. And once he asked Joanne, who was the table monitor, to go fetch a pail of milk from the kitchen. And the minute she got up, he started hatching a plot, trying to get the kids to hide her peanut butter sandwich and put spiders in her soup. I had to remind everyone at the table that Joanne was my first cousin by blood, and I would be forced to waste the first bum that laid a hand on her plate. And ole George says, "Oh don't be a dumbhead, Harriet. Jo's so stupid she won't even notice." And I told him right then and there that I was not his play girlfriend anymore and would rather marry the wolfman than grow up and be his wife. And just in case he didn't get the message, that night around campfire when we were all playing Little Sally Walker sittin' in a saucer and it was my turn to shake it to the east and to shake it to the west and to shake it to the very one that I loved the best—I shook straight for Mr. Nelson the lifeguard, who was not only the ugliest person in camp but the arch enemy of ole George.

And that very first day of camp last summer when Willie came running up to me to get in line for lunch, here comes George talking some simple stuff about "What a beautiful head you have, Willie. A long, smooth, streamlined head. A sure sign of superior gifts. Definitely genius proportions." And poor Willie went for it, grinning and carrying on and touching his head, which if you want to know the truth is a bullet head and that's all there is to it. And he's turning to me every which way, like he's modeling his head in a fashion show. And the minute his back is turned, ole George makes a face about Willie's head and all the kids in the line bust out laughing. So I had to beat up a few right then and there and finish off the rest later in the shower for being so stupid, laughing at a kid with a romantic heart.

One night in the last week of August when the big campfire party is held, it was very dark and the moon was all smoky, and I just couldn't help myself and started in with a story about the great caterpillar who was going to prowl through the tents and nibble off everybody's toes. And Willie started this whimpering in the back of his throat so I had to switch the story real quick to something cheerful. But before I could do that, ole George picked up my story and added a wicked witch who put spells on city kids who come to camp, and a hunchback dwarf that chopped up tents and bunk beds, and a one-eyed phantom giant who gobbled up the hearts of underprivileged kids. And every time he got to the part where the phantom ripped out a heart, poor Willie would get louder and louder until finally he started rolling around in the grass and screaming and all the kids went crazy and scattered behind the rocks almost kicking the fire completely out as they dashed off into the darkness yelling bloody murder. And the counselors could hardly round us all up—me, too, I'm not going to lie about it. Their little circles of flashlight bobbing in and out of the bushes along the patches of pine, bumping into each other as they scrambled for us kids. And poor Willie rolling around something awful, so they took him to the infirmary.

I was sneaking some ginger snaps in to him later that night when I hear Mary and another senior counselor fussing at ole George in the hallway.

"You've been picking on that kid ever since he got here, George. But tonight was the limit——"

"I wasn't picking on him, I was just trying to tell a story——"

"All that talk about hearts, gobblin' up hearts, and underpriv——"

"Yeh, you were directing it all at the little kid. You should be——"

"I wasn't talking about him. They're all underprivileged kids, after all. I mean all the kids are underprivileged."

I huddled back into the shadows and almost banged into Willie's iron bed. I was hoping he'd open his eyes and wink at me and tell me he was just fooling. That it wasn't so bad to have an underprivileged heart. But he just slept. "I'm an underprivileged kid too," I thought to myself. I knew it was a special camp, but I'd never realized. No wonder Aunt Hazel screamed so about my scary stories and my mother flicked off the TV when the monsters came on and Mary was always shushing me. We all had bad hearts. I crawled into the supply cabinet to wait for Willie to wake up so I could ask him about it all. I ate all the ginger snaps but I didn't feel any better. You have a romantic heart, I whispered to myself settling down among the bandages. You will have to be very careful.

It didn't make any difference to Aunt Hazel that I had changed, that I no longer told scary stories or dragged my schoolmates to the latest creature movie, or raced my friends to the edge of the roof, or held my breath, or ran under the train rail when the train was already in sight. As far as she was concerned, I was still the same ole spooky kid I'd always been. So Joanne was kept at home. My mother noticed the difference, but she said over the phone to my grandmother, "She's acting very ladylike these days, growing up." I didn't tell her about my secret, that I knew about my heart. And I was kind of glad Joanne wasn't around 'cause I would have blabbed it all to her and scared her to death. When school starts again, I decided, I'll ask my teacher how to outgrow my underprivileged heart. I'll train myself, just like I did with the Fly family.

"Well, I guess you'll want some change to go to the fair again, hunh?" my mother said coming into my room dumping things in her pocketbook.

"No," I said. "I'm too grown up for circuses."

She put the money on the dresser anyway. I was lying, of course. I was thinking what a terrible strain it would be for Mrs. Perez and everybody else if while sitting there, with the Fly family zooming around in the open air a million miles above the ground, little Harriet Watkins should drop dead with a fatal heart attack behind them.

"I lost," I said out loud.

"Lost what?"

"The battle with the Fly family."

She just stood there a long time looking at me, trying to figure me out, the way mothers are always doing but should know better. Then she kissed me goodbye and left for work.

THINK AND DISCUSS

Understanding

1. Why does Joanne no longer attend camp with Harriet?
2. How does Harriet get ready for the Fly family's performance?
3. What is physically wrong with Willie?
4. How does George treat Willie? How does Harriet treat Willie?

Analyzing

5. What causes the narrator to think that she too has heart trouble?
6. What does Harriet mean when she says she lost her battle with the Fly family?

Extending

7. Most of us have misunderstood conversations. If you can, think of an example from your childhood. What was said? What was your reaction?

REVIEWING: Satire

See Handbook of Literary Terms, p. 684.

   Satire is a technique that ridicules people and institutions in an effort to expose their weaknesses and evils. The purpose of satire is to cause change.

1. What does George do at the bonfire that upsets the campers?
2. What does Harriet overhear George tell the other counselors?
3. What is satirical about a person such as George being a camp counselor?

COMPOSITION

Writing a Journal Entry

   Assume that you are Harriet and while you're at camp you keep a journal. Write a few paragraphs about the day you learn you have a "heart condition."

Changing Point of View

   Because this story is told from the first-person point of view, Harriet is able to give her own opinion of herself. How does she appear to you? Write a paragraph in which you describe Harriet from the third-person view.

BIOGRAPHY

Toni Cade Bambara
1939–

   Toni Cade Bambara's stories reflect the many interests and experiences found in her active and varied life. She has been a dancer, a teacher, and a director of educational projects. Beginning as a part-time writer in the early 1960s, Bambara became well known ten years later, when she edited and wrote for the anthologies *The Black Woman* and *Tales and Stories for Black Folks*. A number of Bambara's stories are about the everyday lives of young people.

See FORESHADOWING in the Handbook of Literary Terms, page 667

Flowers for Algernon

Daniel Keyes

Before, they laughed at Charlie Gordon for his ignorance and dullness; now, they hate him for his knowledge and understanding. What do they want of him?

Progris riport 1—martch 5

Dr. Strauss says I shud rite down what I think and every thing that happins to me from now on. I dont know why but he says its importint so they will see if they will use me. I hope they use me. Miss Kinnian says maybe they can make me smart. I want to be smart. My name is Charlie Gordon. I am 37 years old. I have nuthing more to rite now so I will close for today.

progris riport 2—martch 6

I had a test today. I think I faled it. And I think maybe now they wont use me. What happind is a nice young man was in the room and he had some white cards and ink spillled all over them. He sed Charlie what do yo see on this card. I was very skared even tho I had my rabits foot in my pockit because when I was a kid I always faled tests in school and I spillled ink to.

I told him I saw a inkblot. He said yes and it made me feel good. I thot that was all but when I got up to go he said Charlie we are not thru yet. Then I dont remember so good but he wantid me to say what was in the ink. I dint see nuthing in the ink but he said there was picturs there other pepul saw some picturs. I couldnt see any picturs. I reely tryed. I held the card close up and then far away. Then I said if I had my glases I coud see better I usally only ware my glases in the movies or TV but I said they are in the closit in the hall. I got them. Then I said let me see that card agen I bet Ill find it now.

I tryed hard but I only saw the ink. I told him maybe I need new glases. He rote something down on a paper and I got skared of faling the test. I told him it was a very nice

Slightly abridged from "Flowers for Algernon" by Daniel Keyes. Copyright 1959 by Mercury Press, Inc.; originally appeared in the *Magazine of Fantasy and Science Fiction;* reprinted by permission of the author and his agent, Robert P. Mills.

inkblot with littel points all around the edges. He looked very sad so that wasnt it. I said please let me try agen. Ill get it in a few min-its becaus Im not so fast somtimes. Im a slow reeder too in Miss Kinnians class for slow adults but I'm trying very hard.

He gave me a chance with another card that had 2 kinds of ink spilled on it red and blue.

He was very nice and talked slow like Miss Kinnian does and he explaned it to me that it was a *raw shok*.[1] He said pepul see things in the ink. I said show me where. He said think. I told him I think a inkblot but that wasn't rite eather. He said what does it remind you—pretend something. I closed my eyes for a long time to pretend. I told him I pretend a fowntan pen with ink leeking all over a table cloth.

I dont think I passed the *raw shok* test.

progris riport 3—martch 7

Dr Strauss and Dr Nemur say it dont mat-ter about the inkblots. They said that maybe they will still use me. I said Miss Kinnian never gave me tests like that one only spelling and reading. They said Miss Kinnian told that I was her bestist pupil in the adult nite school because I tryed the hardist and I reely wantid to lern. They said how come you went to the adult nite scool all by yourself Charlie. How did you find it. I said I asked pepul and sumbody told me where I shud go to lern to read and spell good. They said why did you want to. I told them becaus all my life I wantid to be smart and not dumb. But its very hard to be smart. They said you know it will probly be tempirery. I said yes. Miss Kinnian told me. I dont care if it herts.

Later I had more crazy tests today. The nice lady who gave it to me told me the name and I asked her how do you spellit so I can rite it my progris riport. THEMATIC AP-PERCEPTION TEST.[2] I dont know the frist 2 words but I know what *test* means. You got to pass it or you get bad marks. This test lookd easy becaus I coud see the picturs. Only this time she dint want me to tell her the picturs. That mixd me up. She said make up storys about the pepul in the picturs.

I told her how can you tell storys about pepul you never met. I said why shud I make up lies. I never tell lies any more becaus I always get caut.

She told me this test and the other one the raw-shok was for getting personality. I laffed so hard. I said how can you get that thing from inkblots and fotos. She got sore and put her picturs away. I don't care. It was sily. I gess I faled that test too.

Later some men in white coats took me to a difernt part of the hospitil and gave me a game to play. It was like a race with a white mouse. They called the mouse Algernon. Algernon was in a box with a lot of twists and turns like all kinds of walls and they gave me a pencil and paper with lines and lots of boxes. On one side it said START and on the other end it said FINISH. They said it was *amazed*[3] and that Algernon and me had the same *amazed* to do. I dint see how we could have the same *amazed* if Algernon had a box and I had a paper but I dint say nothing.

---

1. *raw shok,* Rorschach (rôr′ shäk) test, a psychological test used to measure personality traits and general intelligence.
2. *Thematic Apperception Test,* another psychological test.
3. *amazed,* a maze, a network of paths through which one must find one's way.

Anyway there wasnt time because the race started.

One of the men had a watch he was trying to hide so I wouldn't see it so I tryed not to look and that made me nervus.

Anyway that test made me feel worser than all the others because they did it over 10 times with different *amazeds* and Algernon won everytime. I dint know that mice were so smart. Maybe thats because Algernon is a white mouse. Maybe white mice are smarter than other mice.

progris riport 4—Mar 8

Their going to use me! Im so exited I can hardly write. Dr Nemur and Dr Strauss had a argament about it first. Dr Nemur was in the office when Dr Strauss brot me in. Dr Nemur was worryed about using me but Dr Strauss told him Miss Kinnian rekemmended me the best from all the people who she was teaching. I like Miss Kinnian becaus shes a very smart teacher. And she said Charlie your going to have a second chance. If you volenteer for this experament you mite get smart. They dont know if it will be perminint but theirs a chance. Thats why I said ok even when I was scared because she said it was an operashun. She said dont be scared Charlie you done so much with so little I think you deserv it most of all.

So I got scaird when Dr. Nemur and Dr. Strauss argud about it. Dr. Strauss said I had something that was very good. He said I had a good *motorvation*. I never even knew I had that. I felt proud when he said that not every body with an eye-q of 68[4] had that thing. I dont know what it is or where I got it but he said Algernon had it too. Algernons *motorva-*

tion is the cheese they put in his box. But it cant be that because I didn't eat any cheese this week.

Then he told Dr Nemur something I dint understand so while they were talking I wrote down some of the words.

He said Dr. Nemur I know Charlie is not what you had in mind as the first of your new brede of intelek** (coudnt get the word) superman. But most people of his low ment** are host** and uncoop** they are usually dull apath** and hard to reach. He has a good natcher hes intristed and eager to please.

Dr Nemur said remember he will be the first human beeng ever to have his intellijence tripled by surgicle meens.

Dr. Strauss said exakly. Look at how well hes lerned to read and write for his low mentel age its as grate an acheve** as you and I lerning einstines therey of **vity without help. That shows the inteness motorvation. Its comparat** a tremen** achev** I say we use Charlie.

I dint get all the words but it sounded like Dr Strauss was on my side and like the other one wasnt.

Then Dr Nemur nodded he said all right maybe your right. We will use Charlie. When he said that I got so exited I jumped up and shook his hand for being so good to me. I told him thank you doc you wont be sorry for giving me a second chance. And I mean it like I told him. After the operashun Im gonna try to be smart. Im gonna try awful hard.

progris riport 5—Mar 10

Im skared. Lots of the nurses and the peo-

---

4. *eye-q of 68.* An average I.Q. is 100.

ple who gave me the tests came to bring me candy and wish me luck. I hope I have luck. I got my rabits foot and my lucky penny. Only a black cat crossed me when I was comming to the hospitil. Dr Strauss says dont be supersitis Charlie this is science. Anyway Im keeping my rabits foot with me.

I asked Dr Strauss if Ill beat Algernon in the race after the operashun and he said maybe. If the operashun works Ill show that mouse I can be as smart as he is. Maybe smarter. Then Ill be abel to read better and spell the words good and know lots of things and be like other people. I want to be smart like other people. If it works perminint they will make everybody smart all over the wurld.

They dint give me anything to eat this morning. I dont know what that eating has to do with getting smart. Im very hungry and Dr. Nemur took away my box of candy. That Dr Nemur is a grouch. Dr Strauss says I can have it back after the operashun. You cant eat befor a operashun. . . .

progress report 6—Mar 15

The operashun dint hurt. He did it while I was sleeping. They took off the bandijis from my head today so I can make a PROGRESS REPORT. Dr. Nemur who looked at some of my other ones says I spell PROGRESS wrong and told me how to spell it and REPORT too. I got to try and remember that.

I have a very bad memary for spelling. Dr. Strauss says its ok to tell about all the things that happin to me but he says I should tell more about what I feel and what I think. When I told him I dont know how to think he said try. All the time when the bandijis were on my eyes I tryed to think. Nothing happened. I dont know what to think about. Maybe if I ask him he will tell me how I can think now that Im suppose to get smart. What do smart people think about. Fancy things I suppose. I wish I knew some fancy things alredy.

progress report 7—Mar 19

Nothing is happining. I had lots of tests and different kinds of races with Algernon. I hate that mouse. He always beats me. Dr. Strauss said I got to play those games. And he said some time I got to take those tests over again. Those inkblots are stupid. And those pictures are stupid too. I like to draw a picture of a man and a woman but I wont make up lies about people.

I got a headache from trying to think so much. I thot Dr Strauss was my frend but he dont help me. He dont tell me what to think or when Ill get smart. Miss Kinnian dint come to see me. I think writing these progress reports are stupid too.

progress report 8—Mar 23

Im going back to work at the factory. They said it was better I shud go back to work but I cant tell anyone what the operashun was for and I have to come to the hospitil for an hour evry night after work. They are gonna pay me mony every month for learning to be smart.

Im glad Im going back to work because I miss my job and all my frends and all the fun we have there.

Dr Strauss says I shud keep writing things down but I dont have to do it every day just when I think of something or something speshul happins. He says dont get discoridged because it takes time and it happins slow. He says it took a long time with Algernon before he got 3 times smarter than he was before. Thats why Algernon beats me all the time because he had that operashun too. That makes me feel better. I coud probly do that *amazed* faster than a reglar mouse. Maybe some day Ill beat him. That would be something. So far Algernon looks smart perminent.

Mar 25 (I dont have to write PROGRESS REPORT on top any more just when I hand it in once a week to Dr Nemur. I just have to put the date on. That saves time)

We had a lot of fun at the factery today. Joe Carp said hey look where Charlie had his operashun what did they do Charlie put some brains in. I was going to tell him but I remembered Dr Strauss said no. Then Frank Reilly said what did you do Charlie forget your key and open your door the hard way. That made me laff. Their really my friends and they like me.

Sometimes somebody will say hey look at Joe or Frank or George he really pulled a Charlie Gordon. I dont know why they say that but they always laff. This morning Amos Borg who is the 4 man at Donnegans used my name when he shouted at Ernie the office boy. Ernie lost a packige. He said Ernie what are you trying to be a Charlie Gordon. I dont understand why he said that.

Mar 28. Dr. Strauss came to my room tonight to see why I dint come in like I was suppose to. I told him I dont like to race with Algernon any more. He said I dont have to for a while but I shud come in. He had a present for me. I thot it was a little television but it wasnt. He said I got to turn it on when I go to sleep. I said your kidding why shud I turn it on when Im going to sleep. Who ever herd of a thing like that. But he said if I want to get smart I got to do what he says. I told him I dint think I was going to get smart and he puts his hand on my sholder and said Charlie you dont know it yet but your getting smarter all the time. You wont notice for a while. I think he was just being nice to make me feel good because I dont look any smarter.

Oh yes I almost forgot. I asked him when I can go back to the class at Miss Kinnians school. He said I wont go their. He said that soon Miss Kinnian will come to the hospitil to start and teach me speshul.

Mar 29 That crazy TV kept up all night. How can I sleep with something yelling crazy things all night in my ears. And the nutty pictures. Wow. I don't know what it says when Im up so how am I going to know when Im sleeping.

Dr Strauss says its ok. He says my brains are lerning when I sleep and that will help me when Miss Kinnian starts my lessons in the hospitl (only I found out it isn't a hospitil its a labatory.) I think its all crazy. If you can get smart when your sleeping why do people go to school. That thing I don't think will work. I use to watch the late show and the late late show on TV all the time and it never made me smart. Maybe you have to sleep while you watch it.

progress report 9—April 3

Dr Strauss showed me how to keep the TV turned low so now I can sleep. I don't hear a

Kristen Müller, "The Last Door" (detail), *Yolanda, The Gallery for Naifs/Folk Art*

thing. And I still dont understand what it says. A few times I play it over in the morning to find out what I lerned when I was sleeping and I don't think so. Miss Kinnian says Maybe its another langwidge. But most times it sounds american. It talks faster than even Miss Gold who was my teacher in 6 grade.

I told Dr. Strauss what good is it to get smart in my sleep. I want to be smart when Im awake. He says its the same thing and I have two minds. Theres the *subconscious* and the *conscious* (thats how you spell it). And one dont tell the other one what its doing. They dont even talk to each other. Thats why I dream. And boy have I been having crazy dreams. Wow. Ever since that night TV. The late late late show. I forgot to ask him if it was only me or if everybody had those two minds.

(I just looked up the word in the dictionary Dr. Strauss gave me. The word is *subconscious. adj. Of the nature of mental operations not yet present in consciousness; as, subconscious conflict of desires.*) There's more but I still dont know what it means. This isnt a very good dictionary for dumb people like me.

Anyway the headache is from the party. My friends from the factery Joe Carp and Frank Reilly invited me to go to Muggsys Saloon for some drinks. I don't like to drink but they said we will have lots of fun. I had a good time.

Joe Carp said I shoud show the girls how I mop out the toilet in the factory and he got me a mop. I showed them and everyone laffed when I told that Mr. Donnegan said I was the best janiter he ever had because I like my job and do it good and never miss a day except for my operashun.

I said Miss Kinnian always said Charlie be proud of your job because you do it good.

Everybody laffed and we had a good time and they gave me lots of drinks and Joe said Charlie is a card when hes potted. I dont know what that means but everybody likes me and we have fun. I cant wait to be smart like my best friends Joe Carp and Frank Reilly.

I dont remember how the party was over but I think I went out to buy a newspaper and coffe for Joe and Frank and when I came back there was no one their. I looked for them all over till late. Then I dont remember so good but I think I got sleepy or sick. A nice cop brot me back home Thats what my landlady Mrs Flynn says.

But I got a headache and a big lump on my head. I think maybe I fell but Joe Carp says it was the cop they beat up drunks some times. I don't think so. Miss Kinnian says cops are to help people. Anyway I got a bad headache and Im sick and hurt all over. I dont think Ill drink anymore.

April 6 I beat Algernon! I dint even know I beat him until Burt the tester told me. Then the second time I lost because I got so exited I fell off the chair before I finished. But after that I beat him 8 more times. I must be getting smart to beat a smart mouse like Algernon. But I don't *feel* smarter.

I wanted to race Algernon some more but Burt said thats enough for one day. They let me hold him for a minit. Hes not so bad. Hes soft like a ball of cotton. He blinks and when he opens his eyes their black and pink on the eges.

I said can I feed him because I felt bad to beat him and I wanted to be nice and make friends. Burt said no Algernon is a very specshul mouse with an operashun like mine, and he was the first of all the animals to stay smart so long. He told me Algernon is so smart that every day he has to solve a test to get his food. Its a thing like a lock on a door that changes every time Algernon goes in to eat so he has to lern something new to get his food. That made me sad because if he couldn't lern he would be hungry.

I don't think its right to make you pass a test to eat. How would Dr Nemur like it to have to pass a test every time he wants to eat. I think Ill be friends with Algernon.

April 9 Tonight after work Miss Kinnian was at the laboratory. She looked like she was glad to see me but scared. I told her dont worry Miss Kinnian Im not smart yet and she laffed. She said I have confidence in you Charlie the way you struggled so hard to read and right better than all the others. At werst you will have it for a littel wile and your doing somthing for science.

We are reading a very hard book. Its called *Robinson Crusoe* about a man who gets merooned on a dessert Iland. Hes smart and figers out all kinds of things so he can have a house and food and hes a good swimmer. Only I feel sorry because hes all alone and has no frends. But I think their must be somebody else on the iland because theres a picture with his funny umbrella looking at footprints. I hope he gets a frend and not be lonly.

April 10 Miss Kinnian teaches me to spell better. She says look at a word and close your eyes and say it over and over until you remember. I have lots of truble with *through* that you say *threw* and *enough* and *tough* that you dont say *enew* and *tew*. You got to say *enuff* and *tuff*. Thats how I use to write it before I started to get smart. Im confused but Miss Kinnian says theres no reason in spelling.

April 14 Finished *Robinson Crusoe.* I want to find out more about what happens to him but Miss Kinnian says thats all there is. *Why.*

Apr 15 Miss Kinnian says Im lerning fast. She read some of the Progress Reports and she looked at me kind of funny. She says Im a fine person and Ill show them all. I asked her why. She said never mind but I shouldnt feel bad if I find out everybody isnt nice like I think. She said for a person who god gave so little to you done more then a lot of people with brains they never even used. I said all my friends are smart people but there good. They like me and they never did anything that wasnt nice. Then she got something in her eye and she had to run out to the ladys room.

Apr 16 Today, I lerned, the *comma,* this is a comma (,) a period, with a tail, Miss Kinnian, says its importent, because, it makes writing, better, she said, somebody, coud lose, a lot of money, if a comma, isnt, in the, right place, I dont have, any money, and I dont see, how a comma, keeps you, from losing it,

Apr 17 I used the comma wrong. Its punctuation. Miss Kinnian told me to look up long words in the dictionary to lern to spell them. I said whats the difference if you can read it anyway. She said its part of your education so now on Ill look up all the words Im not sure how to spell. It takes a long time to write that way but I only have to look up once and after that I get it right.

You got to mix them up, she showed? me" how. to mix! them (and now; I can! mix up all kinds" of punctuation, in! my writing? There, are lots! of rules? to lern; but Im gettin'g them in my head.

One thing I like about, Dear Miss Kinnian: (thats the way it goes in a business letter if I ever go into business) is she, always gives me' a reason" when—I ask. She's a gen'ius! I wish I cou'd be smart" like, her;

(Puncuation, is; fun!)

April 18 What a dope I am! I didn't even understand what she was talking about. I read the grammar book last night and it explanes the whole thing. Then I saw it was the same way as Miss Kinnian was trying to tell me, but I didn't get it.

Miss Kinnian said that the TV working in my sleep helped out. She and I reached a plateau. Thats a flat hill.

After I figured out how punctuation worked, I read over all my old Progress Reports from the beginning. Boy, did I have crazy spelling and punctuation! I told Miss Kinnian I ought to go over the pages and fix all the mistakes but she said, "No, Charlie, Dr. Nemur wants them just as they are. That's why he let you keep them after they were photostated, to see your own progress. You're coming along fast, Charlie."

That made me feel good. After the lesson I went down and played with Algernon. We don't race any more.

April 20 I feel sick inside. Not sick like for a doctor, but inside my chest it feels empty like getting punched and a heartburn at the same time. I wasn't going to write about it, but I guess I got to, because its important. Today was the first time I ever stayed home from work.

Last night Joe Carp and Frank Reilly invited me to a party. There were lots of girls and some men from the factory. I remembered how sick I got last time I drank too much, so I told Joe I didn't want anything to drink. He gave me a plain coke instead.

We had a lot of fun for a while. Joe said I should dance with Ellen and she would teach me the steps. I fell a few times and I couldn't understand why because no one else was dancing besides Ellen and me. And all the time I was tripping because somebody's foot was always sticking out.

Then when I got up I saw the look on Joe's face and it gave me a funny feeling in my stomach. "He's a scream," one of the girls said. Everybody was laughing.

"Look at him. He's blushing. Charlie is blushing."

"Hey, Ellen, what'd you do to Charlie? I never saw him act like that before."

I didn't know what to do or where to turn. Everyone was looking at me and laughing and I felt naked. I wanted to hide. I ran outside and I threw up. Then I walked home. It's a funny thing I never knew that Joe and Frank and the others liked to have me around all the time to make fun of me.

Now I know what it means when they say "to pull a Charlie Gordon."

I'm ashamed.

progress report 11

April 21 Still didn't go into the factory. I told Mrs. Flynn my landlady to call and tell Mr. Donnegan I was sick. Mrs. Flynn looks at me very funny lately like she's scared.

I think it's a good thing about finding out how everybody laughs at me. I thought about it a lot. It's because I'm so dumb and I don't even know when I'm doing something dumb. People think it's funny when a dumb person can't do things the same way they can.

Anyway, now I know I'm getting smarter every day. I know punctuation and I can spell good. I like to look up all the hard words in the dictionary and I remember them. I'm reading a lot now, and Miss Kinnian says I read very fast. Sometimes I even understand what I'm reading about, and it stays in my mind. There are times when I can close my eyes and think of a page and it all comes back like a picture.

Besides history, geography, and arithmetic, Miss Kinnian said I should start to learn foreign languages. Dr. Strauss gave me some more tapes to play while I sleep. I still don't understand how that conscious and unconscious mind works, but Dr. Strauss says not to worry yet. He asked me to promise that when I start learning college subjects next week I wouldn't read any books on psychology—that is, until he gives me permission.

I feel a lot better today, but I guess I'm still a little angry that all the time people were laughing and making fun of me because I wasn't so smart. When I become intelligent like Dr. Strauss says, with three times my I.Q. of 68, then maybe I'll be like everyone else and people will like me.

I'm not sure what an I.Q. is. Dr. Nemur said it was something that measured how intelligent you were—like a scale in the drugstore weighs pounds. But Dr. Strauss had a big argument with him and said an I.Q. didn't weigh intelligence at all. He said an I.Q. showed how much intelligence you could get, like the numbers on the outside of a measuring cup. You still had to fill the cup up with stuff.

Then when I asked Burt, who gives me my intelligence tests and works with Algernon, he said that both of them were wrong (only I had to promise not to tell them he said so). Burt says that the I.Q. measures a lot of different things including some of the things you learned already, and it really isn't any good at all.

So I still don't know what I.Q. is except that mine is going to be over 200 soon. I didn't want to say anything, but I don't see how if they don't know *what* it is, or *where* it is—I don't see how they know *how much* of it you've got.

Dr. Nemur says I have to take a *Rorschach Test* tomorrow. I wonder what *that* is.

April 22 I found out what a Rorschach is. It's the test I took before the operation—the one with the inkblots on the pieces of cardboard.

I was scared to death of those inkblots. I knew the man was going to ask me to find the pictures and I knew I couldn't. I was thinking to myself, if only there was some way of knowing what kind of pictures were hidden there. Maybe there weren't any pictures at all. Maybe it was just a trick to see if I was dumb enough to look for something that wasn't there. Just thinking about that made me sore at him.

"All right, Charlie," he said, "you've seen these cards before, remember?"

"Of course I remember."

The way I said it, he knew I was angry, and he looked surprised. "Yes, of course. Now I want you to look at this. What might this be? What do you see on this card? People see all sorts of things in these inkblots. Tell me what it might be for you—what it makes you think of."

I was shocked. That wasn't what I had expected him to say. "You mean there are no pictures hidden in those inkblots?"

He frowned and took off his glasses. "What?"

"Pictures. Hidden in the inkblots. Last time you told me everyone could see them and you wanted me to find them too."

He explained to me that the last time he had used almost the exact same words he was using now. I didn't believe it, and I still have the suspicion that he misled me at the time just for the fun of it. Unless—I don't know any more—could I have been *that* feeble-minded?

We went through the cards slowly. One looked like a pair of bats tugging at something. Another one looked like two men fencing with swords. I imagined all sorts of things. I guess I got carried away. But I didn't trust him any more, and I kept turning them around, even looking on the back to see if there was anything there I was supposed to catch. While he was making his notes, I peeked out of the corner of my eye to read it. But it was all in code that looked like this:

$$WF + A \quad DdF - Ad \text{ orig.} \quad WF - A$$
$$SF + obj$$

The test still doesn't make sense to me. It seems to me that anyone could make up lies

Charles Sheeler, "Ballardvale,"
Addison Gallery of American Art

about things that they didn't really imagine? Maybe I'll understand it when Dr. Strauss lets me read up on psychology.

April 25 I figured out a new way to line up the machines in the factory, and Mr. Donnegan says it will save him ten thousand dollars a year in labor and increased production. He gave me a $25 bonus.

I wanted to take Joe Carp and Frank Reilly out to lunch to celebrate, but Joe said he had to buy some things for his wife, and Frank said he was meeting his cousin for lunch. I guess it'll take a little time for them to get used to the changes in me. Everybody seems to be frightened of me. When I went over to Amos Borg and tapped him, he jumped up in the air.

People don't talk to me much any more or kid around the way they used to. It makes the job kind of lonely.

April 27 I got up the nerve today to ask Miss Kinnian to have dinner with me tomorrow night to celebrate my bonus.

At first she wasn't sure it was right, but I asked Dr. Strauss and he said it was okay. Dr. Strauss and Dr. Nemur don't seem to be getting along so well. They're arguing all the time. This evening I heard them shouting. Dr. Nemur was saying that it was *his* experiment and *his* research, and Dr. Strauss shouted back that he contributed just as much, because he found me through Miss Kinnian and he performed the operation. Dr. Strauss said that someday thousands of neurosurgeons might be using his technique all over the world.

Dr. Nemur wanted to publish the results of the experiment at the end of this month. Dr. Strauss wanted to wait a while to be sure. Dr. Strauss said Dr. Nemur was more interested in the Chair of Psychology at Princeton[5] than he was in the experiment. Dr. Nemur said Dr. Strauss was nothing but an opportunist trying to ride to glory on *his* coattails.

When I left afterwards, I found myself trembling. I don't know why for sure, but it was as if I'd seen both men clearly for the first time. I remember hearing Burt say Dr. Nemur had a shrew of a wife who was pushing him all the time to get things published so he could become famous. Burt said that the dream of her life was to have a big-shot husband.

April 28 I don't understand why I never noticed how beautiful Miss Kinnian really is. She has brown eyes and feathery brown hair that comes to the top of her neck. She's only thirty-four! I think from the beginning I had the feeling that she was an unreachable genius—and very, very old. Now, every time I see her she grows younger and more lovely.

We had dinner and a long talk. When she said I was coming along so fast I'd be leaving her behind, I laughed.

"It's true, Charlie. You're already a better reader than I am. You can read a whole page at a glance while I can take in only a few lines at a time. And you remember every single thing you read. I'm lucky if I can recall the main thoughts and the general meaning."

"I don't feel intelligent. There are so many things I don't understand."

She took out a cigarette and I lit it for her. "You've got to be a *little* patient. You're accomplishing in days and weeks what it takes normal people to do in a lifetime. That's what makes it so amazing. You're like a giant sponge now, soaking things in. Facts, figures, general knowledge. And soon you'll begin to connect them, too. You'll see how different branches of learning are related. There are many levels, Charlie, like steps on a giant ladder that take you up higher and higher to see more and more of the world around you.

"I can see only a little bit of that, Charlie, and I won't go much higher than I am now, but you'll keep climbing up and up, and see more and more, and each step will open new worlds that you never even knew existed." She frowned. "I hope . . . I just hope——"

"What?"

"Never mind, Charles. I just hope I wasn't wrong to advise you to go into this in the first place."

I laughed. "How could that be? It worked, didn't it? Even Algernon is still smart."

We sat there silently for a while and I knew what she was thinking about as she watched me toying with the chain of my rabbit's foot and my keys. I didn't want to think of that possibility any more than elderly people want to think of death. I *knew* that this was only the beginning. I knew what she meant about levels because I'd seen some of them already. The thought of leaving her behind made me sad.

I'm in love with Miss Kinnian.

---

5. *Chair of Psychology at Princeton,* an appointment as professor of psychology at Princeton University.

progress report 12

April 30 I've quit my job with Donnegan's Plastic Box Company. Mr. Donnegan insisted it would be better for all concerned if I left. What did I do to make them hate me so?

The first I knew of it was when Mr. Donnegan showed me the petition. Eight hundred names, everyone in the factory, except Fanny Girden. Scanning the list quickly, I saw at once that hers was the only missing name. All the rest demanded that I be fired.

Joe Carp and Frank Reilly wouldn't talk to me about it. No one else would either, except Fanny. She was one of the few people I'd known who set her mind to something and believed it no matter what the rest of the world proved, said or did—and Fanny did not believe that I should have been fired. She had been against the petition on principle and despite the pressure and threats she'd held out.

"Which don't mean to say," she remarked, "that I don't think there's something mighty strange about you, Charlie. Them changes. I don't know. You used to be a good, dependable, ordinary man—not too bright maybe, but honest. Who knows what you done to yourself to get so smart all of a sudden. Like everybody around here's been saying, Charlie, it's not right."

"But how can you say that, Fanny? What's wrong with a man becoming intelligent and wanting to acquire knowledge and understanding of the world around him?"

She stared down at her work and I turned to leave. Without looking at me, she said: "It was evil when Eve listened to the snake and ate from the tree of knowledge. It was evil when she saw that she was naked. If not for

that none of us would ever have to grow old and sick, and die."[6]

Once again, now, I have the feeling of shame burning inside me. This intelligence has driven a wedge between me and all the people I once knew and loved. Before, they laughed at me and despised me for my ignorance and dullness; now, they hate me for my knowledge and understanding. What do they want of me?

They've driven me out of the factory. Now I'm more alone than ever before. . . .

May 15 Dr. Strauss is very angry at me for not having written any progress reports in two weeks. He's justified because the lab is now paying me a regular salary. I told him I was too busy thinking and reading. When I pointed out that writing was such a slow process that it made me impatient with my poor handwriting, he suggested I learn to type. It's much easier to write now because I can type seventy-five words a minute. Dr. Strauss continually reminds me of the need to speak and write simply so people will be able to understand me.

I'll try to review all the things that happened to me during the last two weeks. Algernon and I were presented to the *American Psychological Association* sitting in convention with the *World Psychological Association*. We created quite a sensation. Dr. Nemur and Dr. Strauss were proud of us.

I suspect that Dr. Nemur, who is sixty—ten years older than Dr. Strauss—finds it necessary to see tangible results of his work.

---

6. *"It was evil . . . die."* Fanny is referring to the biblical story of the fall of Adam and Eve and their expulsion by God from the Garden of Eden. [Genesis 2]

Undoubtedly the result of pressure by Mrs. Nemur.

Contrary to my earlier impressions of him, I realize that Dr. Nemur is not at all a genius. He has a very good mind, but it struggles under the spectre of self-doubt. He wants people to take him for a genius. Therefore it is important for him to feel that his work is accepted by the world. I believe that Dr. Nemur was afraid of further delay because he worried that someone else might make a discovery along these lines and take the credit from him.

Dr. Strauss on the other hand might be called a genius, although I feel his areas of knowledge are too limited. He was educated in the tradition of narrow specialization; the broader aspects of background were neglected far more than necessary—even for a neurosurgeon.

I was shocked to learn the only ancient languages he could read were Latin, Greek, and Hebrew, and that he knows almost nothing of mathematics beyond the elementary levels of the calculus of variations. When he admitted this to me, I found myself almost annoyed. It was as if he'd hidden this part of himself in order to deceive me, pretending—as do many people I've discovered—to be what he is not. No one I've ever known is what he appears to be on the surface.

Dr. Nemur appears to be uncomfortable around me. Sometimes when I try to talk to him, he just looks at me strangely and turns away. I was angry at first when Dr. Strauss told me I was giving Dr. Nemur an inferiority complex. I thought he was mocking me and I'm oversensitive at being made fun of.

How was I to know that a highly respected psycho-experimentalist like Nemur was unacquainted with Hindustani and Chinese? It's absurd when you consider the work that is being done in India and China today in the very field of his study.

I asked Dr. Strauss how Nemur could refute Rahajamati's attacks on his method if Nemur couldn't even read them in the first place. That strange look on Strauss's face can mean only one of two things. Either he doesn't want to tell Nemur what they're saying in India, or else—and this worries me—Dr. Strauss doesn't know either. I must be careful to speak and write clearly and simply so people won't laugh.

May 18 I am very disturbed. I saw Miss Kinnian last night for the first time in over a week. I tried to avoid all discussions of intellectual concepts and to keep the conversation on a simple, everyday level, but she just stared at me blankly and asked me what I meant about the mathematical variance equivalent in Dorbermann's *Fifth Concerto*.

When I tried to explain she stopped me and laughed. I guess I got angry, but I suspect I'm approaching her on the wrong level. No matter what I try to discuss with her, I am unable to communicate. I must review Vrostadt's equations on *Levels of Semantic Progression*. I find I don't communicate with people much any more. Thank God for books and music and things I can think about. I am alone at Mrs. Flynn's boarding house most of the time and seldom speak to anyone.

May 20 I would not have noticed the new dishwasher, a boy of about sixteen, at the corner diner where I take my evening meals if not for the incident of the broken dishes.

They crashed to the floor, sending bits of white china under the tables. The boy stood there, dazed and frightened, holding the empty tray in his hand. The catcalls from the customers (the cries of "hey, there go the profits!" . . . "*Mazeltov!*"[7] . . . and "well, *he* didn't work here very long . . . " which invariably seem to follow the breaking of glass or dishware in a public restaurant) all seemed to confuse him.

When the owner came to see what the excitement was about, the boy cowered as if he expected to be struck. "All right! All right, you dope," shouted the owner, "don't just stand there! Get the broom and sweep that mess up. A broom . . . a broom, you idiot! It's in the kitchen!"

The boy saw he was not going to be punished. His frightened expression disappeared and he smiled as he came back with the broom to sweep the floor. A few of the rowdier customers kept up the remarks, amusing themselves at his expense.

"Here, sonny, over here there's a nice piece behind you . . . "

"He's not so dumb. It's easier to break 'em than wash 'em!"

As his vacant eyes moved across the crowd of onlookers, he slowly mirrored their smiles and finally broke into an uncertain grin at the joke he obviously did not understand.

I felt sick inside as I looked at his dull, vacuous smile, the wide, bright eyes of a child, uncertain but eager to please. They were laughing at him because he was mentally retarded.

And I had been laughing at him too.

Suddenly I was furious at myself and all those who were smirking at him. I jumped up and shouted, "Shut up! Leave him alone! It's not his fault he can't understand! He can't help what he is! But he's still a human being!"

The room grew silent. I cursed myself for losing control. I tried not to look at the boy as I walked out without touching my food. I felt ashamed for both of us.

How strange that people of honest feelings and sensibility, who would not take advantage of a man born without arms or eyes—how such people think nothing of abusing a man born with low intelligence. It infuriated me to think that not too long ago I had foolishly played the clown.

And I had almost forgotten.

I'd hidden the picture of the old Charlie Gordon from myself because now that I was intelligent it was something that had to be pushed out of my mind. But today in looking at that boy, for the first time I saw what I had been. *I was just like him!*

Only a short time ago, I learned that people laughed at me. Now I can see that unknowingly I joined with them in laughing at myself. That hurts most of all.

I have often reread my progress reports and seen the illiteracy, the childish naïveté, the mind of low intelligence peering from a dark room through the keyhole at the dazzling light outside. I see that even in my dullness I knew I was inferior, and that other people had something I lacked—something denied me. In my mental blindness, I thought it was somehow connected with the ability to read and write, and I was sure that

---

7. *Mazeltov!* a Yiddish expression meaning, in this case, "May you have better luck in the future."

if I could get those skills I would automatically have intelligence too.

Even a feeble-minded man wants to be like other men.

A child may not know how to feed itself, or what to eat, yet it knows of hunger.

This then is what I was like. I never knew. Even with my gift of intellectual awareness, I never really knew.

This day was good for me. Seeing the past more clearly, I've decided to use my knowledge and skills to work in the field of increasing human intelligence levels. Who is better equipped for this work? Who else has lived in both worlds? These are my people. Let me use my gift to do something for them.

Tomorrow, I will discuss with Dr. Strauss how I can work in this area. I may be able to help him work out the problems of widespread use of the technique which was used on me. I have several good ideas of my own.

There is so much that might be done with this technique. If I could be made into a genius, what about thousands of others like myself? What fantastic levels might be achieved by using this technique on normal people? On *geniuses?*

There are so many doors to open. I am impatient to begin.

progress report 13

May 23 It happened today. Algernon bit me. I visited the lab to see him as I do occasionally, and when I took him out of his cage, he snapped at my hand. I put him back and watched him for a while. He was unusually disturbed and vicious.

May 24 Burt, who is in charge of the experimental animals, tells me that Algernon is changing. He is less cooperative; he refuses to run the maze any more; general motivation has decreased. And he hasn't been eating. Everyone is upset about what this may mean.

May 25 They've been feeding Algernon who now refuses to work the shifting-lock problem. Everyone identifies me with Algernon. In a way we're both the first of our kind. They're all pretending that Algernon's behavior is not necessarily significant for me. But it's hard to hide the fact that some of the other animals who were used in this experiment are showing strange behavior.

Dr. Strauss and Dr. Nemur have asked me not to come to the lab any more. I know what they're thinking but I can't accept it. I am going ahead with my plans to carry their research forward. With all due respect to both these fine scientists, I am well aware of their limitations. If there is an answer, I'll have to find it out for myself. Suddenly, time has become very important to me.

May 29 I have been given a lab of my own and permission to go ahead with the research. I'm on to something. Working day and night. I've had a cot moved into the lab. Most of my writing time is spent on the notes which I keep in a separate folder, but from time to time I feel it necessary to put down my moods and thoughts from sheer habit.

I find the *calculus of intelligence* to be a fascinating study. Here is the place for the application of all the knowledge I have acquired.

May 31 Dr. Strauss thinks I'm working too hard. Dr. Nemur says I'm trying to cram a lifetime of research and thought into a few weeks. I know I should rest, but I'm driven on by something inside that won't let me stop. I've got to find the reason for the sharp regression in Algernon. I've got to know *if* and *when* it will happen to me.

June 4
LETTER TO DR. STRAUSS (*copy*)
Dear Dr. Strauss:

Under separate cover I am sending you a copy of my report entitled, "The Algernon-Gordon Effect: A Study of Structure and Function of Increased Intelligence," which I would like to have published.

As you see, my experiments are completed. I have included in my report all of my formulae, as well as mathematical analysis in the appendix. Of course, these should be verified.

Because of its importance to both you and Dr. Nemur (and need I say to myself, too?) I have checked and rechecked my results a dozen times in the hope of finding an error. I am sorry to say the results must stand. Yet for the sake of science, I am grateful for the little bit that I here add to the knowledge of the function of the human mind and of the laws governing the artificial increase of human intelligence.

I recall your once saying to me that an experimental *failure* or the *disproving* of a theory was as important to the advancement of learning as a success would be. I know now that this is true. I am sorry, however, that my own contribution to the field must rest upon the ashes of the work of two men I regard so highly.

Yours truly,
Charles Gordon

June 5
I must not become emotional. The facts and the results of my experiments are clear, and the more sensational aspects of my own rapid climb cannot obscure the fact that the tripling of intelligence by the surgical technique developed by Drs. Strauss and Nemur must be viewed as having little or no practical applicability (at the present time) to the increase of human intelligence.

As I review the records and data on Algernon, I see that although he is still in his physical infancy, he has regressed mentally. Motor activity is impaired; there is a general reduction of glandular activity; there is an accelerated loss of coordination.

There are also strong indications of progressive amnesia.

As will be seen by my report, these and other physical and mental deterioration syndromes can be predicted with significant results by the application of my formula.

The surgical stimulus to which we were both subjected has resulted in an intensification and acceleration of all mental processes. The unforeseen development, which I have taken the liberty of calling the *Algernon-Gordon Effect*, is the logical extension of the entire intelligence speed-up. The hypothesis here proven may be described simply in the following terms: Artificially increased intelligence deteriorates at a rate of time directly proportional to the quantity of the increase.

I feel that this, in itself, is an important discovery.

As long as I am able to write, I will continue to record my thoughts in these progress reports. It is one of my few pleasures. However, by all indications, my own mental deterioration will be very rapid.

I have already begun to notice signs of emotional instability and forgetfulness, the first symptoms of the burnout.

June 10 Deterioration progressing. I have become absent-minded. Algernon died two days ago. Dissection shows my predictions were right. His brain had decreased in weight and there was a general smoothing out of cerebral convolutions, as well as a deepening and broadening of brain fissures.[8]

I guess the same thing is or will soon be happening to me. Now that it's definite, I don't want it to happen.

I put Algernon's body in a cheese box and buried him in the back yard. I cried.

June 15 Dr. Strauss came to see me again. I wouldn't open the door and I told him to go away. I want to be left to myself. I am touchy and irritable. I feel the darkness closing in. It's hard to throw off thoughts of suicide. I keep telling myself how important this journal will be.

It's a strange sensation to pick up a book you enjoyed just a few months ago and discover you don't remember it. I remembered how great I thought John Milton was, but when I picked up *Paradise Lost* I couldn't understand it at all. I got so angry I threw the book across the room.

I've got to try to hold on to some of it. Some of the things I've learned. Oh, God, please don't take it all away.

June 19 Sometimes, at night, I go out for a walk. Last night, I couldn't remember where I lived. A policeman took me home. I have the strange feeling that this has all happened to me before—a long time ago. I keep telling myself I'm the only person in the world who can describe what's happening to me.

June 21 Why can't I remember? I've got to fight. I lie in bed for days and I don't know who or where I am. Then it all comes back to me in a flash. Fugues of amnesia. Symptoms of senility—second childhood. I can watch them coming on. It's so cruelly logical. I learned so much and so fast. Now my mind is deteriorating rapidly. I won't let it happen. I'll fight it. I can't help thinking of the boy in the restaurant, the blank expression, the silly smile, the people laughing at him. No—please—not that again. . . .

June 22 I'm forgetting things that I learned recently. It seems to be following the classic pattern—the last things learned are the first things forgotten. Or is that the pattern? I'd better look it up again. . . .

I reread my paper on the *Algernon-Gordon Effect* and I get the strange feeling that it was written by someone else. There are parts I don't even understand.

Motor activity impaired. I keep tripping over things, and it becomes increasingly difficult to type.

June 23 I've given up using the typewriter. My coordination is bad. I feel I'm moving slower and slower. Had a terrible shock today. I picked up a copy of an article I used in my research, Krueger's *Uber psychische Ganzheit*, to see if it would help me under-

---

8. *His brain . . . fissures.* There seems to be a direct relationship between intelligence and brain size, and between intelligence and the number of cerebral convolutions (folds or ridges on the surface of the brain).

stand what I had done. First I thought there was something wrong with my eyes. Then I realized I could no longer read German. I tested myself in other languages. All gone.

June 30 A week since I dared to write again. It's slipping away like sand through my fingers. Most of the books I have are too hard for me now. I get angry with them because I know that I read and understood them just a few weeks ago.

I keep telling myself I must keep writing these reports so that somebody will know what is happening to me. But it gets harder to form the words and remember spellings. I have to look up even simple words in the dictionary now and it makes me impatient with myself.

Dr. Strauss comes around almost every day, but I told him I wouldn't see or speak to anybody. He feels guilty. They all do. But I don't blame anyone. I knew what might happen. But how it hurts.

July 7 I don't know where the week went. Todays Sunday I know because I can see through my window people going to church. I think I stayed in bed all week but I remember Mrs. Flynn bringing food to me a few times. I keep saying over and over I've got to do something but then I forget or maybe its just easier not to do what I say I'm going to do.

I think of my mother and father a lot these days. I found a picture of them with me taken at a beach. My father has a big ball under his arm and my mother is holding me by the hand. I dont remember them the way they are in the picture. All I remember is my fa-ther drunk most of the time and arguing with mom about money.

He never shaved much and he used to scratch my face when he hugged me. My Mother said he died but Cousin Miltie said he heard his dad say that my father ran away with another woman. When I asked my mother she slapped me and said my father was dead. I dont think I ever found out the truth but I dont care much. (He said he was going to take me to see cows on a farm once but he never did. He never kept his promises. . . .)

July 10 My landlady Mrs. Flynn is very worried about me. She says the way I lay around all day and dont do anything I remind her of her son before she threw him out of the house. She said she doesn't like loafers. If Im sick its one thing, but if Im a loafer thats another thing and she won't have it. I told her I think Im sick.

I try to read a little bit every day, mostly stories, but sometimes I have to read the same thing over and over again because I don't know what it means. And its hard to write. I know I should look up all the words in the dictionary but its so hard and Im so tired all the time.

Then I got the idea that I would only use the easy words instead of the long hard ones. That saves time. I put flowers on Algernons grave about once a week. Mrs. Flynn thinks Im crazy to put flowers on a mouses grave but I told her that Algernon was special.

July 14 Its sunday again. I dont have anything to do to keep me busy now because my television set is broke and I dont have any money to get it fixed. (I think I lost this months check from the lab. I don't remember)

I get awful headaches and asperin doesnt help me much. Mrs. Flynn knows Im really sick and she feels very sorry for me. Shes a wonderful woman whenever someone is sick.

July 22 Mrs. Flynn called a strange doctor to see me. She was afraid I was going to die. I told the doctor I wasnt too sick and I only forget sometimes. He asked me did I have any friends or relatives and I said no I dont have any. I told him I had a friend called Algernon once but he was a mouse and we used to run races together. He looked at me kind of funny like he thought I was crazy. He smiled when I told him I used to be a genius. He talked to me like I was a baby and he winked at Mrs. Flynn. I got mad and chased him out because he was making fun of me the way they all used to.

July 24 I have no more money and Mrs. Flynn says I got to go to work somewhere and pay the rent because I havent paid for two months. I dont know any work but the job I used to have at Donnegans Box Company. I dont want to go back because they all knew me when I was smart and maybe they'll laugh at me. But I dont know what else to do to get money.

July 25 I was looking at some of my old progress reports and its very funny but I cant read what I wrote. I can make out some of the words but they dont make sense.

Miss Kinnian came to the door but I said go away I don't want to see you. She cried and I cried too but I wouldnt let her in because I didn't want her to laugh at me. I told her I didnt like her any more. I told her I didnt want to be smart any more. That's not true. I still love her and I still want to be smart but I had to say that so shed go away. She gave Mrs. Flynn money to pay the rent. I dont want that. I got to get a job.

Please . . . please let me not forget how to read and write. . . .

July 27 Mr. Donnegan was very nice when I came back and asked him for my old job of janitor. First he was very suspicious but I told him what happened to me and he looked very sad and put his hand on my shoulder and said Charlie Gordon you got guts.

Everybody looked at me when I came downstairs and started working in the toilet sweeping it out like I used to. I told myself Charlie if they make fun of you dont get sore because you remember their not so smart as you once thot they were. And besides they were once your friends and if they laughted at you that doesnt meant anything because they liked you too.

One of the new men who came to work there after I went away made a nasty crack he said hey Charlie I hear your a very smart fella a real quiz kid. Say something intelligent. I felt bad but Joe Carp came over and grabbed him by the shirt and said leave him alone you lousy cracker or I'll break your neck. I didnt expect Joe to take my part so I guess hes really my friend.

Later Frank Reilly came over and said Charlie if anybody bothers you or trys to take advantage you call me or Joe and we will set em straight. I said thanks Frank and I got

Kristen Müller, "The Last Door," *Yolanda, The Gallery for Naïfs/Folk Art*

choked up so I had to turn around and go into the supply room so he wouldnt see me cry. Its good to have friends.

July 28 I did a dumb thing today I forgot I wasn't in Miss Kinnians class at the adult center any more like I use to be. I went in and sat down in my old seat in the back of the room and she looked at me funny and she said Charles. I dint remember she ever called me that before only Charlie so I said hello Miss Kinnian Im redy for my lesin today only I lost my reader that we was using. She startid to cry and run out of the room and everybody looked at me and I saw they wasnt the same pepul who use to be in my class.

Then all of a suddin I remembered some things about the operashun and me getting smart and I said holy smoke I reely pulled a Charlie Gordon that time. I went away before she come back to the room.

Thats why Im going away from New York for good. I dont want to do nothing like that agen. I dont want Miss Kinnian to feel sorry for me. Evry body feels sorry at the factery and I dont want that eather so Im going someplace where nobody knows that Charlie Gordon was once a genus and now he cant even reed a book or rite good.

Im taking a cuple of books along and even if I cant reed them Ill practise hard and maybe I wont forget every thing I lerned. If I try reel hard maybe Ill be a littel bit smarter then I was before the operashun. I got my rabits foot and my luky penny and maybe they will help me.

If you ever reed this Miss Kinnian dont be sorry for me Im glad I got a second chanse to be smart becaus I lerned a lot of things that I never even new were in this world and Im grateful that I saw it all for a littel bit. I dont know why Im dumb agen or what I did wrong maybe its because I dint try hard enuff. But if I try and practis very hard maybe Ill get a littl smarter and know what all the words are. I remember a littel bit how nice I had a feeling with the blue book that has the torn cover when I red it. Thats why Im gonna keep trying to get smart so I can have that feeling agen. Its a good feeling to know things and be smart. I wish I had it rite now if I did I would sit down and reed all the time. Anyway I bet Im the first dumb person in the world who ever found out somthing importent for science. I remember I did somthing but I dont remember what. So I gess its like I did it for all the dumb pepul like me.

Goodbye Miss Kinnian and Dr. Strauss and evreybody. And P.S. please tell Dr Nemur not to be such a grouch when pepul laff at him and he would have more frends. Its easy to make frends if you let pepul laff at you. Im going to have lots of frends where I go.

P.P.S. Please if you get a chanse put some flowrs on Algernons grave in the bak yard. . . .

THINK AND DISCUSS
Understanding
1. How does Charlie come to be considered for the operation? What qualities, apart from low intelligence, are reasons for his being chosen?
2. What is Charlie's attitude toward Algernon at the start of their association? How and why does this attitude change?
3. What is the first indication that Algernon is deteriorating?
4. How does Algernon change physically and mentally?
5. What happens to Algernon?

Analyzing
6. Miss Kinnian, Charlie's landlady, and the factory workers all have different attitudes toward Charlie at different times in the story. Explain how each feels about Charlie before his operation, as his intelligence increases, and as his intelligence slips away.
7. As a result of his increased understanding, Charlie sees people in a new light. Explain the changes in Charlie's view of Joe Carp and Frank Reilly; Dr. Nemur and Dr. Strauss; Miss Kinnian.
8. What is **ironic** about Charlie's laughter during the incident involving the dishwasher at the restaurant?
9. How is Charlie's deterioration similar to Algernon's?

Extending
10. To what event in the story does the title refer? In light of Charlie's relation to Algernon, how might the title be symbolic?
11. What do you think is the theme of this story?

APPLYING: Foreshadowing HT
See Handbook of Literary Terms, p. 667.

Foreshadowing occurs when a writer hints at what is to happen later as the plot unfolds.
1. When Miss Kinnian tells Charlie that she hopes she wasn't wrong in urging him to take part in the experiment, he assumes she's worried that he will soon "leave behind" someone of her intelligence. What else might she mean? What might this foreshadow?
2. What might Algernon's decline and death foreshadow?

VOCABULARY
Combining Forms
A *combining form* is a word part that combines with words or with other combining forms to make new words. The combining form *psycho-* comes from the Greek word for *psyche*, "mind." The Vocabulary word *psycho-experimentalist*, then, means "one who does experiments on the mind or about the mind." Another common combining form is *-logy*, meaning "science of," as in *volcanology*, "the science or study of volcanoes."

On a separate sheet, write the words

from Column A. After each word, write the correct definition from Column B.

Column A	Column B
psychoanalysis	mental therapy
psychology	analysis of the mind
psychohistory	science of the mind
psychotherapy	measurement of mental function
psychometrics	history written from a psychological point of view

COMPOSITION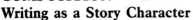

Writing as a Story Character

Write a one-page progress report as if you were Charlie Gordon at some point after your operation. After you have written your progress report, you might have classmates read it to see if they can discover at what point after the operation you are presenting Charlie's ideas and feelings. Before you begin your composition, see "Writing as a Story Character" in the Writer's Handbook.

Writing a Personal Essay

Imagine that you have been given unlimited intelligence. In return, you must devote some of that intelligence to solving one problem that plagues the human race. Which problem would you choose? Why? Write a paragraph in which you name your choice and give specific examples of why you feel it is the best choice possible.

BIOGRAPHY

Daniel Keyes

1927–

Of "Flowers for Algernon" Daniel Keyes writes, "I recall clearly the brief note in my 'idea folder,' something like: 'What would happen if a person's intelligence could be increased by surgery or something like that?' But that's all it was—an idea—until more than five years later a retarded boy said to me: 'Mr. Keyes, if I try hard and become smart will they put me into a regular class and let me be like everyone else?' The impact of those words stayed with me for a long time afterwards, until one day idea fused with character and I began to write 'Flowers for Algernon.'"

Since its first publication, the short story has appeared in numerous books and magazines, has been translated into several languages, and has been adapted for television under the title "The Two Worlds of Charlie Gordon." The story won the Science Fiction Writers of America Hugo Award in 1959. In 1966 Keyes published a novel-length version of the story which won the Nebula Award, and in 1968 the movie version, *Charly*, was produced. In 1980, the musical play *Charlie and Algernon* was produced in New York City.

See **FLASHBACK** in the Handbook of Literary Terms, page 665

The Last Boast

Dorothy Johnson

Each packing box had a rope tied to it by which it would be pulled away at the signal; the nooses were ready.

hen the time came for them to die, Pete Gossard cursed and Knife Hilton cried, but Wolfer Joe Kennedy yawned in the face of the hangman.

What he wanted to do was spit, to show he was not afraid, because he knew men would talk about him later and describe the end he made. But even Wolfer Joe could not raise enough saliva for spitting when he had a noose around his neck. The yawn was the next best thing.

Barney Gallagher, the United States deputy marshal, finished adjusting the rope and asked half-admiringly, "Are we keeping you up?"

"Hanging me up, they told me," Wolfer Joe answered.

On a packing box between his companions, he stood glaring out at the crowd of miners, with his lips pulled back from his teeth in the grin that was his trademark. He had foreseen the hour of his death, but not

the way of it. He had felt the jar of the bullet, heard the Cheyenne arrow whir, gone down screaming under a grizzly's claws—all these were probabilities for a man who had lived as he had lived, and a man had to die sometime.

But he had always seen himself fighting to the end. He had not dreamed of an end by hanging, helpless, with his hands tied behind him. He would not give his executioners the satisfaction of knowing he was astonished. They were going to get satisfaction enough without that.

Knife Hilton stopped crying and stood drooping on his packing box, snuffing like a baby. Pete Gossard stopped yelling curses, and thinking he had figured out a way to delay the performance, shouted earnestly, "I want a preacher! You wouldn't deny a man a preacher, would you?"

The Vigilantes had thought of that, too,

From *The Hanging Tree* by Dorothy M. Johnson. Copyright © 1957 by Dorothy M. Johnson. Reprinted by permission of Ballantine Books, a Division of Random House, Inc. and McIntosh & Otis, Inc.

H. W. Hansen, "The Outlaws"
Collection of Harrison Eiteljorg

and had a preacher there. They knew, by this time, about all the tricks a man could think of to make delay. Pete Gossard had nothing to say to the preacher, after all, except the frantic plea: "Tell 'em to give me a good drop."

"They will, Pete," the preacher promised. He shivered and added, "They always have. May God have mercy!"

There was still a lot of noise from the crowd of miners—the seven or eight hundred of them who had constituted the jury and had filed solemnly between two wagons to vote. Fourteen men had voted for acquittal, and after four hundred voted "guilty," the Vigilanters had stopped the farce of tallying. The noise was far out on the edge of the crowd, where those who could not see clearly were milling around, but in the center, at the hanging place, there was hardly any sound. Here death was, and the men who would beckon to it had nothing much to say.

The three packing boxes were sturdy; each had a rope tied to it by which it would be pulled away at the signal; the nooses were soundly wound. The Vigilanters, Wolfer Joe recollected, had had plenty of practice.

He felt a shudder coming over him, and to disguise it, he threw back his head and laughed.

He had few illusions about himself. Once he had said, grinning, "Reckon I was born bad." More accurately, he might have said,

"I was born outside the law, and mostly I've stayed outside it." He had kept moving westward to places where the law was not. And what caught up with him at last was not law but anger. The angry men at the diggings could not wait for the law to catch up; they set up the Vigilance Committee to enforce ruthless justice.

Barney Gallagher frowned at that laugh. He stepped down from the box, wiping his hands on his pants, and said reflectively, "I was wondering—did you ever do one good thing in your life?"

Wolfer Joe looked into his eyes and answered with his lips pulled back from his teeth, "Yeah. Once. I betrayed a woman."

At the hangman's signal, men pulled the ropes on the packing box.

The word *love* was in the language he used with women, but its meaning was not in his understanding when he met Annie. Even when he left her, he was not sure he knew the meaning, and after that he never had much chance to find out.

She stood with her arms outspread, her hands touching the barn wall, trembling, withdrawing not so much from Wolfer Joe as from life itself pressing toward her.

"You don't really like me," he insisted. "Bet you don't."

"Maybe I do," Annie answered, breathless. "I got to go in now." She could have ducked under his arm, but she only glanced up at him with a scared smile. She was seventeen years old. Wolfer Joe was twenty-nine.

"You go in now," he said, "and I'll know you don't love me." He said the word lightly; he had said it before. The shape of it was easy in his mouth.

She looked away desperately, and the color rose on her neck. "I do so l-love you," she said. "You could just as well stay here, instead of going on."

Oh, no, not at twenty-nine. He could not stay in the settlements for long at a time. The law was creeping westward too fast. He was not sure what the law was, but he knew that he and his like had better keep ahead of it.

"Nothing here to keep me," he said. The words hurt her as he had meant them to hurt, and she drew back. "I got to go on," he said. He added boldly, suddenly seeing a dream, "Going to move on and settle down somewheres. Where I'm going, a girl like you wouldn't go. You wouldn't go with me."

She was pressed tight against the barn wall. "Maybe I would, if I wanted to."

"Your pa wouldn't let you," he scoffed.

"Pa couldn't stop me. Now let me be—let me go!" She struggled against him, but his arms were an iron cage, and his heart pounded against hers.

"Tonight, at the fork of the trail," he said when he let her go, when he loosed her arms from their clinging. "Wait for me there—But you won't come."

"I will!" she said. "Because I l-love you."

That was the last thing she ever said to him.

"I believe you mean it," he answered, and found his voice was hushed with wonder. "I guess you really do," he said, trying to laugh.

The wonder was still on him when he waited where the trail forked. But Doubt hovered there too, and roosting on his shoulder, Suspicion watched the trail with cold, yellow eyes.

If she came, he could take her west and

build a soddy, get a bunch of cattle started—he knew how to swing a long loop on someone else's beef. He had done it before, for pay.

"What makes you think she'll come?" hooted Doubt, circling over him.

"What reason would she have if she did?" croaked Suspicion, with claws sharp in his shoulder.

"There's no reward out for me around here," argued Wolfer Joe. "Supposing she does come, her reason's her own business. It's her I want, not her reasons. I'll settle down somewheres. If she comes."

He watched the trail from up above, belly-down on a flat rock. He jerked when he saw her ride to the meeting place and look anxiously around. She had a little bundle of clothing tied to the saddle. He saw her dismount and look around again. But she didn't call out or say a word. She simply sat down to wait.

He was furious, with an unreasoning anger. "Little fool!" he whispered. "Running off with a man she don't hardly know! What she'll get is no more'n she's got coming."

He remembered that he himself was the man, and he lay there grinning at his own nonsense.

He would wait a while. When she gave up, he would appear and accuse her: "I knowed it was just a notion. You never meant what you said. You start but you can't finish."

Then he would let her go home weeping—or on with him, to do her crying later, when she knew what a fool she was.

But she did not give up. When darkness came, she built a little fire to keep the night away. With his heart pounding, with his lips pulled back from his teeth, Wolfer Joe lay on the flat rock, watching her. She had come so far; she had been so faithful. How long would she wait there for him? How far could he trust her?

Suspicion whispered, "There'll come a day when she'll go crying to the law and say, 'I know where Wolfer Joe is if you want him.'"

He answered, "You don't know my Annie."

He watched her head bend forward on her knees as she waited and dozed. He saw it snap up again when a night sound scared her. After a while the fire burned low, and he knew she was sleeping. She awoke and fed it, and it blazed.

Then he knew he wasn't going down there. He saw not the girl, but her patience. He saw not the red glow of the fire, but faith abiding.

He saw love by the fire, and he could not endure looking for fear he might see it end, during that night or some year to come.

He crept back off the rock and slid silently into the darkness to where his horse was waiting.

He lived for fourteen years after that. He was said to have seventeen notches on his gun, but that wasn't true. He never notched his gun butt for anything he did.

He was justly sentenced to hang for helping to murder two miners whom he and Pete Gossard and Knife Hilton had dry-gulched when the miners tried to take their gold out.

Wolfer Joe made an ending that earned him grim respect, and he left Barney Gallagher puzzling about how betraying a woman could be a thing a man might boast of with the last words he ever had a chance to speak.

THINK AND DISCUSS

Understanding
1. For what crime is Wolfer Joe hanged?
2. What is Wolfer Joe's last boast?

Analyzing
3. What is the main conflict of the story?
4. Joe says his betrayal of Annie was good. How might this be true?
5. Why does Wolfer Joe's boast earn him "grim respect"?

Extending
6. How does Wolfer Joe react to the Vigilanters' justice? Is it fair?

APPLYING: Flashback H𝒯
See Handbook of Literary Terms, p. 665.

An interruption in the major action of a story to show an episode that happened at an earlier time is called a **flashback.** Put these events in chronological order, the order in which they happened. (**a**) Wolfer Joe says that the one good thing he ever did was to betray Annie; (**b**) Wolfer Joe is sentenced to die because he murdered two miners; (**c**) Wolfer Joe betrays Annie.

COMPOSITION

Reading/Writing Log
Dorothy Johnson uses comparisons in describing Wolfer Joe's thoughts as he waits to see whether Annie will meet him. Johnson's description gives the qualities of living things to human emotions. Find this passage and copy it in your reading/writing log. Choose an emotion and decide what sort of creature you'll use to describe that emotion. Then write several sentences describing the emotion.

Stating an Opinion
If you had to boast about the best thing you ever did, what would it be? Use this boast as the title of a short composition. Explain in your composition what it was you did or did not do, and why your action (or inaction) was so significant.

Writing an Obituary
An obituary is a notice of death, with a brief account of a person's life. Write an obituary for Wolfer Joe. Assume, however, that he had married Annie. Be sure to state the cause of death, as well as a summary of his life and a list of any survivors.

BIOGRAPHY

Dorothy Johnson
1905–1984

A native of Iowa and a graduate of the University of Montana, Dorothy Johnson published many Western novels and collections of stories. Johnson won the Spur Award of the Western Writers of America in 1957; she was also made an honorary member of the Blackfoot tribe in Montana.

UNIT 5   SHORT STORY 2

■ CONCEPT REVIEW

The selection that ends this unit is designed to review the important ideas and literary elements that have been presented in the unit. It also contains notes and questions to help you think critically about your reading. A page number in parentheses indicates an Application. For more discussion of the literary terms covered in this unit, see the Handbook of Literary Terms.

The Bracelet

Yoshiko Uchida

"Mama, is it time to go?"

I hadn't planned to cry, but the tears came suddenly, and I wiped them away with the back of my hand. I didn't want my older sister to see me crying.

"It's almost time, Ruri," my mother said gently. Her face was filled with a kind of sadness I had never seen before.

I looked around at my empty room. The clothes that Mama always told me to hang up in the closet, the junk piled on my dresser, the old rag doll I could never bear to part with; they were all gone. There was nothing left in my room, and there was nothing left in the rest of the house. The rugs and furniture were gone, the pictures and drapes were down, and the closets and cupboards were empty. The house was like a gift box after the nice thing inside was gone; just a lot of nothingness.

■ Ruri (rü rē).

■ **Mood** (page 386): The first three paragraphs establish the mood of the story.

It was almost time to leave our home, but we weren't moving to a nicer house or to a new town. It was April 21, 1942. The United States and Japan were at war, and every Japanese person on the West Coast was being evacuated by the government to a concentration camp. Mama, my sister Keiko, and I were being sent from our home, and out of Berkeley, and eventually, out of California.

■ Keiko (kā kō)

The doorbell rang, and I ran to answer it before my sister could. I thought maybe by some miracle, a messenger from the government might be standing there, tall and proper and buttoned into a uniform, come to tell us it was all a terrible mistake; that we wouldn't have to leave after all. Or maybe the messenger would have a telegram from Papa, who was interned in a prisoner-of-war camp in Montana because he had worked for a Japanese business firm.

The FBI had come to pick up Papa and hundreds of other Japanese community leaders on the very day that Japanese planes had bombed Pearl Harbor. The government thought they were dangerous enemy aliens. If it weren't so sad, it would have been funny. Papa could no more be dangerous than the mayor of our city, and he was every bit as loyal to the United States. He had lived here since 1917.

■ *Pearl Harbor,* The Japanese attack on Pearl Harbor, a U.S. naval base in Hawaii, on December 7, 1941, was the immediate cause of American entry into World War II.

When I opened the door, it wasn't a messenger from anywhere. It was my best friend, Laurie Madison, from next door. She was holding a package wrapped up like a birthday present, but she wasn't wearing her party dress, and her face drooped like a wilted tulip.

"Hi," she said. "I came to say goodbye."

She thrust the present at me and told me it was something to take to camp. "It's a bracelet," she said before I could open the package. "Put it on so you won't have to pack it." She knew I didn't have one inch of space left in my suitcase. We had been instructed to take only what we could carry into camp, and Mama had told us that we could each take only two suitcases.

"Then how are we ever going to pack the dishes and blankets and sheets they've told us to bring with us?" Keiko worried.

"I don't really know," Mama said, and she simply began packing those big impossible things into an enormous duffel bag—along with umbrellas, boots, a kettle, hot plate, and flashlight.

"Who's going to carry that huge sack?" I asked.

But Mama didn't worry about things like that. "Someone will help us," she said. "Don't worry." So I didn't.

Laurie wanted me to open her package and put on the bracelet before she left. It was a thin gold chain with a heart dangling on it. She helped me put it on, and I told her I'd never take it off, ever.

"Well, good-bye then," Laurie said awkwardly. "Come home soon."

"I will," I said, although I didn't know if I would ever get back to Berkeley again.

I watched Laurie go down the block, her long blond pigtails bouncing as she walked. I wondered who would be sitting in my desk at Lincoln Junior High now that I was gone. Laurie kept turning and waving, even walking backwards for a while, until she got to the corner. I didn't want to watch anymore, and I slammed the door shut.

The next time the doorbell rang, it was Mrs. Simpson, our other neighbor. She was going to drive us to the Congregational church, which was the Civil Control Station where all the Japanese of Berkeley were supposed to report.

It was time to go. "Come on, Ruri. Get your things," my sister called to me.

It was a warm day, but I put on a sweater and my coat so I wouldn't have to carry them, and I picked up my two suitcases. Each one had a tag with my name and our family number on it. Every Japanese family had to register and get a number. We were Family Number 13453.

Mama was taking one last look around our house. She was going from room to room, as though she were trying to take a mental picture of the house she had lived in for fifteen years, so she would never forget it.

I saw her take a long last look at the garden that Papa loved. The irises beside the fish pond were just beginning to bloom. If Papa had been home, he would have cut the first iris blossom and brought it inside to Mama. "This one is for you," he would have said. And Mama would have smiled and said, "Thank you, Papa San," and put it in her favorite cut-glass vase.

■ *Papa San* (pä pä sän), *San* is often added to the names of both men and women as a polite form of address.

But the garden looked shabby and forsaken now that Papa was gone and Mama was too busy to take care of it. It looked the way I felt, sort of empty and lonely and abandoned.

When Mrs. Simpson took us to the Civil Control Station, I felt even worse. I was scared, and for a minute I thought I was going to lose my breakfast right in front of everybody. There must have been over a thousand Japanese people gathered at the church. Some were old and some were young. Some were talking and laughing, and some were crying. I guess everybody else was scared too. No one knew exactly what was going to happen to us. We just knew we were being taken to the Tanforan Racetracks, which the army had turned into a camp for the Japanese. There were fourteen other camps like ours along the West Coast.

What scared me the most were the soldiers standing at the doorway of the church hall. They were carrying guns with mounted bayonets. I wondered if they thought we would try to run away, and whether they'd shoot us or come after us with their bayonets if we did.

A long line of buses waited to take us to camp. There were trucks, too, for our baggage. And Mama was right; some men were there to help us load our duffel bag. When it was time to board the buses, I sat with Keiko and Mama sat behind us. The bus went down Grove Street and passed the small Japanese food store where Mama used to order her bean-curd cakes and pickled radish. The windows were all boarded up, but there was a sign still hanging on the door that read, "We are loyal Americans."

The crazy thing about the whole evacuation was that we were all loyal Americans. Most of us were citizens because we had been born here. But our parents, who had come from Japan, couldn't become citizens because there was a law that prevented any Asian from becoming a citizen. Now everybody with a Japanese face was being shipped off to concentration camps.

"It's stupid," Keiko muttered as we saw the racetrack looming up beside the highway. "If there were any Japanese spies around, they'd have gone back to Japan long ago."

"I'll say," I agreed. My sister was in high school and she ought to know, I thought.

When the bus turned into Tanforan, there were more armed guards at the gate, and I saw barbed wire strung around the entire grounds. I felt as though I were going into a prison, but I hadn't done anything wrong.

We streamed off the buses and poured into a huge room, where doctors looked down our throats and peeled back our eyelids to see if we had any diseases. Then we were given our housing assignments. The man in charge gave Mama a slip of paper. We were in Barrack 16, Apartment 40.

"Mama!" I said. "We're going to live in an apartment!" The only apartment I had ever seen was the one my piano teacher lived in. It

■ **Tone** (page 372): We see the confused families guarded by soldiers with bayonets from Ruri's point of view. The description also helps convey the author's attitude toward the subject of this story.

■ **theme** (page 356): This paragraph suggests theme.

was in an enormous building in San Francisco with an elevator and thick carpeted hallways. I thought how wonderful it would be to have our own elevator. A house was all right, but an apartment seemed elegant and special.

We walked down the racetrack looking for Barrack 16. Mr. Noma, a friend of Papa's, helped us carry our bags. I was so busy looking around, I slipped and almost fell on the muddy track. Army barracks had been built everywhere, all around the racetrack and even in the center oval.

Mr. Noma pointed beyond the track toward the horse stables. "I think your barrack is out there."

He was right. We came to a long stable that had once housed the horses of Tanforan, and we climbed up the wide ramp. Each stall had a number painted on it, and when we got to 40, Mr. Noma pushed open the door.

"Well, here it is," he said, "Apartment 40."

The stall was narrow and empty and dark. There were two small windows on each side of the door. Three folded army cots were on the dust-covered floor and one light bulb dangled from the ceiling. That was all. This was our apartment, and it still smelled of horses.

Mama looked at my sister and then at me. "It won't be so bad when we fix it up," she began. "I'll ask Mrs. Simpson to send me some material for curtains. I could make some cushions too, and . . . well . . . ." She stopped. She couldn't think of anything more to say.

Mr. Noma said he'd go get some mattresses for us. "I'd better hurry before they're all gone." He rushed off. I think he wanted to leave so that he wouldn't have to see Mama cry. But he needn't have run off, because Mama didn't cry. She just went out to borrow a broom and began sweeping out the dust and dirt. "Will you girls set up the cots?" she asked.

It was only after we'd put up the last cot that I noticed my bracelet was gone. "I've lost Laurie's bracelet!" I screamed. "My bracelet's gone!"

We looked all over the stall and even down the ramp. I wanted to run back down the track and go over every inch of ground we'd walked on, but it was getting dark and Mama wouldn't let me.

I thought of what I'd promised Laurie. I wasn't ever going to take the bracelet off, not even when I went to take a shower. And now I had lost it on my very first day in camp. I wanted to cry.

I kept looking for it all the time we were in Tanforan. I didn't stop looking until the day we were sent to another camp, called Topaz, in the middle of a desert in Utah. And then I gave up.

But Mama told me never mind. She said I didn't need a bracelet to remember Laurie, just as I didn't need anything to remember Papa or our home in Berkeley or all the people and things we loved and had left behind.

"Those are things we can carry in our hearts and take with us no matter where we are sent," she said.

And I guess she was right. I've never forgotten Laurie, even now.

THINK AND DISCUSS
Understanding
1. To what does Ruri compare her empty house?
2. How do Ruri's neighbors react to the family's situation?
3. Who visits Ruri just before the family leaves?
4. At the camp, where does the family discover they will be living?
5. What is Ruri's first reaction to the loss of the bracelet?

Analyzing
6. How does Ruri characterize her father?
7. Before leaving, Ruri looks at her father's garden. How does this garden make her feel?
8. Why do Ruri and the others feel they are being treated unjustly?
9. How does Ruri feel about her sister's opinion of the evacuation?
10. How is Ruri's mother characterized?

Extending
11. What might have led to the incarceration of people of Japanese descent during World War II? Were people of German descent treated similarly?

REVIEWING LITERARY TERMS
Theme
1. What is the theme of "The Bracelet"?

Tone
2. Describe the tone of "The Bracelet." Is it casual, bitter, furious, or something else?

Mood
3. Is the mood in the first three paragraphs one of fear, anger, sadness, or jealousy?

■ CONTENT REVIEW
THINKING SKILLS
Classifying
1. A number of the stories in this unit involve people who are taught something. List these.
2. Review the list you made for item 1. For each story on the list, tell what was taught, who taught it and how it was taught, and whether those who received the teaching learned from it.

Generalizing
3. Several of the people in this unit are characterized by their sensitivity to others. How do the narrator in "Old Man at the Bridge," Harriet Watkins in "My Delicate Heart Condition," and Miss Kinnian in "Flowers for Algernon" illustrate this quality?
4. Compare and contrast Grandpa in "The Medicine Bag" and the old man in "Old Man at the Bridge." Consider not only their character but also the situations they face.

Synthesizing
5. Several stories in this unit give clearly drawn pictures of life in the United States at various points in history. Discuss the pictures from American history that you see in "Upon the Waters," "The Last Boast," "The Medicine Bag," and "The Bracelet."

Evaluating
6. Which character do you consider to be the most sympathetic, or the one for whom you feel most strongly, Charlie in "Flowers for Algernon," Cephas in "Upon the Waters," Grandpa in "The Medicine Bag," or the young man in "The Lady, or the Tiger?" Give reasons for your choice.

■ COMPOSITION REVIEW
Stating Your Opinion
Do you think one generation can understand another, or must they forever be strangers because of differences in age and experience? Write an essay defending your view on this issue, using specific examples from at least two stories in this unit to support the points you make. During prewriting jot down your own opinion, and then list the selections and the characters that you will use to support it.

Analyzing Mood
Mood plays an important part in several of the selections in this unit. Select any short story in the unit and write an essay in which you (a) identify the mood created by the author; (b) discuss how the author created the mood; and (c) give your opinion on how successful the author is in creating the effect.

Reviewing Writer's Craft: Use Comparisons
Now try your hand at using comparisons to make your writing more lively and interesting. Write a paragraph describing a place that is especially beautiful, ugly, frightening, or whatever. Use at least two comparisons in your paragraph. If you have been keeping a reading/writing log, review your entries before you begin this composition.

RAMA 2

Boris Aronson, set design for New York production of *The Diary of Anne Frank, Private Collection*

THE DIARY OF ANNE FRANK

PREVIEW

UNIT 6 DRAMA 2

Play
The Diary of Anne Frank / Frances Goodrich and Albert Hackett
from **The Pen of My Aunt** / Gordon Daviot

Features
Reading a Full-Length Play
The Writer's Craft: Use a Voice
  That Suits Purpose
Comment: Dramatic License
Comment: The Aftermath
Comment: Miep

Review of Literary Terms
foreshadowing
flashback

Reading Literature Skillfully
sequence

Vocabulary Skills
dictionary
context
idioms

Thinking Skills
generalizing
synthesizing
evaluating

Composition
Reading/Writing Log
Rewriting a Dialogue
Describing Characters' Attitudes
Writing About Characters

Enrichment
Oral Interpretation
Research
Oral Reading

Thinking Critically About Literature
Concept Review
Content Review
Composition Review

INTRODUCTION

When Anne Frank was thirteen years old, her family had to leave their own home in Amsterdam, the Netherlands. The Franks were Jews, and, during World War II, no Jew was safe in lands controlled by the Nazis (nä′tsēs)—the German National Socialist Party that sought to conquer Europe.

Earlier Otto Frank, his wife Edith, and their two daughters Margot and Anne had fled Frankfort, Germany. In Amsterdam Mr. Frank became an importer for Travis, Inc. In May, 1940, the Nazi army captured the Netherlands, and in July, 1942, the Franks went into hiding in Amsterdam in a secret apartment to escape persecution.

On her thirteenth birthday, Anne received a diary from her father. Into the diary Anne recorded the hopes, fears, joys, and frustrations of living for twenty-five months in cramped quarters under constant tension. That diary, on which this drama is based, remains a living tribute to the dignity, courage, and perseverance of the human spirit.

Anne Frank (in light coat and hat) with family and friends

Reading A FULL-LENGTH PLAY

In Unit 2 you read three short plays. In this unit, you will read *The Diary of Anne Frank*, a full-length play written to be performed on the stage. Like most full-length plays, it is divided into acts and scenes that mark stages in the development of the plot. In each scene, events occur in **sequence,** each event growing out of, or happening because of, an event that has taken place earlier.

Notice that early in the play you meet the characters and learn about the conflict, the problems and obstacles the characters face. As the play continues, you see the conflict develop in a sequence of events that builds toward a climax. At the end, you learn the outcome, or resolution.

When you watch a play, you can see and hear characters, and you can see changes in the setting that help to convey changes in mood. When you read a play, you must pay attention both to the dialogue, lines the actors speak, and to stage directions, descriptions of setting and of how characters look, speak, and behave.

Stage directions suggest to the actors, director, and technicians what the play should look and sound like on the stage. Stage directions can be used (1) to describe the setting, (2) to describe the characters, (3) to tell the actors how to speak their lines, (4) to tell the actors when, where, and how to move. As you read this play, watch for information in stage directions.

Look also for ways that the characters change from the beginning to the end of the play. Playwrights make use of several methods of characterization. Pay attention to these methods:

Learn about character from the author's statements about the way a character looks, feels, or behaves.

(ANNE *comes running up the stairs. She is thirteen, quick in her movements, interested in everything, mercurial in her emotions. She wears a cape, long wool socks and carries a schoolbag.*)

Learn about character from what a person says about himself or herself.

PETER: I'm sort of a lone wolf.

Learn about character from what others say about a person.

MR. FRANK: That's a nice boy, Peter.
ANNE: He's awfully shy, isn't he?

Learn about character from what people do and the way they do it.

ANNE (*pulling out a pasteboard-bound book*): A diary! (*She throws her arms around her father.*) I've always longed for one. (She looks around the room.) Pencil, pencil, pencil. (She starts down the stairs.) I'm going down to the office to get a pencil.

As you read this or any other play, note plot development, description of setting, clues to character. All will add to your understanding and enjoyment of the world on stage.

The Diary of Anne Frank

Dramatized by Frances Goodrich and Albert Hackett
(based upon the book, *Anne Frank: The Diary of a Young Girl*)

"I see the eight of us . . . as if we were a little piece of blue heaven, surrounded by heavy black rain clouds. The round, clearly defined spot where we stand is still safe, but the clouds gather more closely about us and the circle which separates us from the approaching danger closes more and more tightly."[1]

CHARACTERS

MR. OTTO FRANK (frängk)

MIEP (mēp) GIES (Hēs)

MR. VAN DAAN (fän dän′)

MRS. PETRONELLA (pet′rə nel′ə) VAN DAAN

PETER VAN DAAN

MRS. EDITH FRANK

MARGOT (mär′gət) FRANK

ANNE FRANK

MR. KRALER (krä′lər)

MR. DUSSEL (düs′əl)

The Time: During the years of World War II and immediately thereafter.

The Place: Amsterdam.

There are two acts.

1. From Anne Frank: *The Diary of a Young Girl.* Copyright 1952 by Otto H. Frank. Reprinted by permission of Doubleday & Company, Inc. and Vallentine, Mitchell & Co. Ltd.

Slightly abridged from *The Diary of Anne Frank* by Frances Goodrich and Albert Hackett. Copyright 1954, 1956 as an unpublished work, and copyright © 1956 by Albert Hackett, Frances Goodrich and Otto Frank; copyright renewed © 1986 by Albert Hackett, David Huntoon, and Frances Neuwirth. Reprinted by permission of Random House, Inc. and Flora Roberts, Inc.

ACT ONE

SCENE ONE

The scene remains the same throughout the play. It is the top floor of a warehouse and office building in Amsterdam, Holland. The sharply peaked roof of the building is outlined against a sea of other rooftops, stretching away into the distance. Nearby is the belfry of a church tower, the Westertoren, whose carillon rings out the hours. Occasionally faint sounds float up from below: the voices of children playing in the street, the tramp of marching feet, a boat whistle from the canal.

The three rooms of the top floor and a small attic space above are exposed to our view. The largest of the rooms is in the center, with two small rooms, slightly raised, on either side. On the right is a bathroom, out of sight. A narrow steep flight of stairs at the back leads up to the attic. The rooms are sparsely furnished with a few chairs, cots, a table or two. The windows are painted over, or covered with makeshift blackout curtains. In the main room there is a sink, a gas ring for cooking, and a woodburning stove for warmth.

The room on the left is hardly more than a closet. There is a skylight in the sloping ceiling. Directly under this room is a small steep stairwell, with steps leading down to a door. This is the only entrance from the building below. When the door is opened we see that it has been concealed on the outer side by a bookcase attached to it.

The curtain rises on an empty stage. It is late afternoon, November, 1945.

The rooms are dusty, the curtains in rags. Chairs and tables are overturned.

The door at the foot of the small stairwell swings open. MR. FRANK *comes up the steps into view. He is a gentle, cultured European in his middle years. There is still a trace of a German accent in his speech.*

He stands looking slowly around, making a supreme effort at self-control. He is weak, ill. His clothes are threadbare.

After a second he drops his rucksack on the couch and moves slowly about. He opens the door to one of the smaller rooms, and then abruptly closes it again, turning away. He goes to the window at the back, looking off at the Westertoren as its carillon strikes the hour of six; then he moves restlessly on.

From the street below we hear the sound of a barrel organ and children's voices at play. There is a many-colored scarf hanging from a nail. MR. FRANK *takes it, putting it around his neck. As he starts back for his rucksack, his eye is caught by something lying on the floor. It is a woman's white glove. He holds it in his hand and suddenly all of his self-control is gone. He breaks down, crying.*

We hear footsteps on the stairs. MIEP GIES *comes up, looking for* MR. FRANK. MIEP *is a Dutch girl of about twenty-two. She wears a coat and hat, ready to go home. She is pregnant. Her attitude toward* MR. FRANK *is protective, compassionate.*

MIEP. Are you all right, Mr. Frank?

MR. FRANK (*quickly controlling himself*). Yes, Miep, yes.

MIEP. Everyone in the office has gone home . . . It's after six. (*Then pleading*) Don't stay up here, Mr. Frank. What's the use of torturing yourself like this?

MR. FRANK. I've come to say good-by . . . I'm leaving here, Miep.

MIEP. What do you mean? Where are you going? Where?

MR. FRANK. I don't know yet. I haven't decided.

MIEP. Mr. Frank, you can't leave here! This is your home! Amsterdam is your home. Your business is here, waiting for you . . . You're needed here . . . Now that the war is over, there are things that . . .

MR. FRANK. I can't stay in Amsterdam, Miep. It has too many memories for me. Everywhere there's something . . . the house we lived in . . . the school . . . that street organ playing out there . . . I'm not the person you used to know, Miep. I'm a bitter old man. (*Breaking off*) Forgive me. I shouldn't speak to you like this . . . after all that you did for us . . . the suffering . . .

MIEP. No. No. It wasn't suffering. You can't say we suffered. (*As she speaks, she straightens a chair which is overturned.*)

MR. FRANK. I know what you went through, you and Mr. Kraler. I'll remember it as long as I live. (*He gives one last look around.*) Come, Miep. (*He starts for the steps, then remembers his rucksack, going back to get it.*)

MIEP (*hurrying up to a cupboard*). Mr. Frank, did you see? There are some of your papers here. (*She brings a bundle of papers to him.*) We found them in a heap of rubbish on the floor . . . after you left.

MR. FRANK. Burn them. (*He opens his rucksack to put the glove in it.*)

MIEP. But, Mr. Frank, there are letters, notes . . .

MR. FRANK. Burn them. All of them.

MIEP. Burn *this*? (*She hands him a paperbound notebook.*)

MR. FRANK (*quietly*). Anne's diary. (*He opens the diary and begins to read.*) "Monday, the sixth of July, nineteen forty-two." (*To* MIEP) Nineteen forty-two. Is it possible, Miep? . . . Only three years ago. (*As he continues his reading, he sits down on the couch.*) "Dear Diary, since you and I are going to be great friends, I will start by telling you about myself. My name is Anne Frank. I am thirteen years old. I was born in Germany the twelfth of June, nineteen twenty-nine. As my family is Jewish, we emigrated to Holland when Hitler[1] came to power."

(*As* MR. FRANK *reads on, another voice joins*

Anne's diary

---

1. **Hitler,** Adolph Hitler (ā′dôlf hit′lər), 1889–1945, German National Socialist leader, dictator of Germany from 1933 to 1945.

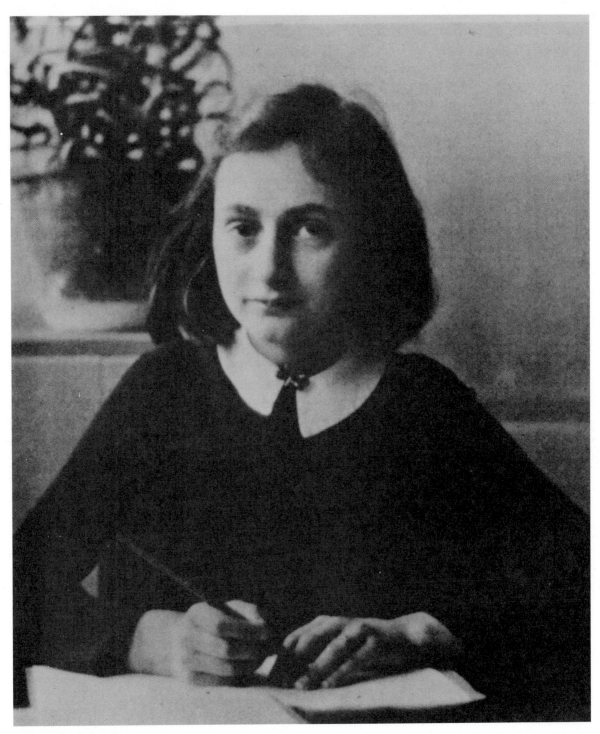

Anne writing in her diary

his, as if coming from the air. It is ANNE'S VOICE.)

MR. FRANK *and* ANNE. "My father started a business, importing spice and herbs. Things went well for us until nineteen forty. Then the war came, and the Dutch capitulation, followed by the arrival of the Germans. Then things got very bad for the Jews."

(MR. FRANK'S VOICE *dies out.* ANNE'S VOICE *continues alone. The lights dim slowly to darkness. The curtain falls on the scene.*)

ANNE'S VOICE. You could not do this and you could not do that. They forced Father out of his business. We had to wear yellow stars. I had to turn in my bike. I couldn't go to a Dutch school any more. I couldn't go to the movies, or ride in an automobile, or even on a streetcar, and a million other things. But somehow we children still managed to have fun. Yesterday Father told me we were going into hiding. Where, he wouldn't say. At five o'clock this morning Mother woke me and told me to hurry and get dressed. I was to put on as many clothes as I could. It would look too suspicious if we walked along carrying suitcases. It wasn't until we were on our way that I learned where we were going. Our hiding place was to be upstairs in the building where Father used to have his business. Three other people were coming in with us . . . the Van Daans and their son Peter . . . Father knew the Van Daans but we had never met them . . .

(*During the last lines the curtain rises on the scene. The lights dim on.* ANNE'S VOICE *fades out.*)

THINK AND DISCUSS
Understanding
1. At what time does this scene take place?
2. Describe the appearance of the rooms.
3. What reason does Mr. Frank give Miep for his decision to leave Amsterdam?
4. What information do you get about Anne from the first entry in her diary?

Analyzing
5. What do you learn about Mr. Frank from his reactions to his surroundings? from his treatment of Miep?

6. What do you learn from Anne's diary about the Nazis' attitude toward the Jews?

Extending
7. What questions does this scene raise that will probably be answered in future scenes?
8. What problems do you predict the Franks and the Van Daans might encounter as they live in hiding?

SCENE TWO

It is early morning, July, 1942. The rooms are bare, as before, but they are now clean and orderly.

MR. VAN DAAN, *a tall, portly man in his late forties, is in the main room, pacing up and down, nervously smoking a cigarette. His clothes and overcoat are expensive and well cut.*

MRS. VAN DAAN *sits on the couch, clutching her possessions, a hatbox, bags, etc. She is a pretty woman in her early forties. She wears a fur coat over her other clothes.*

PETER VAN DAAN *is standing at the window of the room on the right, looking down at the street below. He is a shy, awkward boy of sixteen. He wears a cap, a raincoat, and long Dutch trousers, like "plus fours."[1] At his feet is a black case, a carrier for his cat.*

The yellow Star of David[2] is conspicuous on all of their clothes.

MRS. VAN DAAN (*rising, nervous, excited*). Something's happened to them! I know it!

MR. VAN DAAN. Now, Kerli![3]

MRS. VAN DAAN. Mr. Frank said they'd be here at seven o'clock. He said . . .

MR. VAN DAAN. They have two miles to walk. You can't expect . . .

MRS. VAN DAAN. They've been picked up. That's what happened. They've been taken . . .

(MR. VAN DAAN *indicates that he hears someone coming.*)

MR. VAN DAAN. You see?

(PETER *takes up his carrier and his schoolbag, etc. and goes into the main room as* MR. FRANK *comes up the stairwell from below.* MR. FRANK *looks much younger now. His movements are brisk, his manner confident.*

He wears an overcoat and carries his hat and a small cardboard box. He crosses to the VAN DAANS, *shaking hands with each of them.*)

MR. FRANK. Mrs. Van Daan, Mr. Van Daan, Peter. (*Then, in explanation of their lateness*) There were too many of the Green Police[4] on the streets . . . We had to take the long way around.

(*Up the steps come* MARGOT FRANK, MRS. FRANK, MIEP—*not pregnant now—and* MR. KRALER. *All of them carry bags, packages, and so forth. The Star of David is conspicuous on all of the* FRANKS' *clothing.* MARGOT *is eighteen, beautiful, quiet, shy.* MRS. FRANK *is a young mother, gently bred, reserved. She, like* MR. FRANK, *has a slight German accent.* MR. KRALER *is a Dutchman, dependable, kindly.*

As MR. KRALER *and* MIEP *go upstage[5] to put down their parcels,* MRS. FRANK *turns back to call* ANNE.)

MRS. FRANK. Anne?

(ANNE *comes running up the stairs. She is thirteen, quick in her movements, interested in everything, mercurial in her emotions. She wears a cape, long wool socks and carries a schoolbag.*)

MR. FRANK (*introducing them*). My wife, Edith. Mr. and Mrs. Van Daan (MRS. FRANK *hurries over, shaking hands with*

---

1. *plus fours,* loose knickers that come down below the knee.

2. *Star of David,* a six-pointed star, a religious symbol of the Jewish people. In Nazi-occupied countries all Jews were required to wear a Star of David prominently displayed on their clothing.

3. *Kerli* (ker'lē).

4. *Green Police,* a branch of the Nazi police who wore green uniforms.

5. *upstage,* toward the back of the stage. *Down,* or *downstage,* means toward the front of the stage.

them.) . . . their son, Peter . . . my daughters, Margot and Anne.

(ANNE *gives a polite little curtsy as she shakes* MR. VAN DAAN'S *hand. Then she immediately starts off on a tour of investigation of her new home, going upstairs to the attic room.* MIEP *and* MR. KRALER *are putting the various things they have brought on the shelves.*)

MR. KRALER. I'm sorry there is still so much confusion.

MR. FRANK. Please. Don't think of it. After all, we'll have plenty of leisure to arrange everything ourselves.

MIEP (*to* MRS. FRANK). We put the stores of food you sent in here. Your drugs are here . . . soap, linen here.

MR. FRANK. Thank you, Miep.

MIEP. I made up the beds . . . the way Mr. Frank and Mr. Kraler said. (*She starts out.*) I have to hurry. I've got to go to the other side of town to get some ration books[6] for you.

MRS. VAN DAAN. Ration books? If they see our names on ration books, they'll know we're here.

MR. KRALER. There isn't anything . . .

MIEP. Don't worry. Your names won't be on them. (*As she hurries out*) I'll be up later.

MR. FRANK. Thank you, Miep.

(*Together*)

MRS. FRANK (*to* MR. KRALER). It's illegal, then, the ration books? We've never done anything illegal.

MR. FRANK. We won't be living here exactly according to regulations.

(*As* MR. KRALER *reassures* MRS. FRANK, *he takes various small things, such as matches,*

soap, etc., *from his pockets, handing them to her.*)

MR. KRALER. This isn't the black market, Mrs. Frank. This is what we call the white market[7] . . . helping all of the hundreds and hundreds who are hiding out in Amsterdam.

(*The carillon is heard playing the quarter-hour before eight.* MR. KRALER *looks at his watch.* ANNE *stops at the window as she comes down the stairs.*)

ANNE. It's the Westertoren!

MR. KRALER. I must go. I must be out of here and downstairs in the office before the workmen get here. (*He starts for the stairs leading out.*) Miep or I, or both of us, will be up each day to bring you food and news and find out what your needs are. Tomorrow I'll get you a better bolt for the door at the foot of the stairs. It needs a bolt that you can throw yourself and open only at our signal. (*To* MR. FRANK) Oh . . . You'll tell them about the noise?

MR. FRANK. I'll tell them.

MR. KRALER. Good-by then for the moment. I'll come up again, after the workmen leave.

MR. FRANK. Good-by, Mr. Kraler.

MRS. FRANK (*shaking his hand*). How can we thank you?

(*The others murmur their good-bys.*)

MR. KRALER. I never thought I'd live to see the day when a man like Mr. Frank would

---

6. *ration books,* books of coupons which allowed the bearer to buy a fixed amount of provisions or food.

7. *black market . . . white market.* Black market goods are sold illegally, usually at a very high price. The goods the Franks were receiving (white market) were donated by people wishing to help the Jews.

have to go into hiding. When you think—
(*He breaks off, going out.* MR. FRANK *follows him down the steps, bolting the door after him. In the interval before he returns,* PETER *goes over to* MARGOT, *shaking hands with her. As* MR. FRANK *comes back up the steps,* MRS. FRANK *questions him anxiously.*)

MRS. FRANK. What did he mean, about the noise?

MR. FRANK. First let us take off some of these clothes.

(*They all start to take off garment after garment. On each of their coats, sweaters, blouses, suits, dresses, is another yellow Star*

The doorway and stairs leading to the secret annex.

A bookcase on hinges and a large wall map hid the door and stairs.

of David. MR. *and* MRS. FRANK *are under-dressed quite simply. The others wear several things—sweaters, extra dresses, bathrobes, aprons, nightgowns, etc.)*

MR. VAN DAAN. It's a wonder we weren't arrested, walking along the streets . . . Petronella with a fur coat in July . . . and that cat of Peter's crying all the way.

ANNE (*as she is removing a pair of panties*). A cat?

MRS. FRANK (*shocked*). Anne, please!

ANNE. It's all right. I've got on three more. (*She pulls off two more. Finally, as they have all removed their surplus clothes, they look to* MR. FRANK, *waiting for him to speak.*)

MR. FRANK. Now. About the noise. While the men are in the building below, we must have complete quiet. Every sound can be heard down there, not only in the workrooms, but in the offices too. The men come at about eight-thirty, and leave at about five-thirty. So, to be perfectly safe, from eight in the morning until six in the evening we must move only when it is necessary, and then in stockinged feet. We must not speak above a whisper. We must not run any water. We cannot use the sink, or even, forgive me, the w.c.[8] The pipes go down through the workrooms. It would be heard. No trash . . . (MR. FRANK *stops abruptly as he hears the sound of marching feet from the street below. Everyone is motionless, paralyzed with fear.* MR. FRANK *goes quietly into the room on the right to look down out of the window.* ANNE *runs after him, peering out with him. The tramping feet pass without stopping. The tension is relieved.* MR. FRANK, *followed by* ANNE, *returns to the main room and resumes his instructions to the*

group.) . . . No trash must ever be thrown out which might reveal that someone is living up here . . . not even a potato paring. We must burn everything in the stove at night. This is the way we must live until it is over, if we are to survive.

(*There is silence for a second.*)

MRS. FRANK. Until it is over.

MR. FRANK (*reassuringly*). After six we can move about . . . we can talk and laugh and have our supper and read and play games . . . just as we would at home. (*He looks at his watch.*) And now I think it would be wise if we all went to our rooms, and were settled before eight o'clock. Mrs. Van Daan, you and your husband will be upstairs. I regret that there's no place up there for Peter. But he will be here, near us. This will be our common room, where we'll meet to talk and eat and read, like one family.

MR. VAN DAAN. And where do you and Mrs. Frank sleep?

MR. FRANK. This room is also our bedroom.

MRS. VAN DAAN. That isn't right. We'll sleep here and you take the room upstairs. ⎤
                                                                          ⎬ (*Together*)
MR. VAN DAAN. It's your place. ⎦

MR. FRANK. Please. I've thought this out for weeks. It's the best arrangement. The only arrangement.

MRS. VAN DAAN (*to* MR. FRANK). Never, never can we thank you. (*Then to* MRS. FRANK) I don't know what would have happened to us, if it hadn't been for Mr. Frank.

MR. FRANK. You don't know how your hus-

---

8. *w.c.,* water closet, the bathroom.

band helped me when I came to this country . . . knowing no one . . . not able to speak the language. I can never repay him for that. (*Going to* VAN DAAN) May I help you with your things?

MR. VAN DAAN. No. No. (*To* MRS. VAN DAAN) Come along, *liefje.*[9]

MRS. VAN DAAN. You'll be all right, Peter? You're not afraid?

PETER (*embarrassed*). Please, Mother.

(*They start up the stairs to the attic room above.* MR. FRANK *turns to* MRS. FRANK.)

MR. FRANK. You too must have some rest, Edith. You didn't close your eyes last night. Nor you, Margot.

ANNE. I slept, Father. Wasn't that funny? I knew it was the last night in my own bed, and yet I slept soundly.

MR. FRANK. I'm glad, Anne. Now you'll be able to help me straighten things in here. (*To* MRS. FRANK *and* MARGOT) Come with me . . . You and Margot rest in this room for the time being. (*He picks up their clothes, starting for the room on the right.*)

MRS. FRANK. You're sure . . . ? I could help . . . And Anne hasn't had her milk . . .

MR. FRANK. I'll give it to her. (*To* ANNE *and* PETER) Anne, Peter . . . it's best that you take off your shoes now, before you forget. (*He leads the way to the room, followed by* MARGOT.)

MRS. FRANK. You're sure you're not tired, Anne?

ANNE. I feel fine. I'm going to help Father.

MRS. FRANK. Peter, I'm glad you are to be with us.

PETER. Yes, Mrs. Frank.

(MRS. FRANK *goes to join* MR. FRANK *and* MARGOT.

During the following scene MR. FRANK *helps* MARGOT *and* MRS. FRANK *to hang up their clothes. Then he persuades them both to lie down and rest. The* VAN DAANS *in their room above settle themselves. In the main room* ANNE *and* PETER *remove their shoes.* PETER *takes his cat out of the carrier.*)

ANNE. What's your cat's name?

PETER. Mouschi.[10]

ANNE. Mouschi! Mouschi! Mouschi! (*She picks up the cat, walking away with it. To* PETER) I love cats. I have one . . . a darling little cat. But they made me leave her behind. I left some food and a note for the neighbors to take care of her . . . I'm going to miss her terribly. What is yours? A him or a her?

PETER. He's a tom. He doesn't like strangers. (*He takes the cat from her, putting it back in its carrier.*)

ANNE (*unabashed*). Then I'll have to stop being a stranger, won't I? Is he fixed?

PETER (*startled*). Huh?

ANNE. Did you have him fixed?

PETER. No.

ANNE. Oh, you ought to have him fixed—to keep him from—you know, fighting. Where did you go to school?

PETER. Jewish Secondary.

ANNE. But that's where Margot and I go! I never saw you around.

PETER. I used to see you . . . sometimes . . .

ANNE. You did?

PETER. . . . in the school yard. You were always in the middle of a bunch of kids. (*He takes a penknife from his pocket.*)

---

9. *liefje* (lēt′ʜyə), darling.

10. *Mouschi* (müs′kē).

ANNE. Why didn't you ever come over?

PETER. I'm sort of a lone wolf. (*He starts to rip off his Star of David.*)

ANNE. What are you doing?

PETER. Taking it off.

ANNE. But you can't do that. They'll arrest you if you go out without your star. (*He tosses his knife on the table.*)

PETER. Who's going out?

ANNE. Why, of course! You're right! Of course we don't need them any more. (*She picks up his knife and starts to take her star off.*) I wonder what our friends will think when we don't show up today?

PETER. I didn't have any dates with anyone.

ANNE. Oh, I did. I had a date with Jopie to go and play ping-pong at her house. Do you know Jopie deWaal?[11]

PETER. No.

ANNE. Jopie's my best friend. I wonder what she'll think when she telephones and there's no answer? . . . Probably she'll go over to the house . . . I wonder what she'll think . . . we left everything as if we'd suddenly been called away . . . breakfast dishes in the sink . . . beds not made . . . (*As she pulls off her star the cloth underneath shows clearly the color and form of the star.*) Look! It's still there! (PETER *goes over to the stove with his star.*) What're you going to do with yours?

PETER. Burn it.

ANNE. (*She starts to throw hers in, and cannot.*) It's funny, I can't throw mine away. I don't know why.

PETER. You can't throw . . . ? Something they branded you with . . . ? That they made you wear so they could spit on you?

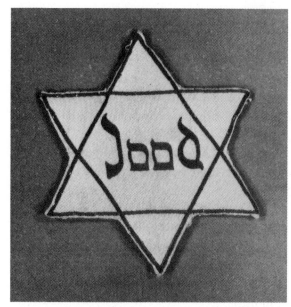

The yellow star of David, which all Jews were forced to wear

ANNE. I know. I know. But after all, it *is* the Star of David, isn't it?

(*In the bedroom, right,* MARGOT *and* MRS. FRANK *are lying down.* MR. FRANK *starts quietly out.*)

PETER. Maybe it's different for a girl.

(MR. FRANK *comes into the main room.*)

MR. FRANK. Forgive me, Peter. Now let me see. We must find a bed for your cat. (*He goes to a cupboard.*) I'm glad you brought your cat. Anne was feeling so badly about hers. (*Getting a used small washtub.*) Here we are. Will it be comfortable in that?

PETER (*gathering up his things*). Thanks.

MR. FRANK (*opening the door of the room on the left*). And here is your room. But I warn you, Peter, you can't grow any more. Not an inch, or you'll have to sleep with your feet out of the skylight. Are you hungry?

---

11. *Jopie deWaal* (yo′pē də väl′).

PETER. No.

MR. FRANK. We have some bread and butter.

PETER. No, thank you.

MR. FRANK. You can have it for luncheon then. And tonight we will have a real supper . . . our first supper together.

PETER. Thanks. Thanks.

(*He goes into his room. During the following scene he arranges his possessions in his new room.*)

MR. FRANK. That's a nice boy, Peter.

ANNE. He's awfully shy, isn't he?

MR. FRANK. You'll like him, I know.

ANNE. I certainly hope so, since he's the only boy I'm likely to see for months and months.

(MR. FRANK *sits down, taking off his shoes.*)

MR. FRANK. Annele,[12] there's a box there. Will you open it?

(*He indicates a carton on the couch.* ANNE *brings it to the center table. In the street below there is the sound of children playing.*)

ANNE (*as she opens the carton*). You know the way I'm going to think of it here? I'm going to think of it as a boarding house. A very peculiar summer boarding house, like the one that we—(*She breaks off as she pulls out some photographs.*) Father! My movie stars! I was wondering where they were! I was looking for them this morning . . . and Queen Wilhelmina![13] How wonderful!

MR. FRANK. There's something more. Go on. Look further.

(*He goes over to the sink, pouring a glass of milk from a thermos bottle.*)

ANNE (*pulling out a pasteboard-bound book*). A diary! (*She throws her arms around her father.*) I've never had a diary. And I've al-

ways longed for one. (*She looks around the room.*) Pencil, pencil, pencil. (*She starts down the stairs.*) I'm going down to the office to get a pencil.

MR. FRANK. Anne! No!

(*He goes after her, catching her by the arm and pulling her back.*)

ANNE (*startled*). But there's no one in the building now.

MR. FRANK. It doesn't matter. I don't want you ever to go beyond that door.

ANNE (*sobered*). Never . . . ? Not even at night time, when everyone is gone? Or on Sundays? Can't I go down to listen to the radio?

MR. FRANK. Never. I am sorry, Anneke. It isn't safe. No, you must never go beyond that door.

(*For the first time* ANNE *realizes what "going into hiding" means.*)

ANNE. I see.

MR. FRANK. It'll be hard, I know. But always remember this, Anneke. There are no walls, there are no bolts, no locks that anyone can put on your mind. Miep will bring us books. We will read history, poetry, mythology. (*He gives her the glass of milk.*) Here's your milk. (*With his arm about her, they go over to the couch, sitting down side by side.*) As a matter of fact, between us, Anne, being here has certain advantages for you. For instance, you remember the battle you had with your mother the other

---

12. **Annele** (än'ə lə), little Anne. *Anneke* (än'ə kə), used later, is a similar term of endearment.

13. **Queen Wilhelmina** (wil'hel mē'nə), queen of Netherlands from 1890 to 1948.

day on the subject of overshoes? You said you'd rather die than wear overshoes? But in the end you had to wear them? Well now, you see, for as long as we are here you will never have to wear overshoes! Isn't that good? And the coat that you inherited from Margot, you won't have to wear that any more. And the piano! You won't have to practice on the piano. I tell you, this is going to be a fine life for you!

(ANNE'S *panic is gone.* PETER *appears in the doorway of his room, with a saucer in his hand. He is carrying his cat.*)

PETER. I . . . I . . . I thought I'd better get some water for Mouschi before . . .

MR. FRANK. Of course.

(*As he starts toward the sink the carillon begins to chime the hour of eight. He tiptoes to the window at the back and looks down at the street below. He turns to* PETER, *indicating in pantomime that it is too late.* PETER *starts back for his room. He steps on a creaking board. The three of them are frozen for a minute in fear. As* PETER *starts away again,* ANNE *tiptoes over to him and pours some of the milk from her glass into the saucer for the cat.* PETER *squats on the floor, putting the milk before the cat.* MR. FRANK *gives* ANNE *his fountain pen, and then goes into the room at the right. For a second* ANNE *watches the cat, then she goes over to the center table, and opens her diary.*

In the room at the right, MRS. FRANK *has sat up quickly at the sound of the carillon.* MR. FRANK *comes in and sits down beside her on the settee, his arm comfortingly around her.*

Upstairs, in the attic room, MR. *and* MRS. VAN DAAN *have hung their clothes in the closet and are now seated on the iron bed.* MRS. VAN DAAN *leans back exhausted.* MR. VAN DAAN *fans her with a newspaper.*

ANNE *starts to write in her diary. The lights dim out, the curtain falls.*

In the darkness ANNE'S VOICE *comes to us again, faintly at first, and then with growing strength.*)

ANNE'S VOICE. I expect I should be describing what it feels like to go into hiding. But I really don't know yet myself. I only know it's funny never to be able to go outdoors . . . never to breathe fresh air . . . never to run and shout and jump. It's the silence in the nights that frightens me most. Every time I hear a creak in the house, or a step on the street outside, I'm sure they're coming for us. The days aren't so bad. At least we know that Miep and Mr. Kraler are down there below us in the office. Our protectors, we call them. I asked Father what would happen to them if the Nazis found out they were hiding us. Pim[14] said that they would suffer the same fate that we would . . . Imagine! They know this, and yet when they come up here, they're always cheerful and gay as if there were nothing in the world to bother them . . . Friday, the twenty-first of August, nineteen forty-two. Today I'm going to tell you our general news. Mother is unbearable. She insists on treating me like a baby, which I loathe. Otherwise things are going better. The weather is . . .

(*As* ANNE'S VOICE *is fading out the curtain rises on the scene.*)

---

14. *Pim,* a nickname Anne gave to her father.

THINK AND DISCUSS
Understanding
1. What is the time setting for this scene?
2. In what ways will Miep and Mr. Kraler help the Franks and Van Daans?
3. Why has Mr. Frank invited the Van Daans to join his family in hiding?
4. Who is assigned to each room?

Analyzing
5. What conditions make the Secret Annex a dangerous hiding place?
6. In what ways does Mr. Frank show that he intends to keep life in the annex as normal as possible?
7. How does Mr. Frank try to reconcile Anne to "going into hiding"?

Extending
8. Peter burns the Star of David, but Anne does not. What do you think he means when he says, "Maybe it's different for a girl"?
9. Peter has Mouschi and Anne has a new diary. How well do these things suit Anne and Peter as you know them so far?
10. Given what she writes in her diary, what problems do you **predict** will grow increasingly difficult for Anne?
11. What purposes are served by having Anne's voice reading from her diary at the end of the scene?

REVIEWING: Foreshadowing Handbook
See Handbook of Literary Terms, p. 667.

Foreshadowing is the use of hints or clues to suggest what may happen later. Discuss what each of these events might foreshadow: the Franks' and Van Daans' reactions to the sound of marching feet; Anne's saying that she hopes she and Peter will get along; the tension between Anne and her mother.

VOCABULARY
Dictionary
Use your Glossary to answer the following questions:
1. Of what two words is the compound *blackout* formed?
2. Of what did a *carillon* originally consist?
3. Does the accented syllable in *mercurial* rhyme with *her, pure,* or *tea?*
4. From what language does *rucksack* come? What does it mean?
5. Write the definition of *reserved* as it is used in this sentence: Her *reserved* manner in dealing with the unfair criticism won much admiration.

THINKING SKILLS
Generalizing
1. What were conditions in Europe like at the time of this play? Back up your generalization with specific information from Scene Two.
2. Based on what Anne tells us about Miep, what kind of person is she?

Use a Voice That Suits Purpose

Whatever its form—letter, story, novel, play, biography, or essay—good writing has a distinctive, personal *voice*. Good writers and the characters they create sound as if they were speaking directly to readers; they sound natural, like real people. Skillful writers, ones aware of audience, are able to convey any **tone** they desire—sarcastic, friendly, forceful, matter-of-fact. This personal voice is important in all writing, from the essay you write for history class to a play such as this one.

In *The Diary of Anne Frank,* the authors use several voices. When the purpose is to convey information, as in stage directions, the voice is matter-of-fact.

The scene . . . is the top floor of a warehouse and office building in Amsterdam, Holland. The sharply peaked roof of the building is outlined against a sea of other rooftops. . . . Nearby is the belfry of a church tower, the Westertoren, whose carillon rings out the hours.

When the purpose is to show characters' feelings, the tone of a speech suits the situation. Listen to the calm, rational voice of Mr. Frank. Notice his sharp focus on the topic. Note his short, clear statements. Listen to his persuasive tone.

MR. FRANK: About the noise. While the men are in the building below, we must have complete quiet. Every sound can be heard down there, not only in the workrooms, but in the offices too. The men come at about eight-thirty, and leave about five-thirty. So, to be perfectly safe, from eight in the morning until six in the evening we must move only when it is necessary, and then in stockinged feet. We must not speak above a whisper.

When we meet Anne and Peter, we hear two voices—one eager and friendly, the other reserved and shy. Notice her questions and exclamations and his flat, fragmentary answers. Listen to the chatty tone of her voice and the guarded tone of his.

ANNE: What's your cat's name?
PETER: Mouschi.
ANNE: Mouschi! Mouschi! I love cats. I have one . . . a darling little cat. But they made me leave her behind. I left some food and a note for the neighbors to take care of her. . . . I'm going to miss her terribly. What is yours? A him or a her?
PETER: He's a tom. He doesn't like strangers.
ANNE: Then I'll have to stop being a stranger, won't I? Is he fixed?
PETER: Huh?

In the scenes that follow, listen to the various speeches and notice how each one reflects attitude and emotion.

When you read, listen to voice.
When you write, choose your voice.

SCENE THREE

It is a little after six o'clock in the evening, two months later.

MARGOT is in the bedroom at the right, studying. MR. VAN DAAN is lying down in the attic room above.

The rest of the "family" is in the main room. ANNE and PETER sit opposite each other at the center table, where they have been doing their lessons. MRS. FRANK is on the couch. MRS. VAN DAAN is seated with her fur coat, on which she has been sewing, in her lap. None of them are wearing their shoes.

Their eyes are on MR. FRANK, waiting for him to give them the signal which will release them from their day-long quiet. MR. FRANK, his shoes in his hand, stands looking down out of the window at the back, watching to be sure that all of the workmen have left the building below.

After a few seconds of motionless silence, MR. FRANK turns from the window.

MR. FRANK (*quietly to the group*). It's safe now. The last workman has left.

(*There is an immediate stir of relief.*)

ANNE. (*Her pent-up energy explodes.*) WHEE!

MRS. FRANK (*startled, amused*). Anne!

MRS. VAN DAAN. I'm first for the w.c.

(*She hurries off to the bathroom. MRS. FRANK puts on her shoes and starts up to the sink to prepare supper. ANNE sneaks PETER'S shoes from under the table and hides them behind her back. MR. FRANK goes into MARGOT'S room.*)

MR. FRANK (*to MARGOT*). Six o'clock. School's over.

(*MARGOT gets up, stretching. MR. FRANK sits down to put on his shoes. In the main room PETER tries to find his.*)

PETER (*to ANNE*). Have you seen my shoes?

ANNE (*innocently*). Your shoes?

PETER. You've taken them, haven't you?

ANNE. I don't know what you're talking about.

PETER. You're going to be sorry!

ANNE. Am I?

(*PETER goes after her. ANNE, with his shoes in her hand, runs from him, dodging behind her mother.*)

MRS. FRANK (*protesting*). Anne, dear!

PETER. Wait till I get you!

ANNE. I'm waiting! (*PETER makes a lunge for her. They both fall to the floor. PETER pins her down, wrestling with her to get the shoes.*) Don't! Don't! Peter, stop it. Ouch!

MRS. FRANK. Anne! . . . Peter!

(*Suddenly PETER becomes self-conscious. He grabs his shoes roughly and starts for his room.*)

ANNE (*following him*). Peter, where are you going? Come dance with me.

PETER. I tell you I don't know how.

ANNE. I'll teach you.

PETER. I'm going to give Mouschi his dinner.

ANNE. Can I watch?

PETER. He doesn't like people around while he eats.

ANNE. Peter, please.

PETER. No!

(*He goes into his room. ANNE slams his door after him.*)

MRS. FRANK. Anne, dear. I think you shouldn't play like that with Peter. It's not dignified.

ANNE. Who cares if it's dignified? I don't want to be dignified.

(*MR. FRANK and MARGOT come from the room on the right. MARGOT goes to help her mother.*

MR. FRANK *starts for the center table to correct* MARGOT'S *school papers.*)

MRS. FRANK (*to* ANNE). You complain that I don't treat you like a grownup. But when I do, you resent it.

ANNE. I only want some fun . . . someone to laugh and clown with . . . After you've sat still all day and hardly moved, you've got to have some fun. I don't know what's the matter with that boy.

MR. FRANK. He isn't used to girls. Give him a little time.

ANNE. Time? Isn't two months time? I could cry. (*Catching hold of* MARGOT) Come on, Margot . . . dance with me. Come on, please.

MARGOT. I have to help with supper.

ANNE. You know we're going to forget how to dance . . . When we get out we won't remember a thing.

(*She starts to sing and dance by herself.* MR. FRANK *takes her in his arms, waltzing with her.* MRS. VAN DAAN *comes in from the bathroom.*)

MRS. VAN DAAN. Next? (*She looks around as she starts putting on her shoes.*) Where's Peter?

ANNE (*as they are dancing*). Where would he be!

MRS. VAN DAAN. He hasn't finished his lessons, has he? His father'll kill him if he catches him in there with that cat and his work not done. (MR. FRANK *and* ANNE *finish their dance. They bow to each other with extravagant formality.*) Anne, get him out of there, will you?

ANNE (*at* PETER'S *door*). Peter? Peter?

PETER (*opening the door a crack*). What is it?

ANNE. Your mother says to come out.

PETER. I'm giving Mouschi his dinner.

MRS. VAN DAAN. You know what your father says.
(*She sits on the couch, sewing on the lining of her fur coat.*)

PETER. For heaven's sake, I haven't even looked at him since lunch.

MRS. VAN DAAN. I'm just telling you, that's all.

ANNE. I'll feed him.

PETER. I don't want you in there.

MRS. VAN DAAN. Peter!

PETER (*to* ANNE). Then give him his dinner and come right out, you hear?
(*He comes back to the table.* ANNE *shuts the door of* PETER'S *room after her and disappears behind the curtain covering his closet.*)

MRS. VAN DAAN (*to* PETER). Now is that any way to talk to your little girl friend?

PETER. Mother . . . for heaven's sake . . . will you please stop saying that?

MRS. VAN DAAN. Look at him blush! Look at him!

PETER. Please! I'm not . . . anyway . . . let me alone, will you?

MRS. VAN DAAN. He acts like it was something to be ashamed of. It's nothing to be ashamed of, to have a little girl friend.

PETER. You're crazy. She's only thirteen.

MRS. VAN DAAN. So what? And you're sixteen. Just perfect. Your father's ten years older than I am. (*To* MR. FRANK) I warn you, Mr. Frank, if this war lasts much longer, we're going to be related and then . . .

MR. FRANK. *Mazeltov!*[1]

---

1. *Mazeltov* (mä′zəl tof), an expression used among Jews to express congratulations or wish good luck.

MRS. FRANK (*deliberately changing the conversation*). I wonder where Miep is. She's usually so prompt.

(*Suddenly everything else is forgotten as they hear the sound of an automobile coming to a screeching stop in the street below. They are tense, motionless in their terror. The car starts away. A wave of relief sweeps over them. They pick up their occupations again.* ANNE *flings open the door of* PETER'S *room, making a dramatic entrance. She is dressed in* PETER'S *clothes.* PETER *looks at her in fury. The others are amused.*)

ANNE. Good evening, everyone. Forgive me if I don't stay. (*She jumps up on a chair.*) I have a friend waiting for me in there. My friend Tom. Tom Cat. Some people say that we look alike. But Tom has the most beautiful whiskers, and I have only a little fuzz. I am hoping . . . in time . . .

PETER. All right, Mrs. Quack Quack!

ANNE (*outraged—jumping down*). Peter!

PETER. I heard about you . . . How you talked so much in class they called you Mrs. Quack Quack. How Mr. Smitter made you write a composition . . . "'Quack, quack,' said Mrs. Quack Quack."

ANNE. Well, go on. Tell them the rest. How it was so good he read it out loud to the class and then read it to all his other classes!

PETER. Quack! Quack! Quack . . . Quack . . . Quack . . .

(ANNE *pulls off the coat and trousers.*)

ANNE. You are the most intolerable, insufferable boy I've ever met!

(*She throws the clothes down the stairwell.* PETER *goes down after them.*)

PETER. Quack, quack, quack!

MRS. VAN DAAN (*to* ANNE). That's right, Anneke! Give it to him!

ANNE. With all the boys in the world . . . Why I had to get locked up with one like you! . . .

PETER. Quack, quack, quack, and from now on stay out of my room!

(*As* PETER *passes her,* ANNE *puts out her foot, tripping him. He picks himself up, and goes on into his room.*)

MRS. FRANK (*quietly*). Anne, dear . . . your hair. (*She feels* ANNE'S *forehead.*) You're warm. Are you feeling all right?

ANNE. Please, Mother.

(*She goes over to the center table, slipping into her shoes.*)

MRS. FRANK (*following her*). You haven't a fever, have you?

ANNE (*pulling away*). No. No.

MRS. FRANK. You know we can't call a doctor here, ever. There's only one thing to do . . . watch carefully. Prevent an illness before it comes. Let me see your tongue.

ANNE. Mother, this is perfectly absurd.

MRS. FRANK. Anne, dear, don't be such a baby. Let me see your tongue. (*As* ANNE *refuses,* MRS. FRANK *appeals to* MR. FRANK.) Otto . . . ?

MR. FRANK. You hear your mother, Anne. (ANNE *flicks out her tongue for a second, then turns away.*)

MRS. FRANK. Come on—open up! (*As* ANNE *opens her mouth very wide*) You seem all right . . . but perhaps an aspirin . . .

MRS. VAN DAAN. For heaven's sake, don't give that child any pills. I waited for fifteen minutes this morning for her to come out of the w.c.

ANNE. I was washing my hair!

MRS. FRANK. I think there's nothing the matter with our Anne that a ride on her bike, or a visit with her friend Jopie deWaal wouldn't cure. Isn't that so, Anne?

(MR. VAN DAAN *comes down into the room. From outside we hear faint sounds of bombers going over and a burst of ack-ack.*[2])

MR. VAN DAAN. Miep not come yet?

MRS. VAN DAAN. The workmen just left, a little while ago.

MR. VAN DAAN. What's for dinner tonight?

MRS. VAN DAAN. Beans.

MR. VAN DAAN. Not again!

MRS. VAN DAAN. Poor Putti![3] I know. But what can we do? That's all that Miep brought us.

(MR. VAN DAAN *starts to pace, his hands behind his back.* ANNE *follows behind him, imitating him.*)

ANNE. We are now in what is known as the "bean cycle." Beans boiled, beans *en casserole*,[4] beans with strings, beans without strings . . .

(PETER *has come out of his room. He slides into his place at the table, becoming immediately absorbed in his studies.*)

MR. VAN DAAN (*to* PETER). I saw you . . . in there, playing with your cat.

MRS. VAN DAAN. He just went in for a second, putting his coat away. He's been out here all the time, doing his lessons.

MR. FRANK (*looking up from the paper*). Anne, you got an excellent in your history paper today . . . and very good in Latin.

ANNE (*sitting beside him*). How about algebra?

MR. FRANK. I'll have to make a confession. Up until now I've managed to stay ahead of you in algebra. Today you caught up with me. We'll leave it to Margot to correct.

Otto Frank, Anne's father

ANNE. Isn't algebra *vile*, Pim!

MR. FRANK. Vile!

MARGOT (*to* MR. FRANK). How did I do?

ANNE (*getting up*). Excellent, excellent, excellent, excellent!

MR. FRANK (*to* MARGOT). You should have used the subjunctive here . . .

MARGOT. Should I? . . . I thought . . . look here . . . I didn't use it here . . .

(*The two become absorbed in the papers.*)

ANNE. Mrs. Van Daan, may I try on your coat?

MRS. FRANK. No, Anne.

---

2. *ack-ack,* antiaircraft fire.
3. *Putti* (pŭt′ē).
4. *en casserole* (aN käs rôl′), prepared and served in a covered baking dish.

MRS. VAN DAAN (*giving it to* ANNE). It's all right . . . but careful with it. (ANNE *puts it on and struts with it.*) My father gave me that the year before he died. He always bought the best that money could buy.

ANNE. Mrs. Van Daan, did you have a lot of boy friends before you were married?

MRS. FRANK. Anne, that's a personal question. It's not courteous to ask personal questions.

MRS. VAN DAAN. Oh, I don't mind. (*To* ANNE) Our house was always swarming with boys. When I was a girl we had . . .

MR. VAN DAAN. Oh, God. Not again!

MRS. VAN DAAN (*good-humored*). Shut up! (*Without a pause, to* ANNE, MR. VAN DAAN *mimics* MRS. VAN DAAN, *speaking the first few words in unison with her.*) One summer we had a big house in Hilversum.[5] The boys came buzzing round like bees around a jam pot. And when I was sixteen! . . . We were wearing our skirts very short those days and I had good-looking legs. (*She pulls up her skirt, going to* MR. FRANK.) I still have 'em. I may not be as pretty as I used to be, but I still have my legs. How about it, Mr. Frank?

MR. VAN DAAN. All right. All right. We see them.

MRS. VAN DAAN. I'm not asking you. I'm asking Mr. Frank.

PETER. Mother, for heaven's sake.

MRS. VAN DAAN. Oh, I embarrass you, do I? Well, I just hope the girl you marry has as good. (*Then to* ANNE) My father used to worry about me, with so many boys hanging round. He told me, if any of them gets fresh, you say to him . . . "Remember, Mr. So-and-So, remember I'm a lady."

ANNE. "Remember, Mr. So-and-So, remember I'm a lady."
(*She gives* MRS. VAN DAAN *her coat.*)

MR. VAN DAAN. Look at you, talking that way in front of her! Don't you know she puts it all down in that diary?

MRS. VAN DAAN. So, if she does? I'm only telling the truth!
(ANNE *stretches out, putting her ear to the floor, listening to what is going on below. The sound of the bombers fades away.*)

MRS. FRANK (*setting the table*). Would you mind, Peter, if I moved you over to the couch?

ANNE (*listening*). Miep must have the radio on.
(PETER *picks up his papers, going over to the couch beside* MRS. VAN DAAN.)

MR. VAN DAAN (*accusingly, to* PETER). Haven't you finished yet?

PETER. No.

MR. VAN DAAN. You ought to be ashamed of yourself.

PETER. All right. All right. I'm a dunce. I'm a hopeless case. Why do I go on?

MRS. VAN DAAN. You're not hopeless. Don't talk that way. It's just that you haven't anyone to help you, like the girls have. (*To* MR. FRANK) Maybe you could help him, Mr. Frank?

MR. FRANK. I'm sure that his father . . . ?

MR. VAN DAAN. Not me. I can't do anything with him. He won't listen to me. You go ahead . . . if you want.

MR. FRANK (*going to* PETER). What about it,

---

5. *Hilversum* (hil′vər səm), a health resort and residential area some miles from Amsterdam.

Peter? Shall we make our school coeducational?

MRS. VAN DAAN (*kissing* MR. FRANK). You're an angel, Mr. Frank. An angel. I don't know why I didn't meet you before I met that one there. Here, sit down, Mr. Frank . . . (*She forces him down on the couch beside* PETER.) Now, Peter, you listen to Mr. Frank.

MR. FRANK. It might be better for us to go into Peter's room.

(PETER *jumps up eagerly, leading the way.*)

MRS. VAN DAAN. That's right. You go in there, Peter. You listen to Mr. Frank. Mr. Frank is a highly educated man.

(As MR. FRANK *is about to follow* PETER *into his room,* MRS. FRANK *stops him and wipes the lipstick from his lips. Then she closes the door after them.*)

ANNE (*on the floor, listening*). Shh! I can hear a man's voice talking.

Peter Van Daan

MR. VAN DAAN (*to* ANNE). Isn't it bad enough here without your sprawling all over the place?

(ANNE *sits up.*)

MRS. VAN DAAN (*to* MR. VAN DAAN). If you didn't smoke so much, you wouldn't be so bad-tempered.

MR. VAN DAAN. Am I smoking? Do you see me smoking?

MRS. VAN DAAN. Don't tell me you've used up all those cigarettes.

MR. VAN DAAN. One package. Miep only brought me one package.

MRS. VAN DAAN. It's a filthy habit anyway. It's a good time to break yourself.

MR. VAN DAAN. Oh, stop it, please.

MRS. VAN DAAN. You're smoking up all our money. You know that, don't you?

MR. VAN DAAN. Will you shut up? (*During this,* MRS. FRANK *and* MARGOT *have studiously kept their eyes down. But* ANNE, *seated on the floor, has been following the discussion interestedly.* MR. VAN DAAN *turns to see her staring at him.*) And what are you staring at?

ANNE. I never heard grownups quarrel before. I thought only children quarreled.

MR. VAN DAAN. This isn't a quarrel! It's a discussion. And I never heard children so rude before.

ANNE (*rising, indignantly*). I, rude!

MR. VAN DAAN. Yes!

MRS. FRANK (*quickly*). Anne, will you get me my knitting? (ANNE *goes to get it.*) I must remember, when Miep comes, to ask her to bring me some more wool.

MARGOT (*going to her room*). I need some hairpins and some soap. I made a list.

(*She goes into her bedroom to get the list.*)

MRS. FRANK (*to* ANNE). Have you some library books for Miep when she comes?

ANNE. It's a wonder that Miep has a life of her own, the way we make her run errands for us. Please, Miep, get me some starch. Please take my hair out and have it cut. Tell me all the latest news, Miep.

(*She goes over, kneeling on the couch beside* MRS. VAN DAAN.) Did you know she was engaged? His name is Dirk, and Miep's afraid the Nazis will ship him off to Germany to work in one of their war plants. That's what they're doing with some of the young Dutchmen . . . they pick them up off the streets—

MR. VAN DAAN (*interrupting*). Don't you ever get tired of talking? Suppose you try keeping still for five minutes. Just five minutes. (*He starts to pace again. Again* ANNE *follows him, mimicking him.* MRS. FRANK *jumps up and takes her by the arm up to the sink, and gives her a glass of milk.*)

MRS. FRANK. Come here, Anne. It's time for your glass of milk.

MR. VAN DAAN. Talk, talk, talk. I never heard such a child. Where is my . . . ? Every evening it's the same, talk, talk, talk. (*He looks around.*) Where is my . . . ?

MRS. VAN DAAN. What're you looking for?

MR. VAN DAAN. My pipe. Have you seen my pipe?

MRS. VAN DAAN. What good's a pipe? You haven't got any tobacco.

MR. VAN DAAN. At least I'll have something to hold in my mouth! (*Opening* MARGOT's *bedroom door*) Margot, have you seen my pipe?

MARGOT. It was on the table last night.

(ANNE *puts her glass of milk on the table and picks up his pipe, hiding it behind her back.*)

MR. VAN DAAN. I know. I know. Anne, did you see my pipe? . . . Anne!

MRS. FRANK. Anne, Mr. Van Daan is speaking to you.

ANNE. Am I allowed to talk now?

MR. VAN DAAN. You're the most aggravating . . . The trouble with you is, you've been spoiled. What you need is a good old-fashioned spanking.

ANNE (*mimicking* MRS. VAN DAAN). "Remember, Mr. So-and-So, remember I'm a lady."

(*She thrusts the pipe into his mouth, then picks up her glass of milk.*)

MR. VAN DAAN (*restraining himself with difficulty*). Why aren't you nice and quiet like your sister Margot? Why do you have to show off all the time? Let me give you a little advice, young lady. Men don't like that kind of thing in a girl. You know that? A man likes a girl who'll listen to him once in a while . . . a domestic girl, who'll keep her house shining for her husband . . . who loves to cook and sew and . . .

ANNE. I'd cut my throat first! I'd open my veins! I'm going to be remarkable! I'm going to Paris . . .

MR. VAN DAAN (*scoffingly*). Paris!

ANNE. . . . to study music and art.

MR. VAN DAAN. Yeah! Yeah!

ANNE. I'm going to be a famous dancer or singer . . . or something wonderful.

(*She makes a wide gesture, spilling the glass of milk on the fur coat in* MRS. VAN DAAN's *lap.* MARGOT *rushes quickly over with a towel.* ANNE *tries to brush the milk off with her skirt.*)

MRS. VAN DAAN. Now look what you've done . . . you clumsy little fool! My beautiful fur coat my father gave me . . .

ANNE. I'm so sorry.

MRS. VAN DAAN. What do you care? It isn't yours . . . So go on, ruin it! Do you know what that coat cost? Do you? And now look at it! Look at it!

ANNE. I'm very, very sorry.

MRS. VAN DAAN. I could kill you for this. I could just kill you!

(MRS. VAN DAAN *goes up the stairs, clutching the coat.* MR. VAN DAAN *starts after her.*)

MR. VAN DAAN. Petronella . . . *liefje! Liefje!* . . . Come back . . . the supper . . . come back!

MRS. FRANK. Anne, you must not behave in that way.

ANNE. It was an accident. Anyone can have an accident.

MRS. FRANK. I don't mean that. I mean the answering back. You must not answer back. They are our guests. We must always show the greatest courtesy to them. We're all living under terrible tension.

(She stops as MARGOT *indicates that* VAN DAAN *can hear. When he is gone, she continues.*) That's why we must control ourselves . . . You don't hear Margot getting into arguments with them, do you? Watch Margot. She's always courteous with them. Never familiar. She keeps her distance. And they respect her for it. Try to be like Margot.

ANNE. And have them walk all over me, the way they do her? No, thanks!

MRS. FRANK. I'm not afraid that anyone is going to walk all over you, Anne. I'm afraid for other people, that you'll walk on them. I don't know what happens to you, Anne. You are wild, self-willed. If I had ever talked to my mother as you talk to me . . .

ANNE. Things have changed. People aren't like that any more. "Yes, Mother." "No, Mother." "Anything you say, Mother." I've got to fight things out for myself! Make something of myself!

MRS. FRANK. It isn't necessary to fight to do it. Margot doesn't fight, and isn't she . . . ?

ANNE (*violently rebellious*). Margot! Margot! Margot! That's all I hear from everyone . . . how wonderful Margot is . . . "Why aren't you like Margot?"

MARGOT (*protesting*). Oh, come on, Anne, don't be so . . .

ANNE (*paying no attention*). Everything she does is right, and everything I do is wrong! I'm the goat around here! . . . You're all against me! . . . And you worst of all!

(She rushes off into her room and throws herself down on the settee, stifling her sobs. MRS. FRANK *sighs and starts toward the stove.*)

MRS. FRANK (*to* MARGOT). Let's put the soup on the stove . . . if there's anyone who cares to eat. Margot, will you take the bread out? (MARGOT *gets the bread from the cupboard.*) I don't know how we can go on living this way . . . I can't say a word to Anne . . . she flies at me . . .

MARGOT. You know Anne. In half an hour she'll be out here, laughing and joking.

MRS. FRANK. And . . . (She makes a motion upwards, indicating the VAN DAANS.) . . . I told your father it wouldn't work . . . but no . . . he had to ask them, he said . . . he owed it to him, he said. Well, he knows now that I was right! These quarrels! . . . This bickering!

MARGOT (*with a warning look*). Shush. Shush. (*The buzzer for the door sounds.* MRS. FRANK *gasps, startled.*)

MRS. FRANK. Every time I hear that sound, my heart stops!

MARGOT (*starting for* PETER'S *door*). It's Miep. (*She knocks at the door.*) Father?

(MR. FRANK *comes quickly from* PETER'S *room.*)

MR. FRANK. Thank you, Margot. (*As he goes down the steps to open the outer door*) Has everyone his list?

MARGOT. I'll get my books. (*Giving her mother a list*) Here's your list. (MARGOT *goes into her and* ANNE'S *bedroom on the right.* ANNE *sits up, hiding her tears, as* MARGOT *comes in.*) Miep's here.

(MARGOT *picks up her books and goes back.* ANNE *hurries over to the mirror, smoothing her hair.*)

MR. VAN DAAN (*coming down the stairs*). Is it Miep?

MARGOT. Yes. Father's gone down to let her in.

MR. VAN DAAN. At last I'll have some cigarettes!

MRS. FRANK (*to* MR. VAN DAAN). I can't tell you how unhappy I am about Mrs. Van Daan's coat. Anne should never have touched it.

MR. VAN DAAN. She'll be all right.

MRS. FRANK. Is there anything I can do?

MR. VAN DAAN. Don't worry.

(*He turns to meet* MIEP. *But it is not* MIEP *who comes up the steps. It is* MR. KRALER *followed by* MR. FRANK. *Their faces are grave.* ANNE *comes from the bedroom.* PETER *comes from his room.*)

MRS. FRANK. Mr. Kraler!

MR. VAN DAAN. How are you, Mr. Kraler?

MARGOT. This is a surprise.

MRS. FRANK. When Mr. Kraler comes, the sun begins to shine.

MR. VAN DAAN. Miep is coming?

MR. KRALER. Not tonight.

(KRALER *goes to* MARGOT *and* MRS. FRANK *and* ANNE, *shaking hands with them.*)

MRS. FRANK. Wouldn't you like a cup of coffee? . . . Or, better still, will you have supper with us?

MR. FRANK. Mr. Kraler has something to talk over with us. Something has happened, he says, which demands an immediate decision.

MRS. FRANK (*fearful*). What is it?

(MR. KRALER *sits down on the couch. As he talks he takes bread, cabbages, milk, etc., from his briefcase, giving them to* MARGOT *and* ANNE *to put away.*)

MR. KRALER. Usually, when I come up here, I try to bring you some bit of good news. What's the use of telling you the bad news when there's nothing that you can do about it? But today something has happened . . . Dirk . . . Miep's Dirk, you know, came to me just now. He tells me that he has a Jewish friend living near him. A dentist. He says he's in trouble. He begged me, could I do anything for this man? Could I find him a hiding place? . . . So I've come to you . . . I know it's a terrible thing to ask of you, living as you are, but would you take him in with you?

MR. FRANK. Of course we will.

MR. KRALER (*rising*). It'll be just for a night or two . . . until I find some other place. This happened so suddenly that I didn't know where to turn.

MR. FRANK. Where is he?

MR. KRALER. Downstairs in the office.

MR. FRANK. Good. Bring him up.

MR. KRALER. His name is Dussel . . . Jan Dussel.

MR. FRANK. Dussel . . . I think I know him.

MR. KRALER. I'll get him.

(*He goes quickly down the steps and out. MR. FRANK suddenly becomes conscious of the others.*)

MR. FRANK. Forgive me. I spoke without consulting you. But I knew you'd feel as I do.

MR. VAN DAAN. There's no reason for you to consult anyone. This is your place. You have a right to do exactly as you please. The only thing I feel . . . there's so little food as it is . . . and to take in another person . . .

(PETER *turns away, ashamed of his father.*)

MR. FRANK. We can stretch the food a little. It's only for a few days.

MR. VAN DAAN. You want to make a bet?

MRS. FRANK. I think it's fine to have him. But, Otto, where are you going to put him? Where?

PETER. He can have my bed. I can sleep on the floor. I wouldn't mind.

MR. FRANK. That's good of you, Peter. But your room's too small . . . even for *you*.

ANNE. I have a much better idea. I'll come in here with you and Mother, and Margot can take Peter's room and Peter can go in our room with Mr. Dussel.

MARGOT. That's right. We could do that.

MR. FRANK. No, Margot. You mustn't sleep

Mr. Dussel

in that room . . . neither you nor Anne. Mouschi has caught some rats in there. Peter's brave. He doesn't mind.

ANNE. Then how about *this?* I'll come in here with you and Mother, and Mr. Dussel can have my bed.

MRS. FRANK. No. No. *No!* Margot will come in here with us and he can have her bed. It's the only way. Margot, bring your things in here. Help her, Anne.

(MARGOT *hurries into her room to get her things.*)

ANNE (*to her mother*). Why Margot? Why can't I come in here?

MRS. FRANK. Because it wouldn't be proper for Margot to sleep with a . . . Please, Anne. Don't argue. Please.

(ANNE *starts slowly away.*)

MR. FRANK (*to* ANNE). You don't mind sharing your room with Mr. Dussel, do you, Anne?

ANNE. No. No, of course not.

MR. FRANK. Good. (ANNE *goes off into her bedroom helping* MARGOT. MR. FRANK *starts to search in the cupboards.*) Where's the cognac?

MRS. FRANK. It's there. But, Otto, I was saving it in case of illness.

MR. FRANK. I think we couldn't find a better time to use it. Peter, will you get five glasses for me?

(PETER *goes for the glasses.* MARGOT *comes out of her bedroom, carrying her possessions, which she hangs behind a curtain in the main room.* MR. FRANK *finds the cognac and pours it into the five glasses that* PETER *brings him.* MR. VAN DAAN *stands looking on sourly.* MRS. VAN DAAN *comes downstairs and looks around at all of the bustle.*)

MRS. VAN DAAN. What's happening? What's going on?

MR. VAN DAAN. Someone's moving in with us.

MRS. VAN DAAN. In here? You're joking.

MARGOT. It's only for a night or two . . . until Mr. Kraler finds him another place.

MR. VAN DAAN. Yeah! Yeah!

(MR. FRANK *hurries over as* MR. KRALER *and* DUSSEL *come up.* DUSSEL *is a man in his late fifties, meticulous, finicky . . . bewildered now. He wears a raincoat. He carries a briefcase, stuffed full, and a small medicine case.*)

MR. FRANK. Come in, Mr. Dussel.

MR. KRALER. This is Mr. Frank.

DUSSEL. Mr. Otto Frank?

MR. FRANK. Yes. Let me take your things. (*He takes the hat and briefcase, but* DUSSEL *clings to his medicine case.*) This is my wife Edith . . . Mr. and Mrs. Van Daan . . . their son, Peter . . . and my daughters, Margot and Anne.

(DUSSEL *shakes hands with everyone.*)

MR. KRALER. Thank you, Mr. Frank. Thank you all. Mr. Dussel, I leave you in good hands. Oh . . . Dirk's coat.

(DUSSEL *hurriedly takes off the raincoat, giving it to* MR. KRALER. *Underneath is his white dentist's jacket, with a yellow Star of David on it.*)

DUSSEL (*to* MR. KRALER). What can I say to thank you . . . ?

MRS. FRANK (*to* DUSSEL). Mr. Kraler and Miep . . . They're our life line. Without them we couldn't live.

MR. KRALER. Please, please. You make us seem very heroic. It isn't that at all. We simply don't like the Nazis. (*To* MR. FRANK, *who offers him a drink*) No, thanks. (*Then going on*) We don't like their methods. We don't like . . .

MR. FRANK (*smiling*). I know. I know. "No one's going to tell us Dutchmen what to do with our damn Jews!"

MR. KRALER (*to* DUSSEL). Pay no attention to Mr. Frank. I'll be up tomorrow to see that they're treating you right. (*To* MR. FRANK) Don't trouble to come down again. Peter will bolt the door after me, won't you, Peter?

PETER. Yes, sir.

MR. FRANK. Thank you, Peter. I'll do it.

MR. KRALER. Good night. Good night.

GROUP. Good night, Mr. Kraler. We'll see you tomorrow . . . *etc., etc.*

(MR. KRALER *goes out with* MR. FRANK. MRS. FRANK *gives each one of the "grown-ups" a glass of cognac.*)

MRS. FRANK. Please, Mr. Dussel, sit down.

(MR. DUSSEL *sinks into a chair.* MRS. FRANK *gives him a glass of cognac.*)

DUSSEL. I'm dreaming. I know it. I don't believe my eyes. Mr. Otto Frank here! (To MRS. FRANK) You're not in Switzerland then? A woman told me . . . She said she'd gone to your house . . . the door was open, everything was in disorder, dishes in the sink. She said she found a piece of paper in the wastebasket with an address scribbled on it . . . an address in Zurich. She said you must have escaped to Zurich.

ANNE. Father put that there purposely . . . just so people would think that very thing!

DUSSEL. And you've been *here* all the time?

MRS. FRANK. All the time . . . ever since July.

(ANNE *speaks to her father as he comes back.*)

ANNE. It worked, Pim . . . the address you left! Mr. Dussel says that people believe we escaped to Switzerland.

MR. FRANK. I'm glad . . . And now let's have a little drink to welcome Mr. Dussel. (*Before they can drink,* MR. DUSSEL *bolts his drink.* MR. FRANK *smiles and raises his glass.*) To Mr. Dussel. Welcome. We're very honored to have you with us.

MRS. FRANK. To Mr. Dussel, welcome.

(*The* VAN DAANS *murmur a welcome. The "grownups" drink.*)

MRS. VAN DAAN. Um. That was good.

MR. VAN DAAN. Did Mr. Kraler warn you that you won't get much to eat here? You can imagine . . . three ration books among the seven of us . . . and now you make eight. (PETER *walks away, humiliated. Outside a street organ is heard dimly.*)

DUSSEL (*rising*). Mr. Van Daan, you don't realize what is happening outside that you should warn me of a thing like that. You don't realize what's going on . . .

(As MR. VAN DAAN *starts his characteristic pacing,* DUSSEL *turns to speak to the others.*) Right here in Amsterdam every day hundreds of Jews disappear . . . They surround a block and search house by house. Children come home from school to find their parents gone. Hundreds are being deported . . . people that you and I know . . . the Hallensteins . . . the Wessels . . .

MRS. FRANK (*in tears*). Oh, no. No!

DUSSEL. They get their call-up notice . . . come to the Jewish theatre on such and such a day and hour . . . bring only what you can carry in a rucksack. And if you refuse the call-up notice, then they come and drag you from your home and ship you off to Mauthausen.[6] The death camp!

MRS. FRANK. We didn't know that things had got so much worse.

DUSSEL. Forgive me for speaking so.

ANNE (*coming to* DUSSEL). Do you know the deWaals? . . . What's become of them? Their daughter Jopie and I are in the same class. Jopie's my best friend.

DUSSEL. They are gone.

ANNE. Gone?

DUSSEL. With all the others.

ANNE. Oh, no. Not Jopie!

(*She turns away, in tears.* MRS. FRANK *motions to* MARGOT *to comfort her.* MARGOT *goes to* ANNE, *putting her arms comfortingly around her.*)

MRS. VAN DAAN. There were some people called Wagner. They lived near us . . . ?

MR. FRANK (*interrupting with a glance at* ANNE). I think we should put this off until

---

6. *Mauthausen* (mout'houz ən), a Nazi concentration camp located in Austria.

The building containing Mr. Frank's business and the secret annex.

later. We all have many questions we want to ask . . . But I'm sure that Mr. Dussel would like to get settled before supper.

DUSSEL. Thank you, I would. I brought very little with me.

MR. FRANK (*giving him his hat and briefcase*). I'm sorry we can't give you a room alone. But I hope you won't be too uncomfortable. We've had to make strict rules here . . . a schedule of hours . . . We'll tell you after supper. Anne, would you like to take Mr. Dussel to his room?

ANNE (*controlling her tears*). If you'll come with me, Mr. Dussel?

(*She starts for her room.*)

DUSSEL (*shaking hands with each in turn*). Forgive me if I haven't really expressed my gratitude to all of you. This has been such a shock to me. I'd always thought of myself as Dutch. I was born in Holland. My father was born in Holland, and my grandfather. And now . . . after all these years . . . (*He breaks off.*) If you'll excuse me.

(DUSSEL *gives a little bow and hurries off after* ANNE. MR. FRANK *and the others are subdued.*)

ANNE (*turning on the light*). Well, here we are.

(DUSSEL *looks around the room. In the main room* MARGOT *speaks to her mother.*)

MARGOT. The news sounds pretty bad, doesn't it? It's so different from what Mr. Kraler tells us. Mr. Kraler says things are improving.

MR. VAN DAAN. I like it better the way Kraler tells it.

(*They resume their occupations, quietly.* PETER *goes off into his room. In* ANNE'S *room,* ANNE *turns to* DUSSEL.)

ANNE. You're going to share the room with me.

DUSSEL. I'm a man who always lived alone. I haven't had to adjust myself to others. I hope you'll bear with me until I learn.

ANNE. Let me help you. (*She takes his briefcase.*) Do you always live all alone? Have you no family at all?

DUSSEL. No one.

(*He opens his medicine case and spreads his bottles on the dressing table.*)

ANNE. How dreadful. You must be terribly lonely.

DUSSEL. I'm used to it.

ANNE. I don't think I could ever get used to

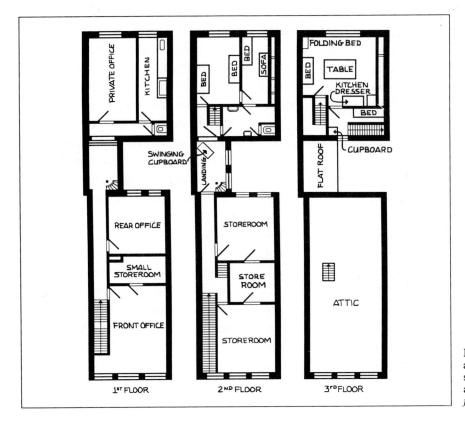

Floor plans of house and annex. (Europeans refer to street level as *ground floor*, and second floor as *first floor*.)

it. Didn't you even have a pet? A cat, or a dog?

DUSSEL. I have an allergy for fur-bearing animals. They give me asthma.

ANNE. Oh, dear. Peter has a cat.

DUSSEL. Here? He has it here?

ANNE. Yes. But we hardly ever see it. He keeps it in his room all the time. I'm sure it will be all right.

DUSSEL. Let us hope so. (*He takes some pills to fortify himself.*)

ANNE. That's Margot's bed, where you're going to sleep. I sleep on the sofa there. (*Indicating the clothes hooks on the wall.*) We cleared these off for your things. (*She goes over to the window.*) The best part about this room . . . you can look down and see a bit of the street and the canal. There's a houseboat . . . you can see the end of it . . . a bargeman lives there with his family . . . They have a baby and he's just beginning to walk and I'm so afraid he's going to fall into the canal some day. I watch him . . .

DUSSEL (*interrupting*). Your father spoke of a schedule.

ANNE (*coming away from the window*). Oh, yes. It's mostly about the times we have to be quiet. And times for the w.c. You can use it now if you like.

DUSSEL (*stiffly*). No, thank you.

ANNE. I suppose you think it's awful, my

talking about a thing like that. But you don't know how important it can get to be, especially when you're frightened . . . About this room, the way Margot and I did . . . she had it to herself in the afternoons for studying, reading . . . lessons, you know . . . and I took the mornings. Would that be all right with you?

DUSSEL. I'm not at my best in the morning.

ANNE. You stay here in the mornings then. I'll take the room in the afternoons.

DUSSEL. Tell me, when you're in here, what happens to me? Where am I spending my time? In there, with all the people?

ANNE. Yes.

DUSSEL. I see. I see.

ANNE. We have supper at half past six.

DUSSEL (*going over to the sofa*). Then, if you don't mind . . . I like to lie down quietly for ten minutes before eating. I find it helps the digestion.

ANNE. Of course. I hope I'm not going to be too much of a bother to you. I seem to be able to get everyone's back up.

(DUSSEL *lies down on the sofa, curled up, his back to her.*)

DUSSEL. I always get along very well with children. My patients all bring their children to me, because they know I get on well with them. So don't worry about that.

(ANNE *leans over him, taking his hand and shaking it gratefully.*)

ANNE. Thank you. Thank you, Mr. Dussel. (*The lights dim to darkness. The curtain falls on the scene.* ANNE'S VOICE *comes to us faintly at first, and then with increasing power.*)

ANNE'S VOICE. . . . And yesterday I finished Cissy Van Marxvelt's latest book. I think she is a first-class writer. I shall definitely let my children read her. Monday the twenty-first of September, nineteen forty-two. Mr. Dussel and I had another battle yesterday. Yes, Mr. Dussel! According to him, nothing, I repeat . . . nothing, is right about me . . . my appearance, my character, my manners. While he was going on at me I thought . . . sometime I'll give you such a smack that you'll fly right up to the ceiling! Why is it that every grownup thinks he knows the way to bring up children? Particularly the grownups that never had any. I keep wishing that Peter was a girl instead of a boy. Then I would have someone to talk to. Margot's a darling, but she takes everything too seriously. To pause for a moment on the subject of Mrs. Van Daan. I must tell you that her attempts to flirt with Father are getting her nowhere. Pim, thank goodness, won't play.

(*As she is saying the last lines, the curtain rises on the darkened scene.* ANNE'S VOICE *fades out.*)

THINK AND DISCUSS

Understanding

1. Early in this scene, what reminders of the war and the Nazis' persecution of Jews do stage directions provide?

2. Near the end of this scene, what information about the outside world does Mr. Dussel provide?

Analyzing

3. Describe the relationship that has developed between Anne and Peter during the two months they have lived in the Secret Annex. Give examples to support your description.

4. **Compare** and **contrast** the way the Franks treat their children with the way the Van Daans treat Peter.

5. What is the typical tone of voice used by Mr. and Mrs. Van Daan? by Mr. and Mrs. Frank? Quote or summarize speeches to support your answer.

6. What inferences about the character of Mr. and Mrs. Van Daan do you draw from the way they treat each other, Anne, and Mr. Dussel?

7. In what ways does the conversation between Mr. Dussel and Anne **foreshadow** the conflict that quickly develops between them?

8. What more do you learn about Anne from this scene? Cite incidents that illustrate her character traits.

Extending

9. Does Anne seem to you a typical thirteen-year-old girl? Why or why not?

10. Who seems to you to be bearing up best under the tension of living in the Secret Annex? Give evidence to support your judgment.

11. Which adult is likely to be most severely tested by changes needed to accommodate Mr. Dussel in the annex? Explain the reasons for your **prediction**.

VOCABULARY

Context

"This isn't a quarrel!" Mr. Van Daan tells Anne. "It's a discussion." Although synonyms have the same or nearly the same meaning, each may have a connotation or shade of meaning that makes it more appropriate in one context than in another.

For each of the following sentences, look up the word listed *first* in parentheses in the Glossary and read the synonym study following the entry. Decide which of the three words in parentheses is most appropriate in the sentence; write that word on your paper.

1. Coach Ridley reminded us that it is not good sportsmanship to (scoff/jeer/sneer) when an opposing player fumbles the ball.

2. Jeffery's excuse for not showing up was some (absurd/ridiculous/preposterous) tale about being kidnaped by a flying saucer.

3. It is customary to (deport/banish/exile) foreign embassy officials who are caught spying and to send them back to their own countries.

4. The diet and daily workout that Bonnie must follow in her Olympic training are

too (strict/rigid/rigorous) for the unstructured lifestyle I prefer.

5. The scenes of cruelty and torture in that movie, according to the reviewer, were the most (vile/base/low) of anything she had ever seen.

COMPOSITION ✒
Reading/Writing Log

Characters reveal their traits by what they say and how they say it. Copy the headings and examples below in your reading/writing log. Then reread Scene Three to find more examples to write under each of the other headings. Write the page and column where you find each example.

How Characters Speak

Mr. Van Daan—complaining, critical, accusing

To his wife when learning they will have beans for supper: Not again! (page 469, column 1)

To Anne, when she tries to hear what is going on downstairs, by putting her ear to the floor: Isn't it bad enough here without your sprawling all over the place? (page 471, column 2)

To Peter, about his studies: Haven't you finished yet? You ought to be ashamed of yourself. (page 470, column 2)

Mr. and Mrs. Frank—calm, polite, tactful, kind

To Mr. and Mrs. Van Daan:
To Peter:
To Anne and Margot:

SCENE FOUR

It is the middle of the night, several months later. The stage is dark except for a little light which comes through the skylight in PETER'S *room.*

Everyone is in bed. MR. *and* MRS. FRANK *lie on the couch in the main room, which has been pulled out to serve as a makeshift double bed.*

MARGOT *is sleeping on a mattress on the floor in the main room, behind a curtain stretched across for privacy. The others are all in their accustomed rooms.*

From outside we hear two drunken soldiers singing "Lili Marlene." A girl's high giggle is heard. The sound of running feet is heard coming closer and then fading in the distance. Throughout the scene there is the distant sound of airplanes passing overhead.

A match suddenly flares up in the attic. We dimly see MR. VAN DAAN. *He is getting his bearings. He comes quickly down the stairs, and goes to the cupboard where the food is stored. Again the match flares up, and is as quickly blown out. The dim figure is seen to steal back up the stairs.*

There is quiet for a second or two, broken only by the sound of airplanes, and running feet on the street below.

Suddenly, out of the silence and the dark, we hear ANNE *scream.*

ANNE (*screaming*). No! No! Don't . . . don't take me!

(*She moans, tossing and crying in her sleep. The other people wake, terrified.* DUSSEL *sits up in bed, furious.*)

DUSSEL. Shush! Anne! Anne, for God's sake, shush!

ANNE (*still in her nightmare*). Save me! Save me!

(*She screams and screams.* DUSSEL *gets out of bed, going over to her, trying to wake her.*)

DUSSEL. For God's sake! Quiet! Quiet! You want someone to hear?

(*In the main room* MRS. FRANK *grabs a shawl and pulls it around her. She rushes in to* ANNE, *taking her in her arms.* MR. FRANK *hurriedly gets up, putting on his overcoat.* MARGOT *sits up, terrified.* PETER'S *light goes on in his room.*)

MRS. FRANK (*to* ANNE, *in her room*). Hush, darling, hush. It's all right. It's all right. (*Over her shoulder to* DUSSEL) Will you be kind enough to turn on the light, Mr. Dussel? (*Back to* ANNE) It's nothing, my darling. It was just a dream.

(DUSSEL *turns on the light in the bedroom.* MRS. FRANK *holds* ANNE *in her arms. Gradually* ANNE *comes out of her nightmare, still trembling with horror.* MR. FRANK *comes into the room, and goes quickly to the window, looking out to be sure that no one outside has heard* ANNE'S *screams.* MRS. FRANK *holds* ANNE, *talking softly to her. In the main room* MARGOT *stands on a chair, turning on the center hanging lamp. A light goes on in the* VAN DAANS' *room overhead.* PETER *puts his robe on, coming out of his room.*)

DUSSEL (*to* MRS. FRANK, *blowing his nose*). Something must be done about that child, Mrs. Frank. Yelling like that! Who knows but there's somebody on the streets? She's endangering all our lives.

MRS. FRANK. Anne, darling.

DUSSEL. Every night she twists and turns. I don't sleep. I spend half my night shushing her. And now it's nightmares!

(MARGOT *comes to the door of* ANNE'S *room, followed by* PETER. MR. FRANK *goes to them, indicating that everything is all right.* PETER *takes* MARGOT *back.*)

MRS. FRANK (*to* ANNE). You're here, safe, you see? Nothing has happened. (*To* DUSSEL) Please, Mr. Dussel, go back to bed. She'll be herself in a minute or two. Won't you Anne?

DUSSEL (*picking up a book and a pillow*). Thank you, but I'm going to the w.c. The one place where there's peace!

(*He stalks out.* MR. VAN DAAN, *in underwear and trousers, comes down the stairs.*)

MR. VAN DAAN (*to* DUSSEL). What is it? What happened?

DUSSEL. A nightmare. She was having a nightmare!

MR. VAN DAAN. I thought someone was murdering her.

DUSSEL. Unfortunately, no.

(*He goes into the bathroom.* MR. VAN DAAN *goes back up the stairs.* MR. FRANK, *in the main room, sends* PETER *back to his own bedroom.*)

MR. FRANK. Thank you, Peter. Go back to bed.

(PETER *goes back to his room.* MR. FRANK *follows him turning out the light and looking out the window. Then he goes back to the main room and gets up on a chair, turning out the center hanging lamp.*)

MRS. FRANK (*to* ANNE). Would you like some water? (ANNE *shakes her head.*) Was it a very bad dream? Perhaps if you told me . . . ?

ANNE. I'd rather not talk about it.

MRS. FRANK. Poor darling. Try to sleep then. I'll sit right here beside you until you fall asleep. *(She brings a stool over, sitting there.)*

ANNE. You don't have to.

MRS. FRANK. But I'd like to stay with you . . . very much. Really.

ANNE. I'd rather you didn't.

MRS. FRANK. Good night, then. *(She leans down to kiss* ANNE. ANNE *throws her arm up over her face, turning away.* MRS. FRANK, *hiding her hurt, kisses* ANNE'S *arm.)* You'll be all right? There's nothing that you want?

ANNE. Will you please ask Father to come?

MRS. FRANK *(after a second).* Of course, Anne dear. *(She hurries out into the other room.* MR. FRANK *comes to her as she comes in.) Sie verlangt nach Dir!*[1]

MR. FRANK *(sensing her hurt).* Edith, *Liebe, schau . . .*[2]

MRS. FRANK. *Es macht nichts! Ich danke dem lieben Herrgott, dass sie sich wenigstens an Dich wendet, wenn sie Trost braucht! Geh hinein, Otto, sie ist ganz hysterisch vor Angst.*[3] *(As* MR. FRANK *hesitates) Geh zu ihr.*[4] *(He looks at her for a second and then goes to get a cup of water for* ANNE. MRS. FRANK *sinks down on the bed, her face in her hands, trying to keep from sobbing aloud.* MARGOT *comes over to her, putting her arms around her.)* She wants nothing of me. She pulled away when I leaned down to kiss her.

MARGOT. It's a phase . . . You heard Father . . . Most girls go through it . . . they turn to their fathers at this age . . . they give all their love to their fathers.

MRS. FRANK. You weren't like this. You didn't shut me out.

MARGOT. She'll get over it . . .

(She smooths the bed for MRS. FRANK *and sits beside her a moment as* MRS. FRANK *lies*

Edith Frank, Anne's mother

down. *In* ANNE'S *room* MR. FRANK *comes in, sitting down by* ANNE. ANNE *flings her arms around him, clinging to him. In the distance we hear the sound of ack-ack.)*

ANNE. Oh, Pim. I dreamed that they came to get us! The Green Police! They broke down the door and grabbed me and started to drag me out the way they did Jopie.

MR. FRANK. I want you to take this pill.

ANNE. What is it?

MR. FRANK. Something to quiet you.

(She takes it and drinks the water. In the main room MARGOT *turns out the light and goes back to her room.)*

MR. FRANK *(to* ANNE*).* Do you want me to read to you for a while?

---

1. *Sie verlangt nach Dir!* She wants to see you.
2. *Edith, Liebe, schau . . .* Edith, my dear, look . . .
3. *Es macht nichts! . . . vor Angst.* It doesn't matter. Thank God that she at least turns to you when she is in need of consolation. Go, Otto, she is hysterical with fear.
4. *Geh zu ihr.* Go to her.

ANNE. No. Just sit with me for a minute. Was I awful? Did I yell terribly loud? Do you think anyone outside could have heard?

MR. FRANK. No. No. Lie quietly now. Try to sleep.

ANNE. I'm a terrible coward. I'm so disappointed in myself. I think I've conquered my fear . . . I think I'm really grown-up . . . and then something happens . . . and I run to you like a baby . . . I love you, Father. I don't love anyone but you.

MR. FRANK (*reproachfully*). Annele!

ANNE. It's true. I've been thinking about it for a long time. You're the only one I love.

MR. FRANK. It's fine to hear you tell me that you love me. But I'd be happier if you said you loved your mother as well . . . She needs your help so much . . . your love . . .

ANNE. We have nothing in common. She doesn't understand me. Whenever I try to explain my views on life to her she asks me if I'm constipated.

MR. FRANK. You hurt her very much now. She's crying. She's in there crying.

ANNE. I can't help it. I only told the truth. I didn't want her here . . . (*Then, with sudden change*) Oh, Pim, I was horrible, wasn't I? And the worst of it is, I can stand off and look at myself doing it and know it's cruel and yet I can't stop doing it. What's the matter with me? Tell me. Don't say it's just a phase! Help me.

MR. FRANK. There is so little we parents can do to help our children. We can only try to set a good example . . . point the way. The rest you must do yourself. You must build your own character.

ANNE. I'm trying. Really I am. Every night I think back over all of the things I did that day that were wrong . . . like putting the wet mop in Mr. Dussel's bed . . . and this thing now with Mother. I say to myself, that was wrong. I make up my mind, I'm never going to do that again. Never! Of course I may do something worse . . . but at least I'll never do *that* again . . . I have a nicer side, Father . . . a sweeter, nicer side. But I'm scared to show it. I'm afraid that people are going to laugh at me if I'm serious. So the mean Anne comes to the outside and the good Anne stays on the inside, and I keep on trying to switch them around and have the good Anne outside and the bad Anne inside and be what I'd like to be . . . and might be . . . if only . . . only . . .

(*She is asleep.* MR. FRANK *watches her for a*

Margot Frank

moment and then turns off the light, and starts out. The lights dim out. The curtain falls on the scene. ANNE'S VOICE *is heard dimly at first, and then with growing strength.)*

ANNE'S VOICE. . . . The air raids are getting worse. They come over day and night. The noise is terrifying. Pim says it should be music to our ears. The more planes, the sooner will come the end of the war. Mrs. Van Daan pretends to be a fatalist. What will be, will be. But when the planes come over, who is the most frightened? No one else but Petronella! . . . Monday, the ninth of November, nineteen forty-two. Wonderful news! The Allies[5] have landed in Africa. Pim says that we can look for an early finish to the war. Just for fun he asked each of us what was the first thing we wanted to do when we got out of here. Mrs. Van Daan longs to be home with her own things, her needlepoint chairs, the Bechstein piano her father gave her . . . the best that money could buy. Peter would like to go to a movie. Mr. Dussel wants to get back to his dentist's drill. He's afraid he is losing his touch. For myself, there are so many things . . . to ride a bike again . . . to laugh till my belly aches . . . to have new clothes from the skin out . . . to have a hot tub filled to overflowing and wallow in it for hours . . . to be back in school with my friends . . .

(As the last lines are being said, the curtain rises on the scene. The lights dim on as ANNE'S VOICE *fades away.)*

---

5. **The Allies** (al'īz), the countries, including Britain and the United States, that fought against Germany, Italy, and Japan in World War II.

THINK AND DISCUSS
Understanding
1. Just before Anne's nightmare, what does Mr. Van Daan do?
2. What clues in earlier scenes foreshadowed this kind of action on his part? Explain.
3. How does Mrs. Frank react to Anne's asking for her father?

Analyzing
4. What do you think prompted Anne's nightmare?
5. What do you think her nightmare might **foreshadow**?
6. What does this scene reveal about the feelings of Mr. Dussel toward Anne? Anne toward her mother? her mother toward Anne? Describe each character's tone of voice and find lines from the play to support your generalizations.

Extending
7. Anne knows that she has treated her mother cruelly. Do you think she gives her father a satisfactory explanation for her behavior? Explain.
8. Would Anne and her mother be likely to express the same feelings toward each other if they were living under normal circumstances? Explain.
9. Mrs. Van Daan, Peter, Mr. Dussel, and Anne tell what they want to do when they get out of the annex. How well do their wishes fit your impression of each person?

SCENE FIVE

It is the first night of the Hanukkah[1] celebration. MR. FRANK *is standing at the head of the table on which is the Menorah.[2] He lights the Shamos, or servant candle, and holds it as he says the blessing. Seated listening is all of the "family," dressed in their best. The men wear hats;* PETER *wears his cap.*

MR. FRANK (*reading from a prayer book*). "Praised be Thou, oh Lord our God, Ruler of the universe, who has sanctified us with Thy commandments and bidden us kindle the Hanukkah lights. Praised be Thou, oh Lord our God, Ruler of the universe, who has wrought wondrous deliverances for our fathers in days of old. Praised be Thou, oh Lord our God, Ruler of the universe, that Thou has given us life and sustenance and brought us to this happy season." (MR. FRANK *lights the one candle of the Menorah as he continues.*) "We kindle this Hanukkah light to celebrate the great and wonderful deeds wrought through the zeal with which God filled the hearts of the heroic Maccabees, two thousand years ago. They fought against indifference, against tyranny and oppression, and they restored our Temple to us. May these lights remind us that we should ever look to God, whence cometh our help." Amen. (*Pronounced O-mayn.*)

ALL. Amen.

(MR. FRANK *hands* MRS. FRANK *the prayer book.*)

MRS. FRANK (*reading*). "I lift up mine eyes unto the mountains, from whence cometh my help. My help cometh from the Lord who made heaven and earth. He will not suffer thy foot to be moved. He that keepeth thee will not slumber. He that keepeth Israel doth neither slumber nor sleep. The Lord is thy keeper. The Lord is thy shade upon thy right hand. The sun shall not smite thee by day, nor the moon by night. The Lord shall keep thee from all evil. He shall keep thy soul. The Lord shall guard thy going out and thy coming in, from this time forth and forevermore." Amen.

ALL. Amen.

(MRS. FRANK *puts down the prayer book and goes to get the food and wine.* MARGOT *helps her.* MR. FRANK *takes the men's hats and puts them aside.*)

DUSSEL (*rising*). That was very moving.

ANNE (*pulling him back*). It isn't over yet!

MRS. VAN DAAN. Sit down! Sit down!

ANNE. There's a lot more, songs and presents.

DUSSEL. Presents?

MRS. FRANK. Not this year, unfortunately.

MRS. VAN DAAN. But always on Hanukkah everyone gives presents . . . everyone!

DUSSEL. Like our St. Nicholas' Day.[3]

(*There is a chorus of "no's" from the group.*)

MRS. VAN DAAN. No! Not like St. Nicholas!

---

1. Hanukkah (hä'nə kə), a Jewish festival usually held in December. The festival commemorates the rededication of the temple in Jerusalem after the Maccabees (mak'ə bēz'), a family of Jewish patriots, led the Jews to victory over the Syrians in 165 B.C.
2. Menorah (mə nôr'ə), a candlestick with various numbers of branches used primarily in Jewish religious services. The Shamos (shäm'əs), or servant candle, is lit first, then used to light the Menorah.
3. St. Nicholas' Day. On December 6, the feast of St. Nicholas, Dutch children are given gifts. St. Nicholas, actually a fourth-century saint, is today a figure like Santa Claus. The feast has no real religious significance.

What kind of a Jew are you that you don't know Hanukkah?

MRS. FRANK (*as she brings the food*). I remember particularly the candles . . . First one, as we have tonight. Then the second night you light two candles, the next night three . . . and so on until you have eight candles burning. When there are eight candles it is truly beautiful.

MRS. VAN DAAN. And the potato pancakes.

MR. VAN DAAN. Don't talk about them!

MRS. VAN DAAN. I make the best *latkes*[4] you ever tasted!

MRS. FRANK. Invite us all next year . . . in your own home.

MR. FRANK. God willing!

MRS. VAN DAAN. God willing.

MARGOT. What I remember best is the presents we used to get when we were little . . . eight days of presents . . . and each day they got better and better.

MRS. FRANK (*sitting down*). We are all here, alive. That is present enough.

ANNE. No, it isn't. I've got something . . . (*She rushes into her room, hurriedly puts on a little hat improvised from the lamp shade, grabs a satchel bulging with parcels and comes running back.*)

MRS. FRANK. What is it?

ANNE. Presents!

MRS. VAN DAAN. Presents!

DUSSEL. Look!

MRS. VAN DAAN. What's she got on her head?

PETER. A lamp shade!

ANNE. (*She picks out one at random.*) This is for Margot. (*She hands it to* MARGOT, *pulling her to her feet.*) Read it out loud.

MARGOT (*reading*).

"You have never lost your temper.
You never will, I fear,
You are so good.
But if you should,
Put all your cross words here."
(*She tears open the package.*) A new cross-word puzzle book! Where did you get it?

ANNE. It isn't new. It's one that you've done. But I rubbed it all out, and if you wait a little and forget, you can do it all over again.

MARGOT (*sitting*). It's wonderful, Anne. Thank you. You'd never know it wasn't new.
(*From outside we hear the sound of a streetcar passing.*)

ANNE (*with another gift*). Mrs. Van Daan.

MRS. VAN DAAN (*taking it*). This is awful . . . I haven't anything for anyone . . . I never thought . . .

MR. FRANK. This is all Anne's idea.

MRS. VAN DAAN (*holding up a bottle*). What is it?

ANNE. It's hair shampoo. I took all the odds and ends of soap and mixed them with the last of my toilet water.

MRS. VAN DAAN. Oh, Anneke!

ANNE. I wanted to write a poem for all of them, but I didn't have time. (*Offering a large box to* MR. VAN DAAN) Yours, Mr. Van Daan, is *really* something . . . something you want more than anything. (*As she waits for him to open it*) Look! Cigarettes!

MR. VAN DAAN. Cigarettes!

ANNE. Two of them! Pim found some old pipe tobacco in the pocket lining of his coat

---

4. *latkes* (lät′kəs), potato pancakes.

. . . and we made them . . . or rather, Pim did.

MRS. VAN DAAN. Let me see . . . Well, look at that! Light it, Putti! Light it.

(MR. VAN DAAN *hesitates*.)

ANNE. It's tobacco, really it is! There's a little fluff in it, but not much.

(*Everyone watches as* MR. VAN DAAN *cautiously lights it. The cigarette flares up. Everyone laughs.*)

PETER. It works!

MRS. VAN DAAN. Look at him.

MR. VAN DAAN (*spluttering*). Thank you, Anne. Thank you.

(ANNE *rushes back to her satchel for another present.*)

ANNE (*handing her mother a piece of paper*). For Mother, Hanukkah greeting.

(*She pulls her mother to her feet.*)

MRS. FRANK. (*She reads.*) "Here's an I.O.U. that I promise to pay. Ten hours of doing whatever you say. Signed, Anne Frank."

(MRS. FRANK, *touched, takes* ANNE *in her arms, holding her close.*)

DUSSEL (*to* ANNE). Ten hours of doing what you're told? *Anything* you're told?

ANNE. That's right.

DUSSEL. You wouldn't want to sell that, Mrs. Frank?

MRS. FRANK. Never! This is the most precious gift I've ever had!

(*She sits, showing her present to the others.* ANNE *hurries back to the satchel and pulls out a scarf, the scarf that* MR. FRANK *found in the first scene.*)

ANNE (*offering it to her father*). For Pim.

MR. FRANK. Anneke . . . I wasn't supposed to have a present!

(*He takes it, unfolding it and showing it to the others.*)

ANNE. It's a muffler . . . to put round your neck . . . like an ascot, you know. I made it myself out of odds and ends . . . I knitted it in the dark each night, after I'd gone to bed. I'm afraid it looks better in the dark!

MR. FRANK (*putting it on*). It's fine. It fits me perfectly. Thank you, Annele.

(ANNE *hands* PETER *a ball of paper, with a string attached to it.*)

ANNE. That's for Mouschi.

PETER (*rising to bow*). On behalf of Mouschi, I thank you.

ANNE (*hesitant, handing him a gift*). And . . . this is yours . . . from Mrs. Quack Quack. (*As he holds it gingerly in his hands*) Well . . . open it . . . Aren't you going to open it?

PETER. I'm scared to. I know something's going to jump out and hit me.

ANNE. No. It's nothing like that, really.

MRS. VAN DAAN (*as he is opening it*). What is it, Peter? Go on. Show it.

ANNE (*excitedly*). It's a safety razor!

DUSSEL. A what?

ANNE. A razor!

MRS. VAN DAAN (*looking at it*). You didn't make that out of odds and ends.

ANNE (*to* PETER). Miep got it for me. It's not new. It's a second-hand. But you really do need a razor now.

DUSSEL. For what?

ANNE. Look on his upper lip . . . you can see the beginning of a mustache.

DUSSEL. He wants to get rid of that? Put a little milk on it and let the cat lick it off.

PETER (*starting for his room*). Think you're funny, don't you.

DUSSEL. Look! He can't wait! He's going in to try it!

PETER. I'm going to give Mouschi his present!

(*He goes into his room, slamming the door behind him.*)

MR. VAN DAAN (*disgustedly*). Mouschi, Mouschi, Mouschi.

(*In the distance we hear a dog persistently barking.* ANNE *brings a gift to* DUSSEL.)

ANNE. And last but never least, my roommate, Mr. Dussel.

DUSSEL. For me? You have something for me? (*He opens the small box she gives him.*)

ANNE. I made them myself.

DUSSEL (*puzzled*). Capsules! Two capsules!

ANNE. They're ear-plugs!

DUSSEL. Ear-plugs?

ANNE. To put in your ears so you won't hear me when I thrash around at night. I saw them advertised in a magazine. They're not real ones . . . I made them out of cotton and candle wax. Try them . . . See if they don't work . . . see if you can hear me talk . . .

DUSSEL (*putting them in his ears*). Wait now until I get them in . . . so.

ANNE. Are you ready?

DUSSEL. Huh?

ANNE. Are you ready?

DUSSEL. Good God! They've gone inside! I can't get them out! (*They laugh as* MR. DUSSEL *jumps about, trying to shake the plugs out of his ears. Finally he gets them out. Putting them away.*) Thank you, Anne! Thank you!

MR. VAN DAAN. A real Hanukkah! ⎫
MRS. VAN DAAN. Wasn't it cute of her? ⎬ (*Together*)
⎭

MRS. FRANK. I don't know when she did it.

MARGOT. I love my present.

ANNE (*sitting at the table*). And now let's have the song, Father . . . please . . . (*To* DUSSEL) Have you heard the Hanukkah song, Mr. Dussel? The song is the whole thing! (*She sings*) "Oh, Hanukkah! Oh, Hanukkah! The sweet celebration . . . "

MR. FRANK (*quieting her*). I'm afraid, Anne, we shouldn't sing that song tonight. (*To* DUSSEL) It's a song of jubilation, of rejoicing. One is apt to become too enthusiastic.

ANNE. Oh, please, please. Let's sing the song. I promise not to shout!

MR. FRANK. Very well. But quietly now . . . I'll keep an eye on you and when . . . (*As* ANNE *starts to sing, she is interrupted by* DUSSEL, *who is snorting and wheezing.*)

DUSSEL (*pointing to* PETER). You . . . You! (PETER *is coming from his bedroom, ostentatiously holding a bulge in his coat as if he were holding his cat, and dangling* ANNE'S *present before it.*) How many times . . . I told you . . . Out! Out!

MR. VAN DAAN (*going to* PETER). What's the matter with you? Haven't you any sense? Get that cat out of here.

PETER (*innocently*). Cat?

MR. VAN DAAN. You heard me. Get it out of here!

PETER. I have no cat. (*Delighted with his joke, he opens his coat and pulls out a bath towel. The group at the table laugh, enjoying the joke.*)

DUSSEL (*still wheezing*). It doesn't need to be the cat . . . his clothes are enough . . . when he comes out of that room . . .

MR. VAN DAAN. Don't worry. You won't be bothered any more. We're getting rid of it.

DUSSEL. At last you listen to me.

(*He goes off into his bedroom.*)

MR. VAN DAAN (*calling after him*). I'm not doing it for you. That's all in your mind . . . all of it! (*He starts back to his place at the table.*) I'm doing it because I'm sick of seeing that cat eat all our food.

PETER. That's not true! I only give him bones . . . scraps . . .

MR. VAN DAAN. Don't tell me! He gets fatter every day! Damn cat looks better than any of us. Out he goes tonight!

PETER. No! No!

ANNE. Mr. Van Daan, you can't do that! That's Peter's cat. Peter loves that cat.

MRS. FRANK (*quietly*). Anne.

PETER (*to* MR. VAN DAAN). If he goes, I go.

MR. VAN DAAN. Go! Go!

MRS. VAN DAAN. You're not going and the cat's not going! Now please . . . this is Hanukkah . . . Hanukkah . . . this is the time to celebrate . . . What's the matter with all of you? Come on, Anne. Let's have the song.

ANNE (*singing*).
"Oh, Hanukkah! Oh, Hanukkah!
The sweet celebration."

MR. FRANK (*rising*). I think we should first blow out the candle . . . then we'll have something for tomorrow night.

MARGOT. But, Father, you're supposed to let it burn itself out.

MR. FRANK. I'm sure that God understands shortages. (*Before blowing it out*) "Praised be Thou, oh Lord our God, who hast sustained us and permitted us to celebrate this joyous festival."

(*He is about to blow out the candle when suddenly there is a crash of something falling below. They all freeze in horror, motionless. For a few seconds there is complete silence.* MR. FRANK *slips off his shoes. The others noiselessly follow his example.* MR. FRANK *turns out a light near him. He motions to* PETER *to turn off the center lamp.* PETER *tries to reach it, realizes he cannot and gets up on a chair. Just as he is touching the lamp he loses his balance. The chair goes out from under him. He falls. The iron lamp shade crashes to the floor. There is a sound of feet below, running down the stairs.*)

MR. VAN DAAN (*under his breath*). God almighty! (*The only light left comes from the Hanukkah candle.* DUSSEL *comes from his room.* MR. FRANK *creeps over to the stairwell and stands listening. The dog is heard barking excitedly.*) Do you hear anything?

MR. FRANK (*in a whisper*). No. I think they've gone.

MRS. VAN DAAN. It's the Green Police. They've found us.

MR. FRANK. If they had, they wouldn't have left. They'd be up here by now.

MRS. VAN DAAN. I know it's the Green Police. They've gone to get help. That's all, they'll be back.

MR. VAN DAAN. Or it may have been the Gestapo[5] looking for papers . . .

---

5. *Gestapo* (gə stä′pō), the Secret Police of Nazi Germany.

MR. FRANK (*interrupting*). Or a thief, looking for money.

MRS. VAN DAAN. We've got to do something . . . Quick! Quick! Before they come back.

MR. VAN DAAN. There isn't anything to do. Just wait.

(MR. FRANK *holds up his hand for them to be quiet. He is listening intently. There is complete silence as they all strain to hear any sound from below. Suddenly* ANNE *begins to sway. With a low cry she falls to the floor in a faint.* MRS. FRANK *goes to her quickly, sitting beside her on the floor and taking her in her arms.*)

MRS. FRANK. Get some water, please! Get some water!

(MARGOT *starts for the sink.*)

MR. VAN DAAN (*grabbing* MARGOT). No! No! No one's going to run water!

MR. FRANK. If they've found us, they've found us. Get the water. (MARGOT *starts again for the sink.* MR. FRANK *getting a flashlight*) I'm going down.

(MARGOT *rushes to him, clinging to him.* ANNE *struggles to consciousness.*)

MARGOT. No, Father, no! There may be someone there, waiting . . . It may be a trap!

MR. FRANK. This is Saturday. There is no way for us to know what has happened until Miep or Mr. Kraler comes on Monday morning. We cannot live with this uncertainty.

MARGOT. Don't go, Father!

MRS. FRANK. Hush, darling, hush. (MR. FRANK *slips quietly out, down the steps and out through the door below.*) Margot! Stay close to me.

(MARGOT *goes to her mother.*)

MR. VAN DAAN. Shush! Shush!

(MRS. FRANK *whispers to* MARGOT *to get the water.* MARGOT *goes for it.*)

MRS. VAN DAAN. Putti, where's our money? Get our money. I hear you can buy the Green Police off, so much a head. Go upstairs quick! Get the money!

MR. VAN DAAN. Keep still!

MRS. VAN DAAN (*kneeling before him, pleading*). Do you want to be dragged off to a concentration camp? Are you going to stand there and wait for them to come up and get you? Do something, I tell you!

MR. VAN DAAN (*pushing her aside*). Will you keep still!

(*He goes over to the stairwell to listen.* PETER *goes to his mother, helping her up onto the sofa. There is a second of silence. Then* ANNE *can stand it no longer.*)

ANNE. Someone go after Father! Make Father come back!

PETER (*starting for the door*). I'll go.

MR. VAN DAAN. Haven't you done enough?

(*He pushes* PETER *roughly away. In his anger against his father* PETER *grabs a chair as if to hit him with it, then puts it down, burying his face in his hands.* MRS. FRANK *begins to pray softly.*)

ANNE. Please, please, Mr. Van Daan. Get Father.

MR. VAN DAAN. Quiet! Quiet!

(ANNE *is shocked into silence.* MRS. FRANK *pulls her closer, holding her protectively in her arms.*)

MRS. FRANK (*softly, praying*). "I lift up mine eyes unto the mountains, from whence cometh my help. My help cometh from the Lord who made heaven and earth. He will not suffer thy foot to be moved . . . He that keepeth thee will not slumber . . ." (*She stops as she hears someone coming. They all watch the door tensely.* MR. FRANK *comes quietly in.* ANNE *rushes to him, holding him tight.*)

MR. FRANK. It was a thief. That noise must have scared him away.

MRS. VAN DAAN. Thank God.

MR. FRANK. He took the cash box. And the radio. He ran away in such a hurry that he didn't stop to shut the street door. It was swinging wide open. (*A breath of relief sweeps over them.*) I think it would be good to have some light.

MARGOT. Are you sure it's all right?

MR. FRANK. The danger has passed. (MARGOT *goes to light the small lamp.*) Don't be so terrified, Anne. We're safe.

DUSSEL. Who says the danger has passed? Don't you realize we are in greater danger than ever?

MR. FRANK. Mr. Dussel, will you be still! (MR. FRANK *takes* ANNE *back to the table, making her sit down with him, trying to calm her.*)

DUSSEL (*pointing to* PETER). Thanks to this clumsy fool, there's someone now who knows we're up here! Someone now knows we're up here, hiding!

MRS. VAN DAAN (*going to* DUSSEL). Someone knows we're here, yes. But who is the someone? A thief! A thief! You think a thief is going to go to the Green Police and say . . . I was robbing a place the other night and I heard a noise up over my head? You think a thief is going to do that?

DUSSEL. Yes. I think he will.

MRS. VAN DAAN (*hysterically*). You're crazy!

(*She stumbles back to her seat at the table.* PETER *follows protectively, pushing* DUSSEL *aside.*)

DUSSEL. I think some day he'll be caught and then he'll make a bargain with the Green Police . . . if they'll let him off, he'll tell them where some Jews are hiding! (*He goes off into the bedroom. There is a second of appalled silence.*)

MR. VAN DAAN. He's right.

ANNE. Father, let's get out of here! We can't stay here now . . . Let's go . . .

MR. VAN DAAN. Go! Where?

MRS. FRANK (*sinking into her chair at the table*). Yes. Where?

MR. FRANK (*rising, to them all*). Have we lost all faith? All courage? A moment ago we thought that they'd come for us. We were sure it was the end. But it wasn't the end. We're alive, safe. (MR. VAN DAAN *goes to the table and sits.* MR. FRANK *prays.*) "We thank Thee, oh Lord our God, that in Thy infinite mercy Thou hast again seen fit to spare us." (*He blows out the candle, then turns to* ANNE.) Come on, Anne. The song! Let's have the song!

(*He starts to sing.* ANNE *finally starts falteringly to sing, as* MR. FRANK *urges her on. Her voice is hardly audible at first.*)

ANNE (*singing*).

"Oh, Hanukkah! Oh, Hanukkah!
The sweet . . . celebration . . ."

(*As she goes on singing, the others gradually join in, their voices still shaking with fear.* MRS. VAN DAAN *sobs as she sings.*)

GROUP.

"Around the feast . . . we . . . gather
In complete . . . jubilation . . .
Happiest of sea . . . sons

Now is here.
Many are the reasons for good cheer."
(DUSSEL *comes from the bedroom. He comes over to the table, standing beside* MARGOT, *listening to them as they sing.*)
"Together
We'll weather
Whatever tomorrow may bring."
(*As they sing on with growing courage, the lights start to dim.*)
"So hear us rejoicing

And merrily voicing
The Hanukkah song that we sing.
Hoy!"
(*The lights are out. The curtain starts slowly to fall.*)
"Hear us rejoicing
And merrily voicing
The Hanukkah song that we sing."
(*They are still singing, as the curtain falls.*)
CURTAIN

THINK AND DISCUSS
Understanding
1. How did members of the "family" celebrate Hanukkah in the years before they went into hiding?
2. How do they celebrate this year?
3. What event abruptly ends the celebration?

Analyzing
4. In what ways does Anne's behavior throughout the scene show that she is striving for greater maturity?
5. What decisions does Mr. Frank make throughout the scene that show him still to be the person in charge?
6. At first Mr. Frank does not want Anne to sing the Hanukkah song. At the end of the scene, why does he urge her to sing?

Extending
7. Review the article on **irony** in the Handbook of Literary Terms. Of the three kinds of irony, which is present in this scene? Give two or three examples to support your answers.
8. How do you think the various characters will behave toward each other in Act Two? Explain.
9. What events do you predict will occur in Act Two? Explain.

READING LITERATURE SKILLFULLY
Sequence
The last scene in Act One is especially important in the development of the plot of the play. Answer these questions about the sequence of events in Act One, Scene Five.
1. What is the cause of Anne's good humor at the beginning of the scene?
2. What happens to put the people in the annex in more danger than ever before?

3. Why is Peter trying to turn out the light?

4. Discuss the reactions of these characters after each realizes the danger: Anne, Margot, Mr. Van Daan, Mrs. Van Daan, Mr. Frank.

COMPOSITION
Rewriting a Dialogue

Imagine that Anne could take back the cruel words she spoke to her mother in Act One, Scene 4. Beginning with Mrs. Frank's speech in which she asks Anne to tell her dream, rewrite the dialogue as if the "sweeter, nicer" Anne were talking. Continue by rewriting the dialogue between Mrs. and Mr. Frank to reflect the consequent change in their *voices*. End with a few lines between Mrs. Frank and Margot.

Describing Characters' Attitudes

In paragraph one of a five-paragraph essay, explain how their *speeches* reveal Mr. and Mrs. Van Daan's attitude toward each other; in paragraph two, their attitude toward Peter. In paragraph three, explain how their *speeches* reveal Mr. and Mrs. Frank's attitude toward each other; in paragraph four, their attitude toward their children. End your essay with a brief comment about your findings. If you are keeping a reading/writing log, review it before making prewriting notes. For additional help in prewriting and in revising, see "Writing About Literature" in the Writer's Handbook.

Comment

Dramatic License

Because a drama is a series of events to be acted out, Frances Goodrich and Albert Hackett had to adapt Anne's diary entries to make them suitable for presentation on a stage. Making such changes, usually for the sake of the overall effect desired by the dramatists, is called using *dramatic license.*

From Anne's descriptions of events in the annex, the dramatists had to create dialogue for the persons involved. Too, they had to compress journal entries to provide necessary exposition, or background, for the play. For example, the first diary entry, which Mr. Frank begins

to read aloud on stage, was drawn from parts of a number of entries. Finally, so as not to crowd the stage unduly with actors, in Miep and Mr. Kraler they created composite characters. The personalities of Miep Gies and Elli Vossen, both of whom worked in the warehouse building and were friends of Anne, merge on stage in Miep; Mr. Kraler and Mr. Koophuis, both business friends of Mr. Frank and both associated with Travis, Inc., become the single character of Mr. Kraler.

In reality, the people living in the Secret Annex had more freedom to move around than do the characters in the play. In the diary, Anne frequently mentions the trips to the "private office" on the first floor of the building where the inhabitants of the annex listened to news broadcasts, speeches, and concerts on the radio. The playwrights, however, realizing the difficulties in staging different settings, have confined the action and the characters to one set, the Secret Annex itself.

During the two years the Franks and the Van Daans occupied the Secret Annex, there were several burglaries in the office below. None of them occurred during the Hanukkah season. Again, the playwrights have used dramatic license in presenting only one of these burglaries. By having the burglary occur during the Hanukkah celebration, the playwrights have created an extremely dramatic situation; the hope and strength which the inhabitants receive from the religious ceremony contrast sharply with the ever present danger of discovery, brought into focus by the intrusion of the unknown thief.

Much of Anne's diary reveals her thoughts about herself, the special problems with which she, as a teenager, is faced. The following diary entry reveals an important aspect of Anne's personality:

Saturday, 15 July, 1944. . . . I have one outstanding trait in my character, which must strike anyone who knows me for any length of time and that is my knowledge of myself. I can watch myself and my actions, just like an outsider. The Anne of every day I can face entirely without prejudice, without making excuses for her, and watch what's good and what's bad about her. This "self-consciousness" haunts me, and every time I open my mouth I know as soon as I have spoken whether "that ought to have been different" or "that was right as it was." There are so many things about myself that I condemn; I couldn't begin to name them all. I understand more and more how true Daddy's words were when he said: "All children must look after their own upbringing." Parents can only give good advice or put them on the right paths, but the final forming of a person's character lies in their own hands.[1]

This is the type of personal, intimate revelation that Anne made only in her diary. To reveal this aspect of Anne's personality to the audience, the dramatists incorporated the entry into Scene Four in which Anne, still frightened and overwrought from her nightmare, confesses to her father things that in actuality she revealed to no one.

Frances Goodrich and Albert Hackett, through their careful selections and adaptations of diary entries, have succeeded in presenting vivid portraits of the inhabitants of the Secret Annex. At the same time, they have preserved the spirit of reality found in the historical source from which they had to work, the diary of a young girl.

---

1. From *Anne Frank: The Diary of a Young Girl*. Copyright 1952 by Otto H. Frank. Reprinted by permission of Doubleday & Company, Inc. and Vallentine, Mitchell & Co., Ltd.

ACT TWO

SCENE ONE

In the darkness we hear ANNE'S VOICE, *again reading from the diary.*

ANNE'S VOICE. Saturday, the first of January, nineteen forty-four. Another new year has begun and we find ourselves still in our hiding place. We have been here now for one year, five months and twenty-five days. It seems that our life is at a standstill. *(The curtain rises on the scene. It is afternoon. Everyone is bundled up against the cold. In the main room* MRS. FRANK *is taking down the laundry, which is hung across the back.* MR.

A page from Anne's diary, where she had pasted her photo

FRANK *sits in the chair down left, reading.* MARGOT *is lying on the couch with a blanket over her and the many-colored knitted scarf around her throat.* ANNE *is seated at the center table, writing in her diary.* PETER, MR. *and* MRS. VAN DAAN, *and* DUSSEL *are all in their own rooms, reading or lying down.*

As the lights dim on, ANNE'S VOICE *continues, without a break.)*

ANNE'S VOICE. We are all a little thinner. The Van Daans' "discussions" are as violent as ever. Mother still does not understand me. But then I don't understand her either. There is one great change, however. A change in myself. I read somewhere that girls of my age don't feel quite certain of themselves. . . .

(The buzzer of the door below suddenly sounds. Everyone is startled; MR. FRANK *tiptoes cautiously to the top of the steps and listens. Again the buzzer sounds, in* MIEP'S *V-for-Victory signal.*[1]*)*

MR. FRANK. It's Miep! *(He goes quickly down the steps to unbolt the door.* MRS. FRANK *calls upstairs to the* VAN DAANS *and then to* PETER.*)*

MRS. FRANK. Wake up, everyone! Miep is here! *(*ANNE *quickly puts her diary away.* MARGOT *sits up, pulling the blanket around her shoulders.* MR. DUSSEL *sits on the edge of his bed, listening, disgruntled.* MIEP *comes up the steps, followed by* MR. KRALER. *They bring flowers, books, newspapers, etc.* ANNE *rushes to* MIEP, *throwing her arms affectionately around her.)* Miep . . . and Mr. Kraler . . . What a delightful surprise!

---

1. *V-for-Victory signal,* three short buzzes followed by a long one. In the Morse Code the letter V is transmitted by three dots and a dash. It was widely used as a victory symbol during World War II.

MR. KRALER. We came to bring you New Year's greetings.

MRS. FRANK. You shouldn't . . . you should have at least one day to yourselves. (*She goes quickly to the stove and brings down teacups and tea for all of them.*)

ANNE. Don't say that, it's so wonderful to see them! (*Sniffing at* MIEP'S *coat*) I can smell the wind and the cold on your clothes.

MIEP (*giving her the flowers*). There you are. (*Then to* MARGOT, *feeling her forehead*) How are you, Margot? . . . Feeling any better?

MARGOT. I'm all right.

ANNE. We filled her full of every kind of pill so she won't cough and make a noise.

(*She runs into her room to put the flowers in water.* MR. *and* MRS. VAN DAAN *come from upstairs. Outside there is the sound of a band playing.*)

MRS. VAN DAAN. Well, hello, Miep. Mr. Kraler.

MR. KRALER (*giving a bouquet of flowers to* MRS. VAN DAAN). With my hope for peace in the New Year.

PETER (*anxiously*). Miep, have you seen Mouschi? Have you seen him anywhere around?

MIEP. I'm sorry, Peter. I asked everyone in the neighborhood had they seen a gray cat. But they said no.

(MRS. FRANK *gives* MIEP *a cup of tea.* MR. FRANK *comes up the steps, carrying a small cake on a plate.*)

MR. FRANK. Look what Miep's brought for us!

MRS. FRANK (*taking it*). A cake!

MR. VAN DAAN. A cake! (*He pinches* MIEP'S *cheeks gaily and hurries up to the cupboard.*) I'll get some plates.

(DUSSEL, *in his room, hastily puts a coat on and starts out to join the others.*)

MRS. FRANK. Thank you, Miepia.[2] You shouldn't have done it. You must have used all of your sugar ration for weeks. (*Giving it to* MRS. VAN DAAN) It's beautiful, isn't it?

MRS. VAN DAAN. It's been ages since I even saw a cake. Not since you brought us one last year. (*Without looking at the cake, to* MIEP) Remember? Don't you remember, you gave us one on New Year's Day? Just this time last year? I'll never forget it because you had "Peace in nineteen forty-three" on it. (*She looks at the cake and reads.*) "Peace in nineteen forty-four!"

MIEP. Well, it has to come sometime, you know. (*As* DUSSEL *comes from his room*) Hello, Mr. Dussel.

MR. KRALER. How are you?

MR. VAN DAAN (*bringing plates and a knife*). Here's the knife, *liefje*. Now, how many of us are there?

MIEP. None for me, thank you.

MR. FRANK. Oh, please. You must.

MIEP. I couldn't.

MR. VAN DAAN. Good! That leaves one . . . two . . . three . . . seven of us.

DUSSEL. Eight! Eight! It's the same number as it always is!

MR. VAN DAAN. I left Margot out. I take it for granted Margot won't eat any.

ANNE. Why wouldn't she!

MRS. FRANK. I think it won't harm her.

MR. VAN DAAN. All right! All right! I just didn't want her to start coughing again, that's all.

---

2. *Miepia* (mēp′нуə).

DUSSEL. And please, Mrs. Frank should cut the cake.

MR. VAN DAAN. What's the difference?

MRS. VAN DAAN. It's not Mrs. Frank's cake, is it, Miep? It's for all of us. *(Together)*

DUSSEL. Mrs. Frank divides things better.

MRS. VAN DAAN *(going to* DUSSEL*)*. What are you trying to say?

MR. VAN DAAN. Oh, come on! Stop wasting time! *(Together)*

MRS. VAN DAAN *(to* DUSSEL*)*. Don't I always give everybody exactly the same? Don't I?

MR. VAN DAAN. Forget it, Kerli.

MRS. VAN DAAN. No. I want an answer! Don't I?

DUSSEL. Yes. Yes. Everybody gets exactly the same . . . except Mr. Van Daan always gets a little bit more.

(VAN DAAN advances on DUSSEL, *the knife still in his hand.)*

MR. VAN DAAN. That's a lie!

(DUSSEL retreats before the onslaught of the VAN DAANS.)

MR. FRANK. Please, please! *(Then to* MIEP*)* You see what a little sugar cake does to us? It goes right to our heads!

MR. VAN DAAN *(handing* MRS. FRANK *the knife).* Here you are, Mrs. Frank.

MRS. FRANK. Thank you. *(Then to* MIEP *as she goes to the table to cut the cake)* Are you sure you won't have some?

MIEP *(drinking her tea).* No, really, I have to go in a minute.

(The sound of the band fades out in the distance.)

PETER *(to* MIEP*).* Maybe Mouschi went back to our house . . . they say that cats . . . Do you ever get over there . . . ? I mean . . . do you suppose you could . . . ?

MIEP. I'll try, Peter. The first minute I get I'll try. But I'm afraid, with him gone a week . . .

DUSSEL. Make up your mind, already someone has had a nice big dinner from that cat! *(PETER is furious, inarticulate. He starts toward DUSSEL as if to hit him. MR. FRANK stops him. MRS. FRANK speaks quickly to ease the situation.)*

MRS. FRANK *(to* MIEP*).* This is delicious, Miep!

MRS. VAN DAAN *(eating hers).* Delicious!

MR. VAN DAAN *(finishing it in one gulp).* Dirk's in luck to get a girl who can bake like this!

MIEP *(putting down her empty teacup).* I have to run. Dirk's taking me to a party tonight.

ANNE. How heavenly! Remember now what everyone is wearing, and what you have to eat and everything, so you can tell us tomorrow.

MIEP. I'll give you a full report! Good-by, everyone!

MR. VAN DAAN *(to* MIEP*).* Just a minute. There's something I'd like you to do for me.

(He hurries off up the stairs to his room.)

MRS. VAN DAAN *(sharply).* Putti, where are you going? *(She rushes up the stairs after him, calling hysterically.)* What do you want? Putti, what are you going to do?

MIEP *(to* PETER*).* What's wrong?

PETER. *(His sympathy is with his mother.)* Father says he's going to sell her fur coat. She's crazy about that old fur coat.

DUSSEL. Is it possible? Is it possible that anyone is so silly as to worry about a fur coat in times like this?

PETER. It's none of your darn business . . . and if you say one more thing . . . I'll, I'll take you and I'll . . . I mean it . . . I'll . . .

(*There is a piercing scream from* MRS. VAN DAAN *above. She grabs at the fur coat as* MR. VAN DAAN *is starting downstairs with it.*)

MRS. VAN DAAN. No! No! No! Don't you dare take that! You hear? It's mine! (*Downstairs* PETER *turns away, embarrassed, miserable.*) My father gave me that! You didn't give it to me. You have no right. Let go of it . . . you hear?

(MR. VAN DAAN *pulls the coat from her hands and hurries downstairs.* MRS. VAN DAAN *sinks to the floor, sobbing. As* MR. VAN DAAN *comes into the main room the others look away, embarrassed for him.*)

MR. VAN DAAN (*to* MR. KRALER). Just a little—discussion over the advisability of selling this coat. As I have often reminded Mrs. Van Daan, it's very selfish of her to keep it when people outside are in such desperate need of clothing . . . (*He gives the coat to* MIEP.) So if you will please to sell it for us? It should fetch a good price. And by the way, will you get me cigarettes. I don't care what kind they are . . . get all you can.

MIEP. It's terribly difficult to get them, Mr. Van Daan. But I'll try. Good-by.

(*She goes.* MR. FRANK *follows her down the steps to bolt the door after her.* MRS. FRANK *gives* MR. KRALER *a cup of tea.*)

MRS. FRANK. Are you sure you won't have some cake, Mr. Kraler?

MR. KRALER. I'd better not.

MR. VAN DAAN. You're still feeling badly? What does your doctor say?

MR. KRALER. I haven't been to him.

MRS. FRANK. Now, Mr. Kraler! . . .

MR. KRALER (*sitting at the table*). Oh, I tried. But you can't get near a doctor these days . . . they're so busy. After weeks I finally managed to get one on the telephone. I told him I'd like an appointment . . . I wasn't feeling very well. You know what he answers . . . over the telephone . . . Stick out your tongue! (*They laugh. He turns to* MR. FRANK *as* MR. FRANK *comes back.*) I have some contracts here . . . I wonder if you'd look over them with me . . .

MR. FRANK (*putting out his hand*). Of course.

MR. KRALER. (*He rises.*) If we could go downstairs . . . (MR. FRANK *starts ahead,* MR. KRALER *speaks to the others.*) Will you forgive us? I won't keep him but a minute. (*He starts to follow* MR. FRANK *down the steps.*)

MARGOT (*with sudden foreboding*). What's happened? Something's happened! Hasn't it, Mr. Kraler?

(MR. KRALER *stops and comes back, trying to reassure* MARGOT *with a pretense of casualness.*)

MR. KRALER. No, really. I want your father's advice . . .

MARGOT. Something's gone wrong! I know it!

MR. FRANK (*coming back, to* MR. KRALER). If it's something that concerns us here, it's better that we all hear it.

MR. KRALER. (*turning to him, quietly*). But . . . the children . . . ?

MR. FRANK. What they'd imagine would be worse than any reality.

(*As* MR. KRALER *speaks, they all listen with*

intense apprehension. MRS. VAN DAAN *comes down the stairs and sits on the bottom step.*)

MR. KRALER. It's a man in the storeroom . . . I don't know whether or not you remember him . . . Carl, about fifty, heavy-set, near-sighted . . . He came with us just before you left.

MR. FRANK. He was from Utrecht?

MR. KRALER. That's the man. A couple of weeks ago, when I was in the storeroom, he closed the door and asked me . . . how's Mr. Frank? What do you hear from Mr. Frank? I told him I only knew there was a rumor that you were in Switzerland. He said he'd heard that rumor too, but he thought I might know something more. I didn't pay any attention to it . . . but then a thing happened yesterday . . . He'd brought some invoices to the office for me to sign. As I was going through them, I looked up. He was standing staring at the bookcase . . . your bookcase. He said he thought he remembered a door there . . . Wasn't there a door there that used to go up to the loft? Then he told me he wanted more money. Twenty guilders[3] more a week.

MR. VAN DAAN. Blackmail!

MR. FRANK. Twenty guilders? Very modest blackmail.

MR. VAN DAAN. That's just the beginning.

DUSSEL (*coming to* MR. FRANK). You know what I think? He was the thief who was down there that night. That's how he knows we're here.

MR. FRANK (*to* MR. KRALER). How was it left? What did you tell him?

MR. KRALER. I said I had to think about it. What shall I do? Pay him the money? . . .

The back of the building, showing the secret annex

Take a chance on firing him . . . or what? I don't know.

DUSSEL (*frantic*). For God's sake don't fire him! Pay him what he asks . . . keep him here where you can have your eye on him.

MR. FRANK. Is it so much that he's asking? What are they paying nowadays?

MR. KRALER. He could get it in a war plant. But this isn't a war plant. Mind you, I don't know if he really knows . . . or if he doesn't know.

---

3. *Twenty guilders,* a little over $5.00 in American money. The guilder (gil′dər) is the monetary unit of the Netherlands.

MR. FRANK. Offer him half. Then we'll soon find out if it's blackmail or not.

DUSSEL. And if it is? We've got to pay it, haven't we? Anything he asks we've got to pay!

MR. FRANK. Let's decide that when the time comes.

MR. KRALER. This may be all imagination. You get to a point, these days, where you suspect everyone and everything. Again and again . . . on some simple look or word, I've found myself . . .

(*The telephone rings in the office below.*)

MRS. VAN DAAN (*hurrying to* MR. KRALER). There's the telephone! What does that mean, the telephone ringing on a holiday?

MR. KRALER. That's my wife. I told her I had to go over some papers in my office . . . to call me there when she got out of church. (*He starts out.*) I'll offer him half then. Good-by . . . we'll hope for the best!

(*The group call their good-bys halfheartedly.* MR. FRANK *follows* MR. KRALER, *to bolt the door below. During the following scene,* MR. FRANK *comes back up and stands listening, disturbed.*)

DUSSEL (*to* MR. VAN DAAN). You can thank your son for this . . . smashing the light! I tell you, it's just a question of time now. (*He goes to the window at the back and stands looking out.*)

MARGOT. Sometimes I wish the end would come . . . whatever it is.

MRS. FRANK (*shocked*). Margot!

(ANNE *goes to* MARGOT, *sitting beside her on the couch with her arms around her.*)

MARGOT. Then at least we'd know where we were.

MRS. FRANK. You should be ashamed of your-self! Talking that way! Think how lucky we are! Think of the thousands dying in the war, every day. Think of the people in concentration camps.

ANNE (*interrupting*). What's the good of that? What's the good of thinking of misery when you're already miserable? That's stupid!

MRS. FRANK. Anne!

(*As* ANNE *goes on raging at her mother,* MR. FRANK *tries to break in, in an effort to quiet her.*)

ANNE. We're young. Margot and Peter and I! You grownups have had your chance! But look at us . . . If we begin thinking of all the horror in the world, we're lost! We're trying to hold onto some kind of ideals . . . when everything . . . ideals, hopes . . . everything, are being destroyed! It isn't our fault that the world is in such a mess! We weren't around when all this started! So don't try to take it out on us! (*She rushes off to her room, slamming the door after her. She picks up a brush from the chest and hurls it to the floor. Then she sits on the settee, trying to control her anger.*)

MR. VAN DAAN. She talks as if we started the war! Did we start the war?

(*He spots* ANNE'S *cake. As he starts to take it,* PETER *anticipates him.*)

PETER. She left her cake. (*He starts for* ANNE'S *room with the cake. There is silence in the main room.* MRS. VAN DAAN *goes up to her room, followed by* MR. VAN DAAN. DUSSEL *stays looking out the window.* MR. FRANK *brings* MRS. FRANK *her cake. She eats it slowly, without relish.* MR. FRANK *takes his cake to* MARGOT *and sits quietly on the sofa beside her.* PETER *stands in the doorway of*

ANNE'S *darkened room, looking at her, then makes a little movement to let her know he is there.* ANNE *sits up, quickly, trying to hide the signs of her tears.* PETER *holds out the cake to her.*) You left this.

ANNE (*dully*). Thanks.

(PETER *starts to go out, then comes back.*)

PETER. I thought you were fine just now. You know just how to talk to them. You know just how to say it. I'm no good . . . I never can think . . . especially when I'm mad . . . That Dussel . . . when he said that about Mouschi . . . someone eating him . . . all I could think is . . . I wanted to hit him. I wanted to give him such a . . . a . . . that he'd . . . That's what I used to do when there was an argument at school . . . That's the way I . . . but here . . . And an old man like that . . . it wouldn't be so good.

ANNE. You're making a big mistake about me. I do it all wrong. I say too much. I go too far. I hurt people's feelings . . .

(DUSSEL *leaves the window, going to his room.*)

PETER. I think you're just fine . . . What I want to say . . . if it wasn't for you around here, I don't know. What I mean . . .

(PETER *is interrupted by* DUSSEL'S *turning on the light.* DUSSEL *stands in the doorway, startled to see* PETER. PETER *advances toward him forbiddingly.* DUSSEL *backs out of the room.* PETER *closes the door on him.*)

ANNE. Do you mean it, Peter? Do you really mean it?

PETER. I said it, didn't I?

ANNE. Thank you, Peter!

(*In the main room* MR. *and* MRS. FRANK *collect the dishes and take them to the sink, washing them.* MARGOT *lies down again on the couch.* DUSSEL, *lost, wanders into* PETER'S *room and takes up a book, starting to read.*)

PETER (*looking at the photographs on the wall*). You've got quite a collection.

ANNE. Wouldn't you like some in your room? I could give you some. Heaven knows you spend enough time in there . . . doing heaven knows what. . . .

PETER. It's easier. A fight starts, or an argument . . . I duck in there.

ANNE. You're lucky, having a room to go to. His lordship is always here . . . I hardly ever get a minute alone. When they start in on me, I can't duck away. I have to stand there and take it.

PETER. You gave some of it back just now.

ANNE. I get so mad. They've formed their opinions . . . about everything . . . but we . . . we're still trying to find out . . . We have problems here that no other people our age have ever had. And just as you think you've solved them, something comes along and bang! You have to start all over again.

PETER. At least you've got someone you can talk to.

ANNE. Not really. Mother . . . I never discuss anything serious with her. She doesn't understand. Father's all right. We can talk about everything . . . everything but one thing, Mother. He simply won't talk about her. I don't think you can be really intimate with anyone if he holds something back, do you?

PETER. I think your father's fine.

ANNE. Oh, he is, Peter! He is! He's the only one who's ever given me the feeling that I have any sense. But anyway, nothing can take the place of school and play and friends of your own age . . . or near your age . . . can it?

PETER. I suppose you miss your friends and all.

ANNE. It isn't just . . . (*She breaks off, staring up at him for a second.*) Isn't it funny, you and I? Here we've been seeing each other every minute for almost a year and a half, and this is the first time we've ever really talked. It helps a lot to have someone to talk to, don't you think? It helps you to let off steam.

PETER (*going to the door*). Well, any time you want to let off steam, you can come into my room.

ANNE (*following him*). I can get up an awful lot of steam. You'll have to be careful how you say that.

PETER. It's all right with me.

ANNE. Do you really mean it?

PETER. I said it, didn't I?

(*He goes out.* ANNE *stands in her doorway looking after him. As* PETER *gets to his door he stands for a minute looking back at her. Then he goes into his room.* DUSSEL *rises as he comes in, and quickly passes him, going out. He starts across for his room.* ANNE *sees him coming, and pulls her door shut.* DUSSEL *turns back toward* PETER'S *room.* PETER *pulls his door shut.* DUSSEL *stands there, bewildered, forlorn.*

The scene slowly dims out. The curtain falls on the scene. ANNE'S VOICE *comes over in the darkness . . . faintly at first, and then with growing strength.*)

ANNE'S VOICE. We've had bad news. The people from whom Miep got our ration books have been arrested. So we have had to cut down on our food. Our stomachs are so empty that they rumble and make strange noises, all in different keys. Mr. Van Daan's is deep and low, like a bass fiddle. Mine is high, whistling like a flute. As we all sit around waiting for supper, it's like an orchestra tuning up. It only needs Toscanini to raise his baton and we'd be off in the Ride of the Valkyries.[4] Monday, the sixth of March, nineteen forty-four. Mr. Kraler is in the hospital. It seems he has ulcers. Pim says we are his ulcers. Miep has to run the business and us too. The Americans have landed on the southern tip of Italy. Father looks for a quick finish to the war. Mr. Dussel is waiting every day for the warehouse man to demand more money. Have I been skipping too much from one subject to another? I can't help it. I feel that spring is coming. I feel it in my whole body and soul. I feel utterly confused. I am longing . . . so longing . . . for everything . . . for friends . . . for someone to talk to . . . someone who understands . . . someone young, who feels as I do . . .

(*As these last lines are being said, the curtain rises on the scene. The lights dim on.* ANNE'S VOICE *fades out.*)

---

4. *Toscanini . . . Ride of the Valkyries.* Toscanini (tos'kə nē'nē), 1867–1957, was a world-famous Italian musical conductor. "Ride of the Valkyries" (val kir'ēz) is a vigorous musical composition by nineteenth-century German composer Richard Wagner (väg'nər).

THINK AND DISCUSS

Understanding

1. How long have Anne and the others been in hiding?

2. From Anne's point of view, what has stayed the same?

3. What does the group decide to do about the workman who wants a raise in his salary?

4. What does Margot say that upsets Mrs. Frank?

5. How much time has elapsed between the diary entry Anne reads at the beginning of this scene and the one she reads at the end?

Analyzing

6. What does the scene with the fur coat reveal about the **characters** of Mr. and Mrs. Van Daan?

7. What effect does Anne's outburst to her mother have on Peter?

8. What do you learn about Mr. Frank and Mr. Dussell from their reactions to Mr. Kraler's story?

9. What does Anne mean when she tells Peter that "this is the first time we've ever really talked"?

Extending

10. Does the diary entry that closes this scene make you feel more or less hopeful about the group's ability to survive the war? Explain.

VOCABULARY

Idioms

An idiom (id'ē əm) is a phrase or expression whose meaning cannot be understood from only the ordinary meanings of the words in it. For example, Peter tells Anne that she can always use his room when she needs to *let off steam*. Look up *steam* in the Glossary. You will find the phrase *let off steam* in dark type in the middle of the entry. Which of the two definitions that follow—a or b—fits the use of the word in the context of *The Diary of Anne Frank?*

Locate each of the following italicized idioms in the Glossary by looking under the most important word. (You may have to try more than one word.) Look for the phrase in dark type in the middle of the entry or at the end. Then rewrite the sentence on your paper, substituting for the idiom a definition written in your own words.

1. Anne refuses to let people *walk all over her*, the way they do Margot.

2. Mr. Dussel hopes Anne *will bear with him* because he is used to living by himself.

3. Miep's sugar cake goes *right to their heads*, Mr. Frank claims.

4. Having someone to talk to, Anne tells Peter, helps her *let off steam*.

COMPOSITION

Reading/Writing Log

Peter's voice contrasts sharply with Anne's during their first real talk. Copy the headings below in your reading/writing log. Then find and copy several examples for each heading. After each example, write the page and column where you found it. The first one has been done for you.

Reading/Writing Log
Peter (halting, uncertain)
Examples:

> I think you're just fine . . . what I want to say . . . if it wasn't for you around

here, I don't know. What I mean . . . (page 503, column 1, paragraph 3)

Peter (flattering)
Examples:

Anne (disturbed)
Examples:

Anne (personal, confiding)
Examples:

SCENE TWO

It is evening, after supper. From the outside we hear the sound of children playing. The "grownups," with the exception of MR. VAN DAAN, *are all in the main room.* MRS. FRANK *is doing some mending,* MRS. VAN DAAN *is reading a fashion magazine.* MR. FRANK *is going over business accounts.* DUSSEL, *in his dentist's jacket, is pacing up and down, impatient to get into his bedroom.* MRS. VAN DAAN *is upstairs working on a piece of embroidery in an embroidery frame.*

In his room PETER *is sitting before the mirror, smoothing his hair. As the scene goes on, he puts on his tie, brushes his coat and puts it on preparing himself meticulously for a visit from* ANNE. *On his wall are now hung some of* ANNE'S *motion picture stars.*

In her room ANNE *too is getting dressed. She stands before the mirror in her slip, trying various ways of dressing her hair.* MARGOT *is seated on the sofa, hemming a skirt for* ANNE *to wear.*

In the main room DUSSEL *can stand it no longer. He comes over, rapping sharply on the door of his and* ANNE'S *bedroom.*

ANNE (*calling to him*). No, no, Mr. Dussel! I am not dressed yet. (DUSSEL *walks away, furious, sitting down and burying his head in his hands.* ANNE *turns to* MARGOT.) How is that? How does that look?
MARGOT (*glancing at her briefly*). Fine.
ANNE. You didn't even look.
MARGOT. Of course I did. It's fine.
ANNE. Margot, tell me, am I terribly ugly?
MARGOT. Oh, stop fishing.
ANNE. No. No. Tell me.
MARGOT. Of course you're not. You've got nice eyes . . . and a lot of animation, and . . .
ANNE. A little vague, aren't you?
(*She reaches over and takes a brassière out of* MARGOT'S *sewing basket. She holds it up to herself, studying the effect in the mirror. Outside,* MRS. FRANK, *feeling sorry for* DUSSEL, *comes over, knocking at the girls' door.*)
MRS. FRANK (*outside*). May I come in?
MARGOT. Come in, Mother.
MRS. FRANK (*shutting the door behind her*). Mr. Dussel's impatient to get in here.

ANNE (*still with the brassière*). Heavens, he takes the room for himself the entire day.

MRS. FRANK (*gently*). Anne, dear, you're not going in again tonight to see Peter?

ANNE (*dignified*). That is my intention.

MRS. FRANK. But you've already spent a great deal of time in there today.

ANNE. I was in there exactly twice. Once to get the dictionary, and then three-quarters of an hour before supper.

MRS. FRANK. Aren't you afraid you're disturbing him?

ANNE. Mother, I have some intuition.

MRS. FRANK. Then may I ask you this much, Anne. Please don't shut the door when you go in.

ANNE. You sound like Mrs. Van Daan! (*She throws the brassière back in* MARGOT'S *sewing basket and picks up her blouse, putting it on.*)

MRS. FRANK. No. No. I don't mean to suggest anything wrong. I only wish that you wouldn't expose yourself to criticism . . . that you wouldn't give Mrs. Van Daan the opportunity to be unpleasant.

ANNE. Mrs. Van Daan doesn't need an opportunity to be unpleasant!

MRS. FRANK. Everyone's on edge, worried about Mr. Kraler. This is one more thing . . .

ANNE. I'm sorry, Mother. I'm going to Peter's room. I'm not going to let Petronella Van Daan spoil our friendship.

(MRS. FRANK *hesitates for a second, then goes out, closing the door after her. She gets a pack of playing cards and sits at the center table, playing solitaire. In* ANNE'S *room* MARGOT *hands the finished skirt to* ANNE. *As* ANNE *is putting it on,* MARGOT *takes off her high-heeled shoes and stuffs paper in the toes so that* ANNE *can wear them.*)

MARGOT (*to* ANNE). Why don't you two talk in the main room? It'd save a lot of trouble. It's hard on Mother, having to listen to those remarks from Mrs. Van Daan and not say a word.

ANNE. Why doesn't she say a word? I think it's ridiculous to take it and take it.

MARGOT. You don't understand Mother at all, do you? She can't talk back. She's not like you. It's just not in her nature to fight back.

ANNE. Anyway . . . the only one I worry about is you. I feel awfully guilty about you. (*She sits on the stool near* MARGOT, *putting on* MARGOT'S *high-heeled shoes.*)

MARGOT. What about?

ANNE. I mean, every time I go into Peter's room, I have a feeling I may be hurting you. (MARGOT *shakes her head.*) I know if it were me, I'd be wild. I'd be desperately jealous, if it were me.

MARGOT. Well, I'm not.

ANNE. You don't feel badly? Really? Truly? You're not jealous?

MARGOT. Of course I'm jealous . . . jealous that you've got something to get up in the morning for . . . But jealous of you and Peter? No.

(ANNE *goes back to the mirror.*)

ANNE. Maybe there's nothing to be jealous of. Maybe he doesn't really like me. Maybe I'm just taking the place of his cat . . . (*She picks up a pair of short, white gloves, putting them on.*) Wouldn't you like to come in with us?

MARGOT. I have a book.

(*The sound of the children playing outside*

fades out. In the main room DUSSEL *can stand it no longer. He jumps up, going to the bedroom door and knocking sharply.*)

DUSSEL. Will you please let me in my room!

ANNE. Just a minute, dear, dear Mr. Dussel. (*She picks up her Mother's pink stole and adjusts it elegantly over her shoulder, then gives a last look in the mirror.*) Well, here I go . . . to run the gauntlet. (*She starts out, followed by* MARGOT.)

DUSSEL (*as she appears—sarcastic*). Thank you so much.

(DUSSEL *goes into his room.* ANNE *goes toward* PETER'S *room, passing* MRS. VAN DAAN *and her parents at the center table.*)

MRS. VAN DAAN. My God, look at her! (ANNE *pays no attention. She knocks at* PETER'S *door.*) I don't know what good it is to have a son. I never see him. He wouldn't care if I killed myself. (PETER *opens the door and stands aside for* ANNE *to come in.*) Just a minute, Anne. (*She goes to them at the door.*) I'd like to say a few words to my son. Do you mind? (PETER *and* ANNE *stand waiting.*) Peter, I don't want you staying up till all hours tonight. You've got to have your sleep. You're a growing boy. You hear?

MRS. FRANK. Anne won't stay late. She's going to bed promptly at nine. Aren't you, Anne?

ANNE. Yes, Mother . . . (*To* MRS. VAN DAAN) May we go now?

MRS. VAN DAAN. Are you asking me? I didn't know I had anything to say about it.

MRS. FRANK. Listen for the chimes, Anne dear.

(*The two young people go off into* PETER'S *room, shutting the door after them.*)

MRS. VAN DAAN (*to* MRS. FRANK). In my day it was the boys who called on the girls. Not the girls on the boys.

MRS. FRANK. You know how young people like to feel that they have secrets. Peter's room is the only place where they can talk.

MRS. VAN DAAN. Talk! That's not what they called it when I was young.

(MRS. VAN DAAN *goes off to the bathroom.* MARGOT *settles down to read her book.* MR. FRANK *puts his papers away and brings a chess game to the center table. He and* MRS. FRANK *start to play. In* PETER'S *room,* ANNE *speaks to* PETER, *indignant, humiliated.*)

ANNE. Aren't they awful? Aren't they impossible? Treating us as if we were still in the nursery. (*She sits on the cot.* PETER *gets a bottle of pop and two glasses.*)

PETER. Don't let it bother you. It doesn't bother me.

ANNE. I suppose you can't really blame them . . . *they* think back to what they were like at our age. They don't realize how much more advanced we are . . . When you think what wonderful discussions we've had! . . . Oh, I forgot. I was going to bring you some more pictures.

PETER. Oh, these are fine, thanks.

ANNE. Don't you want some more? Miep just brought me some new ones.

PETER. Maybe later. (*He gives her a glass of pop and taking some for himself, sits down facing her.*)

ANNE (*looking up at one of the photographs*). I remember when I got that . . . I won it. I bet Jopie that I could eat five ice-cream cones. We'd all been playing ping-pong . . . We used to have heavenly times . . . we'd finish up with ice cream at the Delphi, or the Oasis, where Jews were allowed

Anne's bedroom wall in the secret annex, decorated with her collection of movie stars.

. . . there'd always be a lot of boys . . . we'd laugh and joke . . . I'd like to go back to it for a few days or a week. But after that I know I'd be bored to death. I think more seriously about life now. I want to be a journalist . . . or something. I love to write. What do you want to do?

PETER. I thought I might go off some place . . . work on a farm or something . . . some job that doesn't take much brains.

ANNE. You shouldn't talk that way. You've got the most awful inferiority complex.

PETER. I know I'm not smart.

ANNE. That isn't true. You're much better than I am in dozens of things . . . arithmetic and algebra and . . . well, you're a million times better than I am in algebra. (*With sudden directness*) You like Margot, don't you? Right from the start you liked her, liked her much better than me.

PETER (*uncomfortably*). Oh, I don't know.

(*In the main room* MRS. VAN DAAN *comes from the bathroom and goes over to the sink, polishing a coffeepot.*)

ANNE. It's all right. Everyone feels that way. Margot's so good. She's sweet and bright and beautiful and I'm not.

PETER. I wouldn't say that.

ANNE. Oh, no, I'm not. I know that. I know quite well that I'm not a beauty. I never have been and never shall be.

PETER. I don't agree at all. I think you're pretty.

ANNE. That's not true!

PETER. And another thing. You've changed . . . from at first, I mean.

ANNE. I have?

PETER. I used to think you were awful noisy.

ANNE. And what do you think now, Peter? How have I changed?

PETER. Well . . . er . . . you're . . . quieter.

(*In his room* DUSSEL *takes his pajamas and*

toilet articles and goes into the bathroom to change.)

ANNE. I'm glad you don't just hate me.

PETER. I never said that.

ANNE. I bet when you get out of here you'll never think of me again.

PETER. That's crazy.

ANNE. When you get back with all of your friends, you're going to say . . . now what did I ever see in that Mrs. Quack Quack.

PETER. I haven't got any friends.

ANNE. Oh, Peter, of course you have. Everyone has friends.

PETER. Not me. I don't want any. I get along all right without them.

ANNE. Does that mean you can get along without me? I think of myself as your friend.

PETER. No. If they were all like you, it'd be different.

(*He takes the glasses and the bottle and puts them away. There is a second's silence and then* ANNE *speaks, hesitantly, shyly.*)

ANNE. Peter, did you ever kiss a girl?

PETER. Yes. Once.

ANNE (*to cover her feelings*). That picture's crooked. (PETER *goes over, straightening the photograph.*) Was she pretty?

PETER. Huh?

ANNE. The girl that you kissed.

PETER. I don't know. I was blindfolded. (*He comes back and sits down again.*) It was a party. One of those kissing games.

ANNE (*relieved*). Oh, I don't suppose that really counts, does it?

PETER. It didn't with me.

ANNE. I've been kissed twice. Once a man I'd never seen before kissed me on the cheek when he picked me up off the ice and I was crying. And the other was Mr. Koophuis,[1] a friend of Father's who kissed my hand. You wouldn't say those counted, would you?

PETER. I wouldn't say so.

ANNE. I know almost for certain that Margot would never kiss anyone unless she was engaged to them. And I'm sure too that Mother never touched a man before Pim. But I don't know . . . things are so different now. . . . What do you think? Do you think a girl shouldn't kiss anyone except if she's engaged or something? It's so hard to try to think what to do, when here we are with the whole world falling around our ears and you think . . . well . . . you don't know what's going to happen tomorrow and . . . What do you think?

PETER. I suppose it'd depend on the girl. Some girls, anything they do's wrong. But others . . . well . . . it wouldn't necessarily be wrong with them. (*The carillon starts to strike nine o'clock.*) I've always thought that when two people . . .

ANNE. Nine o'clock. I have to go.

PETER. That's right.

ANNE (*without moving*). Good night.

(*There is a second's pause, then* PETER *gets up and moves toward the door.*)

PETER. You won't let them stop you coming?

ANNE. No. (*She rises and starts for the door.*) Sometime I might bring my diary. There are so many things in it that I want to talk over with you. There's a lot about you.

PETER. What kind of things?

---

1. *Mr. Koophuis* (kōp′hous).

ANNE. I wouldn't want you to see some of it. I thought you were a nothing, just the way you thought about me.

PETER. Did you change your mind, the way I changed my mind about you?

ANNE. Well . . . You'll see . . .

(*For a second* ANNE *stands looking up at* PETER, *longing for him to kiss her. As he makes no move she turns away. Then suddenly* PETER *grabs her awkwardly in his arms, kissing her on the cheek.* ANNE *walks out dazed. She stands for a minute, her back to the people in the main room. As she regains her poise she goes to her mother and father and* MARGOT *silently kissing them. They murmur their good nights to her. As she is about to open her bedroom door, she catches sight of* MRS. VAN DAAN. *She goes quickly to her, taking her face in her hands and kissing her first on one cheek and then on the other. Then she hurries off into her room.* MRS. VAN DAAN *looks after her, and then looks over at* PETER'S *room. Her suspicions are confirmed.*)

MRS. VAN DAAN. (*She knows.*) Ah hah!

(*The lights dim out. The curtain falls on the scene. In the darkness* ANNE'S VOICE *comes faintly at first and then with growing strength.*)

ANNE'S VOICE. By this time we all know each other so well that if anyone starts to tell a story, the rest can finish it for him. We're having to cut down still further on our meals. What makes it worse, the rats have been at work again. They've carried off some of our precious food. Even Mr. Dussel wishes now that Mouschi was here. Thursday, the twentieth of April, nineteen forty-four. Invasion fever[2] is mounting every day. Miep tells us that people outside talk of nothing else. For myself, life has become much more pleasant. I often go to Peter's room after supper. Oh, don't think I'm in love, because I'm not. But it does make life more bearable to have someone with whom you can exchange views. No more tonight. P.S. . . . I must be honest. I must confess that I actually live for the next meeting. Is there anything lovelier than to sit under the skylight and feel the sun on your cheeks and have a darling boy in your arms? I admit now that I'm glad the Van Daans had a son and not a daughter. I've outgrown another dress. That's the third. I'm having to wear Margot's clothes after all. I'm working hard on my French and am now reading *La Belle Nivernaise*.[3]

(*As she is saying the last lines, the curtain rises on the scene. The lights dim on, as* ANNE'S VOICE *fades out.*)

---

2. *Invasion fever*, the expectation that the Allies would invade Europe to free it from German occupation. The invasion actually began on June 6, 1944, known as "D-Day."

3. *La Belle Nivernaise* (lä bel′ niv ər nez′), a tale by Alphonse Daudet, a nineteenth-century French novelist.

THINK AND DISCUSS
Understanding
1. Why is Mrs. Frank concerned about Anne's behavior?
2. How does Margot explain the difference between their mother and Anne?
3. How does Mrs. Van Daan feel about Anne's visits to Peter's room?
4. What are some of the things Peter and Anne talk about?

Analyzing
5. In what ways are Anne and Margot different?
6. What feelings exist between Mrs. Frank and each of her daughters?
7. How do you account for the closer relationship between Mrs. Frank and Margot?
8. How does the relationship between Anne and Peter seem to have affected each of them? Give examples to support your opinions.

THINKING SKILLS
Evaluating
1. Does the relationship between Anne and Margot seem to be a realistic one? Give reasons to support your answer.
2. Are the concerns of Anne and Peter typical for people their age? Explain.
3. Are the attitudes of Mrs. Frank and Mrs. Van Daan believable? Explain.

SCENE THREE

It is night, a few weeks later. Everyone is in bed. There is complete quiet. In the VAN DAANS' *room a match flares up for a moment and then is quickly put out.* MR. VAN DAAN, *in bare feet, dressed in underwear and trousers, is dimly seen coming stealthily down the stairs and into the main room, where* MR. *and* MRS. FRANK *and* MARGOT *are sleeping. He goes to the food safe and again lights a match. Then he cautiously opens the safe, taking out a half-loaf of bread. As he closes the safe, it creaks. He stands rigid.* MRS. FRANK *sits up in bed. She sees him.*

MRS. FRANK (*screaming*). Otto! Otto! *Komme schnell.*[1]

(*The rest of the people wake, hurriedly getting up.*)

MR. FRANK. *Was ist los? Was ist passiert?*[2]

(DUSSEL, *followed by* ANNE, *comes from his room.*)

MRS. FRANK (*as she rushes over to* MR. VAN DAAN). *Er stiehlt das Essen!*[3]

DUSSEL (*grabbing* MR. VAN DAAN). You! You! Give me that.

MRS. VAN DAAN (*coming down the stairs*). Putti . . . Putti . . . what is it?

DUSSEL (*his hands on* VAN DAAN'S *neck*). You dirty thief . . . stealing food . . . you good-for-nothing . . .

MR. FRANK. Mr. Dussel! For God's sake! Help me, Peter!

(PETER *comes over, trying, with* MR. FRANK, *to separate the two struggling men.*)

PETER. Let him go! Let go!

(DUSSEL *drops* MR. VAN DAAN, *pushing him*

---

1. *Komme schnell!* Hurry!
2. *Was ist los? Was ist passiert?* What's the matter? What happened?
3. *Er stiehlt das Essen!* He is stealing food.

away. He shows them the end of a loaf of bread that he has taken from VAN DAAN.)

DUSSEL. You greedy, selfish . . . !

(MARGOT *turns on the lights.*)

MRS. VAN DAAN. Putti . . . what is it?

(*All of* MRS. FRANK'S *gentleness, her self-control, is gone. She is outraged, in a frenzy of indignation.*)

MRS. FRANK. The bread! He was stealing the bread!

DUSSEL. It was you, and all the time we thought it was the rats!

MR. FRANK. Mr. Van Daan, how could you!

MR. VAN DAAN. I'm hungry.

MRS. FRANK. We're all of us hungry! I see the children getting thinner and thinner. Your own son Peter . . . I've heard him moan in his sleep, he's so hungry. And you come in the night and steal food that should go to them . . . to the children!

MRS. VAN DAAN (*going to* MR. VAN DAAN *protectively*). He needs more food than the rest of us. He's used to more. He's a big man. (MR. VAN DAAN *breaks away, going over and sitting on the couch.*)

MRS. FRANK (*turning on* MRS. VAN DAAN). And you . . . you're worse than he is! You're a mother, and yet you sacrifice your child to this man . . . this . . . this . . .

MR. FRANK. Edith! Edith!

(MARGOT *picks up the pink woolen stole, putting it over her mother's shoulders.*)

MRS. FRANK (*paying no attention, going on to* MRS. VAN DAAN). Don't think I haven't seen you! Always saving the choicest bits for him! I've watched you day after day and I've held my tongue. But not any longer! Not after this! Now I want him to go! I want him to get out of here!

MR. FRANK. Edith!

MR. VAN DAAN. Get out of here? } (*Together*)

MRS. VAN DAAN. What do you mean?

MRS. FRANK. Just that! Take your things and get out!

MR. FRANK (*to* MRS. FRANK). You're speaking in anger. You cannot mean what you are saying.

MRS. FRANK. I mean exactly that!

(MRS. VAN DAAN *takes a cover from the* FRANKS' *bed, pulling it about her.*)

MR. FRANK. For two long years we have lived here, side by side. We have respected each other's rights . . . we have managed to live in peace. Are we now going to throw it all away? I know this will never happen again, will it, Mr. Van Daan?

MR. VAN DAAN. No. No.

MRS. FRANK. He steals once! He'll steal again!

(MR. VAN DAAN, *holding his stomach, starts for the bathroom.* ANNE *puts her arms around him, helping him up the step.*)

MR. FRANK. Edith, please. Let us be calm. We'll all go to our rooms . . . and afterwards we'll sit down quietly and talk this out . . . we'll find some way . . .

MRS. FRANK. No! No! No more talk! I want them to leave!

MRS. VAN DAAN. You'd put us out, on the streets?

MRS. FRANK. There are other hiding places.

MRS. VAN DAAN. A cellar . . . a closet. I know. And we have no money left even to pay for that.

MRS. FRANK. I'll give you money. Out of my own pocket I'll give it gladly.

(*She gets her purse from a shelf and comes back with it.*)

MRS. VAN DAAN. Mr. Frank, you told Putti

you'd never forget what he'd done for you when you came to Amsterdam. You said you could never repay him, that you . . .

MRS. FRANK (*counting out money*). If my husband had any obligation to you, he's paid, over and over.

MR. FRANK. Edith, I've never seen you like this before. I don't know you.

MRS. FRANK. I should have spoken out long ago.

DUSSEL. You can't be nice to some people.

MRS. VAN DAAN (*turning on* DUSSEL). There would have been plenty for all of us, if *you* hadn't come here!

MR. FRANK. We don't need the Nazis to destroy us. We're destroying ourselves.

(*He sits down, with his head in his hands. MRS. FRANK goes to MRS. VAN DAAN.*)

MRS. FRANK (*giving* MRS. VAN DAAN *some money*). Give this to Miep. She'll find you a place.

ANNE. Mother, you're not putting *Peter* out. Peter hasn't done anything.

MRS. FRANK. He'll stay, of course. When I say I must protect the children, I mean Peter too.

(PETER *rises from the steps where he has been sitting.*)

PETER. I'd have to go if Father goes.

(MR. VAN DAAN *comes from the bathroom. MRS. VAN DAAN hurries to him and takes him to the couch. Then she gets water from the sink to bathe his face.*)

MRS. FRANK (*while this is going on*). He's no father to you . . . that man! He doesn't know what it is to be a father!

PETER (*starting for his room*). I wouldn't feel right. I couldn't stay.

MRS. FRANK. Very well, then. I'm sorry.

ANNE (*rushing over to* PETER). No, Peter! No! (PETER *goes into his room, closing the door after him.* ANNE *turns back to her mother, crying.*) I don't care about the food. They can have mine! I don't want it! Only don't send them away. It'll be daylight soon. They'll be caught . . .

MARGOT (*putting her arms comfortingly around* ANNE). Please, Mother!

MRS. FRANK. They're not going now. They'll stay here until Miep finds them a place. (*To* MRS. VAN DAAN) But one thing I insist on! He must never come down here again! He must never come to this room where the food is stored! We'll divide what we have . . . an equal share for each! (DUSSEL *hurries over to get a sack of potatoes from the food safe.* MRS. FRANK *goes on, to* MRS. VAN DAAN). You can cook it here and take it up to him.

(DUSSEL *brings the sack of potatoes back to the center table.*)

MARGOT. Oh, no. No. We haven't sunk so far that we're going to fight over a handful of rotten potatoes.

DUSSEL (*dividing the potatoes into piles*). Mrs. Frank, Mr. Frank, Margot, Anne, Peter, Mrs. Van Daan, Mr. Van Daan, myself . . . Mrs. Frank . . .

(*The buzzer sounds in* MIEP'S *signal.*)

MR. FRANK. It's Miep! (*He hurries over, getting his overcoat and putting it on.*)

MARGOT. At this hour?

MRS. FRANK. It is trouble.

MR. FRANK (*as he starts down to unbolt the door*). I beg you, don't let her see a thing like this!

DUSSEL (*counting without stopping*). . . .

Anne, Peter, Mrs. Van Daan, Mr. Van Daan, myself . . .

MARGOT (*to* DUSSEL). Stop it! Stop it!

DUSSEL. . . . Mr. Frank, Margot, Anne, Peter, Mrs. Van Daan, Mr. Van Daan, myself, Mrs. Frank . . .

MRS. VAN DAAN. You're keeping the big ones for yourself! All the big ones . . . Look at the size of that! . . . And that!

(DUSSEL *continues on with his dividing.* PETER, *with his shirt and trousers on, comes from his room.*)

MARGOT. Stop it! Stop it!

(*We hear* MIEP'S *excited voice speaking to* MR. FRANK *below.*)

MIEP. Mr. Frank . . . the most wonderful news! . . . The invasion has begun.

MR. FRANK. Go on, tell them! Tell them!

(MIEP *comes running up the steps, ahead of* MR. FRANK. *She has a man's raincoat on over her nightclothes and a bunch of orange-colored flowers in her hand.*)

MIEP. Did you hear that, everybody? Did you hear what I said? The invasion has begun! The invasion!

(*They all stare at* MIEP, *unable to grasp what she is telling them.* PETER *is the first to recover his wits.*)

PETER. Where?

MRS. VAN DAAN. When? When, Miep?

MIEP. It began early this morning . . .

(*As she talks on, the realization of what she has said begins to dawn on them. Everyone goes crazy. A wild demonstration takes place.* MRS. FRANK *hugs* MR. VAN DAAN.)

MRS. FRANK. Oh, Mr. Van Daan, did you hear that?

(DUSSEL *embraces* MRS. VAN DAAN. PETER *grabs a frying pan and parades around the room, beating on it, singing the Dutch National Anthem.* ANNE *and* MARGOT *follow him, singing, weaving in and out among the excited grownups.* MARGOT *breaks away to take the flowers from* MIEP *and distribute them to everyone. While this pandemonium is going on* MRS. FRANK *tries to make herself heard above the excitement.*)

MRS. FRANK (*to* MIEP). How do you know?

MIEP. The radio . . . The B.B.C.![4] They said they landed on the coast of Normandy!

PETER. The British?

MIEP. British, Americans, French, Dutch, Poles, Norwegians . . . all of them! More than four thousand ships! Churchill spoke, and General Eisenhower![5] D-Day they call it!

MR. FRANK. Thank God, it's come!

MRS. VAN DAAN. At last!

MIEP (*starting out*). I'm going to tell Mr. Kraler. This'll be better than any blood transfusion.

MR. FRANK (*stopping her*). What part of Normandy did they land, did they say?

MIEP. Normandy . . . that's all I know now . . . I'll be up the minute I hear some more! (*She goes hurriedly out.*)

MR. FRANK (*to* MRS. FRANK). What did I tell you? What did I tell you?

(MRS. FRANK *indicates that he has forgotten to bolt the door after* MIEP. *He hurries down the steps.* MR. VAN DAAN, *sitting on the couch, suddenly breaks into a convulsive sob. Everybody looks at him, bewildered.*)

MRS. VAN DAAN (*hurrying to him*). Putti! Putti! What is it? What happened?

---

4. **B.B.C.**, the British Broadcasting Corporation.
5. **Churchill . . . Eisenhower.** Churchill was Prime Minister of England. Eisenhower was supreme commander of the Allied forces. He later became President of the U.S.

MR. VAN DAAN. Please. I'm so ashamed. (MR. FRANK *comes back up the steps.*)

DUSSEL. Oh, for God's sake!

MRS. VAN DAAN. Don't, Putti.

MARGOT. It doesn't matter now!

MR. FRANK (*going to* MR. VAN DAAN). Didn't you hear what Miep said? The invasion has come! We're going to be liberated! This is a time to celebrate! (*He embraces* MRS. FRANK *and then hurries to the cupboard and gets the cognac and a glass.*)

MR. VAN DAAN. To steal bread from children!

MRS. FRANK. We've all done things that we're ashamed of.

ANNE. Look at me, the way I've treated Mother . . . so mean and horrid to her.

MRS. FRANK. No, Anneke, no.

(ANNE *runs to her mother, putting her arms around her.*)

ANNE. Oh, Mother, I was. I was awful.

MR. VAN DAAN. Not like me. No one is as bad as me!

DUSSEL (*to* MR. VAN DAAN). Stop it now! Let's be happy!

MR. FRANK (*giving* MR. VAN DAAN *a glass of cognac*). Here! Here! *Schnapps! Locheim.*[6]

(VAN DAAN *takes the cognac. They all watch him. He gives them a feeble smile.* ANNE *puts up her fingers in a V-for-Victory sign. As* VAN DAAN *gives an answering V-sign, they are startled to hear a loud sob from behind them. It is* MRS. FRANK, *stricken with remorse. She is sitting on the other side of the room.*)

MRS. FRANK (*through her sobs*). When I think of the terrible things I said . . .

(MR. FRANK, ANNE, *and* MARGOT *hurry to her, trying to comfort her.* MR. VAN DAAN *brings her his glass of cognac.*)

MR. VAN DAAN. No! No! You were right!

MRS. FRANK. That I should speak that way to you! . . . Our friends! . . . Our guests! (*She starts to cry again.*)

DUSSEL. Stop it, you're spoiling the whole invasion!

(*As they are comforting her, the lights dim out. The curtain falls.*)

ANNE'S VOICE (*faintly at first and then with growing strength*). We're all in much better spirits these days. There's still excellent news of the invasion. The best part about it is that I have a feeling that friends are coming. Who knows? Maybe I'll be back in school by fall. Ha, ha! The joke is on us! The warehouse man doesn't know a thing and we are paying him all that money! . . . Wednesday, the second of July, nineteen forty-four. The invasion seems temporarily to be bogged down. Mr. Kraler has to have an operation, which looks bad. The Gestapo have found the radio that was stolen. Mr. Drussel says they'll trace it back and back to the thief, and then, it's just a matter of time till they get to us. Everyone is low. Even poor Pim can't raise their spirits. I have often been downcast myself . . . but never in despair. I can shake off everything if I write. But . . . and that is the great question . . . will I ever be able to write well? I want to so much. I want to go on living even after my death. Another birthday has gone by, so now I am fifteen. Already I know what I want. I have a goal, an opinion.

(*As this is being said—the curtain rises on the scene, the lights dim on, and* ANNE'S VOICE *fades out.*)

---

6. *Schnapps!* (schnäps) *Locheim!* (lə HĪ′əm). Mr. Frank is proposing a toast to life.

THINK AND DISCUSS

Understanding

1. What event causes Mrs. Frank's rage?
2. What reason does Mrs. Van Daan give for her husband's behavior?
3. What causes an abrupt change in everyone's mood?

Analyzing

4. Why do you think Mrs. Frank reacts to Mr. Van Daan as she does?
5. Consider Peter's previous attitude toward his father. Why do you think he shows loyalty now?
6. During this scene Mr. Frank says, "We don't need the Nazis to destroy us. We're destroying ourselves." What attitudes and actions of various characters justify his conclusion?

Extending

7. If Miep hadn't come with her news, what do you think might have happened? Give reasons why you think as you do.
8. Is the general reconciliation prompted by Miep's news likely to last? Support your opinion.
9. What might Anne's closing diary entry foreshadow?

SCENE FOUR

It is an afternoon a few weeks later . . . Everyone but MARGOT *is in the main room. There is a sense of great tension.*

Both MRS. FRANK *and* MR. VAN DAAN *are nervously pacing back and forth,* DUSSEL *is standing at the window, looking down fixedly at the street below.* PETER *is at the center table, trying to do his lessons.* ANNE *sits opposite him, writing in her diary.* MRS. VAN DAAN *is seated on the couch, her eyes on* MR. FRANK *as he sits reading.*

The sound of a telephone ringing comes from the office below. They all are rigid, listening tensely. MR. DUSSEL *rushes down to* MR. FRANK.

DUSSEL. There it goes again, the telephone! Mr. Frank, do you hear?

MR. FRANK (*quietly*). Yes. I hear.

DUSSEL (*pleading, insistent*). But this is the third time, Mr. Frank! The third time in quick succession! It's a signal! I tell you it's Miep, trying to get us! For some reason she can't come to us and she's trying to warn us of something!

MR. FRANK. Please. Please.

MR. VAN DAAN (*to* DUSSEL). You're wasting your breath.

DUSSEL. Something has happened, Mr. Frank. For three days now Miep hasn't been to see us! And today not a man has come to work. There hasn't been a sound in the building!

MRS. FRANK. Perhaps it's Sunday. We may have lost track of the days.

MR. VAN DAAN (*to* ANNE). You with the diary there. What day is it?

DUSSEL (*going to* MRS. FRANK). I don't lose track of the days! I know exactly what day it is! It's Friday, the fourth of August. Friday, and not a man at work. (*He rushes back to* MR. FRANK, *pleading with him, almost in tears.*) I tell you Mr. Kraler's dead. That's the only explanation. He's dead and they've closed down the building, and Miep's trying to tell us!

MR. FRANK. She'd never telephone us.

DUSSEL (*frantic*). Mr. Frank, answer that! I beg you, answer it!

MR. FRANK. No.

MR. VAN DAAN. Just pick it up and listen. You don't have to speak. Just listen and see if it's Miep.

DUSSEL (*speaking at the same time*). For God's sake . . . I ask you.

MR. FRANK. No. I've told you, no. I'll do nothing that might let anyone know we're in the building.

PETER. Mr. Frank's right.

MR. VAN DAAN. There's no need to tell us what side you're on.

MR. FRANK. If we wait patiently, quietly, I believe that help will come.

(*There is silence for a minute as they all listen to the telephone ringing.*)

DUSSEL. I'm going down. (*He rushes down the steps.* MR. FRANK *tries ineffectually to hold him.* DUSSEL *runs to the lower door, unbolting it. The telephone stops ringing.* DUSSEL *bolts the door and comes slowly back up the steps.*) Too late. (MR. FRANK *goes to* MARGOT *in* ANNE'S *bedroom.*)

MR. VAN DAAN. So we just wait here until we die.

MRS. VAN DAAN (*hysterically*). I can't stand it! I'll kill myself! I'll kill myself!

MR. VAN DAAN. For God's sake, stop it!

(*In the distance, a German military band is heard playing a Viennese waltz.*)

Anne

MRS. VAN DAAN. I think you'd be glad if I did! I think you want me to die!

MR. VAN DAAN. Whose fault is it we're here? (MRS. VAN DAAN *starts for her room. He follows, talking at her.*) We could've been safe somewhere . . . in America or Switzerland. But no! No! You wouldn't leave when I wanted to. You couldn't leave your things. You couldn't leave your precious furniture.

MRS. VAN DAAN. Don't touch me!

(*She hurries up the stairs, followed by* MR. VAN DAAN. PETER, *unable to bear it, goes to his room.* ANNE *looks after him, deeply concerned.* DUSSEL *returns to his post at the window.* MR. FRANK *comes back into the main room and takes a book, trying to read.* MRS. FRANK *sits near the sink, starting to peel some potatoes.* ANNE *quietly goes to* PETER'S *room, closing the door after her.* PETER *is lying face down on the cot.* ANNE *leans over him, holding him in her arms, trying to bring him out of his despair.*)

ANNE. Look, Peter, the sky. (*She looks up through the skylight.*) What a lovely, lovely day! Aren't the clouds beautiful? You know what I do when it seems as if I couldn't stand being cooped up for one more minute? I *think* myself out. I think myself on a walk in the park where I used to go with Pim. Where the jonquils and the crocus and violets grow down the slopes. You know the most wonderful part about *thinking* yourself out? You can have it any way you like. You can have roses and violets and chrysanthemums all blooming at the same time . . . It's funny . . . I used to take it all for granted . . . and now I've gone crazy about everything to do with nature. Haven't you?

PETER. I've just gone crazy. I think if something doesn't happen soon . . . if we don't get out of here . . . I can't stand much more of it!

ANNE (*softly*). I wish you had a religion, Peter.

PETER. No thanks! Not me!

ANNE. Oh, I don't mean you have to be Orthodox[1] . . . or believe in heaven and hell and purgatory and things . . . I just mean some religion . . . it doesn't matter what. Just to believe in something! When I think of all that's out there . . . the trees . . . and flowers . . . and seagulls . . . when I think of the dearness of you, Peter, . . . and the goodness of the people we know . . . Mr. Kraler, Miep, Dirk, the vegetable man, all risking their lives for us every day . . . When I think of these good things, I'm not afraid any more . . . I find myself, and God, and I . . .

(PETER *interrupts, getting up and walking away.*)

PETER. That's fine! But when I begin to think, I get mad! Look at us, hiding out for two years. Not able to move! Caught here like . . . waiting for them to come and get us . . . and all for what?

ANNE. We're not the only people that've had to suffer. There've always been people that've had to . . . sometimes one race . . . sometimes another . . . and yet . . .

PETER. That doesn't make me feel any better!

ANNE (*going to him*). I know it's terrible, trying to have any faith . . . when people are doing such horrible . . . But you know what I sometimes think? I think the world may be going through a phase, the way I was with Mother. It'll pass, maybe not for hundreds of years, but some day . . . I still believe, in spite of everything, that people are really good at heart.

PETER. I want to see something now . . . Not a thousand years from now!

(*He goes over, sitting down again on the cot.*)

ANNE. But, Peter, if you'd only look at it as part of a great pattern . . . that we're just a little minute in the life . . . (*She breaks off.*) Listen to us, going at each other like a couple of stupid grownups! Look at the sky now. Isn't it lovely? (*She holds out her*

---

1. **Orthodox,** a follower of the branch of Judaism that keeps most closely to ancient ritual, customs, and traditions.

hand to him. PETER *takes it and rises, stand-*
ing with her at the window looking out, his
arms around her.) Some day, when we're
outside again, I'm going to . . .
(*She breaks off as she hears the sound of a*
car, its brakes squealing as it comes to a sud-
den stop. The people in the other rooms also
become aware of the sound. They listen
tensely. Another car roars up to a screeching
stop. ANNE *and* PETER *come from* PETER'S
room. MR. *and* MRS. VAN DAAN *creep down*
the stairs. DUSSEL *comes out from his room.*
Everyone is listening, hardly breathing. A
doorbell clangs again and again in the build-
ing below. MR. FRANK *starts quietly down the*
steps to the door. DUSSEL *and* PETER *follow*
him. The others stand rigid, waiting, terrified.

   In a few seconds DUSSEL *comes stumbling*
back up the steps. He shakes off PETER'S *help*
and goes to his room. MR. FRANK *bolts the*
door below, and comes slowly back up the
steps. Their eyes are all on him as he stands
there for a minute. They realize that what they
feared has happened. MRS. VAN DAAN *starts to*
whimper. MR. VAN DAAN *puts her gently in a*
chair, and then hurries off up the stairs to their
room to collect their things. PETER *goes to*
comfort his mother. There is a sound of violent
pounding on a door below.)

MR. FRANK (*quietly*). For the past two years
we have lived in fear. Now we can live in
hope.

(*The pounding below becomes more insistent.*
There are muffled sounds of voices, shouting
commands.)

MEN'S VOICES. *Auf machen! Da drinnen! Auf*
machen! Schnell! Schnell! Schnell![2] *etc., etc.*
(*The street door below is forced open. We hear*
the heavy tread of footsteps coming up. MR.

View from the attic window of the annex, showing the bell
tower of the Westertoren

FRANK *gets two school-bags from the shelves,*
and gives one to ANNE *and the other to*
MARGOT. *He goes to get a bag for* MRS.
FRANK. *The sound of feet coming up grows*
louder. PETER *comes to* ANNE, *kissing her*
good-by, then he goes to his room to collect his
things. The buzzer of their door starts to ring.
MR. FRANK *brings* MRS. FRANK *a bag. They*
stand together, waiting. We hear the thud of
gun butts on the door, trying to break it down.

   ANNE *stands, holding her school satchel,*
looking over at her father and mother with a
soft, reassuring smile. She is no longer a child,

---

2. *Auf machen . . . Schnell!* Open up in there! Hurry up!

but a woman with courage to meet whatever lies ahead.

The lights dim out. The curtain falls on the scene. We hear a mighty crash as the door is shattered. After a second ANNE'S VOICE *is heard.)*

ANNE'S VOICE. And so it seems our stay is over. They are waiting for us now. They've allowed us five minutes to get our things. We can each take a bag and whatever it will hold of clothing. Nothing else. So, dear Diary, that means I must leave you behind. Good-by for a while. P.S. Please, please, Miep, or Mr. Kraler, or anyone else. If you should find this diary, will you please keep it safe for me, because some day I hope . . .

(Her voice stops abruptly. There is silence. After a second the curtain rises.)

THINK AND DISCUSS
Understanding
1. Why does Mr. Dussel plead with Mr. Frank to answer the phone?
2. Why does Mr. Frank refuse to answer it?
3. In what ways do we learn that the Nazis have found the Secret Annex?

Analyzing
4. What does Anne say to Peter in their last talk?
5. How does Peter respond to Anne's ideas?

6. How do the inhabitants behave when the police arrive?

Extending
7. Mr. Frank says, "For the past two years we have lived in fear. Now we can live in hope." What is your reaction to this statement?
8. The last entry in Anne's diary is a plea to Miep, or Mr. Kraler, or anyone who should find her diary to "keep it safe for me, because some day I hope . . ." How do you think Anne might have finished this entry?

SCENE FIVE

It is again the afternoon in November, 1945.
The rooms are as we saw them in the first scene.
MR. KRALER *has joined* MIEP *and* MR. FRANK.
There are coffee cups on the table. We see a great
change in MR. FRANK. *He is calm now. His bit-*
terness is gone. He slowly turns a few pages of
the diary. They are blank.

MR. FRANK. No more. (*He closes the diary and*
puts it down on the couch beside him.)

MIEP. I'd gone to the country to find food.
When I got back the block was surrounded
by police . . .

MR. KRALER. We made it our business to
learn how they knew. It was the thief . . .
the thief who told them.

(MIEP *goes up to the gas burner, bringing back*
a pot of coffee.)

MR. FRANK (*after a pause*). It seems strange to
say this, that anyone could be happy in a
concentration camp. But Anne was happy
in the camp in Holland where they first
took us. After two years of being shut up in
these rooms, she could be out . . . out in
the sunshine and the fresh air that she
loved.

MIEP (*offering the coffee to* MR. FRANK). A little
more?

MR. FRANK (*holding out his cup to her*). The
news of the war was good. The British and
Americans were sweeping through France.
We felt sure that they would get to us in
time. In September we were told that we
were to be shipped to Poland . . . The men
to one camp. The women to another. I was
sent to Auschwitz. They went to Belsen.[1]
In January we were freed, the few of us
who were left. The war wasn't yet over, so
it took us a long time to get home. We'd be
sent here and there behind the lines where
we'd be safe. Each time our train would
stop . . . at a siding, or a crossing . . .
we'd all get out and go from group to
group . . . Where were you? Were you at
Belsen? At Buchenwald? At Mauthausen?
Is it possible that you knew my wife? Did
you ever see my husband? My son? My
daughter? That's how I found out about
my wife's death . . . of Margot, the Van
Daans . . . Dussel. But Anne . . . I still
hoped. . . . Yesterday I went to Rotterdam. I'd heard of a woman there. . . .
She'd been in Belsen with Anne . . . I
know now.

(*He picks up the diary again, and turns the*
pages back to find a certain passage. As he
finds it we hear ANNE'S VOICE.)

ANNE'S VOICE. In spite of everything, I still
believe that people are really good at heart.

(MR. FRANK *slowly closes the diary.*)

MR. FRANK. She puts me to shame.

(*They are silent.*)

The CURTAIN *falls.*

---

1. *Auschwitz* (oush'vits) . . . *Belsen,* Nazi concentration
camps in Poland and Germany, respectively. Buchenwald
(bü'ʜən vält'), mentioned later, was in Germany.

THINK AND DISCUSS

Understanding

1. What happened to the Van Daans, Dussel, Mrs. Frank, and Margot?

Analyzing

2. Why does Mr. Frank go to Rotterdam and what does he learn there?

Extending

3. Anne says, "In spite of everything, I still believe that people are really good at heart." What is your reaction to this statement? Explain.

4. What is implied by Mr. Frank's reading Anne's diary entry and then saying, "She puts me to shame."

REVIEWING: Flashback HT
See Handbook of Literary Terms, p. 665.

A **flashback** shows action that happened at an earlier time. Flashback can shed light on characters and events of the present by providing background information on them.

1. What is the time relationship between Act One, Scene One, and Act Two, Scene Five?
2. What has Mr. Frank been doing during the time between these scenes?
3. How much of this play is a flashback?

COMPOSITION ✎

Reading/Writing Log

During their last real talk, Anne and Peter speak in *voices* that are very different from each other. As you think about (or reread) their conversation (page 519, column 1, paragraph 1, to page 520, line 3), pay special attention to *how* they talk as well as to what they say. Then copy the headings below in your reading/writing log. Provide the information to complete each heading.

Reading/Writing Log

Anne's attitude/tone of voice
Examples:

Peter's attitude/tone of voice
Examples:

Writing a Dialogue

Imagine that Anne and Peter talk for two of the five minutes allowed them by the police. Use what you have learned about their voices to write a dialogue. *Choose a voice* for Anne and one for Peter that reflect their attitudes. If you are keeping a **reading/writing log,** review what you recorded earlier about their voices. Before you begin, see "Writing Dialogue" in the Writer's Handbook.

Writing About Characters

Choose one of the following pairs of characters: (a) Mr. Frank and Mr. Van Daan; (b) Mrs. Frank and Mrs. Van Daan; (c) Dussel and Mr. Frank. In five paragraphs, describe how each character reacts to being in hiding. Consider their reactions to the shortages and inconvenience they have to bear, to moments of fear, and to the behavior of other characters throughout the play. In paragraph one, briefly introduce the general topic. In paragraph two, three, and four, discuss each of the main points listed above, and mention at least one specific example for each point. In paragraph five, explain briefly how their reactions influence the way you feel about each character. For help in prewriting and revising, see "Writing About Characters" in the Writer's Handbook.

ENRICHMENT
Oral Interpretation

Choose one of the entries from Anne's diary that ends a scene. Read it aloud the way you think she would have read it.

Group Oral Interpretation

Your class will be divided into ten groups, one for each scene in the play. Each member of your group will be assigned the role of one character. Practice reading your role until your group can read clearly enough to be understood, loudly enough to be heard, and smoothly enough to make your reading easy to listen to. When you are the listener, listen carefully to the way others read speeches by the same character whose speeches you read.

Research

To help you better understand the background and scope of the Holocaust (the systematic annihilation by the Nazis of about six million European Jews between 1933 and 1945) your class will be divided into five groups. Each group will examine one of the following topics: "The Organization of Concentration Camps," "Living Conditions in Concentration Camps," "Nazi War Criminals," "The Nuremberg Trials," and "The Resistance: Those Who Helped the Jews." Each member of your group will independently research the group's assigned topic. Then, as a group, you will discuss the information you gathered, select and organize your major points, and assign parts of the report for each person to present orally to the class.

Oral Reading

Select two or three excerpts from Anne's original diary that show her sense of humor. Read them to the class.

 ## BIOGRAPHY

Frances Goodrich (1890–1984) and
Albert Hackett (1900–   )

Both Frances Goodrich and Albert Hackett began their careers as actors. Later they wrote plays for both the stage and the screen. For more information on how this husband-and-wife team made Anne Frank's diary a successful stage play, see the Comment article, page 495.

Comment

The Aftermath

After the inhabitants of the annex were captured on August 4, 1944, they were first sent to Westerbork, a concentration camp in Holland, about eighty miles from Amsterdam. On the morning of September 3, they began the long journey to Auschwitz, the infamous camp in Poland where 4,000,000 Jews died in the gas chambers. For three days they traveled, packed into freight cars. At the camp the men were separated from the women. Mrs. Frank died in the women's camp on January 6, 1945, after her daughters had been sent on to Bergen-Belsen.

It was October 30 when Anne and Margot began the journey to Bergen-Belsen in a cattle car. This camp, where 30,000 prisoners died, was located in Germany. In late 1944 it was in a disorganized state. The Allies were approaching. Food was scarce, and typhus was raging. Here Margot died at the end of February or the beginning of March, 1945, probably of a combination of typhus and starvation. Anne, already ill of typhus, died soon after. Three weeks later British troops liberated the camp.

Mrs. Van Daan also died during the typhus epidemic at Bergen-Belsen. Mr. Van Daan died in the gas chambers at Auschwitz. When the Nazis left Auschwitz in January, 1945, they took Peter Van Daan with them. He survived the forced march and was put in a camp at Mauthausen. He died on the same day that American troops liberated the camp. Mr. Dussel was sent back to Germany and died in Neuengamme. Only Mr. Frank, who remained at Auschwitz until its liberation, survived.

A fuller record of the aftermath of the capture of Anne Frank can be found in Ernst Schnabel's book, *Anne Frank: A Portrait in Courage.*

Anne Frank

Comment

Miep

The Frank family's link with the outside world, their source of food, information, and hope was Miep. When the Nazis occupied Holland, Miep Gies had worked for Otto Frank for several years. She had become his office manager and a close friend of the Frank family. When Frank made plans for hiding his family, Miep was one of the first people he confided in. More than forty-five years after the Frank family "disappeared" into the attic rooms above his business, Miep published a book about what those years were like and how she and many other people helped the Franks (*Anne Frank Remembered* by Miep Gies with Alison Leslie Gold, Simon and Schuster, 1987).

In the prologue to *Anne Frank Remembered*, Miep Gies argues that she is not a hero, that there were many Dutch people who acted as she did by defying the Nazis. It is estimated that more than twenty thousand Dutch people hid Jews, Dutch resistance fighters, and other people in danger during the years of the German occupation of Holland. Over one-third of the Jews hidden survived.

Of the people who helped the Franks while they were in the annex, Miep was in charge of getting food. As shortages increased, she often stood in long lines at several grocers before getting enough for her own family and the residents of the Secret Annex. The Nazi government had declared it a crime to come to the aid of Jews, so Miep daily faced the likelihood of her own death or imprisonment.

When the annex was discovered and its inhabitants arrested, Miep herself narrowly escaped. In a final desperate and heroic effort to save her friends, Miep boldly approached the German command and attempted to buy their lives from the Nazis with money donated by Mr. Frank's employees. When he returned from the concentration camp, Mr. Frank lived for several years with Miep, her husband, and their baby son.

Of Anne Frank and the others from the annex who died in the concentration camps, Miep says, "Not a day goes by that I do not grieve for them."

Miep Gies in 1987, reading Anne's diary

THINKING CRITICALLY
ABOUT LITERATURE

UNIT 6   DRAMA 2

■ CONCEPT REVIEW

The selection that ends this unit contains many of the important ideas
and literary terms found in the play you have just studied. It also
contains notes designed to help you think critically about your reading.
For a more extensive discussion of literary terms, see the Handbook of
Literary Terms.

The setting is a French country house; the time is a day during World
War II. France, like the Netherlands and other European countries, has
been invaded and occupied by Nazi troops. As the scene opens, Madame
and her servant Simone (sē mōn') have been watching out their window
as two German soldiers escort a young stranger to their door.

from The Pen of My Aunt

Gordon Daviot

STRANGER (*in a bright, confident, casual tone*). Ah, there you are, my
  dear Aunt. I am so glad. Come in, my friend, come in. My dear
  Aunt, this gentleman wants you to identify me.

MADAME. Identify you?

CORPORAL. We found this man wandering in the woods——

STRANGER. The Corporal found it inexplicable that anyone should
  wander in a wood.

CORPORAL. And he had no papers on him——

STRANGER. And I rightly pointed out that if I carry all the papers one
  is supposed to these days, I am no good to God or man. If I put

From "The Pen of My Aunt" by Gordon Daviot. Copyright 1954 by Gordon Daviot. Reprinted by
permission of Watkins/Loomis Agency, Inc.

them in a hip pocket, I can't bend forward; if I put them in a front pocket, I can't bend at all.

CORPORAL. He said that he was your nephew, Madame, but that did not seem to us very likely, so we brought him here.

(*There is the slightest pause; just one moment of silence.*)

MADAME. But of course this is my nephew.

CORPORAL. He is?

MADAME. Certainly.

CORPORAL. He lives here?

MADAME (*assenting*). My nephew lives here.

CORPORAL. So! (*Recovering*) My apologies, Madame. But you will admit that appearances were against the young gentleman.

MADAME. Alas, Corporal, my nephew belongs to a generation who delight in flouting appearances. It is what they call "expressing their personality," I understand.

CORPORAL (*with contempt*). No doubt, Madame.

MADAME. Convention is anathema to them, and there is no sin like conformity. Even a collar is an offense against their liberty, and a discipline not to be borne by free necks.

CORPORAL. Ah yes, Madame. A little more discipline among your nephew's generation, and we might not be occupying your country today.

STRANGER. You think it was that collar of yours that conquered my country? You flatter yourself, Corporal. The only result of wearing a collar like that is varicose veins in the head.

MADAME (*repressive*). Please! My dear boy. Let us not descend to personalities.

STRANGER. The matter is not personal, my good Aunt, but scientific. Wearing a collar like that retards the flow of fresh blood to the head, with the most disastrous consequences to the grey matter of the brain. The hypothetical grey matter. In fact, I have a theory——

CORPORAL. Monsieur, your theories do not interest me.

STRANGER. No? You do not find speculation interesting? . . .

CORPORAL. I have only one desire, Monsieur, and that is to see your papers.

STRANGER (*taken off-guard and filling in time*). My papers?

MADAME. But is that necessary, Corporal? I have already told you that——

CORPORAL. I know that Madame is a very good collaborator and in good standing——

■ The Stranger's tone mocks the Corporal.

■ Madame's ability to play her part gives insight into her character.

■ *convention is* anathema (a nath′ə mə) **to them.** Anything conventional or customary is intensely disliked by Madame's nephew and his generation.

■ The Corporal is characterized by his lack of humor and his obsession with rules and regulations.

■ In stalling for time, the Stranger also becomes insulting. Madame's attempts to keep the conversation civil add to the development of the plot.

■ The remark helps to characterize the Corporal.

■ *collaborator* (kə lab′rā′ tər), person who gives help to or cooperates with the enemy, in this case the Nazis.

MADAME. In that case——

CORPORAL. But when we begin an affair we like to finish it. I have asked to see Monsieur's papers, and the matter will not be finished until I have seen them.

MADAME. You acknowledge that I am in "good standing," Corporal?

CORPORAL. So I have heard, Madame.

MADAME. Then I must consider it a discourtesy on your part to demand my nephew's credentials.

CORPORAL. It is no reflection on Madame. It is a matter of routine, nothing more.

STRANGER (murmuring). The great god Routine.

MADAME. To ask for his papers was routine; to insist on their production is discourtesy. I shall say so to your commanding officer.

CORPORAL. Very good, Madame. In the meantime, I shall inspect your nephew's papers.

MADAME. And what if I——

STRANGER (quietly). You may as well give it up, my dear. You could as easily turn a steamroller. They have only one idea at a time. If the Corporal's heart is set on seeing my papers, he shall see them. (Moving towards the door) I left them in the pocket of my coat.

SIMONE (unexpectedly, from the background). Not in your linen coat?

STRANGER (pausing). Yes. Why?

SIMONE (with apparently growing anxiety). Your cream linen coat? The one you were wearing yesterday?

STRANGER. Certainly.

SIMONE. Merciful Heaven! I sent it to the laundry!

STRANGER. To the laundry!

SIMONE. Yes, monsieur; this morning; in the basket.

STRANGER (in incredulous anger). You sent my coat, with my papers in the pocket, to the laundry!

SIMONE (defensive and combatant). I didn't know Monsieur's papers were in the pocket.

STRANGER. You didn't know! You didn't know that a packet of documents weighing half a ton were in the pocket. An identity card, a laisser passer, a food card, a drink card, an army discharge, a permission to wear civilian clothes, a permission to go farther than ten miles to the east, a permission to go more than ten miles to the west, a permission to——

SIMONE (breaking in with spirit). How was I to know the coat was

■ The request to see the stranger's papers **foreshadows** what possible difficulty?

■ **generalizing:** The Corporal is typical of bureaucrats, concerned solely with following the letter of the law.

■ Madame's continuing to play word games with the soldier suggests her courage.

■ **evaluating:** The Stranger knows there are no papers. What might he be planning to do?

■ Simone's speaking up adds to the development of the plot.

■ This and the following speeches help characterize Simone as clever and brave.

■ *laisser passer* (les′ā pä sā′), a document that allows one to go past a military guard.

heavy! I picked it up with the rest of the bundle that was lying on the floor.

STRANGER (*snapping her head off*). My coat was on the back of the chair.

SIMONE. It was on the floor.

STRANGER. On the back of the chair!

SIMONE. It was on the floor with your dirty shirt and your pajamas, and a towel and what not. I put my arms round the whole thing and then—woof! into the basket with them.

STRANGER. I tell you that coat was on the back of the chair. It was quite clean and was not going to the laundry for two weeks yet—if then. I hung it there myself, and——

MADAME. My dear boy, what does it matter? The damage is done now. In any case, they will find the papers when they unpack the basket, and return them tomorrow.

STRANGER. If someone doesn't steal them. There are a lot of people who would like to lay hold of a complete set of papers, believe me.

■ Coming from one who has no papers, this statement is ironic.

MADAME (*reassuring*). Oh, no. Old Fleureau is the soul of honesty. You have no need to worry about them. They will be back first thing tomorrow, you shall see; and then we shall have much pleasure in sending them to the Administration Office for the Corporal's inspection. Unless, of course, the Corporal insists on your personal appearance at the office.

CORPORAL (*cold and indignant*). I have seen Monsieur. All that I want now is to see his papers.

STRANGER. You shall see them, Corporal, you shall see them. The whole half-ton of them. You may inspect them at your leisure. Provided, that is, that they come back from the laundry to which this idiot has consigned them.

MADAME (*again reassuring*). They will come back, never fear. And you must not blame Simone. She is a good child and does her best.

SIMONE (*with an air of belated virtue*). I am not one to pry into pockets.

MADAME. Simone, show the Corporal out, if you please.

SIMONE (*natural feeling overcoming her for a moment*). He knows the way out. (*Recovering*) Yes, Madame.

MADAME. And Corporal, try to take your duties a little less literally in future. My countrymen appreciate the spirit rather than the letter.

CORPORAL. I have my instructions, Madame, and I obey them. Good day, Madame. Monsieur.

(*He goes, followed by* SIMONE—*door closes. There is a moment of silence.*)

STRANGER. For a good collaborator, that was a remarkably quick adoption.

MADAME. Sit down, young man. I will give you something to drink. I expect your knees are none too well.

STRANGER. My knees, Madame, are pure gelatine. As for my stomach, it seems to have disappeared.

MADAME (*offering him the drink she has poured out*). This will recall it, I hope.

STRANGER. You are not drinking, Madame.

MADAME. Thank you, no.

STRANGER. Not with strangers. It is certainly no time to drink with strangers. Nevertheless, I drink the health of a collaborator. (*He drinks.*) Tell me, Madame, what will happen tomorrow when they find that you have no nephew?

MADAME (*surprised*). But of course I have a nephew. I tell lies, my friend; but not *silly* lies. My charming nephew has gone to Bonneval for the day. He finds country life dull.

STRANGER. Dull? This—this heaven?

MADAME (*dryly*). He likes to talk and here there is no audience. At Headquarters in Bonneval he finds the audience sympathetic.

STRANGER (*understanding the implication*). Ah.

MADAME. He believes in the Brotherhood of Man—if you can credit it.

STRANGER. After the last six months?

MADAME. His mother was American, so he has half the Balkans in his blood. To say nothing of Italy, Russia, and the Levant.

STRANGER (*half-amused*). I see.

MADAME. A silly and worthless creature, but useful.

STRANGER. Useful?

MADAME. I—borrow his cloak.

STRANGER. I see.

MADAME. Tonight I shall borrow his identity papers, and tomorrow they will go to the office in St. Estephe.

STRANGER. But—he will have to know.

MADAME (*placidly*). Oh, yes, he will know, of course.

STRANGER. And how will you persuade such an enthusiastic collaborator to deceive his friends?

MADAME. Oh, that is easy. He is my heir.

■ **generalizing:** The behavior of the Nazi conquerors during the last six months makes believing in the brotherhood of man impossible.

■ Madame is using **figurative language.** She explains in her next speech.

THINK AND DISCUSS
Understanding
1. Where and when is this play set?
2. Why have the Germans brought the Stranger to Madame's house?
3. How does Madame act when the Corporal asks to see the Stranger's identity papers?
4. According to Simone, what has happened to the papers?
5. What does Madame promise to do the next day?

Analyzing
6. By identifying the Stranger as her relative, what does Madame indicate to him that she will do?
7. Why does the Stranger talk so much about collars?
8. What can you infer about the story that the coat was sent to the laundry?
9. When the Corporal calls Madame a "good collaborator," he is characterizing her as someone who agrees with and aids her conquerors. In what ways is this statement ironic?
10. After learning that the nephew is Madame's heir, what can you infer he will do with his identity papers?

Extending
11. What do you think the Stranger will do now?
12. After Germany lost the war, people in countries it had occupied who had collaborated with the Nazis were imprisoned or forced to flee. What do you think will happen to Madame when the war is over?

REVIEWING LITERARY TERMS
Foreshadowing
1. Are Simone's actions foreshadowed?
2. What is the first hint that Madame will help the stranger?

■ CONTENT REVIEW
THINKING SKILLS
Classifying
1. Anne's first diary entry describes some of the laws enacted against Jews by the Nazis. Throughout the play, residents of the Secret Annex learn additional details of the Nazi persecution of the Jews. Beginning with Anne's first entry (page 455, column 1, paragraph 3) skim the play for these details; list as many as you can find.

Generalizing
2. Examine the list you made for question 1. In what ways do the early repressive measures (for example, forcing Jews to turn in their bicycles, making them wear yellow stars) pave the way for the later deportations to concentration camps?
3. Since Anne's diary supplied the source materials for the play, people and incidents are seen from her point of view. What different pictures of the various inhabitants of the annex, including Anne, might be presented if the diary had been written by Mr. Dussel? Mrs. Frank? Mrs. Van Daan?

Synthesizing

4. Do you believe that works such as Anne's diary and the play and motion picture based upon it can be influential in preventing future persecution of innocent people? Discuss.

Evaluating

5. The Introduction to the unit speaks of the diary of Anne Frank as "a living tribute to the dignity, courage, and perseverance of the human spirit." Do these words seem an accurate description of the play you have just read? Defend your answer by referring to specific scenes and passages.

6. Consider the following statement: *"The Diary of Anne Frank* is not dramatic enough. The last scene should show Anne's death in a concentration camp. Then we would really feel the tragedy." Explain why you agree or disagree with this viewpoint.

■ COMPOSITION REVIEW

Changing Point of View

The Diary of Anne Frank presents clear pictures of several characters besides Anne. Imagine that you are one of these other characters. Consider this character's attitudes and way of talking. Write a diary entry a page or two long about the events in one scene from the play. Because your character is different from Anne, your account of the same events will use a different way of speaking and may take on a completely different meaning.

Supporting a Statement

One of the most significant statements made by Anne Frank is "In spite of everything, I still believe that people are really good at heart." In a separate paragraph for each pair of characters, discuss how Anne's statement is proved by Miep and Mr. Kraler, and (in *The Pen of My Aunt*) by Madame and Simone. In a third paragraph, explain why you think these people help others. Is it simply because they are "good at heart," or might they have other reasons as well? Use specific speeches and actions from both plays to support your points.

Expressing Your Opinion

Do you believe that people are really good at heart? Express your opinion in a diary entry; a letter; a monologue; a dialogue; an editorial for television, radio, or newspaper; or an essay for a magazine.

Reviewing Writer's Craft: Use a Voice That Suits Purpose

Try your hand at creating a voice to suit your purpose. Choose (**a**) or (**b**). (**a**) Write a letter to someone with whom you disagree strongly. The person may be someone you know in daily life or someone in public life who has done something that deeply angers you. Talk directly to that person. Make your letter reflect your anger. (**b**) Write a letter to someone you feel sorry for—someone in your daily life or in public life who needs comfort. Talk directly to that person. Make your letter quiet and comforting.

GREEK MYTHS

Persephone seated at the foot of Hades' couch. Hades is holding a cornucopia, or horn of plenty.

Decoration from a Greek vase, *The British Museum*

PREVIEW

UNIT 7   GREEK MYTHS

Zeus / Bernard Evslin
Poseidon / Bernard Evslin
Persephone / Anne Terry White
Arachne / Olivia Coolidge
Daedalus / Anne Terry White
Phaëthon / Edith Hamilton
Baucis and Philemon / Olivia Coolidge

Features
Reading a Greek Myth
The Writer's Craft: Use Good Endings
Comment: Transformations in Myth
Glossary of Proper Names

Review of Literary Terms
theme
tone

Reading Literature Skillfully
summary
conclusions

Vocabulary Skills
structure

Thinking Skills
classifying
synthesizing

Composition Assignments Include
Writing a Play
Writing a Speech
Discussing a Plot
Changing Point of View
Reading/Writing Log
Writing a News Story
Writing an Ending

Enrichment
Creative Project
Research Project

Thinking Critically About Literature
Concept Review
Content Review
Composition Review

INTRODUCTION

A series of feathery clouds moves in formation across the sky. After a heavy downpour, a rainbow appears near the horizon. Lightning flashes, and a tree—or a person—is destroyed. The seasons change regularly in a never ending cycle. Night follows day, the tide is high for six hours, then low for six. Today we see these phenomena and explain them through science. Ancient peoples saw them too, and wondered. Their wonder led to the composition of myths—stories that offer explanations for the marvels of nature and often involve gods and goddesses in those explanations.

By the time the civilization of Greece had become established, these myths, thousands of years older, had become more detailed. The sky, the earth, the sea, the underworld—each had its own gods who had responsibilities that were more or less clearly defined.

Myths were passed by word of mouth from person to person and region to region, often carried by professional storytellers. With the passage of time, as different storytellers retold the myths, the details sometimes blurred or came into conflict, so that there are often several different versions of the same basic story.

In addition, some of the myths became more sophisticated as the storytellers included elements of symbolism and philosophy. For example, one myth tells us that Zeus,[1] who ruled the gods, developed a dreadful headache. To give him relief, another god split open his head, and out sprang Athene, adult and fully clad in armor. We can marvel, or we can laugh. But Athene was the Greek goddess of wisdom—and where should wisdom have its source, if not in the mind of the ruler of the gods?

It may surprise us that some Greek myths show the gods in a comic, irreverent, even unfavorable light. The ancient Greeks saw their gods as complete beings, possessing both good and bad traits, and they did not limit their myths to the good traits.

The major gods, called the Olympians, were twelve in number, headed by Zeus. Most of them dwelt with Zeus in a huge palace, enveloped by clouds, on the top of Mount Olympus, the highest mountain in Greece. Lesser deities lived on earth, in the sea, and in the underworld. Sometimes the gods fell in love with humans. Their children could then be either human or immortal. The word *demigod* is usually used to describe one of those half-human, half-divine beings who had attained immortal status. On the other hand, the

---

1. See **Glossary of Proper Names** on page 567 for pronunciation and identification of characters and places mentioned in the introduction and in all the selections in this unit.

Horses relief, from a stone coffin, 400 B.C.
Istanbul Museum of Archaeology

familiar word *hero* was originally used to identify those half-human, half-divine beings who retained their mortal status but were unusually strong and brave.

Greek mythology also provided creatures that were part human, part animal. Almost always these were dangerous monsters like the Minotaur, part man and part bull, who devoured sacrificial victims. On rare occasions these monsters could be relatively harmless, like the mischievous Pan, half human and half goat.

Whatever the origin or meaning of individual myths, they do show us that the ancient Greeks had great curiosity and excellent imaginations.

We no longer believe that the sun is a golden chariot, that lightning is a spear, that the constellations were once living beings. And yet the heritage of myth that has come down to us across the centuries remains fascinating.

The ancient Greeks believed their gods to be immortal. In a way that they might not have expected, they were right, for the gods live on in our language, in our literature, and most of all in those timeless stories, the myths themselves.

Review THEME in the Handbook of Literary Terms, page 690

Zeus

as told by **Bernard Evslin**

Huge, twisted creatures taller than trees attacked the young gods furiously.

ronos, father of the gods, who gave his name to time, married his sister Rhea, goddess of earth. Now, Cronos had become king of the gods by killing his father, Oranos, the First One. The dying Oranos had prophesied, saying, "You murder me now and steal my throne—but one of your own sons will dethrone you, for crime begets crime."

So Cronos was very careful. One by one, he swallowed his children as they were born. First three daughters—Hestia, Demeter, and Hera; then two sons—Hades and Poseidon. One by one, he swallowed them all.

Rhea was furious. She was determined that he should not eat her next child, who she felt sure would be a son. When her time came, she crept down the slope of Olympus to a dark place to have her baby. It was a son, and she named him Zeus. She hung a golden cradle from the branches of an olive tree and put him to sleep there. Then she went back to the top of the mountain. She took a rock and wrapped it in swaddling clothes and held it to her breast, humming a lullaby. Cronos came snorting and bellowing out of his great bed, snatched the bundle from her and swallowed it, clothes and all.

Rhea stole down the mountainside to the swinging golden cradle and took her son down into the fields. She gave him to a shepherd family to raise, promising that their sheep would never be eaten by wolves.

Here Zeus grew to be a beautiful young boy, and Cronos, his father, knew nothing about him. Finally, however, Rhea became lonely for him and brought him back to the court of the gods, introducing him to Cronos as the new cupbearer. Cronos was pleased because the boy was beautiful.

One night Rhea and Zeus prepared a special drink. They mixed mustard and salt with the nectar. Next morning, after a mighty

Benvenuto Cellini, "Jupiter" (detail)
The Italian sculptor used the god's Roman name.

swallow, Cronos vomited up first a stone, and then Hestia, Demeter, Hera, Hades, and Poseidon—who, being gods, were still undigested, still alive. They thanked Zeus and immediately chose him to be their leader.

Then a mighty battle raged. Cronos was joined by the Titans, his half-brothers, huge, twisted, dark creatures taller than trees, whom he kept pent up in the mountains until there was fighting to be done. They attacked the young gods furiously. But Zeus had allies too. He had gone to darker caverns—caves under caves under caves, deep in the mountainside—formed by the first bubbles of the cooling earth. Here Cronos thousands of centuries before (a short time in the life of a god) had pent up other monsters, the one-eyed Cyclopes and the Hundred-handed Ones. Zeus unshackled these ugly cousins and led them against the Titans.

There was a great rushing and tumult in the skies. The people on earth heard mighty thunder and saw mountains shatter. The earth quaked and tidal waves rolled as the gods fought. The Titans were tall as trees, and old Cronos was a crafty leader. He attacked fiercely, driving the young gods before him. But Zeus had laid a trap. Halfway up the slope of Olympus, he whistled for his cousins, the Hundred-handed Ones, who had been lying in ambush. They took up huge boulders, a hundred each, and hurled them downhill at the Titans. The Titans thought the mountain itself was falling on them. They broke ranks and fled.

The young goat-god Pan was shouting with joy. Later he said that it was his shout that made the Titans flee. That is where we get the word "panic."

Now the young gods climbed to Olympus, took over the castle, and Zeus became their king. No one knows what happened to Cronos and his Titans. But sometimes mountains still explode in fire and the earth still quakes, and no one knows exactly why.

THINK AND DISCUSS
Understanding
1. Why does Cronos swallow his children?
2. How is the infant Zeus spared?
3. How is the earth affected by the battle of the gods?

Analyzing
4. Does the prophecy made by the father of Cronos come true? Explain.
5. Explain whether strength or cleverness determines who wins the battle between the young gods and the old.
6. At the end of the myth, what inference can you make about Cronos and the Titans?

7. What natural phenomena, or events, are explained in this myth?

Extending
8. Cronos was king for thousands of centuries. Now Zeus is king. Based on what you know about Zeus from this myth, predict what kind of king he will be.

REVIEWING: Theme HↃ
See Handbook of Literary Terms, p. 690.
   Theme is the main idea or underlying meaning of a literary work. Decide which of the following statements is true.

1. The theme of "Zeus" is that disloyalty among family members can have serious consequences.
2. The main idea of "Zeus" deals with how volcanos and earthquakes came to be.

COMPOSITION
Writing a Scene for a Play

Rewrite a scene from "Zeus" to be performed on stage. Use the scene when young Zeus is brought to Cronos's court. Remember, Zeus is presented only as a handsome young stranger who will serve as cupbearer. Do any members of the court suspect who he really is? What do Zeus and Cronos say to each other? Write both dialogue and the stage directions for this scene.

Writing a Speech

Imagine that you are Zeus, and write a speech to deliver to your followers the night before the great battle with Cronos. The speech should inspire the army to fight for your cause, provide reasons why they should defeat Cronos, and include a promise of how you will be a better king than your father. See "Writing as a Story Character" in the Writer's Handbook before you begin to write.

BIOGRAPHY

Bernard Evslin
1922–

In his book *Greeks Bearing Gifts* (1976), Bernard Evslin writes with an irreverent style that combines wit and tradition. Not only has Evslin retold Greek myths; he also has written a variety of books including *Signs and Wonders: Tales from the Old Testament* (1979) and plays such as *Step on a Crack* (1962) and *Geranium Hat* (1969). He has produced a number of television documentaries, one of which, "Face of the Land," won the *Variety* poll in 1959 for the best TV film.

Reading A GREEK MYTH

As you read the myths in this unit, notice that they contain many of the same elements found in the short stories you have studied. Paying attention to elements such as plot, character, and setting will help you understand and appreciate these stories of Greek gods and goddesses. For example, later in this unit, you will read a myth about a boy who is able to soar through the air like a bird. As you read, pay close attention to the events that lead up to the boy's flight and to what finally happens to him. In "Poseidon," you will meet Poseidon, god of the sea. Pay particular attention to the way his character is drawn. Ask yourself whether he appears to be a god who is like a complete human being, one possessing both good traits and bad. In still another myth, you will go with a young girl who is carried off to the kingdom of the underworld. Noting details of this setting and comparing and contrasting it with the world above ground will help you understand and sympathize with the girl's near-fatal homesickness.

Notice, too, that many of these myths contain summaries of what has happened earlier. A **summary** is a short statement telling the main points of an event. "Zeus" begins with a summary about Cronos, including who his wife is and why he swallows up his children. Without this summary, much of the action in the story—events such as Cronos's vomiting up three children—would not make sense. Note that Bernard Evslin, the author, delivers this summary with few words and very little descriptive detail. The facts are presented in chronological order so that readers can easily follow the action. Once Evslin has provided this background, he can move on with the story.

Reading myths, like reading short stories, often requires that you draw conclusions about characters and events. A **conclusion** is a decision or opinion you reach after thinking about the facts and details you have read. A myth may not tell you what you should think about a particular character or event in it. Writers present facts and let you draw your own conclusions. Based on the facts Evslin gives, what conclusion did you reach about the character of Cronos? Once you formed an opinion of Cronos, you probably also had formed one about Zeus. How do these two differ? Are you glad the battle ended as it did?

The next myth you will read is about Poseidon. As you read, notice that some of his adventures are told only in summary. These summaries give you more information than a short myth could possibly contain. Pay close attention to the facts and details provided in "Poseidon" so that any conclusions you make when you are finished reading are based on as many facts and details as possible.

If you use these reading techniques as you read other myths, you will increase your understanding and enjoyment of them.

Poseidon

as told by **Bernard Evslin**

Poseidon's character is unpredictable—like the wild sea that he chose for his kingdom.

---

fter Cronos was deposed, the three sons threw dice for his empire. Zeus, the youngest, won and chose the sky. Poseidon smiled to himself because the sky was empty, and he knew that the impulsive Zeus had chosen it because it looked so high. And now, he, Poseidon, could choose as he would have done if he had won. He chose the sea. He had always wanted it; it is the best place for adventures and secrets and makes claim on land and sky. Hades, who was always unlucky, had to take the underworld. The earth was held as a commonwealth and left to the goddesses to manage.

Poseidon left Olympus and came to his kingdom. He immediately set about building a huge underwater palace with a great pearl and coral throne. He needed a queen and chose Thetis, a beautiful Nereid, or water nymph. But it was prophesied that any son born to Thetis would be greater than his father, so Poseidon decided to try elsewhere. The prophecy came true. The son of Thetis was Achilles.

Poseidon chose another Nereid named Amphitrite. But like his brother Zeus, he was a great traveler and had hundreds of children in different places. He was a very difficult god, changeful and quarrelsome. He did bear grudges; but he could be pleased, and then his smile was radiant. He liked jokes and thought up very curious forms for his creatures. He liked to startle nymphs with monsters, and concocted the octopus, the squid, the sea-polyp or jellyfish, the swordfish, blowfish, sea cow, and many others. Once, trying to appease Amphitrite's jealous rage, he thought up the dolphin and gave it to her as a gift.

He was greedy and aggressive, always trying to add to his kingdom. Once he claimed Attica as his own and stabbed his trident into the hillside where the Acropolis still stands, and a spring of salt water spouted. Now, the people of Athens did not want to belong to the kingdom of the sea. They were afraid of Poseidon, who had a habit of seizing all the youth of a town when he was in the mood. So they prayed to be put under the protection of another god. Athene heard their prayers. She came down and planted an olive tree by the side of the spring. Poseidon was enraged. His

Reprinted by permission of Scholastic Magazines, Inc. from *Heroes, Gods, and Monsters of the Greek Myths* by Bernard Evslin. Copyright © 1966, 1967 by Scholastic Magazines, Inc.

"Poseidon"

face darkened, and he roared with fury, raising a storm. A fishing fleet was blown off the sea and never came to port. He challenged Athene to single combat and threatened to stir up a tidal wave to break over the city if she refused. She accepted. But Zeus heard the sound of this quarreling and came down and decreed a truce. Then all the gods sat in council to hear the rival claims. After hearing both Athene and Poseidon, they voted to award the city to Athene because her olive tree was the better gift. After that, Athenians had to be very careful when they went to sea, and were often unfortunate in their naval battles.

Poseidon was very fond of Demeter and pursued her persistently.

Finally Demeter said, "Give me a gift. You have made creatures for the sea; now make me a land animal. But a beautiful one, the most beautiful ever seen."

She thought she was safe, because she believed he could make only monsters. She was amazed when he made her a horse, and gasped with delight when she saw it. And Poseidon was so struck by his handiwork that he swiftly made a herd of horses that began to gallop about the meadow, tossing their heads, flirting their tails, kicking up their back legs, and neighing joyously. And he was so fascinated by the horses that he forgot all about Demeter and leaped on one and rode off. Later he made another herd of green ones for his undersea stables. But Demeter kept the first herd; from that all the horses in the world have descended.

Another story says it took Poseidon a full week to make the horse. During that time he made and cast aside many other creatures that didn't come out right. But he simply threw them away without killing them, and they made their way into the world. From them have come the camel, the hippopotamus, the giraffe, the donkey, and the zebra.

THINK AND DISCUSS
Understanding
1. How was Cronos's empire divided?
2. How does Poseidon feel about the division?
3. Why does Poseidon decide not to marry Thetis?
4. Whom does he marry?
5. What special creature does Poseidon make for his queen?
6. When Poseidon makes creatures, what does he do with his mistakes?

Analyzing
7. Explain how Athene became the protector of Athens.
8. This myth explains the origin of some natural phenomena, or things that occur in nature. Cite at least two explanations of natural phenomena in this myth.

Extending
9. In what ways does the behavior of the sea suggest Poseidon's personality?

VOCABULARY
Structure
The *trident* that Poseidon carries is a particular kind of spear. Look up *trident* in the Glossary. What are the meanings of *tri-* and *dent*, the prefix and root from which *trident* is formed?

Use your Glossary to answer the questions about the italicized words, all of which contain either *tri-* or *dent*.
1. How many languages does a *trilingual* person speak?
2. Name at least three things that one can *indent*.
3. According to its etymology, what is *dentifrice* used for?
4. A *dandelion* is so named because of the resemblance of its leaves to what?
5. Which italicized words in this exercise are *trisyllabic*?

THINKING SKILLS
Classifying
Poseidon classifies creatures by either giving them as gifts or "letting them go." Discuss into which of these categories each of the animals listed below might fall.

kangaroo	fox
white-tailed deer	flamingo
moose	duck
anteater	sparrow
opossum	canary
raccoon	persian cat

COMPOSITION
Writing a Description
Imagine Poseidon has allowed you to make one special animal. What kind would it be? Write a one-paragraph description of this animal. Include specific details about its size, shape, color, where it lives, what it eats, and what its abilities are. See "Writing a Clear Description" in the Writer's Handbook before you begin.

Writing an Argument
Imagine that you are either Athene or Poseidon. Write a speech that you will give before the council of gods telling why you deserve to be the protector of Athens.

Persephone

retold by **Anne Terry White**

**When the goddess of the harvest mourned for her lost daughter,
the earth withered.**

---

eep under Mt. Aetna, the gods had buried alive a number of fearful, fire-breathing giants. The monsters heaved and struggled to get free. And so mightily did they shake the earth that Hades, the king of the underworld, was alarmed.

"They may tear the rocks asunder and leave the realm of the dead open to the light of day," he thought. And mounting his golden chariot, he went up to see what damage had been done.

Now the goddess of love and beauty, fair Aphrodite, was sitting on a mountainside playing with her son, Eros. She saw Hades as he drove around with his coal-black horses and she said:

"My son, there is one who defies your power and mine. Quick! Take up your darts! Send an arrow into the breast of that dark monarch. Let him, too, feel the pangs of love. Why should he alone escape them?"

At his mother's words, Eros leaped lightly to his feet. He chose from his quiver his sharpest and truest arrow, fitted it to his bow, drew the string, and shot straight into Hades' heart.

The grim King had seen fair maids enough in the gloomy underworld over which he ruled. But never had his heart been touched. Now an unaccustomed warmth stole through his veins. His stern eyes softened. Before him was a blossoming valley, and along its edge a charming girl was gathering flowers. She was Persephone, daughter of Demeter, goddess of the harvest. She had strayed from her companions, and now that her basket overflowed with blossoms, she was filling her apron with lilies and violets. The god looked at Persephone and loved her at once. With one sweep of his arm he caught her up and drove swiftly away.

"Mother!" she screamed, while the flowers fell from her apron and strewed the ground. "Mother!"

And she called on her companions by name. But already they were out of sight, so fast did Hades urge the horses on. In a few moments they were at the River Cyane. Persephone struggled, her loosened girdle fell to the ground, but the god held her tight. He struck the bank with his trident. The earth opened, and darkness swallowed them all—

---

horses, chariot, Hades, and weeping Persephone.

From end to end of the earth Demeter sought her daughter. But none could tell her where Persephone was. At last, worn out and despairing, the goddess returned to Sicily. She stood by the River Cyane, where Hades had cleft the earth and gone down into his own dominions.

Now a river nymph had seen him carry off his prize. She wanted to tell Demeter where her daughter was, but fear of Hades kept her dumb. Yet she had picked up the girdle Persephone had dropped, and this the nymph wafted on the waves to the feet of Demeter.

The goddess knew then that her daughter was gone indeed, but she did not suspect Hades of carrying her off. She laid the blame on the innocent land.

"Ungrateful soil!" she said. "I made you fertile. I clothed you in grass and nourishing grain, and this is how you reward me. No more shall you enjoy my favors!"

That year was the most cruel mankind had ever known. Nothing prospered, nothing grew. The cattle died, the seed would not come up, men and oxen toiled in vain. There was too much sun. There was too much rain. Thistles and weeds were the only things that grew. It seemed that all mankind would die of hunger.

"This cannot go on," said mighty Zeus. "I see that I must intervene." And one by one he sent the gods and goddesses to plead with Demeter.

But she had the same answer for all: "Not till I see my daughter shall the earth bear fruit again."

Zeus, of course, knew well where Persephone was. He did not like to take from his brother the one joyful thing in his life, but he saw that he must if the race of man was to be preserved. So he called Hermes to him and said:

"Descend to the underworld, my son. Bid Hades release his bride. Provided she has not tasted food in the realm of the dead, she may return to her mother forever."

Down sped Hermes on his winged feet, and there in the dim palace of the king, he found Persephone by Hades' side. She was pale and joyless. Not all the glittering treasures of the underworld could bring a smile to her lips.

"You have no flowers here," she would say to her husband when he pressed gems upon her. "Jewels have no fragrance. I do not want them."

When she saw Hermes and heard his message, her heart leaped within her. Her cheeks grew rosy and her eyes sparkled, for she knew that Hades would not dare to disobey his brother's command. She sprang up, ready to go at once. Only one thing troubled her— that she could not leave the underworld forever. For she had accepted a pomegranate from Hades and sucked the sweet pulp from four of the seeds.[1]

With a heavy heart Hades made ready his golden car. He helped Persephone in while Hermes took up the reins.

"Dear wife," said the King, and his voice trembled as he spoke, "think kindly of me, I pray you. For indeed I love you truly. It will

---

1. *four of the seeds.* Technically, Persephone would have to remain in the underworld permanently because she had eaten those seeds. But Zeus arranged a compromise allowing her to leave, on condition that she spend a portion of each year with Hades.

be lonely here these eight months you are away. And if you think mine is a gloomy palace to return to, at least remember that your husband is great among the immortals. So fare you well—and get your fill of flowers!"

Straight to the temple of Demeter at Eleusis, Hermes drove the black horses. The goddess heard the chariot wheels and, as a deer bounds over the hills, she ran out swiftly to meet her daughter. Persephone flew to her mother's arms. And the sad tale of each turned into joy in the telling.

So it is to this day. One third of the year Persephone spends in the gloomy abode of Hades—one month for each seed that she tasted. Then Nature dies, the leaves fall, the earth stops bringing forth. In spring Persephone returns, and with her come the flowers, followed by summer's fruitfulness and the rich harvest of fall.

THINK AND DISCUSS
Understanding
1. Why does Hades kidnap Persephone?
2. How does Demeter react to her daughter's disappearance?
3. Why does Zeus send gods and goddesses to plead with Demeter?
4. How does Demeter learn where her daughter is?
5. Why must Persephone return to the underworld each year?

Analyzing
6. Describe Persephone's reaction to her new home.
7. Give three or four examples of the gods and goddesses showing "human" emotions.
8. What yearly occurrence does this myth explain?

Extending
9. In this version of the myth, Persephone eats four seeds. Other retellings have her eating five, six, or seven seeds. How might this difference be accounted for?

READING LITERATURE SKILLFULLY
Summarizing

A **summary** is a short statement that tells what happened in a story. The events in a summary are presented briefly and in chronological order. Which one of the following is a good summary of the events that led up to the marriage of Persephone and Hades?

1. Persephone never wanted to marry Hades. Eros shot an arrow into Hades, so he fell in love with her. He was actually outside of his kingdom looking at a mountain that was in danger of exploding. Eros was sitting on the mountain with Aphrodite, his mother. Neither liked Hades because he seemed unemotional so Aphrodite decided to make him fall in love.
2. One day as Hades was out riding on earth, Eros shot an arrow into his heart. He fell in love with Persephone, the first woman he saw. He picked her up,

and, ignoring her cries, drove quickly back to his kingdom.

3. Demeter was the goddess of crops and the earth's fertility. When she could not find Persephone one day, she became very angry and punished the earth for the loss of her daughter.

COMPOSITION
Writing a Myth

Write your own myth explaining some occurrence in nature. In it, describe what the earth was like before the events you will relate; then, tell how the earth was changed. Either make up your own characters or use Greek gods and goddesses from the Glossary of Proper Names on page 567. Before you begin to plan your composition, see "Writing a Story" in the Writer's Handbook.

Writing to Compare and Contrast

In a composition of one or two paragraphs, compare and contrast the characters of Hades and Persephone, explaining why these two are such unlikely candidates for a happy marriage. Use specific examples from the myth to support your ideas.

ENRICHMENT
Creative Project

Work as a class to produce a one-act play based on the events in "Persephone." Work in small groups with classmates to write dialogue and stage directions, choose and coach actors, design and make costumes, and design programs and a poster advertising the production. You might perform your play for another class or for a group of younger students.

BIOGRAPHY

Anne Terry White
1896–

Born in Russia, Anne Terry White came to the United States with her family at the age of eight. She has been both a teacher and a social worker, but she is best known as a writer. Her interest in teaching is evident in her "All About . . ." series, such as *All About Archaeology* (1959) and *All About Mountains and Mountaineering* (1962). She writes on a wide variety of topics, including history, biography, and nature. She has translated a number of books from Russian to English.

Write Good Endings

Good writers leave their readers with something more than a mere "the end." The endings that follow are from selections you have read earlier in this book.

Instead I went upstairs and took out the electric razor Annie gave me for Christmas and shaved off my moustache.

He stepped inside the back door. The Morophus, with a carrot top and a hank of juicy grass hanging from its hairy lips, gazed after him sadly but trustfully.

Beauty is pervasive, and fills, like perfume, more than the object that contains it. Because I had known intimately a river, the earth pulsed under me. The Creek was home. Oleanders were sweet past bearing, and my own shabby fields, weed-tangled, were newly dear. I knew, for a moment, that the only nightmare is the masochistic human mind.

. . . that this nation, under God, shall have a new birth of freedom—and that government of the people, by the people, and for the people shall not perish from the earth.

All good endings create lasting impressions. Such impressions can cause readers to reflect upon what has been read, to feel a strong emotion such as joy or sadness, or to gain a new insight. Note the ending of "Persephone."

So it is to this day. One third of the year Persephone spends in the gloomy abode of Hades—one month for each seed that she tasted. Then nature dies, the leaves fall, the earth stops bringing forth. In spring Persephone returns, and with her come the flowers, followed by summer's fruitfulness and the rich harvest of fall.

White's ending sums up for the reader the purpose of the myth—to explain the changing of the seasons.

Endings usually tie up loose ends. But sometimes a writer can create a lasting impression by leaving readers with unanswered questions. In "Zeus," Bernard Evslin concludes the myth with information about the new rulers of Olympus and hints at what happened to Cronos.

. . . No one knows what happened to Cronos and his Titans. But sometimes mountains still explode in fire and the earth still quakes, and no one knows exactly why.

An ending must be more than just a way to stop the story. If you have put effort into writing a good introduction, including specific details and precise words, appealing to your readers' senses, then you don't want to lose readers at the end.

When you read, look for good endings. When you write, use good endings.

Review TONE in the Handbook of Literary Terms, page 691

Arachne

as told by **Olivia Coolidge**

Arachne believed that her skill was greater than that of anyone— even a goddess.

rachne was a maiden who became famous throughout Greece, though she was neither wellborn nor beautiful and came from no great city. She lived in an obscure little village, and her father was a humble dyer of wool. In this he was very skillful, producing many varied shades, while above all he was famous for the clear, bright scarlet which is made from shellfish, and which was the most glorious of all the colors used in ancient Greece. Even more skillful than her father was Arachne. It was her task to spin the fleecy wool into a fine, soft thread and to weave it into cloth on the high-standing loom within the cottage. Arachne was small and pale from much working. Her eyes were light and her hair was a dusty brown, yet she was quick and graceful, and her fingers, roughened as they were, went so fast that it was hard to follow their flickering movements. So soft and even was her thread, so fine her cloth, so gorgeous her embroidery, that soon her products were known all over Greece. No one had ever seen the like of them before.

At last Arachne's fame became so great that people used to come from far and wide to watch her working. Even the graceful nymphs would steal in from stream or forest and peep shyly through the dark doorway, watching in wonder the white arms of Arachne as she stood at the loom and threw the shuttle from hand to hand between the hanging threads, or drew out the long wool, fine as a hair, from the distaff[1] as she sat spinning. "Surely Athene herself must have taught her," people would murmur to one another. "Who else could know the secret of such marvelous skill?"

Arachne was used to being wondered at, and she was immensely proud of the skill that

---

1. *distaff,* a stick, slit at one end, to hold wool or flax for spinning into thread by hand.

Athene changing Arachne into a spider
Painting by Paolo Veronese (1528–1588)

had brought so many to look on her. Praise was all she lived for, and it displeased her greatly that people should think anyone, even a goddess, could teach her anything. Therefore when she heard them murmur, she would stop her work and turn around indignantly to say, "With my own ten fingers I gained this skill, and by hard practice from early morning till night. I never had time to stand looking as you people do while another maiden worked. Nor if I had, would I give Athene credit because the girl was more skillful than I. As for Athene's weaving, how could there be finer cloth or more beautiful embroidery than mine? If Athene herself were to come down and compete with me, she could do no better than I."

One day when Arachne turned round with such words, an old woman answered her, a grey old woman, bent and very poor, who stood leaning on a staff and peering at Arachne amid the crowd of onlookers. "Reckless girl," she said, "how dare you claim to be equal to the immortal gods themselves? I am an old woman and have seen much. Take my advice and ask pardon of Athene for your words. Rest content with your fame of being the best spinner and weaver that mortal eyes have ever beheld."

"Stupid old woman," said Arachne indignantly, "who gave you a right to speak in this way to me? It is easy to see that you were never good for anything in your day, or you would not come here in poverty and rags to gaze at my skill. If Athene resents my words, let her answer them herself. I have challenged her to a contest, but she, of course, will not come. It is easy for the gods to avoid matching their skill with that of men."

At these words the old woman threw down her staff and stood erect. The wondering onlookers saw her grow tall and fair and stand clad in long robes of dazzling white. They were terribly afraid as they realized that they stood in the presence of Athene. Arachne herself flushed red for a moment, for she had never really believed that the goddess would hear her. Before the group that was gathered there she would not give in; so pressing her pale lips together in obstinacy and pride, she led the goddess to one of the great looms and set herself before the other. Without a word both began to thread the long woolen strands that hang from the rollers, and between which the shuttle moves back and forth. Many skeins lay heaped beside them to use, bleached white, and gold, and scarlet, and other shades, varied as the rainbow. Arachne had never thought of giving credit for her success to her father's skill in dyeing, though in actual truth the colors were as remarkable as the cloth itself.

Soon there was no sound in the room but the breathing of the onlookers, the whirring of the shuttles, and the creaking of the wooden frames as each pressed the thread up into place or tightened the pegs by which the whole was held straight. The excited crowd in the doorway began to see that the skill of both in truth was very nearly equal, but that, however the cloth might turn out, the goddess was the quicker of the two. A pattern of many pictures was growing on her loom. There was a border of twined branches of the olive, Athene's favorite tree, while in the middle, figures began to appear. As they looked at the glowing colors, the spectators realized that Athene was weaving into her pattern a last warning to Arachne. The central figure was the goddess herself competing with Poseidon for possession of the city of Athens; but in the four corners were mortals who had tried to strive with gods and pictures of the awful fate that had overtaken them. The goddess ended a little before Arachne and stood back from her marvelous work to see what the maiden was doing.

Never before had Arachne been matched against anyone whose skill was equal, or even nearly equal to her own. As she stole glances from time to time at Athene and saw the goddess working swiftly, calmly, and always a little faster than herself, she became angry instead of frightened, and an evil thought came into her head. Thus as Athene stepped back a pace to watch Arachne finishing her work, she saw that the maiden had taken for her design a pattern of scenes which showed evil or unworthy actions of the gods, how they had deceived fair maidens, resorted to trickery, and appeared on earth from time to time in the form of poor and humble people. When the goddess saw this insult glowing in bright colors on Arachne's loom, she did not wait while the cloth was judged, but stepped forward, her grey eyes blazing with anger, and tore Arachne's work across. Then she struck Arachne across the face. Arachne stood there a moment, struggling with anger, fear, and pride. "I will not live under this insult," she cried, and seizing a rope from the wall, she made a noose and would have hanged herself.

The goddess touched the rope and touched the maiden. "Live on, wicked girl," she said. "Live on and spin, both you and your descendants. When men look at you they may remember that it is not wise to strive with Athene." At that the body of Arachne shrivelled up; and her legs grew tiny, spindly, and distorted. There before the eyes of the spectators hung a little dusty brown spider on a slender thread.

All spiders descend from Arachne, and as the Greeks watched them spinning their thread wonderfully fine, they remembered the contest with Athene and thought that it was not right for even the best of men to claim equality with the gods.

THINK AND DISCUSS
Understanding
1. Why is Arachne famous?
2. What is Athene's advice to Arachne?
3. Describe Arachne's response to Athene's advice.
4. Describe the patterns that Athene and Arachne weave.
5. Summarize how the weaving contest ends.

Analyzing
6. To whom does Arachne give credit for her success?

7. Why do you think Athene has chosen to visit Arachne disguised as a poor, old woman?

8. Explain why Athene and Arachne choose the designs they do.

9. To the ancient Greeks, one of the greatest sins was *hubris* (hyü′bris), excessive pride or arrogance. Is Arachne guilty of hubris? Explain.

Extending

10. Do you think that Arachne deserves her fate? Why or why not?

REVIEWING: Tone HT
See Handbook of Literary Terms, p. 691.

Tone is the author's attitude toward the subject or audience. An author may view a subject with seriousness, sympathy, irony, displeasure, humor, or indignation. An author reveals the tone by the choice of words and details. Describe the author's attitude toward Arachne and her fate. Give at least four examples from the myth to support your answer.

COMPOSITION
Discussing a Plot

Write a composition in which you discuss the plot of this myth. In your discussion, include all the elements necessary to constructing a plot. Be sure to state where the climax of the myth occurs. You may want to review the article on plot in the Handbook of Literary Terms before you begin to write.

Changing Point of View

Rewrite the story of Arachne from her point of view. To be sure that your composition is "in character," review the myth, noting examples of Arachne's speech and actions. End your composition with Arachne's reaction to her fate. Is she angry, sorry, outraged, ashamed?

BIOGRAPHY

Olivia Coolidge
1908–

Olivia Coolidge was born in London, England, where she became a teacher of Latin and Greek. She also taught in Germany and in the United States. In addition to her deep interest in mythology, she has a love of history. The large number of history books she has written include *Roman People* (1959), *Gandhi* (1971), and *The Presidency of Abraham Lincoln* (1976).

Comment

Transformations in Myth

Arachne was transformed, and thus spiders were created. Throughout Greek mythology runs a theme of such magical changes of shape. Transformation myths account for the origins of certain animals, flowers, trees, mountains—even stars.

Narcissus (när sis′əs) was such a beautiful young man that all the women who saw him longed to be his. Not interested in them or their broken hearts, Narcissus went on his cruel way, scorning love. Those he had wounded prayed to the gods that Narcissus be punished, and the prayer was answered. One day as he knelt by a pool to drink, he saw in the clear water a beautiful face and form and immediately fell in love with it. He could not reach the object of his love, but he could not bear to leave it. So there he remained, leaning over the pool, gazing at his own reflection until at length he turned into the flower that is called narcissus.

One of those who loved Narcissus was Echo, a nymph condemned never to use her voice except to repeat what was said to her. Unable to express her love or to say anything but others' words, she hid herself in a lonely cave and wasted away from longing until only her voice remained. To this day, Echo's voice lingers in caves and on mountainsides, echoing whatever is said to her.

Zeus once fell in love with a young woman named Callisto (kə lis′ tō), who bore him a son. Hera, in a fit of jealousy, turned Callisto into a bear. Later when the son was grown, he encountered the bear one day when he was hunting. Not knowing who she was, he was about to shoot his mother when Zeus carried her up to the sky and placed her among the stars, where she is known as the Great Bear (Ursa Major, also called the Big Dipper). Her son was placed near her and called the Lesser Bear. Hera, still jealous, forbade the Bears ever to descend into the ocean; of all the constellations, they alone never set below the horizon.

A fisherman named Glaucus (glô′kəs) one day spread his catch out on a grassy meadow near the shore. As they touched the grass, the fish began to jump about and dive back into the sea. Amazed, Galucus tasted the grass and immediately felt possessed to jump into the water. The gods of the sea saved him by turning him into a merman with green flowing hair and beard and a body tapering to a fish-like tail. His new form did not prevent him from falling in love with the nymph Scylla (sil′ə), but she was frightened and fled from him. Glaucus then asked Circe (sër′sē), the enchantress, for a potion to cause Scylla to love him. Circe fell in love with Glaucus herself, however, and instead of a love potion mixed a powerful poison, which she poured into the bay where Scylla swam. When Scylla entered the water her body became covered with horrible growths of barking heads. In that spot the monster Scylla remained, destroying in her rage the sailors on ships that passed. At last she was transformed into a rock; in this new form she is still dangerous to sailors and their ships.

Daedalus

retold by **Anne Terry White**

"Not even the eagle soars as high as this!" the boy thought.

In the days when King Minos ruled Crete and his mighty navy ranged the seas, there lived in Athens a man by the name of Daedalus. And his name was known as far and wide as that of Minos. For Daedalus was the greatest architect and sculptor of his time. There was nothing his ingenious mind could not design or his skillful hands execute. And his statues were so real that people said they lived. It seemed that at any moment they might move a hand or take a step or open their lips and speak.

His young nephew, Talus, also had clever hands and a creative mind. So his mother placed him with her brother that the boy might learn his marvelous skills. But Talus had a genius of his own and even more imagination. Walking on the shore one day, he picked up the backbone of a fish. Idly he drew the strong, sharp spines forward and back across a piece of driftwood. They cut deep into the wood. He went home and notched a metal blade all along one edge—and he had a saw. Another time he fixed two iron rods together at the tip. He held one firmly upright against the earth and moved the other slowly around. It made a perfect circle—he had invented the compass.

Talus was a pupil to make any teacher excited and proud. But not Daedalus. Instead of being pleased, he was frightened and sorely jealous.

"Talus will soon surpass me!" he thought.

He could not bear the idea of a rival, and came to hate the boy. And one day, when they stood together on a height, Daedalus pushed Talus off to his death.

He had not planned the deed. It had been a sudden, crazy impulse. The next instant, horrified at what he had done, he rushed down to the boy. But it was too late. Talus was dead, and not all the wonderful skills of Daedalus could call him back. Clearly, if Daedalus wished to save his own life, he must flee. So he left Athens and wandered miserably from place to place, until at last he left Greece altogether and crossed the sea to Crete.

King Minos was delighted to have the Athenian in his realm. The King had something in mind that called for the genius of Daedalus. Minos possessed a fearful monster, with the head and shoulders of a bull and the legs and trunk of a man. The creature

---

was called the Minotaur—that is, the Bull of Minos. The King wanted a suitable place to keep the Minotaur. The building must be such that neither the monster himself nor any victim sent in to be devoured by him could possibly escape from it.

So, at the King's command, Daedalus designed the labyrinth. The building was a bewildering maze of passages. They turned back upon themselves, crisscrossed, and went round and round without leading anywhere. Once inside the labyrinth, it was all but impossible to find the way out again. Even Daedalus himself was once nearly lost.

King Minos was delighted with Daedalus's work and held him in highest favor. Yet Daedalus was less than pleased, for he felt himself to be no better than a prisoner in Crete. The King was so afraid Daedalus would reveal the secret of the labyrinth that he would not let him leave the island. And for that very reason Daedalus yearned to go. With what envy he watched the birds winging their way through the sky!

One day, as his eyes followed the graceful sea birds cleaving the ocean of air, an idea came to him.

"King Minos may shut my way out by land and by sea," he thought, "but he does not control the air."

And he began to study the flight of birds and to observe how their wings are fashioned. He watched the little song birds fold and unfold their wings, watched how they rose from the ground, flew down from the trees, and went to and fro. He also watched the herons slowly flapping their great wings. He watched the eagles soar and swoop. He saw, too, how their feathers overlapped one an-

other—where they were large and where they were small.

When he thought he understood the secrets of flight, Daedalus went to a nesting place he knew of and gathered feathers of various sizes. And in a chamber close to the roof he began to build wings. First he laid down a row of the tiniest feathers, then a row of larger ones overlapping them, and yet larger ones beyond these. He fastened the feathers together in the middle with thread and at the bottom with wax. And when he had built on enough rows, he bent them around into a gentle curve to look like real birds' wings.

His young son Icarus stood by and watched his father work. Laughing, the boy caught the feathers when they blew away in the wind. He pressed his thumb into the yellow wax to soften it for his father, hindering more than he helped.

When Daedalus had finished the pair of wings, he put them on. He raised himself in the air and hovered there. He moved the wings just as he had seen birds do, and lo! he could fly. Icarus clapped his hands together in delight.

"Make me a pair of wings, too, father!" he cried.

Then Daedalus made a second pair of wings and prepared his son to fly.

"Now I warn you, Icarus," Daedalus said, "not to be reckless. Be wise, not bold. Take a course midway between heaven and earth. For if you fly too high, the sun will scorch your feathers. And if you fly too low, the sea will wet them. Take me for your guide. Follow me and you will be safe."

All the time he was speaking, Daedalus

was fastening the wings to his son's shoulders. His hands trembled as he thought of the great adventure before them. At the same time, he was worried about the boy. He did not know whether he could quite trust Icarus to obey. As he adjusted his own wings and kissed the excited child, tears ran down Daedalus's face.

"Remember," he repeated for the last time. "Heed my words and stay close to me!"

Then he rose on his wings and flew from the housetop. Icarus followed.

Daedalus kept a watchful eye on the boy, even as a mother bird does when she has brought a fledgling out of its nest in the treetops and launched it in the air. It was early morning. Few people were about. But here and there a plowman in the field or a fisherman tending his nets caught sight of them.

"They must be gods!" the simple toilers cried, and they bent their bodies in reverent worship.

Father and son flew far out over the sea. Daedalus was no longer worried about Icarus, who managed his wings as easily as a bird. Already the islands of Delos and Paros were behind them. Calymne, rich in honey, was on their right hand. But now Icarus began to yield to the full delight of his new-found powers. He wanted to soar and swoop. How thrilling it was to rise to a height, close his wings, and speed down, down, like a thunderbolt, then turn and rise again!

Time after time Icarus tried it, each time daring greater heights. Then, forgetting his father's warning, he soared higher still, far up into the cloudless sky.

"Not even the eagle soars as high as this!" the boy thought. "I am like the gods that keep the wide heaven."

As the words crossed his mind, he felt a warm stream flow over his shoulders. He had come too close to the blazing sun, and the sweet-smelling wax that bound the feathers was melting. With a shock of terror he felt himself hurtling downward. His wings, broken in a thousand parts, were hurtling downward, too. In vain Icarus moved his arms up and down—he could get no hold on the air.

"Father!" he shrieked. "Father! Help! I am falling."

Even as he cried, the deep blue water of the sea—that ever since has been called Icarian—closed over him.

"Icarus! Icarus! Where are you?" Daedalus cried, turning in every direction and searching the air behind, above, and all around. Then his eyes fell on the sea. Tufts of feathers were floating on the crest of the waves.

Too well he understood their meaning. Folding his great wings, he came to earth on the nearest island and fixed his streaming eyes upon the sea. He beat his breast. Wildly he clutched his hair.

"O Icarus, my son!" he wailed. "Even so fell Talus whom my envy slew! The gods have avenged him." He ripped off his glorious wings and stamped upon them. "Cursed be the skill that wrought my son's destruction!" he cried.

Days afterwards, the body of Icarus washed to the shore. There, on the lonely island which bears the boy's name, Daedalus buried his only son.

THINK AND DISCUSS

Understanding

1. Why must Daedalus flee Athens?
2. Why does King Minos welcome him?
3. How does Daedalus plan to escape?

Analyzing

4. This myth touches on two concepts important to the Greeks. The first is *hubris*. Explain whether Daedalus and Icarus are guilty of hubris.
5. A second concept important to the Greeks is *nemesis* (nem′ə sis), by which an evil deed is appropriately punished. (Nemesis was the goddess of vengeance or divine punishment.) In what sense might the story of Daedalus serve as an illustration of nemesis?

Extending

6. Do you think myths such as that of Daedalus and Icarus would encourage or discourage progress and invention? Explain.
7. How might Daedalus's warning to Icarus be updated to apply to advice given by modern parents to their children?

READING LITERATURE SKILLFULLY

Conclusions

A **conclusion** is a decision or opinion reached after thinking about facts and details. Often, authors don't tell you what to think about a character or an event they create. They give you the information you need to form your own conclusions. The following are conclusions. For each one, tell whether it is supported by the facts given in "Daedalus."

1. Minos was an evil king.
2. Daedalus was an indulgent father.
3. Icarus was as talented as his father.
4. Icarus is punished for hubris.

COMPOSITION

Reading/Writing Log

The myths of Arachne and Daedalus have very different endings, both in the information given and in **mood**. The ending of "Arachne" explains something in nature and provides a moral or lesson. Copy this ending in your reading/writing log. Now copy the ending of "Daedalus." Discuss ways in which the mood of the ending of "Daedalus" is different from the mood of the ending of "Arachne."

Writing to Express an Opinion

Skim this textbook to review endings of selections you have already studied. Choose three of these and copy them in your reading/writing log. After each one, write one sentence telling how the ending affected you.

Writing a News Story

Imagine that you are a newspaper reporter assigned to write a report about the death of Icarus. You interview Daedalus and other people who may have witnessed any of the events leading up to and including Icarus's death. Then write a short news story on your subject.

Phaëthon

retold by **Edith Hamilton**

For a few thrilling moments, Phaëthon felt like the Lord of the Sky. But suddenly the chariot was swinging to and fro—he had lost control!

he palace of the Sun was a radiant place. It shone with gold and gleamed with ivory and sparkled with jewels. Everything without and within flashed and glowed and glittered. It was always high noon there. Shadowy twilight never dimmed the brightness. Darkness and night were unknown. Few among mortals could have long endured that unchanging brilliancy of light, but few had ever found their way thither.

Nevertheless, one day a youth, mortal on his mother's side, dared to approach. Often he had to pause and clear his dazzled eyes, but the errand which had brought him was so urgent that his purpose held fast and he pressed on, up to the palace, through the burnished doors, and into the throneroom where surrounded by a blinding, blazing splendor the Sun-god sat. There the lad was forced to halt. He could bear no more.

Nothing escapes the eyes of the Sun. He saw the boy instantly and he looked at him very kindly. "What brought you here?" he asked. "I have come," the other answered boldly, "to find out if you are my father or not. My mother said you were, but the boys at school laugh when I tell them I am your son. They will not believe me. I told my mother and she said I had better go and ask you." Smiling, the Sun took off his crown of burning light so that the lad could look at him without distress. "Come here, Phaëthon," he said. "You are my son. Clymene told you the truth. I expect you will not doubt my word too? But I will give you a proof. Ask anything you want of me and you shall have it. I call the Styx to be witness to my promise, the river of the oath of the Gods."

No doubt Phaëthon had often watched the Sun riding through the heavens and had told himself with a feeling, half awe, half excitement, "It is my father up there." And then he would wonder what it would be like to be in that chariot, guiding the steeds along that dizzy course, giving light to the world. Now at his father's words this wild dream had become possible. Instantly he cried, "I choose to take your place, Father. That is the only thing I want. Just for a day, a single day, let me have your car to drive."

Peter Paul Rubens, "The Fall of Phäethon" (detail), *Musées Royaux des Beaux-Arts de Belgique*

The Sun realized his own folly. Why had he taken that fatal oath and bound himself to give in to anything that happened to enter a boy's rash young head? "Dear lad," he said, "this is the only thing I would have refused you. I know I cannot refuse. I have sworn by the Styx. I must yield if you persist. But I do not believe you will. Listen while I tell you what this is you want. You are Clymene's son as well as mine. You are mortal and no mortal could drive my chariot. Indeed, no god except myself can do that. The ruler of the gods cannot. Consider the road. It rises up from the sea so steeply that the horses can hardly climb it, fresh though they are in the early morning. In midheaven it is so high that even I do not like to look down. Worst of all is the descent, so precipitous that the Sea-gods waiting to receive me wonder how I can avoid falling headlong. To guide the horses, too, is a perpetual struggle. Their fiery spirits grow hotter as they climb and they scarcely suffer my control. What would they do with you?

"Are you fancying that there are all sorts of wonders up there, cities of the gods full of beautiful things? Nothing of the kind. You will have to pass beasts, fierce beasts of prey, and they are all that you will see. The Bull, the Lion, the Scorpion, the great Crab,[1] each will try to harm you. Be persuaded. Look around you. See all the goods the rich world holds. Choose from them your heart's desire and it shall be yours. If what you want is to be proved my son, my fears for you are proof enough that I am your father."

But none of all this wise talk meant anything to the boy. A glorious prospect opened before him. He saw himself proudly standing in that wondrous car, his hands triumphantly guiding those steeds which Jove himself could not master. He did not give a thought to the dangers his father detailed. He felt not a quiver of fear, not a doubt of his own powers. At last the Sun gave up trying to dissuade him. It was hopeless, as he saw. Besides, there was not time. The moment for starting was at hand. Already the gates of the east glowed purple, and Dawn had opened her courts full of rosy light. The stars were leaving the sky; even the lingering morning star was dim.

There was need for haste, but all was ready. The seasons, the gatekeepers of Olympus, stood waiting to fling the doors wide. The horses had been bridled and yoked to the car. Proudly and joyously Phaëthon mounted it and they were off. He had made his choice. Whatever came of it he could not change now. Not that he wanted to in that first exhilarating rush through the air, so swift that the East Wind was outstripped and left far behind. The horses' flying feet went through the low-banked clouds near the ocean as through a thin sea mist and then up and up in the clear air, climbing the height of heaven. For a few ecstatic moments Phaëthon felt himself the Lord of the Sky. But suddenly there was a change. The chariot was swinging wildly to and fro; the pace was faster; he had lost control. Not he, but the horses were directing the course. That light weight in the car, those feeble hands clutching the reins, had told them their own driver was not there. They were the masters then. No one else could command them. They left the road and rushed where they chose, up, down, to the right, to the left. They nearly wrecked the chariot against the Scorpion; they brought up short and almost ran into the Crab. By this time the poor charioteer was half fainting with terror, and he let the reins fall.

That was the signal for still more mad and reckless running. The horses soared up to the very top of the sky and then, plunging headlong down, they set the world on fire. The highest mountains were the first to burn, Ida and Helicon, where the Muses dwell, Parnassus, and heaven-piercing Olympus. Down their slopes the flame ran to the low-lying valleys and the dark forest lands, until all things everywhere were ablaze. The springs turned into steam; the rivers shrank. It is said that it was then the Nile fled and hid his head, which still is hidden.

In the car Phaëthon, hardly keeping his place there, was wrapped in thick smoke and heat as if from a fiery furnace. He wanted nothing except to have this torment and terror ended. He would have welcomed death. Mother Earth, too, could bear no more. She uttered a great cry which reached up to the gods. Looking down from Olympus they saw that they must act quickly if the world was to be saved. Jove seized his thunderbolt and hurled it at the rash, repentant driver. It struck him dead, shattered the chariot, and made the maddened horses rush down into the sea.

Phaëthon all on fire fell from the car through the air to the earth. The mysterious river Eridanus, which no mortal eyes have ever seen, received him and put out the flames and cooled the body. The naiads, in pity for him, so bold and so young to die, buried him and carved upon the tomb:—

Here Phaëthon lies
    who drove the Sun-god's car.
Greatly he failed,
    but he had greatly dared.

His sisters, the Heliades, the daughters of Helios, the Sun, came to his grave to mourn for him. There they were turned into poplar trees, on the bank of the Eridanus,

Where sorrowing they weep into the
    stream forever.
And each tear as it falls shines in
    the water
A glistening drop of amber.

---

1. *the Bull . . . the great Crab,* the constellations of Taurus, Leo, Scorpio, and Cancer, respectively.

THINK AND DISCUSS
Understanding
1. Why does Phaëthon go to the palace of the sun?
2. What does he ask of the Sun?
3. What does the Sun warn Phaëthon about?
4. Why does the Sun give in to Phaëthon's request?
5. Describe what happens to Phaëthon. Why does it happen?

Analyzing

6. What are the "beasts" that Phaëthon encounters in the sky?

7. What natural phenomenon does this myth explain?

Extending

8. The Sun offers Phaëthon anything he wishes. What do you think he might have chosen that would have been wonderful, but less deadly?

THINKING SKILLS
Synthesizing

Drama critics, looking back at the dramatic productions on television during the 1950s and early 1960s, named that era the "Golden Age of Television." In doing this they synthesized historical events, their knowledge of plays produced for television before and since then, and their own tastes and standards. Given what you have learned in this unit about the ancient Greeks and the myths they created, decide on a name for that period in history.

COMPOSITION
Reading/Writing Log

Edith Hamilton has chosen to end her retelling of this myth with a few lines of poetry. Copy this ending in your reading/writing log. Then discuss this type of ending. Do you think it is effective?

Writing an Ending

Change the ending of one of the myths in this unit by replacing it with a few lines of poetry.

Writing an Essay

Do you think the punishment Phaëthon receives is an example of poetic justice? Write a short essay defending your opinion. Before you begin your essay, see "Using Evidence Effectively" in the Writer's Handbook.

ENRICHMENT
Research Project

Working with a classmate, choose a constellation. Do the research necessary to learn about it, and present your findings to the class. Use at least two visual aids in your report. These might be drawings, slides, photographs, or anything else available to you.

BIOGRAPHY

Edith Hamilton
1867–1963

For Edith Hamilton, the classics were part life as early as age seven, when she was already reading Latin. Receiving both her B.A. and M.A. in the same year from Bryn Mawr College in Maryland, she later became headmistress of Bryn Mawr School. Her first book, *The Greek Way*, was published after her retirement.

GLOSSARY OF PROPER NAMES

Aetna (et′nə), **Mount,** volcano located in northeast Sicily. It is still active.

Amphitrite (am′fə trī′tē), wife of Poseidon.

Aphrodite (af′rə dī′tē), goddess of love and beauty. Roman name: Venus.

Apollo (ə pol′ō), god of the sun, poetry, music, prophecy, and healing. Also called Helios. Roman name: Phoebus (fē′ bəs) Apollo.

Arachne (ə rak′nē), lost a weaving contest to Athene and was changed into a spider.

Athene (ə thē′nē), goddess of wisdom, of weaving and other household arts, and of warfare. Roman name: Minerva (mə nėr′və).

Attica (at′ə kə), southern region of Greece.

Baucis (bô′sis), old peasant woman who entertained Zeus and Hermes.

Clymene (klim′ə nē), mother of Phaëthon.

Cronos (krō′nəs), father of the gods of Olympus.

Cyclops (sī′klops), *pl.* **Cyclopes** (sī klō′pēz), a race of giants, children of Oranos, each having one eye in the center of the forehead.

Daedalus (ded′l əs), skilled workman who constructed the labyrinth in Crete; with his son Icarus he escaped from imprisonment by using wings he built of feathers fastened by wax.

Demeter (di mē′tər), goddess of agriculture and the harvest. Roman name: Ceres (sir′ēz).

Eros (ir′os, er′os), son of Aphrodite. Roman name: Cupid.

Hades (hā′dēz), god of the underworld, which is often called by his name. Roman name: Pluto.

Heliades (hē li′ ə dēz), daughters of Helios.

Helios (hē′lē os), god of the sun, pictured driving a chariot drawn by four horses through the heavens. Also called Apollo.

Hera (hir′ə), wife of Zeus and queen of the gods; goddess of women and marriage. Roman name: Juno (jü′nō).

Hermes (hėr′mēz), messenger of the gods and guide of dead souls to the underworld; god of travel, business, invention, and cunning. Roman name: Mercury ("Quicksilver").

Icarian (i ker′ē ən, ī ker′ē ən) **Sea,** named for Icarus, who drowned in it.

Icarus (ik′ər əs), son of Daedalus. While escaping from Crete on wings that Daedalus made, Icarus flew so high that the sun melted the wax on his wings, and he drowned in the sea.

Oranus (ôr ān′əs), "First One," ancestor of all gods.

Pan (pan), god of flocks, forests, and shepherds. His body was half human, with the legs, horns, and ears of a goat.

Persephone (pər sef′ə nē), daughter of Demeter. Hades fell in love with her and carried her off to rule the underworld with him. Roman name: Proserpina (prō sėr′pə nə).

Phaëthon (fā′ə thon), son of Helios who tried unsuccessfully to drive the sun chariot.

Philemon (fi lē′mon), old peasant man who entertained Zeus and Hermes.

Poseidon (pə sīd′n), god of the sea. Roman name: Neptune.

Rhea (rē′ə), goddess of the earth.

Styx (stiks), river in the underworld that the souls of the dead must cross to reach Hades.

Titan (tīt′n), any one of the gigantic offspring of Oranos; called the "first race."

Zeus (züs), chief god of Olympus, ruler of gods and humans. Roman names: Jupiter, Jove.

a hat	**i** it	**oi** oil	**ch** child	a in about
ā age	**ī** ice	**ou** out	**ng** long	e in taken
ä far	**o** hot	**u** cup	**sh** she	ə = { i in pencil
e let	**ō** open	**u̇** put	**th** thin	o in lemon
ē equal	**ô** order	**ü** rule	**ᴛʜ** then	u in circus
ėr term			**zh** measure	**<** = derived from

THINKING CRITICALLY
ABOUT LITERATURE

UNIT 7   GREEK MYTHS

■ CONCEPT REVIEW

The myth that ends this unit contains many of the important ideas and literary terms found in the myths you have just studied. The notes and questions in the margin are designed to help you think critically about what you are reading. For a more extensive discussion of literary terms, see the Handbook of Literary Terms.

Baucis and Philemon

retold by   **Olivia Coolidge**

One time Zeus and Hermes came down to earth in human form and traveled through a certain district, asking for food and shelter as they went. For a long time they found nothing but refusals from both rich and poor until at last they came to a little, one-room cottage rudely thatched with reeds from the nearby marsh, where dwelled a poor old couple, Baucis and Philemon.

The two had little to offer, since they lived entirely from the produce of their plot of land and a few goats, fowl, and pigs. Nevertheless they were prompt to ask the strangers in and to set their best before them. The couch that they pulled forward for their guests was roughly put together from willow boughs, and the cushions on it were stuffed with straw. One table leg had to be propped up with a piece of broken pot, but Baucis scrubbed the top with fragrant mint and set some water on the fire. Meanwhile Philemon ran out into the garden to

■ **generalizing:** The ancient Greeks considered hospitality a virtue.

■ Both the setting and the character of Baucis and Philemon are established in this paragraph and the one that follows.

"Baucis and Philemon" from *Greek Myths* by Olivia E. Coolidge. Copyright 1949 and © renewed 1977 by Olivia E. Coolidge. Reprinted by permission of Houghton Mifflin Company.

fetch a cabbage and then lifted down a piece of home-cured bacon from the blackened beam where it hung. While these were cooking, Baucis set out her best delicacies on the table. There were ripe olives, sour cherries pickled in wine, fresh onions and radishes, cream cheese, and eggs baked in the ashes of the fire. There was a big earthenware bowl in the midst of the table to mix their crude, homemade wine with water.

The second course had to be fruit, but there were nuts, figs, dried dates, plums, grapes, and apples, for this was their best season of the year. Philemon had even had it in mind to kill their only goose for dinner, and there was a great squawking and cackling that went on for a long time. Poor old Philemon wore himself out trying to catch that goose, but somehow the animal always got away from him until the guests bade him let it be, for they were well served as it was. It was a good meal, and the old couple kept pressing their guests to eat and drink, caring nothing that they were now consuming in one day what would ordinarily last them a week.

■ You can infer that the goose is getting some help from the gods.

At last the wine sank low in the mixing bowl, and Philemon rose to fetch some more. But to his astonishment as he lifted the wineskin to pour, he found the bowl was full again as though it had not been touched at all. Then he knew the two strangers must be gods, and he and Baucis were awed and afraid. But the gods smiled kindly at them, and the younger, who seemed to do most of the talking, said, "Philemon, you have welcomed us beneath your roof this day when richer men refused us shelter. Be sure those shall be punished who would not help the wandering stranger, but you shall have whatever reward you choose. Tell us what you will have."

■ tone (page 556): Note how this statement helps to establish the tone.

The old man thought for a little with his eyes bent on the ground, and then he said: "We have lived together here for many years, happy even though the times have been hard. But never yet did we see fit to turn a stranger from our gate or to seek a reward for entertaining him. To have spoken with the immortals face to face is a thing few men can boast of. In this small cottage, humble though it is, the gods have sat at meat. It is as unworthy of the honor as we are. If, therefore, you will do something for us, turn this cottage into a temple where the gods may always be served and where we may live out the remainder of our days in worship of them."

■ These requests are in keeping with what we know about the characters of Baucis and Philemon.

■ theme (page 541): Hospitality, respect for the gods, and lack of greed are qualities pleasing to the gods.

"You have spoken well," said Hermes, "and you shall have your wish. Yet is there not anything that you would desire for yourselves?"

Philemon thought again at this, stroking his straggly beard, and he glanced over at old Baucis with her thin, grey hair and her rough hands as she served at the table, her feet bare on the floor of trodden earth. "We have lived together for many years," he said again, "and in all that time there has never been a word of anger between us. Now, at last, we are growing old and our long companionship is coming to an end. It is the only thing that has helped us in the bad times and the source of our joy in the good. Grant us this one request, that when we come to die, we may perish in the same hour and neither of us be left without the other."

He looked at Baucis and she nodded in approval, so the old couple turned their eyes on the gods.

"It shall be as you desire," said Hermes. "Few men would have made such a good and moderate request."

Thereafter the house became a temple, and the neighbors, amazed at the change, came often to worship and left offerings for the support of the aged priest and priestess there. For many years Baucis and Philemon lived in peace, passing from old to extreme old age. At last, they were so old and bowed that it seemed they could only walk at all if they clutched one another. But still every evening they would shuffle a little way down the path that they might turn and look together at the beautiful little temple and praise the gods for the honor bestowed on them. One evening it took them longer than ever to reach the usual spot, and there they turned arm in arm to look back, thinking perhaps that it was the last time their limbs would support them so far. There as they stood, each one felt the other stiffen and change and only had time to turn and say once, "Farewell," before they disappeared. In their place stood two tall trees growing closely side by side with branches interlaced. They seemed to nod and whisper to each other in the passing breeze.

■ Evaluate this ending according to what you have learned about good endings.

THINK AND DISCUSS
Understanding
1. What gods visit earth? What form do they take?
2. What kinds of people refuse these gods shelter?
3. Describe the people who finally take the gods in. How do they treat the gods? Who do they think their guests are?
4. What two gifts do Baucis and Philemon ask for?
5. What happens to the old couple?

Analyzing

6. What quality did the ancient Greeks value highly? How do you know?

Extending

7. How would Baucis and Philemon have behaved if they had possessed hubris?

REVIEWING LITERARY TERMS
Theme

1. In one sentence, state the theme of "Baucis and Philemon."

Tone

2. Describe the tone of the myth.

■ CONTENT REVIEW
THINKING SKILLS
Classifying

1. Classify the myths you have read in this unit according to whether they explain a natural phenomenon or tell how mortals should behave.

Generalizing

2. Compare and contrast the tone of "Poseidon" with the tone of "Phaëthon."

3. Of all those described in this unit, which would you most like to challenge and defeat? Why?

Synthesizing

4. Our society also creates mythic figures. Think about people in public life, books, plays, and movies. Are any of these similar to characters you have met in this unit? Give details to support your answer.

Evaluating

5. If you could be transported to ancient Greece and given the chance to meet one of the gods, which would you choose? Why?

6. Many of these myths tell how mortals should behave. Of all the advice given, what do you think would be most useful today? Explain.

■ COMPOSITION REVIEW
Writing a Myth

Choose a modern situation that you think should be changed or done away with. Then write a myth that shows this situation and what happens to people who take part in it. Use one or more of the Greek gods and goddesses in your myth. Be sure to describe the fates of mortals taking part in the situation that you would like to correct.

Writing to Compare and Contrast

Choose two characters from the myths you have read. In a composition of four paragraphs, compare and contrast these characters. In the first paragraph, introduce the characters and briefly describe them. In the second paragraph, tell how the characters are alike. In the third, tell how they are different. The last paragraph should be a summary of points made in the first three.

Reviewing Writer's Craft: Write Good Endings

Write a composition describing a battle between two of the creatures you read about in this unit, a creature from one of the myths and a creature you make up, or two creatures you make up. If you are keeping a reading/writing log, review it before you write your ending.

# NOVEL

Frank E. Schoonover, "Breaking Trail" (detail), *Glenbow Museum*

PREVIEW

UNIT 8   NOVEL

The Call of the Wild / Jack London
from **Homesick** / Jean Fritz

Features
Reading a Novel
The Writer's Craft: Build Emphasis
Comment: He Inspired Jack London
Comment: Buck's Wild World: The
   World of Wolves

Reviewing Literary Terms
connotation/denotation

Reading Literature Skillfully
main idea and supporting details

Vocabulary Skills
context

Thinking Skills
classifying
synthesizing

Composition
Reading/Writing Log
Writing a Description
Writing as a Story Character
Starting a Novel
Writing to Persuade
Writing a Bill of Rights
Writing to Compare and Contrast

Enrichment
Research Project
Group Report
Panel Presentation

Thinking Critically About Literature
Concept Review
Content Review
Composition Review

Reading A NOVEL

When you read a novel, you respond to the same elements that are present in a short story. You develop a sense of the **theme,** the main idea that emerges from the struggle of characters to resolve a **conflict.** You pay attention to how the **supporting details** of **plot, character,** and **setting** work together to convey theme.

The title of a novel usually suggests the theme. Before you start to read, ask yourself:

• What does the title of the novel suggest?

For example, in *The Call of the Wild,* what are the denotations and connotations of the key words, *call* and *wild*?

Most novels are divided into chapters, and the theme of each chapter contributes to the theme of the novel. Often the theme of a chapter is signaled by its title. As you begin each chapter, ask:

• What main idea is suggested by the chapter title?
• How might this chapter contribute to the main idea of the entire novel?

When you read a novel, you should also watch for conflicts. Ask yourself these questions about any novel you read:

• What seems to be the major conflict?
• How is this conflict resolved?
• What is the most important idea that the author states or implies about this major conflict?

In *The Call of the Wild,* for example, the human characters are involved in a rush to find gold in the Alaskan wilderness; the animal characters are the dogs that pull sleds over the frozen trails. Of these animals, the main character is Buck. As you read, ask these questions:

• What conflicts does Buck have with people? with other animals? within himself?
• What is Buck's major conflict?
• How is this conflict resolved?
• Which conflict seems to be most important to Jack London?
• Does this conflict occur only in animals?

Setting can also affect your understanding of theme. For example, *The Call of the Wild* takes place in 1897 during the Klondike gold rush—before dehydrated food, walkie-talkies, helicopters, and a host of other technological advances that can today reduce the hazards of arctic travel. As you read this or any novel, ask:

• How does this setting affect characters?
• How does setting affect the outcome?

If you keep all these questions in mind as you read, you will understand and see the world the novelist is creating. In *The Call of the Wild,* you will enter a world that is sometimes civilized—a world that shows the power of love—and a world that is more often savage—one that shows the power of force. You will learn how people and animals respond to the calls from both worlds.

Review CONNOTATION/DENOTATION in the Handbook of Literary Terms, page 661

The Call of the Wild

Jack London

1 Into the Primitive

"Old longings nomadic leap,
   Chafing at custom's chain;
Again from its brumal sleep
   Wakens the ferine strain."

Buck did not read the newspapers, or he would have known that trouble was brewing, not alone for himself, but for every tidewater dog, strong of muscle and with warm, long hair, from Puget Sound to San Diego. Because men, groping in the Arctic darkness, had found a yellow metal, and because steamship and transportation companies were booming the find, thousands of men were rushing into the Northland. These men wanted dogs, and the dogs they wanted were heavy dogs, with strong muscles by which to toil, and furry coats to protect them from the frost.

Buck lived at a big house in the sun-kissed Santa Clara Valley.[1] Judge Miller's place, it was called. It stood back from the road, half hidden among the trees, through which glimpses could be caught of the wide cool veranda that ran around its four sides. The house was approached by gravelled driveways which wound about through wide-spreading lawns and under the interlacing boughs of tall poplars. At the rear things were on even a more spacious scale than at the front. There were great stables, where a dozen grooms and boys held forth, rows of vine-clad servants' cottages, an endless and orderly array of outhouses, long grape arbors, green pastures, orchards, and berry patches. Then there was the pumping plant for the artesian well, and the big cement tank where Judge Miller's boys took their morning plunge and kept cool in the hot afternoon.

And over this great demesne Buck ruled. Here he was born, and here he had lived the four years of his life. It was true, there were

---

1. **Santa Clara Valley.** The Santa Clara Valley is in western California, near San Francisco.

Jack London, *The Call of the Wild*, 1903. (Slightly abridged.)

other dogs. There could not but be other dogs on so vast a place, but they did not count. They came and went, resided in the populous kennels, or lived obscurely in the recesses of the house after the fashion of Toots, the Japanese pug, or Ysabel, the Mexican hairless—strange creatures that rarely put nose out of doors or set foot to ground. On the other hand, there were the fox terriers, a score of them at least, who yelped fearful promises at Toots and Ysabel looking out of the windows at them and protected by a legion of housemaids armed with brooms and mops.

But Buck was neither house-dog nor kennel dog. The whole realm was his. He plunged into the swimming tank or went hunting with the Judge's sons; he escorted Mollie and Alice, the Judge's daughters, on long twilight or early morning rambles; on wintry nights he lay at the Judge's feet before the roaring library fire; he carried the Judge's grandsons on his back, or rolled them in the grass, and guarded their footsteps through wild adventures down to the fountain in the stable yard, and even beyond, where the paddocks were, and the berry patches. Among the terriers he stalked imperiously, and Toots and Ysabel he utterly ignored, for he was king—king over all creeping, crawling, flying things of Judge Miller's place, humans included.

His father, Elmo, a huge St. Bernard, had been the Judge's inseparable companion, and Buck bid fair to follow in the way of his father. He was not so large—he weighed only one hundred and forty pounds—for his mother, Shep, had been a Scotch shepherd dog. Nevertheless, one hundred and forty pounds, to which was added the dignity that comes of good living and universal respect, enabled him to carry himself in right royal fashion. During the four years since his puppyhood he had lived the life of a sated aristocrat; he had a fine pride in himself, was ever a trifle egotistical, as country gentlemen sometimes become because of their insular situation. But he had saved himself by not becoming a mere pampered house-dog. Hunting and kindred outdoor delights had kept down the fat and hardened his muscles; and to him, as to the cold-tubbing races, the love of water had been a tonic and a health preserver.

And this was the manner of dog Buck was in the fall of 1897, when the Klondike strike dragged men from all the world into the frozen North. But Buck did not read the newspapers, and he did not know that Manuel, one of the gardener's helpers, was an undesirable acquaintance. Manuel had one besetting sin. He loved to play Chinese lottery. Also, in his gambling, he had one besetting weakness—faith in a system; and this made his damnation certain. For to play a system requires money, while the wages of a gardener's helper do not lap over the needs of a wife and numerous progeny.

The Judge was at a meeting of the Raisin Growers' Association, and the boys were busy organizing an athletic club, on the memorable night of Manuel's treachery. No one saw him and Buck go off through the orchard on what Buck imagined was merely a stroll. And with the exception of a solitary man, no one saw them arrive at the little flag station known as College Park. This man talked with Manuel, and money chinked between them.

"You might wrap up the goods before you deliver 'm," the stranger said gruffly, and Manuel doubled a piece of stout rope around Buck's neck under the collar.

"Twist it, an' you'll choke 'm plentee," said Manuel, and the stranger grunted a ready affirmative.

Buck had accepted the rope with quiet dignity. To be sure, it was an unwonted performance: but he had learned to trust in men he knew, and to give them credit for a wisdom that outreached his own. But when the ends of the rope were placed in the stranger's hands, he growled menacingly. He had merely intimated his displeasure, in his pride believing that to intimate was to command. But to his surprise the rope tightened around his neck, shutting off his breath. In quick rage he sprang at the man, who met him halfway, grappled him close by the throat, and with a deft twist threw him over on his back. Then the rope tightened mercilessly, while Buck struggled in a fury, his tongue lolling out of his mouth and his great chest panting futilely. Never in all his life had he been so vilely treated, and never in all his life had he been so angry. But his strength ebbed, his eyes glazed, and he knew nothing when the train was flagged and the two men threw him into the baggage car.

The next he knew, he was dimly aware that his tongue was hurting and that he was being jolted along in some kind of a conveyance. The hoarse shriek of a locomotive whistling a crossing told him where he was. He had traveled too often with the Judge not to know the sensation of riding in a baggage car. He opened his eyes, and into them came the unbridled anger of a kidnapped king. The man sprang for his throat, but Buck was too quick for him. His jaws closed on the hand, nor did they relax till his senses were choked out of him once more.

"Yep, has fits," the man said, hiding his mangled hand from the baggageman, who had been attracted by the sounds of struggle. "I'm takin' 'm up for the boss to 'Frisco. A crack dog-doctor there thinks that he can cure 'em."

Concerning that night's ride, the man spoke most eloquently for himself, in a little shed back of a saloon on the San Francisco water front.

"All I get is fifty for it," he grumbled; "an' I wouldn't do it over for a thousand, cold cash."

His hand was wrapped in a bloody handkerchief, and the right trouser leg was ripped from knee to ankle.

"How much did the other mug get?" the saloon-keeper demanded.

"A hundred," was the reply. "Wouldn't take a sou less, so help me."

"That makes a hundred and fifty," the saloon-keeper calculated; "and he's worth it, or I'm a squarehead."

The kidnapper undid the bloody wrappings and looked at his lacerated hand. "If I don't get the hydrophoby—."

"It'll be because you was born to hang," laughed the saloon-keeper. "Here lend me a hand before you pull your freight," he added.

Dazed, suffering intolerable pain from throat and tongue, with the life half throttled out of him, Buck attempted to face his tormentors. But he was thrown down and choked repeatedly, till they succeeded in fil-ing the heavy brass collar from off his neck. Then the rope was removed, and he was flung into a cagelike crate.

There he lay for the remainder of the weary night, nursing his wrath and wounded pride. He could not understand what it all meant. What did they want with him, these strange men? Why were they keeping him pent up in this narrow crate? He did not know why, but he felt oppressed by the vague sense of impending calamity. Several times during the night he sprang to his feet when the shed door rattled open, expecting to see the Judge, or the boys at least. But each time it was the bulging face of the saloon-keeper that peered in at him by the sickly light of a tallow candle. And each time the joyful bark that trembled in Buck's throat was twisted into a savage growl.

But the saloon-keeper let him alone, and in the morning four men entered and picked up the crate. More tormentors, Buck decided, for they were evil-looking creatures, ragged and unkempt; and he stormed and raged at them through the bars. They only laughed and poked sticks at him, which he promptly assailed with his teeth till he realized that that was what they wanted. Whereupon he lay down sullenly and allowed the crate to be lifted into a wagon. Then he, and the crate in which he was imprisoned, began a passage through many hands. Clerks in the express office took charge of him; he was carted about in another wagon; a truck carried him, with an assortment of boxes and parcels, upon a ferry steamer; he was trucked off the steamer into a great railway depot, and finally he was deposited in an express car.

For two days and nights this express car

Frank Schoonover, "Sockeye,"
Private Collection

was dragged along at the tail of shrieking locomotives; and for two days and nights Buck neither ate nor drank. In his anger he had met the first advances of the express messengers with growls, and they had retaliated by teasing him. When he flung himself against the bars, quivering and frothing, they laughed at him and taunted him. They growled and barked like detestable dogs, mewed, and flapped their arms and crowed. It was all very silly, he knew; but therefore the more outrage to his dignity, and his anger waxed and waxed. He did not mind the hunger so much, but the lack of water caused him severe suffering and fanned his wrath to fever-pitch. For that matter, high-strung and finely sensitive, the ill treatment had flung him into a fever, which was fed by the inflammation of his parched and swollen throat and tongue.

He was glad for one thing: the rope was off his neck. That had given them an unfair advantage; but now that it was off, he would show them. They would never get another rope around his neck. Upon that he was resolved. For two days and nights he neither ate nor drank, and during those two days and nights of torment, he accumulated a fund of wrath that boded ill for whoever first fell foul of him. His eyes turned blood-shot, and he was metamorphosed into a raging fiend. So changed was he that the Judge himself would not have recognized him; and the express messengers breathed with relief when they bundled him off the train at Seattle.

Four men gingerly carried the crate from the wagon into a small, high-walled back yard. A stout man, with a red sweater that sagged generously at the neck, came out and signed the book for the driver. That was the man, Buck divined, the next tormentor, and he hurled himself savagely against the bars. The man smiled grimly, and brought a hatchet and a club.

"You ain't going to take him out now?" the driver asked.

"Sure," the man replied, driving the hatchet into the crate for a pry.

There was an instantaneous scattering of the four men who had carried it in, and from safe perches on top the wall they prepared to watch the performance.

Buck rushed at the splintering wood, sinking his teeth into it, surging and wrestling with it. Wherever the hatchet fell on the outside, he was there on the inside, snarling and growling, as furiously anxious to get out as the man in the red sweater was calmly intent on getting him out.

"Now, you red-eyed devil," he said, when he had made an opening sufficient for the passage of Buck's body. At the same time he dropped the hatchet and shifted the club to his right hand.

And Buck was truly a red-eyed devil, as he drew himself together for the spring, hair bristling, mouth foaming, a mad glitter in his blood-shot eyes. Straight at the man he launched his one hundred and forty pounds of fury, surcharged with the pent passion of two days and nights. In mid air, just as his jaws were about to close on the man, he received a shock that checked his body and brought his teeth together with an agonizing clip. He whirled over, fetching the ground on his back and side. He had never been struck by a club in his life, and did not understand. With a snarl that was part bark and more scream he was again on his feet and launched into the air. And again the shock came and he was brought crushingly to the ground. This time he was aware that it was the club, but his madness knew no caution. A dozen times he charged, and as often the club broke the charge and smashed him down.

After a particularly fierce blow he crawled to his feet, too dazed to rush. He staggered limply about, the blood flowing from nose and mouth and ears, his beautiful coat sprayed and flecked with bloody slaver. Then the man advanced and deliberately dealt him a frightful blow on the nose. All the pain he had endured was as nothing compared with the exquisite agony of this. With a roar that was almost lionlike in its ferocity, he again hurled himself at the man. But the man, shifting the club from right to left, coolly caught him by the under jaw, at the same time wrenching downward and backward. Buck described a complete circle in the air, and half of another, then crashed to the ground on his head and chest.

For the last time he rushed. The man struck the shrewd blow he had purposely withheld for so long, and Buck crumpled up and went down, knocked utterly senseless.

"He's no slouch at dog-breakin', that's wot I say," one of the men on the wall cried enthusiastically.

"Druther break cayuses any day, and twice on Sundays," was the reply of the driver, as he climbed on the wagon and started the horses.

Buck's senses came back to him, but not his strength. He lay where he had fallen, and from there he watched the man in the red sweater.

"'Answers to the name of Buck,'" the man soliloquized, quoting from the saloon-keeper's letter which had announced the consignment of the crate and contents. "Well, Buck, my boy," he went on in a genial voice, "we've had our little ruction, and the best thing we can do is to let it go at that. You've learned your place, and I know mine. Be a good dog and all 'll go well and the goose hang high. Be a bad dog, and I'll whale the stuffin' outa you. Understand?"

As he spoke he fearlessly patted the head he had so mercilessly pounded, and though Buck's hair involuntarily bristled at touch of the hand, he endured it without protest. When the man brought him water he drank eagerly, and later bolted a generous meal of raw meat, chunk by chunk, from the man's hand.

He was beaten (he knew that); but he was not broken. He saw, once for all, that he stood no chance against a man with a club. He had learned the lesson, and in all his after life he never forgot it. That club was a revelation. It was his introduction to the reign of primitive law, and he met the introduction halfway. The facts of life took on a fiercer aspect; and while he faced that aspect uncowed, he faced it with all the latent cunning of his nature aroused. As the days went by, other dogs came, in crates and at the ends of ropes, some docilely, and some raging and roaring as he had come; and one and all, he watched them pass under the dominion of the man in the red sweater. Again and again, as he looked at each brutal performance, the lesson was driven home to Buck: a man with a club was a law-giver, a master to be obeyed, though not necessarily conciliated. Of this last Buck was never guilty, though he did see beaten dogs that fawned upon the man, and wagged their tails, and licked his hand. Also he saw one dog, that would neither conciliate nor obey, finally killed in the struggle for mastery.

Now and again men came, strangers, who talked excitedly, wheedling, and in all kinds of fashions to the man in the red sweater. And at such times that money passed between them the strangers took one or more of the dogs away with them. Buck wondered where they went, for they never came back; but the fear of the future was strong upon him, and he was glad each time when he was not selected.

Yet his time came, in the end, in the form

you ain't got no kick coming, eh, Perrault?"

Perrault grinned. Considering that the price of dogs had been boomed skyward by the unwonted demand, it was not an unfair sum for so fine an animal. The Canadian Government would be no loser, nor would its dispatches travel the slower. Perrault knew dogs, and when he looked at Buck he knew that he was one in a thousand—"One in ten t'ousand," he commented mentally.

Buck saw money pass between them, and was not surprised when Curly, a good-natured Newfoundland, and he were led away by the little weazened man. That was the last he saw of the man in the red sweater, and as Curly and he looked at receding Seattle from the deck of the *Narwhal*, it was the last he saw of the warm Southland. Curly and he were taken below by Perrault and turned over to a . . . giant called François. . . . They were a new kind of men to Buck (of which he was destined to see many more), and while he developed no affection for them, he none the less grew honestly to respect them. He speedily learned that Perrault and François were fair men, calm and impartial in administering justice, and too wise in the way of dogs to be fooled by dogs.

In the 'tween-decks of the *Narwhal*, Buck and Curly joined two other dogs. One of them was a big, snow-white fellow from Spitzbergen who had been brought away by a whaling captain, and who had later accompanied a Geological Survey into the Barrens.

He was friendly, in a treacherous sort of way, smiling into one's face the while he

Frank Schoonover, "Trapper with Christmas Tree" (detail), *Private Collection*

of a little weazened man who spat broken English and many strange and uncouth exclamations which Buck could not understand.

"Sacredam!"[2] he cried, when his eyes lit upon Buck. "Dat one dam bully dog! Eh? How moch?"

"Three hundred, and a present at that," was the prompt reply of the man in the red sweater. "And seein' it's government money,

_____

2. *Sacredam,* Holy Mother, a mild oath.

meditated some underhand trick, as, for instance, when he stole from Buck's food at the first meal. As Buck sprang to punish him, the lash of François's whip sang through the air, reaching the culprit first; and nothing remained to Buck but to recover the bone. That was fair of François, he decided, and that man began his rise in Buck's estimation.

The other dog made no advances, nor received any; also, he did not attempt to steal from the newcomers. He was a gloomy, morose fellow, and he showed Curly plainly that all he desired was to be left alone, and further, that there would be trouble if he were not left alone. "Dave" he was called, and he ate and slept, or yawned between times, and took interest in nothing, not even when the Narwhal crossed Queen Charlotte Sound and rolled and pitched and bucked like a thing possessed. When Buck and Curly grew excited, half wild with fear, he raised his head as though annoyed, favored them with an incurious glance, yawned, and went to sleep again.

Day and night the ship throbbed to the tireless pulse of the propeller, and though one day was very like another, it was apparent to Buck that the weather was steadily growing colder. At last, one morning, the propeller was quiet, and the Narwhal was pervaded with an atmosphere of excitement. He felt it, as did the other dogs, and knew that a change was at hand. François leashed them and brought them on deck. At the first step upon the cold surface, Buck's feet sank into white mushy something very like mud. He sprang back with a snort. More of this white stuff was falling through the air. He shook himself, but more of it fell upon him. He sniffed it curiously, then licked some up on his tongue. It bit like fire, and the next instant was gone. This puzzled him. He tried it again, with the same result. The onlookers laughed uproariously, and he felt ashamed, he knew not why, for it was his first snow.

THINK AND DISCUSS
Understanding
1. Describe Judge Miller's place.
2. Why does Buck let Manuel put a rope around his neck?
3. How does Buck react to his tormentors?

Analyzing
4. What lesson does Buck learn from the man with the club?
5. Why does Buck respect Perrault and François?

Extending
6. After having read this chapter, how would you define *tame* and *wild?*
7. What main ideas connect the title of the novel and the events in Chapter 1?

REVIEWING:
Connotation/Denotation Hℤ
See Handbook of Literary Terms, p. 661.

A word's dictionary meaning is its **denotation.** The feeling or mental picture it creates is its **connotation.** Think about the connotations of each of the following meanings of *wild*: (**a**) wild animals in general; (**b**) a beast, or beasts; (**c**) an uninhabited region.

In all likelihood, your mental picture of "wild animals in general" is more positive than it is for "beasts," and your mental picture of "an uninhabited region" is neutral.

Copy the following words. Use **+, −,** or **0** to signify whether each underlined word has a positive, negative, or neutral

connotation. Then look up each word in your Glossary. Which meanings given for each word are positive, negative, neutral? Discuss differences of opinion.

1. The *Call* of the Wild
2. Buck ruled over this great *demesne.*
3. As a puppy, he lived like an *aristocrat.*
4. Buck's every need was *sated.*
5. He was proud, and a bit *egotistical.*
6. His beautiful coat was sprayed with *slaver.*
7. A little *weazened* man bought Buck.
8. Buck met a *morose* dog named Dave.
9. Into the *Primitive.*

2 The Law of Club and Fang

Buck's first day on the Dyea beach was like a nightmare. Every hour was filled with shock and surprise. He had been suddenly jerked from the heart of civilization and flung into the heart of things primordial. No lazy, sun-kissed life was this, with nothing to do but loaf and be bored. Here was neither peace, nor rest, nor a moment's safety. All was confusion and action, and every moment life and limb were in peril. There was imperative need to be constantly alert; for these dogs and men were not town dogs and men. They were savages, all of them, who knew no law but the law of club and fang.

He had never seen dogs fight as these wolfish creatures fought, and his first experience taught him an unforgettable lesson. It is true, it was a vicarious experience, else he would not have lived to profit by it. Curly was the victim. They were camped near the log store, where she, in her friendly way, made advances to a husky dog the size of a full-grown wolf, though not half so large as she. There was no warning, only a leap in like a flash, a metallic clip of teeth, a leap out equally swift . . . .

It was the wolf manner of fighting, to strike and leap away; but there was more to it than this. Thirty or forty huskies ran to the spot and surrounded the combatants in an intent and silent circle. Buck did not comprehend that silent intentness, nor the eager way with which they were licking their chops. Curly rushed her antagonist, who struck again and leaped aside. He met her next rush with his chest, in a peculiar fashion that tumbled her off her feet. She never regained them. This was what the onlooking huskies had waited for. They closed in upon her, snarling and yelping, and she was buried . . . beneath the bristling mass of bodies.

So sudden was it, and so unexpected, that Buck was taken aback. He saw Spitz run out his scarlet tongue in a way he had of laughing; and he saw François, swinging an axe, spring into the mess of dogs. Three men with clubs were helping to scatter them. It did not take long. Two minutes from the time Curly went down, the last of her assailants were clubbed off. But she lay there limp and lifeless in the bloody, trampled snow, almost literally torn to pieces, François standing over her and cursing horribly. The scene often came back to Buck to trouble him in his sleep. So that was the way. No fair play. Once down, that was the end of you. Well, he would see to it that he never went down. Spitz ran out his tongue and laughed again, and from that moment Buck hated him with a bitter and deathless hatred.

Before he had recovered from the shock caused by the tragic passing of Curly, he received another shock. François fastened upon him an arrangement of straps and buckles. It was a harness, such as he had seen the grooms put on the horses at home. And as he had seen horses work, so he was set to work, hauling François on a sled to the forest that fringed the valley, and returning with a load of firewood. Though his dignity was sorely hurt by thus being made a draught animal, he was too wise to rebel. He buckled down with a will and did his best, though it was all new and strange. François was stern, demanding instant obedience, and by virtue of his whip receiving instant obedience; while Dave, who was an experienced wheeler, nipped Buck's hind quarters whenever he was in error. Spitz was the leader, likewise experienced, and while he could not always get at Buck, he growled sharp reproof now and again, or cunningly threw his weight in the traces to jerk Buck into the way he should go. Buck learned easily, and under the combined tuition of his two mates and François made remarkable progress. Ere they returned to camp he knew enough to stop at "ho," to go ahead at "mush," to swing wide on the bends, and to keep clear of the wheeler when the loaded sled shot downhill at their heels.

"T'ree vair' good dogs," François told Perrault. "Dat Buck, heem pool lak hell. I tich heem queek as anyt'ing."

By afternoon, Perrault, who was in a hurry to be on the trail with his dispatches, returned with two more dogs. "Billee" and "Joe," he called them, two brothers, and true huskies both. Sons of the one mother though they were, they were as different as day and night. Billee's one fault was his excessive good nature, while Joe was the very opposite, sour and introspective, with a perpetual snarl and a malignant eye. Buck received them in comradely fashion. Dave ignored them, while Spitz proceeded to thrash first one and then the other. Billee wagged his tail appeasingly, turned to run when he saw that appeasement was of no avail, and cried (still appeasingly) when Spitz's sharp teeth scored his flank. But no matter how Spitz circled, Joe whirled around on his heels to face him, mane bristling, ears laid back, lips writhing and snarling, jaws clipping together as fast as he could snap, and eyes diabolically gleaming—the incarnation of belligerent fear. So terrible was his appearance that Spitz was

Frank Schoonover, "In the Whirling Blizzard" (detail)
Private Collection

forced to forego disciplining him; but to cover his own discomfiture he turned upon the inoffensive and wailing Billee and drove him to the confines of the camp.

By evening Perrault secured another dog, an old husky, long and lean and gaunt, with a battle-scarred face and a single eye which flashed a warning of prowess that commanded respect. He was called Sol-leks, which means the Angry One. Like Dave, he asked nothing, gave nothing, expected nothing: and when he marched slowly and deliberately into their midst, even Spitz left him alone. He had one peculiarity which Buck was unlucky enough to discover. He did not like to be approached on his blind side. Of this offence Buck was unwittingly guilty, and the first knowledge he had of his indiscretion was when Sol-leks whirled upon him and slashed his shoulder to the bone for three inches up and down. Forever after Buck avoided his blind side, and to the last of their comradeship had no more trouble. His only apparent ambition, like Dave's, was to be left alone, though, as Buck was afterward to learn, each of them possessed one other and even more vital ambition.

That night Buck faced the great problem of sleeping. The tent, illuminated by a candle, glowed warmly in the midst of the white plain; and when he, as a matter of course, entered it, both Perrault and François bombarded him with curses and cooking utensils, till he recovered from his consternation and fled ignominiously into the outer cold. A chill wind was blowing that nipped him sharply and bit with especial venom into his wounded shoulder. He lay down on the snow and attempted to sleep, but the frost soon drove him shivering to his feet. Miserable and disconsolate, he wandered about among the many tents, only to find that one place was as cold as another. Here and there savage dogs rushed upon him, but he bristled his neck-hair and snarled (for he was learning fast), and they let him go his way unmolested.

Finally an idea came to him. He would return and see how his own team mates were making out. To his astonishment, they had disappeared. Again he wandered about through the great camp, looking for them, and again he returned. Were they in the tent? No, that could not be, else he would not have been driven out. Then where could they possibly be? With drooping tail and shivering body, very forlorn indeed, he aimlessly circled the tent. Suddenly the snow gave way beneath his forelegs and he sank down. Something wriggled under his feet. He sprang back, bristling and snarling, fearful of the unseen and unknown. But a friendly little yelp reassured him, and he went back to investigate. A whiff of warm air ascended to his nostrils, and there, curled up under the snow in a snug ball, lay Billee. He whined placatingly, squirmed and wriggled to show his good will and intentions, and even ventured, as a bribe for peace, to lick Buck's face with his warm wet tongue.

Another lesson. So that was the way they did it, eh? Buck confidently selected a spot, and with much fuss and wasted effort proceeded to dig a hole for himself. In a trice the heat from his body filled the confined space and he was asleep. The day had been long and arduous, and he slept soundly and comfortably, though he growled and barked and wrestled with bad dreams.

Nor did he open his eyes till roused by the noises of the waking camp. At first he did not know where he was. It had snowed during the night and he was completely buried. The snow walls pressed him on every side, and a great surge of fear swept through him—the fear of the wild thing for the trap. It was a token that he was harking back through his own life to the lives of his forebears, for he was a civilized dog, an unduly civilized dog and of his own experience knew no trap and so could not of himself fear it. The muscles of his whole body contracted spasmodically and instinctively, the hair on his neck and shoulders stood on end, and with a ferocious snarl

he bounded straight up into the blinding day, the snow flying about him in a flashing cloud. Ere he landed on his feet, he saw the white camp spread out before him and knew where he was and remembered all that had passed from the time he went for a stroll with Manuel to the hole he had dug for himself the night before.

A shout from François hailed his appearance. "Wot I say?" the dog driver cried to Perrault. "Dat Buck for sure learn queek as anyt'ing."

Perrault nodded gravely. As courier for the Canadian Government, bearing important dispatches, he was anxious to secure the best dogs, and he was particularly gladdened by the possession of Buck.

Three more huskies were added to the team inside an hour, making a total of nine, and before another quarter of an hour had passed they were in harness and swinging up the trail toward the Dyea Cañon. Buck was glad to be gone, and though the work was hard he found he did not particularly despise it. He was surprised at the eagerness which animated the whole team and which was communicated to him; but still more surprising was the change wrought in Dave and Solleks. They were new dogs, utterly transformed by the harness. All passiveness and unconcern had dropped from them. They were alert and active, anxious that the work should go well, and fiercely irritable with whatever, by delay or confusion, retarded that work. The toil of the traces seemed the supreme expression of their being and all that they lived for, and the only thing in which they took delight.

Dave was wheeler or sled dog, pulling in

Frank Schoonover, "Breaking Trail" (detail)
Glenbow Museum, Calgary

front of him was Buck, then came Sol-leks; the rest of the team was strung out ahead, single file, to the leader, which position was filled by Spitz.

Buck had been purposely placed between Dave and Sol-leks so that he might receive instruction. Apt scholar that he was, they were equally apt teachers, never allowing him to linger long in error, and enforcing their teaching with their sharp teeth. Dave was fair and very wise. He never nipped Buck without cause, and he never failed to nip him when he stood in need of it. As François's whip backed him up, Buck found it to be cheaper to mend his ways than to retaliate. Once, during a brief halt, when he got tangled in the traces and delayed the start, both Dave and Sol-leks flew at him and administered a sound trouncing. The resulting tangle was even worse, but Buck took good care to keep the traces clear thereafter; and ere the day was done, so well had he mastered his work, his mates about ceased nagging him. François's whip snapped less frequently, and

Perrault even honored Buck by lifting up his feet and carefully examining them.

It was a hard day's run, up the cañon, through Sheep Camp, past the Scales and the timber line, across glaciers and snowdrifts hundreds of feet deep, and over the great Chilkoot Divide, which stands between the salt water and the fresh and guards forbiddingly the sad and lonely North. They made good time down the chain of lakes which fills the craters of extinct volcanoes, and late that night pulled into the huge camp at the head of Lake Bennett, where thousands of goldseekers were building boats against the breakup of the ice in the spring. Buck made his hole in the snow and slept the sleep of the exhausted just, but all too early was routed out in the cold darkness and harnessed with his mates to the sled.

That day they made forty miles, the trail being packed; but the next day, and for many days to follow, they broke their own trail, worked harder, and made poorer time. As a rule, Perrault traveled ahead of the team, packing the snow with webbed shoes to make it easier for them. Francois, guiding the sled at the gee-pole, sometimes exchanged places with him but not often. Perrault was in a hurry, and he prided himself on his knowledge of ice, which knowledge was indispensable, for the fall ice was very thin, and where there was swift water, there was no ice at all.

Day after day, for days unending, Buck toiled in the traces. Always, they broke camp in the dark, and the first gray of dawn found them hitting the trail with fresh miles reeled off behind them. And always they pitched camp after dark, eating their bit of fish, and crawling to sleep into the snow. Buck was ravenous. The pound and a half of sun-dried salmon, which was his ration for each day, seemed to go nowhere. He never had enough, and suffered from perpetual hunger pangs. Yet the other dogs, because they weighed less and were born to the life, received a pound only of the fish and managed to keep in good condition.

He swiftly lost the fastidiousness which had characterized his old life. A dainty eater, he found that his mates, finishing first, robbed him of his unfinished ration. There was no defending it. While he was fighting off two or three, it was disappearing down the throats of the others. To remedy this, he ate as fast as they; and, so greatly did hunger compel him, he was not above taking what did not belong to him. He watched and learned. When he saw Pike, one of the new dogs, a clever malingerer and thief, slyly steal a slice of bacon when Perrault's back was turned, he duplicated the performance the following day, getting away with the whole chunk. A great uproar was raised, but he was unsuspected, while Dub, an awkward blunderer who was always getting caught, was punished for Buck's misdeed.

This first theft marked Buck as fit to survive in the hostile Northland environment. It marked his adaptability, his capacity to adjust himself to changing conditions, the lack of which would have meant swift and terrible death. It marked, further, the decay or going to pieces of his moral nature, a vain thing and a handicap in the ruthless struggle for existence. It was all well enough in the Southland, under the law of love and fellowship, to respect private property and personal feelings; but in the Northland, under the law of club and fang, whoso took such things into account was a fool, and in so far as he observed them he would fail to prosper.

Not that Buck reasoned it out. He was fit, that was all, and unconsciously he accommodated himself to the new mode of life. All his days, no matter what the odds, he had never run from a fight. But the club of the man in the red sweater had beaten into him a more fundamental and primitive code. Civilized, he could have died for a moral consideration, say the defence of Judge Miller's riding whip; but the completeness of his decivilization was now evidenced by his ability to flee from the defence of a moral consideration and so save his hide. He did not steal for joy of it, but because of the clamor of his stomach. He did not rob openly, but stole secretly and cunningly, out of respect for club and fang. In short, the things he did were done because it was easier to do them than not to do them.

His development (or retrogression) was rapid. His muscles became hard as iron and he grew callous to all ordinary pain. He achieved an internal as well as external economy. He could eat anything, no matter how loathsome or indigestible; and, once eaten, the juices of his stomach extracted the last least particle of nutriment; and his blood carried it to the farthest reaches of his body, building it into the toughest and stoutest of tissues. Sight and scent became remarkably keen, while his hearing developed such acuteness that in his sleep he heard the faintest sound and knew whether it heralded peace or peril. He learned to bite the ice out with his teeth when it collected between his toes; and when he was thirsty and there was a thick scum of ice over the water hole, he would break it by rearing and striking it with stiff forelegs. His most conspicuous trait was an ability to scent the wind and forecast it a night in advance. No matter how breathless the air when he dug his nest by tree or bank, the wind that later blew inevitably found him to leeward, sheltered and snug.

And not only did he learn by experience, but instincts long dead became alive again. The domesticated generations fell from him. In vague ways he remembered back to the youth of the breed, to the time the wild dogs ranged in packs through the primeval forest, and killed their meat as they ran it down. It was no task for him to learn to fight with cut and slash and the quick wolf snap. In this manner had fought forgotten ancestors. They quickened the old life within him, and the old tricks which they had stamped into the heredity of the breed were his tricks. They came to him without effort or discovery, as though they had been his always. And when, on the still cold nights, he pointed his nose at a star and howled long and wolflike, it was his ancestors, dead and dust, pointing nose at star and howling down through the centuries and through him. And his cadences were their cadences, the cadences which voiced their woe and what to them was the meaning of the stillness, and the cold, and dark.

Thus, as token of what a puppet thing life is, the ancient song surged through him and he came into his own again; and he came because men had found a yellow metal in the North, and because Manuel was a gardener's helper whose wages did not lap over the needs of his wife and divers small copies of himself.

THINK AND DISCUSS
Understanding
1. Why does the husky attack Curly?
2. What lesson does Buck learn from Curly's death?
3. How do Dave and Sol-leks behave when they are put in harness?

Analyzing
4. What important changes are taking place within Buck?
5. What is the difference between the law of love and fellowship in the Southland and the law of club and fang in the Northland?

Extending

6. After rereading page 589, column 2, paragraph 2, how would you define *civilized* and *decivilization?*
7. In your opinion, has Buck developed or regressed (gone backward)? Explain.

VOCABULARY

Context

When you encounter an unfamiliar word, you can often use its *context*, or surroundings, to determine its meaning. Other words, ideas, or examples provide clues to meaning, as is shown below by the word *primordial.*

> Buck had been jerked from the heart of civilization and flung into the heart of things *primordial.* No lazy, sun-kissed life was this. . . . Here was neither peace, nor rest, nor a moment's safety.

Without looking in the dictionary, you can guess that *primordial* means *uncivilized* or *primitive.*

Find these words in context: *introspective* (585); *discomfiture* (586); *prowess* (586). Then choose the letter of the word that best matches the meaning of each word as it is used in the story.

1. *introspective*: (**a**) cautious; (**b**) outgoing; (**c**) thoughtful; (**d**) uneasy.
2. *discomfiture*: (**a**) embarrassment; (**b**) uncertainty; (**c**) fright; (**d**) cowardice.
3. *prowess*: (**a**) incompetence; (**b**) anger; (**c**) extraordinary ability; (**d**) danger.

---

3 The Dominant Primordial Beast

The dominant primordial[3] beast was strong in Buck, and under the fierce conditions of trail life it grew and grew. Yet it was a secret growth. His newborn cunning gave him poise and control. He was too busy adjusting himself to the new life to feel at ease, and not only did he not pick fights, but he avoided them whenever possible. A certain deliberateness characterized his attitude. He was not prone to rashness and precipitate action; and in the bitter hatred between him and Spitz he betrayed no impatience, shunned all offensive acts.

On the other hand, possibly because he divined in Buck a dangerous rival, Spitz never lost an opportunity of showing his teeth. He even went out of his way to bully Buck, striving constantly to start the fight which could end only in the death of one or the other.

Early in the trip this might have taken place had it not been for an unwonted accident. At the end of this day they made a bleak and miserable camp on the shore of Lake Le Barge. Driving snow, a wind that cut like a white-hot knife, and darkness, had forced them to grope for a camping place. They could hardly have fared worse. At their backs rose a perpendicular wall of rock, and Perrault and François were compelled to make their fire and spread their sleeping

---

3. *primordial* (prī môr′dē əl), existing at the very beginning, primitive.

John Clymer, "Night Visitors" (detail), 1972
Private Collection

robes on the ice of the lake itself. The tent they had discarded at Dyea in order to travel light. A few sticks of driftwood furnished them with a fire that thawed down through the ice and left them to eat supper in the dark.

Close in under the sheltering rock Buck made his nest. So snug and warm was it, that he was loath to leave it when François distributed the fish which he had first thawed over the fire. But when Buck finished his ration and returned, he found his nest occupied. A warning snarl told him that the trespasser was Spitz. Till now Buck had avoided trouble with his enemy, but this was too much. The beast in him roared. He sprang upon Spitz with a fury which surprised them both, and Spitz particularly, for his whole experience with Buck had gone to teach him that his rival was an unusually timid dog, who managed to hold his own only because of his great weight and size.

François was surprised, too, when they shot out in a tangle from the disrupted nest and he divined the cause of the trouble. "A-a-ah!" he cried to Buck. "Gif it to heem, by Gar! Gif it to heem, the dirty t'eef!"

Spitz was equally willing. He was crying with sheer rage and eagerness as he circled back and forth for a chance to spring in. Buck was no less eager, and no less cautious, as he likewise circled back and forth for the advantage. But it was then that the unexpected happened, the thing which projected their struggle for supremacy far into the future, past many a weary mile of trail and toil.

An oath from Perrault, the resounding impact of a club upon a bony frame, and a shrill yelp of pain, heralded the breaking forth of pandemonium. The camp was suddenly discovered to be alive with skulking furry forms,—starving huskies, four or five score of them, who had scented the camp from some Indian village. They had crept in while Buck and Spitz were fighting, and when the two men sprang among them with stout clubs they showed their teeth and fought back. They were crazed by the smell of the food. Perrault found one with head buried in the grub-box. His club landed heavily on the gaunt ribs, and the grub-box was capsized on the ground. On the instant a score of the famished brutes were scrambling for the bread and bacon. The clubs fell upon them unheeded. They yelped and howled under the rain of blows, but struggled none the less madly till the last crumb had been devoured.

In the meantime the astonished team-dogs had burst out of their nests only to be set upon by the fierce invaders. Never had Buck seen such dogs. It seemed as though their bones would burst through their skins. They were mere skeletons, draped loosely in draggled hides, with blazing eyes and slavered fangs. But the hunger-madness made them terrifying, irresistible. There was no opposing them. The team-dogs were swept back against the cliff at the first onset. Buck was beset by three huskies, and in a trice his head and shoulders were ripped and slashed. The din was frightful. Billee was crying as usual. Dave and Sol-leks, dripping blood from a score of wounds, were fighting bravely side by side. Joe was snapping like a demon. Once, his teeth closed on the foreleg of a husky, and he crunched down through the bone. Pike, the malingerer, leaped upon the crippled animal, breaking its neck with a quick dash of teeth and a jerk. Buck got a frothing adversary by the throat, and was sprayed with blood when his teeth sank through the jugular. The warm taste of it in his mouth goaded him to greater fierceness. He flung himself upon another, and at the same time felt teeth sink into his own throat. It was Spitz treacherously attacking from the side.

Perrault and François, having cleaned out their part of the camp, hurried to save their sled-dogs. The wild wave of famished beasts rolled back before them, and Buck shook himself free. But it was only for a moment. The two men were compelled to run back to save the grub, upon which the huskies returned to the attack on the team. Billee, terrified into bravery, sprang through the savage circle and fled away over the ice. Pike and Dub followed on his heels, with the rest of the team behind. As Buck drew himself together to spring after them, out of the trail of his eye he saw Spitz rush upon him with the evident intention of overthrowing him. Once off his feet and under that mass of huskies, there was no hope for him. But he braced himself to the shock of Spitz's charge, then joined the flight out on the lake.

Later, the nine team-dogs gathered together and sought shelter in the forest. Though unpursued, they were in a sorry plight. There was not one who was not wounded in four or five places, while some were wounded grievously. Dub was badly injured in a hind leg; Dolly, the last husky added to the team at Dyea, had a badly torn throat; Joe had lost an eye; while Billee, the good-natured, with an ear chewed and rent to ribbons, cried and whimpered throughout the night. At daybreak they limped warily back to camp, to find the marauders gone and the two men in bad tempers. Fully half their grub supply was gone. The huskies had chewed through the sled lashings and canvas coverings. In fact, nothing, no matter how remotely eatable, had escaped them. They had eaten a pair of Perrault's moose-hide moccasins, chunks out of the leather traces, and even two feet of lash from the end of François's whip. He broke from a mournful contemplation of it to look over his wounded dogs.

"Ah, my frien's," he said softly, "mebbe it mek you mad dog, dose many bites. Mebbe all mad dog, sacredam! Wot you t'ink, eh, Perrault?"

The courier shook his head dubiously. With four hundred miles of trail still between him and Dawson, he could ill afford to have madness break out among his dogs. Two hours of cursing and exertion got the harnesses into shape, and the wound-stiffened team was under way, struggling painfully over the hardest part of the trail they had yet encountered, and for that matter, the hardest between them and Dawson.

The Thirty Mile River was wide open. Its wild water defied the frost, and it was in the eddies only and in the quiet places that the ice held at all. Six days of exhausting toil were required to cover those thirty terrible miles. And terrible they were, for every foot of them was accomplished at the risk of life to dog and man. A dozen times, Perrault, nos-ing the way, broke through the ice bridges, being saved by the long pole he carried, which he so held that it fell each time across the hole made by his body. But a cold snap was on, the thermometer registering fifty below zero, and each time he broke through he was compelled for very life to build a fire and dry his garments.

Nothing daunted him. It was because nothing daunted him that he had been chosen for government courier. He took all manner of risks, resolutely thrusting his little weazened face into the frost and struggling on from dim dawn to dark. He skirted the frowning shores on rim ice that bent and crackled under foot and on which they dared not halt. Once, the sled broke through, with Dave and Buck, and they were half-frozen and all but drowned by the time they were dragged out. The usual fire was necessary to save them. They were coated solidly with ice, and the two men kept them on the run around the fire, sweating and thawing, so close that they were singed by the flames.

At another time Spitz went through, dragging the whole team after him up to Buck, who strained backward with all his strength, his forepaws on the slippery edge and the ice quivering and snapping all around. But behind him was Dave, likewise straining backward, and behind the sled was François, pulling till his tendons cracked.

Again, the rim ice broke away before and behind, and there was no escape except up the cliff. Perrault scaled it by a miracle, while François prayed for just that miracle; and with every thong and sled-lashing and the last bit of harness rove into a long rope, the dogs were hoisted, one by one, to the cliff crest.

François came up last, after the sled and load. Then came the search for a place to descend, which descent was ultimately made by the aid of the rope, and night found them back on the river with a quarter of a mile to the day's credit.

By the time they made the Houtalinqua and good ice, Buck was played out. The rest of the dogs were in like condition; but Perrault, to make up lost time, pushed them late and early. The first day they covered thirty-five miles to the Big Salmon; the next day thirty-five more to the Little Salmon; the third day forty miles, which brought them well up toward the Five Fingers.

Buck's feet were not so compact and hard as the feet of the huskies. His had softened during the many generations since the day his last wild ancestor was tamed. . . . All day long he limped in agony, and camp once made, lay down like a dead dog. Hungry as he was, he would not move to receive his ration of fish, which François had to bring to him. Also, the dog-driver rubbed Buck's feet for half an hour each night after supper, and sacrificed the tops of his own moccasins to make four moccasins for Buck. This was a great relief, and Buck caused even the weazened face of Perrault to twist itself into a grin one morning, when François forgot the moccasins and Buck lay on his back, his four feet waving appealingly in the air, and refused to budge without them. Later his feet grew hard to the trail, and the worn-out footgear was thrown away.

At the Pelly one morning, as they were harnessing up, Dolly, who had never been conspicuous for anything, went suddenly mad. She announced her condition by a long, heart-breaking wolf howl that sent every dog bristling with fear, then sprang straight for Buck. He had never seen a dog go mad, nor did he have any reason to fear madness; yet he knew that here was horror, and fled away from it in panic. Straight away he raced, with Dolly, panting and frothing, one leap behind; nor could she gain on him, so great was his terror, nor could he leave her, so great was her madness. He plunged through the wooded breast of the island, flew down to the lower end, crossed a back channel filled with rough ice to another island, gained a third island, curved back to the main river, and in desperation started to cross it. And all the time, though he did not look, he could hear her snarling just one leap behind. François called to him a quarter of a mile away and he doubled back, still one leap ahead, gasping painfully for air and putting all his faith in that François would save him. The dog-driver held the axe poised in his hand, and as Buck shot past him the axe crashed down upon mad Dolly's head.

Buck staggered over against the sled, exhausted, sobbing for breath, helpless. This was Spitz's opportunity. He sprang upon Buck, and twice his teeth sank into his unresisting foe and ripped and tore the flesh to the bone. Then François's lash descended, and Buck had the satisfaction of watching Spitz receive the worst whipping as yet administered to any of the team.

"One devil, dat Spitz," remarked Perrault. "Some dam day heem keel dat Buck."

"Dat Buck two devils," was François's rejoinder. "All de tam I watch dat Buck I know for sure. Lissen: some dam fine day heem get mad lak hell an' den heem chew dat Spitz all

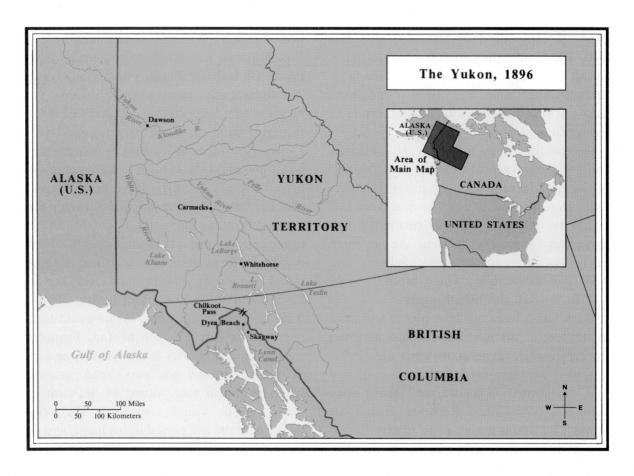

The Yukon, 1896

up an' spit heem out on de snow. Sure. I know."

From then on it was war between them. Spitz, as lead-dog and acknowledged master of the team, felt his supremacy threatened by this strange Southland dog. And strange Buck was to him, for of the many Southland dogs he had known, not one had shown up worthily in camp and on the trail. They were all too soft, dying under the toil, the frost, and starvation. Buck was the exception. He alone endured and prospered, matching the husky in strength, savagery, and cunning. Then he was a masterful dog, and what made him dangerous was the fact that the club of

the man in the red sweater had knocked all blind pluck and rashness out of his desire for mastery. He was preëminently cunning, and could bide his time with a patience that was nothing less than primitive.

It was inevitable that the clash for leadership should come. Buck wanted it. He wanted it because it was his nature, because he had been gripped tight by that nameless, incomprehensible pride of the trail and trace— that pride which holds dogs in the toil to the last gasp, which lures them to die joyfully in the harness, and breaks their hearts if they are cut out of the harness. This was the pride of Dave as wheel-dog, of Sol-leks as he pulled with all his strength; the pride that laid hold of them at break of camp, transforming them from sour and sullen brutes into straining, eager, ambitious creatures; the pride that spurred them on all day and dropped them at pitch of camp at night, letting them fall into gloomy unrest and uncontent. This was the pride that bore up Spitz and made him thrash the sled-dogs who blundered and shirked in the traces or hid away at harness-up time in the morning. Likewise it was this pride that made him fear Buck as a possible lead-dog. And this was Buck's pride, too.

He openly threatened the other's leadership. He came between him and the shirks he should have punished. And he did it deliberately. One night there was a heavy snowfall, and in the morning Pike, the malingerer, did not appear. He was securely hidden in his nest under a foot of snow. François called him and sought him in vain. Spitz was wild with wrath. He raged through the camp, smelling and digging in every likely place, snarling so frightfully that Pike heard and shivered in his hiding-place.

But when he was at last unearthed, and Spitz flew at him to punish him, Buck flew, with equal rage, in between. So unexpected was it, and so shrewdly managed, that Spitz was hurled backward and off his feet. Pike, who had been trembling abjectly, took heart at this open mutiny, and sprang upon his overthrown leader. Buck, to whom fair-play was a forgotten code, likewise sprang upon Spitz. But François, chuckling at the incident while unswerving in the administration of justice, brought his lash down upon Buck with all his might. This failed to drive Buck from his prostrate rival, and the butt of the whip was brought into play. Half-stunned by the blow, Buck was knocked backward and the lash laid upon him again and again, while Spitz soundly punished the many times offending Pike.

In the days that followed, as Dawson grew closer and closer, Buck still continued to interfere between Spitz and the culprits; but he did it craftily, when François was not around. With the covert mutiny of Buck, a general insubordination sprang up and increased. Dave and Sol-leks were unaffected, but the rest of the team went from bad to worse. Things no longer went right. There was continual bickering and jangling. Trouble was always afoot, and at the bottom of it was Buck. He kept François busy, for the dog-driver was in constant apprehension of the life-and-death struggle between the two which he knew must take place sooner or later; and on more than one night the sounds of quarreling and strife among the other dogs turned him out of his sleeping robe, fearful that Buck and Spitz were at it.

But the opportunity did not present itself, and they pulled into Dawson one dreary afternoon with the great fight still to come. Here were many men, and countless dogs, and Buck found them all at work. It seemed the ordained order of things that dogs should work. All day they swung up and down the main street in long teams, and in the night their jingling bells still went by. They hauled cabin logs and firewood, freighted up to the mines, and did all manner of work that horses did in the Santa Clara Valley. Here and there Buck met Southland dogs, but in the main they were the wild wolf husky breed. Every night, regularly, at nine, at twelve, at three, they lifted a nocturnal song, a weird and eerie chant, in which it was Buck's delight to join.

With the aurora borealis[4] flaming coldly overhead, or the stars leaping in the frost dance, and the land numb and frozen under its pall of snow, this song of the huskies might have been the defiance of life, only it was pitched in minor key, with long-drawn wailings and half-sobs, and was more the pleading of life, the articulate travail of existence. It was an old song, old as the breed itself—one of the first songs of the younger world in a day when songs were sad. It was invested with the woe of unnumbered generations, this plaint[5] by which Buck was so strangely stirred. When he moaned and sobbed, it was with the pain of living that was of old the pain of his wild fathers, and the fear and mystery of the cold and dark that was to them fear and mystery. . . .

Seven days from the time they pulled into Dawson, they dropped down the steep bank by the Barracks to the Yukon Trail, and pulled for Dyea and Salt Water. Perrault was carrying dispatches if anything more urgent than those he had brought in; also, the travel pride had gripped him, and he purposed to make the record trip of the year. Several things favored him in this. The week's rest had recuperated the dogs and put them in thorough trim. The trail they had broken into the country was packed hard by later journeyers. And further, the police had arranged in two or three places deposits of grub for dog and man, and he was traveling light.

They made Sixty Mile, which is a fifty-mile run, on the first day; and the second day saw them booming up the Yukon well on their way to Pelly. But such splendid running was achieved not without great trouble and vexation on the part of François. The insidious revolt led by Buck had destroyed the solidarity of the team. It no longer was as one dog leaping in the traces. The encouragement Buck gave the rebels led them into all kinds of petty misdemeanors. No more was Spitz a leader greatly to be feared. The old awe departed, and they grew equal to challenging his authority. Pike robbed him of half a fish one night, and gulped it down under the protection of Buck. Another night Dub and Joe fought Spitz and made him forego the punishment they deserved. And even Billee, the good-natured, was less good-natured, and whined not half so placatingly as in former days. Buck never came near Spitz without snarling and bristling menacingly. In fact, his conduct approached that of a bully, and he was given to swaggering up and down before Spitz's very nose.

The breaking down of discipline likewise affected the dogs in their relations with one another. They quarreled and bickered more than ever among themselves, till at times the camp was a howling bedlam. Dave and Solleks alone were unaltered, though they were made irritable by the unending squabbling. François swore strange barbarous oaths, and stamped the snow in futile rage, and tore his hair. His lash was always singing among the dogs, but it was of small avail. Directly his back was turned they were at it again. He

---

4. **aurora borealis** (ô rôr′ə bôr′ē al′is), northern lights, streamers or bands of light that appear in the sky at night, especially in northern regions.

5. **plaint** (plānt), complaint, a lament.

backed up Spitz with his whip, while Buck backed up the remainder of the team. François knew he was behind all the trouble, and Buck knew he knew; but Buck was too clever ever again to be caught red-handed. He worked faithfully in the harness, for the toil had become a delight to him; yet it was a greater delight slyly to precipitate a fight amongst his mates and tangle the traces.

At the mouth of the Tahkeena, one night after supper, Dub turned up a snowshoe rabbit, blundered it, and missed. In a second the whole team was in full cry. A hundred yards away was a camp of the Northwest Police, with fifty dogs, huskies all, who joined the chase. The rabbit sped down the river, turned off into a small creek, up the frozen bed of which it held steadily. It ran lightly on the surface of the snow, while the dogs ploughed through by main strength. Buck led the pack, sixty strong, around bend after bend, but he could not gain. He lay down low to the race, whining eagerly, his splendid body flashing forward, leap by leap, in the wan white moonlight. And leap by leap, like some pale frost wraith, the snowshoe rabbit flashed on ahead.

All that stirring of old instincts which at stated periods drives men out from the sounding cities to forest and plain to kill things by chemically propelled leaden pellets, the blood lust, the joy to kill—all this was Buck's, only it was infinitely more intimate. He was ranging at the head of the pack, running the wild thing down. . . .

There is an ecstasy that marks the summit of life, and beyond which life cannot rise. And such is the paradox of living, this ecstasy comes when one is most alive, and it comes as a complete forgetfulness that one is alive. This ecstasy, this forgetfulness of living, comes to the artist, caught up and out of himself in a sheet of flame; it comes to the soldier, war-mad on a stricken field and refusing quarter; and it came to Buck, leading the pack, sounding the old wolf-cry, straining after the food that was alive and that fled swiftly before him through the moonlight. He was sounding the deeps of his nature, and of the parts of his nature that were deeper than he, going back into the womb of Time. He was mastered by the sheer surging of life, the tidal wave of being, the perfect joy of each separate muscle, joint, and sinew and that it was everything that was not death, that it was aglow and rampant, expressing itself in movement, flying exultantly under the stars and over the face of dead matter that did not move.

But Spitz, cold and calculating even in his supreme moods, left the pack and cut across a narrow neck of land where the creek made a long bend around. Buck did not know of this, and as he rounded the bend, the frost wraith of a rabbit still flitting before him, he saw another and larger frost wraith leap from the overhanging bank into the immediate path of the rabbit. It was Spitz. The rabbit could not turn, and as the white teeth broke its back in mid air it shrieked as loudly as a stricken man may shriek. At sound of this . . . the full pack at Buck's heels raised a hell's chorus . . . .

Buck did not cry out. He did not check himself, but drove in upon Spitz, shoulder to shoulder, so hard that he missed the throat. They rolled over and over in the powdery snow. Spitz gained his feet almost as though he had not been overthrown, slashing Buck down the shoulder and leaping clear. Twice his teeth clipped together, like the steel jaws of a trap, as he backed away for better footing, with lean and lifting lips that writhed and snarled.

In a flash Buck knew it. The time had come. It was to the death. As they circled about, snarling, ears laid back, keenly watchful for the advantage, the scene came to Buck with a sense of familiarity. He seemed to remember it all,—the white woods, and earth, and moonlight, and the thrill of battle. Over the whiteness and silence brooded a ghostly calm. There was not the faintest whisper of air—nothing moved, not a leaf quivered, the visible breaths of the dogs rising slowly and lingering in the frosty air. They had made short work of the snowshoe rabbit, these dogs that were ill-tamed wolves; and they were now drawn up in an expectant circle. They, too, were silent, their eyes only gleaming and their breaths drifting slowly upward. To Buck it was nothing new or strange, this scene of old time. It was as though it had always been, the wonted way of things.

Spitz was a practised fighter. From Spitzbergen through the Arctic, and across Canada and the Barrens, he had held his own with all manner of dogs and achieved to mastery over them. Bitter rage was his, but never blind rage. In passion to rend and destroy, he never forgot that his enemy was in like passion to rend and destroy. He never rushed till he was prepared to receive a rush; never attacked till he had first defended that attack.

In vain Buck strove to sink his teeth in the neck of the big white dog. Wherever his fangs struck for the softer flesh, they were countered by the fangs of Spitz. Fang clashed fang, and lips were cut and bleeding, but Buck could not penetrate his enemy's guard. Then he warmed up and enveloped Spitz in a whirlwind of rushes. Time and time again he tried for the snow-white throat, where life bubbled near to the surface, and each time and every time Spitz slashed him and got away. Then Buck took to rushing, as though for the throat, when, suddenly drawing back his head and curving in from the side, he would drive his shoulder at the shoulder of Spitz, as a ram by which to overthrow him. But instead, Buck's shoulder was slashed down each time as Spitz leaped lightly away.

Spitz was untouched, while Buck was streaming with blood and panting hard. The fight was growing desperate. And all the while the silent and wolfish circle waited to finish off whichever dog went down. As Buck grew winded, Spitz took to rushing, and he kept him staggering for footing. Once Buck went over, and the whole circle of sixty dogs started up; but he recovered himself, almost in mid air, and the circle sank down again and waited.

But Buck possessed a quality that made for greatness—imagination. He fought by instinct, but he could fight by head as well. He rushed, as though attempting the old shoulder trick, but at the last instant swept low to the snow and in. His teeth closed on Spitz's left foreleg. There was a crunch of breaking bone, and the white dog faced him on three legs. Thrice he tried to knock him over, then repeated the trick and broke the right foreleg. Despite the pain and helplessness, Spitz struggled madly to keep up. He saw the silent circle, with gleaming eyes, lolling tongues, and silvery breaths drifting upward, closing in upon him as he had seen similar circles close in upon beaten antagonists in the past. Only this time he was the one who was beaten.

There was no hope for him. Buck was inexorable. Mercy was a thing reserved for gentler climes. He maneuvered for the final rush. The circle had tightened till he could feel the breaths of the huskies on his flanks. He could see them, beyond Spitz and to either side, half crouching for the spring, their eyes fixed upon him. A pause seemed to fall. Every animal was motionless as though turned to stone. Only Spitz quivered and bristled as he staggered back and forth, snarling with horrible menace, as though to frighten off impending death. Then Buck sprang in and out, but while he was in, shoulder had at last squarely met shoulder. The dark circle became a dot on the moon-flooded snow as Spitz disappeared from view. Buck stood and looked on, the successful champion, the dominant primordial beast who had made his kill and found it good.

THINK AND DISCUSS
Understanding
1. Why does the pack of huskies attack the camp?
2. What does Spitz try to do to Buck during the confusion of the attack?
3. Why does Perrault continue to drive the team instead of letting them recover from their wounds?
4. What does François do to help Buck endure the pain caused by their hard travel?
5. Why does the team spend only a week in Dawson?

Analyzing
6. How does Buck show his great cunning in leading the revolt against Spitz?
7. In their fight to the death, why is Buck able to defeat Spitz?
8. On the map on page 596, find Dyea, where Buck is unloaded. What nearby town marks the southern end of the courier's run? What town marks the northern end of the run?

Extending
9. Every story, novel, or play develops around one or more struggles or **conflicts.** What conflicts occur in this chapter?
10. In your opinion, which of these conflicts poses the greatest challenge to François and Perrault? Explain.
11. Which of the conflicts in this chapter is most challenging for the animals, excluding Buck? Explain.
12. Which conflict is most challenging for Buck? Explain.

Writer's Craft

Build Emphasis

Good writers emphasize what is most important. An effective way to make important ideas or feelings stand out clearly, is to use contrasts; another is to use repetition.

Jack London uses contrast to emphasize the difference between the tame world of Judge Miller's estate and the wild and frozen world of the North. In California Buck is a king.

> The whole realm was his. He plunged into the swimming tank or went hunting with the Judge's sons; he escorted Mollie and Alice, the Judge's daughters, on long twilight or early morning rambles; on wintry nights he lay at the Judge's feet before the roaring library fire; he carried the Judge's grandsons on his back, or rolled them in the grass, and guarded their footsteps through wild adventures down to the fountain in the stable yard. . . .

When Buck is unloaded at a camp on a beach in Alaska, he rules nothing.

> He had been suddenly jerked from the heart of civilization and flung into the heart of things primordial. . . . . Here was neither peace, nor rest, nor a moment's safety. All was confusion and action, and every moment life and limb were in peril. There was imperative need to be constantly alert; for these dogs and men were not town dogs and men. They were savages, all of them, who knew no law but the law of club and fang. . . .

London also uses repetition to build emphasis. After Buck is choked, caged, and deposited in an express car, London repeats words and phrases to emphasize the duration and extent of Buck's torment.

> For two days and nights this express car was dragged along at the tail of shrieking locomotives; and for two days and nights Buck neither ate nor drank. For two days and nights he neither ate nor drank, and during those two days and nights of torment, he accumulated a fund of wrath that boded ill for whoever first fell foul of him.

Later, London builds up the competition between Buck and Spitz by emphasizing, through repetition, the intense pride of the sled dogs.

> It was inevitable that the clash for leadership should come. Buck wanted it. He wanted it because. . . . he had been gripped tight by that nameless, incomprehensible pride of the trail and trace—that pride which holds dogs in the toil to the last gasp. . . . This was the pride that bore up Spitz and made him thrash the sled-dogs who blundered. . . . Likewise it was this pride that made him fear Buck as a possible lead-dog. And this was Buck's pride too.

When you read, look for emphasis.
When you write, build emphasis.

---

4 Who Has Won to Mastership

"Eh? Wot I say? I spik true w'en I say dat Buck two devils."

This was François's speech next morning when he discovered Spitz missing and Buck covered with wounds. He drew him to the fire and by its light pointed them out.

"Dat Spitz fight lak hell," said Perrault, as he surveyed the gaping rips and cuts.

"An' dat Buck fight lak two hells," was François's answer. "An' now we make good time. No more Spitz, no more trouble, sure."

While Perrault packed the camp outfit and loaded the sled, the dog-driver proceeded to harness the dogs. Buck trotted up to the place Spitz would have occupied as leader, but François, not noticing him, brought Sol-leks to the coveted position. In his judgment, Sol-leks was the best lead-dog left. Buck sprang upon Sol-leks in a fury, driving him back and standing in his place.

"Eh? eh?" François cried, slapping his thighs gleefully. "Look at dat Buck. Heem keel dat Spitz, heem t'ink to take de job."

"Go 'way, Chook!" he cried, but Buck refused to budge.

He took Buck by the scruff of the neck, and though the dog growled threateningly, dragged him to one side and replaced Sol-leks. The old dog did not like it, and showed plainly that he was afraid of Buck. François was obdurate, but when he turned his back Buck again displaced Sol-leks who was not at all unwilling to go.

François was angry. "Now, by Gar, I feex you!" he cried, coming back with a heavy club in his hand.

Buck remembered the man in the red sweater, and retreated slowly; nor did he attempt to charge in when Sol-leks was once more brought forward. But he circled just beyond the range of the club, snarling with bitterness and rage; and while he circled he watched the club so as to dodge it if thrown by François, for he was become wise in the way of clubs.

The driver went about his work, and he called to Buck when he was ready to put him in his old place in front of Dave. Buck retreated two or three steps. François followed him up, whereupon he again retreated. After some time of this, François threw down the club, thinking that Buck feared a thrashing. But Buck was in open revolt. He wanted, not to escape a clubbing, but to have the leadership. It was his by right. He had earned it, and he would not be content with less.

Perrault took a hand. Between them they ran him about for the better part of an hour. They threw clubs at him. He dodged. They cursed him, and his fathers and mothers before him, and all his seed to come after him down to the remotest generation, and every hair on his body and drop of blood in his veins; and he answered curse with snarl and kept out of their reach. He did not try to run away, but retreated around and around the camp, advertising plainly that when his desire was met, he would come in and be good.

François sat down and scratched his head. Perrault looked at his watch and swore. Time was flying, and they should have been on the trail an hour gone. Francois scratched his head again. He shook it and grinned sheepishly at the courier, who shrugged his shoulders in sign that they were beaten. Then François went up to where Sol-leks stood and called to Buck. Buck laughed, as dogs laugh, yet kept his distance. François unfastened Sol-leks's traces and put him back in his old place. The team stood harnessed to the sled in an unbroken line, ready for the trail. There was no place for Buck save at the front. Once more François called, and once more Buck laughed and kept away.

"T'row down de club," Perrault commanded.

François complied, whereupon Buck trotted in, laughing triumphantly, and swung around into position at the head of the team. His traces were fastened, the sled broken out, and with both men running they dashed out on to the river trail.

Highly as the dog-driver had forevalued Buck, with his two devils, he found, while the day was yet young, that he had undervalued. At a bound Buck took up the duties of leadership; and where judgment was required, and quick thinking and quick acting, he showed himself the superior even to Spitz, of whom François had never seen an equal.

But it was in giving the law and making his mates live up to it, that Buck excelled. Dave and Sol-leks did not mind the change in leadership. It was none of their business. Their business was to toil, and toil mightily, in the traces. So long as that were not interfered with, they did not care what happened. Billee, the good-natured, could lead for all they cared so long as he kept order. The rest of the team, however, had grown unruly during the last days of Spitz, and their surprise was great now that Buck proceeded to lick them into shape.

Pike, who pulled at Buck's heels, and who never put an ounce more of his weight against the breast band than he was compelled to do, was swiftly and repeatedly shaken for loafing, and ere the first day was done he was pulling more than ever before in his life. The first night in camp, Joe, the sour one, was punished roundly—a thing that Spitz had never succeeded in doing. Buck simply smothered him by virtue of superior weight, and cut him up till he ceased snapping and began to whine for mercy.

The general tone of the team picked up immediately. It recovered its old-time solidarity, and once more the dogs leaped as one dog in the traces. At the Rink Rapids two native huskies, Teek and Koona, were added; and the celerity with which Buck broke them in took away François's breath.

"Nevaire such a dog as dat Buck!" he cried. "No, nevaire! Heem worth one t'ousan' dollair, by Gar! Eh? Wot you say, Perrault?"

And Perrault nodded. He was ahead of the record then, and gaining day by day. The trail was in excellent condition, well packed and hard, and there was no new-fallen snow with which to contend. It was not too cold. The temperature dropped to fifty below zero and remained there the whole trip. The men rode and ran by turn, and the dogs were kept on the jump, with but infrequent stoppages.

The Thirty Mile River was comparatively coated with ice, and they covered in one day going out what had taken them ten days coming in. In one run they made a sixty-mile dash from the foot of Lake Le Barge to the White Horse Rapids. Across Marsh, Tagish, and Bennett (seventy miles of lakes), they flew so fast that the man whose turn it was to run towed behind the sled at the end of a rope. And on the last night of the second week they topped White Pass and dropped down the sea slope with the lights of Skagway and of the shipping at their feet.

It was a record run. Each day for fourteen days they had averaged forty miles. For three days Perrault and François threw chests up and down the main street of Skagway and were deluged with invitations to drink, while the team was the constant centre of a worshipful crowd of dog-busters and mushers. Then three or four Western bad men aspired to clean out the town, were riddled like timber boxes for their pains, and public interest turned to other idols. Next came official orders. François called Buck to him, threw his arms around him, wept over him. And that was the last of François and Perrault. Like other men, they passed out of Buck's life for good.

A Scotsman took charge of him and his mates, and in company with a dozen other dog-teams he started back over the weary trail to Dawson. It was no light running now, nor record time, but heavy toil each day, with a heavy load behind; for this was the mail train, carrying word from the world to the men who sought gold under the shadow of the Pole.

Buck did not like it, but he bore up well to the work, taking pride in it after the manner of Dave and Sol-leks, and seeing that his mates, whether they prided in it or not, did their fair share. It was a monotonous life, operating with machine-like regularity. One day was very like another. At a certain time each morning the cooks turned out, fires were built, and breakfast was eaten. Then while some broke camp, others harnessed the dogs, and they were under way an hour or so before the darkness which gave warning of dawn. At night, camp was made. Some pitched the flies, others cut firewood and pine boughs for the beds, and still others carried water or ice for the cooks. Also, the dogs were fed. To them, this was the one feature of the day, though it was good to loaf around, after the fish was eaten, for an hour or so with the other dogs, of which there were fivescore and odd. There were fierce fighters among them, but three battles with the fiercest brought Buck to mastery, so that when he bristled and showed his teeth they got out of his way.

Best of all, perhaps, he loved to lie near the fire, hind legs crouched under him, forelegs stretched out in front, head raised, and eyes blinking dreamily at the flames. Sometimes he thought of Judge Miller's big house in the sun-kissed Santa Clara Valley, and of the cement swimming-tank, and Ysabel, the Mexican hairless, and Toots, the Japanese pug; but oftener he remembered the man in the red sweater, the death of Curly, the great fight with Spitz, and the good things he had eaten or would like to eat. He was not homesick. The Sunland was very dim and distant, and such memories had no power over him. Far more potent were the memories of his heredity that gave things he had never seen before a seeming familiarity; the instincts (which were but the memories of his ancestors become habits) which had lapsed in later days, and still later, in him, quickened and became alive again.

Sometimes as he crouched there, blinking dreamily at the flames, it seemed that the flames were of another fire, and that as he crouched by this other fire he saw another and different man from the cook before him. . . . And beyond that fire, in the circling darkness, Buck could see many gleaming coals, two by two, always two by two, which he knew to be the eyes of great beasts of prey. And he could hear the crashing of their bodies through the undergrowth, and the noises they made in the night. And dreaming there by the Yukon bank, with lazy eyes blinking at the fire, these sounds and sights of another world would make the hair to rise along his back and stand on end across his shoulders and up his neck, till he whimpered low and suppressedly, or growled softly, and the cook shouted at him, "Hey, you Buck, wake up!" . . . .

It was a hard trip, with the mail behind them, and the heavy work wore them down. They were short of weight and in poor condition when they made Dawson, and should have had a ten days' or a week's rest at least. But in two days' time they dropped down the Yukon bank from the Barracks, loaded with letters for the outside. The dogs were tired, the drivers grumbling, and to make matters worse, it snowed every day. This meant a soft trail, greater friction on the runners, and heavier pulling for the dogs; yet the drivers were fair through it all, and did their best for the animals.

Each night the dogs were attended to first. They ate before the drivers ate, and no man sought his sleeping-robe till he had seen to the feet of the dogs he drove. Still, their strength went down. Since the beginning of the winter they had traveled eighteen hundred miles, dragging sleds the whole weary distance; and eighteen hundred miles will tell upon life of the toughest. Buck stood it, keeping his mates up to their work and maintaining discipline, though he too was very tired. Billee cried and whimpered regularly in his sleep each night. Joe was sourer than ever, and Sol-leks was unapproachable, blind side or other side.

But it was Dave who suffered most of all. Something had gone wrong with him. He became more morose and irritable, and when camp was pitched at once made his nest, where his driver fed him. Once out of the harness and down, he did not get on his feet again till harness-up time in the morning. Sometimes, in the traces, when jerked by a sudden stoppage of the sled, or by straining to start it, he would cry out with pain. The driver examined him, but could find nothing. All the drivers became interested in his case. They talked it over at mealtime, and over their last pipes before going to bed, and one night they held a consultation. He was brought from his nest to the fire and was pressed and prodded till he cried out many times. Something was wrong inside, but they could locate no broken bones, could not make it out.

By the time Cassiar Bar was reached, he was so weak that he was falling repeatedly in the traces. The Scotsman called a halt and took him out of the team, making the next dog, Sol-leks, fast to the sled. His intention was to rest Dave, letting him run free behind the sled. Sick as he was, Dave resented being taken out, grunting and growling while the traces were unfastened, and whimpering broken-heartedly when he saw Sol-leks in the position he had held and served so long. For the pride of trace and trail was his, and sick unto death, he could not bear that another dog should do his work.

When the sled started, he floundered in the soft snow alongside the beaten trail, attacking Sol-leks with his teeth, rushing against him and trying to thrust him off into the soft snow on the other side, striving to leap inside his traces and get between him and the sled, and all the while whining and yelping and crying with grief and pain. The Scotsman tried to drive him away with the whip; but he paid no heed to the stinging lash, and the man had not the heart to strike harder. Dave refused to run quietly on the trail behind the sled, where the going was easy, but continued to flounder alongside in the soft snow, where the going was most difficult, till exhausted, then he fell, and lay where he fell, howling lugubriously as the long train of sleds churned by.

With the last remnant of his strength he managed to stagger along behind till the train made another stop, when he floundered past the sleds to his own, where he stood alongside Sol-leks. His driver lingered a moment to get a light for his pipe from the man behind. Then he returned and started his dogs. They swung out on the trail with remarkable lack of exertion, turned their heads uneasily, and stopped in surprise. The driver was surprised, too; the sled had not moved. He called his comrades to witness the sight. Dave had bitten through both of Sol-leks's traces, and was standing directly in front of the sled in his proper place.

He pleaded with his eyes to remain there. The driver was perplexed. His comrades talked of how a dog could break its heart through being denied the work that killed it, and recalled instances they had known, where dogs, too old for the toil, or injured, had died because they were cut out of the traces. Also, they held it a mercy, since Dave was to die anyway, that he should die in the traces, heart-easy and content. So he was harnessed in again, and proudly he pulled as of old, though more than once he cried out involuntarily from the bite of his inward hurt. Several times he fell down and was dragged in the traces, and once the sled ran upon him so that he limped thereafter on one of his hind legs.

But he held out till camp was reached, when his driver made a place for him by the fire. Morning found him too weak to travel. At harness-up time he tried to crawl to his driver. By convulsive efforts he got on his feet, staggered, and fell. Then he wormed his way forward slowly toward where the harnesses were being put on his mates. He would advance his forelegs and drag up his body with a sort of hitching movement, when he would advance his forelegs and hitch ahead again for a few more inches. His strength left him, and the last his mates saw of him he lay gasping in the snow and yearning toward them. But they could hear him mournfully howling till they passed out of sight behind a belt of river timber.

Here the train was halted. The Scotsman slowly retraced his steps to the camp they had left. The men ceased talking. A revolver-shot rang out. The man came back hurriedly. The whips snapped, the bells tinkled merrily, the sleds churned along the trail; but Buck knew, and every dog knew, what had taken place behind the belt of river trees.

THINK AND DISCUSS

Understanding

1. How does Buck assert mastery over François and Perrault?
2. How do the other dogs react to Buck?
3. What happens to Dave?

Analyzing

4. How is the mail run different from the record run?
5. How do Buck's reactions to the work of the mail run **contrast** with Dave's?
6. Contrast the beginning and the end of this chapter. What is **ironic** about the way the chapter ends?

Extending

7. Can you see any similarities between the way Dave reacts when he cannot work and the way humans behave? Explain.

COMPOSITION

Reading/Writing Log

Jack London uses contrasts to emphasize changes in situations and characters. Copy the headings and examples below in your reading/writing log. Then find examples in Chapter 4 to write after the other headings. Quote key words and phrases; summarize longer examples.

Contrasts

1. **Conditions for Record Run**
   a. General tone of team—solid unit, "leaped as one dog in the traces."
   b. The trail—excellent, "well-packed and hard," no new snow.
   c. Load—light, courier dispatches
   d. Speed—"they flew so fast that the man whose turn it was to run towed behind the sled at the end of a rope."
   e. Mood of dogs and men—excited, proud

vs.

Conditions of the Mail Run
   a. General tone of team
   b. the trail
   c. Load
   d. Speed
   e. Mood of dogs and men

Contrasts

2. **Buck's Reactions to the Mail Run**
   a. How he behaves
   b. What he is concerned about

vs.

Dave's Reactions to the Mail Run
   a. How he behaves
   b. What he is concerned about

---

5 The Toil of Trace and Trail

Thirty days from the time it left Dawson, the Salt Water Mail, with Buck and his mates at the fore, arrived at Skagway. They were in a wretched state, worn out and worn down. Buck's one hundred and forty pounds had dwindled to one hundred and fifteen. The rest of his mates, though lighter dogs, had relatively lost more weight than he. Pike, the malingerer, who, in his lifetime of deceit, had often successfully feigned a hurt leg, was now limping in earnest. Sol-leks was limping, and Dub was suffering from a wrenched shoulder blade.

They were all terribly footsore. No spring or rebound was left in them. Their feet fell heavily on the trail, jarring their bodies and doubling the fatigue of a day's travel. There was nothing the matter with them except that they were dead tired. It was not the dead-tiredness that comes through brief and excessive effort, from which recovery is a matter of hours; but it was the dead-tiredness that comes through the slow and prolonged strength drainage of months of toil. There was no power of recuperation left, no reserve strength to call upon. It had been all used, the last least bit of it. Every muscle, every fibre, every cell, was tired, dead tired. And there was reason for it. In less than five months they had travelled twenty-five hundred miles, during the last eighteen hundred of which they had had but five days' rest. When they arrived at Skagway they were apparently on their last legs. They could barely keep the traces taut, and on the down grades just managed to keep out of the way of the sled.

"Mush on, poor sore feets," the driver encouraged them as they tottered down the main street of Skagway. "Dis is de las'. Den we get one long res'. Eh? For sure. One bully long res'."

The drivers confidently expected a long stop-over. Themselves, they had covered twelve hundred miles with two days' rest, and in the nature of reason and common justice they deserved an interval of loafing. But

so many were the men who had rushed into the Klondike, and so many were the sweethearts, wives, and kin that had not rushed in, that the congested mail was taking on Alpine proportions; also, there were official orders. Fresh batches of Hudson Bay dogs were to take the places of those worthless for the trail. The worthless ones were to be got rid of, and, since dogs count for little against dollars, they were to be sold.

Three days passed, by which time Buck and his mates found how really tired and weak they were. Then, on the morning of the fourth day, two men from the States came along and bought them, harness and all, for a song. The men addressed each other as "Hal" and "Charles." Charles was a middle-aged, lightish-colored man, with weak and watery eyes and a mustache that twisted fiercely and vigorously up, giving the lie to the limply drooping lip it concealed. Hal was a youngster of nineteen or twenty, with a big Colt's revolver and a hunting knife strapped about him on a belt that fairly bristled with cartridges. This belt was the most salient thing about him. It advertised his callowness—a callowness sheer and unutterable. Both men were manifestly out of place, and why such as they should adventure the North is part of the mystery of things that passes understanding.

Buck heard the chaffering, saw the money pass between the man and the Government agent, and knew that the Scotsman and the mail-train drivers were passing out of his life on the heels of Perrault and François and the others who had gone before. When driven with his mates to the new owners' camp, Buck saw a slipshod and slovenly affair, tent half stretched, dishes unwashed, everything in disorder; also, he saw a woman. "Mercedes" the men called her. She was Charles's wife and Hal's sister—a nice family party.

Buck watched them apprehensively as they proceeded to take down the tent and load the sled. There was a great deal of effort about their manner, but no businesslike method. The tent was rolled into an awkward bundle three times as large as it should have been. The tin dishes were packed away unwashed. Mercedes continually fluttered in the way of her men and kept up an unbroken chattering of remonstrance and advice. When they put a clothes-sack on the front of the sled, she suggested it should go on the back; and when they had it put on the back, and covered it over with a couple of other bundles, she discovered overlooked articles which could abide nowhere else but in that very sack, and they unloaded again.

Three men from a neighboring tent came out and looked on, grinning and winking at one another.

"You've got a right smart load as it is," said one of them; "and it's not me should tell you your business, but I wouldn't tote that tent along if I was you."

"Undreamed of!" cried Mercedes, throwing up her hands in dainty dismay. "However in the world could I manage without a tent?"

"It's springtime, and you won't get any more cold weather," the man replied.

She shook her head decidedly, and Charles and Hal put the last odds and ends on top the mountainous load.

"Think it'll ride?" one of the men asked.

"Why shouldn't it?" Charles demanded rather shortly.

"Oh, that's all right, that's all right," the man hastened meekly to say. "I was just a-wonderin', that is all. It seemed a mite top-heavy."

Charles turned his back and drew the lashings down as well as he could, which was not in the least well.

"An' of course the dogs can hike along all day with that contraption behind them," affirmed a second of the men.

"Certainly," said Hal, with freezing politeness, taking hold of the gee-pole with one hand and swinging his whip from the other. "Mush!" he shouted. "Mush on there!"

The dogs sprang against the breastbands, strained hard for a few moments, then relaxed. They were unable to move the sled.

"The lazy brutes, I'll show them," he cried, preparing to lash out at them with the whip.

But Mercedes interfered, crying, "Oh, Hal, you mustn't," as she caught hold of the whip and wrenched it from him. "The poor dears! Now you must promise you won't be harsh with them for the rest of the trip, or I won't go a step."

"Precious lot you know about dogs," her brother sneered; "and I wish you'd leave me alone. They're lazy, I tell you, and you've got to whip them to get anything out of them. That's their way. You ask any one. Ask one of those men."

Mercedes looked at them imploringly, untold repugnance at sight of pain written in her pretty face.

"They're weak as water, if you want to know," came the reply from one of the men.

"Plumb tuckered out, that's what's the matter. They need a rest."

"Rest be blanked," said Hal with his beardless lips; and Mercedes said, "Oh!" in pain and sorrow at the oath.

But she was a clannish creature, and rushed at once to the defense of her brother. "Never mind that man," she said pointedly. "You're driving our dogs and you do what you think best with them."

Again Hal's whip fell upon the dogs. They threw themselves against the breastbands, dug their feet into the packed snow, got down low to it, and put forth all their strength. The sled held as though it were an anchor. After two efforts, they stood still, panting. The whip was whistling savagely, when once more Mercedes interfered. She dropped on her knees before Buck, with tears in her eyes, and put her arms around his neck.

"You poor, poor dears," she cried sympathetically, "why don't you pull hard?—then you wouldn't be whipped." Buck did not like her, but he was feeling too miserable to resist her, taking it as part of the day's miserable work.

One of the onlookers, who had been clenching his teeth to suppress hot speech, now spoke up:—

"It's not that I care a whoop what becomes of you, but for the dogs' sakes I just want to tell you, you can help them a mighty lot by breaking out that sled. The runners are froze fast. Throw your weight against the gee-pole, right and left, and break it out."

A third time the attempt was made, but this time, following the advice, Hal broke out the runners which had been frozen to the snow. The overloaded and unwieldy sled forged ahead, Buck and his mates struggling frantically under the rain of blows. A hundred yards ahead the path turned and sloped steeply into the main street. It would have required an experienced man to keep the top-heavy sled upright, and Hal was not such a man. As they swung on the turn the sled went over, spilling half its load through the loose lashings. The dogs never stopped. The lightened sled bounded on its side behind them. They were angry because of the ill treatment they had received and the unjust load. Buck was raging. He broke into a run, the team following his lead. Hal cried, "Whoa! whoa!" but they gave no heed. He tripped and was pulled off his feet. The capsized sled ground over him, and the dogs dashed on up the street, adding to the gaiety of Skagway as they scattered the remainder of the outfit along its chief thoroughfare.

Kind hearted citizens caught the dogs and gathered up the scattered belongings. Also, they gave advice. Half the load and twice the dogs, if they ever expected to reach Dawson, was what was said. Hal and his sister and brother-in-law listened unwillingly, pitched tent, and overhauled the outfit; canned goods were turned out that made men laugh, for canned goods on the Long Trail is a thing to dream about. "Blankets for a hotel," quoth one of the men who laughed and helped. "Half as many is too much; get rid of them. Throw away that tent, and all those dishes— who's going to wash them anyway? Good Lord, do you think you're traveling on a Pullman?"

And so it went, the inexorable elimination of the superfluous. Mercedes cried when her clothes-bags were dumped on the ground and article after article was thrown out. She cried in general, and she cried in particular over each discarded thing. She clasped hands about knees, rocking back and forth broken-heartedly. She averred she would not go an inch, not for a dozen Charleses. She appealed to everybody and to everything, finally wiping her eyes and proceeding to cast out even articles of apparel that were imperative necessaries. And in her zeal, when she had finished with her own, she attacked the belongings of her men and went through them like a tornado.

This accomplished, the outfit, though cut in half, was still a formidable bulk. Charles and Hal went out in the evening and bought six Outside dogs. These, added to the six of the original team, and Teek and Koona, the huskies obtained at the Rink Rapids on the record trip, brought the team up to fourteen. But the Outside dogs, though practically broken in since their landing, did not amount to much. Three were short-haired pointers, one was a Newfoundland, and the other two were mongrels of indeterminate breed. They did not seem to know anything, these newcomers. Buck and his comrades looked upon them with disgust, and though he speedily taught them their places and what not to do, he could not teach them what to do. They did not take kindly to trace and trail. With the exception of the two mongrels, they were bewildered and spirit-broken by the strange savage environment in which they found themselves and by ill treatment they had received. The two mongrels were without spirit at all; bones were the only things breakable about them.

With the newcomers hopeless and forlorn, and the old team worn out by twenty-five hundred miles of continuous trail, the outlook was anything but bright. The two men, however, were quite cheerful. And they were proud, too. They were doing the thing in style, with fourteen dogs. They had seen other sleds depart over the Pass for Dawson or come in from Dawson, but never had they seen a sled with so many as fourteen dogs. In the nature of Arctic travel there was a reason why fourteen dogs should not drag one sled, and that was that one sled could not carry the food for fourteen dogs. But Charles and Hal did not know this. They had worked the trip out with a pencil, so much to a dog, so many dogs, and so many days, Q.E.D.[6] Mercedes looked over their shoulders and nodded comprehensively, it was all so very simple.

Late next morning Buck led the long team up the street. There was nothing lively about it, no snap or go in him and his fellows. They were starting dead weary. Four times he had covered the distance between Salt Water and Dawson, and the knowledge that, jaded and tired, he was facing the same trail once more, made him bitter. His heart was not in the work, nor was the heart of any dog. The Outsides were timid and frightened, the Insides without confidence in their masters.

Buck felt vaguely that there was no depending upon these two men and the woman. They did not know how to do anything, and as the days went by it became apparent that they could not learn. They were slack in all things, without order or discipline. It took them half the night to pitch a slovenly camp,

_____

6. *Q.E.D.*, which was to be proved (Latin).

and half the morning to break that camp and get the sled loaded in fashion so slovenly that for the rest of the day they were occupied in stopping and rearranging the load. Some days they did not make ten miles. On other days they were unable to get started at all. And on no day did they succeed in making more than half the distance used by the men as a basis in their dog-food computation.

It was inevitable that they should go short on dog-food. But they hastened it by overfeeding, bringing the day nearer when underfeeding would commence. The Outside dogs, whose digestions had not been trained by chronic famine to make the most of little, had voracious appetites. And when, in addition to this, the worn-out huskies pulled weakly, Hal decided that the orthodox ration was too small. He doubled it. And to cap it all, when Mercedes, with tears in her pretty eyes and a quaver in her throat, could not cajole him into giving the dogs still more, she stole from the fish-sacks and fed them slyly. But it was not food that Buck and the huskies needed, but rest. And though they were making poor time, the heavy load they dragged sapped their strength severely.

Then came the underfeeding. Hal awoke one day to the fact that his dog-food was half gone and the distance only quarter covered; further, that for love or money no additional dog-food was to be obtained. So he cut down even the orthodox ration and tried to increase the day's travel. His sister and brother-in-law seconded him; but they were frustrated by their heavy outfit and their own incompetence. It was a simple matter to give the dogs less food; but it was impossible to make the dogs travel faster, while their own inability to

get under way earlier in the morning prevented them from traveling longer hours. Not only did they not know how to work dogs, but they did not know how to work themselves.

The first to go was Dub. Poor blundering thief that he was, always getting caught and punished, he had nonetheless been a faithful worker. His wrenched shoulder blade, untreated and unrested, went from bad to worse, till finally Hal shot him with the big Colt's revolver. It is a saying of the country that an Outside dog starves to death on the ration of the husky, so the six Outside dogs under Buck could do no less than die on half the ration of the husky. The Newfoundland went first, followed by the three short-haired pointers, the two mongrels hanging more grittily on to life, but going in the end.

By this time all the amenities and gentlenesses of the Southland had fallen away from the three people. Shorn of its glamour and romance, Arctic travel became to them a reality too harsh for their manhood and womanhood. Mercedes ceased weeping over the dogs, being too occupied with weeping over herself and with quarreling with her husband and brother. To quarrel was the one thing they were never too weary to do. Their irritability arose out of their misery, increased with it, doubled upon it, outdistanced it. The wonderful patience of the trail which comes to men who toil hard and suffer sore, and remain sweet of speech and kindly, did not come to these two men and the woman. They had no inkling of such a patience. They were stiff and in pain; their muscles ached, their bones ached, their very hearts ached; and because of this they became sharp of speech, and hard words were first on their lips in the morning and last at night.

Charles and Hal wrangled whenever Mercedes gave them a chance. It was the cherished belief of each that he did more than his share of the work, and neither forbore to speak this belief at every opportunity. Sometimes Mercedes sided with her husband, sometimes with her brother. The result was a beautiful and unending family quarrel. Starting from a dispute as to which should chop a few sticks for the fire (a dispute which concerned only Charles and Hal), presently would be lugged in the rest of the family, fathers, mothers, uncles, cousins, people thousands of miles away, and some of them dead. That Hal's views on art, or the sort of society plays his mother's brother wrote, should have anything to do with the chopping of a few sticks of firewood, passes comprehension; nevertheless the quarrel was as likely to tend in that direction as in the direction of Charles's political prejudices. And that Charles's sister's tale-bearing tongue should be relevant to the building of a Yukon fire, was apparent only to Mercedes, who disburdened herself of copious opinions upon that topic, and incidentally upon a few other traits unpleasantly peculiar to her husband's family. In the meantime the fire remained unbuilt, the camp half pitched, and the dogs unfed.

Mercedes nursed a special grievance—the grievance of sex. She was pretty and soft, and had been chivalrously treated all her days. But the present treatment by her husband and brother was everything save chivalrous. It was her custom to be helpless. They complained. Upon which impeachment of what to her was her most essential sex prerogative, she made their lives unendurable. She no longer considered the dogs, and because she was sore and tired, she persisted in riding on the sled. She was pretty and soft, but she weighed one hundred and twenty pounds—a lusty last straw to the load dragged by the weak and starving animals. She rode for days, till they fell in the traces and the sled stood still. Charles and Hal begged her to get off and walk, pleaded with her, entreated, the while she wept and importuned Heaven with a recital of their brutality.

On one occasion they took her off the sled by main strength. They never did it again. She let her legs go limp like a spoiled child, and sat down on the trail. They went on their way, but she did not move. After they had traveled three miles they unloaded the sled, came back for her, and by main strength put her on the sled again.

In the excess of their own misery they were callous to the suffering of their animals. Hal's theory which he practiced on others, was that one must get hardened. He had started out preaching it to his sister and brother-in-law. Failing there, he hammered it into the dogs with a club. At the Five Fingers the dog food gave out, and a toothless old Indian woman offered to trade them a few pounds of frozen horsehide for the Colt's revolver that kept the big hunting knife company at Hal's hip. A poor substitute for food was this hide, just as it had been stripped from the starved horses of the cattlemen six months back. In its frozen state it was more like strips of galvanized iron, and when a dog wrestled it into his stomach it thawed into thin and innutritious leathery strings and into a mass of short hair, irritating and indigestible.

And through it all Buck staggered along at the head of the team as in a nightmare. He pulled when he could; when he could no longer pull, he fell down and remained down till blows from whip or club drove him to his feet again. All the stiffness and gloss had gone out of his beautiful furry coat. The hair hung down, limp and draggled, or matted with dried blood where Hal's club had bruised him. His muscles had wasted away to knotty strings, and the flesh pads had disappeared, so that each rib and every bone in his frame were outlined cleanly through the loose hide that was wrinkled in folds of emptiness. It was heartbreaking, only Buck's heart was unbreakable. The man in the red sweater had proved that.

As it was with Buck, so was it with his mates. They were perambulating skeletons. There were seven all together, including him. In their very great misery they had become insensible to the bite of the lash or the bruise of the club. The pain of the beating was dull and distant, just as the things their eyes saw and their ears heard seemed dull and distant. They were not half living, or quarter living. They were simply so many bags of bones in which sparks of life fluttered faintly. When a halt was made, they dropped down in the traces like dead dogs, and the spark dimmed and paled and seemed to go out. And when the club or whip fell upon them, the spark fluttered feebly up, and they tottered to their feet and staggered on.

There came a day when Billee, the good-natured, fell and could not rise. Hal had traded off his revolver, so he took the axe and knocked Billee on the head as he lay in the traces, then cut the carcass out of the harness and dragged it to one side. Buck saw, and his mates saw, and they knew that this thing was very close to them. In the next day Koona went, and but five of them remained: Joe, too far gone to be malignant; Pike, crippled and limping, only half conscious and not conscious enough longer to malinger; Sol-leks, the one-eyed, still faithful to the toil of trace and trail, and mournful in that he had so little strength with which to pull; Teek, who had not traveled so far that winter and who was now beaten more than the others because he was fresher; and Buck, still at the head of the team, but no longer enforcing discipline or striving to enforce it, blind with weakness half the time and keeping the trail by the loom of it and by the dim feel of his feet.

It was beautiful spring weather, but neither dogs nor humans were aware of it. Each day the sun rose earlier and set later. It was dawn by three in the morning, and twilight lingered till nine at night. The whole long day was a blaze of sunshine. The ghostly winter silence had given way to the great spring murmur of awakening life. This murmur arose from all the land, fraught with the joy of living. It came from the things that lived and moved again, things which had been as dead and which had not moved during the long months of frost. The sap was rising in the pines. The willows and aspens were bursting out in young buds. Shrubs and vines were putting on fresh garbs of green. Crickets sang in the nights, and in the days all manner of creeping, crawling things rustled forth into the sun. Partridges and woodpeckers were booming and knocking in the forest.

Frank Schoonover, "As Darkness Closed Over the North Country" (detail) *Private Collection*

Squirrels were chattering, birds singing, and overhead honked the wildfowl driving up from the South in cunning wedges that split the air.

From every hill slope came the trickle of running water, the music of unseen fountains. All things were thawing, bending, snapping. The Yukon was straining to break loose the ice that bound it down. It ate away from beneath; the sun ate from above. Airholes formed, fissures[7] sprang and spread apart, while thin sections of ice fell through bodily into the river. And amid all this bursting, rending, throbbing of awakening life, under the blazing sun and through the soft-sighing breezes, like wayfarers to death, staggered the two men, the woman, and the huskies.

With the dogs falling, Mercedes weeping and riding, Hal swearing innocuously, and Charles's eyes wistfully watering, they staggered into John Thornton's camp at the mouth of White River. When they halted, the dogs dropped down as though they had all been struck dead. Mercedes dried her eyes and looked at John Thornton. Charles sat down on a log to rest. He sat down very slowly and painstakingly what of his great stiffness. Hal did the talking. John Thornton was whittling the last touches on an ax handle he had made from a stick of birch. He whittled and listened, gave monosyllabic replies, and, when it was asked, terse advice. He knew the breed, and he gave his advice in the certainty that it would not be followed.

"They told us up above that the bottom was dropping out of the trail and that the best thing for us to do was to lay over," Hal said in response to Thornton's warning to take no more chances on the rotten ice. "They told us we couldn't make White River, and here we are." This last with a sneering ring of triumph in it.

"And they told you true," John Thornton answered. "The bottom's likely to drop out at any moment. Only fools, with the blind luck of fools, could have made it. I tell you straight, I wouldn't risk my carcass on that ice for all the gold in Alaska."

"That's because you're not a fool, I suppose," said Hal. "All the same, we'll go on to Dawson." He uncoiled his whip. "Get up there, Buck! Hi! Get up there! Mush on!"

Thornton went on whittling. It was idle, he knew, to get between a fool and his folly; while two or three fools more or less would not alter the scheme of things.

But the team did not get up at the command. It had long since passed into the stage where blows were required to rouse it. The

7. **fissure** (fish′ər), a long, narrow opening; split; crack.

whip flashed out, here and there, on its merciless errands. John Thornton compressed his lips. Sol-leks was the first to crawl to his feet. Teek followed. Joe came next, yelping with pain. Pike made painful efforts. Twice he fell over, when half up, and on the third attempt managed to rise. Buck made no effort. He lay quietly where he had fallen. The lash bit into him again and again, but he neither whined nor struggled. Several times Thornton started, as though to speak, but changed his mind. A moisture came into his eyes, and, as the whipping continued, he arose and walked irresolutely up and down.

This was the first time Buck had failed, in itself a sufficient reason to drive Hal into a rage. He exchanged the whip for the customary club. Buck refused to move under the rain of heavier blows which now fell upon him. Like his mates, he was barely able to get up, but, unlike them, he had made up his mind not to get up. He had a vague feeling of impending doom. This had been strong upon him when he pulled into the bank, and it had not departed from him. What of the thin and rotten ice he had felt under his feet all day, it seemed that he sensed disaster close at hand, out there ahead on the ice where his master was trying to drive him. He refused to stir. So greatly had he suffered, and so far gone was he, that the blows did not hurt much. And as they continued to fall upon him, the spark of life within flickered and went down. It was nearly out. He felt strangely numb. As though from a great distance, he was aware that he was being beaten. The last sensations of pain left him. He no longer felt anything, though very faintly he could hear the impact of the club upon his body. But it was no longer his body, it seemed so far away.

And then, suddenly, without warning, uttering a cry that was inarticulate and more like the cry of an animal, John Thornton sprang upon the man who wielded the club. Hal was hurled backward, as though struck by a falling tree. Mercedes screamed. Charles looked on wistfully, wiped his watery eyes, but did not get up because of his stiffness.

John Thornton stood over Buck, struggling to control himself, too convulsed with rage to speak.

"If you strike that dog again, I'll kill you," he at last managed to say in a choking voice.

"It's my dog," Hal replied, wiping the blood from his mouth as he came back. "Get out of my way, or I'll fix you. I'm going to Dawson."

Thornton stood between him and Buck and evinced no intention of getting out of the way. Hal drew his long hunting knife. Mercedes screamed, cried, laughed, and manifested the chaotic abandonment of hysteria. Thornton rapped Hal's knuckles with the ax handle, knocking the knife to the ground. He rapped his knuckles again as he tried to pick it up. Then he stooped, picked it up himself, and with two strokes cut Buck's traces.

Hal had no fight left in him. Besides, his hands were full with his sister, or his arms, rather; while Buck was too near death to be of further use in hauling the sled. A few minutes later they pulled out from the bank and down the river. Buck heard them go and raised his head to see. Pike was leading, Sol-leks was at the wheel, and between were Joe and Teek. They were limping and staggering. Mercedes was riding the loaded sled. Hal guided at the gee-pole, and Charles stumbled along in the rear.

As Buck watched them, Thornton knelt beside him and with rough, kindly hands searched for broken bones. By the time his search had disclosed nothing more than many bruises and a state of terrible starvation, the sled was a quarter of a mile away. Dog and man watched it crawling along over the ice. Suddenly, they saw its back end drop down, as into a rut, and the gee-pole, with Hal clinging to it, jerk into the air. Mercedes's scream came to their ears. They saw Charles turn and make one step to run back, and then a whole section of ice give way and the dogs and humans disappear. A yawning hole was all that was to be seen. The bottom had dropped out of the trail.

John Thornton and Buck looked at each other.

"You poor devil," said John Thornton and Buck licked his hand.

THINK AND DISCUSS
Understanding
1. How much rest did the dogs have during their last run?
2. What do Hal and Charles attempt to do against the advice of the men from the neighboring tent?
3. Describe how the party is equipped when it finally sets out for Dawson.
4. What instinct or fear makes Buck refuse to get up when he is ordered to?
5. What happens to the team and its owners?
6. How is Buck spared?

Analyzing
7. In what ways do Hal, Charles, and Mercedes show their shallowness, incompetence, and cruelty in the way they treat the dogs?
8. Why are neither the dogs nor the humans aware of the spring weather?

Extending
9. Do you think that Hal, Charles, and Mercedes deserve their fate? Explain.

THINKING SKILLS
Classifying
Jack London has shown readers two distinct types of people who have been drawn to the North by the gold. One type is competent, businesslike, and ambitious, but fair in its treatment of the work animals and seems, in fact, to grow fond of these animals. The other type falls apart physically, emotionally, and morally in the face of Arctic conditions. Classify the humans introduced so far into one or the other of these categories.

COMPOSITION ◆━
Reading/Writing Log
Earlier London used repetition to emphasize the dogs' pride. He uses this technique again in describing their exhaustion.

From paragraph 1, column 1, page 609, copy the sentences that either use the word *tired* or illustrate its meaning. Then underline the words and phrases that repeat the idea of the dogs' being *dead tired*.

6 For the Love of a Man

When John Thornton froze his feet in the previous December, his partners had made him comfortable and left him to get well, going on themselves up the river to get out a raft of saw-logs for Dawson. He was still limping slightly at the time he rescued Buck, but with the continued warm weather even the slight limp left him. And here, lying by the river bank through the long spring days, watching the running water, listening lazily to the songs of birds and the hum of nature, Buck slowly won back his strength.

A rest comes very good after one has travelled three thousand miles, and it must be confessed that Buck waxed lazy as his wounds healed, his muscles swelled out, and the flesh came back to cover his bones. For that matter, they were all loafing—Buck, John Thornton, and Skeet and Nig—waiting for the raft to come that was to carry them down to Dawson. Skeet was a little Irish setter who early made friends with Buck, who in a dying condition, was unable to resent her first advances. She had the doctor trait which some dogs possess, and as a mother cat washes her kittens, so she washed and cleansed Buck's wounds. Regularly, each morning after he had finished his breakfast, she performed her self-appointed task, till he came to look for her ministrations as much as he did for Thornton's. Nig, equally friendly though less demonstrative, was a huge dog, half bloodhound and half deerhound, with eyes that laughed and a boundless good nature.

To Buck's surprise these dogs manifested no jealousy toward him. They seemed to share the kindliness and largeness of John Thornton. As Buck grew stronger they enticed him into all sorts of ridiculous games, in which Thornton himself could not forbear to join, and in this fashion Buck romped through his convalescence and into a new existence. Love, genuine passionate love, was his for the first time. This he had never experienced at Judge Miller's down in the sun-kissed Santa Clara Valley. With the Judge's sons, hunting and tramping, it had been a working partnership; with the Judge's grandsons, a sort of pompous guardianship; and with the Judge himself, a stately and dignified friendship. But love that was feverish and burning, that was adoration, that was madness, it had taken John Thornton to arouse.

This man had saved his life, which was something; but, further, he was the ideal master. Other men saw to the welfare of their dogs from a sense of duty and business expediency; he saw to the welfare of his as if they were his own children, because he could not help it. And he saw further. He never forgot a kindly greeting or a cheering word, and to sit down for a long talk with them ("gas" he called it) was as much his delight as theirs. He had a way of taking Buck's head roughly between his hands, and resting his own head upon Buck's, of shaking him back and forth, the while calling him ill names that to Buck were love names. Buck knew no greater joy than that rough embrace and the sound of murmured oaths, and at each jerk back and forth it seemed that his heart would be shaken out of his body so great was its ecstasy. And when, released, he sprang to his feet, his mouth laughing, his eyes eloquent, his throat vibrant with unuttered sound, and in that fashion remained without movement,

John Thornton would reverently exclaim, "God! you can all but speak!"

Buck had a trick of love expression that was akin to hurt. He would often seize Thornton's hand in his mouth and close so fiercely that the flesh bore the impress of his teeth for some time afterward. And as Buck understood the oaths to be love words, so the man understood this feigned bite for a caress.

For the most part, however, Buck's love was expressed in adoration. While he went wild with happiness when Thornton touched him or spoke to him, he did not seek these tokens. Unlike Skeet, who was wont to shove her nose under Thornton's hand and nudge and nudge till petted, or Nig, who would stalk up and rest his great head on Thornton's knee, Buck was content to adore at a distance. He would lie by the hour, eager, alert, at Thornton's feet, looking up into his face, dwelling upon it, studying it, following with keenest interest each fleeting expression, every movement or change of feature. Or, as chance might have it, he would lie farther away, to the side or rear, watching the outlines of the man and the occasional movements of his body. And often, such was the communion in which they lived, the strength of Buck's gaze would draw John Thornton's head around, and he would return the gaze, without speech, his heart shining out of his eyes as Buck's heart shone out.

For a long time after his rescue, Buck did not like Thornton to get out of his sight. From the moment he left the tent to when he entered it again, Buck would follow at his heels. His transient masters since he had come into the Northland had bred in him a fear that no master could be permanent. He was afraid that Thornton would pass out of his life as Perrault and François and the Scotsman had passed out. Even in the night, in his dreams, he was haunted by this fear. At such times he would shake off sleep and creep through the chill to the flap of the tent, where he would stand and listen to the sound of his master's breathing.

But in spite of this great love he bore John Thornton, which seemed to bespeak the soft civilizing influence, the strain of the primitive, which the Northland had aroused in him, remained alive and active. Faithfulness and devotion, things born of fire and roof, were his; yet he retained his wildness and wiliness. He was a thing of the wild, come in from the wild to sit by John Thornton's fire, rather than a dog of the soft Southland stamped with the marks of generations of civilization. Because of his very great love, he could not steal from this man, but from any other man, in any other camp, he did not hesitate an instant, while the cunning with which he stole enabled him to escape detection.

His face and body were scored by the teeth of many dogs, and he fought as fiercely as ever and more shrewdly. Skeet and Nig were too good-natured for quarrelling—besides, they belonged to John Thornton; but the strange dog, no matter what the breed or valor, swiftly acknowledged Buck's supremacy or found himself struggling for life with a terrible antagonist. And Buck was merciless. He had learned well the law of club and fang, and he never forewent an advantage or drew back from a foe he had started on the way to Death. He had lessoned from Spitz, and from the chief fighting dogs of the police and mail, and knew there was no middle course. He must master or be mastered; while to show mercy was a weakness. Mercy did not exist in the primordial life. It was misunderstood for fear, and such misunderstandings made for death. Kill or be killed, eat or be eaten, was the law; and this mandate, down out of the depths of Time, he obeyed.

He was older than the days he had seen and the breaths he had drawn. He linked the past with the present, and the eternity behind him throbbed through him in a mighty rhythm to which he swayed as the tides and seasons swayed. He sat by John Thornton's fire, a broad-breasted dog, white-fanged and long-furred; but behind him were the shades of all manner of dogs, half-wolves and wild wolves, urgent and prompting, tasting the savor of the meat he ate, thirsting for the water he drank, scenting the wind with him, listening with him and telling him the sounds made by the wild life in the forest, dictating his moods, directing his actions, lying down to sleep with him when he lay down, and dreaming with him and beyond him and becoming themselves the stuff of his dreams.

So peremptorily did these shades beckon him, that each day mankind and the claims of mankind slipped farther from him. Deep in the forest a call was sounding, and as often as he heard this call, mysteriously thrilling and luring, he felt compelled to turn his back upon the fire and the beaten earth around it, and to plunge into the forest, and on and on, he knew not where or why; nor did he wonder where or why, the call sounding imperiously, deep in the forest. But as often as he gained the soft unbroken earth and the green shade, the love for John Thornton drew him back to the fire again.

Thornton alone held him. The rest of mankind was as nothing. Chance travellers might praise or pet him; but he was cold under it all, and from a too demonstrative man he would get up and walk away. When Thornton's partners, Hans and Pete, arrived on the long-expected raft, Buck refused to notice them till he learned they were close to Thornton; after that he tolerated them in a passive sort of way, accepting favors from them as though he favored them by accepting. They were of the same large type as Thornton, living close to the earth, thinking simply and seeing clearly; and ere they swung the raft into the big eddy by the sawmill at Dawson, they understood Buck and his ways, and did not insist upon an intimacy such as obtained with Skeet and Nig.

For Thornton, however, his love seemed to grow and grow. He alone among men could put a pack upon Buck's back in the summer traveling. Nothing was too great for Buck to do, when Thornton commanded. One day (they had grub-staked themselves from the proceeds of the raft and left Dawson for the headwaters of the Tanana) the men and dogs were sitting on the crest of a cliff which fell away, straight down, to naked bed-rock three hundred feet below. John Thornton was sitting near the edge, Buck at his shoulder. A thoughtless whim seized Thornton, and he drew the attention of Hans and Pete to the experiment he had in mind. "Jump, Buck!" he commanded, sweeping his arm out and over the chasm. The next instant he was grappling with Buck on the extreme edge, while Hans and Pete were dragging them back into safety.

"It's uncanny," Pete said, after it was over and they had caught their speech.

Thornton shook his head. "No, it is splendid, and it is terrible, too. Do you know, it sometimes makes me afraid."

"I'm not hankering to be the man that lays hands on you while he's around," Pete announced conclusively, nodding his head toward Buck.

"Py Jingo!" was Hans's contribution. "Not mineself either."

It was at Circle City, ere the year was out, that Pete's apprehensions were realized. "Black" Burton, a man evil-tempered and malicious, had been picking a quarrel with a tenderfoot at the bar, when Thornton stepped good-naturedly between. Buck, as was his custom, was lying in a corner, head on paws, watching his master's every action. Burton struck out, without warning, straight from the shoulder. Thornton was sent spinning, and saved himself from falling only by clutching the rail of the bar.

Those who were looking on heard what was neither bark nor yelp, but a something which is best described as a roar, and they saw Buck's body rise up in the air as he left the floor for Burton's throat. The man saved his life by instinctively throwing out his arm, but was hurled backward to the floor with Buck on top of him. Buck loosed his teeth from the flesh of the arm and drove in again for the throat. This time the man succeeded only in partly blocking, and his throat was torn open. Then the crowd was upon Buck, and he was driven off; but while a surgeon checked the bleeding, he prowled up and down, growling furiously, attempting to rush in, and being forced back by an array of hostile clubs. A "miners' meeting," called on the spot, decided that the dog had sufficient provocation, and Buck was discharged. But his reputation was made, and from that day his name spread through every camp in Alaska.

Later on, in the fall of the year, he saved John Thornton's life in quite another fashion. The three partners were lining a long and narrow poling-boat down a bad stretch of rapids on the Forty Mile Creek. Hans and Pete moved along the bank, snubbing with a thin manila rope from tree to tree, while Thornton remained in the boat, helping its descent by means of a pole, and shouting directions to the shore. Buck, on the bank, worried and anxious, kept abreast of the boat, his eyes never off his master.

At a particularly bad spot, where a ledge of barely submerged rocks jutted out into the river, Hans cast off the rope, and, while Thornton poled the boat out into the stream, ran down the bank with the end in his hand to snub the boat when it had cleared the ledge. This it did, and was flying downstream in a current as swift as a millrace, when Hans checked it with the rope and checked too suddenly. The boat flirted over and snubbed in to the bank bottom up, while Thornton, flung sheer out of it, was carried downstream toward the worst part of the rapids, a stretch of wild water in which no swimmer could live.

Buck had sprung in on the instant; and at the end of three hundred yards, amid a mad swirl of water, he overhauled Thornton. When he felt him grasp his tail, Buck headed for the bank, swimming with all his splendid strength. But the progress shoreward was slow; the progress down-stream amazingly rapid. From below came the fatal roaring where the wild current went wilder and was rent in shreds and spray by the rocks which thrust through like the teeth of an enormous comb. The suck of the water as it took the beginning of the last steep pitch was frightful, and Thornton knew that the shore was impossible. He scraped furiously over a rock, bruised across a second, and struck a third with crushing force. He clutched its slippery top with both hands, releasing Buck, and above the roar of the churning water shouted: "Go, Buck! Go!"

Buck could not hold his own, and swept on down-stream, struggling desperately, but unable to win back. When he heard Thornton's command repeated, he partly reared out of the water, throwing his head high, as though for a last look, then turned obediently toward the bank. He swam powerfully and was dragged ashore by Pete and Hans at the very point where swimming ceased to be possible and destruction began.

They knew that the time a man could cling to a slippery rock in the face of that driving current was a matter of minutes, and they ran as fast as they could up the bank to a point far above where Thornton was hanging on. They attached the line with which they had been snubbing the boat to Buck's neck and shoulders, being careful that it should neither strangle him nor impede his swimming, and launched him into the stream. He struck out boldly, but not straight enough into the stream. He discovered the mistake too late, when Thornton was abreast of him and a bare half-dozen strokes away while he was being carried helplessly past.

Hans promptly snubbed with the rope, as though Buck were a boat. The rope thus tightening on him in the sweep of the current, he was jerked under the surface, and under the surface he remained till his body struck against the bank and he was hauled out. He was half drowned, and Hans and Pete threw themselves upon him, pounding the breath into him and the water out of him. He staggered to his feet and fell down. The faint sound of Thornton's voice came to them, and though they could not make out the words of it, they knew that he was in his extremity. His master's voice acted on Buck like an electric shock. He sprang to his feet and ran up the bank ahead of the men to the point of his previous departure.

Again the rope was attached and he was launched, and again he struck out, but this time straight into the stream. He had miscalculated once, but he would not be guilty of it a second time. Hans paid out the rope, permitting no slack, while Pete kept it clear of coils. Buck held on till he was on a line straight above Thornton; then he turned, and with the speed of an express train headed down upon him. Thornton saw him coming, and, as Buck struck him like a battering ram, with the whole force of the current behind him, he reached up and closed with both arms around the shaggy neck. Hans snubbed the rope around the tree, and Buck and Thornton were jerked under the water. Strangling, suffocating, sometimes one upper-most and sometimes the other, dragging over the jagged bottom, smashing against rocks and snags, they veered in to the bank.

Thornton came to, belly downward and being violently propelled back and forth across a drift log by Hans and Pete. His first glance was for Buck, over whose limp and apparently lifeless body Nig was setting up a

Frank Schoonover, "The Edge of the Wilderness" (detail),
1924 *Private Collection*

howl, while Skeet was licking the wet face and closed eyes. Thornton was himself bruised and battered, and he went carefully over Buck's body, when he had been brought around, finding three broken ribs.

"That settles it," he announced. "We camp right here." And camp they did, till Buck's ribs knitted and he was able to travel.

That winter, at Dawson, Buck performed another exploit, not so heroic, perhaps, but one that put his name many notches higher on the totem-pole of Alaskan fame. This exploit was particularly gratifying to the three men; for they stood in need of the outfit which it furnished, and were enabled to make a long-desired trip into the virgin East, where miners had not yet appeared. It was brought about by a conversation in the Eldorado Saloon, in which men waxed boastful of their favorite dogs. Buck, because of his record, was the target for these men, and Thornton was driven stoutly to defend him. At the end of half an hour one man stated that his dog could start a sled with five hundred pounds and walk off with it; a second bragged six hundred for his dog; and a third, seven hundred.

"Pooh! Pooh!" said John Thornton. "Buck can start a thousand pounds."

"And break it out? And walk off with it for a hundred yards?" demanded Matthewson, a Bonanza king, he of the seven hundred vaunt.

"And break it out, and walk off with it for a hundred yards," John Thornton said coolly.

"Well," Matthewson said, slowly and deliberately, so that all could hear, "I've got a thousand dollars that says he can't. And there it is." So saying, he slammed a sack of gold dust of the size of a bologna sausage down upon the bar.

Nobody spoke. Thornton's bluff, if bluff it was, had been called. He could feel a flush of warm blood creeping up his face. His tongue had tricked him. He did not know whether Buck could start a thousand pounds. Half a ton! The enormousness of it appalled him. He had great faith in Buck's strength and had often thought him capable of starting such a load; but never, as now, had he faced the possibility of it, the eyes of a dozen men fixed upon him, silent and waiting. Further, he had no thousand dollars; nor had Hans or Pete.

"I've got a sled standing outside now, with twenty fifty-pound sacks of flour on it," Matthewson went on with brutal directness, "so don't let that hinder you."

Thornton did not reply. He did not know what to say. He glanced from face to face in the absent way of a man who has lost the power of thought and is seeking somewhere to find the thing that will start it going again. The face of Jim O'Brien, a Mastodon king and old-time comrade, caught his eyes. It was a cue to him, seeming to rouse him to do what he would never have dreamed of doing.

"Can you lend me a thousand?" he asked, almost in a whisper.

"Sure," answered O'Brien, thumping down a plethoric[8] sack by the side of Matthewson's. "Though it's little faith I'm having, John, that the beast can do the trick."

The Eldorado emptied its occupants into the street to see the test. The tables were deserted, and the dealers and gamekeepers came forth to see the outcome of the wager and to lay odds. Several hundred men, furred and mittened, banked around the sled within easy distance. Matthewson's sled, loaded with a thousand pounds of flour, had been standing for a couple of hours, and in the intense cold (it was sixty below zero) the runners had frozen fast to the hard-packed snow. Men offered odds of two to one that Buck could not budge the sled. A quibble arose concerning the phrase "break out." O'Brien contended it was Thornton's privilege to knock the runners loose, leaving Buck to "break it out" from a dead standstill. Matthewson insisted that the phrase included

---

8. *plethoric* (plə thôr′ik), too full, inflated.

breaking the runners from the frozen grip of the snow. A majority of the men who had witnessed the making of the bet decided in his favor, whereat the odds went up to three to one against Buck. There were no takers. Not a man believed him capable of the feat. Thornton had been hurried into the wager, heavy with doubt; and now that he looked at the sled itself, the concrete fact, with the regular team of ten dogs curled up in the snow before it, the more impossible the task appeared. Matthewson waxed jubilant.

"Three to one!" he proclaimed. "I'll lay you another thousand at that figure, Thornton. What d'ye say?"

Thornton's doubt was strong in his face, but his fighting spirit was aroused—the fighting spirit that soars above odds, fails to recognize the impossible, and is deaf to all save the clamor for battle. He called Hans and Pete to him. Their sacks were slim, and with his own the three partners could rake together only two hundred dollars. In the ebb of their fortunes, this sum was their total capital; yet they laid it unhesitatingly against Matthewson's six hundred.

The team of ten dogs was unhitched, and Buck, with his own harness, was put into the sled. He had caught the contagion of the excitement, and he felt that in some way he must do a great thing for John Thornton. Murmurs of admiration at his splendid appearance went up. He was in perfect condition, without an ounce of superfluous flesh, and the one hundred and fifty pounds that he weighed were so many pounds of grit and virility. His furry coat shone with the sheen of silk. Down the neck and across the shoulders, his mane, in repose as it was, half bristled and seemed to lift with every movement, as though excess of vigor made each particular hair alive and active. The great breast and heavy fore legs were no more than in proportion with the rest of the body where the muscles showed in tight rolls underneath the skin. Men felt these muscles and proclaimed them hard as iron, and the odds went down to two to one.

"Gad, sir! Gad, sir!" stuttered a member of the latest dynasty, a king of the Skookum Benches. "I offer you eight hundred for him, sir, before the test, sir; eight hundred just as he stands."

Thornton shook his head and stepped to Buck's side.

"You must stand off from him," Matthewson protested. "Free play and plenty of room."

The crowd fell silent; only could be heard the voices of the gamblers vainly offering two to one. Everybody acknowledged Buck a magnificent animal, but twenty fifty-pound sacks of flour bulked too large in their eyes for them to loosen their pouch-strings.

Thornton knelt down by Buck's side. He took his head in his two hands and rested cheek on cheek. He did not playfully shake him, as was his wont, or murmur soft love curses; but he whispered in his ear. "As you love me, Buck. As you love me," was what he whispered. Buck whined with suppressed eagerness.

The crowd was watching curiously. The affair was growing mysterious. It seemed like a conjuration. As Thornton got to his feet, Buck seized his mittened hand between his jaws, pressing in with his teeth and releasing slowly, half-reluctantly. It was the answer, in terms, not of speech, but of love. Thornton stepped well back.

"Now, Buck," he said.

Buck tightened the traces, then slacked them for a matter of several inches. It was the way he had learned.

"Gee!" Thornton's voice rang out, sharp in the tense silence.

Buck swung to the right, ending the movement in a plunge that took up the slack and with a sudden jerk arrested his one hundred and fifty pounds. The load quivered, and from under the runners arose a crisp crackling.

"Haw!" Thornton commanded.

Buck duplicated the manœuvre, this time to the left. The crackling turned into a snapping, the sled pivoting and the runners slipping and grating several inches to the side. The sled was broken out. Men were holding their breaths, intensely unconscious of the fact.

"Now, MUSH!"

Thornton's command cracked out like a pistol-shot. Buck threw himself forward, tightening the traces with a jarring lunge. His whole body was gathered compactly together in the tremendous effort, the muscles writhing and knotting like live things under the silky fur. His great chest was low to the ground, his head forward and down, while his feet were flying like mad, the claws scarring the hard-packed snow in parallel grooves. The sled swayed and trembled, half-started forward. One of his feet slipped, and one man groaned aloud. Then the sled lurched ahead in what appeared a rapid succession of jerks, though it never really came to a dead stop again . . . half an inch . . . an inch . . . two inches. . . . The jerks perceptibly diminished; as the sled gained momentum, he caught them up, till it was moving steadily along.

Men gasped and began to breathe again, unaware that for a moment they had ceased to breathe. Thornton was running behind, encouraging Buck with short, cheery words. The distance had been measured off, and as he neared the pile of firewood which marked the end of the hundred yards, a cheer began to grow and grow, which burst into a roar as he passed the firewood and halted at command. Every man was tearing himself loose, even Matthewson. Hats and mittens were flying in the air. Men were shaking hands, it did not matter with whom, and bubbling over in a general incoherent babel.

But Thornton fell on his knees beside Buck. Head was against head, and he was shaking him back and forth. Those who hurried up heard him cursing Buck, and he cursed him long and fervently, and softly and lovingly.

"Gad, sir! Gad, sir!" spluttered the Skookum Bench king. "I'll give you a thousand for him, sir, a thousand, sir—twelve hundred, sir."

Thornton rose to his feet. His eyes were wet. The tears were streaming frankly down his cheeks. "Sir," he said to the Skookum Bench king, "no, sir. You can go to hell, sir. It's the best I can do for you, sir."

Buck seized Thornton's hand in his teeth. Thornton shook him back and forth. As though animated by a common impulse, the onlookers drew back to a respectful distance, nor were they again indiscreet enough to interrupt.

THINK AND DISCUSS
Understanding
1. How is Buck's feeling for Thornton different from his feelings for the Millers?
2. What gesture does Thornton use to express his love to Buck?
3. What gesture does Buck use to express his love to Thornton?
4. Why does Buck choose the civilized world over the world of the wild?

Analyzing
5. What inner conflict begins to trouble Buck?
6. How does Buck demonstrate both civilized and wild traits in his love for Thornton?

Extending
7. What do you consider to be Buck's most admirable trait?

READING LITERATURE SKILLFULLY
Main Idea and Supporting Details
Earlier in this unit, you learned that determining the **main idea**—of a paragraph, a story, an article, a chapter, or an entire novel—and finding **details** that support that main idea can help you better understand what you are reading. Now answer the questions that follow about Chapter 6.

1. What is the title of this chapter?
2. In your own words, give the main idea of the chapter.
3. Give at least five details from Chapter 6 that support the main idea.

COMPOSITION
Reading/Writing Log
In this chapter, London uses **contrast** to emphasize the conflict within Buck between the civilized world and the wild world. The chart below lists words and phrases associated with the civilized world. Copy it in your reading/writing log. Then find examples in the chapter that are associated with the wild world. Write them in your log.

Contrasts
Civilized World
love for John Thornton
faithfulness and devotion
fire and roof (man-made shelter)
softness (easier life)
no stealing from Thornton
no fighting with Thornton's dogs
show mercy
vs.

What the wild world means to Buck

Comment

He Inspired Jack London

Belinda Mulrooney reached Alaska just after the discovery of gold in 1896. She built a hotel in the Yukon, and around it grew the boom town of Grand Forks. She was noted for her kindness to animals, especially the working dogs.

It was Nero [a St. Bernard that Belinda had bought from a man who could not afford to feed him] who was Belinda's pride and joy. One spring when Belinda left on a business trip to Seattle, she had one of her employees keep Nero tied up in Dawson until her boat left. She boarded a steamer and was on the first few minutes of the long journey Outside when miners aboard noticed an animal on the shore running parallel to the ship.

Once he got several hundred feet ahead of the bow, the dog leaped into the water and began swimming toward the boat. The miners cheered when they realized it was Nero, calling to the captain to stop. He refused, fearing the boat would be caught in the strong current and dragged into shore. But the miners were insistent and the captain relented. The boat stopped—without mishap—and the miners hauled the dripping dog on board and took him to

Nero, the Model for Buck
photo courtesy Seattle Times

Belinda's cabin. She took Nero to Seattle with her, booking two rooms in a hotel—one for her and the adjoining one for Nero. Nero was bathed and fed, and his stay in Seattle was as comfortable as any hotel guest's.

It was one of Belinda's customers at the Grand Forks Hotel who immortalized Nero for the rest of the world: Jack London used him as a model for Buck in *The Call of the Wild*.

From *Klondike Lost: A Decade of Photographs by Kinsey & Kinsey* by Norm Bolotin. Copyright © 1980 by Norm Bolotin. Reprinted by permission of Alaska Northwest Publishing Company.

7   The Sounding of the Call

When Buck earned sixteen hundred dollars in five minutes for John Thornton, he made it possible for his master to pay off certain debts and to journey with his partners into the East after a fabled lost mine, the history of which was as old as the history of the country. Many men had sought it; few had found it; and more than a few there were who had never returned from the quest. This lost mine was steeped in tragedy and shrouded in mystery. No one knew of the first man. The oldest tradition stopped before it got back to him. From the beginning there had been an ancient and ramshackle cabin. Dying men had sworn to it, and to the mine the site of which it marked, clinching their testimony with nuggets that were unlike any known grade of gold in the Northland.

But no living man had looted this treasure house, and the dead were dead; wherefore John Thornton and Pete and Hans, with Buck and half a dozen other dogs, faced into the East on an unknown trail to achieve where men and dogs as good as themselves had failed. They sledded seventy miles up the Yukon, swung to the left into the Stewart River, passed the Mayo and the McQueston, and held on until the Stewart itself became a streamlet, threading the upstanding peaks which marked the backbone of the continent.

John Thornton asked little of man or nature. He was unafraid of the wild. With a handful of salt and a rifle he could plunge into the wilderness and fare wherever he pleased and as long as he pleased. Being in no haste, Indian fashion, he hunted his dinner in the course of the day's travel; and if he failed to find it, like the Indian, he kept on traveling, secure in the knowledge that sooner or later he would come to it. So, on this great journey into the East, straight meat was the bill of fare, ammunition and tools principally made up the load on the sled, and the time-card was drawn upon the limitless future.

To Buck it was boundless delight, this hunting, fishing, and indefinite wandering through strange places. For weeks at a time they would hold on steadily, day after day; and for weeks upon end they would camp, here and there, the dogs loafing and the men burning holes through frozen muck and gravel and washing countless pans of dirt by the heat of the fire. Sometimes they went hungry, sometimes they feasted riotously, all according to the abundance of game and the fortune of hunting. Summer arrived, and dogs and men packed on their backs, rafted across blue mountain lakes, and descended or ascended unknown rivers in slender boats whipsawed from the standing forest.

The months came and went, and back and forth they twisted through the uncharted vastness, where no men were and yet where men had been if the Lost Cabin were true. They went across divides in summer blizzards, shivered under the midnight sun on naked mountains between the timber line and the eternal snows, dropped into summer valleys amid swarming gnats and flies, and in the shadows of glaciers picked strawberries and flowers as ripe and fair as any the Southland could boast. In the fall of the year they penetrated a weird lake country, sad and silent, where wildfowl had been, but where then there was no life nor sign of life—only the blowing of chill winds, the forming of ice in sheltered places, and the melancholy rippling of waves on lonely beaches.

And through another winter they wandered on the obliterated trails of men who had gone before. Once, they came upon a path blazed through the forest, an ancient path, and the Lost Cabin seemed very near. But the path began nowhere and ended nowhere, and it remained mystery, as the man who made it and the reason he made it remained mystery. Another time they chanced upon the time-graven wreckage of a hunting lodge, and amid the shreds of rotted blankets John Thornton found a long-barreled flintlock. He knew it for a Hudson Bay Company gun of the young days in the Northwest, when such a gun was worth its height in beaver skins packed flat. And that was all—no hint as to the man who in an early day had reared the lodge and left the gun among the blankets.

Spring came on once more, and at the end of all their wandering they found, not the Lost Cabin, but a shallow placer[9] in a broad valley where the gold showed like yellow butter across the bottom of the washing-pan. They sought no farther. Each day they worked earned them thousands of dollars in clean dust and nuggets, and they worked every day. The gold was sacked in moose-hide bags, fifty pounds to the bag, and piled like so much fire-wood outside the spruce-bough lodge. Like giants they toiled, days flashing on the heels of days like dreams as they heaped the treasure up.

There was nothing for the dogs to do save the hauling in of meat now and again that Thornton killed, and Buck spent long hours musing by the fire. . . . The call still sounded in the depths of the forest. It filled him with a great unrest and strange desires. It caused him to feel a vague, sweet gladness, and he was aware of wild yearnings and stirrings for he knew not what. Sometimes he pursued the call into the forest, looking for it as though it were a tangible thing, barking softly or defiantly, as the mood might dictate. He would thrust his nose into the cool wood moss, or into the black soil where long grasses grew, and snort with joy at the fat earth smells; or he would crouch for hours, as if in concealment, behind fungus-covered trunks of fallen trees, wide-eyed and wide-eared to all that moved and sounded about him. It might be, lying thus, that he hoped to surprise this call he could not understand. But he did not know why he did these various things. He was impelled to do them, and did not reason about them at all.

Irresistible impulses seized him. He would be lying in camp, dozing lazily in the heat of the day, when suddenly his head would lift and his ears cock up, intent and listening, and he would spring to his feet and dash away, and on and on, for hours, through the forest aisles and across the open spaces where the grasses bunched. He loved to run down dry watercourses, and to creep and spy upon the bird life in the woods. For a day at a time he would lie in the underbrush where he could watch the partridges drumming and strutting up and down. But especially he loved to run in the dim twilight of the summer midnights, listening to the subdued and sleepy murmurs of the forest, reading signs and sounds as man may read a book, and seeking for the mysterious something that called—called, waking or sleeping, at all times, for him to come.

One night he sprang from sleep with a start, eager-eyed, nostrils quivering and scenting, his mane bristling in recurrent waves. From the forest came the call (or one note of it, for the call was many-noted), distinct and definite as never before—a long-

---

9. *placer* (plas′ər), deposit of sand, gravel or earth in the bed of a stream containing particles of gold or other valuable minerals.

drawn howl, like, yet unlike, any noise made by husky dog. And he knew it, in the old familiar way, as a sound heard before. He sprang through the sleeping camp and in swift silence dashed through the woods. As he drew closer to the cry he went more slowly, with caution in every movement, till he came to an open place among the trees, and looking out saw, erect on haunches, with nose pointed to the sky, a long, lean, timber wolf.

He had made no noise, yet it ceased from its howling and tried to sense his presence. Buck stalked into the open, half crouching, body gathered compactly together, tail straight and stiff, feet falling with unwonted care. Every movement advertised commingled threatening and overture of friendliness. It was the menacing truce that marks the meeting of wild beasts that prey. But the wolf fled at sight of him. He followed, with wild leapings, in a frenzy to overtake. He ran him into a blind channel, in the bed of the creek, where a timber jam barred the way. The wolf whirled about, pivoting on his hind legs after the fashion of Joe and of all cornered husky dogs, snarling and bristling, clipping his teeth together in a continuous and rapid succession of snaps.

Buck did not attack, but circled him about and hedged him in with friendly advances. The wolf was suspicious and afraid; for Buck made three of him in weight, while his head barely reached Buck's shoulder. Watching his chance, he darted away, and the chase was resumed. Time and again he was cornered and the thing repeated, though he was in poor condition or Buck could not so easily have overtaken him. He would run till

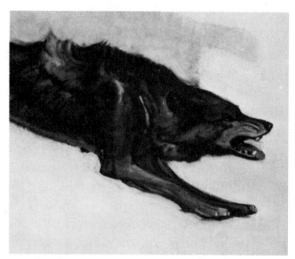

Frank Schoonover, "Pack of Running Wolves" (detail)
Private Collection

Buck's head was even with his flank, when he would whirl around at bay, only to dash away again at the first opportunity.

But in the end Buck's pertinacity was rewarded; for the wolf, finding that no harm was intended, finally sniffed noses with him. Then they became friendly, and played about in the nervous, half-coy way with which fierce beasts belie their fierceness. After some time of this the wolf started off at an easy lope in a manner that plainly showed he was going somewhere. He made it clear to Buck that he was to come, and they ran side by side through the sombre twilight, straight up the creek bed, into the gorge from which it issued, and across the bleak divide where it took its rise.

On the opposite slope of the watershed they came down into a level country where were great stretches of forest and many streams, and through these great stretches they ran steadily, hour after hour, the sun rising higher and the day growing warmer. Buck was wildly glad. He knew he was at last answering the call, running by the side of his wood brother toward the place from where the call surely came. Old memories were coming upon him fast, and he was stirring to them as of old he stirred to the realities of which they were the shadows. He had done this thing before, somewhere in that other and dimly remembered world, and he was doing it again now, running free in the open, the unpacked earth underfoot, the wide sky overhead.

They stopped by a running stream to drink, and, stopping, Buck remembered John Thornton. He sat down. The wolf started on toward the place from where the call surely came, then returned to him, sniffing noses and making actions as though to encourage him. But Buck turned about and started slowly on the back track. For the better part of an hour the wild brother ran by his side, whining softly. Then he sat down, pointed his nose upward, and howled. It was a mournful howl, and as Buck held steadily on his way he heard it grow faint and fainter until it was lost in the distance.

John Thornton was eating dinner when Buck dashed into camp and sprang upon him, in a frenzy of affection, overturning him, scrambling upon him, licking his face, biting his hand—"playing the general tom-fool," as John Thornton characterized it, the while he shook Buck back and forth and cursed him lovingly.

For two days and nights Buck never left camp, never let Thornton out of his sight. He followed him about at his work, watched him while he ate, saw him into his blankets at night and out of them in the morning. But after two days the call in the forest began to sound more imperiously than ever. Buck's restlessness came back on him, and he was haunted by recollections of the wild brother, and of the smiling land beyond the divide and the run side by side through the wide forest stretches. Once again he took to wandering in the woods, but the wild brother came no more; and though he listened through long vigils, the mournful howl was never raised.

He began to sleep out at night, staying away from camp for days at a time; and once he crossed the divide at the head of the creek and went down into the land of timber and streams. There he wandered for a week, seeking vainly for fresh sign of the wild brother, killing his meat as he traveled and traveling with the long, easy lope that seems never to tire. He fished for salmon in a broad stream that emptied somewhere into the sea, and by this stream he killed a large black bear, blinded by the mosquitoes while likewise fishing, and raging through the forest helpless and terrible. Even so, it was a hard fight, and it aroused the last latent remnants of Buck's ferocity. And two days later, when he returned to his kill and found a dozen wolverines quarreling over the spoil, he scattered them like chaff; and those that fled left two behind who would quarrel no more.

The blood-longing became stronger than ever before. He was a killer, a thing that preyed, living on the things that lived, unaided, alone, by virtue of his own strength and prowess, surviving triumphantly in a hostile environment where only the strong survive. Because of all this he became possessed of a great pride in himself, which communicated itself like a contagion to his physical being. It advertised itself in all his movements, was apparent in the play of every muscle, spoke plainly as speech in the way he carried himself, and made his glorious furry coat if anything more glorious. But for the stray brown on his muzzle and above his eyes, and for the splash of white hair that ran midmost down his chest, he might well have been mistaken for a gigantic wolf, larger than the largest of the breed. From his St. Bernard father he had inherited size and weight, but it was his shepherd mother who had given shape to that size and weight. His muzzle was the long wolf muzzle, save that it was larger than the muzzle of any wolf; and his head somewhat broader, was the wolf head on a massive scale.

His cunning was wolf cunning, and wild cunning; his intelligence, shepherd intelligence and St. Bernard intelligence; and all this, plus an experience gained in the fiercest of schools, made him as formidable a creature as any that roamed the wild. A carnivorous animal, living on a straight meat diet, he was in full flower, at the high tide of his life, overspilling with vigor and virility. When Thornton passed a caressing hand along his back, a snapping and crackling followed the hand, each hair discharging its pent magnetism at the contact. Every part, brain and body, nerve tissue and fibre, was keyed to the most exquisite pitch; and between all the parts there was a perfect equilibrium or adjustment. To sights and sounds and events which required action, he responded with lightning-like rapidity. Quickly as a husky dog could leap to defend from attack or to attack, he could leap twice as quickly. He saw the movement, or heard sound, and responded in less time than another dog required to compass the mere seeing or hearing. He perceived and determined and responded in the same instant. In point of fact the three actions of perceiving, determining, and responding were sequential; but so infinitesimal were the intervals of time between them that they appeared simultaneous. His muscles were surcharged with vitality, and snapped into play sharply, like steel springs. Life streamed through him in splendid flood, glad and rampant, until it seemed that it would burst him asunder in sheer ecstasy and pour forth generously over the world.

"Never was there such a dog," said John Thornton one day, as the partners watched Buck marching out of camp.

"When he was made, the mold was broke," said Pete.

"Py jingo! I t'ink so mineself," Hans affirmed.

They saw him marching out of camp, but they did not see the instant and terrible transformation which took place as soon as he was within the secrecy of the forest. He no longer marched. At once he became a thing of the wild, stealing along softly, cat-footed, a passing shadow that appeared and disappeared among the shadows. He knew how to take advantage of every cover, to crawl on his belly like a snake, and like a snake to leap and strike. He could take a ptarmigan from its nest, kill a rabbit as it slept, and snap in midair the little chipmunks fleeing a second too late for the trees. Fish, in open pools, were not too quick for him; nor were beaver, mending their dams, too wary. He killed to eat, not from wantonness; but he preferred to eat what he killed himself. So a lurking humor ran through his deeds, and it was his delight to steal upon the squirrels, and, when he all but had them, to let them go, chattering in mortal fear to the treetops.

As the fall of the year came on, the moose appeared in greater abundance, moving slowly down to meet the winter in the lower and less rigorous valleys. Buck had already dragged down a stray part-grown calf; but he wished strongly for larger and more formidable quarry, and he came upon it one day on the divide at the head of the creek. A band of twenty moose had crossed over the land of streams and timber, and chief among them was a great bull. He was in a savage temper, and, standing over six feet from the ground, was as formidable an antagonist as ever Buck could desire. Back and forth the bull tossed his great palmated antlers, branching to fourteen points and embracing seven feet within the tips. His small eyes burned with a vicious and bitter light, while he roared with fury at sight of Buck.

From the bull's side, just forward of the flank, protruded a feathered arrow-end, which accounted for his savageness. Guided by that instinct which came from the old hunting days of the primordial world, Buck proceeded to cut the bull out from the herd. It was no slight task. He would bark and dance about in front of the bull, just out of reach of the great antlers and of the terrible splay hoofs which could have stamped his life out with a single blow. Unable to turn his back on the fanged danger and go on, the bull would be driven into paroxysms of rage. At such moments he charged Buck, who re-

treated craftily, luring him on by a simulated inability to escape. But when he was thus separated from his fellows, two or three of the younger bulls would charge back upon Buck and enable the wounded bull to rejoin the herd.

There is a patience of the wild—dogged, tireless, persistent as life itself—that holds motionless for endless hours the spider in its web, the snake in its coils, the panther in its ambuscade; this patience belongs peculiarly to life when it hunts its living food; and it belonged to Buck as he clung to the flank of the herd, retarding its march, irritating the young bulls, worrying the cows with their half-grown calves, and driving the wounded bull mad with helpless rage. For half a day this continued. Buck multiplied himself, attacking from all sides, enveloping the herd in a whirlwind of menace, cutting out his victim as fast as it could rejoin its mates, wearing out the patience of creatures preyed upon, which is a lesser patience than that of creatures preying.

As the day wore along and the sun dropped to its bed in the northwest (the darkness had come back and the fall nights were six hours long), the young bulls retraced their steps more and more reluctantly to the aid of their beset leader. The down-coming winter was harrying them on to the lower levels, and it seemed they could never shake off this tireless creature that held them back. Besides, it was not the life of the herd, or of the young bulls, that was threatened. The life of only one member was demanded, which was a remoter interest than their lives, and in the end they were content to pay the toll.

As twilight fell the old bull stood with lowered head, watching his mates—the cows he had known, the calves he had fathered, the bulls he had mastered—as they shambled on at a rapid pace through the fading light. He could not follow, for before his nose leaped the merciless fanged terror that would not let him go. Three hundred-weight more than half a ton he weighed; he had lived a long, strong life, full of fight and struggle, and at the end he faced death at the teeth of a creature whose head did not reach beyond his great knuckled knees.

From then on, night and day, Buck never left his prey, never gave it a moment's rest, never permitted it to browse the leaves of trees or the shoots of young birch and willow. Nor did he give the wounded bull opportunity to slake his burning thirst in the slender trickling streams they crossed. Often, in desperation, he burst into long stretches of flight. At such times Buck did not attempt to stay him, but loped easily at his heels, satisfied with the way the game was played, lying down when the moose stood still, attacking him fiercely when he strove to eat or drink.

The great head drooped more and more under its tree of horns, and the shambling trot grew weaker and weaker. He took to standing for long periods, with nose to the ground and dejected ears dropped limply; and Buck found more time in which to get water for himself and in which to rest. At such moments, panting with red lolling tongue and with eyes fixed upon the big bull, it appeared to Buck that a change was coming over the face of things. He could feel a new stir in the land. As the moose were coming into the land, other kinds of life were coming in. Forest and stream and air seemed palpitant with their presence. The news of it was borne in upon him, not by sight or sound, or smell, but by some other and subtler sense. He heard nothing, saw nothing, yet knew that the land was somehow different; that through it strange things were afoot and ranging; and he resolved to investigate after he had finished the business in hand.

At last, at the end of the fourth day, he pulled the great moose down. For a day and a night he remained by the kill, eating and sleeping, turn and turn about. Then, rested, refreshed and strong, he turned his face toward camp and John Thornton. He broke into the long easy lope, and went on, hour after hour, never at loss for the tangled way, heading straight home through strange country with a certitude of direction that put man and his magnetic needle to shame.

As he held on he became more and more conscious of the new stir in the land. There was life abroad in it different from the life which had been there throughout the summer. No longer was this fact borne in upon him in some subtle, mysterious way. The birds talked of it, the squirrels chattered about it, the very breeze whispered of it. Several times he stopped and drew in the fresh morning air in great sniffs, reading a message which made him leap on with greater speed. He was oppressed with a sense of calamity happening, if it were not calamity already happened; and as he crossed the last watershed and dropped down into the valley toward camp, he proceeded with greater caution.

Three miles away he came upon a fresh trail that sent his neck hair rippling and bristling. It led straight toward camp and John Thornton. Buck hurried on, swiftly and stealthily, every nerve straining and tense, alert to the multitudinous details which told a story—all but the end. His nose gave him a varying description of the passage of the life on the heels of which he was traveling. He remarked the pregnant silence of the forest. The bird life had flitted. The squirrels were in hiding. One only he saw,—a sleek gray fellow, flattened against a gray dead limb so that he seemed a part of it, a woody excrescence upon the wood itself.

As Buck slid along with the obscureness of a gliding shadow, his nose was jerked suddenly to the side as though a positive force had gripped and pulled it. He followed the new scent into a thicket and found Nig. He was lying on his side, dead where he had dragged himself, an arrow protruding, head and feathers, from either side of his body.

A hundred yards farther on, Buck came upon one of the sled-dogs Thornton had bought in Dawson. This dog was thrashing about in a death-struggle, directly on the trail, and Buck passed around him without stopping. From the camp came the faint sound of many voices, rising and falling in a sing-song chant. Bellying forward to the edge of the clearing, he found Hans, lying on his face, feathered with arrows like a porcupine. At the same instant Buck peered out where the spruce-bough lodge had been and saw what made his hair leap straight up on his neck and shoulders. A gust of overpowering rage swept over him. He did not know that he growled, but he growled aloud with a terrible ferocity. For the last time in his life he allowed passion to usurp cunning and reason, and it was because of his great love for John Thornton that he lost his head.

The Yeehats were dancing about the wreckage of the spruce-bough lodge when they heard a fearful roaring and saw rushing upon them an animal the like of which they had never seen before. It was Buck, a live hurricane of fury, hurling himself upon them in a frenzy to destroy. He sprang at the foremost man (it was the chief of the Yeehats), ripping the throat wide open. . . . He did not pause to worry the victim, but ripped in passing, with the next bound tearing wide the throat of a second man. There was no withstanding him. He plunged about in their very midst, tearing, rending, destroying, in constant and terrific motion which defied the arrows they discharged at him. In fact, so inconceivably rapid were his movements, and so closely were the Indians tangled together, that they shot one another with the arrows; and one young hunter, hurling a spear at Buck in mid air, drove it through the chest of another hunter. . . . Then a panic seized the Yeehats, and they fled in terror to the woods, proclaiming as they fled the advent of the Evil Spirit.

And truly Buck was the Fiend incarnate, raging at their heels and dragging them down like deer as they raced through the trees. It was a fateful day for the Yeehats. They scattered far and wide over the country, and it was not till a week later that the last of the survivors gathered together in a lower valley and counted their losses. As for Buck, wearying of the pursuit, he returned to the desolated camp. He found Pete where he had been killed in his blankets in the first moment of surprise. Thornton's desperate struggle was fresh-written on the earth, and Buck scented every detail of it down to the edge of a deep pool. By the edge, head and forefeet in the water, lay Skeet, faithful to the last. The pool itself, muddy and discolored from the sluice boxes, effectually hid what it contained, and it contained John Thornton; for Buck followed his trace into the water, from which no trace led away.

All day Buck brooded by the pool or roamed restlessly above the camp. Death, as a cessation of movements, as a passing out and away from the lives of the living, he knew, and he knew John Thornton was dead. It left a great void in him, somewhat akin to hunger, but a void which ached and ached, and which food could not fill. At times, when he paused to contemplate the carcasses of the Yeehats, he forgot the pain of it; and at such times he was aware of a great pride in himself—a pride greater than any he had yet experienced. He had killed man . . . and he had killed in the face of the law of club and fang. He sniffed the bodies curiously. They had died so easily. It was harder to kill a husky dog than them. They were no match at all, were it not for their arrows and spears and clubs. Thenceforward he would be unafraid of them except when they bore in their hands their arrows, spears, and clubs.

Night came on, and a full moon rose high over the trees into the sky, lighting the land till it lay bathed in ghostly day. And with the coming of the night, brooding and mourning by the pool, Buck became alive to a stirring of the new life in the forest other than that which the Yeehats had made. He stood up, listening and scenting. From far away drifted a faint, sharp yelp, followed by a chorus of similar sharp yelps. As the moments passed the yelps grew closer and louder. Again Buck knew them as things heard in that other world which persisted in his memory. He walked to the center of the open space and listened. It was the call, the many-noted call, sounding more luringly and compelling than ever before. And as never before, he was ready to obey. John Thornton was dead. The last tie was broken. Man and the claims of man no longer bound him.

Hunting their living meat, as the Yeehats were hunting it, on the flanks of the migrating moose, the wolf pack had at last crossed over from the land of streams and timber and invaded Buck's valley. Into the clearing where the moonlight streamed, they poured in a silvery flood; and in the center of the clearing stood Buck, motionless as a statue, waiting their coming. They were awed, so still and large he stood, and a moment's pause fell, till the boldest one leaped straight for him. Like a flash Buck struck, breaking the neck. Then he stood, without movement, as before, the stricken wolf rolling in agony behind him. Three others tried it in sharp succession; and one after the other they drew back, streaming blood from slashed throats or shoulders.

This was sufficient to fling the whole pack forward, pellmell, crowded together, blocked and confused by its eagerness to pull down the prey. Buck's marvellous quickness and agility stood him in good stead. Pivoting on his hind legs, and snapping and gashing, he was everywhere at once, presenting a front which was apparently unbroken so swiftly did he whirl and guard from side to side. But to prevent them from getting behind him, he was forced back, down past the pool and into a creek bed, till he brought up against a high gravel bank. He worked along to a right angle in the bank which the men had made in the course of mining, and in this angle he came to bay, protected on three sides and with nothing to do but face the front.

And so well did he face it, that at the end of half an hour the wolves drew back discomfited. The tongues of all were out and lolling, the white fangs showing cruelly white in the moonlight. Some were lying down with heads raised and ears pricked forward; others stood on their feet, watching him; and still others were lapping water from the pool. One wolf, long and lean and gray, advanced cautiously, in a friendly manner, and Buck recognized the wild brother with whom he had run for a night and a day. He was whining softly, and, as Buck whined, they touched noses.

Then an old wolf, gaunt and battle-scarred, came forward. Buck writhed his lips into the preliminary of a snarl, but sniffed noses with him. Whereupon the old wolf sat down, pointed nose at the moon, and broke out the long wolf howl. The others sat down and howled. And now the call came to Buck in unmistakable accents. He, too, sat down and howled. This over, he came out of his angle and the pack crowded around him, sniffing in half-friendly, half-savage manner. The leaders lifted the yelp of the pack and sprang away into the woods. The wolves swung in behind, yelping in chorus. And Buck ran with them, side by side with the wild brother, yelping as he ran.

And here may well end the story of Buck. The years were not many when the Yeehats noted a change in the breed of timber wolves; for some were seen with splashes of brown on head and muzzle, and with a rift of white centering down the chest. But more remarkable than this, the Yeehats tell of a Ghost Dog that runs at the head of the pack. They are afraid of this Ghost Dog, for it has cunning greater than they, stealing from their camps in fierce winters, robbing their traps, slaying their dogs, and defying their bravest hunters.

Nay, the tale grows worse. Hunters there are who fail to return to the camp, and hunters there have been whom their tribesmen found with throat slashed cruelly open and with wolf prints about them in the snow greater than the prints of any wolf. Each fall, when the Yeehats follow the movement of the moose, there is a certain valley which they never enter. And women there are who become sad when the word goes over the fire of how the Evil Spirit came to select that valley for an abiding-place.

In the summers there is one visitor, however, to that valley, of which the Yeehats do not know. It is a great, gloriously coated wolf, like, and yet unlike, all other wolves. He crosses alone from the smiling timber land and comes down into an open space among the trees. Here a yellow stream flows from rotted moose-hide sacks and sinks into the ground, with long grasses growing through it and vegetable mold overrunning it and hiding its yellow from the sun; and here he muses for a time, howling once, long and mournfully, ere he departs.

But he is not always alone. When the long winter nights come on and the wolves follow their meat into the lower valleys, he may be seen running at the head of the pack through the pale moonlight or glimmering borealis, leaping gigantic above his fellows, his great throat a-bellow as he sings a song of the younger world, which is the song of the pack.

The Sounding of the Call **639**

THINK AND DISCUSS
Understanding
1. What do Thornton, Pete, and Hans seek?
2. Where does their search end?
3. What does Buck find when he returns to camp? What does he do?
4. What happens to Buck?

Analyzing
5. What qualities does Buck exhibit during his efforts to bring down the great bull moose? during his trip back to camp? when he arrives at the camp? when he sits by the pool?
6. Reconstruct what took place at the camp during Buck's absence.
7. Why does Buck return to the valley each summer?
8. What two Yeehat myths are described in this chapter? In what ways does each myth relate to events in the chapter?

Extending
9. Do you think John Thornton would be pleased about Buck's new life? Explain.

THINKING SKILLS
Synthesizing
John Thornton and his partners go in search of the "fabled lost mine." Along the way they find traces of others who have sought this treasure. Tales of lost and fabulous treasures are found in settings other than the Yukon. What other accounts of searches for these treasures have you read? (Consider folk and fairy tales, novels or movies such as *King Solomon's Mines*, and historical accounts—expeditions to find the seven cities of gold, the fountain of youth, the buried treasure of various pirates.) Then decide what all these accounts have in common. Finally, write a phrase or sentence that might be used as the title of an article on this topic.

COMPOSITION
Writing a Description
Write a description of a particularly beautiful happening in the natural world—a flower bud opening, the wind blowing through a field of ripe corn, the bright yellow flowers of a forsythia bush against the dark red brick of your building. Before you begin to write, review London's description of the Yukon spring and see "Writing a Clear Description" in the Writer's Handbook.

Writing as a Story Character
Imagine that you are one of the Yeehat Indians who escaped Buck. Write one or two paragraphs telling about Buck—how he attacked you, what he did to the other Yeehats, and how you got away.

ENRICHMENT
Research Project
Use your school or public library to find information on the Iditarod, a one-thousand-mile sled-dog race held in Alaska every year. Then prepare an oral report to present to your classmates and teacher.

Group Report
Working in groups, invent a one-hundred-mile race for walkers, runners, or

bicyclists. It should be run near where you live. Invent rules. Describe areas that will be especially challenging and weather conditions that might make the race even more challenging. List the clothing and equipment needed. Tell what the winner will receive. Present your report to your class. Use as many graphic aids as you can find (or draw) to help your audience understand your ideas.

Panel Presentation

Prepare a panel discussion on the various types of dogs found in *The Call of the Wild*. First, review the novel and list the types, beginning with Buck, Ysabel, Toots, and the other dogs at Judge Miller's. When the list is complete, divide the items on it among the members of your group. Then, learn about each dog on your list. During the panel discussion, tell your classmates and teacher what you have learned, using pictures wherever possible. Finally, ask your audience for their opinions about which types are most and least suited to the life Buck lives after he is kidnapped.

For a biography of Jack London, see page 83.

Comment

Buck's Wild World: The World of Wolves

The call that Buck so often hears and finally obeys is the call of wolves, and the song he finally sings with them is their song, the song of the pack—a chorus of long, drawn-out, unforgettable howls that can be heard for miles.

Buck shares some traits with the pack he joins because dogs and wolves are members of the same species. Dogs and wolves will mate, and they have fertile offspring. Thus, London's telling of young wolves with Buck's color and markings is scientifically accurate.

The gray, or timber, wolves that Buck joins resemble large, well-developed German shepherds. Compared to these wolves, whose heads barely reach his shoulder, Buck is indeed gigantic.

There is, however, one extremely important difference between Buck and the wolves (and, indeed, between Buck and most dogs). Buck's killing people is the result of all the extraordinary circumstances that have occurred since his kidnapping. And—despite the fictional accounts of wolves killing and eating human beings, accounts that have been terrifying readers for centuries—there is not a single recorded case of this ever having happened.

In spite of the evidence, over the years wolves have been despised and hunted almost to extinction. In recent years, the Fund for Animals, an organization that works for animals' rights, has run a campaign to educate the public about the true nature of the wolf.

UNIT 8 NOVEL

■ CONCEPT REVIEW

The selection that ends this unit contains many of the important ideas and literary elements found in the novel you have just studied. It also contains notes designed to help you think critically about your reading. For a more extensive discussion of any of the literary terms mentioned, see the *Handbook of Literary Terms*.

This selection is an excerpt from *Homesick: My Own Story*, by Jean Fritz, an award-winning writer of books for young people. She was born in China in 1915 and lived there until she was twelve.

from Homesick

Jean Fritz

■ What is the connotation of *homesick* for you?

In my father's study there was a large globe with all the countries of the world running around it. I could put my finger on the exact spot where I was and had been ever since I'd been born. And I was on the wrong side of the globe. I was in China in a city named Hankow, a dot on a crooked line that seemed to break the country right in two. The line was really the Yangtse River, but who would know by looking at a map what the Yangtse River really was?

Orange-brown, muddy mustard-colored. And wide, wide, wide. With a river smell that was old and came all the way up from the bottom. Sometimes old women knelt on the riverbank, begging the

■ *Hankow* (hän′kō′), a port in east China on the Yangtse River.
■ *Yangtse* (yang′tsē) *River,* a river flowing from Tibet through China to the China Sea. It is the longest river in China. Also spelled *Yangtze.*

River God to return a son or grandson who may have drowned. They would wail and beat the earth to make the River God pay attention, but I knew how busy the River God must be. All those people on the Yangtse River! Men hauling water. Women washing clothes. Houseboats swarming with old people and young, chickens and pigs. Big crooked-sailed junks with eyes painted on their prows so they could see where they were going. I loved the Yangtse River, but, of course, I belonged on the other side of the world. In America with my grandmother.

Twenty-five fluffy little yellow chicks hatched from our eggs today, my grandmother wrote.

I wrote my grandmother that I had watched a Chinese magician swallow three yards of fire.

The trouble with living on the wrong side of the world was that I didn't feel like a *real* American.

For instance. I could never be president of the United States. I didn't want to be president; I wanted to be a writer. Still, why should there be a *law* saying that only a person born in the United States could be president? It was as if I wouldn't be American enough.

Actually, I was American every minute of the day, especially during school hours. I went to a British school and every morning we sang "God Save the King." Of course the British children loved singing about their gracious king. Ian Forbes stuck out his chest and sang as if he were saving the king all by himself. Everyone sang. Even Gina Boss who was Italian. And Vera Sebastian who was so Russian she dressed the way Russian girls did long ago before the Revolution when her family had to run away to keep from being killed.

But I wasn't Vera Sebastian. I asked my mother to write an excuse so I wouldn't have to sing, but she wouldn't do it. "When in Rome," she said, "do as the Romans do." What she meant was, "Don't make trouble. Just sing." So for a long time I did. I sang with my fingers crossed but still I felt like a traitor.

Then one day I thought: If my mother and father were really and truly in Rome, they wouldn't do what the Romans did at all. They'd probably try to get the Romans to do what *they* did, just as they were trying to teach the Chinese to do what Americans did. (My mother even gave classes in American manners.)

So that day I quit singing. I kept my mouth locked tight against the king of England. Our teacher, Miss Williams, didn't notice at first.

■ Note the use of imagery in this description of the setting.

■ *junks* (jungks), Chinese sailing ships.

■ The sharp contrast between these images suggests the gap between Jean's two worlds.

■ In order to run for President, one must be at least thirty-five years old, have been born in the United States and lived there at least fourteen years.

■ *the Revolution,* the Russian Revolution, which overthrew the government of Nicholas II in 1917 and established what later became the Communist government.

■ Her conclusion helps characterize Jean.

She stood in front of the room, using a ruler for a baton, striking each syllable so hard it was as if she were making up for the times she had nothing to strike.

"Make him vic-tor-i-ous," the class sang. It was on the strike of "vic" that Miss Williams noticed. Her eyes lighted on my mouth and when we sat down, she pointed her ruler at me.

"Is there something wrong with your voice today, Jean?" she asked.

"No, Miss Williams."

"You weren't singing."

"No, Miss Williams. It is not my national anthem."

"It is the national anthem we sing here," she snapped. "You have always sung. Even Vera sings it."

I looked at Vera with the big blue bow tied on the top of her head. Usually I felt sorry for her but not today. At recess I might even untie that bow, I thought. Just give it a yank. But if I'd been smart, I wouldn't have been looking at Vera. I would have been looking at Ian Forbes and I would have known that, no matter what Miss Williams said, I wasn't through with the king of England.

Recess at the British School was nothing I looked forward to. Every day we played a game called prisoner's base, which was all running and shouting and shoving and catching. I hated the game, yet everyone played except Vera Sebastian. She sat on the sidelines under her blue bow like someone who had been dropped out of a history book. By recess I had forgotten my plans for that bow. While everyone was getting ready for the game, I was as usual trying to look as if I didn't care if I was the last one picked for a team or not. I was leaning against the high stone wall that ran around the schoolyard. I was looking up at a little white cloud skittering across the sky when all at once someone tramped down hard on my right foot. Ian Forbes. Snarling bulldog face. Heel grinding down on my toes. Head thrust forward the way an animal might before it strikes.

"You wouldn't sing it. So say it," he ordered. "Let me hear you say it."

I tried to pull my foot away but he only ground down harder.

"Say what?" I was telling my face please not to show what my foot felt.

"*God save the king.* Say it. Those four words. I want to hear you say it."

Although Ian Forbes was short, he was solid and tough and built for fighting. What was more, he always won. You had only to look at his bare knees between the top of his socks and his short pants to know that he would win. His knees were square. Bony and unbeatable. So of course it was crazy for me to argue with him.

"Why should I?" I asked. "Americans haven't said that since George the Third."

He grabbed my right arm and twisted it behind my back.

"Say it," he hissed.

I felt the tears come to my eyes and I hated myself for the tears. I hated myself for not staying in Rome the way my mother had told me.

"I'll never say it," I whispered.

They were choosing sides now in the schoolyard and Ian's name was being called—among the first as always.

He gave my arm another twist. "You'll sing tomorrow," he snarled, "or you'll be sorry."

As he ran off, I slid to the ground, my head between my knees. *Oh, Grandma, I thought, why can't I be there with you? I'd feed the chickens for you. I'd pump water from the well, the way my father used to do.*

It would be almost two years before we'd go to America. I was ten years old now; I'd be twelve then. But how could I think about *years?* I didn't even dare to think about the next day. After school I ran all the way home, fast so I couldn't think at all.

Our house stood behind a high stone wall which had chips of broken glass sticking up from the top to keep thieves away. I flung open the iron gate and threw myself through the front door.

"I'm home!" I yelled.

Then I remembered that it was Tuesday, the day my mother taught an English class at the Y.M.C.A. where my father was the director.

I stood in the hall, trying to catch my breath, and as always I began to feel small. It was a huge hall with ceilings so high it was as if they would have nothing to do with people. Certainly not with a mere child, not with me—the only child in the house. Once I asked my best friend, Andrea, if the hall made her feel little too. She said no. She was going to be a dancer and she loved space. She did a high kick to show how grand it was to have room.

Andrea Hull was a year older than I was and knew about everything sooner. She told me about commas, for instance, long before I took punctuation seriously. How could I write letters without commas? She

■ George the Third, king of England from 1760 to 1820. During his reign the American Revolution separated the U.S. from British rule.

asked. She made me so ashamed that for months I hung little wagging comma-tails all over the letters to my grandmother. She told me things that sounded so crazy I had to ask my mother if they were true.

I wished that Andrea were with me now, but she lived out in the country and I didn't see her often. Lin Nai-Nai, my amah, was the only one around, and of course I knew she'd be there. It was her job to stay with me when my parents were out. As soon as she heard me come in, she'd called, "Tsai loushang." which meant that she was upstairs. She might be mending or ironing but most likely she'd be sitting by the window embroidering. And she was. She even had my embroidery laid out, for we had made a bargain. She would teach me to embroider if I would teach her English. I liked embroidering: the cloth stretched tight within my embroidery hoop while I filled in the stamped pattern with cross-stitches and lazy daisy flowers. The trouble was that lazy daisies needed French knots for their centers and I hated making French knots. Mine always fell apart, so I left them to the end. Today I had twenty lazy daisies waiting for their knots.

Lin Nai-Nai had already threaded my needle with embroidery floss.

"Black centers," she said, "for the yellow flowers."

I felt myself glowering. "American flowers don't have centers," I said and gave her back the needle.

Lin Nai-Nai looked at me, puzzled, but she did not argue. She was different from other amahs. She did not even come from the servant class, although this was a secret we had to keep from the other servants, who would have made her life miserable had they known. She had run away from her husband when he had taken a second wife. She would always have been Wife Number One and the Boss no matter how many wives he had, but she would rather be no wife than head of a string of wives. She was modern. She might look old-fashioned, for her feet had been bound up tight when she was a little girl so that they would stay small, and now, like many Chinese women, she walked around on little stumps stuffed into tiny cloth shoes. Lin Nai-Nai's were embroidered with butterflies. Still, she believed in true love and one wife for one husband. We were good friends, Lin Nai-Nai and I, so I didn't know why I felt so mean.

She shrugged. "English lesson?" she asked, smiling.

I tested my arm to see if it still hurt from the twisting. It did. My foot too. "What do you want to know?" I asked.

We had been through the polite phrases—Please, Thank you, I beg

■ *Lin Nai-Nai* (lin nī′nī′). *amah* (ä′mə), maidservant.

■ *Tsai loushang* (tsī lō′shäng′).

your pardon, Excuse me, You're welcome, Merry Christmas (which she had practiced but hadn't had a chance to use since this was only October).

"If I meet an American on the street," she asked, "how do I greet him?"

I looked her straight in the eye and nodded my head in a greeting. "Sewing machine," I said. "You say, 'Sew-ing machine.'"

She repeated after me, making the four syllables into four separate words. She got up and walked across the room, bowing and smiling. "Sew Ing Ma Shing." Part of me wanted to laugh at the thought of Lin Nai-Nai maybe meeting Dr. Carhart, our minister, whose face would surely puff up, the way it always did when he was flustered. But part of me didn't want to laugh at all. I didn't like it when my feelings got tangled, so I ran downstairs and played chopsticks on the piano. Loud and fast. When my sore arm hurt, I just beat on the keys harder.

■ Jean takes out her anger and frustration by teaching her friend the wrong words.

Then I went out to the kitchen to see if Yang Sze-Fu, the cook, would give me something to eat. I found him reading a Chinese newspaper, his eyes going up and down with the characters. (Chinese words don't march across flat surfaces the way ours do; they drop down cliffs, one cliff after another from right to left across a page.)

■ *Yang Sze-Fu* (yäng su'fü').

"Can I have a piece of cinnamon toast?" I asked. "And a cup of cocoa?"

Yang Sze-Fu grunted. He was smoking a cigarette, which he wasn't supposed to do in the kitchen, but Yang Sze-Fu mostly did what he wanted. He considered himself superior to common workers. You could tell because of the fingernails on his pinkies. They were at least two inches long, which was his way of showing that he didn't have to use his hands for rough or dirty work. He didn't seem to care that his fingernails were dirty, but maybe he couldn't keep such long nails clean.

He made my toast while his cigarette dangled out of the corner of his mouth, collecting a long ash that finally fell on the floor. He wouldn't have kept smoking if my mother had been there, although he didn't always pay attention to my mother. Never about butter pagodas, for instance. No matter how many times my mother told him before a dinner party, "No butter pagoda," it made no difference. As soon as everyone was seated, the serving boy, Wong Sze-Fu, would bring in a pagoda and set it on the table. The guests would "oh" and

■ *Wong Sze-Fu* (wông su'fü').

"ah," for it was a masterpiece: a pagoda molded out of butter, curved roofs rising tier upon tier, but my mother could only think how unsanitary it was. For, of course, Yang Sze-Fu had molded the butter with his hands and carved the decorations with one of his long fingernails. Still, we always used the butter, for if my mother sent it back to the kitchen, Yang Sze-Fu would lose face and quit.

When my toast and cocoa were ready, I took them upstairs to my room (the blue room) and while I ate, I began *Sara Crewe* again. Now there was a girl, I thought, who was worth crying over. I wasn't going to think about myself. Or Ian Forbes. Or the next day. I wasn't. I wasn't.

And I didn't. Not all afternoon. Not all evening. Still, I must have decided what I was going to do because the next morning when I started for school and came to the corner where the man sold hot chestnuts, the corner where I always turned to go to school, I didn't turn. I walked straight ahead. I wasn't going to school that day.

I walked toward the Yangtse River. Past the store that sold paper pellets that opened up into flowers when you dropped them in a glass of water. Then up the block where the beggars sat. I never saw anyone give money to a beggar. You couldn't, my father explained, or you'd be mobbed by beggars. They'd follow you everyplace; they'd never leave you alone. I had learned not to look at them when I passed and yet I saw. The running sores, the twisted legs, the mangled faces. What I couldn't get over was that, like me, each one of those beggars had only one life to live. It just happened that they had drawn rotten ones.

Oh, Grandma, I thought, we may be far apart but we're lucky, you and I. Do you even know how lucky? In America do you know?

This part of the city didn't actually belong to the Chinese, even though the beggars sat there, even though upper-class Chinese lived there. A long time ago other countries had just walked into China and divided up part of Hankow (and other cities) into sections, or concessions, which they called their own and used their own rules for governing. We lived in the French concession on Rue de Paris. Then there was the British concession and the Japanese. The Russian and German concessions had been officially returned to China, but the people still called them concessions. The Americans didn't have one, although, like some of the other countries, they had gunboats on the river. In case, my father said. In case what? Just in case. That's all he'd say.

■ *lose face,* lose dignity or self-respect.

■ *Sarah Crewe,* published in 1888 by Frances Hodgson Burnett, a tale of neglected and misunderstood children who finally achieve happiness.

The concessions didn't look like the rest of China. The buildings were solemn and orderly with little plots of grass around them. Not like those in the Chinese part of the city: a jumble of rickety shops with people, vegetables, crates of quacking ducks, yard goods, bamboo baskets, and mangy dogs spilling onto a street so narrow it was hardly there.

The grandest street in Hankow was the Bund, which ran along beside the Yangtse River. When I came to it after passing the beggars, I looked to my left and saw the American flag flying over the American consulate building. I was proud of the flag and I thought maybe today it was proud of me. It flapped in the breeze as if it were saying ha-ha to the king of England.

■ Note that these details suggest the width of the gap between most Chinese and the foreigners.

Then I looked to the right at the Customs House, which stood at the other end of the Bund. The clock on top of the tower said nine-thirty. How would I spend the day?

I crossed the street to the promenade part of the Bund. When people walked here, they weren't usually going anyplace; they were just out for the air. My mother would wear her broad-brimmed beaver hat when we came and my father would swing his cane in that jaunty way that showed how glad he was to be a man. I thought I would just sit on a bench for the morning. I would watch the Customs House clock, and when it was time, I would eat the lunch I had brought along in my schoolbag.

■ *promenade*, a public walkway.

I was the only one sitting on a bench. People did not generally "take the air" on a Wednesday morning and besides, not everyone was allowed here. The British had put a sign on the Bund, NO DOGS, NO CHINESE. This meant that I could never bring Lin Nai-Nai with me. My father couldn't even bring his best friend, Mr. T.K. Hu. Maybe the British wanted a place where they could pretend they weren't in China, I thought. Still, there were always Chinese workers around. In order to load and unload boats in the river, they had to cross the Bund. All day they went back and forth, bent double under their loads, sweating and chanting in a tired, singsong way that seemed to get them from one step to the next.

■ Jean attempts to find an acceptable reason for the presence of such a sign, but she immediately begins to question her conclusion.

To pass the time, I decided to recite poetry. The one good thing about Miss Williams was that she made us learn poems by heart and I liked that. There was one particular poem I didn't want to forget. I looked at the Yangtse River and pretended that all the busy people in the boats were my audience.

"'Breathes there the man, with soul so dead,'" I cried, "'Who never to himself hath said, This is my own, my native land!'"

I was so carried away by my performance that I didn't notice the policeman until he was right in front of me. Like all policemen in the British concession, he was a bushy-bearded Indian with a red turban wrapped around his head.

He pointed to my schoolbag. "Little miss," he said, "why aren't you in school?"

He was tall and mysterious-looking, more like a character in my Arabian Nights book than a man you expected to talk to. I fumbled for an answer. "I'm going on an errand," I said finally. "I just sat down for a rest." I picked up my schoolbag and walked quickly away. When I looked around, he was back on his corner, directing traffic.

So now they were chasing children away too, I thought angrily. Well, I'd like to show them. Someday I'd like to walk a dog down the whole length of the Bund. A Great Dane. I'd have him on a leash—like this—(I put out my hand as if I were holding a leash right then) and he'd be so big and strong I'd have to strain to hold him back (I strained). I was so busy with my Great Dane I was at the end of the Bund before I knew it. I let go of the leash, clapped my hands, and told my dog to go home. Then I left the Bund and the concessions and walked into the Chinese world.

My mother and father and I had walked here but not for many months. This part near the river was called the Mud Flats. Sometimes it was muddier than others, and when the river flooded, the flats disappeared under water. Sometimes even the fishermen's huts were washed away, knocked right off their long-legged stilts and swept down the river. But today the river was fairly low and the mud had dried so that it was cracked and cakey. Most of the men who lived here were out fishing, some not far from the shore, poling their sampans through the shallow water. Only a few people were on the flats: a man cleaning fish on a flat rock at the water's edge, a woman spreading clothes on the dirt to dry, a few small children. But behind the huts was something I had never seen before. Even before I came close, I guessed what it was. Even then, I was excited by the strangeness of it.

It was the beginnings of a boat. The skeleton of a large junk, its ribs lying bare, its backbone running straight and true down the bottom. The outline of the prow was already in place, turning up wide and snubnosed, the way all junks did. I had never thought of boats starting from nothing, of taking on bones under their bodies. The eyes, I

■ Jean's choosing this poem is not surprising, given the way she is feeling.

■ *Arabian Nights book,* a collection of ancient tales from Arabia, Persia, and India.

■ *sampans,* (sam'panz), small boats used in China and throughout southeast Asia. A sampan is sculled by an oar at the stern and usually has a single sail and a cabin made of mats.

■ Personification is used in this description of the boat.

supposed, would be the last thing added. Then the junk would have life.

The builders were not there and I was behind the huts where no one could see me as I walked around and around, marveling. Then I climbed inside and as I did, I knew that something wonderful was happening to me. I was a-tingle, the way a magician must feel when he swallows fire, because suddenly I knew that the boat was mine. No matter who really owned it, it was mine. Even if I never saw it again, it would be my junk sailing up and down the Yangtse River. My junk seeing the river sights with its two eyes, seeing them for me whether I was there or not. Often I had tried to put the Yangtse River into a poem so I could keep it. Sometimes I had tried to draw it, but nothing I did ever came close. But now, *now* I had my junk and somehow that gave me the river too.

I thought I should put my mark on the boat. Perhaps on the side of the spine. Very small. A secret between the boat and me. I opened my schoolbag and took out my folding penknife that I used for sharpening pencils. Very carefully I carved the Chinese character that was our name. Gau. (In China my father was Mr. Gau, my mother was Mrs. Gau, and I was Little Miss Gau.) The builders would paint right over the character, I thought, and would never notice. But I would know. Always and forever I would know.

■ *Gau* (gou).

For a long time I dreamed about the boat, imagining it finished, its sails up, its eyes wide. Someday it might sail all the way down the Yangtse to Shanghai, so I told the boat what it would see along the way because I had been there and the boat hadn't. After a while I got hungry and I ate my egg sandwich. I was in the midst of peeling an orange when all at once I had company.

■ *Shanghai* (shang′hī′), a seaport in east China.

A small boy, not more than four years old, wandered around to the back of the huts, saw me, and stopped still. He was wearing a ragged blue cotton jacket with a red cloth, pincushion-like charm around his neck which was supposed to keep him from getting smallpox. Sticking up straight from the middle of his head was a small pigtail which I knew was to fool the gods and make them think he was a girl. (Gods didn't bother much with girls; it was boys that were important in China.) He walked slowly up to the boat, stared at me, and then nodded as if he'd already guessed what I was. "Foreign devil," he announced gravely.

I shook my head. "No," I said in Chinese. "American friend."

■ **Generalizing:** The boy sees Jean in stereotypical terms. What conditions might have led him to think as he does?

Through the ribs of the boat, I handed him a segment of orange. He ate it slowly, his eyes on the rest of the orange. Segment by segment, I gave it all to him. Then he wiped his hands down the front of his jacket.

"Foreign devil," he repeated.

"American friend," I corrected. Then I asked him about the boat. Who was building it? Where were the builders?

He pointed with his chin upriver. "Not here today. Back tomorrow."

I knew it would only be a question of time before the boy would run off to alert the people in the huts. "Foreign devil, foreign devil," he would cry. So I put my hand on the prow of the boat, wished it luck, and climbing out, I started back toward the Bund. To my surprise the boy walked beside me. When we came to the edge of the Bund, I squatted down so we would be on the same eye level.

"Good-bye," I said. "May the River God protect you."

For a moment the boy stared. When he spoke, it was as if he were trying out a new sound. "American friend," he said slowly.

When I looked back, he was still there, looking soberly toward the foreign world to which I had gone.

■ Jean's speech and actions have helped the boy see that all foreigners are not alike.

The time, according to the Customs House clock, was five after two, which meant that I couldn't go home for two hours. School was dismissed at three-thirty and I was home by three-forty-five unless I had to stay in for talking in class. It took me about fifteen minutes to write "I will not talk in class" fifty times, and so I often came home at four o'clock. (I wrote up and down like the Chinese: fifty "I's," fifty "wills," and right through the sentence so I never had to think what I was writing. It wasn't as if I were making a promise.) Today I planned to arrive home at four, my "staying-in" time, in the hope that I wouldn't meet classmates on the way.

Meanwhile I wandered up and down the streets, in and out of stores. I weighed myself on the big scale in the Hankow Dispensary and found that I was as skinny as ever. I went to the Terminus Hotel and tried out the chairs in the lounge. At first I didn't mind wandering about like this. Half of my mind was still on the river with my junk, but as time went on, my junk began slipping away until I was alone with nothing but questions. Would my mother find out about today? How could I skip school tomorrow? And the next day and the next? Could I get sick? Was there a kind of long lie-abed sickness that didn't hurt?

I arrived home at four, just as I had planned, opened the door, and called out, "I'm home!" Cheery-like and normal. But I was scarely in the house before Lin Nai-Nai ran to me from one side of the hall and my mother from the other.

"Are you all right? Are you all right?" Lin Nai-Nai felt my arms as if she expected them to be broken. My mother's face was white. "What happened?" she asked.

Then I looked through the open door into the living room and saw Miss Williams sitting there. She had beaten me home and asked about my absence, which of course had scared everyone. But now my mother could see that I was in one piece and for some reason this seemed to make her mad. She took me by the hand and led me into the living room. "Miss Williams said you weren't in school," she said. "Why was that?"

I hung my head, just the way cowards do in books.

My mother dropped my hand. "Jean will be in school tomorrow," she said firmly. She walked Miss Williams to the door. "Thank you for stopping by."

As soon as Miss Williams was gone and my mother was sitting down again, I burst into tears. Kneeling on the floor, I buried my head in her lap and poured out the whole miserable story. My mother could see that I really wasn't in one piece after all, so she listened quietly, stroking my hair as I talked, but gradually I could feel her stiffen. I knew she was remembering that she was a Mother.

"You better go up to your room," she said, "and think things over. We'll talk about it after supper."

I flung myself on my bed. What was there to think? Either I went to school and got beaten up. Or I quit.

After supper I explained to my mother and father how simple it was. I could stay at home and my mother could teach me, the way Andrea's mother taught her. Maybe I could even go to Andrea's house and study with her.

My mother shook her head. Yes, it was simple, she agreed. I could go back to the British School, be sensible, and start singing about the king again.

I clutched the edge of the table. Couldn't she understand? I couldn't turn back now. It was too late.

So far my father had not said a word. He was leaning back, teetering on the two hind legs of his chair, the way he always did after a meal, the way that drove my mother crazy. But he was not the kind of person to keep all four legs of a chair on the floor just because someone wanted him to. He wasn't a turning-back person so I hoped maybe he would understand. As I watched him, I saw a twinkle start in his eyes and suddenly he brought his chair down slam-bang flat on the floor. He got up and motioned for us to follow him into the living room. He sat down at the piano and began to pick out the tune for "God Save the King."

A big help, I thought. Was he going to make me practice?

Then he began to sing:

"My country 'tis of thee,

Sweet land of liberty, . . ."

Of course! It was the same tune. Why hadn't I thought of that? Who would know what I was singing as long as I moved my lips? I joined in now, loud and strong.

"Of thee I sing."

My mother laughed in spite of herself. "If you sing that loud," she said, "you'll start a revolution."

"Tomorrow I'll sing softly," I promised. "No one will know." But for now I really let freedom ring.

Then all at once I wanted to see Lin Nai-Nai. I ran out back, through the courtyard that separated the house from the servants' quarters, and upstairs to her room.

"It's me," I called through the door and when she opened up, I threw my arms around her. "Oh, Lin Nai-Nai, I love you," I said. "You haven't said it yet, have you?"

"Said what?"

"Sewing machine. You haven't said it?"

"No," she said, "not yet. I'm still practicing."

"Don't say it, Lin Nai-Nai. Say 'Good day.' It's shorter and easier. Besides, it's more polite."

"Good day?" she repeated.

"Yes, that's right. Good day." I hugged her and ran back to the house.

The next day at school when we rose to sing the British national anthem, everyone stared at me, but as soon as I opened my mouth, the class lost interest. All but Ian Forbes. His eyes never left my face, but I sang softly, carefully, proudly. At recess he sauntered over to where I stood against the wall.

■ Note how the conflict is resolved.

He spat on the ground. "You can be glad you sang today," he said. Then he strutted off as if he and those square knees of his had won again.

And, of course, I was glad.

■ The last line is ironic.

THINK AND DISCUSS
Understanding
1. Why doesn't Jean want to sing "God Save the King"? What happens to her because she won't sing it?
2. What does Jean do the day she skips school?
3. How does Jean solve her problem about singing "God Save the King"?

Analyzing
4. Why do you think Jean taught Lin Nai-Nai to say "Sewing Machine" for "Good Morning"?
5. Why do you think the small boy Jean meets calls her a "foreign devil"? What does his statement tell you about the attitude of the Chinese toward Westerners in China?
6. How does the boy change during the time he spends with Jean? Why does he change?
7. Jean says her father "wasn't a turning-back person." What does she mean? Do you think Jean is more like her mother or her father? Explain.
8. Both Jean and Ian Forbes think they have won the struggle about singing the anthem. Who do you think has won? Why?

Extending
9. Jean's mother believes that "when in Rome do as the Romans do." Do you agree? Imagine you're the "Roman."

How would you feel if a student from another country refused to sing your national anthem? Explain.
10. Would you enjoy living in a country very different from your own?

REVIEWING LITERARY TERMS
Connotation/Denotation
The denotation of *junk* is a Chinese sailing ship. What is the connotation of *junk*, a *boat*, for the narrator?

■ CONTENT REVIEW
THINKING SKILLS
Classifying
1. Put each of the following groups into one of these classifications: highly regarded by the narrator; held in contempt by the narrator; neither praised nor criticized by the narrator. (a) the sled dogs; (b) people who fall apart under the Arctic conditions; (c) small, pampered house dogs; (d) people who learn survival skills and patience from their experiences in the Arctic; (e) the Yeehats.

Generalizing
2. Based on information given in the novel, describe the effects of the gold rush on the Canadian government.

Synthesizing

3. Several of the minor characters in *The Call of the Wild* are stereotypes, representing particular kinds of people who went to the North in search of gold. One example of this is Burton, the bully who picks on a tenderfoot and ends up tangling with Buck (Chapter 6). Burton is the stereotypical "bad man" of the frontier. Find at least two more of these stereotypes.

Evaluating

4. Do you agree with this statement? Give evidence to support your answer: Mercedes is not only a stereotype, but a very negative one. Her presence in the novel is an insult to all women.

■ COMPOSITION REVIEW

Starting a Novel

Write the first five paragraphs of a novel about a wild dog who is transformed into a tame dog. In paragraph one, describe where the dog lives. Use what you have learned about the wild from *The Call of the Wild* to describe the setting. In paragraph two, describe the animals over whom this dog rules. In paragraph three, describe a human who comes into the wild. In paragraph four, describe how this person discovers the dog. In paragraph five, tell how the person feels about the dog and why he or she wants to tame it.

Writing to Persuade

Is mastery or mastership a goal everyone should strive for? Why, or why not? Write three paragraphs in which you do these three things: (1) Explain what *mastery* or *mastership* means. (2) Explain why you think it should or should not be the goal for everyone. (3) Describe the kind of person for whom it is or is not a desirable goal.

Writing a Bill of Rights

Pretend that you have the power to create and enforce laws to protect the sled dogs in Alaska at the time of *The Call of the Wild*. Draw up a bill of rights that will insure humane treatment of these animals.

Writing to Compare and Contrast

Write a three-paragraph comparison of Buck and Dave. In the first paragraph, discuss Buck as a leader. In the second paragraph, discuss Dave as a follower. Support each main idea with details from the chapter, including the role each dog plays in the record run and on the mail run. In the third paragraph, discuss one or more traits that the dogs have in common *or* express and support your opinion about which dog you admire more.

Reviewing Writer's Craft: Build Emphasis

Try your hand at using repetition and contrast to build emphasis. Write one paragraph about a positive feeling or condition of a person or an animal and another paragraph about its opposite—for example, pride in doing well versus complete indifference; feeling full of life versus feeling exhausted. Remember to repeat key words and phrases in each paragraph to build emphasis and heighten the contrast between the two. Before you begin, you may want to review the Writer's Craft article in this unit as well as entries in your reading/writing log.

Jean-Honore Fragonard, "A Young Girl Reading," painted about 1776. *The National Gallery of Art*

HANDBOOK OF LITERARY TERMS

■ ALLITERATION

She sells seashells by the seashore.
Peter Piper picked a peck of pickled peppers.

These tongue twisters have always been enjoyed because people like to play with the sounds of language. Advertisers use them in slogans; poets use them in their writing.

The use of repeated consonant sounds is called *alliteration*. Usually, the repeated, or alliterative, sounds occur at the beginnings of words, as in these lines:

All *d*ay within the *d*reamy house,
The *d*oors upon their hinges creaked . . . .

> *Alfred, Lord Tennyson*
> **from "Mariana"**

But sometimes they are found within words as well.

The gray sea and the *l*ong b*l*ack *l*and;
and the ye*ll*ow half-moon *l*arge and *l*ow . . . .

> *Robert Browning*
> **from "Meeting at Night"**

Alliteration in poetry helps create melody and sounds pleasant to hear. But the sounds should reflect the meaning—the sense—of a line. As you read the following lines, notice how the repeated *h*, *s*, and *sh* sounds echo the noise made by the scythes, or long-handled mowers, that are being swung through tall grass:

Hush, ah hush, the Scythes are saying,
  Hush, and heed not, and fall asleep;
Hush, they say to the grasses swaying,
  Hush, they sing to the clover deep!

> *Andrew Lang*
> **from "Scythe Song"**

Alliteration can also be used to call attention to important words:

Like *trains* of cars on *tracks* of plush
  I hear the level bee . . . .

> *Emily Dickinson*
> **from "The Bee"**

Alliteration can point out contrasts:

Between the *d*ark and the *d*aylight,
  When the night is beginning to lower . . . .

> *Henry Wadsworth Longfellow*
> **from "The Children's Hour"**

Alliteration can link words that are similar in image, thought, and feeling:

We'll talk of *s*unshine and of *s*ong,
And *s*ummer days when we were young . . . .

> *William Wordsworth*
> **from "To a Butterfly"**

Alliteration can affect MOOD.
Sweet and low, sweet and low,
  Wind of the western sea,
Low, low, breathe and blow,
  Wind of the western sea!

> *Alfred, Lord Tennyson*
> **from "Sweet and Low"**

What effect do these sounds create? In what ways are the sounds an "echo to the sense"?

■ ALLITERATION (ə lit′ə rā′shən)

Repeated consonant sounds occurring at the beginning of words or within words.

■ Apply to **"Still Life: Lady with Birds"** on page 321

■ CHARACTERIZATION

In order to create a fictitious character, the author may describe the character:

Karen was small for her age and inclined to plumpness. Her blue eyes viewed the people and events around her with a mixture of curiosity and amusement. She was not a woman, but she was past being a child; too sophisticated for toys, she might still, on impulse, turn a somersault on the living room rug.

1. Approximately how old is Karen?
2. What details help you visualize her?
3. What details reveal something about Karen's personality?

An author may reveal a character's personality through that character's speech and actions:

"But why can't I go?" Karen wailed. "Everyone else is going. You never let me go anywhere! You just don't want me to grow up and have fun!" Karen wheeled around and stormed out of the house, slamming the door behind her.

4. What does Karen reveal about her personality in this speech?
5. What do her actions contribute to your picture of her?

An author may give the reactions and opinions of other characters:

"I've known Karen a long time, ever since first grade. We've been best friends since last year. I like her because . . . well, I guess it's because she's always so happy and sure of herself and she's good at things like baseball and swimming and painting and stuff." Joanie paused, then added, "Everybody at school likes her."

6. What is Joanie's relationship to Karen?

7. What do you learn about Karen from Joanie's comments?

An author may show the character's inner thoughts and feelings:

The sunlight trickled between the slats of the bamboo blinds. Karen stretched luxuriously, pleasantly aware of the tingling sensation in her muscles.

She really ought to get up, she thought. Sally was coming over at eleven. Maybe she should make some sandwiches so they could eat out in the backyard. Mrs. Henley was taking them to the beach in the afternoon. She should also finish that letter to Peggy . . . maybe she would tonight . . . if she remembered . . . and if she had the time.

8. What is Karen thinking about?
9. What do her thoughts tell you about her personality?

Authors may use any one of the four methods of *characterization* illustrated above to bring to life the fictional people they create: (1) describing the character's appearance; (2) reporting the character's speech and behavior; (3) describing the reactions of other characters to the individual; and (4) revealing the character's thoughts and feelings. Most authors, however, use a combination of methods.

In the following novel excerpt, the author uses all four methods to characterize Meg, a teenaged girl who is visiting the principal of her former school. Charles Wallace is Meg's younger brother.

"I need to see you, please, Mr. Jenkins."
"Why aren't you in school?"
"I am. This school."
"Kindly don't be rude, Meg. I see you haven't changed any over the summer. I had hoped you would not be one of my problems this year. Have you informed anybody of your whereabouts?"

The early morning light glinted off his spectacles, veiling his eyes. Meg pushed her own spectacles up her nose, but could not read his expression; as usual, she thought, he looked as though he smelled something unpleasant.

He sniffed. "I will have my secretary drive you to school. That will mean the loss of her services for a full half day."

"I'll hitchhike, thanks."

"Compounding one misdemeanor with another? In this state, hitchhiking happens to be against the law."

"Mr. Jenkins, I didn't come to talk to you about hitchhiking, I came to talk to you about Charles Wallace."

"I don't appreciate your interference, Margaret."

"The bigger boys are bullying him. They'll really hurt him if you don't stop them."

Madeleine L'Engle
from *A Wind in the Door*

Each of the following is a true statement about Meg. For each one point out lines from the excerpt which prove the statement and name the method or methods of characterization used.

1. Meg wears glasses.
2. Meg always finds that Mr. Jenkins looks sour.
3. Meg is concerned about Charles Wallace's safety.
4. Meg has caused problems for Mr. Jenkins in the past.

■ CHARACTERIZATION

The methods an author uses to acquaint the reader with his or her characters. An author may describe the character's physical traits and personality, report the character's speech and behavior, give opinions and reactions of other characters toward this individual, or reveal the character's thoughts and feelings.

From *A Wind in the Door* by Madeleine L'Engle (Farrar, Straus and Giroux, 1980), pages 18–19.

■ Apply to "**Paw Paw**" on page 46

■ CONNOTATION/ DENOTATION

Our new house just wasn't home until Dad's blue rocking chair arrived.

If you were to look up the words *house* and *home* in a dictionary, you would find that both words have approximately the same meaning—"a dwelling place." However, the speaker in the sentence above suggests that *home* has an additional meaning. Aside from the strict dictionary definition, or *denotation*, many people associate such things as comfort, love, security, or privacy with a home but do not necessarily make the same associations with a house. What is the first thing that comes to your mind when you think of a home? of a house? Why do you think that real-estate advertisers use the word *home* more frequently than *house?*

The feelings, images, and memories that surround a word make up its *connotation*. Both *house* and *home* have the same denotation, or dictionary meaning; *home* also has many connotations.

Read the sentences and answer the questions that follow:

Annette was surprised.
Annette was amazed.
Annette was astonished.

1. What is the general meaning of each of the three sentences about Annette? Do the words *surprised*, *amazed*, and *astonished* have approximately the same denotation?
2. What additional meanings are suggested by *astonished?* Would one be more likely to be *surprised* or *astonished* at seeing a ghost?

3. Which word in each pair below has the more favorable connotation to you?

thrifty—penny-pinching
pushy—aggressive
politician—statesman
chef—cook
slender—skinny

Since everyone reacts emotionally to certain words, writers often deliberately select words that they think will influence your reactions and appeal to your emotions. Read the dictionary definition below:

cock roach (kok′rōch′), *n.* any of an order of nocturnal insects, usually brown with flattened oval bodies, some species of which are household pests inhabiting kitchens, areas around water pipes, etc. [<Spanish *cucaracha*]

What does the word *cockroach* mean to you? Is a cockroach merely an insect or is it also a household nuisance and a disgusting creature? Read each of the following poems. As you read, decide what poets Wild and Morley find in roaches. In both poems, pay attention to connotation as well as denotation. Then consider the questions that follow.

Roaches

Last night when I got up
to let the dog out I spied
a cockroach in the bathroom
crouched flat on the cool
5   porcelain,
            delicate
antennae probing the toothpaste cap
   and feasting himself on a gob
      of it in the bowl:
10 I killed him with one unprofessional
          blow,
scattering arms and legs
   and half his body in the sink . . .

I would have no truck with roaches,
15 crouched like lions in the ledges of sewers
their black eyes in the darkness
       alert for tasty slime,
breeding quickly and without design,
laboring up drainpipes through filth
20   to the light;
I read once they are among
   the most antediluvian[1] of creatures,
   surviving everything,
   and in more primitive times
25 thrived to the size of your hand . . .

yet when sinking asleep
   or craning at the stars,
I can feel their light feet
     probing in my veins,
30 their whiskers nibbling
   the insides of my toes;
and neck arched,
   feel their patient scrambling
up the dark tubes of my throat.

Peter Wild

from **Nursery Rhymes for the Tender-hearted**
(*dedicated to Don Marquis*)

Scuttle, scuttle, little roach—
How you run when I approach:
Up above the pantry shelf
Hastening to secrete yourself.

5 Most adventurous of vermin,
How I wish I could determine
How you spend your hours of ease,
Perhaps reclining on the cheese.

Cook has gone, and all is dark—
10 Then the kitchen is your park;
In the garbage heap that she leaves
Do you browse among the tea leaves?

How delightful to suspect
All the places you have trekked:
15 Does your long antenna whisk its
Gentle tip across the biscuits?
Do you linger, little soul,
Drowsing in our sugar bowl?
Or, abandonment most utter,
20 Shake a shimmy on the butter?

Do you chant your simple tunes
Swimming in the baby's prunes?
Then, when dawn comes, do you slink
Homeward to the kitchen sink?

25 Timid roach, why be so shy?
We are brothers, thou and I.
In the midnight, like yourself,
I explore the pantry shelf!

Christopher Morley

---

1. *antediluvian* (an'ti də lü'vē ən), very old.

"Roaches" by Peter Wild from *Poetry of the Desert Southwest* published by The Baleen Press, 1973. Reprinted by permission of the author.

Reread the dictionary definition. Which of the denotative characteristics of a cockroach do both poets include in their poems? What characteristics does Wild give to roaches that are not in the dictionary definition? What additional characteristics does Morley give to roaches?

In each poem, the word *roach* acquires meanings beyond its dictionary definition. Both poets lead us away from a literal view of roaches to a nonliteral one. Which poet succeeds in giving roaches favorable connotations? Which poet comes closer to expressing your own feelings about roaches?

■ CONNOTATION

The emotional, imaginative, cultural, or traditional associations surrounding a word, as opposed to its strict, literal dictionary meaning.

■ DENOTATION

The strict dictionary meaning of a word, presented objectively and without emotional associations.

From *Chimneysmoke* by Christopher Morley. Copyright 1921, 1949 by Christopher Morley. Reprinted by permission of Harper & Row, Publishers, Inc.

■ Apply to "**One Land, Two Worlds**" on page 256

■ FIGURATIVE LANGUAGE

The Eagle

He clasps the crag with crooked hands;
Close to the sun in lonely lands,
Ringed with the azure world, he stands.

The wrinkled sea beneath him crawls;
5 He watches from his mountain walls,
And like a thunderbolt he falls.

Alfred, Lord Tennyson

1. Explain the meaning of each of the following phrases in the context of the poem:
   a. crooked hands
   b. close to the sun in lonely lands
   c. wrinkled sea beneath him crawls
   d. his mountain walls
   e. like a thunderbolt he falls
2. This poem is a description of an eagle, yet it differs greatly from the ordinary dictionary definition of *eagle:* "a large, strong bird of prey that has keen eyes and powerful wings." How does the above poem suggest the eagle's strength? Which lines emphasize his keen vision? Which presents a more colorful description of the eagle, the poem or the dictionary? Explain your answer.

To make his description of the eagle especially clear and appealing, Tennyson uses *figurative language* instead of literal language. In literal language, words are used in their ordinary meaning, without exaggeration or inventiveness. (The dictionary definition of *eagle* is written in literal terms.) Figurative language goes beyond the ordinary meanings of words in order to emphasize ideas or emotions. Whenever you use a *figure of speech* such as "you're eating like a pig" or "he runs like the wind" you are comparing two different things in order to emphasize a similarity. Some of the most common figures of speech are SIMILE, METAPHOR, and HYPERBOLE.

Read the poem below and answer the questions that follow:

Companions

A leaf ran at my heels
Halfway across the dusk.
It rattled like a cough.
It was as curled as an old man's hand around
   a hoe.
5 It was as brown as the apes.
In a gust we parted,
the leaf stumbling one way
and I another.
It was not a decision;
10 we merely went on separate journeys.
The wind rose behind me
and I carried it on my shoulders all the way
like a raving corner of the sea.

Adrien Stoutenburg

1. To what things is the leaf compared?
2. How do the words that describe the leaf's movements make it seem human?
3. In what ways do the leaf and the wind both act as "companions"?

Effective figurative language has several characteristics: it makes its point by being both forceful and brief; it has a quality of freshness about it; it fits the situation; the things being compared must be alike in some recognizable way so that the general effect of the comparison is consistent and appropriate:

But the cruel rocks, they gored her side,
   Like the horns of an angry bull.

Henry Wadsworth Longfellow
from "The Wreck of the Hesperus"

Look at the cartoon below. Has the cartoonist illustrated the literal or the figurative meaning of the expression "work for peanuts"?

"I'm awful tired of working for peanuts!"

Reprinted by permission of Lawrence Lariar.

■ FIGURATIVE LANGUAGE

Any language that goes beyond the literal meaning of words in order to furnish new effects or fresh insights into an idea or a subject. The most common figures of speech are SIMILE, METAPHOR, and HYPERBOLE.

■ Apply to "**Dream Variations**" on page 331

■ FLASHBACK

Read the following narrative, paying particular attention to the order in which events occur. After you've finished reading, do the exercise that follows.

"I'm not going."

"Don't be silly." That's Mother. "Of course you are."

"I'm not."

"Why?"

"I don't believe in all this."

"Some stuff you learn at that fancy boarding school," Jerome, my only brother, can never resist a chance to knock my school.

"Rainy Day Nolan, funerals aren't something you do or don't believe in—like a political party or a religion. They are something you just do." Mother looks up from her oatmeal long enough to catch my eye and hold it.

When mother calls me by my full name, which isn't really my name (I was christened Lorraine Mary, but born on a rainy day), I know she's serious.

I'm the fifth in a family of seven girls and one boy, and the only one with two separate sets of names. I'm also the only one good at foreign languages, which is why I got a scholarship two years ago when I was twelve, and why Jerome gets to make cracks about my fancy boarding-school ideas. It's also why I was the only one in the family who had not been with Pappy Bill, Mother's father, when he died.

"They're awful. People in this town don't go to wakes and funerals to pay respects, they go to visit with each other. And I can't bear the funeral home—pink lights and that carpet with the birds on it. And I can't abide Big Lou."

"Hear that?" Jerome demands. "*Bear! Abide!* Spare me."

"Big Lou was here last winter, every time

Pappy Bill needed him." My sister Jean always tries to look at both sides. She's reminding me that Big Lou always came when Pappy Bill had to go to the hospital. It's a small town, so Big Lou is both paramedic and undertaker.

"Big Lou only looks weird." My little sister Teresa is now a cheerleader, and she's turning catty. I'll have to talk to her about that. "It's all that football he played before he settled down."

Dad comes in, looking tired. "They open at three—three to five—and then seven to ten. We don't all have to be there all the time."

"Rainy ain't going." Martha, the youngest, reminds him.

"*Isn't.*" This from half the table. "Don't be silly," which means Dad will not discuss it.

"She wants to remember Pappy Bill as he was," Teresa mimics my voice.

Dad pours more coffee. Nobody says anything, but it isn't a comfortable silence.

"Excuse me."

Nobody answers, so I leave the table.

The railroad tracks run through the middle of town, and I walk the ties for awhile. It's the warmest May anybody can remember, and along the tracks it already smells like summer. Whatever it is about railroad ties that makes them smell like tar—oily and warm—that's how the sun is making them smell. And those hearty wildflowers and weeds that grow through the cinders on the roadbed are already pushing their way up. And all this reminds me of Pappy Bill.

I'm real little—not more than three or four, and I'm in the backyard near the flower bed, and I'm trying not to cry. I've picked a purple-and-white iris without asking first; and pretty as it is, it doesn't help. Something's wrong, and it's probably my fault.

A few minutes earlier, I'd run into the kitchen and found my mother crying.

"It's almost time for Pappy Bill to come home. Pappy Bill is taking me down to the river."

She doesn't answer me, just reaches down and rumples my hair.

"If you're going to the river, put your sweater on."

I back away, frightened by her voice, how far away she sounds.

"Bye."

"Take a sweater, Rainy," she repeats, her face turned away from me.

It is too warm for a sweater. I wander outside. I wonder what I'd done to make Mother cry. She doesn't seem mad to me. Just sad and far away in her mind, which is even worse.

Pappy Bill comes to find me.

"Come on, Rainy; flowers waiting."

I hold his hand all the way to the river. The big boys have built a pier of railroad ties. Pappy Bill sits on it, on the end nearest the shore, looking out over water so still that it mirrors the hills on the other side.

I don't pick any flowers. I kneel near a patch of white daisies with yellow centers and—my favorite—red clover. I feel sick—so alone, so scared, so certain I've done something wrong. I'm trying so hard not to cry that I don't know he has moved until he is there beside me. He takes my hands and helps me stand up. He stands in front of me, looking down.

"Rainy, I don't know how to say this so a little girl will understand. And if you were a grownup, I wouldn't need to."

I'm crying so hard I can't get my breath.

"Sometimes," he goes on, "people have bad times. And people have these bad times no matter how many other good things they have in their lives. Now you kids are good things— grand things—in your parents' life. But right now, Rainy, your folks are having a bad time. It hasn't got anything at all to do with you."

He clears his throat and then picks me up and swings me onto his shoulder. We stand looking out over the water. I stop crying.

"Darn it, Rainy, I don't know how to tell a little girl that something isn't her fault."

I'm not sure I know what he means, but I feel a lot better.

Arrange these events from the narrative in chronological order.

1. Rainy refuses to attend the funeral.
2. Rainy finds her mother crying.
3. Pappy Bill dies.
4. Rainy picks flowers on the riverbank.
5. Rainy goes for a walk and begins to think about her grandfather.

Did you notice that at the beginning of the excerpt Rainy is fourteen years old, her grandfather has died, and she is unwilling to attend the services? The other events in the passage are not happening as you read them; they happened earlier, and she is recalling them as she walks down the railroad tracks. The author breaks in with a **flashback,** an interruption in the narrative to show an event or events that happened before that particular point.

When you rearrange the events, you put them in chronological order. A flashback can easily cover years of chronological time and give information that helps the reader better understand the story.

■ FLASHBACK

An interruption of the narrative to show an episode that happened before that particular point in the story.

■ Apply to **"The Last Boast"** on page 434

■ FORESHADOWING

It was a perfect day for a picnic. The morning was bright and clear with a few scattered clouds of the white, fluffy variety that kids find pictures in. Roses were in bloom, and birds sang outside my window. Nothing could go wrong on such a perfect day. Or so I, in my childlike innocence, thought.

1. Where is the first suggestion that something is going to happen to spoil the narrator's perfect day?
2. At this point, do you have any definite idea of what may go wrong?

Sometimes an author gives the reader clues or suggestions about events that will happen later. This technique is called *foreshadowing*. In the paragraph above, you know that something will happen to mar the "perfect day," but you don't know whether it will be a humorous incident, such as a cow eating the picnic lunch, or a tragic event, such as a drowning or an automobile accident.

Not all foreshadowing is as obvious as that in the example above. Frequently, future events are merely hinted at through dialogue, description, or the attitudes and reactions of the characters.

In the following novel excerpt the main character, David Copperfield, recounts an event from his childhood. His mother, a young, attractive woman, had been widowed shortly before David was born. Peggotty is a trusted and devoted servant of the Copperfield family. As you read, notice clues that might foreshadow future events:

Peggotty and I were sitting one night by the parlor fire, alone. I had been reading to Peggotty about crocodiles. I remember she had a cloudy impression, after I had done, that they were a sort of vegetable. I was tired of reading, and dead sleepy; but having leave, as a high treat, to sit up until my mother came home from spending the evening at a neighbor's, I would rather have died upon my post (of course) than have gone off to bed. . . .

"Peggotty," says I suddenly, "were you ever married?"

"Lord, Master Davy," replied Peggotty, "what's put marriage in your head?"

She answered with such a start that it quite woke me. And then she stopped in her work, and looked at me, with her needle drawn out to its thread's length.

"But were you ever married, Peggotty?" says I. "You are a very handsome woman, an't you?"

"Me handsome, Davy!" said Peggotty. "Lawk no, my dear! But what put marriage in your head?"

"I don't know! You mustn't marry more than one person at a time, may you, Peggotty?"

"Certainly not," says Peggotty, with the promptest decision.

"But if you marry a person, and the person dies, why then you may marry another person, mayn't you, Peggotty?"

"You may," says Peggotty, "if you choose."

"You an't cross, I suppose, Peggotty, are you?" said I, after sitting quiet for a minute.

I really thought she was, she had been so short with me. But I was quite mistaken; for she laid aside her work (which was a stocking of her own), and opening her arms wide, took my curly head within them, and gave it a good squeeze. I know it was a good squeeze, because, being very plump, whenever she made any little exertion after she was dressed, some of the buttons on the back of her gown flew off. And I recollect two bursting while she was hugging me.

"Now let me hear some more about the crorkindills," said Peggotty, "for I an't heard half enough."

I couldn't quite understand why Peggotty looked so queer, or why she was so ready to go back to the crocodiles. However, we returned to those monsters, with fresh interest on my part; but I had my doubts of Peggotty, who was thoughtfully sticking her needle into various parts of her face and arms all the time.

We had exhausted the crocodiles, and begun with the alligators, when the garden bell rang. We went to the door, and there was my mother, looking unusually pretty, I thought, and with her a gentleman with beautiful black hair and whiskers, who had walked home with us from church last Sunday.

As my mother stepped down on the threshold to take me in her arms and kiss me, the gentleman said I was a more highly privileged little fellow than a monarch.

"What does that mean?" I asked him.

He patted me on the head; but somehow I didn't like him or his deep voice, and I was jealous that his hand should touch my mother's in touching me—which it did. I put it away as well as I could.

"Oh, Davy!" remonstrated my mother.

"Dear boy!" said the gentleman. "I cannot wonder at his devotion. Come, let us shake hands!"

My right hand was in my mother's left, so I gave him the other.

"Why, that's the wrong hand, Davy!" laughed the gentleman.

My mother drew my right hand forward; but I resolved, for my former reason, not to give it to him, and I did not. I gave him the other, and he shook it heartily, and said I was a brave fellow, and went away.

At this minute I see him turn around in the garden, and give us a last look with his ill-omened black eyes, before the door was shut.

Peggotty, who had not said a word or moved a finger, secured the fastenings instantly, and we all went into the parlor. My mother, contrary to her usual habit, instead of coming to the elbow-chair by the fire, remained at the other end of the room, and sat singing to herself.

"Hope you have had a pleasant evening, ma'am," said Peggotty, standing as stiff as a barrel in the center of the room, with a candlestick in her hand.

"Much obliged to you, Peggotty," returned my mother in a cheerful voice, "I have had a very pleasant evening."

"A stranger or so makes an agreeable change," suggested Peggotty.

"A very agreeable change, indeed," returned my mother.

Peggotty continuing to stand motionless in the middle of the room, and my mother resuming her singing, I fell asleep. . . .

Charles Dickens
from *David Copperfield*

1. How does Peggotty's attitude suggest that David's mother is about to remarry? When do you learn whom she will probably marry?
2. Which of Mrs. Copperfield's actions lead you to expect the marriage?
3. What hints are there in the man's attitude that foreshadow the marriage?
4. Find the clues that suggest the man is not as kind as he tries to appear.

Foreshadowing frequently serves two purposes. It builds suspense by raising questions that encourage the reader to go on and find out more about the event that is being foreshadowed. The preceding passage, for example, foretells Mrs. Copperfield's marriage to the blackhaired gentleman. It does not, however, explain how David will fit into this marriage, or what will happen to Peggotty, who obviously does not approve of the marriage.

Foreshadowing is also a means of adding plausibility to a narrative by partially preparing the reader for events to follow. In this passage, the gentleman appears to like David even though the boy dislikes him immediately. The "last look" the gentleman gives them "with his ill-omened black eyes" also suggests that the man is not so kind and generous as he appears to be and that he may be the cause of much future unhappiness for the Copperfields.

■ FORESHADOWING

An author's use of hints or clues to suggest events that will occur later in a narrative.

■ Appy to "**Flowers for Algernon**" on page 410

■ HYPERBOLE

So fair art thou, my bonnie lass,
    So deep in love am I:
And I will love thee still, my dear,
    Till all the seas go dry.

Robert Burns
from "A Red, Red Rose"

According to the last line, how long will the speaker's love last? Do you think the last line is intended to be taken literally or figuratively? What is the effect of the last line?

Hyperbole is an exaggerated statement used to increase or heighten effect. When you say, "I could eat a horse," you are deliberately exaggerating in order to let your listener know that you are extremely hungry.

Read the limerick below and answer the questions that follow:

There was a young lady from Lynn
Who was so exceedingly thin
    That when she essayed
    To drink lemonade
She slid down the straw and fell in.

Author Unknown

1. What is the exaggerated statement in this limerick?
2. What is the purpose of the hyperbole?

■ HYPERBOLE (hī pėr′bə lē)

An exaggerated statement used especially as a figure of speech to heighten effect.

■ Apply to "**My Boss the Cat**" on page 246

■ IMAGERY

The hot July sun beat relentlessly down, casting an orange glare over the farm buildings, the fields, and the pond. Even the usually cool green willows bordering the pond hung wilting and dry. Our sun-baked backs ached for relief. We pulled off our sweaty clothes and plunged into the pond, but the tepid water only stifled us and we soon climbed back onto the brown, dusty bank. Our parched throats longed for something cool—a strawberry ice, a tall frosted glass of lemonade.

We pulled on our clothes and headed through the dense, crackling underbrush, the sharp briars pulling at our damp jeans. At last we reached the watermelon patch. As we began to cut open the nearest melon, we could smell the tang of the pungent skin mingling with the dusty odor of dry earth. Suddenly the melon gave way with a crack, revealing the juicy, deep pink sweetness inside.

1. From the paragraphs above pick out words and phrases that appeal to your sense of (a) sight; (b) sound; (c) smell; (d) taste; (e) touch and feeling.
2. Of those listed in question 1, which sense impression is strongest?

To make descriptions of people, places, and events seem real, writers often use words and phrases that appeal to the senses. These words and phrases, called *images*, help a reader to mentally experience what the characters in the literary selection are actually experiencing. The use of imagery helps bring a fictional world to life.

Well-chosen images arouse a particular response or emotion in the reader's imagination, as they do in the poem in the next column.

Horse

A
quarter horse, no rider
canters through the pasture

thistles raise soft purple burrs
5 her flanks are shiny in the sun

I whistle and she runs
almost sideways toward me

the oats in my hand are sweets to her:

dun mane furling in its breeze,
10 her neck
corseted with muscle,
wet teeth friendly against my hand—
how can I believe
you ran under a low maple limb
15 to knock me off?

Jim Harrison

To what senses does the poet appeal in this poem? Pick out the sensory images which seem most vivid to you.

■ IMAGERY

Concrete details that appeal to the senses of sight, sound, touch, smell, and taste, or to internal feelings.

"Horse" from *Plain Song* by James Harrison. Copyright © 1965 by James Harrison. Reprinted by permission of the author.

■ Apply to "**Snow Sculpture**" on page 307

■ INFERENCE

Help Wanted:
Young person to work at Sox ballpark. Some sales experience helpful but not necessary. Uniform provided. Apply at concession stand, corner Addison and 14th.

1. The person who takes this job will probably be (a) a major-league baseball player; (b) an usher; (c) a hot-dog vendor.
2. What details tell you what kind of job this is?

Study carefully the following cartoon:

"Miss Feiner. Yoo-hoo."

1. Why is the skier calling to Miss Feiner?
2. What do you think happened to Miss Feiner?

A correct conclusion that you draw from just a few hints is called an *inference*.

Many writers do not tell a reader everything outright. Instead they rely on a reader's ability to "read between the lines" and make reasonable inferences from the information presented.

A reader can make inferences from an author's description of a scene or character, from a character's conversation and actions, from the way in which other characters react to a particular individual, and even from an author's choice of words.

In the following novel excerpt the author describes Jo, a young writer, on the day she first takes a manuscript to a publisher:

"There, I've done my best! If this won't suit I shall have to wait till I can do better."

Lying back on the sofa, Jo read the manuscript carefully through, making dashes here and there, and putting in many exclamation points; then she tied it up with a smart red ribbon, and sat a minute looking at it with a sober, wistful expression, which plainly showed how earnest her work had been. Then Jo produced another manuscript; and, putting both in her pocket, crept quietly down the stairs.

She put on her hat and jacket as noiselessly as possible, and, going to the back entry window, got out upon the roof of a low porch, swung herself down to the grassy bank, and took a roundabout way to the road.

If anyone had been watching her, he would have thought her movements decidedly peculiar; for she went off at a great pace till she reached a

From *Little Women* by Louisa May Alcott (The World Publishing Company, 1969), pages 172–173.

certain number in a certain busy street. She went into the doorway, looked up the dirty stairs, and, after standing stock still a minute, suddenly dived into the street, and walked away as rapidly as she came. This maneuver she repeated several times, to the great amusement of a black-eyed young gentleman lounging in the window of a building opposite. On returning for the third time, Jo gave herself a shake, pulled her hat over her eyes, and walked up the stairs, looking as if she were going to have all her teeth out.

There was a dentist's sign, among others, which adorned the entrance, and, after staring a moment at the pair of artificial jaws which slowly opened and shut to draw attention to a fine set of teeth, the young gentleman put on his coat, took his hat, and went down to post himself in the opposite doorway, saying, with a smile and a shiver, "It's like her to come alone, but if she has a bad time she'll need someone to help her home."

Louisa May Alcott
from *Little Women*

1. How can you tell that Jo doesn't want anyone to see her leave the house?
2. How do Jo's actions reveal her nervousness?
3. Where does the "black-eyed gentleman" assume that Jo is going?
4. Does the "black-eyed gentleman" know Jo? How do you know?

■ INFERENCE

A reasonable and intelligent conclusion drawn from hints or other information provided by an author.

■ Apply to "**Charles**" on page 116

■ IRONY

Verbal irony

It was one of those days! The alarm clock failed to go off, John ripped the sleeve of his new shirt, spilled orange juice on his math paper, and missed his ride to school. When he finally climbed on a city bus, he told the driver, "This is certainly going to be a great day!"

1. What does John mean by his statement?
2. Does he actually believe it *is* going to be a great day?

John is using *verbal irony* when he says the opposite of what he really means or feels. Can you recall a situation in which you used verbal irony? Describe it.

Irony of situation

Read the following synopsis of a short story by O. Henry entitled "The Cop and the Anthem":

It is late autumn in New York, and Soapy, a bum, decides that it is time for him to make his usual arrangements for the winter months: he will get himself arrested and sentenced to prison. There he will have food and lodging, at least. To achieve this goal, Soapy plans to eat a large and expensive meal, and then leave without paying for it. However, when he goes into a fashionable restaurant, he is turned away because of his shabby clothes. Next he smashes a store window and immediately confesses his deed to a policeman. But the policeman refuses to believe him. He does get his meal in a not-so-fashionable restaurant, but instead of being arrested when he can't pay, he is merely thrown out onto the street.

Soapy makes several more attempts to be arrested, including stealing an umbrella. But it turns out that the man with the umbrella had himself stolen it earlier. Soapy gives up in despair and heads for the park and his accustomed bench, but on the way he stops before a church. As he stands there listening to the music from within, he is reminded of his happy childhood and the depths to which he has now fallen. He resolves to reform his life, find a job, and to become successful. But as he stands there lost in thought, he is finally arrested—for vagrancy!

1. What does Soapy at first hope will happen to him?
2. Why doesn't it happen?
3. When does the result he hoped for actually occur?
4. Why is the outcome a surprise?

This story, in which things turn out contrary to what is expected, is an example of *irony of situation*. The situation occurs because Soapy does not get arrested when he actually commits crimes but does when he loiters in front of a church making the decision to alter his life for the better.

Dramatic irony

Below is part of a synopsis of a detective mystery. Read it and answer the questions that follow:

Scene One: The play begins in the dimly lighted library of a huge, old house. A tall man wearing gloves enters and crosses to a painting which hangs above a sofa. He removes the painting, revealing a wall safe behind it. With the skill of a professional burglar, he carefully begins twirling the lock until after a few moments he succeeds in opening the safe. Greedily he grabs the jewels he finds within and makes a speedy exit.

Scene Two: The library is now ablaze with light. The wall safe is open as we left it at the close of the last scene. A famous detective has just arrived and has assembled in the library the owners of the house, guests, and various servants. Among those seated on the sofa beneath the safe is the tall man. He appears to be completely calm and collected. One by one, the detective questions each of the servants. The tall man is next. . . .

1. At this point in the action, what do you know that none of the characters in the play (except the tall man) know?
2. Why might the tall man's answers to the detective's questions mean more to you than to the other characters in the play?

Dramatic irony occurs in fiction or drama when the reader or spectator knows more about the true state of affairs than the characters do. Authors often employ dramatic irony to create suspense. For example, dramatic irony is used by Edgar Allan Poe in "The Tell-Tale Heart." When the police arrive, you know that the narrator has just killed and hidden the old man. By allowing you to know more than the police know, the author helps increase your feelings of suspense as the narrator becomes more and more uncomfortable.

■ IRONY

The contrast between what is expected, or what appears to be, and what actually is.

Verbal irony is the contrast between what is said and what is actually meant.

Irony of situation refers to a happening that is the opposite of what is expected or intended.

Dramatic irony occurs when the audience or reader knows more than the characters do.

■ Apply to *Back There* on page 159

■ METAPHOR

Night

Night is a cavalier dauntless and bold;
Riding through clouds on a steed strapped with
    gold,
Sapphires flash from his cloak's sable folds
And each silken pocket a star-baby holds.

Christine Wood Bullwinkle

1. The speaker in the poem above makes a comparison between two essentially different things, night and a cavalier, or horseman. What does this comparison suggest about night?
2. In line 3 what are the sapphires being compared to? In what ways are the two things the same? What is the sable cloak being compared to? What similarities exist between these things?
3. Consider each of the following literal descriptions of night: "the time between evening and morning," "dark," "evening." Which is a more vivid description of night—the poem, or any of the literal descriptions?

In literature and, particularly, in poetry, a writer often expresses one thing in terms of another (night as a cavalier). This use of FIGURATIVE LANGUAGE helps the reader see unexpected, but valid, connections between things that are basically different. When things that are basically unlike are related through implied comparison, these comparisons are called *metaphors*.

In a metaphor there is never a connective such as *like* or *as* to signal that a comparison is being made. (See SIMILE.) As a result, metaphors are not always easy to spot. Explain what makes the following sentence a metaphor: "The tumbleweeds are the children of the desert."

Look for the metaphor in this poem:

For a Hopi Silversmith

he has gathered the windstrength
from the third mesa
into his hand
and cast it into silver

5 i have wanted to see
the motion of wind
for a long time

thank you
for showing me

Joy Harjo

1. What does a silversmith do?
2. What has the silversmith done, according to the speaker, that is so special?
3. How might designing and working a piece of silver remind the speaker of gathering and casting the strength and motion of the wind?

■ METAPHOR

A figure of speech that involves an implied comparison between two relatively unlike things.

Christine Wood Bullwinkle, "Night" from *Poems for the Children's Hour* by Josephine Bouton, ed. (Springfield, Mass.: Milton Bradley Co.), 1927.

"For a Hopi Silversmith" from *The First Skin Around Me* published by Territorial Press. Copyright © 1976 by Joy Harjo. Reprinted by permission.

■ Apply to **"The clouds pass"** on page 304

■ MOOD

The Harbor

Passing through huddled and ugly walls
By doorways where women
Looked from their hunger-deep eyes,
Haunted with shadows of hunger-hands,
5 Out from the huddled and ugly walls,
I came sudden, at the city's edge,
On a blue burst of lake—
Long lake waves breaking under the sun
On a spray-flung curve of shore;
10 And a fluttering storm of gulls,
Masses of great gray wings
And flying white bellies
Veering and wheeling free in the open.

Carl Sandburg

1. What is the setting in lines 1 through 5?
   Is the setting a pleasant one?
2. What is the effect of the poet's use of
   words such as *huddled, ugly, hunger-*
   deep, haunted, shadows, and *hunger-*
   hands? What feelings do these words
   create?
3. In the last eight lines of the poem, what
   words and images help create feelings of
   freedom and optimism?
4. What sort of statement about the lake
   does Sandburg seem to be making?

   In this poem, as in any piece of writing,
the author selects elements such as setting,
specific details, and images to convey the
desired *mood*—in this case one that moves
from an atmosphere of ugliness and
hopelessness to one of beauty, openness,
and optimism. Another poet might have
treated either or both scenes in an entirely
different way, depending on his or her
purpose.

As you read the following poem, pay
particular attention to the mood being
created:

Running—I

What were we playing? Was it prisoner's base?
I ran with whacking keds
Down the cart-road past Rickard's place,
And where it dropped beside the tractor-sheds

5 Leapt out into the air above a blurred
Terrain, through jolted light,
Took two hard lopes, and at the third
Spanked off a hummock-side exactly right,

And made the turn, and with delighted strain
10 Sprinted across the flat
By the bull-pen, and up the lane.
Thinking of happiness, I think of that.

Richard Wilbur

1. What mood does the poem
   communicate to you—happiness,
   excitement, exhaustion?
2. What details in the poem help create
   this mood?

■ MOOD

**The total feeling in a literary work. The
choice of setting, objects, details, images,
and words all contribute to create a
specific mood.**

"The Harbor" from *Chicago Poems* by Carl Sandburg. Copyright
1916 by Holt, Rinehart and Winston, Inc., copyright 1944 by Carl
Sandburg. Reprinted by permission of Harcourt, Brace Jovanovich,
Inc.

"Running—I" copyright © 1968 by Richard Wilbur. Reprinted from
his volume *Walking to Sleep* by permission of Harcourt Brace
Jovanovich, Inc. and Faber and Faber Limited.

■ Apply to "**Old Man at the Bridge**" on page 383

■ ONOMATOPOEIA

Booth led boldly with his big bass drum—
(Are you washed in the blood of the lamb?)

Vachel Lindsay
**from "General William Booth
Enters into Heaven"**

What action is being described in these lines? What words are used to create the sound of marching in time to a drumbeat? What feeling do these lines convey?

The moan of doves in immemorial elms,
And murmuring of innumerable bees.

Alfred, Lord Tennyson
from "The Princess"

Words such as *yelp, moan,* and *bow wow* have sounds that reflect their sense. **Onomatopoeia** is the use of words to imitate sounds. Words such as *hiss, rumble, hush,* and *crack* are onomatopoetic words.
Find onomatopoeia in these lines.

There was silence supreme! Not a shriek, not a
   scream,
Scarcely even a howl or a groan,
As the man they called "Ho!" told his story of
   woe
In an antediluvian tone.

Lewis Carroll
from "The Hunting of the Snark"

■ ONOMATOPOEIA

(on′ə mat′ə pē′ə)

The use of words whose sounds suggest their sense.

■ Apply to **"Dog at Night"** on page 326

676 *Handbook of Literary Terms*

■ PERSONIFICATION

A Word is Dead

A word is dead
When it is said,
Some say.

I say it just
Begins to live
That day.

Emily Dickinson

Can a word die? We often give nonhuman things human characteristics. A cloud "scowls" or "weeps." The sun "smiles."
What is personified in the lines below?

Primer Lesson

Look out how you use proud words.
When you let proud words go, it is not easy to
   call them back.
They wear long boots, hard boots; they walk
   off proud; they can't hear you calling—
Look out how you use proud words.

Carl Sandburg

■ PERSONIFICATION

A figure of speech in which human characteristics are given to nonhuman things and events.

■ Apply to **"Check"** on page 317

■ PLOT

The material following this story deals with *conflict*, *details*, *pattern of events*, *climax*, and *conclusion*. These are all important elements of *plot*.

If Cornered, Scream

On the night it happened she hurried across the hospital parking lot, unlocked her car door, and got in. She started the car, waved to her co-workers, honked to the security guard, and drove the half block to the freeway entrance. The late hour meant light traffic, and though she was a good driver, she was always relieved whenever she had negotiated an entrance ramp. That done, she settled back, driving easily.

Then in the dim dashboard light she saw the gas gauge indicating empty and remembered with annoyance that she hadn't had time to stop for gas. Working a late shift at the hospital was not an ideal situation, but it meant more money and allowed her to attend graduate classes during the days.

As she drove, she found herself gripping the steering wheel and made a conscious effort to relax and think pleasant thoughts. Each night during the drive home, she relived the safety lectures given to the nurses—make sure someone on the ward knows where you are at all times; leave the grounds in groups; avoid isolated places in the hospital; if cornered, scream.

Again she deliberately relaxed her grip on the wheel and took a deep breath.

Funny, she thought, she didn't know why, but she was even more uptight than usual. She was tired and looked forward to a long soak in the tub and her new magazine which had lain unread the last three days.

The gas gauge again caught her attention. She could probably make it home on what was still left in the tank, but she would have to fill up before class in the morning. If she stopped tonight at the station that Gabriel ran on Imperial Highway, she'd have a few extra minutes in the morning and wouldn't have to rush.

She approached Imperial Highway, flicked on the right blinker, headed down the off-ramp, waited at the stoplight, and then made a left turn. She pulled into the station at a pump and rolled down the window as Gabriel walked to the car.

Since he always spoke pleasantly on the nights she stopped for gas, she had automatically discounted the few disturbing rumors that accompanied his sudden appearance in the area.

"Hi, Florence Nightingale. Fill 'er up?"

"Hi, Gabriel. Yes, fill it up, please."

As she handed him the gas-tank key, he asked, "Any more ping-pong playing under the hood?"

"No, no more noise. It stopped when you did whatever you did."

Gabriel filled the tank, cleaned the windows and mirrors, and gave her the change from a twenty. When he finished he said offhandedly, "By the way, my birthday was Sunday. Why don't you step inside the office and see what my sister gave me? You won't believe your eyes!"

"Oh, Gabriel, I'm in a really big hurry. I just can't stop tonight. But I will next time. I promise."

"Aw, come on. It won't be new any more by then. Besides, this is something extra-special. Come on. Only take a second."

As she and Gabriel talked back and forth, she realized she was wasting more time than if she went in and saw the silly gift.

Looking more agreeable than she felt, she said, "Okay, you win, Gabriel. Remember, this better be good!"

"It is. You'll see. Oh, before you get out, angle the car over this way—just in case anyone wants

From "If Cornered, Scream" by Patricia J. Thurmond. First published in *Ellery Queen's Mystery Magazine*, January 1978. Copyright © 1977 by Patricia J. Thurmond.

to pull in." Watching his gestures, she parked the car and followed him to the station office.

Once inside, Gabriel locked the door and quickly took a gun out of the drawer. Through the roar of her heartbeat in her ears she heard him say that there was no birthday and no present. Her fingers tingled. Nausea pitched and rolled through her body like seasickness. Each time the nausea crested, her legs felt like loosened moorings.

Her nose and toes were cold and she knew clinically, almost like an observer, that she was experiencing the symptoms of shock. She was unable to make a self-protective move, or even to scream. She tried to prepare to die, but didn't know how. Crazily, in the midst of her silent hysteria, the absurdity of it struck her, and she had a demented desire to laugh. Gabriel's lips were moving but she still couldn't hear above the roar in her ears.

Finally she heard sounds coming from his mouth. The sounds became words as her head cleared, and the words began to make sense.

". . . sorry I had to scare you by telling you that. But don't feel bad, I was scared myself when I saw that dude on the floor in the back of your car. I had you angle the car that way so that I can see both doors from here. And if he tries to get out, he belongs to me. I'll call the cops now. It's okay. Good thing you stopped for gas tonight."

In a few minutes she was aware of the sirens, the flashing lights of the squad cars, and the bellow of the bullhorn.

Patricia J. Thurmond

Conflict

1. When does the main character first think that her life is in danger? Is she able to make any move to prevent this danger? Is her conflict with Gabriel real or imagined?
2. Has this "danger" been foreshadowed earlier in the story? If so, where?

Every story, novel, or play develops around a struggle or *conflict*. Sometimes there may be only one main conflict. Sometimes, characters may be involved in several conflicts.

Conflicts in literature are of two general types: (1) *external conflict,* in which the character or main figure (sometimes an animal or group) struggles against another character, nature, or society; and (2) *internal conflict,* in which two elements of a character's personality struggle against one another. What is the internal conflict in this story? Is there an external conflict? Explain.

Details

Many details that an author chooses are helpful in developing plot. Why is each of the following details important to the story?

1. the late hour
2. the empty gas gauge
3. the main character's early-morning class

Pattern of Events

1. What purpose does each of the following incidents serve?
   a. The main character drives out of a hospital parking lot.
   b. She looks at her gas gauge.
   c. She turns off the freeway.
   d. Gabriel cleans the windows and mirrors.
   e. Gabriel asks her to look at his birthday present.
   f. The main character finally agrees.
   g. Gabriel tells her to angle the car out of the way of the gas pumps.

h. He takes a gun out of a drawer.

i. He tells her there's a man on the floor in the back of her car.

2. Could any of these incidents be eliminated without damaging the story? Explain.

3. Could the order of these incidents be rearranged without lessening the impact of the story?

4. What is the outcome of the story?

An author writes a story with a specific outcome in mind. Therefore, those incidents that are important to the ending are arranged in a cause-effect relationship. Each incident should logically follow the preceding ones since each is a necessary link to the outcome. In a well-planned story no one incident can be moved or eliminated without damaging or even ruining the effect the writer is trying to achieve.

Climax and Conclusion

In your opinion, where in the story is the highest point of interest or emotional intensity? Does the course of events or the main character's course of action change at this point? Explain.

The *climax* of a story takes place when the reader experiences the greatest emotional response to a character's problem, when the situation is such that the conflict must be resolved one way or another, or when a character starts to take a decisive action to end the conflict.

The climax of "If Cornered, Scream" begins when the main character suffers shock at seeing Gabriel's gun and continues until she starts listening to what he is telling her and realizes that the gun is only meant to protect her. Not every story contains a climax in this sense; sometimes the problem is left unresolved.

The *conclusion* of a story includes the resolution of the conflict and any events following it. Sometimes the conclusion contains a direct or implied comment on the conflict.

What events follow the resolution of the conflict or the climax in this story?

■ PLOT

A series of related events selected by the author to present and bring about the resolution of some *internal* or *external* conflict. In a carefully constructed plot, *details* and incidents are selected and arranged in a cause-effect relationship so that each is a necessary link leading to the outcome of the story. The events usually follow a pattern: a situation is established; a conflict or problem arises; certain events bring about a *climax*, or a character takes a decisive action; the conflict is resolved.

■ Apply to "**The Last Specimen**" on page 13

■ POINT OF VIEW

On Friday, September 13, 1965, I was born to JoAnn and Bob Cheever.

Robert H. Cheever, Jr., was born to JoAnn and Bob Cheever on Friday, September 13, 1965.

What is the only important difference between the two sentences above?

Before beginning to write, an author must decide who the narrator will be; that is, who will tell the story. A story may be told by one of the characters, as in the first sentence, or by an outsider, as in the second sentence. The relationship between the narrator and the story he or she tells is called *point of view*.

The four passages that follow tell the same incident from different points of view. Notice how the amount of information given about each character depends upon the point of view used.

1. As I placed the carefully wrapped package on the park bench, I looked up and saw Molly walking across the street. I hoped that she hadn't seen me.

a. Is the narrator a character in the incident or an outsider?
b. Do you know what the narrator is doing?
c. Do you know what Molly is doing? what she is thinking?

2. As George placed the carefully wrapped package on the park bench, he looked up and saw Molly walking across the street.

a. Is the narrator a character in the incident or an outsider?
b. Do you know what George is doing? what he is thinking?
c. Do you know what Molly is doing? what she is thinking?

3. George, anxiously hoping that no one was watching him, placed a carefully wrapped package on an empty park bench. But when he looked around, he saw Molly watching him from across the street.

a. Is the narrator a character in the incident or an outsider?
b. Do you know what George is doing? what he is thinking?
c. Do you know what Molly is doing? what she is thinking?

4. George, anxiously hoping that no one was watching him, placed a carefully wrapped package on an empty park bench. But Molly, who was walking home, saw him and couldn't help thinking that he was acting strangely.

a. Is the narrator a character in the incident or an outsider?
b. Do you know what George is doing? what he is thinking?
c. Do you know what Molly is doing? what she is thinking?

An author uses a narrator much as a movie director uses a camera. Through choice of point of view (who the narrator is), the author can focus sharply on some details and characters while showing others less clearly.

First-Person Point of View

In example number 1, the narrator is George, a character in the story. In telling the story from his personal point of view, the narrator ("I," or first person) can tell us his own thoughts, but he cannot tell us the thoughts of other characters. Just as you can report what you see others doing, the narrator can tell us only what he sees other characters doing or what he is told by other characters; and just as you cannot enter the minds of other people, the narrator cannot enter the minds of characters other than himself. (For examples of the first-person point of view see "Top Man" and "Not Poor, Just Broke.")

Third-Person Point of View In each of the next three examples, the narrator is not a character in the story but is an outsider, or third person.

Third-Person Objective Point of View Example 2 is written from the third-person objective point of view. This narrator can tell us what is happening, but does not tell us the thoughts of any of the characters. Like a newspaper reporter, this narrator can give only the facts as they occur; he or she cannot enter into the characters' minds.

Third-Person Limited Point of View In the third example the narrator sees into the mind of only one character, George. This is known as the third-person limited point of view. (For examples of the third-person limited point of view see "The Inspiration of Mr. Budd" and "The Treasure of Lemon Brown.")

Third-Person Omniscient (om nish′ənt) **Point of View** In the fourth example, the narrator again is an outsider, a third person. But here the narrator has the ability to see into the minds and record the thoughts of both characters. Like a superhuman being, this narrator is *omniscient* (all-knowing). (For examples of the use of the omniscient point of view see

"Upon the Waters" and "To Build a Fire.")

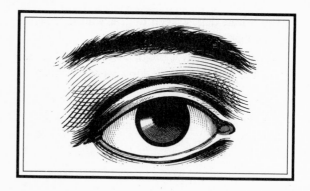

■ POINT OF VIEW

The relationship between the narrator and the story he or she tells. The author's choice of narrator for a story determines the amount of information a reader will be given. The four major points of view are

1. *First Person:* **The narrator ("I") is a character in the story who can reveal only personal thoughts and feelings and what he or she sees and is told by other characters.**

2. *Third-Person Objective:* **The narrator is an outsider who can report only what he or she sees and hears.**

3. *Third-Person Limited:* **The narrator is an outsider who sees into the mind of one of the characters.**

4. *Third-Person Omniscient:* **The narrator is an all-knowing outsider who can enter the minds of more than one of the characters.**

■ Apply to **"Rain, Rain Go Away"** on page 101

■ RHYME

I'm a lean dog, a keen dog, a wild dog and
   lone;
I'm a rough dog, a tough dog, hunting on
   my own;
I'm a bad dog, a mad dog, teasing silly
   sheep;
I love to sit and bay the moon, to keep fat
   souls from sleep.

5 I'll never be a lap dog, licking dirty feet,
A sleek dog, a meek dog, cringing for my
   meat;
Not for me the fireside, the well-filled plate,
But shut door, and sharp stone, and cuff and
   kick and hate.

Irene Rutherford McLeod
from "Lone Dog"

In the first stanza of "Lone Dog," which
words at the ends of lines rhyme? Which
words rhyme in the second stanza?

In poetry, this device of ending two or
more lines with words that sound alike is
called *end rhyming;* end words that share a
particular sound are *end rhymes.*

When used in a poem, end rhymes set
up a pattern of sounds, or a *rhyme scheme.*
You can chart a rhyme scheme with letters
of the alphabet by using the same letter for
end words that rhyme. Consider, for
example, the following limerick:

There was an old man from Peru	*a*
Who dreamed he was eating his shoe.	*a*
He awoke in the night	*b*
And turned on the light	*b*
And found out it was perfectly true.	*a*

The rhyme scheme for this limerick is *a*
(the sound ending line 1); *a* (a sound

rhyming with line 1); *b* (a new, or second
rhyming sound); *b* (a sound rhyming with
the second sound); *a* (a rhyme for the first
sound).

If the limerick had a third rhyming
sound, it would be designated by the letter
c. A fourth rhyme would be labeled *d,* and
so on. By using this method, you can chart
the rhyme scheme of any poem that uses
end rhymes.

1. Make a chart of the rhyme scheme for a
   stanza of McLeod's "Lone Dog."
2. Reread the first line of "Lone Dog."
   Which words *within* the line rhyme?

Rhyming words within a line are called
internal rhymes. Find at least three internal
rhymes in "Lone Dog."

In a second type of internal rhyme, a
word within a line rhymes with the end
word:

For the moon never *beams* without bringing me
   dreams
Of the beautiful Annabel Lee . . . .

Edgar Allan Poe
from "Annabel Lee"

Can you find any internal rhymes of this
type in "Lone Dog"?

■ RHYME

**The repetition of syllable sounds. End
words that share a sound are called *end
rhymes.* Rhyming words within a line of
poetry are called *internal rhymes.***

■ Apply to **"Concord Hymn"** on page 282

■ RHYTHM

I Never Saw a Purple Cow

I never saw a purple cow,
I never hope to see one.
But I can tell you anyhow,
I'd rather see than be one.

Gelett Burgess

Read the above verse aloud. Notice that its author has arranged words in a way that automatically causes you to place greater stress on some words or syllables than on others. This combination of stressed and unstressed words or syllables creates a pattern that gives the line a definite flow, or *rhythm*. In the case of this nonsense rhyme, the rhythm is very regular (capital letters indicate stressed words or syllables):

> i NEVer SAW a PURple COW,
> i NEVer HOPE to SEE one.
> but I can TELL you ANyHOW,
> i'd RATHer SEE than BE one.

The *ti TUM ti TUM ti TUM* rhythm gives the verse a singsong effect. Also, each line of the verse is *end-stopped;* that is, the words are so arranged that a pause, designated by a punctuation mark, is necessary at the end of each line. These pauses, which call attention to the verse's rhymes, strengthen its singsong effect.

In a nonsense verse like "I Never Saw a Purple Cow," the regular rhythm heightens its humorous effect. In most other types of poetry, however, such absolute rhythmic regularity is uncommon. Pay special attention to rhythm as you read the following lines:

The splendor falls on castle walls
    And snowy summits old in story;
The long light shakes across the lakes,
    And the wild cataract leaps in glory.
5 Blow, bugle, blow, set the wild echoes flying,
Blow, bugle; answer, echoes, dying, dying,
dying.

Alfred, Lord Tennyson
from "The Princess"

1. On which words or syllables in the first line do accents fall? in the second line? the third? the fourth? (Notice how the rhythm changes in the last two lines.)
2. Where is the first pause in the stanza? the second pause?

Line 1 of this stanza overflows into the second line; it is a *run-on* line. Because you do not pause at the end of a run-on line, you do not emphasize the rhyme, thus increasing the poem's rhythmical variety. The variety of the rhythm causes the reader to stress the poem's meaning rather than its rhythm.

Rhythm is everywhere. Even the most CASual EVeryday SPEECH FALLS into RHYTHmic PHRASes. But poets do not use rhythm simply because it exists.

First, rhythm is used because it is enjoyable for its own sake. Think of the pleasure young children get from nursery rhymes. And on all the sidewalks of America children jump rope to chants such as this one.

aLONG CAME the DOCtor!
aLONG CAME the NURSE!
aLONG CAME the LAdy
with the BIG, FAT PURSE!

Second, rhythm allows the poet to fit the movement of the poem to the MOOD he or she is trying to create:

WORK—WORK—WORK
Till the BRAIN beGINS to SWIM!
WORK—WORK—WORK
Till the EYES are HEAVy and DIM!
SEAM, and GUSset, and BAND,
BAND, and GUSset, and SEAM,
Till Over the BUTtons I FALL aSLEEP,
And SEW them ON in a DREAM!

Thomas Hood
from "The Song of the Shirt"

Would you describe the mood of these lines as light and cheerful or heavy and weary? Is the rhythm in keeping with the mood of the lines? Explain.

Third, the poet can use rhythm to emphasize important words. Read these lines aloud:

Hang a lantern aloft in the belfry arch
Of the North Church tower as a signal light,—
One, if by land, or two, if by sea;
And I on the opposite shore will be. . . .

Henry Wadsworth Longfellow
from "Paul Revere's Ride"

1. What words are significant to the meaning of these lines?
2. Which syllables do you emphasize?

■ RHYTHM

A series of stressed and unstressed sounds in a group of words. Rhythm may be regular or it may be varied.

■ Apply to **"The Highwayman"** on page 288

■ SATIRE

Rodrigues,
The Late Look Magazine.

"I remember when you could crawl through this desert and feel safe even at three o'clock in the morning. . . ."

1. According to the cartoon, why is it no longer safe to crawl through the desert?
2. Do you think the cartoonist intended this cartoon to be taken literally? Why or why not?
3. What social problem is the cartoonist commenting on?

The author of the poem below is commenting on a different kind of social problem:

The Ingredients of Expedience

There's a new recipe for water
That's caught on to such a degree
I now pass it on to others
The way it was passed on to me:
5   Into an ocean of fluids
Add a roentgen of fallout or two,
Aluminum cans, detergents
(With the phosphates most pleasing to you).
Stir in ground glass, melted plastics,

10　Any leftovers, sewage, rough waste.
　　Thicken with chemical acids
　　And mix to a pliable paste:
　　Mercury, mustard or nerve gas
　　Well blended with plenty of oil,
15　Insecticides, powdered or liquid,
　　Then slowly bring all to a boil.
　　That's it. Oh, yes, one reminder—
　　And forgive me for throwing a curve—
　　Fish die, but children prefer it
20　If you cool before you serve.

Henry Gibson

1. According to the poem, what is the "new recipe for water"?
2. What is the poet's attitude toward this new kind of water?
3. *Expedience* means "personal advantage" or "self-interest." Who might benefit by having water like that described in the poem?

A literary work in which the author makes fun of the vices or follies of society is called a *satire*. A satire can deal with almost any subject, from minor human absurdity (the existence of a particular clothing fad, for example) to major social and political problems (crime, the futility of war). But all satire has one thing in common: it uses humor, which may range from light-hearted to bitter, to comment on the weakness of people and society.

The purpose of much satire is to draw people's attention to serious social problems and to encourage people to think or act in a certain way. What is the author of "The Ingredients of Expedience" satirizing? How is he trying to influence readers' ideas about the state of our water supply?

Sometimes the language, style, or ideas of a literary work are mimicked for satiric or comic effect. This is called *parody* (par′ə dē).

Read the following parody of a Greek myth and answer the questions that come after:

Endremia and Liason
(From the Greek Mythology)

Endremia was the daughter of Polygaminous, the God of Ensilage, and Reba, the Goddess of Licorice. She was the child of a most unhappy union, it later turned out, for when she was a tiny child her father struck her mother with an anvil and turned himself into a lily pad to avoid the vengeance of Jove. But Jove was too sly for Polygaminous and struck him with a bolt of lightning the size of the Merchants Bank Building which threw him completely off his balance so that he toppled over into a chasm and was dashed to death.

In the meantime, Little Endremia found herself alone in the world with nobody but Endrocine, the Goddess of Lettuce, and her son Bilax, the God of Gum Arabic, to look after her. But, as Polygaminous (her father; have you forgotten so soon, you dope?) had turned Endremia into a mushroom before he turned himself into a lily pad, neither of her guardians knew who she was, so their protection did her no good.

But Jove had not so soon forgotten the daughter of his favorite (Reba), and appeared to her one night in the shape of a mushroom gatherer. He asked her how she would like to get off that tree (she was one of those mushrooms which grow on trees) and get into his basket. Endremia, not knowing that it was Jove who was asking her, said not much. Whereupon Jove unloosed his mighty wrath and struck down the whole tree with a bolt of lightning which he had brought with him in case Endremia wouldn't listen to reason.

This is why it is never safe to eat the mushrooms which grow on trees, or to refuse to get into Jove's basket.

Robert Benchley

1. Compare "Endremia and Liason" to other Greek myths you have read. Is the style similar? the characters? the plot? How is it different?
2. In your opinion, what purpose did the author have in mind in writing "Endremia and Liason"?

■ SATIRE

A literary work in which the author ridicules the vices or follies of people and society, usually for the purpose of producing some change in attitude or action. In *parody*, the language, style, or ideas of another literary work are mimicked for comic or satiric effect.

■ Apply to "**The Lady, or the Tiger?**" on page 396

■ SETTING

Below is the first paragraph of a short story. Read it and answer the questions that follow:

One sunny afternoon in the autumn of the year 1861 a soldier lay in a clump of laurel by the side of a road in western Virginia. He lay at full length upon his stomach, his feet resting upon the toes, his head upon the left forearm. His extended right hand loosely grasped his rifle. But for . . . a slight rhythmic movement of the cartridge box at the back of his belt he might have been thought to be dead. He was asleep at his post of duty . . . if detected he would be dead shortly afterward, death being the just and legal penalty of his crime.

Ambrose Bierce
from "A Horseman in the Sky"

1. Where does the story take place? What details tell you this?
2. When do the events of this story take place? What clues tell you so?

The time and place in which the events of a narrative occur form the *setting*. The place may be a region, a city or town, or even a house or room. The time may be a period in history, a time of year, or a time of day. In some narratives, the setting is specific and detailed, as in the paragraph above, but in others, it may be intentionally obscure:

The stranger rode slowly into the dusty town. His wide-brimmed Stetson was pulled forward on his head, casting a shadow over his gaunt face. The sunlight sparkled on his spurs and on the handle of his gun which hung casually by his right side. He headed straight for the stagecoach office and reined his horse.

1. Where does this event take place? What details tell you this?
2. In approximately what period of history does this event occur? How do you know?

Soon after the successful lift-off, Mission Control received its first communication from the spacecraft *Encounter*. "All systems are GO," reported Astronaut Jake Lewis, whose voice came in loud and clear. "Next stop—the planet Mars!"

1. Where does this take place? How do you know?
2. In approximately what period does it take place? What details tell you this?

"Land ho!" shouted the lookout to the other Vikings. "To starboard, about three miles off!"

1. Where does this take place? How do you know?
2. Is there any indication of time of day? of time in history? Explain.

In some narratives the description of setting is either brief or merely suggested through the use of details scattered throughout the story. An author can suggest the setting by references to articles of clothing, famous historical figures, well-known landmarks, or through the dialect and speech patterns of the characters. Not all stories have a setting in which both the time and place are identifiable.

Frequently a setting which is presented in detail forms an important part of the narrative. It may have an effect on the events of the PLOT; it may reveal character; or it may create a certain MOOD or atmosphere, as in the following example:

At Santa Ysabel del Mar the season was at one of those moments when the air rests quiet over land and sea. The old breezes were gone; the new ones were not yet risen. The flowers in the mission garden opened wide; no wind came by day or night to shake the loose petals from their stems. Along the basking, silent, many-colored shore gathered and lingered the crisp odors of the mountains. The dust hung golden and motionless long after the rider was behind the hill, and the Pacific lay like a floor of sapphire, whereon to walk beyond the setting sun into the East.[1] One white sail shone there. Instead of an hour, it had been from dawn till afternoon in sight between the short headlands; and the Padre[2] had hoped that it might be the ship his homesick heart awaited.

Owen Wister
from "Padre Ignacio"

1. What is the setting of this excerpt?
2. How does setting affect the Padre?

■ SETTING

The time and place in which the events of a narrative occur. The setting may be specific and detailed and introduced at the very beginning of the story, or it may be merely suggested through the use of details scattered throughout the story. In some stories the setting is vital to the narrative: it may have an effect on the events of the PLOT, reveal character, or create a certain atmosphere. In other stories the setting is relatively unimportant.

1. *East*, here, the Orient.

2. *Padre* (pä′drä), father. It is used as a name for a priest, especially in regions where Spanish is spoken.

■ Apply to "**To Build a Fire**" on page 68

■ SIMILE

My heart is like an apple-tree
    Whose boughs are bent with thick-set fruit. . . .

Christina Rossetti
from "A Birthday"

And the muscles of his brawny arms
    Are strong as iron bands.

Henry Wadsworth Longfellow
from "The Village Blacksmith"

In both examples above, comparisons are made. What things are being compared in each? What word in each example tells you that a comparison is being made?

A *simile,* one type of FIGURATIVE LANGUAGE, is a stated comparison between two things that are really very different but that share some common quality. To create a vivid picture, a writer points out the quality they share. Similes are introduced by the use of *like* or *as.* If you were to say "Jason runs *like* the wind and is *as* strong as an ox," you would be using similes.

One important thing to remember is that statements comparing things that are essentially alike are not similes. Statements such as "She looks like her mother" or "She skates as well as I do" are not similes. A simile reveals a similar quality in two elements that are otherwise different.

■ SIMILE (sim′ə lē)

A figure of speech that involves a direct comparison between two unlike things, usually with the words *like* or *as.*

■ Apply to "How Tuesday Began" on page 300

■ STEREOTYPE

Does anything surprise you about this photograph? Although it has become more and more common to see women working at jobs that traditionally have been done by men, it still may be unusual to see women working at physically demanding jobs like this one. Perhaps some people expect to see instead a strong-looking man with a tough manner. These people have a fixed idea, or *stereotype,* in their minds of what a typical repairperson looks and acts like.

Stereotypes are helpful to the cartoonist who wants to make us laugh through a simple sketch, to the author who wishes to create a character in as few words as possible, and to the television or film writer who has only a limited time to spend on characterization. Each relies upon commonly held generalizations to characterize a person, group, issue, etc.

Read the descriptions of stereotyped characters. Then from the choices listed, choose the one that fits the stereotype:

1. wears white hat; rides the range; seldom talks; best friend is horse. (**a**) farmer; (**b**) cowboy; (**c**) gambler; (**d**) dancer.
2. rides in a limousine; wears jewelry; throws elegant parties. (**a**) nurse; (**b**) pilot; (**c**) movie star; (**d**) judge.

PLOTS or situations may also be stereotyped. While watching television you may have had the feeling that you have seen a program before, although the names and characters have been changed. Stereotyped situations or plots include those that have become trite or uninteresting from overuse, such as the disabled airplane with at least one ill passenger or the widow who fights to save the ranch. Can you name other stereotyped plots?

Stereotypes can be misleading and potentially damaging if they lead a reader to accept certain highly generalized views about *real* people and situations. In real life, people and situations are much more complicated.

■ STEREOTYPE (ster′ē ə tīp′)

A fixed, generalized idea about a character or situation. An example of a stereotyped character might be the wicked stepmother in fairy tales; a stereotyped situation might be a plot about a small boy and his brave dog.

■ Apply to "**The Three Garridebs**" on page 176

■ SYMBOL

What does this picture of an eagle suggest to you? If your answer is the United States or perhaps a quality such as courage, strength, or independence, you recognize the eagle as a *symbol*. A symbol may be an object, a person, an action, a situation—anything that suggests a meaning beyond its obvious meaning.

While some symbols suggest the same thing to most people (the heart is a universal symbol of love), other symbols have different meanings for different people. What might a gun symbolize to a hunter? a thief? a soldier?

In the poem that follows, the road is more than just a road. Read the poem carefully and answer the questions that come after:

Uphill

Does the road wind uphill all the way?
    Yes, to the very end.
Will the day's journey take the whole long day?
    From morn to night, my friend.

5 But is there for the night a resting place?
    A roof for when the slow dark hours begin.

May not the darkness hide it from my face?
  You cannot miss that inn.

Shall I meet other wayfarers at night?
10 Those who have gone before.
Then must I knock, or call when just in sight?
  They will not keep you standing at that door.

Shall I find comfort, travel-sore and weak?
  Of labor you shall find the sum.
15 Will there be beds for me and all who seek?
  Yea, beds for all who come.

Christina Rossetti

1. What kind of "journey" do you think is
   being discussed?
2. What does each of the following
   elements represent: (**a**) the road; (**b**) the
   uphill climb; (**c**) the day; (**d**) the night;
   (**e**) the journey's end; (**f**) the inn;
   (**g**) the other wayfarers?

■ SYMBOL

**A person, place, event, or object that has
a meaning in itself but suggests other
meanings as well.**

■ Apply to "**Caged Bird**" on page 312

■ THEME

About Crows

The old crow is getting slow.
  The young crow is not.
Of what the young crow does not know
  The old crow knows a lot.

5 At knowing things the old crow
  Is still the young crow's master.
What does the slow old crow not know?
  How to go faster.

The young crow flies above, below,
10 And rings around the slow old crow.
What does the fast young crow not know?
  Where to go.

John Ciardi

1. What is the chief characteristic of the
   young crow in this poem? What is the
   chief characteristic of the old crow?
2. What accounts for the differences
   between the two crows?
3. Is this poem only about birds? Could
   the comment the speaker makes about
   youth and age be applied to people as
   well? Explain.
4. Which of the following statements best
   expresses the main idea of the poem?
   (**a**) Youthful enthusiasm is often a poor
   substitute for the wisdom of experience.
   (**b**) Don't expend too much energy
   without having a destination in mind.
   (**c**) Although the young crow can fly
   much faster than the old crow, the
   young crow does not know in which
   direction to go.

The main idea of a literary work is called the *theme*. The theme, or main idea, of the poem above is best expressed in statement **a**. Statement **b** presents a moral: it tells the reader how to act. It is not the theme because the poem does not tell the reader how to act or behave. Statement **c** gives the PLOT of the poem, not the theme.

The theme of a story might be the idea that fighting solves nothing. This theme might not be stated anywhere in the story but it will be suggested through the events of the plot and the attitudes of the characters.

It is important also to recognize the difference between the *theme* of a literary work and the *subject* of a literary work. The subject is the topic on which an author has chosen to write. The theme, however, makes some statement about or expresses some opinion on that topic. For instance, in the above example the subject of the story might be war while the theme of the story might be the idea that war is futile.

Not every literary work has a theme. Some are written purely to entertain the reader. A mystery story, for example, written primarily to keep the reader in suspense, may not have a theme.

■ THEME

The main idea or underlying meaning of a literary work. A theme may be stated or implied. Theme differs from the *subject*, or topic, of a literary work in that it involves a statement or opinion about the topic. Not every literary work has a theme.

■ Apply to "**A Lesson in Discipline**" on page 352

■ TONE

Afoot and light-hearted I take to the open road,
Healthy, free, the world before me,
The long, brown path before me leading
    wherever I choose.
Henceforth I ask not good-fortune, I myself
    am good-fortune.
5 Henceforth I whimper no more, postpone no
    more, need nothing,
Done with indoor complaints, libraries,
    querulous criticisms.
Strong and content I travel the open road.

Walt Whitman
from "Song of the Open Road"

1. Does the speaker regret leaving the indoors? Explain.
2. What is this poem about? What might the "open road" represent?
3. What is the speaker's attitude as he sets forth? What words and phrases convey his attitude?

To achieve a complete understanding of most literary works, you must determine how the author feels about the subject and audience. An author's attitude toward the subject and audience is called *tone*. The tone of a literary work serves the same basic purpose as a tone of voice; it helps to indicate the speaker's attitude, whether it is one of anger, sadness, amusement, joy, defiance, or some other emotion. The tone may, in fact, reflect a combination of several different emotions.

Sometimes an author will state directly how he or she feels about a character, a situation, an idea, or the reader. The speaker in the poem, for example, states that he feels "light-hearted," "healthy," "free," "strong," and "content." He addresses the audience as if they were his equals. The attitude, or tone, of Whitman's poem is one of enthusiasm and joyful optimism. Read the following novel excerpt to see whether you can determine the author's attitude:

It was Miss Murdstone who was arrived, and a gloomy-looking lady she was; dark, like her brother, whom she greatly resembled in face and voice, and with very heavy eyebrows, nearly meeting over her large nose. She brought with her two uncompromising hard black boxes, with her initials on the lids in hard brass nails. When she paid the coachman she took her money out of a hard steel purse, and she kept the purse in a very jail of a bag which hung upon her arm by a heavy chain, and shut up like a bite. It seemed that there had never been such a metallic lady altogether as Miss Murdstone was.

Charles Dickens
from *David Copperfield*

1. (a) What sort of woman is being described in this paragraph? Cite specific words that the author uses to describe her. (b) How do her possessions contribute to the picture of this woman?
2. (a) What is the author's attitude toward the woman? How do you know? (b) Is this attitude stated or implied?

In most literary works the author's attitude will not be stated directly, as it is in the excerpt from Whitman's "Song of the Open Road," but will be suggested through the author's choice of words and details. In the paragraph above, for example, Charles Dickens never states that this character is not likable. However, by describing her and her possessions as "gloomy-looking," "dark,"

"uncompromising," and "metallic," he implies his opinion of her and draws the reader into sharing his attitude.

■ TONE

The author's attitude, stated or implied, toward a subject and toward the audience. Some possible attitudes are earnestness, seriousness, bitterness, humor, sympathy, indignation, whimsicality, joy, mockery, cynicism, and irony. An author's tone can be revealed through choice of words and details. Tone should not be confused with MOOD, which is the climate of feeling within a literary work. For example, an author may create a mood of mystery around a character or setting but may treat that character or setting in an ironic, serious, or humorous tone.

■ Apply to **"The Ransom of Red Chief"** on page 364

Winslow Homer, "Homework," 1874. *Canajoharie Library and Art Gallery, NY*

WRITER'S HANDBOOK

WRITER'S HANDBOOK

693

Writing About Literature

Writing a composition about a work of literature is not one enormous job but rather a series of little jobs. This article will give you specific tips on how to apply the three steps of the writing process—prewriting, writing, and revising—to literature assignments.

PREWRITING

Here are some guidelines to help you examine this or any other literature assignment.

Sample Assignment

"The Highwayman" is a narrative poem. Write a four- or five-paragraph essay in which you explain for your classmates how the plot of the poem is like the plot of a story. Illustrate ways in which "The Highwayman" is poetic by giving examples of vivid word choices, comparisons, and sound effects.

1. Identify Purpose

Look at writing assignments for words such as the following, and be sure you know what these words mean:

analyze: examine critically in order to determine the key elements of a work
compare/contrast: point out how things are alike and how they are different
illustrate: make clear by examples, illustrations, comparisons, quotations
describe: give a picture or account of something

explain: make clear something not apparent or understood
discuss: consider all sides of a question
interpret: bring out more than the obvious meaning by using special knowledge or imagination
convince: persuade by argument; give proof
create: produce from one's own thought or imagination
imagine: form an image; put oneself in a new situation
defend: write in favor of an opinion
support: prove ideas, claims, or opinions

2. Identify Audience

Your audience determines the amount of background you give and the vocabulary and tone that you use.

3. Write a Thesis Statement

Assignments that can be written in one paragraph can be developed around a topic sentence, a sentence that states the main idea of the paragraph. For longer compositions you may need a thesis statement. It explains the topic of the paper in one or more sentences and may also express your attitude toward the subject.

4. Take Effective Notes

Begin by rereading the work that you are to write about. For a composition on "The Highwayman," make notes on the development of the plot; then read the poem again and make notes about the poetic language. Your notes may be either direct quotations from the poem or paraphrases, which use your own words.

5. Organize Your Notes

For the sample composition, you would organize your notes according to the different kinds of information requested—information about plot and about the use of vivid words, comparisons, and sound effects. Compare the composition on page 697 with the notes prepared for it. Forms such as charts and cluster diagrams can also be used to organize notes.

WRITING

Plan on *not* handing in your first draft. As you write this draft, don't worry about neatness or correctness; just get your ideas on paper as quickly as possible. If you can't think of a first sentence, leave that for later and begin with the second sentence. You will have a chance to revise later.

REVISING

Ideally, you should have time to set your draft aside for several days. Now reread it. Do your ideas still make sense? Read your draft aloud to yourself. How does it sound? You may also find it helpful to discuss improving the draft with a partner or small group before you revise. As you revise, use these checklists.

Content and Organization

- Is the topic of each paragraph developed fully through use of examples?
- Does each sentence in a paragraph relate to the topic sentence?
- Are ideas presented in a reasonable order?
- Are transitional words and phrases used within and between paragraphs?
- Should any information be added?
- Should some information be dropped or moved?
- Does the concluding paragraph provide a good ending?

Style

- Is language simple and direct?
- Are point of view and tone consistent?
- Are there a variety of sentence types?
- Are too many *and*'s used when other ways of combining sentences are appropriate?
- Are verbs active rather than passive?
- Are tenses of the verbs consistent?
- Are pronoun references clear?
- Are any words, such as *nice* and *good*, overused?

Mechanics

- Is each paragraph indented?
- Are words spelled correctly?
- Are capital letters used correctly?
- Is punctuation used correctly?
- Are there sentence fragments that must be revised?

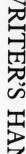

WRITER'S HANDBOOK

1. Introduction (include thesis statement)
2. Plot
   —action-packed
   —major events
     Highwayman promises to return
     Tim betrays him
     Soldiers use Bess as decoy, plan
       ambush
     Bess saves her lover (quote)
     Highwayman dies, seeking revenge
       (quote)
3. Word choices, comparisons
   —characters easy to see
     Highwayman's French cocked hat,
     claret velvet coat, lace, brown doeskin breeches, boots
     Tim, pale, peaked, hollow eyes, mad
     Bess, black hair & eyes, red lips
4. Sound effects, comparisons
   —rhythm fits action
   —words echo meaning (give examples
     about horse and gunshot)
5. Conclusion
   —final examples of good comparisons
     the wind (quote)
     the moon (quote)
     the road (quote)

ASSIGNMENT

Complete either of the assignments on page 22. Follow the steps in the writing process as outlined in this lesson.

The Highwayman

"The Highwayman" is one of my favorite poems because it is like an exciting short, short story. Its plot is easy to follow, and its vivid language, strong comparisons, and sound effects make the characters and events easy to picture.

The plot is action-packed. Tim, a jealous servant, overhears the highwayman promise to come back to Bess after he has stolen some gold. Bess watches for him all day, but at sunset, British soldiers (probably tipped off by Tim) use Bess as a decoy and get ready to shoot the highwayman on sight. Bess, bound and gagged, is tied in a standing position, a musket bound to her side with the barrel pointing to her breast. At midnight, she finally succeeds in working a finger onto the trigger. When she hears the highwayman, "her finger moved in the moonlight/ Her musket shattered the moonlight/ Shattered her breast in the moonlight and warned him—with her death." The highwayman later learns how Bess died and is "shot like a dog on the highway" as he returns seeking his revenge.

The word choices, comparisons, and sound effects make characters and events easy to visualize. The highwayman is a colorful figure, dressed in a French cocked hat, a wine-colored velvet coat with lace at his chin, brown doeskin breeches, and thigh-high boots. Tim has a white and peaked face, hollow and mad eyes, and "hair like moldy hay." Bess is black-eyed and red-lipped. She braids a red love knot into her long, black hair.

When you read the poem aloud, you realize how the fast-paced rhythm fits the fast-paced action and how some words make you hear the sounds they describe. Over the cobbles the highwayman's horse "clattered and clashed." "*Tlot-tlot; tlot-tlot!*" sound the hoofbeats. And when Bess pulls the trigger, the shot "shattered the moonlight."

Even the setting is exciting. When the poem ends, as it began, "when the wind is in the trees/ When the moon is a ghostly galleon tossed upon cloudy seas/ When the road is a ribbon of moonlight over the purple moor," it is easy to see and hear the highwayman riding once more "up to the old inn door."

WRITER'S HANDBOOK

Using Evidence Effectively

When your assignment is to support an idea, you must convince your audience that the idea is sound. You convince them by providing evidence that proves your point.

PREWRITING

Sample Assignment

Read "The Moustache" and then write a short composition in which you evaluate Mike's character, using examples from the story to support your opinion.

Here are some guidelines to help you with the sample assignment.

1. Go to the Source

First, go back and read the piece of writing carefully. As you do, take notes about Mike's appearance, speech, and actions. Note as well how other characters react to him. There are two ways to record these notes.

direct quotations—You might take material directly from the story. In a direct quotation, you copy the author's words exactly as they appear. These words are always enclosed in quotation marks.

paraphrase—You can also note information in your own words. For example, to paraphrase the information from paragraph 2 on page 5, you might write that Mike's reaction to his grandmother's hands shows that he is sensitive both to his own feelings and to other people.

2. Choose Your Examples

Look over the notes you have taken and select the items that will most strongly support your ideas. Ask yourself: Is this evidence convincing? Am I convinced? Will my readers be?

Suppose you want to support the idea that Mike is typical of young people his age and also sensitive, insightful, and caring. You must choose evidence that relates directly to your point. Among your strongest evidence will be information showing Mike's concern about his appearance and his relationship with Cindy, his fondness for his grandmother and his efforts to spare her more hurt, and the understanding he gains from his experience. Your weakest evidence is unsupported opinion: You like this character and so he must have good qualities. Avoid making statements that are true but beside the point: Mike gets along well with his sister's boyfriend.

3. Arrange Your Examples

Arrange your evidence in an order that makes sense. If you plan to prove that Mike is both typical of someone his age and also very sensitive, insightful, and caring, you arrange your evidence in the same order that the qualities are listed, starting with evidence that Mike is typical and going through the other qualities in order.

In other compositions, you might organize chronologically, according to cause and effect, or by order of importance, with the most important evidence placed last.

WRITING

4. Explain Your Idea

State your idea in the first sentence or two. Follow with your examples. Be sure to explain how each piece of evidence relates to your idea.

5. End Forcefully

After presenting your last piece of evidence, bring your composition to a quick and forceful conclusion. You might summarize your evidence and restate your main point, rewording it slightly.

REVISING

When you have completed your first draft, evaluate it by using the checklist of content and organization, style, and mechanics on page 695. In addition, look for the following things.

- Is the idea stated clearly?
- Do the examples support the idea?
- Does the paper end with a summary of the evidence and a restatement of the main idea?

You will find this article helpful in completing the assignments on pages 108, 255, and 566.

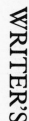

Writing a Clear Description

It would be surprising if a day passed when you did not describe something: the shoes you'd like to buy, a new classmate, a football play. Now you are asked to write a description. Where do you start?

PREWRITING

Sample Assignment

Describe both the appearance and character of Ichabod Crane.

1. Form a Mental Picture

Visualize what you are going to describe. Fill in as much detail as you can.

2. Decide What Impression You Want to Create

What makes your subject special? What do you want readers to see and feel about the subject as they read your description?

3. Choose Details

Jot down all important specific details from the picture you have visualized. If you are writing about a literary selection, reread it to sharpen details. If you are writing about Ichabod, you'd certainly reread the narrator's description of how Ichabod looks, walks, and behaves. You might list these details.

> *Ichabod Crane*
> tall and thin, hands "like shovels"
> sticking "a mile out of his sleeves"
> looks like a walking scarecrow
> greedy (food, Katerina's farm)
> long nose, huge ears, glassy eyes
> (respected because he's the
> schoolteacher)

4. Choose a Method of Presentation

You can arrange details in a number of ways. If you are writing about Ichabod, you might begin with physical description, go on to describe his actions and how others view him, and conclude with your own opinion of the character. If you were describing a dark street at night, you might organize details from near to far, from far to near, from the sidewalk up, or from the tops of the buildings down to the street and sidewalks. Look over your details and choose an arrangement that suits them.

WRITING

5. Create a Picture

Use words that appeal to the five senses. If you are describing a dark street at night, don't simply say that the street is frightening. Show this with your choice of details.

> *sight:* dim streetlights cast only small
> circles of light
> *sound:* rustle of old newspapers blown
> by wind, murmur of distant traffic
> *smell:* dampness, stench of garbage
> *touch:* clammy fog, chilling wind

Another way to convey your ideas is to use precise, forceful words. Streetlights don't *shine* they *cast small circles of light.* Old newspapers don't *move;* they *rustle.*

Use an occasional comparison to make a description more vivid. Notice how effective the narrator is when he tells us that Ichabod looks like a walking scarecrow, that Ichabod's hands are like shovels, that his nose looks like a weathervane.

REVISING

In addition to the checklist questions on page 695, ask yourself:
- Does the description create a main impression?
- Does it show rather than tell?
- Have you used precise, forceful words and comparisons?

You will find this article helpful in completing the assignments on pages 22, 228, and 395.

Writing to Compare and Contrast

Often writing assignments ask you to compare and contrast two characters, incidents, objects, ideas, or selections. With such an assignment, you must do three things: You must find likenesses, you must find differences, and you must find an effective way to organize this material.

PREWRITING

Sample Assignment

After reading "Top Man," compare and contrast Osborn and Nace as mountain climbers.

1. List Points of Comparison

Whether the assignment is general ("Compare the characters of Osborn and Nace") or specific ("Compare Osborn and Nace as mountaineers"), take time to list points of comparison.

For example, if you are comparing the two men as mountain climbers, the points of comparison might be as follows:

background and experience
attitude toward climbing
methods
judgments

As you review the material you are writing about, you probably will drop some points and add others. But starting with such points will help you get organized.

2. Make Charts

Record information from your list on a chart such as this:

MARTIN NACE	PAUL OSBORN
Background and Experience	
Official in Indian Civil Service	1 year out of college
Explored & climbed in Himalayas for 20 years	Many spectacular ascents in Alps & Rockies
Member of 5 British expeditions to K3	Reputation as "most skilled & audacious" of younger American climbers
Attitude	
Matter of fact, cautious, slow	Overwhelming desire to act, to conquer
"The apostle of trial-and-error & watchful waiting"	Wants to take short, straight line
Utter concentration on problem at hand	Becomes irked over difference of opinion
Spirit deep inside him—patient, indomitable	Given to temper
	Thinks Nace is "through"
Methods ("utterly dissimilar")	
Slow, methodical	Magnificent—peerless mountaineer
Unspectacular	Attacks mountain head on
Studies mountain, spars with it, wears it down	Always discovering new routes & short cuts
Judgments	
His instant decision saves lives of men	Rashly eager
Careful approach	Doesn't want to wait & test
Saves Osborn's life	Puts his own life in danger

3. Form an Opinion

Form an opinion on the comparisons you are making. If you write that opinion as a sentence, it might become your thesis statement: Nace [or Osborn] is the better mountaineer.

4. Choose a Pattern of Organization

You might choose to organize your paper by comparing or contrasting your subjects point by point, writing a sentence or two for each item. Or you might discuss one of the subjects first and then turn to the other, or discuss likenesses and then differences.

WRITING

5. Write Your Composition

Begin with a statement that identifies what you will compare and contrast and why. Then follow with details arranged in the pattern you have chosen.

6. Use Words That Signal

Show how your examples are related by using words that signal likenesses: *comparably, both, alike.* Signal differences with *but, yet, on the other hand.*

REVISING

In addition to using the checklist on page 695, consider the following questions:
• Are your points of comparison clear?
• Is your organization pattern consistent?
• Have you used words that emphasize likenesses and differences?

You will find this article helpful in completing the assignments on pages 250, 297, and 550.

Writing to Summarize

Writing book reports, reviews of books or plays, and assignments asking you to tell what happens in a story, poem, or article all require that you be able to write a summary. A good summary is short, concise, and accurate.

PREWRITING

Sample Assignment

Summarize "The Ballad of William Sycamore."

Think It Through

Remember the following information on writing a summary.

Summaries should be short. If you are summarizing events in a short piece of writing, one paragraph is enough. If you are summarizing an entire book, you will need two or three paragraphs.

A summary should also be accurate. If you cannot remember an important piece of information, look back and find it; don't guess. A summary should be written in the present tense.

A summary of a piece of fiction usually follows the plot development and includes only the main events. A summary of nonfiction is made up of main ideas.

WRITING

Here is a summary of the poem, "The Ballad of William Sycamore."

> Born in a cabin on the Appalachian frontier, William Sycamore enjoys a pioneer's childhood. When he is grown and married, his travels follow the westward expansion of the United States. Finally civilization catches up with him, and there is no more unsettled land to move on to. Knowing that there is no place for him now, he chooses to die as he has lived. He is buried in the land he loves so much.

REVISING

In addition to reviewing the checklist on page 695, ask yourself these questions.
• Have I included only the main ideas or the main events in the plot?
• Does the summary tell who did what, when, where, and why?
• Is the summary short?
• Is it accurate?
• Have I used present-tense verbs?
• Have I combined sentences?

You will find this article helpful in completing the assignments on pages 100, 263, and 438.

Writing About Plot

Plot refers to a series of related events selected by the author to present and bring about the resolution of some internal or external conflict. In a carefully constructed plot, details and incidents are selected and arranged so that each is a necessary link leading to the outcome of the story.

PREWRITING

Composition assignments about plot may require that you discuss the plot as a whole or examine only one aspect of it.

Sample Assignment

For a plot to be effective, readers must be presented with a conflict or problem. The events of the plot should be linked in a cause-and-effect pattern that leads to the turning point and then to the resolution of the problem or conflict. "Mr. Mendelsohn" does not contain a great deal of action. Does it have an effective plot? In a three- or four-paragraph composition, discuss the plot of "Mr. Mendelsohn."

1. Examine the Framework of the Plot

Here is one way to chart the plot of "Mr. Mendelsohn."

Conflict
Mr. Mendelsohn and his loneliness
Mr. Mendelsohn and his sisters
 	
Climax
Suarez family moves
Mr. Mendelsohn moves
   to retirement home
 	
Resolution
Mr. Mendelsohn dies
His sister finds
   Tato's picture
	Sequence of Events
	Mr. Mendelsohn often joins the Suarez family for meals; six months later, he is spending more time with the Suarez family than he does at home; gradually, over several years, Mr. Mendelsohn becomes part of the Suarez family, becoming especially close to Tato, the baby

2. Reread the Assignment

Read over the assignment again, asking yourself questions such as these.

- Are the events linked together in a cause-and-effect relationship?
- Does the turning point follow the events naturally, or does it seem forced?
- Is the conclusion satisfactory?

WRITING

Here is the first paragraph of a composition written about the plot of "Mr. Mendelsohn."

The short story "Mr. Mendelsohn" by Nicholasa Mohr contains more internal than external conflict. There is not much physical action in the story, but it does contain an effective plot. Main events in the plot are linked in a cause-and effect relationship that leads to the climax. The turning point of the action leads naturally to the conclusion.

In the rest of the paper, the writer must explain each point made in the opening paragraph.

REVISING

When you have completed your first draft, evaluate it with the checklist on page 695.

Here are some specific points that you should also check.

- Is the connection between events clear?
- Have I used examples from the selection to support my judgment about the effectiveness of the plot?

You will find this article helpful in completing the assignments on pages 114 and 556.

Writing About Characters

Fictional characters can often make a lasting impression on you, just as some real people do. How do writers achieve such effective characterization? When you are asked to write a composition about characters, follow the guidelines in this article.

PREWRITING

Sample Assignment

Choose the most unusual but believable character you have read about in this book. Explain what makes the character both unique and realistic. Give examples from the selection to support your ideas.

1. Think It Through

When you are given an assignment such as this, choose a selection and review it with the specific assignment in mind. Also consider the following questions.

Who are the major characters and who are the minor ones? Most of the attention in a story will center on the main character or characters. In "The Treasure of Lemon Brown," Greg and Lemon Brown are the major characters. Minor characters, though these may not be fully developed, can make a critical difference in what happens to the main characters, as Greg's father does in "The Treasure of Lemon Brown." (If Greg had not quarreled with his father, he would never have met Lemon Brown.)

How does the author create characters on paper? You will remember that writers reveal character through physical description, by showing actions and speech, and by revealing what other characters say. Consider these methods as you review a selection. Make notes of examples that you might use in your composition.

Do the character's motives seem to fit the kind of person the character is shown to be? Well-developed characters act as they do for specific reasons. When writing about a particular character, try to figure out what motivates that character. Are the actions consistent with the kind of person the author has created?

Is the character a stereotype or a unique individual? Story characters come alive when they are like real people. What makes Lemon Brown so special?

2. Organize Details

If you were given the sample assignment, you might choose to write about the character of Lemon Brown. You would then review the story, putting your notes on a chart similar to this one.

Appearance	Behavior	Effect on Other Characters
old, small, frail dressed in rags and castoff clothing a "street person"	challenges Greg when they meet defends himself against the thugs expresses unique philosophy: "If you know your pappy did something . . ." "Every man got a treasure" "What else a man got 'cepting what he can pass on . . ."	son Jesse also valued Lemon's treasure, carried it into battle with him Lemon's pride as a father causes Greg to look again at his own father

WRITING

Here is the first paragraph of a paper written for the sample assignment.

Sweet Lemon Brown, the old man in the short story "The Treasure of Lemon Brown" by Walter Dean Myers, is a memorable character because he thinks and acts in surprising ways. Both Lemon Brown's appearance and the way in which he lives suggest he will be a helpless victim. Yet the reader, like Greg in the story, learns valuable lessons from Lemon's philosophy.

In the other paragraphs in the paper, information from the chart would be used to support each of the points made in the first paragraph.

REVISING

When you have completed the first draft of your composition, evaluate it, either alone or with others, by going through the checklist on page 695. Here are some other points about characters to check.

- Is the character portrayed accurately, as he or she appears in the story?
- Are there examples from the story to support the character traits discussed?

You will find this article helpful in completing the assignments on pages 362, 409, and 523.

Writing Dialogue

A dialogue is a conversation. Dialogue, of course, appears in drama, but it is also used in other kinds of fiction and in nonfiction as well.

PREWRITING
Sample Assignment

Write a dialogue between the speaker in "The Tell-Tale Heart" and the attorney assigned to defend him at his trial for the murder of the old man.

1. Think It Through

Before beginning an assignment asking you to write dialogue, review these important points about good written conversation.

Dialogue imitates the way people talk in real life. People often leave out words or speak in incomplete sentences. Look at these examples from "The Moustache."

"It was never the same after that night, was it, Mike? The glitter was gone. From you. From us. And then the accident . . ."

Dialogue should suit the person who is speaking. Note that Laurie, the kindergartener in Shirley Jackson's story, "Charles," speaks as you would expect a child that age to talk.

"Because she tried to make him color with red crayons," Laurie said. "Charles wanted to color with green crayons, so he hit the teacher and she spanked him and said nobody play with Charles but everybody did."

Dialogue advances the story. Any conversation between characters should move along the action of the story or advance the plot. Note how this dialogue from "A Christmas Memory" provides details of both plot and setting.

"The courthouse bell sounded so cold and clear. And there were no birds singing; they've gone to warmer country, yes indeed. Oh, Buddy, stop stuffing biscuit and fetch our buggy. Help me find my hat. We've thirty cakes to bake."

Dialogue is indicated with the use of quotation marks. Whenever a character speaks, quotation marks are placed around that speaker's words. A new paragraph is used to show a change in speaker. Because plays are made up mostly of dialogue, they are an exception. Quotation marks and indenting are not used, and each speaker's name is printed to the left of the words spoken.

WRITER'S HANDBOOK

WRITING

Here is an example of dialogue written for the sample assignment. Are the man's words in keeping with the way he is characterized in the story?

"Hello, I'm Mary Sotak from the Public Defender's office. I will be the attorney on your case," she said as she offered her hand to the man sitting across from her.

He did not look up. "Miss Sotak, I am not insane, but I fear I shall be unable to speak with you at this time. Why will they not look beneath the planks, tear up the floor, and still the beating of the heart? I cannot think clearly, it beats in my ear so loud."

"I believe they did tear up the floor. But his heart was no longer beating."

"Ah, you. You too make a mockery of me. I hear it still. I swear by all I know, I hear it now. Even as we speak . . ."

"We must discuss an insanity plea."

REVISING

When you have completed the first draft of your dialogue, use the checklist on page 695. In addition, consider the following:
• Are the exact words enclosed in quotation marks?
• Are the words spoken consistent with the character in the story, or with the character created by the writer of the dialogue?
• Is each change of speaker indicated by a new paragraph?

You will find this article helpful in completing the assignments on pages 31, 310, and 373.

Writing a Story

You've read many stories, studied and discussed the elements that make up a good story, and evaluated according to what you learned. Now you get to write one of your own.

PREWRITING

Sample Assignment

Write a brief story on a topic of your choice. Use what you have learned about plot, character, setting, and point of view to make your story as good as it can be.

1. Brainstorm Story Ideas

Brainstorm story ideas with a partner or small group. Make a list of all the possibilities mentioned. Save any ideas you don't use for later assignments. (If you are keeping a reading/writing log, it is an excellent place to put the list. You can then add to it as other ideas occur to you.) To help your brainstorming group get started, you might begin with these headings. List as many possibilities as you can under each.

> People Our Age
> Adults Who Made a Difference
> Imaginary Creatures
> Fictional Characters I Like
> Lessons I've Learned
> Perfect Places
> Victories
> Real Places
> Imaginery Places

2. Consider Your Options

The items in the list above can all be classified according to plot, character, or setting. Which of the three interests you most? Select one of these topics to explore further.

3. Explore Possibilities

Now either list details of character or setting or chart your plot. The order doesn't matter. As you work with each element, consider the following questions. Use the Handbook of Literary Terms to review any terms you are unsure of.

Setting

Where and when does the story take place?

Does setting affect mood?

Is setting important to the action?

Plot

What is the situation at the beginning of the story?

How does the situation change? Why?

What is the climax?

How is the conflict resolved?

Character

What special qualities does the main character have?

What does the main character look like?

Does the character face external or internal struggle?

4. Decide on Point of View

Where do you plan to stand in relation to your characters? Ask yourself these questions.

Will you put yourself in the story as an omniscient (all-seeing) narrator? If so, you can tell everything that all the characters see, feel, think, and do.

Will you limit yourself to *one* character's point of view? If so, you will write only what that one character sees, thinks, feels, and does.

Will one of your characters tell the story? If so, your pronouns will be first-person pronouns.

Will someone outside the action tell the story? If so, your pronouns will be third-person pronouns.

Once you choose a point of view, stay with it throughout your story.

WRITING

Now use your prewriting notes to write the first draft of your story. As you write, use these techniques.

WRITER'S HANDBOOK

5. Tell About Your Characters

Make statements that reveal distinctive characteristics. These statements from "Top Man" are important because they reveal contrasts between two characters who compete for leadership.

> "Osborn was twenty-three and a year out of college, a compact buoyant mass of energy and high spirits."
> "Nace was in his forties—lean, taciturn, introspective."

This description from "Paw Paw" is important because it shares with readers Casey's first sight of Paw Paw.

> ". . . the door swung open and I saw a tiny, pleasant, round-faced woman smiling at me. Her cheeks were a bright red. Her gray hair was all curly and frizzy around her head and a pair of rimless, thick eyeglasses perched on her nose."

6. Use Dialogue

Note how dialogue adds interest and helps readers visualize the characters of "Red Chief," as well as those of Laurie, and "Charles."

> "I like this fine. I never camped out before; but I had a pet 'possum once, and I was nine last birthday. I hate to go to school. Rats ate up sixteen of Jimmy Talbot's aunt's speckled eggs. Are there any real Indians in these woods? I want some more gravy. Does the trees moving make the wind blow? We had five puppies. What makes your nose so red, Hank? My father has lots of money. Are the stars hot?"

> "You know what Charles did today?" Laurie demanded at the lunch table, in a voice slightly awed. "He told a little girl to say a word and she said it and the teacher washed her mouth out with soap and Charles laughed."

7. Show What Characters Do

The emphasis is on showing, not telling. This passage *shows* why Mrs. Luella Bates Washington Jones was not an easy mark for a young purse-snatcher.

> "The strap broke with the tug the boy gave it from behind. But the boy's weight and the weight of the purse caused him to lose his balance. Instead of taking off full blast, the boy fell on his back on the sidewalk, and his legs flew up. The large woman simply turned around and kicked him right square in his blue-jeaned sitter. She shook him until his teeth rattled. Then she reached down and picked the boy up by his shirt."

REVISING

When you have finished your first draft, evaluate it using the checklist on page 695. You should also look for these things.

- Is there a clear pattern of events?
- Is there a turning point in the action and a satisfying conclusion for the story?
- Does the main character come alive?
- If the time and place are important, are they adequately described?

You will find this article helpful as you complete assignments on pages 55, 121, and 550.

Writing About Poetry

Writing a composition about poetry is similar to writing about other types of literature. You follow a series of steps as you plan, write, and revise your assignment.

PREWRITING

Sample Assignment

Discuss and evaluate the effectiveness of imagery in the poem "How Tuesday Began."

1. Identify Purpose

First examine what the assignment asks you to do. If necessary, review the definitions of key words in "Writing About Literature," page 694.

2. Review Literary Terms

When an assignment specifies that you write about a particular literary term, make sure you are certain of what that term means. If necessary, review it in the Handbook of Literary Terms. You might want to note the definition so that you can check it as you plan your composition.

Imagery: Concrete details that appeal to the senses of sight, sound, touch, taste, and smell as well as to internal feelings and emotions.

3. Reread the Poem

Read the poem aloud. Then reread it, looking for examples of the literary technique you are to discuss.

4. Take Notes

If you were asked to write about rhyme in a particular poem, you'd note whether the poem had a regular pattern of end rhyme or whether it contained internal rhyme. If you were asked to write about similes, you'd find and note these.

The notes on the next page were made for the sample assignment.

Character	Image	Sense
Woman	black; green housedress	sight
	large—fills aisle	sight
	sits slowly (lines 18–19)	sight
	sighs	hearing
	unhappy (lines 21, 40–41)	
	rolls fearlessly with the movement of bus, like a "rubber lifeboat" (lines 30–32)	sight, touch
	grabs old woman and seats her safely (lines 37–39, 43)	sight, hearing, touch
	says something kind	hearing
Old Woman	old; slow; trembles	sight, touch
	can't see; "vague" eyes (line 25–26)	sight
	fearful	sight
	stranded; tries to move through bus "seat by seat" (line 29)	sight

WRITING

Here is the first paragraph of a composition written for the sample assignment.

In the first line of "How Tuesday Began" by Kathleen Fraser, the speaker says that she does not want to lose the memory of something that happened as she rode the bus on Tuesday morning. Through her use of imagery in the rest of the poem, Kathleen Fraser both brings that memory to life and preserves it for readers.

In the body of the paper, the writer must discuss images in the poem and how these images help readers to visualize the event. Restating the thesis statement would provide an effective conclusion.

REVISING

Use the checklists on page 695 to check your organization, style, and mechanics. Then look for these points before you write your final draft.
- Have you correctly identified the literary term you are to discuss?
- Have you correctly identified the examples of the term in the poem?
- Does your discussion of the term support the statement you made in your introductory paragraph?

You will find this article helpful in completing assignments on pages 306 and 325.

11

Writing a Poem

In some eighth-grade classrooms, students write every day about what matters to them. Many students turn by choice to writing poetry to express their feelings. That's right, they choose to write poetry.

PREWRITING

If you choose to write a poem, you probably know what you want to write about. If you are asked to write a poem, you may need some help determining your topic. Here's what you might do to get yourself started.

1. Write About What You Know

As you will find when you study Unit 4, poems are written on every topic imaginable. Because there are no suitable and unsuitable topics for poems, you can write on any topic that is familiar to you. One eighth-grader wrote a very good poem on the rules in study hall. Another described her feelings after she had just gotten her hair cut very short. They wrote successfully on what they know. You can do the same.

2. Look Before You Write

If you use general terms to describe your experience, chances are your reader will feel nothing. "Cats are interesting animals. Asleep or awake, quiet or noisy, they are really entertaining pets." But when you observe closely and take careful note of what you are observing, you make your experience come alive. Rosalie Moore tells of cats, and here are cats you can see and hear. Reread "Catalogue," noting the

specific details used. When you write about what you know, observe it closely. Write a list of specifics, using words that appeal to as many senses as possible.

WRITING

As you write the first draft of your poem, keep these points in mind.

3. Let Images Do Your Talking

If you speak about your own special thoughts and feelings in very general terms, you may diminish them, or make them appear less important than they actually are. For example, if you were to write "What would life be like if we didn't have goals and the hope that we will achieve those goals?" This sounds like the beginning of an uninspired sermon. Langston Hughes in "Dreams" uses two images that show such a life: When dreams die, life is a "broken-winged bird" and an empty field "frozen with snow."

4. Try Short Lines

If you are just beginning to write poetry, don't try to force your ideas and images into lines that rhyme or have a set pattern of rhythm. Think of each line as a means you might use to make certain words stand out.

WRITER'S HANDBOOK

For an example of how effective this technique can be, reread "Snow Sculpture" on page 307. In this poem we first look at the slow work of sun and freeze on heaps of snow piled along sides of streets by snowplows; then we see the word "assume"—all by itself—before we see how the snow takes on new and wonderful shapes, like sculpture in a garden.

Use Words That Suggest or Imitate Sounds

If your poem is about a dog barking, you obviously must search for words that either sound like barking or describe this sound. That's what Louis Untermeyer does in "Dog at Night," using words such as *bark, howls, bow-wow,* and *bellowing.*

REVISING

After you have written your poem, evaluate it according to this list.
- Do the words create an experience to which readers will respond?
- Is the rhythm appropriate to the subject and mood of the poem?

You will find this article helpful in completing composition assignments on pages 255, 303, and 340.

12 Writing About Nonfiction

You read many different types of nonfiction—biographies, autobiographies, articles, essays. At times you may be asked to judge whether a particular piece of writing is a good example of the kind of nonfiction it is.

PREWRITING
Sample Assignment

"Treasure Hunt" is an article about the continuing search for buried treasure on Oak Island. Write a composition in which you discuss ways the author conveys information on this subject. Then evaluate whether the author has successfully conveyed this information.

1. Analyze the Assignment

As you would with any composition assignment, think about what you are being asked to do. You might want to restate the assignment, numbering the tasks:

1. Discuss how author conveys information.
2. Did he do a good job?

2. Reread the Selection

Now look back at the selection. Keep in mind what the assignment asks you to do.

Ways of Presenting Information		
Details	**Character Descriptions, Quotations**	**Background, Facts**
Who—is digging for treasure? (Daniel Blankenship) What—a shaft to explore for buried treasure Where—in a shaft 150' deep, Borehole 10-X Where—Oak Island, in Mahone Bay, off Halifax, Nova Scotia Why—to find buried treasure	Daniel Blankenship— cheerful, brave, optimistic, wealthy, Does his own digging David Tobias— older, wealthy, working on this for 20 years C. Brown—impulsive, enthusiastic, wealthy Mildred Restall—bitter (lost family), contemptuous, thinks they are wasting their time	On treasure (might be booty of Sir Francis Drake or Spanish ships) On efforts to reach it Of original discovery of tunnels Of claims on land by various people

3. Take Notes

You might organize notes for the assignment on "Treasure Hunt" on a chart such as this one.

4. Study Your Notes

Look at the headings in the chart. These should tell you what information the writer set out to convey. Now make a judgment: Did the writer do a good job? Would using other techniques have improved the article by making it more informative?

5. Write a Thesis Statement

After evaluating information in your notes, write a thesis statement. This statement will help you organize your paper and may also serve as your opening paragraph.

WRITING

Read the first paragraph of a paper written for the sample assignment.

D'Arcy O'Connor's use of details, character description and quotations, and historical information all help explain what this treasure hunt is about. Using more than one means of conveying information adds variety and interest. If the author had presented only facts, readers would have no idea of the human drama created by this continuing search for buried pirate treasure.

REVISING

Evaluate your first draft by using the checklist on page 695 and these questions:
• Have you stated your thesis clearly?
• Have you included enough information?

You will find this article helpful as you complete assignments on pages 242 and 255.

WRITER'S HANDBOOK

Writing as a Story Character

Understanding characters—how they think, react, and speak—is one of the great pleasures of reading. We learn about characters' various backgrounds, become involved in familiar and unfamiliar situations, discover why they do what they do. When we live their lives, we enrich our own.

PREWRITING
Sample Assignment

Assume that you are Charlie Gordon in "Flowers for Algernon." Describe a meeting between you and a newspaper reporter who is interviewing you about the intelligence you gained after your operation.

Here are some suggestions to help you write as a story character.

1. Examine the Assignment

Assignments may be specific, such as the sample above. Such assignments tell you exactly what to do. If you were given an assignment such as this, you should reread the selection and make notes on what you need in order to write your paper.

Assignments may also be general. ("What do you think Joe Carp and Frank Reilly say about Charlie after Charlie becomes a genius?") If your assignment is general, you have free choice in what you say. You may make up incidents and speeches that fit the characters and the situations.

Whether the assignment to write as a story character is specific or general, you should make notes about the character's background, motivation, and situation.

2. List Background Information

Think about the character's background. Consider sex, age, education, where he or she is from, or anything else that seems relevant. The more you know about your character, the easier it is to understand how that person thinks and acts. Look at these notes for the sample assignment.

Background of Charlie Gordon
Employment: janitor
Place of work: Donnegan's Plastic Box Co.
Education: in a class for slow adults; slow reader, poor grammar, can't spell. All *before* operation.
Friends: Joe and Frank. Charlie thinks they are his friends.

3. Discuss Behavior

What makes the character behave as he or she does? Behavior may be the result of internal thoughts and feelings, such as Charlie Gordon's desire to be smart. It may be dictated by outside forces, such as Dr. Strauss's requirement that Charlie tell no one about the purpose of the operation. Note all motives for a character's behavior.

Charlie's Motives
Wants to be smart like other people
Wants people to like him
Wants to have friends

4. Consider the Situation
People express themselves differently in different situations. For example, a character would feel and speak one way if in danger and quite differently if relaxing after a meal. Consider the situation your character is in.

Situation When Charlie Gordon Is Interviewed
Knows how to read well and write skillfully
Realizes that Joe and Frank have made fun of him
Realizes that people once laughed at him because he was dumb
Fascinated by what he learns from books

5. Decide How Characters Will Speak
People from different backgrounds speak in different ways. Study the selection to see how your character speaks. Does he or she use common everyday words or a more sophisticated vocabulary? Are sentences long or short?

WRITING
You may find it most effective to write from the first-person point of view. Here is the first paragraph of a composition written for the Sample Assignment.

A man from the newspaper came today to interview me. I was worried that he would ask me a lot of questions that were embarrassing, but I actually enjoyed talking to him. I think that's because I never saw him before today. I never knew him when I was stupid. He did not look at me the way others do— half worried, half afraid.

REVISING
Use the checklist on page 695 to evaluate your first draft. In addition, ask yourself the following questions.
- Does the character sound like the person portrayed in the story? Are the ideas and emotions consistent with what I know about the character?
- If I have not used the first-person point of view, would doing so have made my paper more effective?

You will find this article helpful in completing the assignments on pages 43, 108, and 362.

Writing to Persuade

You use persuasion every day—with your family, with your friends, and at school. In order to be effective when you persuade, it is not enough to say "I'm right." You must present reasons or arguments. These arguments must be based on facts and organized in a logical way.

PREWRITING
Sample Assignment

What causes the downfall of the man in "To Build a Fire"? Is it fate, bad luck, inexperience, cold weather, foolishness, or something else? Support your opinion with evidence from the story.

Use these guidelines when you are asked to express and defend an opinion.

1. State Your Opinion

Having already read the story, you may be prepared to write an initial opinion. Write this down as clearly and forcefully as you can.

The downfall of the man was caused not by fate or cold or accident but by his own foolishness.

Do not write:

It seems to me that maybe the man's downfall . . .

You may eventually use your statement of opinion as your thesis statement. For now, it will help you focus on, and organize, your evidence.

2. Reread the Selection

Look for facts and examples that you can use as evidence to support your statement. If you are having trouble finding evidence, reevaluate your statement and, if necessary, change it.

3. Make Notes

Write the details from the selection that support your position. Your notes might look something like these:

man "without imagination"
"not much given to thinking"
"This man did not know cold"
ignored the advice of old timer at
    Sulphur Creek
"It was his own fault, or rather, his
    mistake."

The statements listed are factual. You can look them up. Another source of information is evidence based on inference, generalizing, logic, and common sense. Can you infer that prolonged exposure to the cold had a deadly effect on the man's mind, as well as on his body? Yes. Although the reader is told that the man plans to run until he reaches camp, the weight of the evidence is against his attaining this goal. Note all such inferences that you are able to make.

4. Test the Soundness of Your Opinion

Review your notes, looking for the three or four strongest points to back up your opinion. Avoid words and phrases such as *always, every, never, none, everyone knows,* and *no one believes.* These words usually begin sweeping generalizations. How can you possibly prove that *nobody* thinks in a certain way? Such statements are meant to make your argument more convincing, but in fact will weaken it.

WRITING

5. Arrange your Evidence

Begin your paper with your thesis statement. Then organize a paragraph around each piece of evidence. Start each paragraph with a topic sentence. Save your strongest argument for last. Drive your composition toward a strong conclusion instead of letting it sputter out like an engine out of gas.

6. Finish Strong and Fast

Once you've made your final (and best) point, quickly bring your paper to a close. Summarize your evidence to form your conclusion.

WRITING

Here is the beginning of one writer's sample assignment.

The downfall of the man was caused not by fate or cold or accident but by his own foolishness. Evidence throughout the story suggests that the man is foolish. Readers are told that he is "not much given to thinking." He is also "without imagination." By ignoring the advice of those with experience in arctic travel, he shows his foolishness. By being unable to imagine the effects of extreme cold, he is unprepared to deal with them.

Paragraphs following this introduction would give specific evidence to back up each point made in the thesis statement.

REVISING

Working alone or with a partner, use these questions and the checklists on page 695 to evaluate your first draft.
- Read your draft aloud. Is the evidence convincing? Would more detail from the selection make it more convincing?
- Does the first sentence of each paragraph state the main idea of that paragraph?
- Read the first and last paragraphs. Does the last fulfill the promise of the first?

You will find this article helpful in completing the assignments on pages 100, 395, and 546.

WRITER'S HANDBOOK

GLOSSARY OF LITERARY TERMS

Words in SMALL CAPITAL LETTERS refer you to other entries in the Glossary of Literary Terms.

alliteration (ə lit'ə rā'shən), the REPETITION of consonant sounds at the beginnings of words or within words. "Curiosity killed the cat" is an example of alliteration.

biography (bī og'rə fē), any account of a real person's life written by someone else. *Autobiography* is the story of part or all of a person's life written by the person who lived it.

characterization (kar'ik tər ə zā'shən), the methods an author uses to acquaint a reader with the characters in a work.

connotation (kon'ə tā'shən), the emotional associations surrounding a word, as opposed to its literal meaning. The words *homesick*, *grandfather*, and *Thanksgiving* have emotional associations for most people.

denotation (dē'nō tā'shən), the literal meaning of a word; the definition in a dictionary.

dialogue, the conversation between one or more people in a literary work. Dialogue is the chief means of moving the plot along in a play.

drama, a composition in prose or verse written to be acted on a stage or before motion-picture or television cameras, or in front of a microphone. The story is told through DIALOGUE alone in a radio drama and through dialogue and action in other types of plays.

end rhyme, the rhyming of words at the ends of lines of poetry.

essay, a brief composition that presents a personal point of view. "A Celebration of Grandfathers," page 251, is an essay.

fable, a brief TALE, in which the characters are often animals, told to point out a moral truth.

fantasy, see SCIENCE FICTION.

fiction, a story, novel, or play about imagined people and events. Its purpose is to entertain and often to illustrate some truth about life.

figurative language, language expanded beyond its ordinary literal meaning. It uses comparisons to express a fitting relationship between things essentially unlike. SIMILES, METAPHORS, and HYPERBOLE are figurative language.

flashback, an interruption in the action of a story, play, or piece of nonfiction to show an episode that happened at an earlier time.

foreshadowing, a hint given to the reader of what is to come. In *The Call of the Wild*, page 576, Buck's arctic adventures are foreshadowed when readers are told that the discovery of gold on the Alaskan frontier has created a demand for large, strong dogs with thick warm coats.

free verse, a type of poetry that is "free" from a fixed pattern of RHYTHM or RHYME. "The Clouds Pass," page 304, and "Snow Sculpture," page 307, are examples of free verse.

genre (zhän'rə), a form or type of literary work.

hero/heroine, the main character in a literary work. Sherlock Holmes is the hero in *The Three Garridebs*, page 176.

humor, a literary work that is funny or amusing. "My Boss the Cat," page 246, is an example of humor.

hyperbole (hī pėr'bə lē), an exaggerated statement, sometimes involving FIGURATIVE LANGUAGE.

imagery (im'ij rē), concrete words or details that appeal to the senses of sight, sound, touch, smell, taste, and to internal feelings.

irony (ī'rə nē), a contrast between what appears to be and what really is. (See the Handbook of Literary Terms.)

legend, a story by an unknown author, handed down through the years.

light verse, short poems written chiefly to amuse or entertain.

limerick, a five-line humorous poem. The first, second, and fifth lines rhyme and the third and fourth lines rhyme. Limericks usually have as subjects the manners of people.

metaphor (met'ə fôr), a figure of speech that involves an implied comparison between two basically unlike things. "Her eyes are stars" is a metaphor.

mood, the atmosphere or feeling within a work.

moral, the lesson or teaching in a fable or story. The poem, "Fable for When There's No Way Out," contains a moral.

mystery, a work of fiction that contains a puzzling

problem or an event not explained until the end so as to keep the reader in SUSPENSE.

myth (mith), a traditional story connected with the religion or beliefs of a people, usually attempting to account for something in nature. Unit 7 contains a selection of Greek myths.

narrative, a story or account of an event or a series of happenings. It may be true or fictional.

narrator, the teller of a story. The teller may be a character in the story, as in "My Delicate Heart Condition," page 403, or someone outside the story as in "The Last Specimen, p. 13.

nonfiction, literature about real people and events rather than imaginary ones. Nonfiction can be autobiography, biography, essay, article, speech, or history. Unit 3 is all nonfiction.

novel/novella, long works of FICTION dealing with characters, situations and settings that copy those of real life. A novella (nō vel′ə) is a short novel. *The Call of the Wild*, page 576, is a novel.

onomatopoeia (on′ə mat′ə pē′ə), words used to imitate the sound of a thing. *Hiss, smack, buzz,* and *hum* are onomatopoetic words.

personification (pər son′ə fə kā′shən), a figure of speech or FIGURATIVE LANGUAGE in which human characteristics are given to nonhuman things.

play, see DRAMA.

plot, a series of happenings in a literary work. Plot consists of these elements: a conflict, a pattern of events, a climax, and a conclusion.

poetry, composition in verse. The words in poetry are arranged in lines that have rhythm and, sometimes, rhyme.

point of view, the relationship between the NARRATOR of a story and the characters and action in it. The two most common points of view are first person and third person.

repetition, word or phrase used over and over again for emphasis, especially in poetry.

rhyme, the REPETITION of syllable sounds. End words that share a particular sound are called END RHYMES.

rhyme scheme (skēm), the pattern of END RHYME in a poem.

rhythm (riTH′əm), the arrangement of stressed and unstressed sounds in writing and speech. Rhythm may be regular or irregular.

satire, a kind of writing that makes fun of something, often some human weakness.

science fiction/fantasy. Both science fiction and fantasy are works set wholly or partly in an unreal world. Often, at least one character is unlike a human being. Frequently, the plot concerns events that cannot be scientifically explained. "The Last Specimen," page 13, is an example of science fiction.

setting, the time and place in which the events in a NARRATIVE occur.

short story, a story shorter than a NOVEL. Although it generally describes just one event, it must have a beginning, a middle, and an end. The characters are usually fewer in number and not as fully developed as those in a novel.

simile (sim′ə lē), a comparison in which the word *like* or *as* is used to point out a similarity between two basically unlike things. A simile is a type of FIGURATIVE LANGUAGE.

speaker, the same as a NARRATOR. Often the teller of a story is referred to as the narrator, and the narrator of a poem is called the speaker.

stanza, a group of lines set off visually from the other lines in a poem. "Fifteen," page 279, has four stanzas.

suspense, the method or methods an author uses to maintain a reader's interest. In *The Three Garridebs*, page 176, suspense is achieved by letting readers know that the man who calls himself John Garrideb is lying but not letting them know why he is doing so.

symbol, a person, place, event, or object that has a meaning in itself but suggests other meanings as well. A heart is a symbol of love.

tale, a spoken or written account of some happening. It is usually less complicated than a short story.

theme, the main idea or underlying meaning of a literary work. The theme of "Hyacinth Drift," page 217, is that the world contains enough beauty to cure the worst of emotional illnesses if only a person is able to see that beauty.

tone, an author's attitude toward the subject of a literary work or toward the reader. Paul Gallico's tone in "My Boss, the Cat," page 246, is humorous. The tone of "The Gettysburg Address," (page 262) is formal and serious.

GLOSSARY OF LITERARY TERMS

GLOSSARY

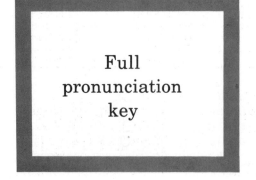

Full pronunciation key

The pronunciation of each word is shown just after the word, in this way: **ab bre vi ate** (ə brē′vē āt). The letters and signs used are pronounced as in the words below. The mark ′ is placed after a syllable with primary or heavy accent, as in the example above. The mark ′ after a syllable shows a secondary or lighter accent, as in **ab bre vi a tion** (ə brē′vē ā′shən).

Some words, taken from foreign languages, are spoken with sounds that do not otherwise occur in English. Symbols for these sounds are given in the key as "foreign sounds."

a	hat, cap	j	jam, enjoy	u	cup, butter	
ā	age, face	k	kind, seek	u̇	full, put	
ä	father, far	l	land, coal	ü	rule, move	
		m	me, am			
b	bad, rob	n	no, in	v	very, save	
ch	child, much	ng	long, bring	w	will, woman	
d	did, red			y	young, yet	
		o	hot, rock	z	zero, breeze	
e	let, best	ō	open, go	zh	measure, seizure	
ē	equal, be	ô	order, all			
ėr	term, learn	oi	oil, voice	ə	represents:	
		ou	house, out		a in about	
f	fat, if				e in taken	
g	go, bag	p	paper, cup		i in pencil	
h	he, how	r	run, try		o in lemon	
		s	say, yes		u in circus	
i	it, pin	sh	she, rush			
ī	ice, five	t	tell, it			
		th	thin, both			
		ŦH	then, smooth			

foreign sounds

Y as in French *du.*
Pronounce (ē) with the lips rounded as for (ü).

a as in French *ami.*
Pronounce (ä) with the lips spread and held tense.

œ as in French *peu.*
Pronounce (ā) with the lips rounded as for (ō).

N as in French *bon.*
The N is not pronounced, but shows that the vowel before it is nasal.

H as in German *ach.*
Pronounce (k) without closing the breath passage.

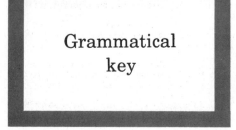

Grammatical key

adj.	adjective	*prep.*	preposition
adv.	adverb	*pron.*	pronoun
conj.	conjunction	*v.*	verb
interj.	interjection	*v.i.*	intransitive verb
n.	noun	*v.t.*	transitive verb
sing.	singular	*pl.*	plural
pt.	past tense	*pp.*	past participle

a bid ing (ə bī′ding), *adj.* permanent; lasting; steadfast.

-able, *suffix forming adjectives from verbs and nouns.* that can be ___ed: *Enjoyable = that can be enjoyed.*

a bode (ə bōd′), *n.,* place of residence; dwelling; house or home. —*v.* a pt. and a pp. of **abide.**

a brupt (ə brupt′), *adj.* **1** characterized by sudden change; unexpected: *an abupt turn.* **2** very steep. **3** short or sudden in speech or manner; blunt. [< Latin *abruptum* broken off < *ab-* off + *rumpere* to break] —**a brupt′ly,** *adv.*

ab scond (ab skond′), *v.i.* go away hurriedly and secretly, especially to avoid punishment; go off and hide.

ab stract (*adj.* ab′strakt, ab strakt′; *v.* ab strakt′) *adj.* **1** thought of apart from any particular object or actual instance; not concrete: *Sweetness is an abstract quality.* **2** not representing any actual object; having little or no resemblance to real or material things: *abstract paintings.* —*v.t.* **1** take away; remove; extract: *Iron is abstracted from ore.* **2** take away secretly, slyly, or dishonestly. —**ab stract′ly,** *adv.*

ab surd (ab sėrd′, ab zėrd′), *adj.* plainly not true, logical, or sensible; ridiculous. See synonym study below. [< Latin *absurdus* out of tune, senseless] —**ab surd′ly,** *adv.* —**ab surd′ness,** *n.*

Syn. Ridiculous, absurd, preposterous mean not sensible or reasonable. **Ridiculous** emphasizes the laughable effect produced by something out of keeping with good sense: *Her attempts to be the life of the party were ridiculous.* **Absurd** emphasizes inconsistency with what is true or sensible: *His belief that he was too clever to be caught in his wrongdoing was absurd.* **Preposterous** suggests extreme absurdity and, often, the idea of being contrary to nature: *The child drew a preposterous man with arms growing from his head.*

a bys mal (ə biz′məl), *adj.* **1** too deep or great to be measured; bottomless. **2** INFORMAL. extremely bad; of very low quality. —**a bys′ mal ly,** *adv.*

a byss (ə bis′), *n.* **1** a bottomless or very great depth. **2** anything too deep or great to be measured; lowest depth. [< Late Latin *abyssus* < Greek *abyssos* < *a-* without + *byssos* bottom]

ac cede (ak sēd′), *v.i.,* **-ced ed, -ced ing.** **1** give in; agree; consent (*to*): *Please accede to my request.* **2** become a party (to): *Our government acceded to the treaty.*

ac claim (ə klām′), *v.t.* **1** welcome with shouts or other signs of approval: *The crowd acclaimed the winning team.* **2** proclaim or announce with approval: *The newspapers acclaimed the results of the election.* [< Latin *acclamare* < *ad-* to + *clamare* cry out]

ac cli mate (ə klī′mit, ak′lə māt), *v.t., v.i.,* **-mat ed, -mat ing.** accustom or become accustomed to a new climate, surroundings, or conditions. —**ac cli ma tion** (ak′lə mā′shən), *n.*

ac cord ance (ə kôrd′ns), *n.* agreement; harmony: *in accordance with the rules.*

ac cord ing ly (ə kôr′ding lē), *adv.* in agreement with what is expected or stated: *These are the rules; you can act accordingly or leave the club.*

ac cus tomed (ə kus′təmd), *adj.* **1** usual; customary. **2** accustomed to, used to; in the habit of: *The farmer was accustomed to hard work and long hours. She is accustomed to jogging dail*·.

ac quit tal (ə kwit′l), *n.* an acquitting; discharge; release.

ac tive (ak′tiv), *adj.* **1** moving or capable of moving rather quickly much of the time; nimble: *as active as a kitten.* **2** showing much or constant action; brisk: *an active market, active trade.* —**ac′tive ly,** *adv.* —**ac′tive ness,** *n.*

a cute (ə kyüt′), *adj.* **1** acting keenly on the senses; sharp; intense: *acute pain.* **2** crucial; critical: *an acute shortage of water.* **3** quick in perceiving and responding to impressions; keen: *an acute sense of smell.* [< Latin *acutum* sharpened < *acuere* sharpen] —**a cute′ly,** *adv.* —**a cute′ness,** *n.*

ad her ence (ad hir′əns), *n.* a holding to and following closely; adhering: *the judge's rigid adherence to rules was greatly respected.*

---

a hat	i it	oi oil	ch child	(a in about
ā age	ī ice	ou out	ng long	e in taken
ä far	o hot	u cup	sh she	ə = { i in pencil
e let	ō open	ů put	th thin	o in lemon
ē equal	ô order	ü rule	ŦH then	(u in circus
ėr term			zh measure	< = derived from

a do be (ə dō′bē), *n.* **1** brick made of sun-dried clay. **2** building made of such bricks or of sun-dried clay. —*adj.* built or made of adobe. [< Spanish < Arabic *at-tūb* the brick]

adobe building and oven

aes thet ic (es thet′ik), *adj.* **1** based on or determined by beauty rather than by practically useful, scientific, or moral considerations. **2** having or showing an appreciation of beauty in nature or art.

af fec ta tion (af′ek tā′shən), *n.* behavior that is not natural, but assumed to impress others; pretense.

a fore (ə fôr′), *adv., prep., conj.* ARCHAIC or DIALECT. before.

a fore men tioned (ə fôr′men′shənd, ə fôr′men′shənd), *adj.,* spoken of before; mentioned earlier.

aft (aft), *adv.* at or toward the stern of a ship, boat, or aircraft.

af ter math (af′tər·math), *n.* result or consequence, especially of something destructive.

a ghast (ə gast′), *adj.* struck with surprise or horror; filled with shocked amazement. [past participle of obsolete *agast* terrify < Old English *on-* on + *gæstan* frighten. Related to GHOST.]

ag i tate (aj′ə tāt), *v.t.,* **-tat ed, -tat ing.** **1** move or shake violently: *A sudden wind agitated the surface of the river.* **2** disturb or upset very much. [< Latin *agitatum* moved to and fro < *agere* to move]

air (er, ar), *n.* **1** the odorless, tasteless, and invisible mixture of gases that surrounds the earth. **2** space overhead; sky: *Birds fly in the air.* **3** a simple melody or tune.

a jar (ə jär′), *adj.* slightly open: *Please leave the door ajar.*

al cove (al′kōv), *n.* **1** a small room opening out of a larger room. **2** recess or large, hollow space in a wall.

al ien ate (ā′lyə nāt, ā′lē ə nāt), *v.t.,* **-at ed, -at ing.** **1** turn away the normal feelings, fondness, or devotion of anyone. **2** transfer (property, a property right, etc.) to the ownership of another.

al le giance (ə lē′jəns), *n.* **1** the loyalty owed to one's country or government. **2** faithfulness to a person, cause, etc.; loyalty.

al lo cate (al′ə kāt), *v.t.,* **-cat ed, -cat ing.** set or lay aside for a special purpose; assign, allot, or apportion.

a main (ə mān′), *adv.* **1** at full speed. **2** with full force; violently.

a mass (ə mas′) *v.t.* heap together; pile up, especially for oneself; accumulate.

am ber (am′bər), *n.* **1** a hard, translucent, yellow or yellowish-brown fossil resin, easily polished and used for jewelry, in making pipe stems, etc. **2** the color of amber; yellow or yellowish brown.

am ble (am′bəl), *n., v.,* **-bled, -bling.** —*n.* gait of a horse or mule when it lifts first the two legs on one side and then the two on the other. —*v.i.* **1** (of a horse or mule) go with such a gait. **2** walk at an easy, slow pace.

a men i ty (ə men′ə tē, ə mē′nə tē), *n., pl.* **-ties. amenities,** *pl.* pleasant ways; polite acts. Saying: *''Thank you''* and holding the door open for a person to pass through are amenities.

a mid ships (ə mid′ships), *adv.* in or toward the middle of a ship; halfway between the bow and stern. *The torpedo hit us amidships.*

am ne sia (am nē′ zhə), *n.* partial or entire loss of memory caused by injury to the brain, or by disease, shock, etc. [< Greek *amnēsia* forgetfulness < *a-* not + *mimnēskesthai* remember]

am phi the a ter (am′fə thē′ə tər), *n.* **1** a circular or oval building with tiers of seats around a central open space. **2** place of public contest; arena.

-an, *suffix forming adjectives and nouns, especially from proper nouns.* **1** of or having to do with ___: *Mohammedan = of or having to do with Mohammed.* **2** native or inhabitant of ___: *American = native or inhabitant of America.* **3** person who knows much about or is skilled in ___: *Magician = person skilled in magic. Historian = person who knows much about history.* Also, **-ian, -ean.**

a nach ro nism (ə nak′rə niz′əm), *n.* **1** error in fixing a date or dates. **2** anything out of keeping with a specified time, especially something proper to a former age but not to the present. [< Greek *anachronismos* < *ana-* back + *chronos* time]

an es thet ic (an′əs thet′ik), *n.* substance that causes anesthesia, or the loss of the feeling of pain, touch, cold, etc.

an guish (ang′gwish), *n.* **1** severe physical pain; great suffering. **2** extreme mental pain or suffering: *the anguish of despair.* —**an′guished,** *adj.*

an hy drite (an hī′drīt), *n.* a white or grayish mineral consisting of anhydrous sulfate of calcium. *Formula:* $CaSO_4$

an hy drous (an hī′drəs), *adj.* without water.

a no rak (ä′nə räk′), *n.* a heavy jacket with a fur hood worn in arctic regions. [< Eskimo (Greenland) *ánorâq* clothing]

an tag o nist (an tag′ə nist), *n.* person who fights, struggles, or contends against another; adversary; opponent.

an thro po log i cal (an′thrə pə loj′ə kəl), *adj.* of anthropology, the science or study of human beings, dealing especially with their fossil remains, physical characteristics, cultures, customs, and beliefs.

ap a thet ic (ap′ə thet′ik), *adj.* **1** lacking interest or desire for action; indifferent. **2** lacking in feeling; unemotional. —**ap′a thet′i cal ly,** *adv.*

a pos tle or **A pos tle** (ə pos′əl), *n.* **1** one of the twelve disciples, **the Apostles,** chosen by Christ to preach the gospel to all the world. **2** leader of any reform movement or new belief who displays great vigor in seeking to popularize it.

ap pall ing (ə pô′ling), *adj.* causing horror; dismaying; terrifying. —**ap pall′ing ly,** *adv.*

ap pa ra tus (ap′ə rā′təs, ap′ə rat′əs), *n., pl.* **-tus** or **-tus es.** **1** the tools, machines, or other equipment necessary to carry out a purpose or for a particular use: *apparatus for an experiment in chemistry, gardening apparatus.* **2** a mechanism or piece of machinery: *My attempts to be an amateur mechanic taught me that an automobile is a complicated apparatus.*

ap pease (ə pēz′), *v.t.,* **-peased, -peas ing. 1** put an end to by satisfying (an appetite or desire): *A good dinner will appease your hunger.* **2** make calm or quiet; pacify. —**ap peas′ing ly,** *adv.*

ap pend age (ə pen′dij), *n.* thing attached to something larger or more important; addition.

ap pen dix (ə pen′diks), *n., pl.* **-dix es** or **-di ces.** addition at the end of a book or document.

ap pli ca bil i ty (ap′lə kə bil′ə tē), *n.* quality of being applicable or appropriate for use.

ap pre hen sion (ap′ri hen′shən), *n.* **1** expectation of misfortune; dread of impending danger; fear. **2** arrest. **3** understanding.

ar a ble (ar′ə bəl), *adj.* (of land) suitable for producing crops which require plowing and tillage. —*n.* arable land.

ar chae o log i cal (är′kē ə loj′ə kəl), *adj.* of or having to do with archaeology. Also, **archeological.** —**ar′chae o log′i cal ly,** *adv.*

ar chae ol o gy (är′kē ol′ə jē), *n.* the scientific study of the people, customs, and life of ancient times, antedating the keeping of historic records.

ar dor (är′dər), *n.* **1** warmth of emotion; passion. **2** great enthusiasm; eagerness; zeal: *patriotic ardor.* [< Latin < *ardere* to burn]

ar du ous (är′jü əs), *adj.* **1** hard to do; requiring much effort; difficult: *an arduous lesson.* **2** using up much energy; strenuous: *an arduous climb.* [< Latin *arduus* steep] —**ar′du ous ly,** *adv.*

a ris to crat (ə ris′tə krat), *n.* **1** person who belongs to the aristocracy; noble. **2** person like an aristocrat in tastes, opinion, and manners.

ar ma da (är mä′də), *n.* **1** a large fleet of warships. **2 the Armada,** the Spanish fleet that was sent to attack England in 1588 but was defeated in the English Channel. **3** any large group of military vehicles. [< Spanish < Medieval Latin *armata* armed force. Doublet of ARMY.]

ar rears (ə rirz′), *n. pl.* money due but not paid; unpaid debts.

art ful (ärt′fəl), *adj.* **1** slyly clever; crafty; deceitful: *a swindler's artful tricks.* **2** skillful; clever. —**art′ful ly,** *adv.* —**art′ful ness,** *n.*

ar tic u late (*adj.* är tik′yə lit; *v.* är tik′yə lāt), *adj., v.,* **-lat ed, -lat ing.** —*adj.* **1** uttered in distinct syllables of words: *A baby cries and gurgles, but does not use articulate sounds.* **2** able to put one's thoughts into words easily and clearly: *She is the most articulate of the sisters. Our guide was both articulate and informed.*

ar til ler y (är til′ər ē), *n.* **1** mounted guns or rocket launchers manned by a crew; guns of larger caliber than machine guns; cannon; ordnance. **2** the part of an army that uses and manages such guns.

as cend (ə send′), *v.i.* go up; rise; move upward: *He watched the airplane ascend.* —*v.t.* go to or toward the top of: *A small party is planning to ascend Mount Everest.*

as cent (ə sent′), *n.* **1** act of going up; upward movement; rising: *early balloon ascents.* **2** act of climbing a ladder, mountain, etc.

as cot (as′kət, as′kot), *n.* necktie with broad ends, resembling a scarf, tied so that the ends may be laid flat, one across the other. [< *Ascot,* English race track]

as pect (as′pekt), *n.* **1** way in which a subject or situation appears to the mind: *The whole aspect of the situation is changing.* **2** way in which an object appears to the eye; appearance: *the general aspect of the countryside.* **3** facial expression; countenance: *the solemn aspect of the judge.*

as pire (ə spīr′), *v.i.,* **-pired, -pir ing. 1** have an ambition for something; desire earnestly; seek: *I aspired to be captain of the team.* **2** rise high. —**as pir′ing ly,** *adv.*

as sert (ə sėrt′), *v.t.* **1** state positively; declare firmly; affirm: *She asserts that she will go whether we do or not.* **2** maintain (a right, a claim, etc.); insist upon: *Assert your independence.* **3 assert oneself,** insist on one's rights; demand recognition: *If you feel you've been treated unfairly, you should assert yourself.*

as sume (ə süm′), *v.t.* **-sumed, -sum ing. 1** take for granted without actual proof; suppose: *She assumed that the train would be on time.* **2** take upon oneself formally; undertake (an office or responsibility): *assume leadership.* **3** take on; put on: *The problem had assumed a new form.*

a sun der (ə sun′dər), *adv.* in pieces; into separate parts: *Lightning split the tree asunder.*

at tain (ə tān′), *v.t.* **1** reach (a state or condition) by living, growing, or developing: *attain the age of 80.* **2** win or acquire by effort: *attain a goal.* **3** reach (a place); arrive at; gain: *attain the top of a hill.* —*v.i.* succeed in coming or getting (to): *attain to a position of great influence.*

at ten tive (ə ten′tiv), *adj.* **1** paying attention; observant. **2** courteous; polite: *an attentive host.* —**at ten′tive ly,** *adv.*

at ti tude (at′ə tüd, at′ə tyüd), *n.* **1** way of thinking, feeling, or acting; feeling or behavior of a person toward a situation: *My attitude toward school has changed.* **2** position of the body appropriate to an action, purpose, emotion, etc.; posture; pose.

au da cious (ô dā′shəs), *adj.* **1** having the courage to take risks; recklessly daring; bold. **2** rudely bold; impudent. **—au da′cious ly,** *adv.* **—au da′cious ness,** *n.*

au dac i ty (ô das′ə tē), *n.* **1** reckless daring. **2** rude boldness. [< Latin *audacia* < *audax* bold < *audere* to dare]

au di ble (ô′də bəl), *adj.* that can be heard; loud enough to be heard. [< Latin *audire* hear]

au ro ra bo re al is (ô rôr′ə bôr′ē al′is; ô rōr′ə bōr′ē al′is), the aurora of the northern sky; northern lights. [< New Latin]

aus tere (ô stir′), *adj.* **1** stern in manner or appearance; harsh: *a silent, austere man.* **2** severe in self-discipline; strict in morals: *The Puritans were austere.* **3** severely simple: *The tall, plain columns stood against the sky in austere beauty.*

au thor i ta tive (ə thôr′ə tā′tiv), *adj.* **1** proceeding from a recognized authority; official: *The president issued an authoritative declaration of policy.* **2** of or characterized by authority.

a venge (ə venj′), *v.,* **a venged, a veng ing. —v.t.** take revenge for or on behalf of: *avenge an insult.*

a ver (ə vėr′), *v.t.,* **a verred, a ver ring.** state positively to be true; assert; affirm.

awe (ô), *n., v.,* **awed, aw ing. —n. 1** a feeling of wonder and reverence inspired by anything of great beauty, majesty, or power: *The young girl stood in awe before the queen.* **2** dread mingled with reverence. *—v.t.* cause to feel awe; fill with awe: *The majesty of the mountains awed us.*

---

back yard (bak′yärd′). *n.* yard behind a house or building.

bade (bad, bād), *v.t.,* a pt. of **bid.** ► **Bade** is used chiefly in formal and literary English: *The king bade her remain.*

bank[1] (bangk), *n.* **1** a long pile or heap. **2** the rising ground bordering a river, lake etc. *—v.i.* (of an airplane) slope to one side, especially when turning.

bank[2] (bangk), *n.* institution whose business is the custody, lending, transmitting, and paying orders for money.

bar bar ic (bär bar′ik), *adj.* **1** like barbarians; suited to an uncivilized people; rough and rude. **2** crudely rich or splendid.

bar ba rism (bär′bə riz′əm), *n.* **1** condition of uncivilized people. **2** a barbarous act, custom, or trait.

bar rage (bə räzh′), *n.* barrier of artillery fire to check the enemy or to protect one's own soldiers when advancing or retreating.

barrel organ, hand organ, or large, portable music box that is made to play tunes by turning a crank.

basket boat, a boat made out of tightly woven fibers.

bas-re lief (bä′ri lēf′), *n.* carving or sculpture in which the figures stand out only slightly from the background. [< French]

bat tal ion (bə tal′yən), *n.* **1** a military unit of infantry, etc. **2** a large division of an army in battle array. **3 battalions,** *pl.* armies; military forces.

bat ter y (bat′ər ē), *n., pl.* **-ter ies. 1** a single electric cell: *a flashlight battery.* **2** a military unit of artillery, usually commanded by a captain.

bay ber ry (bā′ber′ē, bā′bər ē), *n., pl.* **-ries.** a North American shrub of the same genus as the wax myrtle, with clusters of grayish-white berries coated with wax. Candles made from the wax of bayberries burn with a pleasant fragrance.

bay o net (bā′ə nit, bā′ə net′), *n.* a heavy, daggerlike blade for piercing or stabbing, made to be attached to the muzzle of a rifle, etc.

bea con (bē′kən), *n.* **1** fire or light used as a signal to guide or warn. **2** a tall tower for a signal; lighthouse. **3** any thing or person that is a guiding or warning signal.

bear (ber, bar), *v.t.,* **bore, borne, bear ing. 1** take from one place to another; carry. **2** hold up; support. **3** put up with; abide: *She can't bear the noise.*

beck on (bek′ən), *v.i., v.t.* to signal by a motion of the head or

---

a hat	i it	oi oil	ch child	(a in about
ā age	ī ice	ou out	ng long	e in taken
ä far	o hot	u cup	sh she	ə = i in pencil
e let	ō open	u̇ put	th thin	o in lemon
ē equal	ô order	ü rule	₮H then	u in circus
ėr term			zh measure	< = derived from

hand: *He beckoned me to follow him. The tall man beckoned to her.* [Old English *bēcnan* < *bēacen* sign, beacon]

be get (bi get′), *v.t.,* **be got, be got ten, be get ting. 1** become the father of. **2** cause to be; produce.

be lea guer (bi lē′gər), *v.t.* **1** surround with troops. **2** surround. **—be lea′guered,** *adj.*

ben e dic tion (ben′ə dik′shən), *n.* **1** the asking of God's blessing, as at the end of a church service. **2** blessing.

ben e fac tor (ben′ə fak′tər, ben′ə fak′tər), *n.* person who has helped others, either by gifts of money or by some kind act.

be nign (bi nīn′), *adj.* kindly in feeling; benevolent; gracious: *a benign old woman.*

be reft (bi reft′), *adj.* deprived; left alone and desolate.

be seech (bi sēch′), *v.t.,* **-sought** or **-seeched, -seech ing.** ask earnestly; beg; implore.

be stow (bi stō′), *v.t.* **1** give (something) as a gift; give; confer. **2** make use of; apply.

bid (bid), *v.t.,* **bade, bid, bid ding. 1** tell (someone) what to do, where to go, etc.; command; order: *Do as I bid you. You bade me forget what is unforgettable.* **2** say or tell (a greeting, etc.); wish: *My friends came to bid me good-by.*

bil low (bil′ō), *n.* **1** a great, swelling wave or surge of the sea. **2** a great rolling or swelling mass of smoke, flame, air, etc. *—v.i.* **1** rise or roll in big waves; surge. **2** swell out; bulge.

bin dle (bin′dl), *n., v.,* **-dled, -dling. —n.** a bundle; bedroll. *—v.i.* wrap in a bundle or bedroll.

bi sect (bī sekt′), *v.t.* divide into two parts.

black out (blak′out′), *n.* the extinguishing or concealing of all the lights of a city, district, etc., as a protection against an air raid.

blanch (blanch), *v.t.* make white or pale: *Old age blanched his hair. —v.i.* turn white or pale: *blanch with fear.* [< Old French *blanchir* < *blanc* white]

bland (bland), *adj.* **1** gentle or soothing; balmy: *a bland summer breeze.* **2** smoothly agreeable and polite: *a bland smile.* [< Latin *blandus* soft] **—bland′ly,** *adv.* **—bland′ness,** *n.*

blowz y (blou′zē), *adj.,* lacking neatness; untidy; disheveled: *blowzy hair.* Also, **blowsy.**

bolo tie (bō′lō), a necktie of thin cord fastened in front with a decorative clasp.

boo ty (bü′tē), *n., pl.* **-ties. 1** plunder taken from the enemy in war. **2** money, valuables, etc., seized by thieves or robbers; plunder. **3** gains; winnings. [perhaps < Middle Dutch *botye*]

borne (bôrn, bōrn), *v.* a pp. of **bear.** *I have borne it as long as I can.*

► *borne.* **Borne** is the past participle of *bear* in most of its meanings: *The ship was borne along by the breeze. The men had borne these burdens without complaint.*

bound (bound), *adj.* **1** under some obligation; tied down by circumstance, duty, etc.; obliged: *I feel bound by my promise.* **2** certain; sure: *It is bound to get dark soon.* **3** tied fast; fastened: *bound hands.* [Middle English *bounden*]

bound en (boun′dən), *adj.* **1** required; obligatory: *one's bounden duty.* **2** under obligation because of favors received; obliged.

boun ty (boun′tē), *n., pl.* **-ties.** a generous gift.

brake (brāk), *n.* thicket, or clump of small trees growing close together.

bran dish (bran′dish), *v.t.* wave or shake threateningly; flour-

---

ish. —*n.* a threatening shake; flourish. [< Old French *brandiss-,* a form of *brandir* to brand < *brand* sword]

brev i ty (brev′ə tē), *n., pl.* **-ties. 1** shortness in time. **2** shortness in speech or writing; conciseness.

bridge head (brij′hed′), *n.* **1** position obtained and held by advance troops within enemy territory, used as a starting point for further attack. **2** any position taken as a foothold from which to make further advances. **3** fortification protecting the end of a bridge nearer to the enemy.

brim stone (brim′stōn′), *n.* sulfur, a highly flammable, non-metallic element used in making matches and gunpowder.

brin y (brī′nē), *adj.,* **brin i er, brin i est.** of or like brine, or salty water; very salty: *a briny taste.* —**brin′i ness,** *n.*

bru mal (brü′mal), *adj.* wintry.

buc ca neer (buk′ə nir′), *n.* a pirate, especially one who preyed upon Spanish vessels and colonies in America in the 1600's and 1700's. [< French *boucanier,* ultimately < Tupi *boucan* frame for curing meat (early Caribbean pirates preserved meat in this way)]

Bud dha (bü′də, büd′ə), *n.* 563?-483? B.C., a religious teacher of northern India and the founder of Buddhism.

bump er (bum′pər), *n.* **1** any device that protects against damage from bumping. **2** cup or glass filled to the brim. —*adj.* unusually large: *a bumper crop.*

bump kin (bump′kən), *n.* an awkward or naïve person from the country. [perhaps < Middle Dutch *bommekyn* little barrel]

bunch (bunch), *n.* **1** group of things of the same kind growing, fastened, placed, or thought of together: *a bunch of grapes, a bunch of sheep.* **2** INFORMAL. group of people: *They are a friendly bunch.* —*v.i.* come together in one place.

buoy ant (boi′ənt, bü′yənt), *adj.* **1** able to float. **2** hopeful; cheerful; lighthearted. —**buoy′an cy,** *n.* —**buoy′ant ly,** *adv.*

bur gle (bėr′gəl), *v.t.,* **-gled, -gling.** INFORMAL. burglarize; rob. [back-formation < *burglar*]

bur nish (bėr′nish), *v.t.* **1** make (metal) smooth and bright; polish (a surface) by rubbing until shiny: *burnish brass.* **2** make bright and glossy. —**bur′nished,** *adj.*

bust (bust), SLANG. *v.t.* burst; break.

butte (byüt), *n.* (in the western United States) a steep, flat-topped hill standing alone.

cache (kash), *n.* a hiding place, especially of goods, treasure, food, etc. [< French < *cacher* to hide]

ca lam i ty (kə lam′ə tē), *n., pl.* **-ties. 1** a great misfortune, such as a flood, a fire, the loss of one's sight or hearing. **2** serious trouble; misery. [< Latin *calamitatem*]

cal cu lus (kal′kyə ləs), *n., pl.* **-li** (-lī), **-lus es.** system of calculation in advanced mathematics.

call (kôl), *v.* **1** speak or say in a loud voice. **2** rouse; waken. *n.* **1** shout or cry. **2** command or summons.

cal li o pe (kə lī′ə pē, kal′ē ōp), *n.* a musical instrument having a series of steam whistles played by pushing keys.

cal low (kal′ō), *adj.* young and inexperienced: *a callow youth.*

can dor (kan′dər), *n.* **1** a saying openly what one really thinks; honesty in giving one's opinion. **2** fairness; impartiality.

can non ade (kan′ə nād′), *n., v.,* **-ad ed, -ad ing.** —*n.* a continued firing of cannons; barrage. —*v.t.* attack with cannons.

cap i tal (kap′ə təl), *n.* **1** city where the government of a country, state, or province is located. **2** capital letter. **3** amount of money or property that companies or individuals use to increase their wealth: *The Smith Manufacturing Company has capital amounting to $300.000.* **4** source of power or advantage; resources.

ca pit u late (kə pich′ə lāt), *v.i.,* **-lat ed, -lat ing.** surrender on certain terms or conditions: *The men in the fort capitulated*

on condition that they be allowed to go away unharmed. —**ca pit′u la′tion,** *n.* —**ca pit′u la′tor,** *n.*

ca price (kə prēs′), *n.* **1** a sudden change of mind without reason; whim. **2** tendency to change suddenly and without reason.

car i ca ture (kar′ə kə chùr, kar′ə kə chər), *n., v.,* **-tured, -tur ing.** —*n.* picture, cartoon, or description that exaggerates the peculiarities of a person or the defects of a thing.

car il lon (kar′ə lon, kə ril′yən), *n.* **1** set of bells arranged for playing melodies. **2** melody played on such bells. [< French, ultimately < Latin *quattuor* four (because it originally consisted of four bells)]

car nage (kär′nij), *n.* slaughter of a great number of people.

car niv or ous (kär niv′ər əs), *adj.* **1** of or having to do with an order of mammals that feed chiefly on flesh. **2** using other animals as food: flesh-eating: *the strong carnivorous eagle.* [< Latin *carnivorus* < *carnem* flesh + *vorare* devour]

cas cade (ka skād′), *n.* **1** a small waterfall. **2** anything like this: *Her dress had a cascade of ruffles down the front.*

case ment (kās′mənt), *n.* **1** window or part of a window which opens on hinges like a door. **2** any window.

cas sock (kas′ək), *n.* a long outer garment, usually black, worn by a clergyman. [< French *casaque* < Italian *casacca*]

Cau ca sian (kô kā′zhən, kô kā′shən), *n.* member of the division of the human race that includes the original inhabitants of Europe, southwestern Asia, and northern Africa, and their descendants throughout the world.

caulk (kôk), *v.t.* fill up (a seam, crack, or joint) so that it will not leak; make watertight: *Sailors caulk wooden boats with oakum and tar. Plumbers caulk joints in pipe with lead.* Also, **calk.** [< Old French *cauquer* press in, tread < Latin *calcare* < *calcem* heel]

caulk ing (kôk′ing), *n.* material used to fill up a seam or joint so that it will not leak.

cau ter ize (kô′tə rīz′), *v.t.,* **-ized, -iz ing.** burn with a hot iron or a caustic substance. Doctors sometimes cauterize wounds to prevent bleeding or infection. —**cau′ter i za′tion,** *n.*

ca vort (kə vôrt′), *v.* prance about; jump around.

cay use (kī yüs′, kī′üs), *n.* in the western United States: **1** an Indian-bred pony. **2** any pony or horse. [< *Cayuse*]

ce les tial (sə les′chəl), *adj.* **1** of the sky; having to do with the heavens: *The sun, moon, planets, and stars are celestial bodies.* **2** of or belonging to heaven as the place of God and the angels.

cen trif u gal (sen trif′yə gəl, sen trif′ə gəl), *adj.* moving or tending to move away from a center. —**cen trif′u gal ly,** *adv.*

chafe (chāf), *v.,* **chafed, chaf ing,** *n.* —*v.t.* **1** rub so as to wear away, scrape, or make sore: *The stiff collar chafed my neck.* **2** rub to make warm: *She chafed her cold hands.* **3** wear away by rubbing.

chaf fer (chaf′ər), *n.* a disputing about a price; bargaining. —**chaf′fer ing.**

char ac ter (kar′ik tər), *n.* **1** all the qualities or features possessed; sort; nature: *He dislikes people of that character.* **2** moral strength or weakness: *a person of shallow, changeable character.* **3** person or animal in a play, poem, story, or book. **4** letter, mark, or sign used in writing or printing. **5** writing or printing of a certain style: *books in Gothic character.* [< Latin < Greek *charaktēr* instrument for marking, distinctive mark < *charassein* engrave]

chas tise (cha stīz′), *v.t.,* **-tised, -tis ing. 1** inflict punishment or suffering on to improve; punish. **2** criticize severely; rebuke.

check (chek), *v.t.* **1** stop suddenly: *They checked their steps.* **2** hold back; control; restrain: *check one's anger, check a forest fire.*

che mise (shə mēz′), *n.* a loose, shirtlike undergarment worn by women and girls.

chide (chīd), *v.,* **chid ed, chid** or **chid den, chid ing.** —*v.t.* find fault with; reproach or blame; scold: *She chided the little girl for soiling her dress.* —*v.i.* find fault; speak in rebuke.

chiv al rous (shiv′əl rəs), *adj.* **1** having the qualities of an ideal knight; brave, courteous, considerate, helpful, honorable, and devoted to the service of the weak and oppressed. —**chiv al rous ly,** *adv.*

cho ris ter (kôr′ə stər, kor′ə stər), *n.* **1** singer in a choir or chorus. **2** leader of a choir.

chron ic (kron′ik), *adj.* **1** lasting a long time: *Rheumatism is often a chronic disease.* **2** suffering long from an illness: *a chronic invalid.* **3** never stopping; constant; habitual: *a chronic liar.*

cir cum vent (sèr′kəm vent′), *v.t.* **1** get the better of or defeat by trickery; outwit: *circumvent the law.* **2** go around. [< Latin *circumventum* circumvented < *circum* around + *venire* come]

cit ron (sit′rən), *n.* **1** a pale-yellow citrus fruit somewhat like a lemon. **2** its rind, candied and used in fruit cakes, candies, etc. [< Middle French < Italian *citrone* < Latin *citrus* citrus tree]

civ il (siv′əl), *adj.* **1** of citizens. **2** polite or courteous.

clair voy ant (kler voi′ənt, klar voi′ənt), *adj.* supposedly having the power of seeing or knowing things that are out of sight.

clar et (klar′ət), *n.* **1** kind of red wine. **2** a dark purplish-red. —*adj.* dark purplish-red.

claw foot (klô′fùt), *n.* representation of the claws of an animal on the foot of a piece of furniture.

cleave (klēv), *v.t.* **cleft** or **cleaved, cleav ing. 1** cut, divide, or split open. **2** pass through; pierce; penetrate: *The airplane cleft the clouds.*

cock (kok) *n.* an upward turn or bend of the eye, ear, hat, etc.

co gnac (kō′nyak, kon′yak), *n.* a French brandy of superior quality. [< French < *Cognac,* town and region in France]

co her ent (kō hir′ənt), *adj.* **1** logically connected; consistent: *A sentence that is not coherent is hard to understand.* **2** sticking together; holding together.

coiffe (kwäf), *n.* style of arranging the hair. —*v.t.* to dress (the hair) by arranging or styling. [< French]

col lab o rate (kə lab′ə rāt′), *v.i.,* **-rat ed, -rat ing. 1** work together. **2** aid traitorously. —**col lab′o ra′tor,** *n.*

col lec tive (kə lek′tiv), *adj.* **1** of a group; as a group; taken all together: *collective revenues of the government.* **2** of or derived from a number of persons taken or acting together.

com mence (kə mens′), *v.,* **-menced, -menc ing.** —*v.i.* make a start; begin. —*v.t.* begin (an action); enter upon.

com mend (kə mend′), *v.t.* **1** speak well of; praise. **2** recommend. **3** hand over for safekeeping; entrust: *She commended the child to his care.*

com men da tion (kom′ən dā′shən), *n.* **1** praise; approval. **2** recommendation. **3** a handing over to another for safekeeping; entrusting.

com mon place (kom′ən plās′), *adj.* not new or interesting; everyday; ordinary. —**com′mon place′ness,** *n.*

com mon wealth (kom′ən welth′), *n.* **1** the people who make up a nation; citizens of a state. **2** a democratic state; republic.

com mune (*v.* kə myün′; *n.* kom′yün), *v.,* **-muned, -mun ing,** *n.* —*v.i.* talk intimately; communion. —*n.* intimate talk; communion.

com pas sion ate (kəm pash′ə nit), *adj.* desiring to relieve another's suffering; sympathetic.—**com pas′sion ate ly,** *adv.*

com pel (kəm pel′), *v.t.,* **-pelled, -pel ling. 1** drive or urge with force; force: *Rain compelled them to stop.* **2** cause or get by force: *A police officer can compel obedience to the law.* —**com pel′ling ly,** *adv.*

com pen sa tion (kom′pən sā′shən), *n.* **1** something given as an equivalent; something given to make up for a loss, injury, etc. **2** pay: *Equal compensation should be given for equal work.* **3** a balancing by equal power, weight, etc.

com pe tent (kom′pə tənt), *adj.* **1** properly qualified; able; fit. **2** legally qualified.

com ply (kəm plī′), *v.i.,* **-plied, -ply ing.** act in agreement with a request or command: *I will comply with the doctor's request.*

com po sure (kəm pō′zhər), *n.* calmness; quietness; self-control.

con ceive (kən sēv′), *v.,* **-ceived, -ceiv ing.** —*v.t.* **1** form in the mind; think up: *The Wright brothers conceived the design of*

the first successful motor-driven airplane. **2** have (an idea or feeling). —*v.i.* have an idea or feeling; think; imagine: *We cannot conceive of such a thing happening.*

con cep tion (kən sep′shən), *n.* **1** thought; idea; impression: *Your conception of the problem is different from mine.* **2** act or power of conceiving.

con ces sion (kən sesh′ən), *n.* **1** a conceding; granting; yielding. **2** something conceded or granted by a government or controlling authority; grant. Land or privileges given by a government to a business company are called concessions. **3** privilege or space leased for a particular use: *the hot-dog concession at the ballpark.*

con cil i ate (kən sil′ē āt), *v.t.,* **-at ed, -at ing.** win over; soothe: *I conciliated the angry child with a candy bar.*

con coc tion (kon kok′shən, kən kok′shən), *n.* **1** act of concocting. **2** thing concocted.

con cus sion (kən kush′ən), *n.* **1** a sudden, violent shaking; shock. **2** injury to a soft part of the body, especially the brain, caused by a blow, fall, or other physical shock.

con dense (kən dens′), *v.,* **-densed, -dens ing.** —*v.t.* **1** make denser or more compact; compress. **2** put into fewer words; express briefly. —*v.i.* become denser or more compact.

con de scend ing (kon′di sen′ding), *adj.* **1** stooping to the level of one's inferiors. **2** scornful; patronizing.

con fla gra tion (kon′flə grā′shən), *n.* a great and destructive fire: *A conflagration destroyed most of the city.*

con form i ty (kən fôr′mə tē), *n., pl.* **-ties.** action in agreement with generally accepted standards of business, conduct, or worship; fitting oneself and one's actions to the ideas of others; compliance.

con front (kən frunt′), *v.t.* **1** meet face to face; stand facing. **2** face boldly; oppose. **3** bring face to face; place before: *The prosecuting attorney confronted the accused with the forged check.* —**con′fron ta′tion,** *n.*

con jec tur al (kən jek′chər əl), *adj.* involving conjecture or guesswork. —**con jec′tur al ly,** *adv.*

con ju ra tion (kon′jə rā′shən), *n.* **1** an invoking by a sacred name. **2** words used in a magic spell.

con sci en tious (kon′shē en′shəs), *adj.* **1** careful to do what one knows is right; controlled by conscience. **2** done with care to make it right; painstaking: *conscientious work.*

con scious ness (kon′shəs nis), *n.* condition of being conscious; awareness. People and animals have consciousness; plants and stones do not.

con se crate (kon′sə krāt), *v.,* set apart as sacred; make holy; sanctify.

con sole (kən sōl′), *v.t.,* **-soled, -sol ing.** ease the grief or sorrow of; comfort. [< Middle French *consoler* < Latin *consolari* < *com-* + *solari* soothe] —**con sol′a ble,** *adj.*

con sor ti um (kən sôr′shē əm), *n., pl.* **-ti a** (-shē ə). **1** partnership; association. **2** group, association, etc., formed by such an agreement. [< Latin < *consortem* consort]

con spic u ous (kən spik′yü əs), *adj.* **1** easily seen; clearly visible: *A traffic sign should be conspicuous.* **2** worthy of notice; remarkable. —**con spic′u ous ly,** *adv.*

con spir a cy (kən spir′ə sē), *n., pl.* **-cies. 1** act of conspiring; secret planning with others to do something unlawful or wrong, especially against a government, public personage, etc. **2** a plot or intrigue.

con spir a to ri al (kən spir′ə tôr′ē əl, kən spir′ə tōr′ē əl), *adj.* having to do with conspiracy or conspirators. —**con spir′a to′ri al ly,** *adv.*

a hat	i it	oi oil	ch child		a in about
ā age	ī ice	ou out	ng long		e in taken
ä far	o hot	u cup	sh she	ə =	i in pencil
e let	ō open	ù put	th thin		o in lemon
ē equal	ô order	ü rule	ᴛH then		u in circus
èr term			zh measure		< = derived from

GLOSSARY

con sta ble (kon′stə bəl, kun′stə bəl), *n.* a police officer, especially in a district or rural area of the United States.

con tend (kən tend′), *v.i.* **1** work hard against difficulties; fight; struggle. **2** take part in a contest; compete. **3** argue; dispute. —**con tend′er,** *n.*

con tig u ous (kən tig′yü əs), *adj.* **1.** touching. **2** adjoining; near. [< Latin *contiguus* < *contingere* touch closely.]

con va les cence (kon′və les′ns), *n.* the gradual recovery of health and strength after illness.

con ven tion al (kən ven′shə nəl), *adj.* **1** depending on conventions; customary. **2** of the usual type or design; commonly used or seen: *conventional furniture.* **3** (in the arts) following custom and traditional models; formal.

con vic tion (kən vik′shən), *n.* **1** act of proving or declaring guilty. **2** a being convinced. **3** firm belief; certainty.

con vul sive (kən vul′siv), *adj.* **1** violently disturbing. **2** having or producing convulsions or violent spasms. —**con vul′sive ly,** *adv.*

co pi ous (kō′pē əs), *adj.* more than enough; plentiful; abundant: *a copious harvest.*

copse (kops), *n.* thicket of small trees, bushes, shrubs.

cor don (kôrd′n), *n.* line or circle of soldiers, policemen, forts, etc., enclosing or guarding a place. [< French]

cor nice (kôr′nis), *n.* an ornamental, horizontal molding along the top of a wall, pillar, building, etc.

cor pus cle (kôr′pus′əl, kôr′pə səl), *n.* **1** any of the cells that form a large part of the blood, lymph, etc. **2** a very small particle.

cor pus cu lar (kôr pus′kyə lər), *adj.* of, like, or consisting of corpuscles.

coun te nance (koun′tə nəns), *n., v.,* **-nanced, -nanc ing.** —*n.* **1** expression of the face. **2** face; features: *a noble countenance.* —*v.t.* approve or encourage; sanction.

counter-, *prefix.* **1** in opposition to; against: *Counteract = act against.* **2** in return: *Counterattack = attack in return.* **3** corresponding: *Counterpart = corresponding part.*

coun ter bal ance (*n.* koun′tər bal′əns; *v.* koun′tər bal′əns), *n., v.,* **-anced, -anc ing.** —*n.* weight balancing another weight. —*v.t., v.i.* act as a counterbalance to; offset.

coun ter plot (koun′tər plot′), *n., v.,* **-plot ted, -plot ting.** —*n.* a plot to defeat another plot. —*v.i.* plot in opposition. —*v.t.* plot against (another plot or plotter).

cour i er (kėr′ē ər, kůr′ē ər), *n.* **1** messenger sent in haste: *Government dispatches were sent by couriers.* **2** a secret agent who transfers information to and from other agents.

cour ti er (kôr′tē ər), *n.* **1** person often present at a royal court. **2** person who tries to win favor by flattery.

cre scen do (krə shen′dō), *adj., adv., n., pl.* **-dos.** —*adj., adv.* (in music) with a gradual increase in force or loudness. —*n.* a gradual increase in loudness, especially in music.

cre vasse (krə vas′), *n.* a deep crack or crevice in the ice of a glacier, or in the ground after an earthquake. [< French < Old French *crevace.* Doublet of CREVICE.]

crev ice (krev′is), *n.* a narrow split or crack; fissure.

crop (krop), *v.* cut or bite off the top of.

crypt (kript), *n.* an underground room or vault.

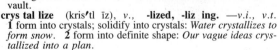

crevasse

crys tal lize (kris′tl īz), *v.,* **-lized, -liz ing.** —*v.i., v.t.* **1** form into crystals; solidify into crystals: *Water crystallizes to form snow.* **2** form into definite shape: *Our vague ideas crystallized into a plan.*

cub (kub), *n.* **1** a young bear, fox, lion, etc. **2** a young or inexperienced person. **3** cub scout. [origin uncertain]

cun ning (kun′ing), *adj.* **1** clever in deceiving; sly: *a cunning fox, a cunning thief.* **2** skillful; clever: *The old watch was a fine example of cunning workmanship.* [Old English *cunning* < *cunnan* know (how).] —**cun′ning ly,** *adv.*

cur (kėr), *n.* a dog of mixed breed; mongrel.

curt (kėrt), *adj.* rudely brief; short; abrupt: *a curt way of talking.* [< Latin *curtus* cut short] —**curt′ly,** *adv.*

cy cle (sī′kəl), *n., v.,* **-cled, -cling.** —*n.* **1** period of time or complete process of growth or action that repeats itself in the same order: *The seasons of the year—spring, summer, autumn, and winter—make a cycle.* **2** bicycle, tricycle, or motorcycle. —*v.i.* pass through a cycle; occur over and over again in the same order. [< Late Latin *cyclus* < Greek *kyklos* wheel, circle, ring]

cyn i cal (sin′ə kəl), *adj.* **1** doubting the sincerity and goodness of others. **2** sneering; sarcastic. —**cyn′i cal ly,** *adv.*

cy press (sī′prəs), *n.* **1** any of a genus of evergreen trees with hard wood and small, dark, scalelike leaves. **2** its wood, used for boards, shingles, and doors.

dan de li on (dan′dl ī′ən), *n.* a common weed with deeply notched leaves and bright, yellow flowers. [< Middle French *dent de lion* lion's tooth; from its toothed leaves]

das tard ly (das′tərd lē), *adj.* like a dastard; mean and cowardly.

deb o nair or **deb o naire** (deb′ə ner′, deb′ə nar′), *adj.* pleasant, courteous, and cheerful. [< Old French *debonaire* < *de bon aire* of good disposition] —**deb′o nair′ly,** *adv.*

de bris or **dé bris** (də brē′, dā′brē′; *British* deb′rē′), *n.* **1** the remains of anything broken down or destroyed; ruins; rubbish: *the debris from an explosion.* **2** (in geology) a mass of large fragments worn away from rock: *the debris left by a glacier.* [< French *débris*]

de cant er (di kan′tər), *n.* a glass bottle with a stopper, used for serving wine, liquor, or other liquids.

de cease (di sēs′), *n., v.,* **-ceased, -ceas ing.** —*n.* act or fact of dying; death. —*v.i.* die. [< Latin *decessus* < *decedere* depart < *de-* away + *cedere* go]

de cree (di krē′), *n., v.,* **-creed, -cree ing.** —*n.* something ordered or settled by authority; official decision. —*v.t.* **1** order or settle by authority. **2** decide; determine.

de cry (di krī′), *v.t.,* **-cried, -cry ing.** **1** express strong disapproval of; condemn. **2** make little of.

ded i cate (ded′ə kāt), *v.t.,* set apart for a sacred or solemn purpose; consecrate.

def er ence (def′ər əns), *n.* **1** respect for the judgment, opinion, wishes, etc., of another. **2** great respect.

def e ren tial (def′ə ren′shəl), *adj.* showing deference; respectful. —**def′e ren′tial ly,** *adv.*

de lir i ous (di lir′ē əs), *adj.* **1** temporarily out of one's senses; wandering in mind; raving. **2** wildly enthusiastic.

de ment ed (di men′tid), *adj.* mentally ill; insane; crazy.

de mesne (di mān′, di mēn′), *n.* house and land belonging to a feudal lord and used by him.

de mure (di myůr′), *adj.,* **-mur er, -mur est. 1** artificially proper; assuming an air of modesty; coy: *a demure smile.* **2** reserved or composed in demeanor; serious and sober. —**de mure′ly,** *adv.*

den ti frice (den′tə fris), *n.* paste, powder, or liquid for cleaning the teeth. [< Latin *dentifricium* < *dentem* tooth + *fricare* to rub]

de ploy (di ploi′), *v.t.* **1** spread out (troops, military units, etc.) from a column into a long battle line. **2** spread out, extend, or place, especially in a planned or strategic position: *deploy offensive missiles, deploy actors on a stage.* **3** use: *deploy one's talents to the best advantage.* —*v.i.* (of troops, military units, etc.) spread out strategically or so as to form a more extended front or line.

de port (di pôrt′, di pōrt′), *v.t.* **1** force to leave a country; banish; expel. See synonym study below. **2** behave or conduct (oneself) in a particular manner. [< Latin *deportare* < *de-* away + *portare* carry] —**de port′a ble,** *adj.*

Syn. 1 Banish, exile, deport mean cause to leave a country. **Banish** means to force a person, by order of authority, to leave his or her own or a foreign country, permanently or for a stated time: *Napoleon was banished to Elba.* **Exile** means either to compel another to leave his or her own country or home or voluntarily to remove oneself from either for a protracted period: *The kaiser was exiled from Germany after World War I. She exiled herself abroad because of her dissatisfaction with the government.* **Deport** usually means to banish a person from a country of which he or she is not a citizen: *Aliens who have entered the United States illegally may be deported.*

de pose (di pōz′), *v.t.,* **-posed, -pos ing.** put out of office or a position of authority, especially a high one like that of king.

de pute (di pyüt′), *v.t.,* **-put ed, -put ing.** appoint to act on one's behalf; appoint as one's substitute or agent; delegate.

de ri sion (di rizh′ən), *n.* scornful laughter; ridicule.

de ter (di ter′), *v.t.,* **-terred, -ter ring.** discourage or prevent from acting or proceeding by fear or consideration of danger or trouble; hinder.

de ter i o rate (di tir′ē ə rāt′), *v.,* **-rat ed, -rat ing.** —*v.i.* become lower in quality or value; depreciate: *Machinery deteriorates rapidly if it is not taken care of.* —*v.t.* make lower in quality or value. [< Latin *deterioratum* worsened < *deterior* worse] —**de ter′i o ra′tion,** *n.* —**de ter′i o ra′tive,** *adj.*

de ter mi nate (di ter′mə nit), *adj.* **1** with exact limits; fixed; definite. **2** settled; positive. **3** determined; resolute.

de vi ous (dē′vē əs), *adj.* **1** out of the direct way; winding. **2** straying from the right course; not straightforward: *a devious scheme, a devious nature.* —**de′vi ous ly,** *adv.*

de vise (di vīz′), *v.t.,* **-vised, -vis ing.** think out; plan or contrive; invent: *I devised a way of raising boards up to my tree house by using a pulley.*

di a tribe (dī′ə trīb), *n.* speech or discussion bitterly and violently directed against some person or thing; denunciation.

di gres sion (də gresh′ən, dī gresh′ən), *n.* a digressing; turning aside from the main subject in talking or writing.

di lap i dat ed (də lap′ə dā′tid), *adj.* fallen into ruin or disrepair; decayed through neglect. [< Latin *dilapidatum* scattered; ruined (as by hailstones) < *dis-* + *lapis* stone]

di min u tive (də min′yə tiv), *adj.* very small; tiny; minute.

din ghy (ding′ē), *n., pl.* **-ghies.** a small rowboat.

Dip per (dip′ər), *n.* either of two groups of stars in the northern sky somewhat resembling the shape of a dipper; Big Dipper or Little Dipper.

dire (dīr), *adj.,* **dir er, dir est.** causing great fear or suffering; dreadful. [< Latin *dirus*] —**dire′ly,** *adv.* —**dire′ness,** *n.*

dis arm (dis ärm′), *v.t.* **1** take weapons away from: *The police disarmed the robbers.* **2** remove anger or suspicion from; make friendly: *The speaker's honesty disarmed the angry crowd.*

dis cern (də zėrn′, də sėrn′), *v.t.* see clearly; perceive the difference between (two or more things); distinguish or recognize: *We discerned the island through the mist. There are too many conflicting opinions for me to discern the truth.* [< Latin *discernere* < *dis-* off + *cernere* to separate] —**dis cern′er,** *n.*

dis cern i ble (də zėr′nə bəl, də sėr′nə bəl), *adj.* capable of being discerned. —**dis cern′i bly,** *adv.*

dis com fi ture (dis kum′fi chùr, dis kum′fi chər), *n.* defeat of plans or hopes; frustration.

dis con so late (dis kon′sə lit), *adj.* without hope; forlorn; unhappy: *disconsolate over the death of a friend.* —**dis con′so late ly,** *adv.*

dis cre tion (dis kresh′ən), *n.* **1** quality of being discreet; great carefulness in speech or action; good judgment; wise caution: *Use your own discretion.* **2** freedom to decide or choose: *It is within the principal's discretion to punish a pupil.*

a hat	i it	oi oil	ch child		a in about
ā age	ī ice	ou out	ng long		e in taken
ä far	o hot	u cup	sh she	ə =	i in pencil
e let	ō open	ù put	th thin		o in lemon
ē equal	ô order	ü rule	ŦH then		u in circus
ėr term			zh measure	< = derived from

dis en tan gle (dis′en tang′gəl), *v.t., v.i.* **-gled, -gling.** free from tangles or complications; untangle.

dis grun tled (dis grun′tld), *adj.* in bad humor; discontented. [< *dis-* + obsolete *gruntle* to grunt, grumble]

dis heart en (dis härt′n), *v.t.* cause to lose hope; discourage; depress. —**dis heart′en ing ly,** *adv.* —**dis heart′en ment,** *n.*

di shev eled or **di shev elled** (də shev′əld), *adj.* not neat; rumpled; mussed; disordered; *disheveled appearance.*

dis mem ber (dis mem′bər), *v.t.* **1** separate or divide into parts: *After the war the defeated country was dismembered.* **2** cut or tear the limbs from; divide limb from limb. —**dis mem′ber ment,** *n.*

dis pose (dis pōz′), *v.,* **1** put in the proper order. **2** make ready or willing.

dis po si tion (dis′pə zish′ən), *n.* **1** one's habitual ways of acting toward others or of thinking about things; nature: *a cheerful disposition.* **2** tendency; inclination: *a disposition to argue.* **3** a settlement: *What disposition did the court make of the case?*

dis qui et (dis kwī′ət), *v.t.* make uneasy or anxious; disturb. —*n.* uneasy feelings; anxiety. —**dis qui′et ing ly,** *adv.*

dis sec tion (di sek′shən, dī sek′shən), *n.* act of cutting apart an animal, plant, etc., in order to examine or study the structure.

dis sem ble (di sem′bəl), *v.,* **-bled, -bling.** —*v.t.* **1** hide (one's real feelings, thoughts, plans, etc.); disguise. **2** pretend; feign. —*v.i.* conceal one's opinions, motives, etc.

dis sim i lar (di sim′ə lər), *adj.* not similar; unlike; different.

dis sim u late (di sim′yə lāt), *v.,* **-lat ed, -lat ing.** —*v.t.* disguise or hide under a pretense; dissemble. —*v.i.* hide the truth; dissemble. —**dis sim′u la′tion,** *n.* —**dis sim′u la′tor,** *n.*

dis suade (di swād′), *v.t.,* **-suad ed, -suad ing.** **1** persuade not to do something. **2** advise against. [< Latin *dissuadere* < *dis-* against + *suadere* to urge]

dis tem per (dis tem′pər), *n.* an infectious viral disease of dogs and other animals, accompanied by fever, a short, dry cough, and a loss of strength.

dis traught (dis trôt′), *adj.* **1** in a state of mental conflict and confusion; distracted. **2** crazed.

di vers (dī′vərz), *adj.* several, various.

di ver si ty (də vėr′sə tē, dī vėr′sə tē), *n., pl.* **-ties. 1** complete difference; unlikeness. **2** point of unlikeness. **3** variety: *a diversity of food on the table.*

di vert (də vėrt′, dī vėrt′), *v.t.* **1** turn aside: *A ditch diverted water from the stream into the fields.* **2** amuse; entertain: *Listening to music diverted me after a hard day's work.*

dog ged (dô′gid, dog′id), *adj.* not giving up; stubborn: *dogged determination.* [< *dog*] —**dog′ged ness,** *n.*

dog ma (dôg′mə, dog′mə), *n., pl.* **-mas, -ma ta** (-mə tə). **1** belief taught or held as true, especially by authority of a church; doctrine. **2** any system of established principles and tenets.

dole ful (dōl′fəl), *adj.* very sad or dreary; mournful; dismal. —**dole′ful ly,** *adv.* —**dole′ful ness,** *n.*

do mes tic (də mes′tik), *adj.* **1** of the home, household, or family affairs: *domestic problems, a domestic scene.* **2** attached to home; devoted to family life. —*n.* servant in a household. [< Latin *domesticus* < *domus* house]

do min ion (də min′yən), *n.* power or right of governing and

GLOSSARY

729

GLOSSARY

controlling; rule; control.

dor mant (dôr′mənt), *adj.* **1** lying asleep; sleeping or apparently sleeping. **2** in a state of rest or inactivity; not in motion.

dote (dōt), *v.i.,* **dot ed, dot ing. 1** be weak-minded and childish because of old age. **2 dote on** or **dote upon,** be foolishly fond of; be too fond of. [Middle English *doten*] —**dot′er,** *n.*

dow dy (dou′dē), *adj.,* **-di er, -di est.** poorly dressed; not neat; not stylish; shabby. [origin uncertain] —**dow′di ly,** *adv.*

down (doun), *n.* Usually, **downs,** *pl.* rolling, grassy land. [Old English *dūn* hill]

dry gulch, 1 to ambush with the intent of killing. **2** to betray by a sudden change of attitude or allegiance.

du bi ous (dü′bē əs, dyü′bē əs), *adj.* **1** filled with or being in doubt; doubtful; uncertain. **2** feeling doubt; hesitating. [< Latin *dubiosus* < *dubius* doubtful] —**du′bi ous ly,** *adv.*

dun (dun), *adj.* dull, grayish-brown. —*n.* a dull, grayish brown.

dys pep tic (dis pep′tik), *adj.* **1** having to do with dyspepsia, or indigestion. **2** suffering from dyspepsia. **3** gloomy; pessimistic.

ebb (eb), *n.* a flowing of the tide away from the shore; fall of the tide. —*v.i.* **1** flow out; fall: *The tide ebbed.* **2** grow less or weaker; decline: *My courage ebbed as I neared the haunted house.*

eb on y (eb′ə nē), *n., pl.* **-on ies,** *adj.* —*n.* **1** a hard, durable black wood. **2** any of a genus of tropical trees that yield this wood.

ec cen tric i ty (ek′sen tris′ə tē), *n., pl.* **-ties.** something strange or out of the ordinary; oddity; peculiarity.

ec sta sy (ek′stə sē), *n., pl.* **-sies. 1** condition of very great joy; thrilling or overwhelming delight. **2** any strong feeling that completely absorbs the mind; uncontrollable emotion.

ec stat ic (ek stat′ik), *adj.* **1** full of ecstasy: *an ecstatic look of pleasure.* **2** caused by ecstasy: *an ecstatic mood.*

edge (ej), *n., v.,* **edged, edg ing.** —*n.* **1** line or place where something ends or begins; part farthest from the middle; side. **2** the extreme border or margin of anything; rim; brink. **3 on edge, a** disturbed; irritated; tense. **b** eager; anxious. **4 take the edge off,** take away the force, strength, or pleasure of. —*v.t.* **1** put an edge on; form an edge on: *edge a path with flowers.* **2** move little by little. —*v.i.* move sideways.

e go is tic (ē′gō is′tik, eg′ō is′tik), *adj.* **1** seeking the welfare of oneself only; selfish. **2** talking too much about oneself; conceited. —**e′go is′ti cal,** *adj.*

e go is ti cal (ē′gō is′tə kəl, eg′ō is′tə kəl), *adj.* egoistic.

e go tism (ē′gə tiz′əm, eg′ə tiz′əm), *n.* **1** habit of thinking, talking, or writing too much of oneself; conceit. **2** selfishness.

e gret (ē′gret, eg′ret), *n.* any of various herons which in mating season grow tufts of beautiful, long plumes.

eke (ēk), *v.t.,* **eked, ek ing. 1 eke out, a** add to; increase. **b** barely manage to make (a living, a profit, etc.). **c** make (something) last longer by careful or economic use. **2** ARCHAIC and DIALECT. increase.

el e va tion (el′ə vā′shən), *n.* **1** a raised place; high place: *A hill is an elevation.* **2** height above the earth's surface: *The airplane cruised at an elevation of 35,000 feet.* **3** height above sea level: *The elevation of Denver is 5300 feet.* **4** dignity; loftiness; nobility. **5** a raising; lifting up: *the elevation of Caesar from general to ruler of Rome.*

e lic it (i lis′it), *v.t.* draw forth; bring out: *elicit the truth by discussion.* [< Latin *elicitum* lured out < *ex-* out + *lacere* entice]

em a nate (em′ə nāt), *v.,* **-nat ed, -nat ing.** —*v.i.* originate from a person or thing as a source; come forth; spread out: *The rumor emanated from Chicago.* —*v.t.* send out; emit. [< Latin *emanatum* flowed out < *ex-* out + *manare* to flow]

em bat tle (em bat′l), *v.t.,* **-tled, -tling. 1** prepare for battle; form into battle order. **2** fortify.

em bed (em bed′), *v.t.,* **-bed ded, -bed ding. 1** fix or enclose in a surrounding mass; fasten firmly: *Precious stones are often found embedded in rock.* **2** plant in a bed: *He embedded the bulbs in a box of sand.* Also, **imbed.**

em i grate (em′ə grāt), *v.i.,* **-grat ed, -grat ing.** leave one's own country or region to settle in another. [< Latin *emigratum* moved out < *ex-* out + *migrare* to move] →**emigrate, immigrate.** *Emigrate* means to move out of a country or region, *immigrate* to move into a country. One who *emigrates* from Norway might *immigrate* to the United States.

e mit (i mit′), *v.t.,* **e mit ted, e mit ting. 1** give off; send out; discharge: *The sun emits light and heat.* **2** put into circulation; issue. **3** utter; express. [< Latin *emittere* < *ex-* out + *mittere* send]

en deav or (en dev′ər), *v.i., v.t.* make an effort; try hard; attempt earnestly; strive: *A runner endeavors to win a race.* —*n.* an earnest attempt; hard try; effort.

en gulf (en gulf′), *v.t.* swallow up; overwhelm: *A wave engulfed the small boat.* —**en gulf′ment,** *n.*

en sue (en sü′), *v.i.,* **-sued, -su ing. 1** come after; follow. **2** happen as a result.

en tan gle (en tang′gəl), *v.t.,* **-gled, -gling. 1** get twisted up and caught; tangle: *I entangled my feet in the coil of rope and fell down.* **2** get into difficulty; involve: *Don't get entangled in their scheme.* **3** perplex; confuse. —**en tan′gle ment,** *n.*

en ter prise (en′tər prīz), *n.* **1** an important, difficult, or dangerous plan to be tried; great or bold undertaking. **2** any undertaking; project; venture: *a business enterprise.*

en thuse (en thüz′), *v.,* **-thused, -thus ing.** INFORMAL. —*v.i.* show enthusiasm. —*v.t.* fill with enthusiasm. [black-formation < *enthusiasm*]

en treat y (en trē′tē), *n., pl.* **-treat ies.** an earnest request; prayer or appeal: *I gave in to the children's entreaties.*

en vel op (en vel′əp), *v.t.* **1** wrap or cover; enfold. **2** hide; conceal: *Fog enveloped the village.* **3** surround; encircle: *envelop the enemy.* [< Old French *enveloper* < *en-* in + *voluper* to wrap]

ep i logue or **ep i log** (ep′ə lôg, ep′ə log), *n.* **1** a concluding section added to a novel, poem, etc., that rounds out or interprets the work. **2** any concluding act or event.

ep i tha la mic (ep′ə thə lā′mik), *adj.* honoring a bride, bridegroom, or newly married couple. [< Latin < Greek *epithalamion* < *epi-* upon + *thalamos* bridal chamber]

ere (er, ar), ARCHAIC. —*prep.* before.

er mine (ėr′mən), *n., pl.* **-mines** or **-mine.** any of several kinds of weasel of northern regions which are brown in summer but white with a black-tipped tail in winter.

ermine

Esq. or **Esqr.,** Esquire, a title of respect.

e ther (ē′thər), *n.* a colorless, volatile, flammable, sweet-smelling liquid, produced by the action of sulfuric acid on ethyl alcohol. Because its fumes cause unconsciousness when deeply inhaled, ether is used as an anesthetic.

e vac u ate (i vak′yü āt), *v.t.,* **-at ed, -at ing. 1** leave empty; withdraw from: *The tenants evacuated the building.* **2** withdraw; remove: *evacuate civilians from a war zone.* [< Latin *evacuatum* emptied out < *ex-* out + *vacuus* empty] —**e vac′u a′tor,** *n.*

e voke (i vōk′), *v.t.,* **e voked, e vok ing.** call forth; bring out; elicit: *A good joke evokes a laugh.*

e volve (i volv′), *v.,* **e volved, e volv ing.** —*v.t.* **1** develop gradually; work out; unfold: *evolve a plan for earning money.* **2** develop by a process of growth and change to a more highly organized condition.

ew er (yü′ər), *n.* a wide-mouthed water pitcher.

ex ceed ing ly (ek sē′ding lē), *adv.* very greatly; extremely.

ex cres cence (ek skres′ns), *n.* **1** an unnatural growth: *Warts are excrescences on the skin.* **2** a natural outgrowth: *Finger-nails are excrescences.*

ex cru ci at ing (ek skrü′shē ā′ting), *adj.* causing great suffering; very painful; torturing. **—ex cru′ci at′ing ly,** *adv.*

ex e cute (ek′sə kyüt), *v.t.,* **-cut ed, -cut ing. 1** carry out; do. **2** make according to a plan or design: *The same artist executed that painting and that statue.*

ex hil a rate (eg zil′ə rāt′), *v.t.,* **-rat ed, -rat ing.** make merry or lively; put into high spirits; cheer.

ex pel (ek spel′), *v.t.,* **-pelled, -pel ling. 1** drive out with much force; force out. **2** dismiss permanently.

ex trav a gant (ek strav′ə gənt), *adj.* spending carelessly and lavishly; wasteful. **—ex trav′a gant ly,** *adv.*

ex trem i ty (ek strem′ə tē), *n., pl.* **-ties. 1** the very end; farthest possible place; last part or point. **2 extremities,** *pl.* the hands and feet. **3** an extreme degree: *Joy is the extremity of happiness.*

ex u ber ant (eg zü′bər ənt), *adj.* **1** very abundant; overflowing; lavish: *exuberant joy, an exuberant welcome.* **2** profuse in growth; luxuriant: *the exuberant vegetation of the jungle.*

fal ter (fôl′tər), *v.i.* **1** hesitate in action from lack of courage. **2** move unsteadily; stumble; totter. **3** come forth in hesitating, broken sounds: *My voice faltered as I stood up to speak.* **—fal′ter er,** *n.* **—fal′ter ing ly,** *adv.*

fan cied (fan′sēd), *adj.* imagined; imaginary; *a fancied insult.*

fan ci er (fan′sē ər), *n.* person who has a liking for or is especially interested in something: *a dog fancier.*

fan cy (fan′sē), *v.,* **-cied, -cy ing,** *n., pl.* **-cies. —v.t. 1** picture to oneself; imagine; conceive: *Can you fancy yourself on the moon?* **2** have an idea or belief; suppose: *I fancy that is right, but I am not sure.* **3** be fond of; like: *I fancy the idea of having a picnic.* **—n. 1** power to imagine; imagination; fantasy: *Dragons and giants are creatures of fancy.* **2** a liking.

fas tid i ous (fa stid′ē əs), *adj.* hard to please; dainty in taste; easily disgusted.

fast ness (fast′nis), *n.* **1** a strong, safe place; stronghold. **2** a being fast or firm. **3** a being quick or rapid; swiftness.

fat (fat), *n., adj.,* **fat ter, fat test,** *v.,* **fat ted, fat ting. —n.** a white or yellow oily substance formed in animal tissue, made up chiefly of carbon, hydrogen, and oxygen **—adj. 1** consisting of or containing fat; oily: *fat meat.* **2** in a well-fed condition; plump: *a fat baby, a fat pig.* **3** fertile: *fat land.* **4** full of good things; plentifully supplied; plentiful.

fa tal ist (fā′tl ist), *n.* believer in fatalism, the belief that fate controls everything that happens.

fa tigue (fə tēg′), *n.* **1** weariness caused by hard work or effort. **2** task or exertion producing weariness.

fee ble (fē′bəl), *adj.,* **-bler, -blest.** lacking strength; weak; frail: *The patient is still feeble.*

fe rine (fēr′īn), *adj.* a wild animal.

fer vent (fėr′vənt), *adj.* showing great warmth of feeling; very earnest; ardent: *fervent devotion.* **—fer′vent ly,** *adv.*

fe ro cious (fə rō′shəs), *adj.* **1** savagely cruel or destructive; fierce. **2** INFORMAL. extremely intense: *a ferocious headache.* [< Latin *ferocem* fierce] **—fe ro′cious ly,** *adv.* **—fe ro′cious ness,** *n.*

fer vid (fėr′vid), *adj.* **1** full of strong feeling; intensely emotional; ardent; spirited. **2** intensely hot. **—fer′vid ly,** *adv.*

fes toon (fe stün′), *n.* a string or chain of flowers, leaves, ribbons, etc., hanging in a curve between two points. **—v.t.** decorate with festoons.

fi as co (fē as′kō), *n., pl.* **-cos** or **-coes.** a complete or ridiculous failure; humiliating breakdown. [< Italian, literally, flask]

fill (fil), *v.t.* **1** make full; put into until there is room for nothing more: *fill a cup.* **—n. 1** enough to fill something. **2** something that fills. Earth and rock used to level uneven land is called fill.

fine-tooth comb, 1 comb with projections very close together.

2 SLANG. look for carefully.

fis sure (fish′ər), *n., v.,* **-sured, -sur ing. —n. 1** a long, narrow opening; split; crack. **2** a splitting apart; division into parts. **—v.t.** split apart; divide into parts. **—v.i.** become split or cleft. [< Latin *fissura* < *findere* cleave]

flag (flag), *n.* **1** a piece of cloth varying in size, color, and design but most frequently oblong or square, attached by one edge to a staff. **—v.t.** stop or signal.

fla min go (flə ming′gō), *n., pl.* **-gos** or **-goes.** any of a family of large, web-footed, aquatic tropical birds with feathers that vary from pink to scarlet. [< Portuguese < Spanish *flamenco,* literally, Flemish (from comparing the ruddy complexion of Flemings to the bird's color)]

flat (flat), *adj.,* **flat ter, flat test,** *n.* **—adj. 1** smooth and level; even; plane: *flat land.* **2** at full length; horizontal: *The storm left the trees flat on the ground.* **3** not very deep or thick: *A plate is flat.* **4** with little air in it; deflated: *a flat tire.* **5** not to be changed; positive; absolute: *a flat refusal.* **6** in music: below the true pitch; too low in pitch. **—n. 1** something flat. **2** flatboat. **3** land that is flat and level. **4** swamp.

flaw (flô), *n.* **1** gust of wind; sudden squall. **2** a short period of rough weather. [origin uncertain]

flaw less (flô′lis), *adj.* without a flaw; perfect. **—flaw′less ly,** *adv.* **—flaw′less ness,** *n.*

fledg ling or **fledge ling** (flej′ling), *n.* **1** a young bird that has just grown feathers needed for flying. **2** a young, inexperienced person.

flim sy (flim′zē), *adj.,* **-si er, -si est,** *n., pl.* **-sies. —adj.** lacking material strength; not solid or substantial; light and thin; slight; frail: *The flimsy grocery bag tore.*

fling (fling), *v.t.,* **flung, fling ing. 1** throw with force; throw: *fling a stone.* **2** throw aside; discard; abandon.

flood (flud), *n.* **1** a great flow of water over what is usually dry land. **2** a large amount of water. **—v.i. 1** pour out or stream like a flood. **2** flow like a flood.

flo rid (flôr′id, flor′id), *adj.* **1** reddish; ruddy: *a florid complexion.* **2** elaborately ornamented; showy; ornate: *florid language.*

floss (flôs, flos), *n.* **1** short, loose, silk fibers. **2** a shiny, untwisted silk thread made from such fibers. It is used for embroidery. **3** soft, silky fluff or fibers. Milkweed pods contain white floss. **—v.i.** use dental floss: *Did you floss this morning?*

flot sam (flot′səm), *n.* **1** wreckage of a ship or its cargo found floating on the sea. **2 flotsam and jetsam, a** wreckage or cargo found floating on the sea or washed ashore. **b** odds and ends.

flu ent (flü′ənt), *adj.* **1** flowing smoothly or easily. **2** speaking or writing easily and rapidly. **—flu′ent ly,** *adv.*

flung (flung), *v.* pt. and pp. of **fling.**

flut ed (flü′tid), *adj.* having long, round grooves.

foe (fō), *n.* person or group that hates and seeks to injure another; enemy.

foil (foil), *v.t.* **1** prevent from carrying out plans, attempts, etc.; get the better of; outwit or defeat: *The hero foiled the villain.* **2** prevent (a scheme, plan, etc.) from being carried out.

fore bod ing (fôr bō′ding, fōr bō′ding), *n.* **1** prediction; warning. **2** a feeling that something bad is going to happen.

fore close (fôr klōz′, fōr klōz′), *v.,* **-closed, -closing, —v.t. 1** shut out; prevent; exclude: *foreclose objections.* **2** take away

---

a hat	**i** it	**oi** oil	**ch** child		(a in about
ā age	**ī** ice	**ou** out	**ng** long		e in taken
ä far	**o** hot	**u** cup	**sh** she	**ə** =	i in pencil
e let	**ō** open	**ù** put	**th** thin		o in lemon
ē equal	**ô** order	**ü** rule	**ŦH** then		(u in circus
ėr term			**zh** measure		< = derived from

the right to redeem (a mortgage). When the conditions of a mortgage are not met, the holder can foreclose and have the property sold to satisfy his or her claim. —**fore clos′er,** *n.*

fore sight (fôr′sīt′, fōr′sīt′), *n.* **1** power to see or know beforehand what is likely to happen. **2** careful thought for the future.

fore stall (fôr stôl′, fōr stôll′), *v.t.* **1** prevent by acting first. **2** act sooner than; get ahead of. [Middle English *forstallen* < Old English *foresteall* prevention]

for lorn (fôr lôrn′), *adj.* **1** left alone and neglected. **2** wretched in feeling or looks; unhappy. **3** hopeless; desperate. —**for lorn′ly,** *adv.*

for mi da ble (fôr′mə də bəl), *adj.* hard to overcome; hard to deal with; to be dreaded: *a formidable opponent.*

foy er (foi′ər, foi′ā), *n.* an entrance hall used as a lounging room in a theater, apartment house, or hotel; lobby.

frail ty (frāl′tē), *n., pl.* **-ties. 1** a being frail; weakness. **2** moral weakness; liability to yield to temptation.

frank furt er (frangk′fər tər), *n.* a reddish smoked sausage made of beef and pork, or of beef alone; wiener. [< German *Frankfurter* of or from Frankfurt]

fraud u lent (frô′jə lənt, frô′dyə lənt), *adj.* **1** guilty of fraud; cheating; dishonest. **2** intended to deceive: *a fraudulent offer.* **3** done by fraud; obtained by trickery. —**fraud′u lent ly,** *adv.*

freight (frāt), *n.* **1** load of goods carried on a train, truck, ship, or aircraft. **2** train for carrying goods. **3** load; burden. —*v.t.* **1** load with freight. **2** load; burden; oppress.

frit il lar y (frit′l er′ē), *n., pl.* **-lar ies. 1** any of a genus of bulbous plants of the lily family, having drooping, bell-shaped flowers spotted with dark green or purple.

froth y (frô′thē, froth′ē), *adj.,* **froth i er, froth i est. 1** foamy. **2** light or trifling; unimportant: *frothy conversation.*

fruit less (früt′lis), *adj.* **1** having no results; of no use; unsuccessful. **2** producing no fruit. —**fruit′less ly,** *adv.*

fugue (fyüg), *n.* in psychiatry, a period during which a patient suffers from loss of memory, often begins a new life, and, upon recovery, remembers nothing of the amnesic period.

fun da men tal (fun′də men′tl), *adj.* of or forming a foundation or basis; essential; basic: *Reading is a fundamental skill.*

fu tur i ty (fyü tûr′ə tē, fyü tyûr′ə tē), *n., pl.* **-ties. 1** future. **2** a future state or event. **3** quality, condition, or fact of being future.

gab ble (gab′əl), *v.,* **-bled, -bling,** *n.* —*v.i.* talk rapidly with little or no meaning; jabber. —*n.* rapid talk with little or no meaning. [probably imitative] —**gab′bler,** *n.*

gait (gāt), *n.* **1** the manner of walking or running: *He has a lame gait because of an injured foot.* **2** (of horses) any one of various manners of stepping or running, as the gallop, trot, pace, etc.

gal le on (gal′ē ən, gal′yən), *n.* a large, high ship with three or four decks, used especially in the 1400's and 1500's. [< Spanish *galeón* < *galea* galley]

gar ish (ger′ish, gar′ish), *adj.* **1** excessively bright; glaring: *a garish yellow.* **2** obtrusively bright in color; gaudy: *a garish suit.*

gar land (gär′lənd), *n.* wreath or string of flowers, leaves, etc. —*v.t.* **1** decorate with garlands. **2** form into garlands. [< Old French *garlande*]

gar ru lous (gar′ə ləs, gar′yə ləs), *adj.* **1** talking too much; talkative. **2** using too many words; wordy. [< Latin *garrulus* < *garrire* to chatter] —**gar′ru lous ly,** *adv.*

gaunt (gônt, gänt), *adj.* **1** very thin and bony; with hollow eyes and a starved look: *Sickness had made him gaunt.*

gaunt let (gônt′lit, gänt′lit), *n.* **1** a former punishment or torture in which the offender had to run between two rows of people who struck him or her with clubs or other weapons. **2 run the gauntlet, a** pass between two rows of people each of whom strikes the runner as he or she passes. **b** be exposed to unfriendly attacks or severe criticism. Also, **gantlet.** [< Swed-

ish *gatlopp* a running through a lane]

gee pole, a pole to direct a team of animals to turn right.

gen ial (jē′nyəl), *adj.* smiling and pleasant; cheerful and friendly; kindly: *a genial welcome.* [< Latin *genialis,* literally, belonging to the genius < *genius* genius] —**ge′ni al′ i ty,** *n.*

ges tic u late (je stik′yə lāt), *v.i.,* **-lat ed, -lat ing.** make or use gestures to show ideas or feeling. [< Latin *gesticulatum* gesticulated, ultimately < *gestus* gesture] —**ges tic′u la′tion,** *n.*

gin ger ly (jin′jər lē), *adv.* with extreme care or caution. —*adj.* extremely cautious or wary. —**gin′ger li ness,** *n.*

gir dle (gėr′dl), *n.* **1** belt, sash, cord, etc., worn around the waist. **2** anything that surrounds: *a girdle of trees around the pond.* **3** a light corset worn about the hips or waist.

glan du lar (glan′jə lər, glan′dyə lər), *adj.* **1** of or like a gland. **2** having glands. **3** made up of glands. —**glan′du lar ly,** *adv.*

glow er (glou′ər), *v.i.* stare angrily; scowl fiercely: *The rivals glowered at each other.* —*n.* an angry stare; fierce scowl.

gnarled (närld), *adj.* containing gnarls; knotted; twisted.

gnash (nash), *v.t.* strike or grind together: *gnash one's teeth.*

goad (gōd), *n.* **1** a sharp-pointed stick for driving cattle; gad. **2** anything which drives or urges one on. —*v.t.* drive or urge on; act as a goad to: *Hunger can goad a person to steal.* [Old English *gād*]

gorge (gôrj), *n.* **1** a deep, narrow valley, usually steep and rocky, especially one with a stream. **2** mass stopping up a narrow passage: *An ice gorge blocked the river.*

graft (graft), *n.* **1** dishonest gains or unlawful profits made by a person in and through an official position. **2** money dishonestly and improperly taken. —*v.i.* make money by dishonest or unlawful means.

griev ous (grē′vəs), *adj.* **1** hard to bear; causing great pain or suffering. **2** very evil or offensive; outrageous.

grope (grōp), *v.,* **groped, grop ing.** —*v.i.* **1** feel about with the hands: *I groped for a flashlight when the lights went out.* **2** search blindly and uncertainly: *The detectives groped for some clue to the mysterious crime.*

gru el ing or **gru el ling** (grü′ə ling), *adj.* very tiring; exhausting: *The marathon is a grueling contest.* —*n.* an exhausting or very tiring experience. —**gru′el ing ly, gru′el ling ly,** *adv.*

guer ril la (gə ril′ə), *n.* member of a band of fighters who harass the enemy by sudden raids, ambushes, etc. Guerrillas are not part of a regular army. —*adj.* of or by guerrillas: *a guerrilla attack.*

haft (haft), *n.* handle, especially that of a knife, sword, etc.

ham let (ham′lit), *n.* a small village; little group of houses in the country.

hand it to you, INFORMAL. give credit or praise to.

hant (haunt), *n.* haunt.

har ry (har′ē), *v.t.,* **-ried, -ry ing. 1** raid and rob with violence; lay waste; pillage. **2** keep troubling; worry; torment.

haunt (hônt, hänt), *v.t.* visit frequently and habitually with manifestations of influence and presence: *People say ghosts haunt that old house.* —*n.* place often gone to or visited: *The swimming pool was the children's favorite haunt.* **2** DIALECT. ghost.

head (hed), *n.* **1** the top part of the human body containing the brain, eyes, nose, ears, and mouth. **2** the top part of anything: *the head of a pin.* **3** the front part of anything: *the head of a procession.* **4** the chief person; leader; commander; director. **5** the source of a river or stream.

go to one's head, a affect one's mind. **b** make one dizzy. **c** make one conceited.

hang one's head, be ashamed and show that one is.

head and shoulders above, considerably better than; much superior to.

heark en (här′kən), *v.i.* pay attention to what is said; listen attentively; listen. Also, **harken.** [Old English *heorcnian*]

hence (hens), *adv.* **1** as a result of this; therefore: *The king died, and hence his son became king.* **2** from now: *years hence.*

hep (hep), *adj.* SLANG. informed about; familiar with.

he red i tar y (hə red′ə ter′ē), *adj.* **1** passing by inheritance from generation to generation: *"Prince" and "princess" are hereditary titles.* **2** transmitted or capable of being transmitted by means of genes from parents to offspring: *Color blindness is hereditary.* **3** derived from one's parents or ancestors: *a hereditary custom, a hereditary enemy to a country.*

here in af ter (hir′ in af′tər), *adv.* afterward in this document, statement, etc.

hi a tus (hī ā′təs), *n., pl.* **-tus es** or **-tus.** an empty space; space from which something necessary to completeness is missing; gap: *A lost or erased part of a manuscript is a hiatus.* [< Latin, gap < *hiare* to gape]

hi er o glyph ic (hī′ər ə glif′ik), *n.* picture, character, or symbol standing for a word, idea, or sound; hieroglyph: *The ancient Egyptians used hieroglyphics instead of an alphabet like ours.* [< Late Latin *hieroglyphicus* < Greek *hieroglyphikos* < *hieros* sacred + *glyphē* a carving]

hilt (hilt), *n.* handle of a sword, dagger, or tool.

hist (hist), *interj.* be still! listen!

hith er (hiŦн′ər), *adv.* **1** to this place; here. **2 hither and thither,** here and there

hith er to (hiŦн′ər tü′), *adv.* until now: *a fact hitherto unknown.*

hoard (hôrd, hōrd), *v.t., v.i.* save and store away (money, goods, etc.) for preservation or future use: *A squirrel hoards nuts for the winter.*

hue (hyü), *n.* that property of color by which it can be distinguished as red, yellow, blue, and other regions of the spectrum; color: *all the hues of the rainbow.*

hum bug (hum′bug′), *n., v.,* **-bugged, -bug ging.** —*n.* person who tries to deceive or cheat; fraud; impostor. —*v.t.* deceive with a sham; cheat. [origin unknown]

hu mil i ate (hyü mil′ē āt), *v.t.,* **-at ed, -at ing.** lower the pride, dignity, or self-respect of; make ashamed. [< Latin *humiliare* < *humilis* low.] —**hu mil′i at′ing ly,** *adv.*

hy a cinth (hī′ə sinth), *n.* **1** plant of the lily family that grows from a bulb and has a spike of small, fragrant, bell-shaped flowers. **2** its flower.

hy drau lic (hī drô′lik), *adj.* **1** having to do with water or other liquids at rest or in motion. **2** operated by the pressure of water or other liquids in motion, especially when forced through an opening or openings: *a hydraulic press.* [< Latin *hydraulicus,* ultimately < Greek *hydōr* water + *aulos* pipe] —**hy drau′li cal ly,** *adv.*

hy dro pho by (hī′drə fō′bē), *n.* rabies.

hyp o crit i cal (hip′ə krit′ə kəl), *adj.* of or like a hypocrite, a person who pretends to be what he or she is not; insincere.

hy poth e sis (hī poth′ə sis), *n., pl.* **-ses** (-sēz′). **1** something assumed because it seems likely to be a true explanation. **2** proposition assumed as a basis for reasoning. [< Greek < *hypo-* under + *thesis* a placing]

-ian, *suffix.* a form of **-an,** as in *mammalian, Italian.*

i bis (ī′bis), *n., pl.* **i bis es** or **i bis.** any of various large, long-legged wading birds of warm regions having long, downward-curving bills.

i de al ism (ī dē′ə liz′əm), *n.* an acting according to one's ideals of what ought to be, regardless of circumstances or of the approval or disapproval of others; a cherishing of fine ideals.

i dle (ī′dl), *adj.,* **i dler, i dlest. 1** doing nothing; not busy; not working: *idle hands.* **2** fond of doing nothing; lazy. —**i′dle ness,** *n.* —**i′dly,** *adv.*

il lit er a cy (i lit′ər ə sē), *n., pl.* **-cies. 1** inability to read and write. **2** lack of education; lack of cultural knowledge. **3** error

in speaking or writing, caused by a lack of education or knowledge.

im mi nent (im′ə nənt), *adj.* likely to happen soon; about to occur: *Black clouds show rain is imminent.* [< Latin *imminentem* overhanging, threatening] —**im′mi nent ly,** *adv.*

im mor tal (i môr′tl), *adj.* **1** living forever; never dying; everlasting. **2** of or having to do with immortal beings or immortality; divine.—**im mor′tal ly,** *adv.*

im pair (im per′, im par′), *v.t.* make worse; damage; harm.

im pal pa ble (im pal′pə bəl), *adj.* **1** that cannot be felt by touching; intangible: *Sunbeams and shadows are impalpable.* **2** very hard to understand; that cannot be grasped by the mind: *impalpable distinctions.* —**im pal′pa bly,** *adv.*

im par tial (im pär′shəl), *adj.* showing no more favor to one side than to the other; fair; just.

im peach (im pēch′), *v.t.* **1** accuse (a public official) of wrong conduct during office before a competent tribunal: *The judge was impeached.* **2** charge with wrongdoing; accuse.

im per a tive (im per′ə tiv), *adj.* not to be avoided; that must be done; urgent; necessary: *It is imperative that this very sick child should stay in bed.* [< Latin *imperativus* < *imperare* to command]

im per cep ti ble (im′pər sep′tə bəl), *adj.* that cannot be perceived or felt; very slight, gradual, subtle, or indistinct. —**im′per cep′ti bly,** *adv.*

im per i ous (im pir′ē əs), *adj.* **1** haughty or arrogant; domineering; overbearing. **2** not to be avoided; necessary; urgent. —**im per′i ous ly,** *adv.* —**im per′i ous ness,** *n.*

im promp tu (im promp′tü, im promp′tyü), *adv.* without previous thought or preparation; offhand: *a speech made impromptu.* —*adj.* made or done without previous thought or preparation: *an impromptu speech, an impromptu party.*

im pro vise (im′prə vīz), *v.t.* **-vised, -vis ing. 1** make up (music, poetry, etc.) on the spur of the moment; sing, recite, speak, etc., without preparation. **2** provide offhand; make for the occasion: *The stranded motorists improvised a tent out of two blankets and some long poles.* —**im′pro vis′er,** *n.*

im pu dent (im′pyə dənt), *adj.* shamelessly bold; very rude; insolent. [<Latin *impudentem* < *in-* not + *pudere* be modest]

im pulse (im′puls), *n.* a sudden, driving force or influence; thrust, push.

im pul sive (im pul′siv), *adj.* acting or done upon impulse; with a sudden inclination or tendency to act: *Impulsive buyers often purchase things they don't need.* —**im pul′sive ly,** *adv.*

in-, *prefix.* not; the opposite of; the absence of: *Inexpensive = not expensive. Inattention = the absence of attention.* Also, **i-, il-, im-,** and **ir-.** [< Latin]

in ac tiv i ty (in′ak tiv′ə tē), *n.* absence of activity; idleness; slowness.

in ad e quate (in ad′ə kwit), *adj.* not adequate; not enough; not as much as is needed: *inadequate preparation for an examination.* —**in ad′e quate ly,** *adv.* —**in ad′e quate ness,** *n.*

in ar tic u late (in′är tik′yə lit), *adj.* **1** not uttered in distinct syllables or words: *an inarticulate mutter.* **2** unable to speak in words; dumb: *inarticulate with grief. Cats and dogs are inarticulate.* **3** not able to put one's thoughts or feelings into words easily and clearly. —**in′ar tic′u late ly,** *adv.*

in au gu rate (in ô′gyə rāt′), *v.t.,* **-rat ed, -rat ing. 1** install in office with formal ceremonies: *A President of the United States is inaugurated every four years.* **2** make a formal beginning of; begin.

Pronunciation key:

a hat	i it	oi oil	ch child	
ā age	ī ice	ou out	ng long	(a in about
ä far	o hot	u cup	sh she	e in taken
e let	ō open	u̇ put	th thin	ə { i in pencil
ē equal	ô order	ü rule	Ŧн then	o in lemon
ėr term			zh measure	(u in circus
				< = derived from

GLOSSARY

733

incarcerate

in car ce rate (in kär′sə rāt′), *v.t.*, **-rat ed, -rat ing.** imprison.

in cal cu la ble (in kal′kyə lə bəl), *adj.* **1** too great in number to be counted; innumerable. **2** impossible to foretell or reckon beforehand. **3** that cannot be relied on; uncertain.

in car nate (*adj.* in kär′nit, in kär′nāt; *v.* in kär′nāt), *adj.*, *v.*, **-nat ed, -nat ing.** —*adj.* embodied in flesh, especially in human form: *the Devil incarnate.* —*v.t.* make incarnate; embody: *Lancelot incarnated the spirit of chivalry.*

in con ti nent (in kon′tə nənt), *adj.* without self-control. —**in con′ti nent ly,** *adv.*

in cor rupt i ble (in′kə rup′tə bəl), *adj.* **1** not to be corrupted; honest. **2** not subject to decay; lasting forever.

in dent (*v.* in dent′; *n.* in′dent, in dent′), *v.t.* **1** make notches or jags in (an edge, line, border, etc.): *an indented coastline.* **2** begin (a line) farther from the left margin than the other lines: *The first line of a paragraph is usually indented.* —*v.i.* form a notch or recess. —*n.* a notch; indentation. [< Old French *endenter* < Late Latin *indenture* to crunch on < Latin *in-* in + *dentem* tooth]

in dig nant (in dig′nənt), *adj.* angry at something unworthy, unjust, unfair, or mean. [< Latin *indignantem* < *in-* not + *dignus* worthy] —**in dig′nant ly,** *adv.*

in dig na tion (in′dig nā′shən), *n.* anger at something unworthy, unjust, unfair, or mean; anger mixed with scorn; righteous anger: *Cruelty to animals aroused our indignation.*

in dom i ta ble (in dom′ə tə bəl), *adj.* that cannot be discouraged, beaten, or conquered; unyielding. [< Late Latin *indomitabilis* < Latin *indomitus* untamed < *in-* not + *domare* to tame]

in duce (in düs′, in dyüs′), *v.t.*, **-duced, -duc ing.** **1** lead on; influence; persuade: *Advertisements induce people to buy.* **2** bring about; cause: *Some drugs induce sleep.*

in dulge (in dulj′), *v.*, **-dulged, -dulg ing.** —*v.i.* give in to one's pleasure; let oneself have, use, or do what one wants: *A smoker indulges in tobacco.* —*v.t.* **1** give in to; let oneself have, use, or do: *She indulged her fondness for candy by eating a whole box.* **2** give in to the wishes or whims of; humor: *We often indulge a sick person.*

in ef fa ble (in ef′ə bəl), *adj.* not to be expressed in words; too great to be described in words. —**in ef′fa ble ness,** *n.*

in ef fec tu al (in′ə fek′chü əl), *adj.* **1** without effect; useless. **2** not able to produce the effect wanted; powerless. —**in′ef fec′tu al ly,** *adv.*

in ert (in ėrt′), *adj.* **1** having no power to move or act; lifeless: *A stone is an inert mass of matter.* **2** inactive; slow; sluggish.

in ev i ta ble (in ev′ə tə bəl), *adj.* not to be avoided; sure to happen; certain to come: *Death is inevitable.* [< Latin *inevitabilis* < *in-* not + *evitare* avoid < *ex-* out + *vitare* shun]

in ex haust i ble (in′ig zô′stə bəl), *adj.* **1** that cannot be exhausted; very abundant. **2** that cannot be wearied; tireless.

in ex or a ble (in ek′sər ə bəl), *adj.* not influenced by pleading or entreaties; relentless; unyielding.

inferiority complex, an abnormal feeling of being inferior to, or not as good as, other people, sometimes made up for by overly aggressive behavior.

in fir ma ry (in fėr′mər ē), *n.*, *pl.* **-mar ies.** **1** place for the care of the infirm, sick, or injured. **2** any hospital.

in fu ri ate (in fyùr′ē āt), *v.t.*, **-at ed, -at ing.** fill with wild, fierce anger; make furious; enrage. —**in fur′i at′ing ly,** *adv.*

in gen ious (in jē′nyəs), *adj.* **1** skillful in making; good at inventing. **2** cleverly planned or made: *This mousetrap is an ingenious device.* [< Latin *ingeniosus* < *ingenium* natural talent < *in-* in + *gignere* beget, be born]

in graft (in graft′), *v.t.* **1** graft (a shoot, etc.) from one tree or plant into another. **2** fix in; implant. Also, **engraft.**

in grat i tude (in grat′ə tüd, in grat′ə tyüd), *n.* lack of gratitude or thankfulness; being ungrateful.

in jec tion (in jek′shən), *n.* **1** act or process of injecting or forcing (liquid, medicine, etc.) into a chamber or passage: *Drugs are often given by injection.* **2** liquid injected: *an injec-*

tion of penicillin.

in noc u ous (i nok′yü əs), *adj.* not hurtful or injurious; harmless. —**in noc′u ous ly,** *adv.*

in sid i ous (in sid′ē əs), *adj.* **1** seeking to entrap or ensnare; wily or sly; crafty; tricky. **2** working secretly or subtly.

in so lent (in′sə lənt), *adj.* boldly rude; intentionally disregarding the feelings of others; insulting. [< Latin *insolentem* arrogant, contrary to custom < *in-* not + *solere* be accustomed] —**in′so lent ly,** *adv.*

inst., instant (of the present month). "The 10th inst." means "the tenth day of the present month."

in sta bil i ty (in′stə bil′ə tē), *n.* lack of firmness; being unstable; unsteadiness.

in sub stan tial (in′səb stan′shəl), *adj.* **1** frail; flimsy: *A cobweb is very insubstantial.* **2** unreal; not actual; imaginary: *Dreams and ghosts are insubstantial.* —**in′sub stan′tial ly,** *adv.*

in suf fer a ble (in suf′ər ə bəl), *adj.* intolerable; unbearable: *insufferable rudeness.* —**in suf′fer a ble ness,** *n.*

in su per a ble (in sü′pər ə bəl), *adj.* that cannot be passed over or overcome; insurmountable: *an insuperable barrier.*

in tan gi ble (in tan′jə bəl), *adj.* **1** not capable of being touched or felt: *Sound and light are intangible.* **2** not easily grasped by the mind; vague: *Charm is an intangible quality.*

in te grate (in′tə grāt), *v.*, **-grat ed, -grat ing.** —*v.t.* **1** make into a whole; complete. **2** put or bring together (parts) into a whole.

in tel li gi ble (in tel′ə jə bəl), *adj.* capable of being understood; clear; comprehensible. —**in tel′li gi bly,** *adv.*

in ten si fy (in ten′sə fī), *v.t.*, *v.i.*, **-fied, -fy ing.** make or become intense; strengthen. —**in ten′si fi ca′tion,** *n.*

in ter lace (in′tər lās′), *v.*, **-laced, -lac ing.** —*v.t.* arrange (threads, strips, or branches) so that they go over and under each other; weave together; intertwine: *Baskets are made by interlacing reeds or fibers.* —*v.i.* cross each other over and under; mingle together in an intricate manner: *interlacing roads and streams.*

in ter mi na ble (in tėr′mə nə bəl), *adj.* **1** never stopping; unceasing; endless. **2** so long as to seem endless; very long and tiring. —**in ter′mi na bly,** *adv.*

in tern (in tėrn′), *v.t.* confine within a country or place; force to stay in a certain place, especially during wartime.

in ter ro gate (in ter′ə gāt), *v.*, **-gat ed, -gat ing.** —*v.t.* ask questions of; examine or get information from by asking questions.

in ter sperse (in′tər spėrs′), *v.t.*, **-spersed, -spers ing.** vary with something put here and there: *The grass was interspersed with beds of flowers.*

in ter vene (in′tər vēn′), *v.i.*, **-vened, -ven ing.** **1** come between; be between: *A week intervenes between my sister's birthday and mine.* **2** come between persons or groups to help settle a dispute; act as an intermediary: *The President was asked to intervene in the coal strike.* [< Latin *intervenire* < *inter-* between + *venire* come] —**in′ter ven′er, in′ter ve′nor,** *n.*

in ti ma cy (in′tə mə sē), *n.*, *pl.* **-cies.** **1** a being intimate; close acquaintance; closeness. **2** a familiar or intimate act.

in tro spect (in′trə spekt′), *v.i.* look inward; be introspective.

in tro spec tive (in′trə spek′tiv), *adj.* characterized by introspection, or examination of one's own thoughts and feelings. —**in′tro spec′tive ly,** *adv.*

in trude (in trüd′), *v.*, **-trud ed, -trud ing.** —*v.i.* force oneself in; come unasked and unwanted. —*v.t.* give unasked and unwanted; force in: *intrude one's opinions upon others.* [< Latin *intrudere* < *in-* in + *trudere* to thrust] —**in trud′er,** *n.*

in tu i tion (in′tü ish′ən, in′tyü ish′ən), *n.* immediate perception or understanding of truths, facts, etc., without reasoning: *By experience with many kinds of people the doctor had developed great powers of intuition.*

in var i a ble (in ver′ē ə bəl, in var′ē ə bəl), *adj.* always the same; unchanging; unchangeable; constant: *an invariable habit.* —**in var′i a ble ness,** *n.* —**in var′i a bly,** *adv.*

in vec tive (in vek′tiv), *n.* a violent attack in words; railing

GLOSSARY

734

speech, writing, or expression; abusive language.

in ven to ry (in′vən tôr′ē, in′vən tōr′ē), *n., pl.* **-ries,** *v.,* **-ried, -ry ing.** —*n.* **1** a complete list of articles with their estimated value. **2** all the articles listed or to be listed; stock. —*v.t.,* make a complete and detailed list of.

in voice (in′vois), *n.* list of goods sent to a purchaser showing prices, amounts, shipping charges, etc.

ir i des cent (ir′ə des′nt), *adj.* displaying changing colors; changing color when moved or turned.

ir re place a ble (ir′i plā′sə bəl), *adj.* not replaceable; impossible to replace with another.

ir ri gate (ir′ə gāt), *v.,* **-gat ed, -gat ing.** —*v.t.* supply (land) with water by using ditches, by sprinkling, etc.

-ity, *suffix forming nouns from adjectives.* quality, condition, or fact of being ___: *Sincerity = quality or condition of being sincere.* Also, **-ty.** [<Old French *-ité* < Latin *-itatem*]

ja pon i ca (jə pon′ə kə), *n.* camellia, a variety of shrubs with glossy leaves and white, red, or pink flowers.

jaun ty (jôn′tē, jän′tē), *adj.,* **-ti er, -ti est. 1** easy and lively; sprightly; carefree: *The happy children walked with jaunty steps.* **2** smart; stylish: *She wore a jaunty little hat.*

jell (jel), *v.i.* **1** become jelly; thicken or congeal. **2** INFORMAL. take definite form; become fixed: *Her hunch soon jelled into a plan.* —*v.t.* cause to jell. —*n.* jelly. [back-formation < *jelly*]

ju bi lant (jü′bə lənt), *adj.* expressing or showing joy; rejoicing. [< Latin *jubilantem* < *jubilum* wild shout] —**ju′bi lant ly,** *adv.* —**ju′bi la′tion,** *n.*

jus ti fy (jus′tə fī), *v.t.,* **-fied, -fy ing. 1** show to be just or right; give a good reason for; defend: *The fine quality of the cloth justifies its high price.* **2** show to be just or right.

kin dle (kin′dl), *v.,* **-dled, -dling.** —*v.t.* **1** set on fire; light. **2** stir up; arouse: *kindle enthusiasm.* —*v.i.* **1** catch fire; begin to burn: *This damp wood will never kindle.* **2** become stirred up or aroused. **3** light up; brighten: *The girl's face kindled as she told about the airplane ride.*

ku chen (kü′kən; GERMAN kü′Hən), *n.* kind of cake, usually topped with cinnamon and sugar or fruit.

la bor (lā′bər), *n.* **1** effort in doing or making something; work; toil. **2** work, especially manual work, done by skilled and unskilled workers for wages. **3** the physical exertions of childbirth prior to delivery: *She was in labor for two hours.*

la bo ri ous (lə bôr′ē əs, lə bōr′ē əs), *adj.* requiring much work; requiring hard work. —**la bo′ri ous ly,** *adv.*

lab y rinth (lab′ə rinth′), *n.* **1** number of connecting passages so arranged that it is hard to find one's way from point to point; maze. **2 Labyrinth** (in Greek legends) the maze built by Daedalus for King Minos of Crete to imprison the Minotaur. **3** any confusing, complicated arrangement: *a labyrinth of dark and narrow streets.* [< Greek *labyrinthos*]

lack a dai si cal (lak′ə dā′zə kəl), *adj.* lacking interest or enthusiasm; languid; listless; dreamy. [< *lackaday* alas, variant of *alack a day!*] —**lack′a dai′si cal ly,** *adv.*

lay a finger on, SLANG. touch; locate; hurt.

lee (lē), *n.* **1** shelter; protection. **2** side or part sheltered or away from the wind: *the lee of a ship.*

le o tard (lē′ə tärd), *n.* Usually, **leotards,** *pl.* a tight-fitting one-piece garment worn by dancers, acrobats, etc. [< French *léotard* < Jules *Léotard,* French aerialist of the 1800s]

-less, *suffix forming adjectives from verbs and nouns.* without a ___; that has no ___: *Homeless = without a home.*

leth ar gy (leth′ər jē), *n., pl.* **-gies.** drowsy dullness; lack of energy; sluggish inactivity. [< Greek *lēthargia* < *lēthē* forgetfulness + *argos* lazy < *a-* not + *ergon* work]

lib e rate (lib′ə rāt′), *v.t.,* **-rat ed, -rat ing.** set free; free or release from slavery, prison, confinement, etc.

li chen (lī′kən), *n.* any of a large group of flowerless organisms that look somewhat like moss and grow in patches on trees, rocks, etc.

lit i gant (lit′ə gənt), *n.* person engaged in a lawsuit.

lit i ga tion (lit′ə gā′shən), *n.* **1** a carrying on of a lawsuit. **2** a going to law. **3** a lawsuit or legal proceeding.

lo (lō), *interj.* Often, **lo and behold.** look! see! behold! [Old English *lā*]

loathe (lōŦH), *v.t.* **loathed, loath ing.** feel strong dislike and disgust for; abhor; hate; detest: *loathe cockroaches.* [Old English *lāthian* to hate < *lāth* hostile]

lodging house, house in which rooms are rented.

lo qua cious (lō kwā′shəs), *adj.* talking much; fond of talking. —**lo qua′cious ly,** *adv.* —**lo qua′cious ness,** *n.*

lu mi nous (lü′mə nəs), *adj.* **1** shining by its own light. **2** full of light; shining; bright. **3** easily understood; clear; enlightening.

mack i naw (mak′ə nô), *n.* **1** kind of short coat made of heavy woolen cloth, often in a plaid pattern. **2** a large, heavy, flat-bottomed boat with a sharp prow and square stern, formerly used on the Great Lakes. [< *Mackinaw* City, town in northern Michigan]

made his pile, INFORMAL. made his fortune.

magic lantern, an early type of projector for showing photographic slides on a screen.

make shift (māk′shift′), *adj.* used for a time instead of the right thing; temporarily substituted.

mal a prop ism (mal′ə prop′iz′əm), *n.* **1** a ridiculous misuse of words, especially a confusion of two words somewhat similar in sound but different in meaning, as a musical *progeny* for a musical *prodigy.* Malapropisms are often used for humorous effect. **2** instance of this; a misused word. [< Mrs. *Malaprop,* character in Richard Sheridan's play *The Rivals,* noted for her absurd misuse of words < *malapropos*]

ma lev o lent (mə lev′ə lənt), *adj.* wishing evil to happen to others; showing ill will; spiteful.

ma lig nant (mə lig′nənt), *adj.* **1** very evil, hateful, or malicious. **2** having an evil influence; very harmful.

ma lin ger (mə ling′gər), *v.i.* pretend to be sick, injured, etc., in order to escape work or duty; shirk. [< French *malingre* sickly] —**ma lin′ger er,** *n.*

man i fest (man′ə fest), *adj.* apparent to the eye or to the mind; plain; clear: *a manifest error.* —**man′i fest′ly,** *adv.*

man tle (man′tl), *n.* **1** a long, loose cloak without sleeves. **2** anything that covers like a mantle: *The ground had a mantle of snow.*

mark (märk), *n.* **1** trace or impression, such as a line, dot, spot, stain, or scar, made by some object on the surface of another. **2** grade or rating. **3** something aimed at; target; goal. —*v.t.* **1** give grades to; rate. **2** show clearly; indicate: *A frown marked her disapproval.* **3** pay attention to; notice; observe: *Mark well my words.* **4** keep (the score); record.

mar row (mar′ō), *n.* **1** the soft tissue that fills the cavities of most bones and is the source of red blood cells and many white blood cells. **2** the inmost or essential part.

marsh (märsh), *n.* low land covered at times by water.

marshal

mar shal (mär′shəl), *n., v.,* **-shaled, -shal ing** or **-shalled, -shal ling.** —*n.* officer of various kinds, especially a police officer. —*v.t.* **1** arrange in proper order: *marshal facts for a debate.* **2** conduct with ceremony: *We were marshaled before the queen.*

mar tyr (mär′tər), *n.* **1** person whose chooses to die or suffer rather than renounce a religious faith. **2** person who is put to death or made to suffer greatly because of a belief, cause, or principle. **3** person who suffers great pain or anguish. —*v.t.* **1** put (a person) to death or torture because of religious or other beliefs. **2** cause to suffer greatly; torture.

mas och ism (mas′ə kiz′əm), *n.* abnormal pleasure derived from being dominated or physically abused.

mas och is tic (mas′ə kis′tik), *adj.* of or having to do with masochists or masochism. —**mas′och is′ti cal ly,** *adv.*

mas tiff (mas′tif), *n.* any of a breed of large, powerful dogs having a short, thick coat, drooping ears, and hanging lips. [< Old French *mastin;* influenced by Old French *mestif* mongrel]

mea ger or **mea gre** (mē′gər), *adj.* **1** lacking fullness or richness; poor or scanty; sparse: *a meager meal.* **2** thin; lean: *a meager face.* [< Old French *maigre* < Latin *macer*] — **mea′ger ly, mea′gre ly,** *adv.* —**mea′ger ness, mea′gre ness,** *n.*

mean¹ (mēn), *v.t.* **meant, mean ing. 1** have as its thought; signify: *What does this word mean?* **2** have in mind; intend: *I do not mean to go.* [Old English *mǣnan* to mean, tell, say]

mean² (mēn), *adj.* **1** of a petty, unkind, small-minded nature: *mean thoughts.* **2** low in quality or grade; poor: *the meanest of gifts.* **3** of little importance or value: *the meanest flower.* **4** SLANG. excellent; clever; skillful: *to play a mean game of tennis.* [Old English *(ge)mǣne* common]

mean³ (mēn), *adj.* **1** halfway between two extremes **2** intermediate in kind, quality, or degree; average. [< Old French *meien* < Latin *medianus* of the middle < *medius* middle]

med i tate (med′ə tāt), *v.,* **-tat ed, -tat ing.** —*v.i.* engage in deep and serious thought; think quietly; reflect. —*v.t.* think about. —**med′i ta′tion,** *n.* —**med′i ta′tor,** *n.*

mel an chol y (mel′ən kol′ē), *n.* condition of sadness and low spirits; gloominess; dejection.

men ace (men′is), *n., v.,* **-aced, -ac ing.** —*n.* something that threatens; threat. —*v.t.* offer a menace to; threaten. —*v.i.* be threatening. —**men′ac ing ly,** *adv.*

mer cu ri al (mər kyùr′ē əl), *adj.* **1** sprightly and animated; quick. **2** changeable; fickle. **3** containing mercury.

met a mor phose (met′ə môr′fōz), *v.,* **-phosed, -phos ing. 1** change in form, structure, or substance by or as if by witchcraft; transform. **2** change the form or structure of by metamorphosis or metamorphism.

me te or ol o gy (mē′tē ə rol′ə jē), *n.* science dealing with the atmosphere and atmospheric conditions or phenomena, especially as they relate to weather. —**me′te or ol′o gist,** *n.*

me tic u lous (mə tik′yə ləs), *adj.* extremely or excessively careful about details. —**me tic′u lous ly,** *adv.*

met ro pol i tan (met′rə pol′ə tən), *adj.* of a metropolis; belonging to a large city or cities: *metropolitan newspapers. n.* person who lives in a large city and has metropolitan ideas.

met tle (met′l), *n.* **1** quality of disposition or temperament. **2** spirit; courage. **3 on one's mettle,** ready to do one's best.

minc ing (min′sing), *adj.* **1** putting on a dainty and refined manner. **2** walking with short steps. —**minc′ing ly,** *adv.*

min now (min′ō), *n.* any very tiny fish. *v.* cut through.

minx (mingks), *n.* a pert girl. [origin uncertain]

mi rac u lous (mə rak′yə ləs), *adj.* **1** constituting a miracle; supernatural. **2** marvelous. —**mi rac′ u lous ly,** *adv.*

mis cre ant (mis′krē ənt), *adj.* having very bad morals; wicked; base. —*n.* a base or wicked person; villain.

mit i gate (mit′ə gāt), *v.t., v.i.,* **-gat ed, -gat ing.** make or become mild or milder; make or become less harsh; soften.

mod er ate (mod′ər it), *adj.* **1** kept or keeping within proper bounds; not extreme. **2** not very large or good; fair; medium.

[< Latin *moderatum* regulated < *modus* measure]

moi e ty (moi′ə tē), *n., pl.* **-ties. 1** half. **2** part.

mol e cule (mol′ə kyül), *n.* **1** the smallest particle into which an element or compound can be divided without changing its chemical and physical properties. **2** a very small particle.

mol li fy (mol′ə fī), *v.t.* **-fied, -fy ing.** soften in temper; calm, pacify, or appease; mitigate.

mo men tar y (mō′mən ter′ē), *adj.* lasting only a moment; fleeting; transitory. —**mo′men tar′i ness,** *n.*

mon arch (mon′ərk), *n.* king, queen, emperor, empress, etc.; ruler. [< Greek *monarchos* < *monos* alone + *archein* to rule]

mo not o nous (mə not′n əs), *adj.* **1** continuing in the same tone or pitch. **2** not varying; without change; uniform. **3** wearying because of its sameness; tedious: *monotonous work.* —**mo not′o nous ly,** *adv.* —**mo not′o nous ness,** *n.*

moor (mùr), *n.* an open wasteland, usually covered with heather.

mo rose (mə rōs′), *adj.* gloomy; sullen; ill-humored.

mor tal (môr′tl), *adj.* **1** sure to die sometime. **2** of human beings; of mortals: *Mortal bodies feel pain.* **3** very great; deadly: *mortal terror.* —*n.* a being that is sure to die sometime. [< Latin *mortalis* < *mortem* death]

mo ti va tion (mō′tə vā′shən), *n.* act or process of furnishing with an incentive or inducement to action.

mo tor (mō′tər), *n.* engine that makes a machine go: *an electric motor.* —*adj.* **1** run by a motor: *a motor vehicle.* **2** causing or having to do with motion or action. **3** (of muscles, impulses, centers, etc.) concerned with or involving motion or activity. **4** of, having to do with, or involving muscular or glandular activity. [<Latin, mover < *movere* to move]

muck (muk), *n.* **1** unclean matter; dirt or filth. **2** a heavy, moist, dark soil made up chiefly of decayed plants.

mul ti tude (mul′tə tüd, mul′tə tyüd), *n.* **1** a great many; crowd; host: *a multitude of enemies.* **2 the multitude,** the common people. [< Latin *multitudo* < *multus* much]

mu tu al (myü′chü əl), *adj.* done, said, felt, etc., by each toward the other; given and received. —**mu′tu al ly,** *adv.*

na ïve or **na ive** (nä ēv′), *adj.* simple in nature; like a child; not sophisticated; artless.

na ï ve té or **na i ve te** (nä ē′və tā′), *n.* quality of being naïve or childlike; unspoiled freshness; artlessness.

nau seous (nô′shəs, nô′zē əs, nô′zhəs), *adj.* **1** causing nausea; sickening. **2** disgusting; loathsome. **3** feeling nausea; nauseated. —**nau′seous ly,** *adv.* —**nau′seous ness,** *n.*

nec tar (nek′tər), *n.* **1** (in Greek and Roman myths) the drink of the gods. **2** any delicious drink. [< Latin < Greek *nektar*]

ne go ti ate (ni gō′shē āt), *v.,* **-at ed, -at ing.** —*v.i.* talk over and arrange terms; confer; consult: *Both countries negotiated for peace.* —*v.t.* **1** arrange for: *They finally negotiated a peace treaty.* **2** get past or over.

neur o sur geon (nùr′ō sėr′jən), *n.* physician who specializes in neurosurgery, surgery involving the brain or other parts of the nervous system.

noc tur nal (nok tėr′nl), *adj.* **1** of the night. **2** in the night.

no mad ic (nō mad′ik), *adj.* of nomads or their life; wandering.

non cha lant (non′shə lənt, non′shə länt′), *adj.* without enthusiasm; coolly unconcerned; indifferent. [< French < *non-* not + *chaloir* care about] —**non′cha lant ly,** *adv.*

non com mit tal (non′kə mit′l), *adj.* not committing oneself; not saying yes or no.

non plus (non plus′, non′plus), *v.,* **-plused, -plus ing** or **-plussed, -plus sing,** *n.* —*v.t.* puzzle completely; make unable to say or do anything; perplex. —*n.* state of being nonplused.

no ta tion (nō tā′shən), *n.* **1** set of signs or symbols used to represent numbers, quantities, or other values. **2** the representing of numbers, quantities, or other values by symbols or signs.

GLOSSARY

nov el (nov′əl), *adj.* of a new kind or nature; strange; new; unfamiliar: *a novel idea.* —*n.* long story with characters and a plot. [< Latin *novellus,* diminutive of *novus* new]

nu cle us (nü′klē əs, nyü′klē əs), *n., pl.* **-cle i** or **-cle us es.** **1** a central part or thing around which other parts or things are collected. **2** a beginning to which additions are to be made. **3** the central part of an atom.

nur ture (nėr′chər), *v.,* **-tured, -tur ing,** *n.* —*v.t.* bring up; care for; foster; rear; train: *They nurtured the child as if he had been their own.* —*n.* a bringing up; rearing; training; education: *The two sisters had received very different nurture.*

ob du rate (ob′dü rit), *adj.,* unmoved by persuasion, pity, or tender feelings; stubborn; unyielding.

o blique (ə blēk′), *adj.* neither perpendicular to nor parallel with a given line or surface; slanting.

ob scure (əb skyůr′), *adj.,* **-scur er, -scur est,** *v.,* **-scured, -scur ing.** —*adj.* **1** not clearly expressed; hard to understand. **2** not well known; attracting no notice: *an obscure little village, an obscure poet.* **3** not distinct; not clear: *an obscure shape, obscure sounds.* **4** dark; dim: *an obscure corner.* —*v.t.* **1** hide from view; make obscure; dim; darken: *Clouds obscure the sun.* **2** make dim or vague to the understanding.

ob se qui ous (əb sē′kwē əs), *adj.* polite or obedient from hope of gain. [< Latin *obsequiosus* < *obsequium* dutiful service < *ob-* after + *sequi* follow] —**ob se′qui ous ly,** *adv.*

ob sti na cy (ob′stə nə sē), *n., pl.* **-cies. 1** a refusal to give in; stubbornness. **2** an obstinate act.

oc a ri na (ok′ə rē′nə), *n.* a small wind instrument, usually made of terra cotta or plastic, with finger holes and a protruding, whistlelike mouthpiece. It produces a soft sound.

oc tave (ok′tiv, ok′tāv), *n.* **1** interval between a musical tone and another tone having twice or half as many vibrations. From middle C to the C above it is an octave. **2** the eighth tone above or below a given tone. [< Latin *octavus* eighth < *octo* eight]

o gle (ō′gəl), *v.,* **o gled, o gling,** *n.* —*v.t., v.i.* look at with desire; make eyes at. —*n.* an ogling look. [probably < Low German *oeglen* < *oegen* look at < *oog* eye] —**o′gler,** *n.*

om i nous (om′ə nəs), *adj.* unfavorable; threatening: *ominous clouds.* —**om′i nous ly,** *adv.* —**om′i nous ness,** *n.*

on slaught (ôn′slôt, on′slôt′), *n.* a vigorous attack. [probably < Dutch *aanslag* an attempt, stroke]

ope (ōp), *v.t., v.i.,* **oped, oping,** *adj.* ARCHAIC. open.

op por tun ist (op′ər tü′nist, op′ər tyü′nist), *n.* person who uses every opportunity to gain advantage, regardless of right or wrong.

op pres sive (ə pres′iv), *adj.* **1** hard to bear; burdensome: *The intense heat was oppressive.* **2** harsh; unjust.

orb (ôrb), *n.* **1** anything round; sphere; globe. **2** sun, moon, planet, or star. **3** the eyeball or eye. [< Latin *orbis* circle]

or bit (ôr′bit), *n.* the curved, usually elliptical path of a heavenly body, planet, or satellite about another body in space: *the earth's orbit about the sun, the moon's orbit about the earth, the orbit of a weather satellite about the earth.*

or ches trate (ôr′kə strāt), *v.t.,* **-trat ed, -trat ing.** compose or arrange (music) for performance by an orchestra. —**or′ches trat′ er, or′ches tra′tor,** *n.* —**or′ches tra′tion,** *n.*

os ten ta tious (os′ten tā′shəs), *adj.* **1** done for display; intended to attract notice. **2** showing off; liking to attract notice. —**os′ten ta′tious ly,** *adv.* —**os′ten ta′tious ness,** *n.*

ost ler (os′lər), *n.* person who takes care of horses at an inn.

o va tion (ō vā′shən), *n.* an enthusiastic public welcome; burst of loud cheering. [< Latin *ovationem* < *ovare* rejoice]

pact (pakt), *n.* agreement between persons or parties; compact; treaty. [< Latin *pactum* < *pacisci* make an agreement]

a hat	i it	oi oil	ch child		a in about
ā age	ī ice	ou out	ng long		e in taken
ä far	o hot	u cup	sh she	ə =	i in pencil
e let	ō open	ů put	th thin		o in lemon
ē equal	ô order	ü rule	ᴛʜ then		u in circus
ėr term			zh measure	< = derived from

pa go da (pə gō′də), *n.* temple or other sacred building having many stories, with a roof curving upward from each story, found in India, China, and other Asian countries. [< Portuguese *pagode* < Tamil *pagavadi* < Sanskrit *bhagavatī* goddess]

pagoda

pal at a ble (pal′ə tə bəl), *adj.* **1** agreeable to the taste; pleasing. **2** acceptable.

pa lav er (pə lav′ər), *n.* **1** unnecessary or idle words; mere talk. **2** smooth, persuading talk; flattery.

pall (pôl), *n.* **1** a heavy cloth of black, purple, or white velvet, spread over a coffin. **2** a dark, gloomy covering: *A pall of smoke shut out the sun.*

pal mate (pal′māt), *adj.* **-ated.** shaped like a hand with the fingers spread out: *a palmate leaf.*

pal met to (pal met′ō), *n., pl.* **-tos** or **-toes.** any of a genus of relatively small palms with fan-shaped leaves, abundant on the southeastern coast of the United States.

pal pi tant (pal′pə tənt), *adj.,* palpitating.

pal pi tate (pal′pə tāt), *v.i.,* **-tat ed, -tat ing.** beat rapidly; throb.

pan de mo ni um (pan′də mō′nē əm), *n.* **1** place of wild disorder or lawless confusion. **2** wild uproar or lawlessness.

pan out, INFORMAL. turnout; work out.

par a dox (par′ə doks), *n.* **1** statement that may be true but seems to say two opposite things. EXAMPLES: "More haste, less speed," "The child is father to the man."

par a pet (par′ə pet, par′ə pit), *n.* **1** a low wall or mound of stone, earth, etc., in front of a walk or platform at the top of a fort, trench, etc., to protect soldiers; rampart. **2** a low wall or barrier at the edge of a balcony, roof, bridge, etc.

par a pher nal ia (par′ə fər nā′lyə), *n., pl. or sing.* **1** personal belongings. **2** equipment; outfit.

par ox ysm (par′ək siz′əm), *n.* **1** a sudden, severe attack of the symptoms of a disease, usually recurring periodically. **2** a sudden outburst of emotion or activity.

pa ter nal (pə tėr′nl), *adj.* **1** of or like a father; fatherly. **2** related on the father's side of the family: *a paternal aunt, paternal grandparents.* [< Latin *paternus* < *pater* father]

peak ed (pē′kid), *adj.* sickly in appearance; thin. [< earlier *peak* look sick; origin uncertain] —**peak′ed ness,** *n.*

peer less (pir′lis), *adj.* without an equal; matchless.

pen non (pen′ən), *n.* **1** a long, narrow flag originally carried on the lance of a knight. **2** any flag or banner.

per am bu late (pə ram′byə lāt), *v.,* **-lated, -lat ing.** —*v.t.* **1** walk through. **2** walk through and examine. —*v.i.* walk or travel about; stroll. [< Latin *perambulatum* walked through < *per-* through + *ambulare* to walk] —**per am′bu la′tion,** *n.*

per ceive (pər sēv′), *v.t.,* **-ceived, -ceiv ing. 1** be aware of through the senses; see, hear, taste, smell, or feel. **2** take in with the mind; observe; understand. [< Old French *perceivre* < Latin *percipere* < *per-* thoroughly + *capere* to grasp]

per cep tion (pər sep′shən), *n.* act of perceiving, seeing, or understanding: *His perception of the change came in a flash.* **2** power of perceiving: *a keen perception.* **3** understanding: *I now have a clear perception of what went wrong.*

pe remp tor y (pə remp′tər ē, per′əmp tôr′ē), *adj.* **1** leaving no choice; decisive; final; absolute. **2** allowing no denial or refusal: *a peremptory command.* —**pe remp′tor i ly,** *adv.*

per i win kle (pėr′ē wing′kəl), *n.* any of a genus of usually low, trailing evergreen plants with blue flowers.

per me ate (pėr′mē āt), *v.t.,* **-at ed, -at ing.** spread through the whole of; pass through; pervade.

per pen dic u lar (pėr′pən dik′yə lər), *adj.* **1** standing straight up; vertical; upright. **2** very steep; precipitous. **3** at right angles to a given line, plane, or surface. —**per′pen dic′u lar ly,** *adv.*

per pet u al (pər pech′ü əl), *adj.* **1** lasting forever; eternal: *the perpetual hills.* **2** never ceasing; continuous; constant: *a perpetual stream of visitors.* —**per pet′u al ly,** *adv.*

per plex (pər pleks′), *v.t.* **1** trouble with doubt; puzzle; bewilder. **2** make difficult to understand or settle; confuse. [< Latin *perplexus* confused < *per-* thoroughly + *plectere* intertwine] —**per plex′ed ly,** *adv.* —**per plex′ing ly,** *adv.*

per sist (pər sist′, pər zist′), *v.i.* **1** continue firmly; refuse to stop or be changed; persevere. **2** remain in existence; last; stay: *On the tops of very high mountains snow persists throughout the year.* **3** say again and again; maintain. [< Latin *persistere* < *per-* to the end + *sistere* to stand] —**per sis′tent,** *n.*

per ti nac i ty (pėrt′n as′ə tē), *n.* great persistence; holding firmly to a purpose, action, or opinion.

per vade (pər vād′), *v.t.,* **-vad ed, -vad ing.** go or spread throughout; be throughout: *The odor of pines pervades the air.* [< Latin *pervadere* < *per-* through + *vadere* go] —**per vad′er,** *n.*

pe ti tion (pə tish′ən), *n.* a formal request to a superior or to one in authority for some privilege, right, benefit. —*v.t., v.i.* ask earnestly; make a petition to: *They petitioned the mayor to use his influence with the city council.*

phys ics (fiz′iks), *n.* science that deals with the properties and interrelationships of matter and energy, excluding chemical and biological change. Physics includes the study of mechanics, heat, light, sound, electricity, magnetism, and atomic energy.

pin na cle (pin′ə kəl), *n.* **1** a high peak or point of rock, ice, etc. **2** the highest point: *at the pinnacle of one's fame.*

pitch pipe, pipe covered with resin from evergreen trees.

plait (plāt, plat *for 1;* plāt, plēt *for 2*), *n., v.t.* **1** braid. **2** pleat. [< Old French *pleit,* ultimately < Latin *plicare* to fold]

plaque (plak), *n.* a thin, flat, ornamental plate or tablet of metal, porcelain, etc., usually intended to be hung up as a wall decoration.

pla teau (pla tō′), *n., pl.* **-teaus** or **-teaux** (-tōz′). **1** large, high plain; tableland. **2** a level, especially the level at which something is unchanged for a period.

poetic justice, ideal justice, with goodness being suitably rewarded and wrongdoing properly punished, as shown often in poetry, drama, and fiction.

poign ant (poi′nyənt), *adj.* **1** very painful; piercing. **2** stimulating to the mind, feelings, or passions; keen; intense: *a subject of poignant interest.*

point (point), *n.* **1** a sharp, tapering end. **2** the interval between any two adjacent points of a compass.

poise (poiz), *n., v.,* **poised, pois ing.** —*n.* mental balance, composure, or self-possession: *She has perfect poise and never seems embarrassed.* —*v.t.* balance. —*v.i.* **1** be balanced. **2** hang supported or suspended. **3** hover, as a bird in the air.

pole ax or **pole axe** (pōl′aks′), *n., pl.* **-ax es, -axed, -ax ing.** —*n.* **1** ax with a long handle and a hook or spike opposite the blade. **2** kind of battle-ax with a short handle. —*v.t.* knock down or kill with or as if with a poleax. [Middle English *pollax* < *polle* head + *ax* ax]

pome gran ate (pom′gran′it), *n.* a reddish-yellow fruit with a thick skin and many seeds, each enveloped in a juicy red pulp which has a pleasant, slightly sour taste. [< Old French *pome grenate* apple with grains]

pom pous (pom′pəs), *adj.* **1** trying to seem very important; vainglorious; self-important: *a pompous manner.* **2** overly flowery or high-flown; inflated: *pompous language.*

pon toon (pon tün′), *n.* **1** a low, flat-bottomed boat. **2** such a boat, or some other floating structure, used as one of the supports of a temporary bridge. **3** either of two air-filled, watertight, boat-shaped parts of an aircraft for landing, floating on, or taking off from water; float. [< French *ponton* < Latin *pontonem* < *pons* bridge]

por tal (pôr′tl, pōr′tl), *n.* door, gate, or entrance, usually an imposing one. [< Medieval Latin *portale* < Latin *porta* gate]

port ly (pôrt′lē, pōrt′lē), *adj.,* **-li er, -li est.** **1** having a large body; stout; corpulent. **2** stately; dignified.

po tent (pōt′nt), *adj.* having great power; powerful; strong.

powder horn, powder flask made of an animal's horn.

pre-, *prefix.* **1** before in time, rank, etc.: *Prewar = before a war.* **2** before in position, space, etc.; in front of: *Premolar = in front of the molars.* **3** beforehand; in advance: *Prepay = pay in advance.* [< Latin *prae-, pre-*]

pre am ble (prē′am′bəl), *n.* **1** introduction to a speech or a writing **2** a preliminary or introductory fact or circumstance.

pre ar range (prē′ə ränj′), *v.t.,* **-ranged, -rang ing.** arrange beforehand. —**pre′ar range′ment,** *n.*

prec i pice (pres′ə pis), *n.* **1** a very steep face of rock; cliff or steep mountainside. **2** situation of great peril.

pre cip i tate (*v.* pri sip′ə tāt; *adj.* pri sip′ə tit, pri sip′ə tāt), *v.,* **-tat ed, -tat ing,** *adj.* —*v.t.* **1** hasten the beginning of; bring about suddenly: *precipitate an argument.* **2** throw headlong; hurl. —*adj.* very hurried. —**pre cip′i tate ly,** *adv.*

pre cip i tous (pri sip′ə təs), *adj.* **1** like a precipice; very steep: *precipitous cliffs.* **2** hasty; rash. **3** rushing headlong; very rapid. —**pre cip′i tous ly,** *adv.*

pre con cep tion (prē′kən sep′shən), *n.* idea or opinion formed beforehand.

pre dom i nance (pri dom′ə nəns), *n.* a being predominant, or having more power or authority than others.

pre em i nent or **pre-em i nent** (prē em′ə nənt), *adj.* standing out above all others; superior. —**pre em′i nent ly,** *adv.*

prem ise (prem′is), *n.* **1** (in logic) a statement assumed to be true and used to draw a conclusion. **2 premises,** *pl.* **a** a house or building with its grounds. **b** (in law) things mentioned previously, such as the names of the parties concerned, a description of the property, the price, grounds for complaint, etc.

pre mo ni tion (prē′mə nish′ən, prem′ə nish′ən), *n.* notification or warning of what is to come; forewarning.

pre rog a tive (pri rog′ə tiv), *n.* **1** right or privilege that nobody else has. **2** special superiority of right.

pre sume (pri züm′), *v.,* **-sumed, -sum ing.** —*v.t.* **1** take for granted without proving; suppose. **2** take upon oneself; venture; dare: *May I presume to tell you you are wrong?* —*v.i.* **2** act with improper boldness; take liberties.

pri mal (prī′məl), *adj.* of early times; first; primeval.

prime (prīm), *v.t.,* **primed, prim ing.** **1** prepare by putting something in or on. **2** supply (a gun) with powder.

prim i tive (prim′ə tiv), *adj.* **1** of early times; of long ago. **2** first of the kind: *primitive spacecraft.* **3** very simple; such as people had early in human history.

pri mor di al (prī môr′dē əl), *adj.* **1** existing at the very beginning; primitive. **2** original. [< Latin *primordium* beginning < *primus* first + *ordiri* begin] —**pri mor′di al ly,** *adv.*

pri or (prī′ər), *adj.* coming before; earlier: *I can't go with you because I have a prior engagement.* [< Latin]

pro cliv i ty (prō kliv′ə tē), *n., pl.* **-ties.** tendency; inclination.

pro cure (prə kyùr′), *v.t.,* **-cured, -cur ing.** **1** obtain by care or effort; secure: *procure a job.* **2** bring about; cause.

pro di gious (prə dij′əs), *adj.* **1** very great; huge; vast. **2** wonderful; marvelous.

prof fer (prof′ər), *v.t.* offer for acceptance; present. —*n.* an offer made. [< Anglo-French *proffrir* < Old French *pro-* forth + *offrir* to offer]

pro found (prə found′), *adj.* **1** very deep: *a profound sigh, a profound sleep.* **2** deeply felt; very great. **3** having or showing great knowledge or understanding: *a profound book.*

GLOSSARY

prog e ny (proj′ə nē), *n.*, *pl.* **-nies.** children or offspring.
pro gres sion (prə gresh′ən), *n.* a moving forward; going ahead: *Creeping is a slow method of progression.*
pro gres sive (prə gres′iv), *adj.* **1** making progress; advancing to something better; improving: *a progressive nation.* **2** favoring progress; wanting improvement or reform in government, business, etc. **3** moving forward; developing: *a progressive disease.* —**pro gres′sive ly,** *adv.* —**pro gres′sive ness,** *n.*
prom e nade (prom′ə nād′, prom′ə näd′), *n.*, *v.*, **-nad ed, -nad ing.** —*n.* **1** walk for pleasure or display: *a promenade in the park.* **2** a public place for such a walk. **3** dance or ball. **4** march of all the guests at the opening of a formal dance. —*v.i.* walk up and down for pleasure or for display: *promenade on a ship's deck.* —*v.t.* **1** walk through. **2** take on a promenade. [< French < *promener* take for a walk < Latin *prominare* drive on < *pro-* forward + *minare* to drive] —**prom′e nad′er,** *n.*
prom i nent (prom′ə nənt), *adj.* **1** well-known or important; distinguished. **2** that catches the eye; easy to see: *A single tree in a field is prominent.* **3** standing out; projecting: *Some insects have prominent eyes.* [< Latin *prominentem* projecting < *pro-* forward + *minere* to jut] —**prom′i nent ly,** *adv.*
prompt (prompt), *adj.* **1** ready and willing; on time; quick; punctual: *Be prompt to obey.* **2** done at once; made without delay. —*v.t.* **1** cause (someone) to do something: *Curiosity prompted me to ask the question.* **2** give rise to; suggest; inspire: *A kind thought prompted the gift.* —**prompt′ly,** *adv.* —**prompt′ness,** *n.*
proph e cy (prof′ə sē), *n.*, *pl.* **-cies.** **1** a telling what will happen; foretelling future events. **2** thing told about the future. **3** a divinely inspired utterance, revelation, writing, etc.
proph e sy (prof′ə sī), *v.*, **-sied, -sy ing.** —*v.i.* **1** tell what will happen. **2** speak when or as if divinely inspired. —*v.t.* **1** foretell; predict. **2** utter in prophecy.
prop o si tion (prop′ə zish′ən), *n.* **1** what is offered to be considered; proposal: *The corporation made a proposition to buy out the small business.* **2** INFORMAL. A business enterprise; an undertaking: *a paying proposition.*
pro sa ic (prō zā′ik), *adj.* matter-of-fact; ordinary.
pros trate (pros′trāt), *v.*, **-trat ed, -trat ing,** *adj.* —*v.t.* lay down flat; cast down. —*adj.* **1** lying flat with face downward: *She was humbly prostrate in prayer.* **2** overcome; helpless.
pro trude (prō trüd′), *v.*, **-trud ed, -trud ing.** —*v.t.* thrust forth; stick out: *The saucy child protruded her tongue.* —*v.i.* be thrust forth; project: *Her teeth protrude too far.* [< Latin *protrudere* < *pro-* forward + *trudere* to thrust]
prov i den tial (prov′ə den′shəl), *adj.* **1** happening by or as if by God's intervention; fortunate. **2** of or proceeding from divine power or influence. —**prov′i den′tial ly,** *adv.*
pro vin cial (prə vin′shəl), *adj.* **1** of a province: *provincial government.* **2** having the manners, speech, dress, point of view, etc., of people living in a province. **3** lacking refinement.
prov o ca tion (prov′ə kā′shən), *n.* **1** act of provoking. **2** something that stirs up or provokes.
prow (prou), *n.* the front part of a ship or boat; bow.
prow ess (prou′is), *n.* **1** bravery; daring. **2** brave acts.
psalm (säm, sälm), *n.* **1** a sacred song or poem. **2 Psalm,** any of the 150 sacred songs or hymns that together form a book of the Old Testament.
psy cho–ex per i men tal ist (sī′kō ek sper′ə men′tə list), *n.* one who does experiments on or about the mind.
psy chol o gy (sī kol′ə jē), *n.*, *pl.* **-gies.** **1** science or study of the mind. **2** the mental states and processes of a person or persons; mental nature and behavior.
pul sa tion (pul sā′shən), *n.* **1** a beating; throbbing. **2** a beat; throb. **3** vibration; quiver.
pulse (puls), *n.*, *v.*, **pulsed, puls ing.** —*n.* **1** the regular beating of the arteries caused by the rush of blood into them after each contraction of the heart. **2** any regular, measured beat: *the pulse in music.* **3** feeling; sentiment: *the pulse of the nation.* —*v.i.* beat; throb; vibrate: *My heart pulsed with excitement.* [< Latin *pulsus* < *pellere* to beat.]

pun cheon (pun′chən), *n.* slab of timber or a piece of a split log, with the face roughly smoothed.
pur ga to ry (pėr′gə tôr′ē, pėr′gə tōr′ē), *n.*, *pl.* **-ries.** **1** (in Roman Catholic belief) a place in which the souls of those who have died penitent are purified from sin. **2** any condition or place of temporary suffering or punishment.

quer y (kwir′ē), *n.*, *pl.* **quer ies,** *v.*, **quer ied, quer y ing.** —*n.* **1** question; inquiry. **2** doubt. —*v.t.* **1** ask about; inquire into; ask. **2** express doubt about. —*v.i.* ask questions.
queue (kyü), *n.*, *v.*, **queued, queu ing** or **queue ing.** —*n.* **1** braid of hair hanging down from the back of the head. **2** a line of people, automobiles, etc. —*v.i.* **1** form or stand in a long line. **2 queue up,** line up. Also, **cue.**
quirk (kwėrk), *n.* **1** a peculiar way of acting. **2** a sudden twist or turn: *a quirk of fate, a mental quirk.*
quiv er (kwiv′ər), *v.i.* shake with a slight but rapid motion; shiver; tremble. —*n.* act of quivering; tremble. [Old English *cwifer* nimble] —**quiv′er er,** *n.* —**quiv′er ing ly,** *adv.*

ra di ant (rā′dē ənt), *adj.* **1** shining; bright; beaming. **2** sending out rays of light or heat. —**ra′di ant ly,** *adv.*
ral ly (ral′ē), *v.*, **-lied, -ly ing,** *n.*, *pl.* **-lies.** —*v.t.* bring together, especially to get in order again: *The commander was able to rally the fleeing troops.* —*v.i.* **1** come together in a body for a common purpose or action. **2** come to help a person, party, or cause. —*n.* **1** a rallying; recovery. **2** a mass meeting or assembly for a common purpose or action: *a political rally.*
rant (rant), *v.i.* speak wildly, extravagantly, violently, or noisily. —*n.* extravagant, violent, or noisy speech.
ra pi er (rā′pē ər), *n.* a long light sword used for thrusting.
rap tur ous (rap′chər əs), *adj.* full of rapture, delight, or great joy. —**rap′tur ous ly,** *adv.* —**rap′tur ous ness,** *n.*
rar e fy (rer′ə fī′, rar′ə fī), *v.t.*, **-fied, -fy ing.** **1** make less dense: *The air on high mountains is rarefied.* **2** refine; purify.
rash er (rash′ər), *n.* a thin slice of bacon or ham for frying or broiling. [origin uncertain]
ra tion al (rash′ə nəl), *adj.* **1** reasoned out; sensible; reasonable: *When very angry, people seldom act in a rational way.* **2** able to think and reason clearly.
ra tion ale (rash′ə nal′, rash′ə nä′lē), *n.* the fundamental reason. [< Latin, neuter of *rationalis* rational]
rau cous (rô′kəs), *adj.* hoarse; harsh-sounding: *the raucous caw of a crow.* [< Latin *raucus*] —**rau′cous ly,** *adv.*
realm (relm), *n.* **1** kingdom. **2** region or sphere in which something rules or prevails. **3** a particular field of something: *the realm of biology.* [< Old French *realme,* ultimately < Latin *regimen* rule. See REGIMEN.]
rea son (rē′zn), *n.* **1** cause or motive for an action, feeling, etc.: *I have my own reasons for doing this.* **2** ability or power to think and draw conclusions. **3** right thinking; good sense.
re as sure (rē′ə shur′), *v.t.*, **-sured, -sur ing.** **1** restore to confidence: *The crew's confidence during the storm reassured the passengers.* **2** assure again or anew. **3** insure again.
re coil (ri koil′), *v.i.* **1** draw back; shrink back: *Most people would recoil at seeing a snake in the path.* **2** spring back: *The*

739

GLOSSARY

Pronunciation key:
a hat, ā age, ä far, e let, ē equal, ėr term; i it, ī ice; o hot, ō open, ô order; oi oil, ou out, u cup, ů put, ü rule; ch child, ng long, sh she, th thin, ŦH then, zh measure; ə = a in about, e in taken, i in pencil, o in lemon, u in circus; < = derived from

gun recoiled after I fired. **3** react.

rec on cil i a tion (rek′ən sil′ē ā′shən), *n.* **1** a bringing together again in friendship. **2** a settlement or adjustment of disagreements or differences.

re con nais sance (ri kon′ə səns), *n.* examination or survey, especially for military purposes. [< French]

rec on noi ter (rek′ə noi′tər, rē′kə noi′tər), *v.t.* approach and examine or observe in order to learn something. —*v.i.* approach a place and make a first survey of it.

red coat (red′kōt′), *n.* (in former times) a British soldier.

re deem (ri dēm′), *v.t.* **1** buy back. **2** pay off. **3** make up for; balance.

red o lent (red′l ənt), *adj.* **1** having a pleasant smell; fragrant; aromatic. **2** smelling strongly: *a house redolent of fresh paint.*

reef (rēf), *n.* a narrow ridge of rocks, sand, or coral at or near the surface of the water.

re flect (ri flekt′), *v.t.* **1** turn back or throw back (light, heat, sound, etc.): *The sidewalks reflect heat on a hot day.* **2** give back a likeness or image of: *The sky was reflected in the still pond.* —*v.i.* **1** cast back light, heat, sound, etc. **2** think carefully; ponder; deliberate.

re flec tive (ri flek′tiv), *adj.* **1** that reflects; reflecting: *the reflective surface of polished metal.* **2** thoughtful: *a reflective look.* —**re flec′tive ly,** *adv.* —**re flec′tive ness,** *n.*

ref or ma tion (ref′ər mā′shən), *n.* a reforming or a being reformed; change for the better; improvement.

re frain¹ (ri frān′), *v.i.* hold oneself back, especially from satisfying a momentary impulse. [< Old French *refrener* < Latin *refrenare* furnish with a bridle, refrain < *re-* back + *frenum* bridle] —**re frain′ment,** *n.*

re frain² (ri frān′), *n.* phrase or verse recurring regularly in a song or poem, especially at the end of each stanza; chorus.

re fute (ri fyüt′), *v.t.,* **-fut ed, -fut ing.** show (a claim, opinion, or argument) to be false or incorrect; prove wrong.

re gal (rē′gəl), *adj.* **1** belonging to a king or queen; royal. **2** fit for a king or queen; stately.

re gress (ri gres′), *v.i.* **1** go back; move in a backward direction. **2** return to an earlier or less advanced state.

re it e rate (rē it′ə rāt′), *v.t.,* **-rat ed, -rat ing.** say or do several times; repeat (an action, demand, etc.) again and again.

re lent less (ri lent′lis), *adj.* without pity; not relenting; unyielding. —**re lent′less ly,** *adv.* —**re lent′less ness,** *n.*

re mand (ri mand′), *v.t.* **1** send back. **2** send back (a prisoner or an accused person) into custody.

rem i nisce (rem′ə nis′), *v.i.,* **-nisced, -nisc ing.** talk or think about past experiences or events.

re morse (ri môrs′), *n.* deep, regret for having done wrong.

rend (rend), *v.t.,* **rent, rend ing. 1** pull apart violently; tear: *Wolves will rend a lamb.* **2** split: *Lightning rent the tree.*

ren der (ren′dər), *v.t.* **1** cause to become; make: *Fright rendered me speechless.* **2** give; do: *render a service, render judgment.* **3** offer for consideration, approval, payment, etc.; hand in; report: *render a bill.* **4** give in return: *render thanks.*

ren e gade (ren′ə gād), *n., adj., v.,* **-gad ed, -gad ing.** —*n.* deserter from a religious faith, a political party, etc.; traitor. —*adj.* like a traitor; deserting; disloyal. —*v.i.* turn renegade.

re nounce (ri nouns′), *v.t.,* **-nounced, -nounc ing. 1** declare that one gives up; give up entirely; give up: *He renounces his claim to the money.* **2** cast off; refuse to recognize as one's own; repudiate; disown. [< Middle French *renoncer* < Latin *renuntiare* < *re-* back + *nuntius* message]

re past (ri past′), *n.* meal; food.

re pent ant (ri pen′tənt), *adj.* feeling repentance or regret; sorry for wrongdoing; repenting. —**re pent′ant ly,** *adv.*

re pose (ri pōz′), *n., v.,* **-posed, -pos ing.** —*n.* **1** rest or sleep: *Do not disturb her repose.* **2** quietness; ease: *repose of manner.* **3** peace; calmness. —*v.i.* **1** lie at rest: *The cat reposed upon the cushion.* **2** lie in a grave.

re pug nance (ri pug′nəns), *n.* strong dislike, distaste, or aversion.

re served (ri zėrvd′), *adj.* **1** kept in reserve; kept by special arrangement: *a reserved seat.* **2** set apart: *a reserved section at the stadium.* **3** self-restrained in action or speech. **4** disposed to keep to oneself.

res ig na tion (rez′ig nā′shən), *n.* **1** act of resigning. **2** a written statement giving notice that one resigns. **3** patient acceptance.

res o lute (rez′ə lüt), *adj.* **1** having a fixed resolve; determined; firm. **2** constant in pursuing a purpose; bold.

re sound (ri zound′), *v.i.* **1** give back sound; echo. **2** sound loudly. **3** be filled with sound.

res pite (res′pit), *n.* **1** time of relief and rest; lull: *a respite from the heat.* **2** a putting off; delay.

ret ri bu tion (ret′rə byü′shən), *n.* a deserved punishment; return for wrongdoing. [< Latin *retributionem,* ultimately < *re-* back + *tribuere* assign]

re un ion (rē yü′nyən), *n.* **1** a coming together again. **2** a social gathering of persons who have been separated or who have interests in common: *a college reunion.*

rev eil le (rev′ə lē), *n.* a signal on a bugle or drum to waken soldiers in the morning. [< French *réveillez(-vous)* awaken!]

rev el (rev′əl), *v.,* **-eled, -el ing** or **-elled, -el ling,** *n.* —*v.t.* make merry. —*n.* a noisy good time; merrymaking. —**rev′el er, rev′el ler,** *n.*

rev er ent (rev′ər ənt), *adj.* feeling or showing reverence, or a feeling of deep respect, awe, and love. —**rev′er ent ly,** *adv.*

rev er ie (rev′ər ē), *n.* **1** dreamy thoughts; dreamy thinking of pleasant things. **2** condition of being lost in dreamy thoughts. Also, **revery.** [< French *rêverie* < *rêver* to dream]

rhap so dy (rap′sə dē), *n., pl.* **-dies. 1** extravagant enthusiasm in speech or writing: *go into rhapsodies over a gift.* **2** (in music) an instrumental composition. **3** a kind of poem suitable for recitation at one time. [< Greek *rhapsōidia* verse composition < *rhaptein* to stitch + *ōidē* song, ode]

rheu mat ic (rü mat′ik), *adj.* **1** of or having to do with rheumatism. **2** having to do with rheumatic fever, a disease that often causes swelling of the heart.

rig ma role (rig′mə rōl′), *n.* foolish talk or activity; words or action without meaning; nonsense. Also, **rigamarole.**

rime (rīm), *n., v.,* **rimed, rim ing.** —*n.* white frost; hoarfrost.

roe (rō), *n.* fish eggs, especially when contained in the ovarian membrane of the female fish.

roil (roil), *v.t.* **1** make (water, etc.) muddy by stirring up sediment. **2** rile. [< Old French *rouiller*]

ro man ti cize (rō man′tə sīz), *v.t.,* **-cized, -ciz ing.** make romantic, or imaginary and unrealistic.

ruck sack (ruk′sak′), *n.* knapsack. [< German *Rucksack*]

ruc tion (ruk′shən), *n.* INFORMAL. disturbance; quarrel; row.

rude (rüd), *adj.,* **1** not courteous; impolite. **2** roughly made.

ru in a tion (rü′ə nā′shən), *n.* ruin; destruction; downfall.

Sab bath (sab′əth), *n.* day of the week used for rest and worship.

sac ri le gious (sak′rə lij′əs, sak′rə lē′jəs), *adj.* injurious or insulting to sacred persons or things.

sac ris ty (sak′ris tē), *n., pl.* **-ties.** place where the sacred vessels, robes, etc., of a church are kept; vestry.

sa gac i ty (sə gas′ə tē), *n.* keen, sound judgment; mental acuteness; shrewdness.

sage (sāj), *n.* a small shrub whose greyish-green leaves are used as seasoning and in medicine.

sa hib (sä′ib, sä′hib), *n.* sir; master (in colonial India, a term of respect used to or about Europeans). [< Hindi *sāhib* < Arabic *ṣāḥib* lord]

sa li ent (sā′lē ənt, sā′lyənt), *adj.* standing out; easily seen or noticed; prominent; striking.

sal low (sal′ō), *adj.* having a sickly, yellowish or brownish-yellow color: *a sallow skin, a sallow complexion.* —*v.t.* make sallow. [Old English *salo*] —**sal′low ness,** *n.*

sa loon (sə lün′), *n.* **1** place where alcoholic drinks are sold and drunk; tavern. **2** a large room for general or public use. **3** a fashionable or stylish shop. [< French *salon* salon.]

sa lu bri ous (sə lü′brē əs), *adj.* favorable or conducive to good health; healthful. [< Latin *salubris* < *salus* good health] —**sa lu′bri ous ly**, *adv.* —**sa lu′bri ous ness**, *n.*

sal u tar y (sal′yə ter′ē), *adj.* **1** beneficial: *give someone salutary advice.* **2** good for the health; wholesome.

sate (sāt), *v.t.,* **sat ed, sat ing.** **1** satisfy fully (any appetite or desire). **2** supply with more than enough, so as to disgust or weary.

sat u rate (sach′ə rāt′), *v.t.,* **-rat ed, -rat ing.** soak thoroughly; fill full: *During the fog, the air was saturated with moisture.* [< Latin *saturatum* filled < *satur* full]

sav age (sav′ij), *adj.* **1** not civilized; barbarous. **2** violently aggressive; fiercely cruel or brutal. **3** wild or rugged: *savage mountain scenery.* **4** undomesticated; untamed. **5** furiously angry; enraged. [< Old French *sauvage* < Late Latin *salvaticus,* ultimately < Latin *silva* forest] —**sav′age ly**, *adv.*

saw horse (sô′hôrs′), *n.* frame for holding wood that is being sawed.

scant ling (skant′ling), *n.* **1** a small beam or piece of timber, often used as an upright piece in the frame of a building. **2** small beams or timbers collectively.

schoon er (skü′nər), *n.* ship with two or more masts and fore-and-aft sails.

scoff (skôf, skof), *v.i.* make fun to show one does not believe something; mock. See synonym study below. —*v.t.* jeer at. —*n.* **1** mocking words or acts. **2** something ridiculed. [< Scandinavian (Danish) *skuffe* deceive] —**scoff′ing ly**, *adv.* **Syn.** *v.i.* **Scoff, jeer, sneer** mean to show scorn or contempt for someone or something. **Scoff** implies scornful irreverence or cynicism: *scoff at religion.* **Jeer** implies mocking laughter: *The mob jeered when the speaker got up to talk.* **Sneer** means to express ill-natured contempt or disparagement by look, tone, or manner of speech: *sneer at everything sentimental.*

score (skôr, skōr), *n.* **1** the record of points made in a game. **2** group or set of twenty.

scru ti ny (skrüt′n ē), *n., pl.* **-nies.** **1** close examination; careful inspection. **2** a looking searchingly at something.

scythe (sīฐH), *n., v.,* **scythed, scyth ing.** —*n.* a long, thin, slightly curved blade on a long handle, for cutting grass, etc. —*v.t.* cut or mow with a scythe. [Old English *sithe;* spelling influenced by Latin *scindere* to cut]

se cur i ty (si kyür′ə tē), *n., pl.* **-ties.** **1** freedom from danger, care, or fear; feeling or condition of being safe. **2** something that secures or makes safe. **3** Usually, **securities,** *pl.* bond or stock certificates.

sed i men tar y (sed′ə men′tər ē), *adj.* in geology: formed by the depositing of sediment, or earth, stones, etc., deposited by water, wind, or ice.

seine (sān), *n., v.,* **seined, sein ing.** —*n.* a fishing net that hangs straight down in the water, with floats at the upper edge and sinkers at the lower.

se man tic (sə man′tik), *adj.* having to do with the meaning of words. —**se man′ti cal ly**, *adv.*

sem blance (sem′bləns), *n.* **1** outward appearance: *Their story had the semblance of truth, but was really false.* **2** likeness. [< Old French < *sembler* seem < Latin *similare* make similar < *similis* similar]

semi-, *prefix.* **1** half: *Semicircle = half a circle.* **2** partly; incompletely: *Semicivilized = partly civilized.*

se nil i ty (sə nil′ə tē), *n.* **1** old age. **2** the mental and physical deterioration often characteristic of old age.

sen si bil i ty (sen′sə bil′ə tē), *n., pl.* **-ties.** **1** ability to feel or perceive: *Some drugs lessen a person's sensibilities.* **2** sensitiveness. **3** fineness of feeling.

sen ti nel (sen′tə nəl), *n.* person stationed to keep watch and guard against surprise attacks.

se rene (sə rēn′), *adj.* **1** peaceful; calm: *a serene smile.* **2** not cloudy; clear; bright: *a serene sky.* —**se rene′ly**, *adv.*

sev er (sev′ər), *v.t.* **1** cut apart; cut off: *sever a rope.* **2** break

a hat	**i** it	**oi** oil	**ch** child		a in about
ā age	**ī** ice	**ou** out	**ng** long		e in taken
ä far	**o** hot	**u** cup	**sh** she	**ə** =	i in pencil
e let	**ō** open	**u̇** put	**th** thin		o in lemon
ē equal	**ô** order	**ü** rule	**ᴛʜ** then		u in circus
ėr term			**zh** measure		< = derived from

off: *The two countries severed friendly relations.* [< Old French *sevrer,* ultimately < Latin *separare* to separate]

shaft (shaft), *n.* **1** the long, slender stem of an arrow, spear. **2** the main part of a column or pillar.

sheath ing (shē′ᴛʜing), *n.* casing; covering.

shied (shīd), *v.* a pt. and a pp. of **shy.** started back or aside suddenly: *The horse shied at the noise.*

shil ling (shil′ing), *n.* **1** a former coin of Great Britain, which was equal to 12 pence or 1/20th of a pound. It was replaced by the 5 new pence piece. **2** unit of money of colonial America corresponding to the British shilling. [Old English *scilling*]

shoal (shōl), *n.* **1** place in a sea, lake, or stream where the water is shallow. **2** sandbank or sandbar.

shorn (shôrn, shōrn), *v.* a pp. of **shear.** —*adj.* sheared, or cut with shears or scissors.

show down (shō′doun′), *n.* a meeting face to face in order to settle an issue or dispute: *The showdown between the mayor and the council resulted in a welcome compromise.*

shroud (shroud), *n.* **1** cloth or garment in which a dead person is wrapped or dressed for burial. **2** something that covers, conceals, or veils: *The fog was a shroud over the city.* **3** Usually, **shrouds,** *pl.* rope from a mast to the side of a ship. Shrouds help support the mast. [Old English *scrūd*]

shut tle (shut′l), *n., v.,* **-tled, -tling.** —*n.* device that carries the thread from one side of the web to the other in weaving.

sid ing (sī′ding), *n.* **1** a short railroad track to which cars can be switched from a main track. **2** boards, shingles, etc., forming the outside walls of a wooden building.

si dle (sī′dl), *v.,* **-dled, -dling,** *n.* —*v.i.* **1** move sideways. **2** move sideways slowly so as not to attract attention: *The little boy shyly sidled up to the visitor.* —*n.* movement sideways.

si mul ta ne ous (sī′məl tā′nē əs, sim′əl tā′nē əs), *adj.* existing, done, or happening at the same time: *The two simultaneous shots sounded like one.* —**si′mul ta′ne ous ly**, *adv.*

sin is ter (sin′ə stər), *adj.* **1** showing ill will; threatening: *a sinister rumor, a sinister look.* **2** bad; evil; dishonest. **3** disastrous; unfortunate. **4** on the left; left. [< Latin; the left side being considered unlucky] —**sin′is ter ly**, *adv.*

sire (sīr), *n.* a male ancestor. —*v.t.* be the father of.

skein (skān), *n.* **1** a small, coiled bundle of yarn or thread. There are 120 yards in a skein of cotton yarn. **2** a confused tangle.

slav er (slav′ər), *v.* let saliva run from the mouth; drool. —*n.* saliva running from the mouth.

slew (slü), *v.* a pt. of **slay.** Killed violently.

slide (slīd), *v.* **1** move smoothly along on a surface. **2** let slide, not bother about; neglect.

slough (slou *for 1 and 3;* slü *for 2*), *n.* **1** a soft, deep, muddy place. **2** a swampy place; marshy inlet; slew; slue.

slue (slü), *v.t., v.i.,* **slued, slu ing,** turn, swing, twist.

smite (smīt), *v.,* **smote, smit ten** or **smote, smit ing.** —*v.t.* **1** give a hard blow to (a person, etc.) with the hand, a stick, or the like; strike. **2** give or strike (a blow, stroke, etc.). **3** attack with a sudden pain, disease, etc.

smote (smōt), *v.* pt. and a pp. of **smite.**

snub (snub), *v.t.,* **snubbed, snub bing,** **1** treat coldly, or with contempt. **2** check or stop (a rope or cable running out) suddenly.

snuff (snuf), *v.t.* draw in through the nose; draw up into the nose. —*n.* powdered tobacco, often scented, taken into the nose.

sol em nize (sol′əm nīz), *v.t.,* **-nized, -niz ing.** **1** hold or perform (a ceremony or service): *The marriage was solemnized in the cathedral.* **2** make serious or grave.

so lil o quize (sə lil′ə kwīz), *v.i.,* **-quized, -quiz ing. 1** talk to oneself. **2** speak a soliloquy. **—so lil′o quiz′er,** *n.*

som ber (som′bər), *adj.* **1** having deep shadows; dark; gloomy. **2** sad; dismal: *His losses made him very somber.*

som no lent (som′nə lənt), *adj.* **1** sleepy; drowsy. **2** tending to produce sleep. [< Latin *somnolentus* < *somnus* sleep] **—som′no lent ly,** *adv.*

so phis ti ca tion (sə fis′tə kā′shən), *n.* **1** a lessening or loss of naturalness, simplicity, or frankness; worldly experience or ideas; artificial ways. **2** sophistry.

sore (sôr, sōr), *adj.,* **sor er, sor est. 1** causing sharp or continuous pain **2** sad; distressed: *The suffering of the poor makes her heart sore.* **3** severe; distressing: *Your going away is a sore grief to us.* **—sore′ly,** *adv.* **—sore′ness,** *n.*

sou sa phone (sü′zə fōn′), *n.* a wind instrument similar to the tuba, with a flaring bell that faces forward. [< John Philip *Sousa,* who designed it]

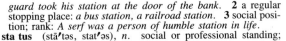

sousaphone

sown (sōn), *v.* a pp. of **sow.** planted.

Spanish Main, 1 (formerly) the NW coast of South America, from which Spanish galleons used to sail with gold for Spain. **2** (in later use) the Caribbean Sea.

spar[1] (spär), *n.* a stout pole used to support or extend the sails of a ship; mast, yard, gaff, etc. [Middle English *sparre* rafter]

spar[2] (spär), *v.i.,* **sparred, spar ring. 1** make motions of attack and defense with the arms and fists; box. **2** dispute.

spare (sper, spar), *v.* **1** show mercy to; refrain from harming. **2** make free from something; relieve or exempt from something. **—adj. 1** in reserve; extra: *a spare tire, a spare room.*

spas mod ic (spaz mod′ik), *adj.* having to do with a spasm, or sudden tightening of the muscles: *a spasmodic cough.*

spat (spat), *v.* a pt. and a pp. of **spit.**

spec i men (spes′ə mən), *n.* **1** one of a group or class taken to show what the others are like; sample: *She collects specimens of all kinds of rocks.* **2** INFORMAL. a human being; person.

spec tre (spek′tər), *n.* **1** phantom or ghost, especially one of a terrifying nature or appearance. **2** thing causing terror or dread. Also, **specter.** [< Latin *spectrum* appearance.]

spec u la tive (spek′yə lā′tiv, spek′yə lə tiv), *adj.* carefully thoughtful; reflective. **—spec′u la′tive ly,** *adv.*

splat (splat), *n.* **1** a sound like that of something splashing, spattering, or slapping. **2** a spot. **—interj.** the making of such a sound. **—adv.** with such a sound. [back-formation < *splatter*]

spright ly (sprīt′lē), *adj.,* **-li er, -li est,** *adv.* **—adj.** lively; gay. **—adv.** in a lively manner. Also, **spritely.**

squan der (skwon′dər), *v.t.* spend foolishly; waste: *squander one's money.* [origin uncertain] **—squan′der er,** *n.*

stac ca to (stə kä′tō), *adj.* **1** (in music) with breaks between the successive tones; disconnected; detached. **2** abrupt: *a staccato manner.* [< Italian, literally, detached]

stalk (stôk), *v.t.* approach or pursue without being seen or heard: *The hunters stalked the lion.* **—v.i. 1** spread silently and steadily: *Disease stalked through the land.* **2** walk with slow, stiff, or haughty strides. **—n. 1** a haughty gait. **2** act of stalking. [Old English *(be)stealcian* steal along] **—stalk′a ble,** *adj.* **—stalk′er,** *n.*

stance (stans), *n.* manner of standing; posture.

stan chion (stan′shən), *n.* an upright bar, post, or support, as for a window, a roof, or the deck of a ship.

sta tion (stā′shən), *n.* **1** place which a person is appointed to occupy in the performance of some duty; assigned post: *The*

guard took his station at the door of the bank. **2** a regular stopping place: *a bus station, a railroad station.* **3** social position; rank: *A serf was a person of humble station in life.*

sta tus (stā′təs, stat′əs), *n.* social or professional standing; position; rank: *lose status.*

stealth y (stel′thē), *adj.,* **stealth i er, stealth i est.** done in a secret manner; secret; sly: *The cat crept in a stealthy way toward the bird.* **—stealth′i ly,** *adv.* **—stealth′i ness,** *n.*

steam (stēm), *n.* **1** the invisible vapor or gas formed when water is heated to the boiling point. **2** the white cloud or mist formed by the condensation, when cooled, of this vapor or gas. **3** INFORMAL. power; force. **4 let off steam,** INFORMAL. **a** get rid of excess energy. **b** relieve one's feelings.

steed (stēd), *n.* **1** horse, especially a riding horse. **2** a high-spirited horse. [Old English *stēda*]

ster e op ti con (ster′ē op′tə kən, stir′ē op′tə kən), *n.* projector arranged to combine two images on a screen so that they gradually become one image with three-dimensional effect.

sti fle (stī′fəl), *v.,* **-fled, -fling. —v.t. 1** stop the breath of; smother. **2** keep back; stop: *stifle a cry, stifle a yawn.*

stim u lus (stim′yə ləs), *n., pl.* **-li. 1** something that stirs to action or effort; incentive. **2** something that excites an organ or part of the body to a specific activity or function; something that produces a response. [< Latin, originally, goad]

stow (stō), *v.t.* **1** put away to be stored; pack: *The cargo was stowed in the ship's hold.* **2** pack things closely in; fill by packing: *stow a pantry with cans of food.*

stren u ous (stren′yü əs), *adj.* **1** very active: *We had a strenuous day moving into our new house.* **2** full of energy: *a strenuous worker.* **3** requiring much energy: *strenuous exercise.*

strict (strikt), *adj.* **1** very careful in following a rule or in making others follow it. **2** harsh; severe: *a strict parent.* See synonym study below. **—strict′ly,** *adv.*

Syn. 1,2 Strict, rigid, rigorous mean severe and unyielding or harsh and stern. **Strict** emphasizes showing or demanding a very careful and close following of a rule, standard, or requirement: *Our teacher is strict and insists that we follow instructions to the letter.* **Rigid** emphasizes being firm and unyielding, not changing or relaxing for anyone or under any conditions: *They maintain a rigid working schedule.* **Rigorous** emphasizes the harshness, or sternness of the demands made, conditions imposed, etc.: *We believe in rigorous enforcement of the laws.*

stride (strīd), *v.,* **strode, strid den, strid ing,** *n.* **—v.i.** walk with long steps: *stride rapidly down the street.*

strive (strīv), *v.i.,* **strove** or **strived, striv en, striv ing. 1** try hard; work hard: *strive for self-control.* **2** struggle; fight: *The swimmer strove against the tide.*

strode (strōd), *v.* pt. of **stride.**

strove (strōv), *v.* a pt. of **strive.**

stul ti fy (stul′tə fī), *v.t.,* **-fied, -fy ing. 1** make futile; frustrate: *stultify a person's efforts.* **2** cause to appear foolish.

sua vi ty (swä′və tē, swav′ə tē), *n., pl.* **-ties.** smoothly agreeable quality or behavior; smooth politeness; blandness.

sub con scious (sub kon′shəs), *adj.* not wholly conscious; existing in the mind but not fully perceived or recognized: *a subconscious fear.* **—n.** thoughts, feelings, etc., that are present in the mind but not fully perceived or recognized.

sub due (səb dü′, səb dyü′), *v.t.,* **-dued, -du ing. 1** overcome by force; conquer. **2** keep down; hold back; suppress: *We subdued a desire to laugh.* **3** tone down; soften.

sub ject (*n., adj.* sub′jikt, sub′jekt; *v.* səb jekt′), *n.* **1** something thought about, discussed, investigated, etc. **2** something learned or taught; course of study. **3** person under the power, control, or influence of another: *the subjects of a monarch.* **4** person or thing that undergoes or experiences something: *Rabbits and mice are often subjects for medical experiments.* **—v.t. 1** bring under some power or influence: *Rome subjected all Italy to its rule.* **2** cause to undergo or experience something: *The lawyer subjected the witness to grueling cross-examination.*

sub or di nate (*adj., n.* sə bôrd′n it; *v.* sə bôrd′n āt), *adj., n., v.,* **-nat ed, -nat ing. —adj. 1** lower in rank: *In the army,* lieutenants are subordinate to captains. **2** lower in importance; secondary. **3** under the control or influence of something else; dependent. —*n.* a subordinate person or thing. —*v.t.* make subordinate: *He subordinated his wishes to those of his guests.* [< Medieval Latin *subordinatum* lowered in rank < Latin *sub-* under + *ordinem* order] —**sub or'di nate ly,** *adv.*

sub ter ra ne an (sub'tə rā'nē ən), *adj.* underground: *A subterranean passage led from the castle to a cave.* [< Latin *subterraneus* < *sub-* under + *terra* earth]

suc ces sion (sək sesh'ən), *n.* **1** group of persons or things coming one after another; series. **2** the coming of one person or thing after another.

suf fuse (sə fyüz'), *v.t.,* **-fused, -fus ing.** overspread (with a liquid, dye, etc.): *eyes suffused with tears. At twilight the sky was suffused with color.*

sulk y (sul'kē), *adj.,* **sulk i er, sulk i est.** silent and bad-humored because of resentment; sullen: *Some children become sulky when they cannot have their own way.*

sul len (sul'ən), *adj.* **1** silent because of bad humor or anger: *The sullen child refused to answer my question.* **2** showing bad humor or anger.

sump tu ous (sump'chü əs), *adj.* lavish and costly; magnificent; rich: *a sumptuous banquet.* —**sump'tu ous ly,** *adv.*

su per nat ur al (sü'pər nach'ər əl), *adj.* above or beyond what is natural. *Ghosts are supernatural beings.* —*n.* **the supernatural,** supernatural influences or phenomena.

sup ple ment (*n.* sup'lə mənt; *v.* sup'lə ment), *n.* **1** something added to complete a thing, or to make it larger or better. **2** something added to supply a deficiency: *a diet supplement.* —*v.t.* supply something additional to.

sup po si tion (sup'ə zish'ən), *n.* **1** act of supposing. **2** thing supposed; belief; opinion.

surge (sėrj), *v.,* **surged, surg ing,** *n.* —*v.i.* **1** rise and fall; move like waves. *The crowd surged through the streets.* **2** rise or swell (up) violently or excitedly, as feelings, thoughts, etc. —*n.* a swelling wave; sweep or rush of waves.

sur mise (sər mīz'), *v.t., v.i.,* **-mised, -mis ing.** infer or guess: *We surmised that the delay was caused by some accident.*

sur pass (sər pas'), *v.t.* do better than; be greater than; excel.

sur rep ti tious (sėr'əp tish'əs), *adj.* **1** stealthy; secret: *a surreptitious glance.* **2** secret and unauthorized: *surreptitious meetings.* —**sur'rep ti'tious ly,** *adv.*

sus te nance (sus'tə nəns), *n.* **1** food; nourishment. **2** means of living; support: *give money for the sustenance of the poor.*

syl van (sil'vən), *adj.* of, in, or having woods. Also, **silvan.** [< Latin *sylvanus, silvanus* < *silva* forest]

sym met ri cal (si met'rə kəl), *adj.* having symmetry; well-proportioned. —**sym met'ri cal ly,** *adv.*

sym pa thy (sim'pə thē), *n., pl.* **-thies. 1** a sharing of another's sorrow or trouble: *We feel sympathy for a person who is ill.* **2** agreement in feeling.

syn di cate (*n.* sin'də kit; *v.* sin'də kāt), *n., v.,* **-cat ed, -cat ing.** —*n.* a combination of persons or companies formed to carry out some undertaking, especially one requiring a large capital investment.

tac i turn (tas'ə tėrn'), *adj.* speaking very little; not fond of talking. —**tac'i turn'ly,** *adv.*

tal ly (tal'ē), *n., pl.* **-lies,** *v.,* **-lied, -ly ing.** —*n.* **1** anything on which a score or account is kept. **2** notch or mark made on a tally; mark made for a certain number of objects in keeping account. —*v.t.* **1** mark on a tally; count up. **2** mark with an identifying label; tag.

tan gi ble (tan'jə bəl), *adj.* **1** that can be touched or felt by touch: *A chair is a tangible object.* **2** real; actual; definite: *a tangible improvement, tangible evidence.* —**tan'gi bil'i ty,** *n.*

tap es try (tap'ə strē), *n., pl.* **-tries. 1** fabric with pictures or designs woven in it, used to hang on walls, cover furniture, etc. **2** a picture in tapestry.

tat too (ta tü'), *n., pl.* **-toos. 1** signal on a bugle, drum, etc., calling soldiers or sailors to their quarters at night. **2** series of raps, taps, etc.: *The hail beat a loud tattoo on the windowpane.* [< Dutch *taptoe* < *tap* taproom + *toe* pull to, shut]

taunt (tônt, tänt), *v.t.* **1** jeer at; mock; reproach; deride. **2** get or drive by taunts; provoke: *taunt someone into taking a dare.* —*n.* a bitter or insulting remark; mocking; jeering. [origin uncertain]

taut (tôt), *adj.* tightly drawn; tense: *a taut rope.*

tem per a men tal (tem'pər ə men'tl), *adj.* **1** subject to moods and whims; easily irritated; sensitive. **2** due to temperament; constitutional.

ten ta tive (ten'tə tiv), *adj.* **1** done as a trial or experiment. **2** hesitating. —**ten'ta tive ly,** *adv.* —**ten'ta tive ness,** *n.*

Ter ti ar y (tėr'shē er'ē, tėr'shər ē), *n., pl.* **-ar ies,** *adj.* —*n.* **1** the period of time from 70 million to 2 million years ago, during which the great mountain systems, such as the Alps, Himalayas, Rocky Mountains, and Andes, appeared, and rapid development of mammals occurred. **2** rocks formed in this period. —*adj.* of or having to do with the Tertiary or its rocks.

teth er (teth'ər), *n.* rope or chain for fastening an animal so that it can move only within a certain limit. —*v.t.* fasten or confine with or as with a tether.

the o ret i cal (thē'ə ret'ə kəl), *adj.* **1** planned or worked out in the mind, not from experience; based on theory, not on fact. **2** dealing with theory only; not practical.

the sis (thē'sis), *n., pl.* **-ses** (-sēz). proposition or statement to be proved or to be maintained against objections.

thith er (thiŦH'ər, ŦHiŦH'ər), *adv.* to that place; there. —*adj.* on that side; farther. [Old English *thider*]

tid al (tī'dl), *adj.* **1** of tides; having tides; caused by tides. A tidal river is affected by the ocean's tide. **2** dependent on the state of the tide as to time of arrival and departure: *a tidal steamer.* —**tid'al ly,** *adv.*

tier (tir), *n.* one of a series of rows arranged one above another: *tiers of seats in a stadium.* —*v.t., v.i.* arrange, or be arranged, in tiers. [< Middle French *tire,* originally, order < *tirer* to draw]

tol er a ble (tol'ər ə bəl), *adj.* **1** able to be borne or endured; bearable. **2** fairly good; passable: *She is in tolerable health.*

tomb (tüm), *n.* grave, vault, mausoleum, or other place of burial for a dead body, often above ground. —**tomb'less,** *adj.* —**tomb'like',** *adj.*

to paz (tō'paz), *n.* **1** a hard, transparent or translucent mineral that occurs in crystals of various forms and colors. It is a compound of aluminum, silica, and fluorine. **2** a yellow variety of sapphire or quartz, used as a gem.

top o graph i cal (top'ə graf'ə kəl), *adj.* of or having to do with the surface features of a place or region. A topographical map shows mountains, rivers, etc.

tor rent (tôr'ənt, tor'ənt), *n.* **1** a violent, rushing stream of water. **2** a heavy downpour: *The rain came down in torrents.* **3** any violent, rushing stream; flood: *a torrent of abuse.*

touch stone (tuch'stōn'), *n.* **1** a black stone used to test the purity of gold or silver. **2** any means of testing; a test.

trace (trās), *n.* either of the two straps, ropes, or chains by which an animal pulls a wagon, carriage.

trans fix (tran sfiks'), *v.t.* **1** pierce through: *The hunter transfixed the lion with a spear.* **2** make motionless or helpless (with

GLOSSARY

amazement, terror, grief, etc.). **—trans fix′ion,** *n.*

trans for ma tion (tran′sfər mā′shən), *n.* a transforming, or a changing of the appearance, shape, or nature of a thing or person.

trans pose (tran spōz′), *v.t.,* **-posed, -pos ing.** **1** change the position or order of; interchange.

tra vail (trə vāl′, trav′āl), *n.* toil; labor.

tra verse (trə vėrs′, trav′ərs), *v.i.,* **-versed, -vers ing.** **1** walk or move in a crosswise direction; move back and forth: *That horse traverses.* **2** ski in a diagonal course.

treach er ous (trech′ər əs), *adj.* **1** not to be trusted; not faithful; disloyal. **2** having a false appearance of strength, security, etc.; not reliable; deceiving: *Thin ice is treacherous.*

treach er y (trech′ər ē), *n., pl.* **-er ies.** **1** a breaking of faith; treacherous behavior; deceit.

tread (tred), *v.,* **trod, trod den** or **trod, tread ing,** *n.* **—v.i.** **1** set the foot down; walk; step: *tread through the meadow.* **2** step heavily; trample: *Don't tread on the flower beds.* **—v.t.** **1** set the feet on; walk on or through; step on: *tread the streets.* **2** tread the measure, dance.

tri bu nal (tri byü′nl, trī byü′nl), *n.* **1** court of justice; place of judgment. **2** place where judges sit in a court of law.

trice (trīs), *n.* **1** a very short time; moment; instant. **2 in a trice,** in an instant; immediately.

tri dent (trīd′nt), *n.* a three-pronged spear. **—adj.** three-pronged. [< Latin *tridentem* < *tri-* three + *dentem* tooth]

tri fle (trī′fəl), *n., v.,* **-fled, -fling. —n. 1** thing having little value or importance. **2** a small amount; little bit: *I was a trifle late.* **—v.i.** talk or act lightly, not seriously: *Don't trifle with serious matters.* [< Old French *trufle* mockery, diminutive of *truffe* deception]

tri lin gual (trī ling′gwəl), *adj.* **1** able to speak three languages. **2** using three languages **3** written or expressed in three languages: *a trilingual text.*

tri syl lab ic (tris′ə lab′ik, trī sə lab′ik), *adj.* having three syllables. **—tri′syl lab′i cal ly,** *adv.*

trough (trôf, trof), *n.* **1** a narrow, open, boxlike container for holding food or water, especially for farm stock or other animals. **2** a channel for carrying water; gutter. **3** a long hollow between two ridges, especially the hollow between two waves.

tru an cy (trü′ən sē), *n., pl.* **-cies.** act or habit of staying away from school without permission.

trumped-up (trumpt′up′), *adj.* made up to deceive; fabricated; spurious: *a trumped-up charge.*

tu mult (tü′mult, tyü′mult), *n.* **1** noise or uproar; commotion: *the tumult of the storm.* **2** a violent disturbance or disorder: *The cry of ''Fire!'' caused a tumult in the theater.* **3** a violent disturbance of mind or feeling; confusion or excitement. [< Latin *tumultus*]

tur ban (tėr′bən), *n.* **1** scarf wound around the head or around a cap, worn by men in parts of India and in some other countries. **2** any hat or headdress like this. [< Middle French *turbant* < Turkish *tülbend.* Doublet of TULIP.]

turban (def. 1)

un-, *prefix.* not ___; the opposite of ___: *Unequal = not equal; the opposite of equal. Unchanged = not changed. Unjust = not just.*

un a bashed (un′ə basht′), *adj.* not embarrassed, ashamed, or awed. **—un′a bash′ed ly,** *adv.*

un bri dled (un brī′dld), *adj.* **1** not having a bridle on. **2** not controlled; not restrained: *unbridled anger.*

un der tow (un′dər tō′), *n.* **1** any strong current below the surface, moving in a direction different from that of the surface current. **2** the backward flow of water from waves breaking.

un du la tion (un′jə lā′shən, un′dyə lā′shən), *n.* **1** a wavelike motion; an undulating. **2** a wavy form. **3** one of a series of wavelike bends, curves, swellings, etc.

un eas y (un ē′zē), *adj.,* **-eas i er, -eas i est.** **1** restless; disturbed; anxious: *an uneasy sleep, be uneasy about a decision.* **2** not comfortable. **3** not easy in manner; awkward. **—un eas′i ly,** *adv.*

un fore seen (un′fôr sēn′, un′fōr sēn′), *adj.* not known beforehand; unexpected.

u ni son (yü′nə sən, yü′nə zən), *n.* **1** harmonious combination or union; agreement: *The feet of marching soldiers move in unison. They spoke in unison.* **2** identity in pitch of two or more sounds, tones, etc. [< Medieval Latin *unisonus* sounding the same < Latin *unus* one + *sonus* sound]

un seem ly (un sēm′lē), *adj.* not seemly; not suitable; improper: *unseemly haste.* **—adv.** improperly; unsuitably.

un tram meled or **un tram melled** (un tram′əld), *adj.* not hindered; not restrained; free.

un wont ed (un wun′tid, un wōn′tid, un wôn′tid), *adj,* **1** not customary; not usual. **2** not accustomed; not used.

va cate (vā′kāt), *v.,* **-cat ed, -cat ing. —v.t. 1** go away from and leave empty or unoccupied; make vacant: *They will vacate the house at the end of the month.* **2** make void; annul; cancel. **—v.i.** go away; leave. [< Latin *vacatum* emptied]

vac u ous (vak′yü əs), *adj.* showing no thought or intelligence; foolish; stupid: *a vacuous smile.* **—vac′u ous ly,** *adv.*

va gar y (və ger′ē, vā′gər ē), *n., pl.* **-gar ies. 1** an odd fancy; extravagant notion: *the vagaries of a dream.* **2** odd action; caprice.

val or (val′ər), *n.* bravery; courage.

var i ance (ver′ē əns, var′ē əns), *n.* **1** difference; disagreement: *variances in the spelling of proper names.* **2** a disagreeing or falling out; discord; quarrel. **3** a varying; change.

var i a tion (ver′ē ā′shən, var′ē ā′shən), *n.* **1** a varying in condition, degree, etc.; change. **2** amount of change. **3** a varied or changed form. **4** (in music) a tune or theme repeated with changes in rhythm, harmony, etc.

vault (vôlt), *v.t.* jump or leap over by using a pole or the hands. **—v.i.** jump or leap. **—n.** act of vaulting.

ve he ment (vē′ə mənt), *adj.* **1** having or showing strong feeling; caused by strong feeling; eager; passionate. **2** forceful; violent. [< Latin *vehementem* being carried away < *vehere* carry] **—ve′he ment ly,** *adv.*

ven ture (ven′chər), *n., v.,* **-tured, -tur ing. —n. 1** a risky or daring undertaking: *courage equal to any venture.* **2** thing risked; stake. **—v.t. 1** expose to risk or danger: *Men venture their lives in war.* **2** dare when embarassment, rejection, or rebuff might follow: *No one ventured to interrupt the speaker.* **—v.i.** dare to come, go, or proceed: *They ventured out on the thin ice and fell through.*

verge (vėrj), *n.* **1** the point at which something begins or happens; brink: *business on the verge of ruin.* **2** a limiting edge, margin, or bound of something; border: *the verge of a cliff.*

ver i fy (ver′ə fī), *v.t.,* **-fied, -fy ing. 1** prove to be true; confirm. **2** test the correctness of; check for accuracy.

vex (veks), *v.t.* **1** anger by trifles; annoy; provoke. **2** worry; trouble; harass. **3** disturb by commotion; agitate.

vi car i ous (vī ker′ē əs, vī ker′ē əs), *adj.* **1** done or suffered for others: *vicarious work.* **2** felt by sharing in others' experience.

vi cin i ty (və sin′ə tē), *n., pl.* **-ties. 1** region near or about a place; surrounding district; neighborhood: *know many people in New York and its vicinity.* **2** nearness in place; being close.

vile (vīl), *adj.*, **vil er, vil est. 1** very bad: *vile weather.* **2** foul; disgusting; obnoxious: *a vile smell.* **3** evil; low; immoral: *vile habits.* See synonym study below.
Syn. *adj.* **1 Base, vile, low** mean morally inferior and contemptible. **Base** means reduced to a low moral state, without honor or without moral standards, usually by selfishness or cowardliness: *Betraying a friend for a reward is base.* **Vile** means evil and without moral standards or decency: *Ill-treatment and torture of helpless prisoners is a vile outrage.* **Low** means without a sense of decency or of what is honorable: *To steal from the collection plate in church is low.*
vir ile (vir′əl), *adj.* **1** of, belonging to, or characteristic of a man; manly; masculine. **2** vigorous; forceful.
vir tue (ver′chü), *n.* moral excellence; goodness. [< Old French *vertu* < Latin *virtutem* manliness, virtue < *vir* man]
vit tles (vit′lz), *n.pl.* DIALECT. food or provisions.
vol ley (vol′ē), *n.*, *pl.* **-leys,** *v.* —*n.* **1** shower of stones, bullets, arrows, etc. **2** the discharge of a number of guns or other weapons firing missiles at once. **3** a rapid outpouring or burst of words, oaths, shouts, cheers, etc.
vo ra cious (və rā′shəs), *adj.* **1** eating much; greedy in eating; ravenous. **2** very eager; unable to be satisfied; insatiable. [< Latin *voracis* greedy]
vo tive (vō′tiv), *adj.* **1** promised by a vow; done, given, etc., because of a vow. **2** made up or expressive of a vow, desire, or wish: *a votive prayer.*
vouch safe (vouch sāf′), *v.t.*, **-safed, -saf ing.** be willing to grant, do, or give: *The proud man vouchsafed no reply when we spoke to him.*

waft (waft, wäft), *v.t.* carry over water or through air: *The waves wafted the boat to shore.* —*v.i.* float. —*n.* **1** a breath or puff of air, wind, scent, etc. **2** a waving movement; wave. **3** act of wafting.
walk (wôk), *v.i.* **1** go on foot. **2** roam. **3** (in baseball) go to first base after the pitcher has thrown four balls. —*v.t.* **1** go over, on, or through: *The captain walked the deck.* **2** (in baseball) allow (a batter) to reach first base by pitching four balls.
walk out, **a** go on strike. **b** leave suddenly.
walk out on, INFORMAL. desert.
walk over, **a** defeat easily and by a wide margin. **b** act without regard for; trample on; override.
wane (wān), *v.,* **waned, wan ing,** *n.* —*v.i.* **1** lose size; become smaller gradually. **2** decline in power, influence, or importance. **3** decline in strength or intensity: *The light of day wanes in the evening.* **4** draw to a close.
war y (wer′ē, war′ē), *adj.*, **war i er, war i est. 1** on one's guard against danger, deception, etc.: *a wary fox.* **2** cautious or careful. **3** wary of, cautious or careful about: *be wary of driving in heavy traffic.* —**war′i ly,** *adv.*
weath er cock (weŦH′ər kok′), *n.* vane to show which way the wind is blowing, especially one in the shape of a rooster.
wea zened (wē′znd), *adj.* wizened.
wel ter weight (wel′tər wāt′), *n.* boxer who weighs more than 135 pounds and less than 147 pounds.
wend (wend), *v.,* **wend ed** or **went, wend ing,** —*v.t.* direct (one's way): *We wended our way home.* —*v.i.* go.
wheel er (hwē′lər), *n.* **1** person or thing that wheels. **2** thing,

a hat	i it	oi oil	ch child		a in about
ā age	ī ice	ou out	ng long		e in taken
ä far	o hot	u cup	sh she	ə =	i in pencil
e let	ō open	ù put	th thin		o in lemon
ē equal	ô order	ü rule	ŦH then		u in circus
ėr term			zh measure	< = derived from

as a vehicle, that has a wheel or wheels. **3** wheel horse or dog.
whence (hwens), *adv.* from what place; from where: *Whence do you come?* —*conj.* **1** from what place, source, or cause: *She told whence she came.* **2** from which: *Let them return to the country whence they came.*
whim si cal (hwim′zə kəl), *adj.* **1** having many odd notions or fancies; capricious; *a whimsical person.* **2** odd; fanciful: *a whimsical expression.*
wick et (wik′it), *n.* **1** a small door or gate: *The big door has a wicket in it.* **2** a small window or opening, often having a grate or grill over it: *Buy your tickets at this wicket.*
wield (wēld), *v.t.* hold and use; manage; control: *wield a hammer.*
wild-goose chase (wīld′güs′), a useless search or attempt; foolish or hopeless quest.
wing (wing), *n.* **1** one of the movable parts of a bird, insect, or bat used in flying, or a corresponding part in a bird or insect that does not fly. **2** either of the spaces to the right or left of the stage of a theater, out of sight of the audience.
wist ful (wist′fəl), *adj.* longing; yearning: *A child stood looking with wistful eyes at the toys in the window.* —**wist′ful ly,** *adv.* —**wist′ful ness,** *n.*
with al (wi ŦHôl′, wi thôl′), *adv.* **1** with it all; as well; besides; also: *I am tired and hungry and hurt withal.* **2** ARCHAIC. **a** in spite of all; nevertheless. **b** therewith. —*prep.* ARCHAIC. with. [Middle English < *with* + *all*]
wiz ened (wiz′nd, wē′znd), *adj.* dried up; withered; shriveled.
wont (wunt, wŏnt, wônt), *adj.* accustomed: *He was wont to read the paper at breakfast.* —*n.* custom; habit: *She rose early, as was her wont.*
wraith (rāth), *n.* **1** ghost of a person seen before or soon after the person's death. **2** specter; ghost.
wrath ful (rath′fəl), *adj.* feeling or showing wrath; very angry. —**wrath′ful ly,** *adv.* —**wrath′ful ness,** *n.*
wrought (rôt), *v.* ARCHAIC. a pt. and a pp. of **work.** worked; brought about.

yeo man ry (yō′mən rē), *n.* yeomen, or (formerly) in Great Britain, a person who owned land and farmed it himself.
yon (yon), *adj., adv.* ARCHAIC. [Old English *geon*]

zeal (zēl), *n.* eager desire or effort; earnest enthusiasm; fervor: *religious zeal, work with zeal for pollution control.*
ze nith (zē′nith), *n.* **1** the point in the heavens directly overhead. **2** the highest point; apex.

GLOSSARY

745

INDEX OF READING AND LITERATURE SKILLS

INDEX OF VOCABULARY EXERCISES

INDEX OF THINKING SKILLS

INDEX OF COMPOSITION ASSIGNMENTS

INDEX OF ENRICHMENT ACTIVITIES

INDEX OF FEATURES

INDEX OF AUTHORS AND TITLES

ILLUSTRATION ACKNOWLEDGMENTS

UNIT 1 1—Photo courtesy Hirschl & Adler Gallery, NY; **7**—Photo courtesy Campanile Galleries, Inc., Chicago; **11**—AP/Wide World Photos; **16**—Photo: Art Resource, NY; **22**—Courtesy Delacorte Press/Photo: © 1979 Jim Kalett; **25**—Courtesy Private Collection; **31**—Courtesy Dell Publishing; **44**—AP/Wide World Photos; **55**—Photo by Francine Ann Yep, Courtesy Harper & Row, Publishers, Inc. **67**—The Bettmann Archive; **73**—Photo courtesy Tatistcheff Gallery, NY; **77**—Photo: © Lisa Ebright; **83**—AP/Wide World Photos; **93**—© Galen Rowell/Mountain Light; **105**—Photo courtesy Marlborough Gallery, NY; **108**—Courtesy Isaac Asimov; **115**—Poe, ms. Manuscripts Department, Lilly Library, Indiana University, Bloomington; **121**—AP/Wide World Photos; **127**—© 1983 by Rodney Smith from *In the Land of Light Israel, a Portrait of Its People,* Houghton Mifflin Company; **135**—Photo: Cindy Grossman; **140**—Courtesy Chicago Historical Society

UNIT 2 144—Museum of Modern Art, New York; **145**—Collection Whitney Museum of American Art, New York, Bequest of Josephine N. Hopper; **149**—National Gallery of Art, Washington. Gift of Edgar William and Bernice Chrysler Garbisch; **157**—Sleepy Hollow Restorations; **163**—Photo: Frederic Lewis; **173**—Courtesy Rod Serling; **174**—Courtesy Brandywine River Museum; **178, 187**—© Paul B. Goode; **194**—National Portrait Gallery, London. Gift of Jean Conan Doyle, 1959

UNIT 3 216—Photo: Alfred Eisenstaedt/courtesy Viking Press, Inc.; **219**—The Brooklyn Museum, Purchase Fund, 1911; **228**—AP/Wide World Photos; **229**—Museum of Modern Art/Film Stills Archive; **233**—AP/Wide World Photos; **245**—Courtesy Yankee Books/Photo: Be Brown; **250**—AP/Wide World Photos; **258**—Rare Book Division, New York Public Library, Astor, Lenox and Tilden Foundation; **259**—Asa Battles; **261**—Lippincott & Crowell Publishers/Photo: Johan Elbers; **263**—Library of Congress; **264, 266**—Institute for Intercultural Studies, NY

UNIT 4 274—Art Institute of Chicago, Gift of Burr Robbins; **275**—Culver Pictures; **276**—Frank Donato/Impact Photo, Inc.; **280**—AP/Wide World Photos; **287**—George Eastman House Collection; **290**—Photo © Dan Morrill; **295**—Photo courtesy Heritage Gallery, L.A.; **298**—(top) AP/Wide World Photos, (bottom) Photo: L.A. Hyder; **301**—Courtesy Louis K. Meisel Gallery; **303**—Photo © Layle Silbert, NY; **303**—Courtesy Robert Francis; **304**—Collection Whitney Museum of American Art, Bequest of Loula D. Lasker; **306**—Photo courtesy Naomi Washington; **309**—© Zoltan Szabo; **311**—(top) Courtesy Margaret Tsuda, (middle) Courtesy Random House/Photo: Bob Fletcher; **313**—Phillips Memorial Gallery, Washington, DC, Collections: E. Weyhe; **316**—(top) Courtesy Gerard W. Purcell Assoc., Ltd., NY, (bottom) Courtesy Vassar College; **320**—Library of Congress; **322**—© Zoltan Szabo;

323—Photo: Myron Miller © 1985; **325, 327**—AP/Wide World Photos; **329**—Courtesy Dr. Irwin Goldstein; **330**—UPI/Bettmann Newsphotos; **335**—© Rollie McKenna; **335**—(bottom) Metropolitan Museum of Art, Bequest of Adele S. Colgate 1962, 63.550.159; **338**—Wadsworth Atheneum, Hartford. In Memory of William Arnold Healy given by his daughter Susie Healy Camp.

UNIT 5 344, 345—Illustration © 1984 Will Barnet; **348**—Columbus Museum of Art, Ohio, Museum Purchase, Howald Fund; **350**—Courtesy Lescher & Lescher, Ltd./Photo: Sigrid Estrada; **357**—Courtesy Teresa Foley; **360**—from *Now Sheba Sings the Songs* by Maya Angelou, with art by Tom Feelings. Art copyright © 1987 by Tom Feelings. Reproduced by permission of the publisher, Dial Books for Young Readers; **367**—Memorial Art Gallery of the University of Rochester, Rochester, NY, Gift of Mrs. Granger A. Hollister/photo: David Henry; **373**—The Bettmann Archive; **377**—Museum of the American Indian, Heye Foundation, NY; **382**—Courtesy Virginia Driving Hawk Sneve; **384**—© Robert Capa/Magnum Photos, Inc.; **386**—UPI/Bettmann Newsphotos; **389**—© Tom Heflin; **395**—Courtesy Henry Holt and Company/Photo: Ron Brown; **399**—© Mark Sabin; **402**—The Bettmann Archive; **405**—Circus World Museum, Baraboo, Wisconsin; **409**—Courtesy Random House/Photo: Carole Dufrechon; **415, 430**—Courtesy Yolanda, The Gallery for Naifs/Folk Art, Chicago; **420**—Addison Gallery of American Art, Phillips Academy, Andover, MA; **433**—AP/Wide World Photos; **435**—Courtesy Harrison Eiteljorg

UNIT 6 446, 447—from *The Theatre Art of Boris Aronson* by Frank Rich and Lisa Aronson, Copyright © 1987 by Frank Rich and Lisa Aronson. Reprinted by permission of Alfred A. Knopf, Inc.; **449–520, 525**—© 1988, Copyright by ANNE FRANK-Fonds/Cosmopress, Genève; **524**—AP/Wide World Photos; **526**—Anne-Marie O'Healy

UNIT 7 540—Scala/Art Resource, NY; **545**—©Erich Lessing/Giraudon, Art Resource, NY; **553**—Scala, Florence; **556**—Courtesy Houghton Mifflin Company; **566**—AP/Wide World Photos

UNIT 8 572, 573, 588—Glenbow Museum, Calgary, Alberta, Canada; **579–586**—Private Collection; **592**—Courtesy John Clymer; **616**—Delaware Art Museum. On long term loan from private collector; **624**—Private Collection; **629**—The Seattle Times; **632**—Private Collection

HANDBOOKS 657—National Gallery of Art, Gift of Mrs. Mellon Bruce in memory of Her Father Andrew W. Mellon 1961; **688**—Courtesy AT&T Phone Center; **693**—Canajoharie Library and Art Gallery, NY

GLOSSARY 723—Stewart/Jeroboam, Inc. **728**—National Film Board of Canada **737**—Courtesy of the Consulate General of Japan, New York. **744**—F. A. O.